HISTORY IN DISPUTE

ADVISORY BOARD

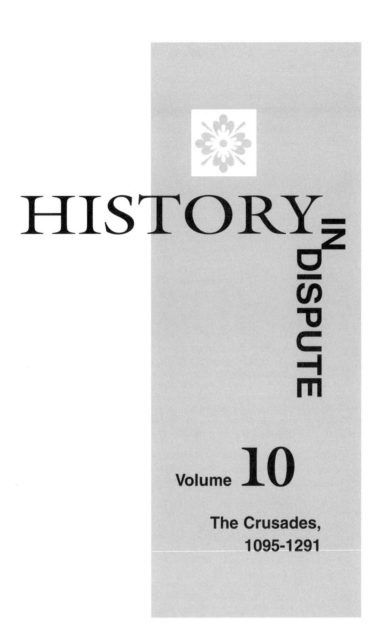

HISTORY IN DISPUTE

Volume **10**

The Crusades,
1095-1291

Edited by **Mark T. Abate**

A MANLY, INC. BOOK

GALE®

THOMSON
✳
TM
GALE

Detroit • New York • San Diego • San Francisco • Cleveland • New Haven, Conn. • Waterville, Maine • London • Munich

History in Dispute
Volume 10: The Crusades, 1095–1291
Mark T. Abate

Editorial Directors
Matthew J. Bruccoli and Richard Layman

Senior Editor
Karen L. Rood

Series Editor
Anthony J. Scotti Jr.

ISBN 1-55862-454-6

Printed in the United States of America
10 9 8 7 6 5 4 3 2 1

CONTENTS

CONTENTS

CONTENTS

ABOUT THE SERIES

History in Dispute is an ongoing series designed to present, in an informative and lively pro-con format, different perspectives on major historical events drawn from all time periods and from all parts of the globe. The series was developed in response to requests from librarians and educators for a history-reference source that will help students hone essential critical-thinking skills while serving as a valuable research tool for class assignments.

Individual volumes in the series concentrate on specific themes, eras, or subjects intended to correspond to the way history is studied at the academic level. For example, early volumes cover such topics as the Cold War, American Social and Political Movements, and World War II. Volume subtitles make it easy for users to identify contents at a glance and facilitate searching for specific subjects in library catalogues.

Each volume of *History in Dispute* includes up to fifty entries, centered on the overall theme of that volume and chosen by an advisory board of historians for their relevance to the curriculum. Entries are arranged alphabetically by the name of the event or issue in its most common form. (Thus, in Volume 1, the issue "Was detente a success?" is presented under the chapter heading "Detente.")

Each entry begins with a brief statement of the opposing points of view on the topic, followed by a short essay summarizing the issue and outlining the controversy. At the heart of the entry, designed to engage students' interest while providing essential information, are the two or more lengthy essays, written specifically for this publication by experts in the field, each presenting one side of the dispute.

In addition to this substantial prose explication, entries also include excerpts from primary-source documents, other useful information typeset in easy-to-locate shaded boxes, detailed entry bibliographies, and photographs or illustrations appropriate to the issue.

Other features of *History in Dispute* volumes include: individual volume introductions by academic experts, tables of contents that identify both the issues and the controversies, chronologies of events, names and credentials of advisers, brief biographies of contributors, thorough volume bibliographies for more information on the topic, and a comprehensive subject index.

ACKNOWLEDGMENTS

James F. Tidd Jr., *Editorial associate.*

Philip B. Dematteis, *Production manager.*

Kathy Lawler Merlette, *Office manager.*

Ann M. Cheschi, Carol A. Cheschi, and Linda Dalton Mullinax, *Administrative support.*

Ann-Marie Holland, *Accounting.*

Sally R. Evans, *Copyediting supervisor.* Phyllis A. Avant, Brenda Carol Blanton, Caryl Brown, Melissa D. Hinton, Philip I. Jones, Rebecca Mayo, Nancy E. Smith, and Elizabeth Jo Ann Sumner, *Copyediting staff.*

Zoe R. Cook, *Series team leader layout and graphics.* Janet E. Hill, *Layout and graphics supervisor.* Sydney E. Hammock, *Graphics and prepress.*

Scott Nemzek and Paul Talbot, *Photography editors.*

Amber L. Coker, *Permissions editor and Database manager.*

Joseph M. Bruccoli and Zoe R. Cook, *Digital photographic copy work.*

Marie L. Parker, *Systems manager.*

Kathleen M. Flanagan, *Typesetting supervisor.* Patricia Marie Flanagan, Mark J. McEwan, and Pamela D. Norton, *Typesetting staff.*

Walter W. Ross, *Library researcher.* Tucker Taylor, *Circulation department head, Thomas Cooper Library, University of South Carolina.* John Brunswick, *Interlibrary-loan department head.* Virginia W. Weathers, *Reference department head.* Brette Barclay, Marilee Birchfield, Paul Cammarata, Gary Geer, Michael Macan, Tom Marcil, and Sharon Verba, *Reference librarians.*

PREFACE

On 27 November 1095 Pope Urban II concluded a Church council at Clermont with an appeal addressed to the French warrior class. Urban proposed a new form of holy war, one initiated by Christ and pronounced by the papacy, which combined the penitential act of pilgrimage to Jerusalem with the sharply honed martial skills of the European aristocracy. The knights were to become pilgrims who would fight their way toward and liberate the site of their devotion: the holy city of Jerusalem, which had been under Islamic control for the past five centuries. Because of the rigors and dangers associated with this armed pilgrimage, God would view it as a satisfactory penance for past sins. The result was the First Crusade (1096–1102) and the beginning of a movement that thundered across three continents for more than seven centuries.

The First Crusade emerged amid a landscape that was saturated by both endemic violence and extreme religious piety. The difficulties that the Carolingians had in maintaining political order hit critical mass in the last decades of the tenth century. Buckling beneath the weight of foreign invasions, the last Carolingians in western Francia (present-day France) became more dependent on the castellan class (lesser nobility) and its mounted retainers to maintain order. Castellans, becoming increasingly independent and competitive concerning land and power, jockeyed ever more aggressively for local dominance. In 987 the warrior aristocracy circumvented the claims of the last Carolin-gian and dubiously "elected" Hugh Capet as their king. Central authority continued to erode at an alarming rate. Localization and fragmentation of power intensified, and the slide into anarchy became ever more steep. With the early Capetians unable to exert much control beyond their own estates clustered around Paris, that bloody free-for-all known as the "castellan revolution" ensued, lasting until about 1030. As foreign invasions subsided at the turn of the millennium, the castellan class turned ferociously upon the people it once protected as well as against each other. Private wars and plunder expeditions proliferated, shredding beyond repair the fabric of the old order. Bulwarks of the now-defunct Carolingian order—dukes, counts, and bishops—retrenched and adapted to the conditions in order to survive. The violence of late-tenth- and early- eleventh-century Europe was nothing less than the birth pangs of "feudal" Europe and its fraternal twin—the First Crusade.

Powerful new expressions of religiosity punctuated the turn of the millennium as well. As noncombatants were increasingly subjected to violence, a mass movement known as the Peace of God emerged to protect the more vulnerable members of society. In large outdoor gatherings, the offenders, surrounded by ecclesiastical leaders, counts, the masses, and even several saints through the palpable presence of their relics, swore oaths to limit the violence. By prohibiting the plundering of churches, attacks on non-combatants, warfare on designated days, even cattle rustling, the Peace sought to restore some modicum of order to a ravaged landscape. Even the most brutal members of the castellan class—though they frequently came into conflict with ecclesiastical leaders over land—possessed a strong sense of religious piety that was nurtured, amplified, and eventually transformed by the Church reform of the eleventh century. Compelling testimony to the powerful hold that religion had on men of the age can be found in the fact that oaths on the relics of saints brought relative peace to such a war-torn environment. Castellans might not have had much respect for local bishops, but they certainly had a healthy fear of the power of saints. Eventually, the Peace of God evolved into the Truce of God, a movement that in turn tried to circumscribe the violence even further by virtually condemning the killing of fellow Christians altogether. Some historians have found seeds of the crusading movement in the Truce of God. If the killing of Christians was to receive such harsh condemnation, particularly in a society that had plunder writ large across its system for redistributing wealth, then external and non-Christian opponents would have to be found. In this sense the First Crusade can be usefully considered as an inverted projection of the Truce of God on to the "infidel." The Council of Clermont, from which Urban launched the First Crusade, had buttressing the Truce of God as an important part of its agenda.

This religious transformation of European society was not limited to the Peace and the Truce of God. Western Europe experienced a sort of "second coming" of Christianity in the eleventh century. Central to this invigorating spiritual rebirth were the transformation of monasticism and the diffusion of its ideals. Before the eleventh century, monks were seen, in a real sense, as the only perfect Christians. Most Christians saw themselves as strangers in a strange land, spiritual beings who were captive to all the temptations and degradations that filled the secular world. Being a "true" Christian entailed a retreat from this strange, brutal, secular world through a social rather than physical death. Sheltered in the cloister, monks could avoid the spiritual pitfalls of worldly existence and focus on the work of God. Living a rigorous life of poverty, chastity, and obedience, monks not only aimed to perfect themselves but also assisted, through their intercessory prayers, in the redemption of those unfortunates who lacked the spiritual fortitude to withdraw from the world. Monks thus played an instrumental role in the division of labor in European society. Fighting sin itself, both personal and communal, they were the original "soldiers of Christ." The great lay magnates who were the patrons of monasteries could find some solace in the fact that a spiritual elite was practicing religious perfection—being true Christians—for them.

Reformers of the eleventh century endeavored to narrow the gap between the ideals of monasticism and the realities of lay behavior. All men were now expected to shoulder more of the weight of their own sins by digesting and implementing modified monastic virtues. The "work of God" was no longer the sole responsibility of monks but a communal effort in which all contributed their specific talents to the best of their abilities. As the ideas of these monastic reformers flowed into the consciousness of the laity, people of all classes—including the castellans—became increasingly aware of and alarmed about their sinful nature. Higher standards of behavior were required, and more outlets for expiating personal sins were needed. Increasing pilgrimage traffic, both to European shrines and the Holy Land itself, was one response to this new spiritual climate. Another response, the armed pilgrimage that the modern world calls the First Crusade, was another. Thus, the rise of crusading can be seen as an alternative to monasticism for laymen who wished to live a more (but not completely perfect) Christian life.

While the eleventh-century reformers tried to narrow the gap between clerical and lay piety, they also aimed to sharpen the distinction between ecclesiastical and secular authority. The extensive use that secular rulers made of high ecclesiastical figures in their administrative apparatus all but blurred the line of demarcation between lay and religious office. Bishops not only had pastoral duties but also ranked high among the great political power brokers. Questions of true loyalties arose, and the answers were not to the liking of the reformers. The emblematic dispute of this confrontation was the Investiture Controversy, a clash over whether secular or ecclesiastical leaders should present bishops with the symbols of their office. Beneath the symbolism of "investiture" lurked the reality of who bestowed the offices themselves, which in turn was as clear an indicator as any of who commanded the allegiance of ecclesiastical magnates. Related to these problems was the growing tension between abbeys and their lay benefactors. When lay lords bequeathed lands to monasteries, they expected something in return—namely, intensive spiritual labor, through prayer and the work of God, for the salvation of their souls. Such benefactors tended to exert a great deal of control over these proprietary religious houses. Part of the reform program was based on liberation of the Church from lay pressures of all sorts. Testimony to the impact this conflict had on the rise of the First Crusade can be found in the fact that Urban II began his pontificate in exile promoting the "liberation" of the Church from imperial control and interference.

During the latter half of the eleventh century the Islamic world was fractured by external pressure, deep-seated divisions, and internal conflicts. In the tenth century the Byzantine Empire awakened from a long, fairly submissive slumber and began regaining lands it had lost during the period of early Islamic expansion two centuries earlier. Also during this century three rival caliphates arose. In 929 the Umayyad emir in Cordoba, descendent from a previous line of caliphs in the East, adopted the title *caliph*. In 968 the Shia Fatimids established a caliphate in Egypt, thereby challenging the Sunni Abbasids in Baghdad over the legitimate claim to the mantle of Muhammad, the "seal of the prophets." Shortly thereafter, much of the eastern Mediterranean, including Jerusalem, fell into the Fatimid orbit. Precarious as the situation was, it was further destabilized in the mid eleventh century by the arrival of the Ghuzz Turks and their most powerful clan—the Seljuks. These sturdy and austere nomadic steppe warriors, freshly converted to Islam and championing the Sunni cause, became energetic defenders of the Abbasids and launched a two-pronged attack against both Byzantines and Fatimids. In 1071 the great Seljuk sultan Alp Arslan soundly defeated the Byzantine emperor at Manzikert; when the dust settled, much of Asia Minor had been detached from the Empire. The Fatimids suffered great losses as well, including Syria and Jerusalem. Centrifugal force, however, soon ravaged Seljuk unity following the death of Alp Arslan's successor. Rocked by civil war over a disputed throne, the Byzantines were unable to capitalize on the opportunity. Emirs in the region became more independent. In 1081, ten years after the disaster at Manzikert, Alexius Comnenus became the ruler of a truncated empire that had an exhausted treasury, a predominantly mercenary army, and enemies on nearly every border.

Byzantine relations with the Latin West were characterized by both cooperation and conflict. Contacts between the two former halves of the Roman Empire, East and West, were never completely severed. Commercial traffic across the Mediterranean significantly grew during the eleventh century as the Italian mercantile states increasingly participated in the lucrative luxury-goods market with both Byzantines and Fatimids. Although the Byzantines occasionally reprimanded Venice for supplying Egypt with military contraband, relations between the two states were tight and grew tighter as the century progressed. In exchange for much-needed military assistance against the

Normans in Italy, the Byzantine Empire granted Venice generous trade concessions in the 1080s. Constantinople became addicted to bands of German, French, English, and Scandinavian mercenaries who defended (and in cases like the Normans, alternatively defended and attacked) imperial or former imperial lands in Asia Minor, Sicily, and southern Italy. Relations between the Latin and Greek churches had been poisoned since the schism of 1054 when Pope Leo IX and Michael Kerularios (the patriarch of Constantinople) hurled mutual excommunications across the Mediterranean at one another. Reconciliation between, and eventual reunion of, the estranged churches was an important goal of the reform papacy. Pope Gregory VII responded to the news of Manzikert with a proposal to assist the browbeaten Byzantines. Twice he called upon Latin Christian warriors to become "soldiers of Christ" or "soldiers of St. Peter," who would march to the East, under his personal leadership, to liberate fellow Christians from Turkish domination. Twice the response was unenthusiastic.

Given the empire's grave situation, Alexius was interested in some form of détente between Greek and Roman churches as a lubricant for military assistance. In March 1095 negotiations between Alexius and Urban culminated at the Council of Piacenza in northern Italy, where an imperial representative asked the Pope for Western assistance against the Islamic threat. Urban then toured French lands: in August he reached Le Puy, whose bishop Adhemar would become the papal legate of the First Crusade, and moved on to Tolouse, whose count Raymond of St. Gilles would become an important lay leader of the expedition. In October, Urban dedicated a new altar at the great abbey of Cluny, itself a ground zero of sorts for the reform movement, and then spent the bulk of November at Clermont, where he officially proclaimed the First Crusade. In addition to personally promoting the Crusade, Urban sent letters to several Italian city-states and urged bishops to recruit soldiers through preaching.

The eastern Mediterranean, however, was not the only theater in which the Christian-Islamic confrontation was taking place. In Spain, Christians and Muslims had been battling since the Islamic conquest of Spain began in 711. The Islamic invasion of Spain, launched from North Africa, quickly became a blitzkrieg. The Christian riposte was slow but gradually quickened in pace. Around the turn of the millennium the caliphate of Cordoba shattered into a plethora of small, weak, independent states. These *taifa* states paid tribute to the strengthening Christian powers until Alfonso VI (the Battler) conquered Toledo in 1085. The following year the Berber Almoravids came to assist

PREFACE

the *taifa* states against the Christian advance. To the dismay of the *taifa* kings the Almoravids began with conquering these "soft" Muslims themselves as a preliminary to making the peninsula safe for Islam. In the south, French warriors were entering Spain to assist in its "reconquest." Quite possibly, Raymond of St. Gilles, Count of Tolouse and one of the leaders of the First Crusade in the East, fought Muslims in Iberia around this time. And of course it should be remembered that the colorful career of Rodrigo Diaz, more commonly known today as "El Cid," was at its height during the years that the First Crusade was preached and launched. Urban, in fact, was concerned that the Crusade to the East might siphon off support for the Spanish campaign, and he urged Spaniards to remain in their own theater. Counts in Catalonia, for example, had taken vows to participate in the Crusade to the East; Urban responded by pointing out that Muslims were oppressing Christians in their own lands, and they had no need to journey to the other side of the world. Urban enthusiastically supported the reconquest in Spain, just as he supported the Norman conquest of Islamic Sicily.

Gregory VII's summons twenty years earlier received a response far too cool to make such an expedition a reality; Urban received a response so heated that it became almost impossible to control. News of the warrior pilgrimage swept across France and spilled into lands beyond, setting in motion the "international" composition that would henceforth characterize the movement. Kinship ties and solidarity played important roles in the exponential recruitment for the expedition—men quickly followed the examples of relatives who had taken the cross, and in many cases the expedition became a family affair: bands of brothers set out together, sons accompanied fathers, and even some wives went on the expedition. Families also made great financial sacrifices to support would-be Crusaders. In the midst of a terrible spell of agricultural troubles, men scrambled to mortgage land, and families pulled together to raise the necessary funds.

Modern historians break down the First Crusade into three main segments, or "waves." The first wave is often called "The Peasant Crusade," since the majority of its participants were noncombatants. Such a rubric, however, is of questionable value since members of the nobility as well as experienced knights were in leadership positions. Thus, the undisciplined conduct of and the particularly grisly atrocities committed by this wave cannot be explained away as the senseless acts of commoners and thugs who had no sound leadership. Still, the first wave rode upon a wave of unbridled and irrational mass enthusiasm. Flocking to the banner of a popular preacher known as Peter the Hermit, the first

wave of the Crusade set out early in the spring of 1096 with little planning or supplies. Several contingents under separate leaders began the long trek by land to Constantinople, where they would meet and cross into the Holy Land. Tragic is far too light a word for describing the course of the first wave; it left a trail of death and misery in its wake. The contingent led by Count Emich of Leiningen took to slaughtering Jews in the Rhineland—an event which has been called "The First Holocaust"—never even made it to Constantinople. After reaching the Hungarian border, rumors that the king of Hungary was prepared to confront them with a massive army caused the contingent to fall apart. Another army led by a man known as Folkmar—about whom scholars know virtually nothing—attacked the Jewish community of Prague before being dispersed by a Hungarian army. Likewise, an unruly army led by a man named Gottschalk was destroyed by Hungarian troops. Peter the Hermit, despite several confrontations with local Christian troops along the way, managed to get the bulk of his army to Constantinople. After receiving a taste of the unruly nature of Peter's troops, Emperor Alexius decided to ferry them across the Bosporus Sea and on to the Holy Land itself as soon as possible. Refusing to wait for the "second wave" of Crusaders, most of Peter's army was destroyed near Nicaea, the Seljuk sultan's capital. Although Peter himself was away negotiating with Alexius at the time and lived to continue playing an important role in the First Crusade, the Peasant Crusade had come to an end.

The second wave was led by some of the most powerful lords in Europe. Hugh of Vermandois, brother of the king of France, ranked among them. Raymond, a knight of advanced age and considerable wealth, led the largest contingent in conjunction with the papal legate Adhemar of Le Puy. Godfrey of Bouillon, the duke of lower Lorraine, set out with his brother Baldwin and later met up with another brother, Eustace, the count of Boulogne, in the East. The family of the recently deceased William the Conqueror was also well represented by his eldest son, Robert, Duke of Normandy, and his son-in-law Count Stephen of Blois. The Italian-Norman Bohemond of Taranto, eldest son of Robert Guiscard and veteran of fighting Muslims in southern Italy, set out for the East with his nephew Tancred. These various contingents planned to meet at Constantinople, find out exactly what role the emperor Alexius would play in the expedition, procure his support, and cross the Bosporus.

Alexius responded to the second wave of Crusaders with caution. His objective was to have the Crusaders recover as much land for the

Byzantines as possible. The Crusaders themselves could pose a threat, particularly the Italian Normans who had been periodically at war with the empire over Italian possessions in recent years. Alexius's strategy of isolating the Crusade leaders from one another and coercing them into taking oaths of fealty to him was not well received. Short on supplies and already weary from the months-long journey to Constantinople, the Latin leaders eventually relented, although for some it was under protest. In exchange for oaths of loyalty and swearing to restore any and all Byzantine lands retrieved from Muslims, the Crusade leaders received much-needed supplies and promises of military support. After being ferried across the Bosporus, the crusading contingents set out for the well-fortified city of Nicaea, the home of the sultan Kilij Arslan and the gateway to the Holy Land.

As luck would have it, the Crusaders arrived at Nicaea while the sultan was away from the city, battling a Muslim rival. Kilij Arslan returned to find his capital under siege. The sultan's forces attacked but failed to break the siege. It ended successfully but unpleasantly for the Crusader host. The Byzantines secretly negotiated surrender terms with the city and in the process deprived the Crusaders of the much-needed plunder that was necessary for financing the rest of the expedition. Plunder was one of the primary means for reprovisioning troops, and the cries of bad faith at Nicaea hit a chord that resonated throughout the remainder of the expedition and—it could be argued—for the crusading movement in its entirety. As the Crusaders continued on into Asia Minor, the sultan laid an ambush at the pass of Dorylaeum. The Crusaders, adapting quite well to Turkish military strategy, smashed the sultan's troops and put them to flight. A few subsequent skirmishes also went well for the Crusaders. With renewed confidence the Crusaders struck out for the next crucial target of the expedition, Antioch.

This confidence ultimately proved to be short-lived. The Crusaders' march through Anatolia to the city of Antioch will forever rank among the most grueling treks in history, comparable to the Native Americans' Trail of Tears, Napoleon's retreat from Russia, or Mao's Long March. The unforgiving terrain offered little in the line of supplies. The human casualties produced by starvation, disease, and exposure were staggering. Some knights, after food became extremely scarce, sustained themselves by drinking blood from incisions made on their horses. Just as problematic as the human toll (if not more so, logistically speaking) was the decimation of horses and pack ani-

mals. Many knights, whose status as well as combat tactics depended on horses, found themselves either walking or mounting surviving beasts of burden; dogs and sheep in turn were used to carry equipment. Such conditions prompted many Crusaders to reassess their decision, thus beginning the trickle of desertions that slowly bled the Crusader ranks. Baldwin of Boulogne, however, escaped these privations and in so doing established the first Crusader State in the East. His raiding of settlements in Armenia eventually led him to Edessa, where he was adopted by its ruler, Thoros. Prince Thoros was murdered by a mob shortly thereafter, and Baldwin rose to take his place, styling himself "count of Edessa."

The crusading host finally reached the city walls of Antioch in October 1097 and settled down for what would become an eight-month siege. The problem of provisions did not improve, and the Crusaders spent an incredible amount of time traveling to foraging sites, some of which were up to fifty miles away. In early June 1098 a conspiracy hatched by Bohemond paid substantial dividends. A traitor within the city lowered a ladder down to Bohemond and some of his men; the band quickly ran to the city gates and threw them open. The Crusaders slaughtered hundred of Turks on sight and, if a chronicler who was present is to be believed, the only way to walk through the city streets was to constantly step over scores of corpses.

Days after Antioch was taken, the Crusaders found themselves besieged by relief forces sent by the governor of Mosul. Starvation once again struck the Crusaders as Turkish forces cut off supply routes to the city. Some men were reduced to eating bark. Disease rose and desertion exploded. With morale hitting rock bottom, it seemed as though the pilgrimage-expedition was coming to a bitter end. Crusader spirits, however, were renewed after St. Andrew visited one of the Crusaders through a series of visions and directed him to the resting site of one of the greatest relics—the lance that pierced the side of Christ. Rumors spread that saints and the ghosts of fallen Crusaders would form a spiritual auxiliary that would help defeat the enemy in battle. Liturgical preparations were made to spiritually fortify the warriors for a massive strike against the Turkish besiegers. That the weakened and starving Crusaders succeeded in defeating the better-supplied Turkish forces seemed to reinforce the validity of the expedition's war cry—"God wills this."

Leadership problems would prove to be a perennial issue for the entire crusading movement; they first came to the fore with full force at Antioch. Crusader contingents were not nearly as rigid, regimented, or organized as modern armies are.

There was no official commander in chief who held ultimate authority or, for that matter, the loyalty of all the participants. Crusader armies were composed of several lords who commanded the loyalty of their own retainers while forming loose associations with other lords. Given this situation, it was just as easy for contingents to compete with one another as it was to cooperate. Generally speaking, the great lords on the expedition were of equal power and unable to dominate one another or assume control. Complicating this situation even further were the throngs of men without lords, frequently but not always of the lower classes, who were "freelance" Crusaders drifting from one patron to the next or, in exceptional circumstances, banding together with others of their kind to promote and protect their own interests. Much of the decision making in the First Crusade was done "town-meeting" style; Adhemar of Le Puy, the papal legate, apparently commanded enough respect to maintain stability. When he died during one of the many epidemics that swept through the Crusader ranks at Antioch, order completely broke down. Other clergymen were unable to fill the leadership vacuum left by Adhemar's death. The great lords quarreled ferociously over possessions and what the next course of action should be. The Crusade bogged down for six months until the poorer participants, outraged by the leaders' inability to act and terrified by the specter of starvation, mobilized themselves and forced the leaders to move on.

In the early months of 1099 the Crusaders began their long march toward Jerusalem. They reached the Holy City itself on 7 June. Although the ranks were rife with disagreements and disputes, the leaders cooperated enough to lay siege to the city. Italian and English ships that landed at the port of Jaffa provided desperately needed materials, and the Crusaders began building siege engines. In early July the Crusaders busied themselves with liturgy: barefoot penitential processions around the city walls and sermons to large audiences at accessible holy sites. Jerusalem's defenses were breached on 15 July, and the wholesale butchering of the Muslim inhabitants by the Crusaders that followed has become legendary. After liberating the city, the majority of the Crusaders fulfilled their vow by visiting the Holy Sepulchre, helping fend off an Egyptian force dispatched to Jerusalem, and then returning home.

The Latin states that the First Crusade left in the eastern Mediterranean have been referred to by some historians as the first genuine European "colonies." Whether colonies or not, the Crusaders established a network of semi-autonomous states along the coast and its hinterland. In the north,

between the Tigris and Euphrates Rivers, was the County of Edessa; its native population was mostly composed of Armenian Christians who saw the Crusaders as natural allies against the dreaded Turks. The Principality of Antioch was also established over a population that was mostly Eastern Christian. The County of Tripoli, established by Raymond of Toulouse, ruled over a population that was mostly Muslim with a sprinkling of Eastern Christians. In the south was the Kingdom of Jerusalem, whose first elected king was Godfrey of Bouillon. The organization was decidedly feudal: the counts of Edessa and Tripoli were vassals of the king of Jerusalem (Antioch was an anomaly as it was held as a fief from the Byzantine emperor), and all the smaller lordships were bound by Jerusalem's high court and owed military service to defend the realm.

Latin settlement was fairly sparse. Efforts were made to attract settlers from western Europe with some degree of success in the early to mid twelfth century. Attractive terms brought some enterprising men who established "new towns" that they cultivated and defended. Yet, these modest migrations did little to alter the demographics of the regions, and Latin Christians remained the vast minority. The Latin failure to colonize the land in earnest resulted in a feudal system that looked much different than the Western model; Latins tended to inhabit the coastal cities and towns, while Muslims and Eastern Christians worked the land in the interior—much as they had under Islamic rule. Trade, however, bustled and made commerce an extremely important part of the economic foundation of the states.

The traditional periodization and numbering of the Crusades is arbitrary and imprecise. Although what has become known as the Second Crusade did not really begin until 1147, there was much crusading activity between the end of the First Crusade and Zengi's capture of Edessa in 1144. Tardy Crusaders, and many who deserted the host and were subsequently driven back by shame or threats of excommunication, constituted the so-called "Crusade of 1101." The expedition was ill-fated: poor strategic decisions, combined with a renewed Turkish unity following the success of the First Crusade, proved to be a recipe for disaster. In 1106 Bohemond toured France in an attempt to drum up support for a Crusade that would strengthen the Principality of Antioch. Significantly, Bohemond envisioned this Crusade as one against both Muslims and Byzantines, each posing a separate threat to Antioch. The legate of Pope Paschal officially proclaimed a Crusade. This Crusade also proved ill-fated; after being defeated by the Byzantine military, Bohemond returned to southern Italy, where he spent the remainder of his days.

The "Crusade of Pope Calixtus II" was prompted by a military disaster for the Principality of Antioch. Rather than waiting for reinforcements from the other Latin states, Antioch sent out its entire military force to repel a Turkish attack in 1119. Antioch's army was smashed at the "Field of Blood," leaving the principality dangerously exposed. The king of Jerusalem quickly sent out pleas for assistance to both the Pope and Venice. Calixtus responded by organizing a Crusade broad in scope, but his efforts were ultimately hampered by the situation in Spain. Christendom was engaged in a two-front war against Islam, and the pressing need for Christian soldiers in both theaters strained resources. Yet, the Venetian response yielded important results. After defeating an Egyptian fleet off the coast of Ascalon, the Venetians played a major role in the conquest of the important coastal city of Tyre. As a reward for its services, Venice received effective control over one-third of the city.

In addition to these campaigns, which clearly bear the marks of a Crusade, many smaller expeditions took place that might have been Crusades. During this early stage of the movement it is often quite difficult to distinguish "Crusade" from "pilgrimage," since the terms were interchangeable. Regardless of whether these smaller pilgrimages were Crusades, clearly, many of their participants were armed and helped defend the kingdom of Jerusalem while visiting its shrines.

Another important development during this period was the rise of the military orders. Probably the greatest innovation of the Latin East was monastic orders that took up the cause of defending Christians by fighting the infidel. The Templars were the first group of this kind. Originating in 1118, the Templars began as a small association of knights dedicated to policing the dangerous pilgrimage routes in the Holy Land. Soon they received the support of the most influential figure in Christendom, Bernard of Clairvaux, who penned a monastic rule for the group and successfully lobbied for their formal recognition as a monastic order, albeit a rather idiosyncratic one in that its "work of God" focused on armed resistance of evil. The Hospital of St. John, an already existing order dedicated to the care of the sick and poor, quickly followed suit by developing a militarized wing. Since the plight of the Holy Land captured the European imagination, the newly formed military orders were flooded with pious donations that fueled their rapid growth. Over time, the power of these orders reached such an extent that they formed the backbone of the Crusader States' defense. As other crusading theaters were established, the military orders spread and multiplied.

On Christmas Eve 1144, Imad al-Din Zengi, the Turkish *atabeg* (governor) of Mosul, captured Edessa. Shock waves rippled throughout the Latin Christian world. Not since the Field of Blood had such a disaster visited the Holy Land. The Field of Blood, moreover, had only placed one Crusader State in a vulnerable position; Zengi's victory signaled the actual fall of a Crusader State and impending danger to the bordering states.

The Second Crusade (1147–1149) got off to a much slower start and initially did not prompt anything close to the enthusiastic reception that marked the First Crusade. On 1 December 1145 the newly elected Pope Eugenius III issued a Crusade encyclical, *Quantum praedecessores,* which gave the most precise explanation of Crusader status and benefits yet and served as the model for subsequent Crusade encyclicals. Shortly thereafter, the king of France, Louis VII, announced his intention to make the journey. His decision met with a cool response from his men. Bernard of Clairvaux, who had already made a great contribution to the history of the Crusades by lobbying for the Templars, took up the preaching mantle. The results were prodigious. When Louis finally took the cross on Easter 1146, the crusading host was so large that Bernard had to shred his own clothes to distribute enough crosses. After concluding his preaching tour in France, Bernard moved into German lands, where he secured the participation of King Conrad III. Once again, news of a Crusade prompted anti-Semitic sentiment, so much so that Bernard had to spend a considerable amount of time and energy quashing it. In addition to introducing the concept of royal leadership into the movement, the Second Crusade was also notable for the magnitude of its undertaking by opening up three crusading fronts simultaneously. The continuing war against the Moors in Spain was now fully equated with crusading in the East, and the battle against the pagan Wends in eastern Germany was transformed into a new crusading theater. Both of these new fronts were mentioned in Eugenius's encyclical *Divina dispensatione.* Italian-Normans, although not officially Crusaders, were battling Muslims in North Africa.

The Crusade to the East was plagued with problems from beginning to end. Near Dorylaeum, the site of a grand Christian victory during the First Crusade, Conrad's army was smashed by the Turks in 1147. The survivors banded together with the French contingents.

The Crusader host was then afflicted by the many ills that characterized the First Crusade: the climate was terrible, the lack of supplies debilitating, and Byzantine support minimal. A fatal logistical oversight moreover proved disastrous: a Byzantine fleet charged with transporting the Crusaders was much smaller than needed. Louis was forced to leave a substantial portion of his army at the docks and, faced with no other means of transportation, these Crusaders had to take the dangerous land route. Most of them died en route, and this development in turn fanned the flames of the already present Crusader suspicions concerning the Byzantines. After reaching Antioch, Louis decided to proceed directly to Jerusalem rather than try to recapture Edessa. Louis and Conrad, taking counsel with the king of Jerusalem, Baldwin III, decided to strike Damascus with their combined resources. The campaign was a disaster. The Crusaders, to avoid the danger of archers and to attack what seemed to be a less fortified section of the city walls, exchanged a cluster of orchards for a site with neither food nor water. Conflict broke out among the ranks concerning who would control Damascus once conquered; this situation, combined with rumors of an Islamic relief force on the way, dealt a serious blow to morale. After breaking the siege and retreating, accusations were hurled back and forth about treachery and bribery.

Over the next three decades several crusading encyclicals were published by the papacy as conditions in the Latin East continued to erode. Responses were marginal, resulting in only small expeditions and some financial relief for the beleaguered Latin settlements. Although the Crusader States made some ambitious bids to extend the borders in the south, including a few invasions of Egypt, they were primarily on the defensive during the aftermath of the Second Crusade. The great lords of the Crusader States were primarily located along the coast, which the Latins dominated, and castles were used as strong-point defenses protecting resources in the interior. Continuing divisions between the Sunni Turks to the north and the Shi'i Fatimids in the south was the saving grace for the Latin states. When this division finally came to an end through the unification of Syria and Egypt, the normal "low-intensity" conflicts that characterized relations between the Latins and their Muslim neighbors gave way to catastrophe for the Crusader settlement and the near obliteration of its military forces.

The word *jihad* had and still has a multiplicity of meanings. Literally, the word means "to struggle," and it can be applied in spiritual, ethical, or military fashions. It is the last of these meanings that concerns the history of the Crusades, and its impact on the movement was substantial from the mid eleventh to the early fourteenth centuries. By and large, the concept of armed struggle against the infidel had gone into a long slumber in the eastern Mediterranean following the early age of Islamic expansion (though it never quite became comatose). Its vigorous reawakening during the twelfth century had much to do with the Seljuk Turks. Although local Muslim religious leaders might have been preaching the armed form of jihad shortly after the Crusader arrival, it was Zengi who first implemented it against the Franks. The result was a genuine turning point in the Islamic-Christian conflict and the fall of the first Crusader State. Zengi's son and successor, Nur al-Din, prosecuted the jihad against the Franks both more aggressively and more systematically. The Crusader States, however, were not alone in feeling the effects of Nur al-Din's jihad. By claiming that he alone was capable of expelling the Franks, and that other Muslim leaders impeded rather than promoted reconquest of the region, Nur al-Din used the jihad to justify aggressive action against Muslim rivals. The most spectacular of these successes was the conquest of Fatimid Egypt in 1169. Dynasty building and the jihad against the Latin states thus became entwined.

Saladin inherited the Zengid dynasty's jihad tradition and put it to similar use against both Frankish and Muslim opponents. Using Egypt as his base, he systematically began eliminating his Zengid rivals to the north, effectively unifying Islamic Syria and Egypt. In many respects Saladin was a diplomat without peer in the latter half of the twelfth century; by shrewdly using truces and treaties in a strategic manner, he managed to make great gains in a short time. Reynald of Chatillon, lord of Transjordan, who was pursuing his own foreign policies, presented Saladin with the casus belli for breaking his truce. Reynald consistently raided Islamic merchant and pilgrimage caravans, launched galleys into the Red Sea, which wreaked havoc with Islamic transports and apparently flirted with taking the war to the heart of the Islamic world itself—Mecca. Saladin swore that he would kill Reynald with his own hands, a vow he made good in the summer of 1187, after much of the Crusader States had fallen to him.

Saladin's large army crossed into Galilee on 30 June 1187 and immediately began laying siege to Tiberias. The Crusader State muster produced approximately twenty thousand men—the largest Latin army ever put into the field—but was still vastly outnumbered by Saladin's massive force of about thirty thousand men. For the Crusaders the question at hand was whether or not to relieve Tiberias immediately. Heated and acrimonious debate broke out; in the end the decision was made to march to Tiberias. The Crusader columns were attacked incessantly by Muslim archers on the flanks; the Templars, who formed the rear guard, were steadily fighting off the skirmishers who were harassing them. Lack of water access, however, doomed the Latin army. It caused panic, and panic led to hasty and ill-conceived acts: thirst and heat exhaustion led to a virtual separation of cavalry and infantry, as well as desperate cavalry charges against superior forces. The campaign ended in disaster for the Crusaders. On 4 July 1187 at the Horns of Hattin the entire Latin army was smashed beyond repair in the most devastating military defeat of the entire Crusade movement. When the dust settled, there no longer was a Latin army. Even the garrisons of fortified sites throughout the Holy Land were now light since their complements had been skimmed to muster the main army.

Saladin then moved quickly to capitalize on his stunning victory. After sweeping through Galilee he focused on important coastal sites and scored more victories—most noteworthy being the conquests of Acre and Ascalon, both of which were extremely important coastal cities. Jerusalem itself fell to Saladin in early October. By 1189 Saladin had control over much of the Holy Land and had seized approximately fifty fortified sites. Significantly, though, he had left some of the strongest and most strategic sites in Crusader hands, most importantly Tyre, Antioch, and Tripoli. These sites would become the beachheads for western Europe's riposte—the Third Crusade (1189–1192).

Pope Gregory VIII responded to Saladin's near complete conquest of the Holy Land with the crusading encyclical, *Audita tremendi,* which initiated the Third Crusade. The reception of this encyclical, unlike those which had met recent papal pleas to support the Latins in the East, was tremendous: the capture of Jerusalem, the loss of the True Cross, and the impending loss of the entire Holy Land generated waves of pious outrage and pledges of support. Although there was royal participation in the Second Crusade, this expedition has been dubbed the "Crusade of Kings" because of the number of rulers who took the cross. Quickest to act was the king of Sicily, William II, who sent a fleet to the eastern Mediterranean, which successfully shored up the remaining strategic sites in the Crusader States—Tyre, Tripoli, and Antioch. Sporadic fleets from various states in Europe set sail to the Holy Land as quickly as they could. Emperor Frederick I (Barbarossa), who as a younger man had participated in the Second Crusade, took the cross. At the advanced age of seventy, Frederick mustered what might well have been the largest crusading contingent to date and began marching to the Holy Land in May 1189. In England, King Henry II and his eldest son, Richard I, the Lion-Hearted, had taken Crusader vows but were currently embroiled in a civil war with one another, a conflict that was further complicated by the participation of the young king of France, Philip Augustus. When Henry died, Richard succeeded to the throne and made preparations for the Crusade. The conflict, however, resulted in the tardy appearance of the French and English kings in the Holy Land.

The barons of the Crusader States focused on Acre as the first target to be recovered. The siege of Acre began in the summer of 1188, and several Crusader contingents from Europe joined in the fray as they arrived. Frederick Barbarossa's large contingent, after heated conflict with the Byzantine emperor, crossed Asia Minor. But when Frederick himself drowned while fording a river in June 1190, his host essentially disintegrated. After finally mobilizing for the Crusade, the kings of England and France wintered in Sicily; in March, Philip sailed for Acre to take part in the siege, while Richard first went to Cyprus. After Acre fell in July 1191, Philip returned to France while Richard prepared for his long march southward down the coast. Enforcing strict discipline in the ranks, despite the constant attacks and harassment dished out by Muslim forces, Richard recovered a good deal of the coastline. His strategic mind was possibly at its best when he resisted the lure of Jerusalem, a city high in spiritual and symbolic value but of little strategic utility. After capturing the important port city of Jaffa and fending off Saladin's rapid bid to reclaim it, Richard visited Ascalon and rebuilt the city's fortifications. Concerned about the fate of his throne, given the intrigues of his brother John and Philip Augustus, Richard made a hasty truce with Saladin before beginning his journey home in the autumn of 1192. As a postscript to the Third Crusade (though an important one), the new German emperor, Henry VI, began preparing a Crusade, possibly as an attempt to redeem the vow of his father Frederick I, who died en route. Henry himself died before the departure date, but the "Crusade of 1197" went on as planned, with the Crusaders managing to capture Beirut and part of Sidon. The new century began with the most important coastal sites in Christian hands.

In the summer of 1198 Innocent III issued a Crusade encyclical that resulted in the

Fourth Crusade (1202–1204). That Innocent's appeal was made directly to the warrior aristocracy rather than monarchs (though the latter's participation was certainly welcome) may indicate that he was trying to tighten papal control over the movement. If so, then the Fourth Crusade came as a bitter disappointment to the young pontiff: rather than giving the badly damaged Crusader States a reprieve by striking Egypt, it veered off course and captured the Byzantine Empire.

The Fourth Crusade was a logistical nightmare from the start. The expedition's main leader, Thibald of Champagne, spent much of his time quarreling with other leaders over organizational issues before his untimely death caused yet more confusion. He was replaced by Boniface, Marquis of Montferrat, a man with an amazing network of political connections. The land route was eventually deemed impractical, and the decision was made to commission the Venetians to build a fleet to transport the Crusaders. A committee of six men was sent to Venice to negotiate terms. The Crusade leaders essentially gave this committee a blank check by preapproving whatever deal the six men struck with Venice. Negotiations closed in the spring of 1201. When the Crusader host finally arrived in October 1202, it was only one-third of its projected size, resulting in too many ships and not enough cash to pay for them. Piety was, more often than not, subordinated to good business sense in Venice. The Crusade was going nowhere until the fleet was paid for. Previous Crusades frequently ran out of cash at one point or another. The Fourth Crusade, however, had the singular distinction of running out of cash before it even began.

The Venetian doge, Enrico Dandalo, made the Crusaders a new offer. In exchange for military support against Zara, an important port city on the Dalmatian coast, the Venetians would not only transport the Crusaders to the East but become partners in the expedition as well. Belated payment for the balance on the fleet, plus a fair share in the financial gains of the Crusade, would be adequate compensation. Left with little other choice for launching the campaign, the Crusader leadership agreed to the Venetians' terms. Zara, however, was under the protection of the king of Hungary, who had taken the cross himself, and many of its inhabitants were Crusaders as well. To better grease the gears of this new partnership, the Venetians sent the papal legate back to Rome. Many men who had taken the cross, disgusted with the direction the Crusade was taking, began deserting. The fleet set sail and arrived at Zara in November 1202. Before the siege began, the Crusaders received the Pope's response to the recent chain of events. Innocent

forbade the Crusaders to attack Zara. Consequently, many Crusaders refused to take part in the attack on the city. The remaining Crusaders and the Venetians laid siege to Zara and divided the plunder. Innocent responded by excommunicating them.

While the Crusaders wintered in Zara, the expedition took yet another turn. Earlier, the Byzantine emperor Isaac Angelus had his eyes put out and was deposed by his brother Alexius III. Isaac's son, Alexius IV, fled to the West in search of assistance in regaining the throne from his uncle. The Crusaders in Zara seemed to be just the sort of assistance Alexius needed. In exchange for helping him, Alexius pledged a large sum of cash, reunion between the Roman and Greek churches, and a large contingent of soldiers to assist in the Crusade. Once again dissension emerged in the Crusader ranks. Most of the Crusade leaders and the Venetians approved of the plan; those who did not broke with the host and set off for the Holy Land on their own. The Crusaders arrived at Constantinople early in the summer of 1203. Though attempts to take the city failed, Alexius III lost his nerve and fled on 17 July. The blind emperor, Isaac, was restored to the throne, and his son was made coemperor. Although the coemperors tried to make good on the promises made to the Crusaders, the animosity that the clergy and inhabitants of Constantinople had for the Latins produced a groundswell of violent protests. This outrage culminated with a palace coup d'etat that removed the emperors from power. The new emperor, Alexius V, was no friend of the Latins, and the position of the Crusaders became even more precarious. After meeting in council, the Crusade leaders decided to take Constantinople. Their effort proved successful and resulted in a series of feudal states owing obligations to the newly elected "Latin emperor." Greek exiles transferred their "empire" to Nicaea where it remained for the next five decades. The Fourth Crusade did nothing to aid the ailing but still extant Crusader States. But without slaying a single Muslim soldier, it created an entire chain of new ones. When it became clear that the Fourth Crusade was not going to reach the Holy Land itself, the king of Jerusalem made a six-year truce with al-Adil.

Of all the crusading Popes, to Innocent III a place of particular distinction must be accorded. His commitment to crusading was relentless, his energy in promoting it prodigious, and his creativity in adapting it remarkable. His pontificate began during the "Crusade of 1197," and there was not one year during his eighteen-year reign that a Crusader army was not in the field. Under Innocent, the

Crusader theaters of operation expanded significantly: in addition to continuing expeditions against Muslims in Spain and in the East, Innocent launched Crusades against secular enemies of the papacy in Italy, pagans in the Baltic, and heretics in southern France.

In addition to being a tireless promoter of the Crusade, Innocent III was also the Pope who extended the doctrine of papal supremacy to its grandest extent. As a corollary to this situation, he also tried to tighten his grip, both theoretically and physically, on central Italy as the patrimony of St. Peter and as land subject to papal control in the temporal as well as spiritual sense. Innocent III was thus one of the greatest architects of the "papal monarchy." Papal interest in southern Italy and Sicily was also intense, and recently it had become joined to the German Empire. When the emperor Henry VI died in 1197, he left behind his infant son, Frederick II, as heir, granting the papacy not only a political reprieve but a wonderful opportunity as well. Innocent was regent for Frederick, but a powerful imperial representative, Markward of Anweiler, claimed to be the legitimate regent for the infant king and Sicily. Markward soon invaded Sicily to press his claim as regent, and the pontiff responded with vigor. In 1199 Innocent became the first (but certainly not the last) Pope to proclaim a fully formed Crusade against a Christian opponent of the papacy. Probably sensing the controversial implications of his innovation, Innocent made every effort to mingle the Crusade against Markward with the upcoming crusade to the East: Markward was viewed as another Saladin, an evil man who conspired with Muslims against Christians. Neutralizing him was a prerequisite for succeeding in the Holy Land. That this Crusade did not amount to much (Markward died suddenly) should not diminish its importance. Innocent's innovation established a precedent that was to have a varied and checkered impact on the movement for the rest of the century.

In the Baltic, Innocent followed the tracks laid down by Celestine III. Celestine granted Crusade indulgences in the 1190s to men willing to defend the fledgling Catholic mission in Livonia. Innocent, however, completely transformed the nature of the effort. In 1202 a new military order, the Livonian Sword-Brothers, was founded and charged with protecting missionaries and battling violent pagans. In 1204 Innocent laid the foundations for the "perpetual Crusade," which ultimately created much of Christian Eastern Europe. Men who had taken the Crusader vow but could not make the journey to the East for financial or health reasons could commute their pledge and fight on the Livonian front while still receiving the indul-

gence in full, just as if they had made the journey to the Holy Land. The Livonian frontier also became the site of annual "summer Crusades" that proved quite successful. Within a few decades the whole of Livonia (present-day Latvia) was secured. Subsequent Popes replicated Innocent's strategy throughout the Baltic. The culmination of this approach, combining military orders with seasonal Crusades, can be seen in Prussia. The Teutonic Knights created their own state, held as a fief from the papacy, which served as a base of operations for waging a "perpetual Crusade" throughout the region.

In January 1208 the assassination of Peter of Castelnau, a papal legate in southwestern France, prompted Innocent to turn the machinery of the Crusade on the Cathars, Christian heretics who had permeated every level of society in the region over the past century. The assassin was a vassal of the count of Tolouse, Raymond VI, who had already been excommunicated himself for his lax approach to the heresy running rampant through his domain. Raymond, alarmed at the enthusiastic response to Innocent's call for a Crusade against Tolouse and the sizable army that was gathering in Lyon, had himself flogged in a local abbey as a sign of penance; he then promised to be more diligent about dealing with heresy in his lands and pleaded for mercy. So the Crusaders struck at the viscount of Beziers and Carcassonne, whose lands had a high density of Cathars. Beziers fell to the Crusaders in July 1209; 15,000 townspeople were massacred, an event that probably played no small role in the quick capitulation of Carcassonne the following month.

The entire region was then subjected to seasonal crusading much as that taking place in the Baltic. Every summer a Crusader host appeared and campaigned; during the "off-season" Simon of Montfort, veteran of the Fourth Crusade (but one who obeyed papal orders) was charged with protecting the gains. In 1211 Simon invaded Tolouse, citing the fact that Raymond had not made good on his promises. Keeping control over gains made during these short, sporadic Crusades in Tolouse was a daunting task; strategic sites loyal to Raymond capitulated during the summer campaigning season only to renege and rejoin the count when the Crusade ended. This game of cat and mouse continued until the summer of 1213, when the king of Aragon, Peter II, marched to assist his brother-in-law Raymond and, no doubt, to look after Aragonese interests north of the Pyrenees. Simon, however, defeated the Aragonese army, and King Peter himself was killed. When Innocent ended the granting of indulgences for crusading against the Cathars (he did not want it competing with the new Crusade to the East he was planning), it sapped much of the virility out of the effort. In the end, it was not really crusading that finally stamped out the heresy but the arrival of the Inquisition.

Just as important as Innocent's expansion of crusading, and his application of it to new purposes, were the modifications he made to its apparatus. Although he drew upon the latent ideas of previous authors, Innocent was the true father of the plenary indulgence, which became the crowning jewel of Crusader rewards. Crusading was no longer seen as a satisfactory penitential act; it was now the divine guarantee of an all-loving God to completely obliterate penalties for sins committed by humans who, however weak they may be, had enough spiritual strength and devotion to perform such an act. The spiritual pot, so to speak, was significantly sweetened for would-be Crusaders. In his *Ad liberandum,* Innocent clarified and codified the traditional privileges Crusaders received, giving a good deal more precision to the boons that helped motivate Crusaders or made their journeys a bit easier. His greatest contributions might well have been in developing new means for financing Crusades. In the past, Crusaders were obligated to finance themselves completely unless they received the largesse of a greater lord to help defray the cost. Crusading, however, had become increasingly expensive, and this situation was complicating recruitment. Innocent devised two solutions to the problem that had tremendous impact on the further development of the movement. First, by instituting a tax upon the clergy, Innocent hoped to generate enough cash to subsidize Crusaders. Second, Innocent proffered vow redemption as another means for financing crusading activity. Able-bodied warriors were no longer the only Christians who could take the cross; the aged, the sick, and women could take the vow, "redeem" it through a cash payment, and receive the indulgence.

Recruitment through preaching also underwent substantive change during Innocent's pontificate. Much of this change was certainly because of the new types of "recruits" who were being targeted for enlistment. Crusade sermons were no longer just focusing on able-bodied, self-financed warriors. The diffusion of the indulgence to noncombatants, who could participate in the Crusade through donations without ever leaving Europe, much less fighting Muslims, transformed the Crusade sermon into a sort of political fund-raiser cum religious revival meeting. Some Crusade preachers tailored their sermons to the nature of a particular audience; those who would fight through force of arms and those who would fight through financial contributions. Innocent also conducted a complete organizational overhaul of Crusade preaching. From the time of Urban II to the eve of Innocent's election, Crusade preaching was conducted through the "great man" approach: a powerful, charismatic figure such as Urban or Bernard of Clairvaux would launch a preaching tour, stop at heavily populated areas to deliver sermons, and win recruits. Innocent bypassed the "great man" approach and adopted a more systematic method for recruitment. Crusade preaching under Innocent was conducted at the local level, a strategy that allowed recruitment sermons to reach more people in a more organized and methodical way. Such an approach also bypassed linguistic and jurisdictional problems. Innocent also solicited the support of Parisian masters for developing better sermons; the result was the creation of the *Brevis ordinacio de praedicacione crucis,* a work that provided Crusade preachers with theological justifications and practical advice for winning recruits.

Nearly every part of crusading went through some sort of alteration, for better or for worse, under Innocent III. It would not be wrong to state that he, more so than any other Pope, transformed crusading from a tradition into an institution. In 1213 he announced his intention to launch another Crusade to the East. This expedition was to be the great test of the new crusading machinery that he so painstakingly constructed over the years. Although he played a tremendous, omnipresent, and tireless role in the preparation of the new Crusade, the aging pontiff died before its departure.

In many respects the course of the Fifth Crusade (1217–1229) was even more bizarre than that of the Fourth. After stunning victories against important strategic sites in Egypt, which were quickly negated by even more stunning reverses, the holy city of Jerusalem was finally recovered by the excommunicated crusading emperor Frederick II through a peace treaty with the Egyptian sultan. The patriarch of Jerusalem responded by placing the holy city itself under interdict.

The first contingents of Crusaders, led by King Andrew of Hungary and Leopold, Duke of Austria, retained the services of the Venetians for transport and planned to depart in August 1217. The logistical nightmare this time was the mirror image of that which hampered the Fourth Crusade; rather than having too many ships for too few Crusaders with too little money, the fleet was not large enough to accommodate the assembled host. Familiar problems greeted the Crusaders when they finally reached Acre. Chief among these was the perennial crisis regarding supplies. A bad annual harvest made it impossible for the Crusader host to be provided with enough food; so perilous was the situation that many Crusaders were being advised to return to Europe. The dreary prospect of hunger and living off the land once again became a harsh reality. Another problem that faced the Crusaders was the tidal nature that characterized the expeditions themselves. Simply put, all those who had taken the cross were never at the same place at the same time; Crusader armies were in a constant state of flux as some contingents set out for home while others were in the process of arriving. Deliberations about what should be done while waiting to be reinforced by incoming contingents was a familiar feature of crusading activity. Yet, from beginning to end, this problem hit the Fifth Crusade with particular force.

The Crusaders spent the winter of 1217–1218 conducting sorties against Islamic forces to keep themselves supplied while harassing the enemy and awaiting reinforcements. Soon the Crusaders focused their efforts on Mt. Tabor—the site of a well-supplied strategic fortress that was specifically mentioned as an essential target in Innocent's crusading bull. Boasting seventy-seven towers and a massive garrison, Mount Tabor regulated access to important roads and posed a substantive threat to the city of Acre itself. Concerned that the attack on Mount Tabor would result in a costly siege that would make a later assault on Egypt impossible, King John of Jerusalem ordered a retreat after a few unsuccessful attempts to take the fortress. King Andrew, despite threats of excommunication, set out for home in January 1218 with many of his troops and the skull of St. Stephen. Many of the remaining Crusaders then busied themselves with the important task of strengthening the fortifications of important coastal cities.

Reinforcements from Germany, the Low Countries, and Italy began arriving at Acre in April 1218, along with a sizable fleet. Leaders of the newly arrived Crusader contingents met in war council with the king and patriarch of Jerusalem, Duke Leopold, and the masters of the military orders. The decision was made to strike at Damietta—"the key to all Egypt." A month later the Crusaders arrived at Damietta and settled down for what turned out to be an eighteen-month siege. Three months into the siege, the Crusaders succeeded in striking a potentially devastating blow to the city's defenses, one of such strategic importance that the sultan al-Adil supposedly died of shock upon hearing of it. Oliver of Paderborn, one of the great preachers of the Fifth Crusade, supervised the construction of a floating siege machine that managed to take the Chain Tower,

a fortified site with ballistae on an island in the middle of the Nile, which used chains to bar unfriendly traffic in the river. Muslims defenders, however, were quick to react and sank several of their own ships to shut out the Crusader fleet. The death of al-Adil, however, whether of shock or not, introduced a complicated political situation for the Egyptians at the worst possible moment. Taking advantage of this political instability, the Crusaders managed to establish themselves on both banks of the Nile. In May 1218 Italian reinforcements arrived under the leadership of Cardinal Pelagius, the papal legate to the Crusade. Disease also struck the Crusaders, depleting their ranks by about one-fifth.

Given the gravity of the new military situation, Egypt put out peace feelers. In exchange for a Crusader withdrawal and thirty-year truce, Egypt would surrender what once was the Kingdom of Jerusalem. The Crusaders were divided over whether or not to accept the terms. Tensions grew to such an extent that King John and Pelagius had a falling out, and the king left the siege altogether. John was in favor of accepting the terms, but Pelagius, confident in the arrival of German reinforcements, wanted to wait. Once again the ebb and flow of troops in the Crusader ranks caused a state of paralysis. Duke Leopold had already returned home. The king of Jerusalem had gone. The remaining Crusader leadership decided to wait until Emperor Frederick II arrived with his host from Germany. Frederick's departure had been delayed for a variety of reasons, but he had promised to send an advance contingent to assist the Crusaders until his arrival. Frederick's promised troops arrived in May. Responding to papal pressure, King John rejoined the Crusader host in July. After a prolonged stalemate, Damietta fell to the Crusaders in November 1219. Squabbling over the division of booty and over who had legitimate claim to the town immediately followed the capture of the city. The sultan continued to make peace overtures and to offer terms, but the Crusade leaders were now under strict orders from both the Pope and Emperor Frederick not to accept any such offer. Eventually, the Crusaders decided to strike the strategic city of Mansurah but soon found themselves captives in the unforgiving geography of the region. Blocked from further advance by a canal and facing an unusually high flood level of the Nile, the Crusade army could not even retreat safely. Supply lines from Damietta were severed, and the sultan ordered the opening of the dikes to flood out the Crusaders. Caught in a hopeless situation, the Crusaders finally surrendered in late August 1221.

Historians have been reluctant to consider Frederick's belated campaign as an actual phase of the Fifth Crusade. After all, Frederick did not depart for the Holy Land until September 1227, twelve years after he first took his crusading vow and six years after the Crusaders surrendered to the sultan in Egypt. Before setting out on his Crusade, Frederick was crowned king of Jerusalem because of his recent marriage to the kingdom's heiress, Yolande. This situation redirected his Crusade away from Egypt and back to Jerusalem itself. Frederick became ill en route to the East and chose the port city of Otranto for his convalescence. Outraged at yet another delay, Pope Gregory IX immediately excommunicated Frederick. When Frederick finally arrived in the East, his situation was extremely weak; much of the Crusader force had already departed, and many of those who remained had misgivings about participating in a Crusade led by an excommunicate. Frederick decided to follow up on his previous diplomatic negotiations with Egypt and penned a treaty in which the emperor recovered Jerusalem.

After the truce negotiated between Frederick and Egypt expired, there were two main bursts of crusading activity before the famous campaigns of the French king Louis IX. The first was directed toward the ailing Latin empire of Constantinople; it succeeded in shoring up its position enough to buy more time. The second, led by Count Thibald of Champagne and Duke Hugh of Burgundy, set out to expand militarily on Frederick's earlier diplomatic gains. This Crusade began ambitiously, waging war as it did against both Damascus in the north and Egypt in the south. During the fighting the city of Jerusalem was once again lost. Many of the problems that haunted the Fifth Crusade faced these Crusaders as well: dissension in the ranks; disputes over whether to negotiate or to fight; and the fact that not all Crusader contingents arrived at the same time, making synchronized military activity impossible. Thibald's Crusade ended much like that of Frederick's—Jerusalem was once again restored to Christendom through diplomacy. Yet, the terms of Thibald's agreement were much more beneficial to the Latins. The Crusader States now possessed more land than they had since Saladin's victories. Frankish possession of Jerusalem, however, was not to last long. The Franks in the East, allied with Damascus against Egypt and its Turkish mercenaries, suffered a major military reversal at the Battle of La Forbie (Harbiyah) in October 1244. The army of the Crusader States was crushed in the battle, and Jerusalem was lost.

Two months after the crushing defeat meted out at La Forbie, Louis IX took the Crusader vow. By almost any measure, Louis's Crusade to the East was the best prepared and organized. Two problems that plagued all previous Crusades—shortages of cash and supplies—were almost nonexistent in Louis's Crusade. The king took it upon himself to subsidize Crusaders' expenses, and it is estimated that about one-half of the knights participating in the expedition received such financial assistance. The royal war chest, moreover, was so substantive that the French king was able to continue lending money to Crusaders throughout most of the expedition. Louis also took it upon himself to personally make arrangements for transporting the bulk of his force to the East, though the greatest magnates of the realm were expected to hire their own transports. As far as supplying the expedition was concerned, Louis's meticulous preparations paid great dividends. Rather than relying on the tender mercies of speculators in the East, Louis made the city of Limassol in Cyprus a forward supply base that stocked massive quantities of food long before the Crusaders even boarded the transport ships. The cost of the expedition was astronomical; the annual royal income averaged only £250,000, while the Crusade cost Louis an estimated £1,500,000. Despite the contribution of one-tenth of the French church's revenue for five years (estimated at about £950,000), raising the necessary cash proved a daunting task. Louis successfully met this fiscal challenge in a variety of ways: most domestic spending was cut while the Crusade was being organized and executed; the crown extracted—with renewed vigor and attentiveness—as much as it possibly could from its possessions; and the king came down particularly hard on the property of Jews and heretics.

Louis set sail for the East late in August 1248 and arrived at his forward base in Cyprus on 17 September. After eight months of preparations, his assembled host sailed to Damietta. The city of Damietta, which was taken during the Fifth Crusade only after a yearlong siege, was captured by King Louis—and with minimal Crusader losses—after a mere day of battle. Five months passed before Louis made his next move. War councils debated whether to follow up the gain of Damietta with the conquest of Alexandria, the great port of Egypt, or to move directly on to Cairo itself. Robert of Artois, the king's brother and the prospective Christian "king of Egypt" if the Crusade succeeded, lobbied intensely for immediately attacking Cairo. Robert's view prevailed, and on 20 November the Crusaders began their march southward, following the same route as had the armies of the Fifth Crusade; and, like the armies of the Fifth Crusade, Louis's troops found the geography of the Nile Valley to be a formidable opponent. Blocked from advancing on Mansurah by a Nile tributary, Louis's engineers began constructing a dike by which to cross and lay siege to the city. Their efforts were frustrated by the steady hail of Greek fire that Muslim defenders unleashed upon the Franks. A local peasant revealed to the Crusaders the location of a dangerous but suitable ford. Louis began the slow process of moving his troops across the ford. The advance guard, under the command of Robert, surprised and dispersed an Egyptian outpost. Emboldened by this victory, Robert, disobeying the direct orders of the king to stay put until the crossing was complete, followed the Egyptian survivors right into the city of Mansurah itself. Caught within the narrow city streets and unable to maneuver properly, the advance guard, including Robert himself, were massacred. Louis and the main force engaged the enemy in a battle outside the city, until the Muslims retreated behind Mansurah's walls. Louis's position rapidly deteriorated. Casualties and disease drastically depleted the Crusader ranks. The Egyptians managed to cut off the Crusader supply lines. In April, Louis began the retreat to Damietta but only made it halfway. The Crusaders were forced to surrender, and Louis was taken prisoner. After paying a hefty ransom, Louis stayed in the Crusader States for another four years, trying to strengthen their position through truces and the refortification of strategic coastal cities.

Louis's Crusade was the last major expedition that set out to save the Latin settlements in the East. The impressive fortifications that he constructed before leaving Acre, however, were not enough to offset the damage done at La Forbie. Making the situation even more perilous was the rise of the Mamluk sultanate in Egypt, a powerful and centralized military monarchy that replaced the squabbling Ayyubid descendents of Saladin. The Mamluke sultanate was forged by the most successful slave revolt in history. Mamluks were originally slaves who, after being purchased as children, were trained by the Ayyubids in Egypt to serve as trusted bodyguards and as an elite military force. Eventually, a faction of Mamluks assassinated the Ayyubid sultan and formed a junta. Despite the factional fighting and assassinations that marred its existence, this new "slave state" succeeded in forging a formidable Islamic empire that ultimately unified Egypt and Syria and placed the Crusader States in the uncomfortable position of needing to deal with two fronts that, for the first time since Saladin's death, could not easily be played against one another. The Mamluks also inherited the Ayyubid jihad tradition that, as it had for Saladin and his successors, played a major role in religiously legitimizing the coup d'etat.

The Crusader States did receive a respite because of the appearance of the Mongols on the scene. Nearly all of Asia and eastern Europe felt the effects of the Mongol expansion that began with Genghis Khan and continued unabated with his immediate successors. The Mongols brought an end to the Abbasid caliphate in Iraq in 1258; after conquering Baghdad, the last Caliph was supposedly rolled up in a carpet and kicked to death by victorious Mongols. The following year the Ilkhan Mongols launched an invasion into Syria. Aleppo was taken in January 1260, followed by Damascus in early March. The northernmost Crusader State, Antioch, along with the Christian kingdom of Armenia, submitted to Mongol overlordship. Ilkhan military efforts, however, were sensitive to events taking place in the Mongol heartland in Asia and its near constant conflict with other khannates. To protect his interests further east after news arrived that the Great Khan had died, Hulegu, the Ilkhan ruler, had to leave for China, along with much of the Mongol force occupying Syria. The Mongols who remained in Syria under Hulegu's deputy Kitbugha, despite their depleted numbers, were charged with preparing for an invasion of Egypt. Rulers of the Crusader States promised Kitbugha that they would remain neutral during the impending conflict, but they allowed the Mamluks safe conduct through their lands and even provided supplies. Mongols and Mamluks engaged each other in a pitched battle at Ayn Jalut (The Springs of Goliath) on 3 September 1260. Although the Mamluks won the battle, it certainly was not a decisive victory. Not only did the Mongols return the following year, but they also reappeared off and on for the next three decades. Yet, the victory at Ayn Jalut did save Syria from Mongol domination and paved the way for its unification with Egypt.

Qutuz, the Mamluke sultan who presided over the victory at Ayn Jalut, was soon murdered by his emirs and replaced with Baybars, a particularly brutal Mamluk whose intuition for military strategy exceeded Saladin's. After storming Galilee in 1263, he proceeded to seize major ports along the Crusader State coastline and several strategic sites in the interior. Acre itself was virtually surrounded by the fortified bases he acquired. By the time Baybars died in 1277, the Crusader States had been completely devastated, reduced mainly to a narrow strip of coastline. Baybars was also quite successful in checking the Ilkhan threat: he made an alliance with a rival khannate, the Golden Horde, and even took the war to the Ilkhans themselves by launching several expeditions into Anatolia. After Baybar's death, the elderly but extremely battle-hardened and still virile emir Qalawun seized the sultanate in 1279. Any immediate action he might have planned against the Crusader States was quickly interrupted by a formidable Mongol invasion of Syria in 1281. On 29 October 1281 the Mongol and Mamluke forces clashed in a major battle outside the city of Homs. Despite the considerable attention the Battle of Ayn Jalut has received, the Battle of Homs was in fact a much more pitched and significant conflict. On one side of the battlefield the Mamluks won while on the other side the Mongols were victorious; throughout the conflict each side believed that it was losing the battle. When the dust settled, the Mamluks scored a marginal victory, but one so questionable that it led an Armenian observer to question whether or not such heavy Mamluk casualties could possibly be considered a victory. The Mongol retreat from Syria and the utter devastation of the Mamluk ranks, however, bought the Crusader States more time. Before any attempt could be made to strike the Franks, Qalawun would first need to rebuild the Egyptian army.

The final fall of the Crusader States in the Latin East was rather anticlimactic. Qalawun negotiated short treaties with the Latins while further solidifying his position as sultan and mending his military machine. In western Europe the political situation was embroiled in the usual conflict and chaos, though in a much more accentuated form since the conflict between the papacy and empire was coming to a head. Qalawun began to move on the Crusaders in the mid 1280s, taking a few important Frankish strongholds, and finally, in 1289 he seized Tripoli. Although the western European political scene was such that the organization of a full-scale Crusade was impossible, Pope Nicholas IV needed to authorize the preaching of a Crusade to protect Acre. His efforts resulted in a mob of leaderless Italians descending upon Acre, who took to butchering Muslim noncombatants and Eastern Christians in the streets. Qalawun demanded that the Franks turn over the murderers and was rebuffed. The sultan, however, died shortly thereafter. Qalawun's son, al-Ashraf, presided over organizing the assault on Acre.

On 5 April 1291 the Mamluk army began laying siege to Acre. Soldiers sent from Cyprus bought the city more time but were not sufficient to turn the course of the siege. The military orders fought heroically and with distinction; when the battle was clearly lost, they focused their efforts upon providing cover for those boarding ships to evacuate the city. The Templar fortress was the last holdout, and it finally fell on 28 May. Those who had not managed to escape from the city were killed or sold into slavery. In what must have been the supreme act of cowardice in the history of the Crusader States, the commander of Tyre, the important fortified city that once served as the beachhead for recovering the coast earlier, deserted his post and left it for the enemy to occupy effortlessly. The Mamluks spent the summer of 1291 seizing those sites that remained in Crusader hands until the last one, the great Templar coastal fortress at Athlit, fell on 14 August 1291. All fortifications on the coast were completely destroyed by the Mamluks to prevent a possible Crusader return.

Despite the definitive and final loss of the Holy Land, its importance to western Europe never dissipated. "Recovery" of the Holy Land remained high on the papacy's priority list for centuries and was discussed at countless councils. An entire literary genre emerged dedicated to various schemes for recapturing the Holy Land. Yet, despite the lingering interest, the Holy Land remained beyond western European control until the nineteenth century. The final loss of the Holy Land, however, should not be seen as an indication that the Crusades, as a movement, were a failure. In an age characterized by fragmented political leadership and primitive military logistics, maintaining the Latin presence on the eastern Mediterranean coast for two centuries was an amazing accomplishment. Furthermore, crusading was not to "die out" in the region for some time; it was redirected to the Aegean and what was referred to at the time as "Romania." In the West the Crusades were ultimately an unqualified success: the Iberian Peninsula was recovered, and Crusades played no small role in the creation of Christian eastern Europe. Crusading continued long past the "classical age" that constitutes the subject matter of this volume, and there are many people in the Islamic world today who believe it is still continuing through Western imperialism and interference in the region.

–MARK T. ABATE, WESTFIELD STATE
COLLEGE, WESTFIELD, MASSACHUSETTS

PREFACE

CHRONOLOGY

Boldface type indicates an entry in this volume.

1095

French monk Peter the Hermit is already preaching that Christians should march to Jerusalem. His quest becomes known as the People's Crusade. (*See* **Peter the Hermit** *and* **Popular Crusades**)

MARCH: Pope Urban II convenes a council in Piacenza, Italy. Attendees discuss possible aid to the Byzantine Empire in response to an appeal made by Emperor Alexius I Comnenus.

27 NOVEMBER: In a sermon given near the end of the Council of Clermont, Urban II calls for a Crusade to free Jerusalem from Muslim control. (*See* **First Crusade, Inventing the Crusades,** *and* **Urban II**)

1096

Jews in the Rhineland are attacked by groups of Crusaders gathering to join the Crusade to the East. Massacres occur in such cities as Worms, Mainz, and Cologne. (*See* **Attacks on Jews** *and* **Treatment of Jews**)

12 APRIL: Bands of followers of Peter the Hermit arrive in Cologne. (*See* **Peter the Hermit** *and* **Popular Crusades**)

SUMMER: The First Crusade (1096–1102) begins. European Crusader knights—their armies, retainers, and even families—begin their trek (fighting pilgrimage) toward the East. (*See* **First Crusade**)

OCTOBER: Remnants of Peter the Hermit's band are destroyed by Muslim Turks in Asia Minor. (*See* **Peter the Hermit** and **Popular Crusades**)

EARLY WINTER: First Crusaders begin arriving in Constantinople and continue to trickle into the city into 1097.

1097

1 JULY: The Crusaders defeat a Seljuk Turk army at the Battle of Dorylaeum in Asia Minor (Turkey).

21 OCTOBER: The siege of Antioch begins.

1098

10 MARCH: Edessa, an ancient Macedonian capital in Asia Minor, falls to Baldwin of Boulogne and becomes the first of the Crusader States.

3 JUNE: Crusaders breach the walls of Antioch, aided by treasonous Turks, but they fail to capture the citadel. A Turkish army arrives and besieges the Crusaders within the walls of the city.

28 JUNE: The Crusader army, led by Bohemond, leaves the city and defeats Turkish infantry and cavalry at the Battle of Antioch. The Crusaders then take the citadel.

1099

15 JULY: After a siege more than a month long, Jerusalem is captured by the Crusaders. Muslims and Jews in the city are massacred.

22 JULY: Godfrey of Bouillon becomes the first Latin king of Jerusalem. (*See* **Crusader States**)

29 JULY: Pope Urban II dies. (*See* **Urban II**)

12 AUGUST: The Crusaders attack an Egyptian army sent to relieve Jerusalem and defeat it at the Battle of Ascalon.

DECEMBER: Pisan ships resupply the Crusaders. (*See* **Maritime States**)

1100

Several lesser Crusader armies march to the East but are defeated by Muslim troops.

18 JULY: Godfrey of Bouillon dies; Baldwin of Boulogne becomes the new king of Jerusalem (Baldwin I) in September, although he is not crowned until Christmas Day. (*See* **Crusader States**)

AUGUST: Bohemond is captured while attacking Sabastea and will not be released until 1103. The Norman crusader Tancred becomes regent of Antioch.

1102

MAY: Baldwin I's smaller army defeats a larger Egyptian force but suffers heavy losses at the First Battle of Ramleh. A larger Egyptian force is later attacked by Crusader cavalry; the knights are wiped out at the Second Battle of Ramleh, although Baldwin escapes. Stephen of Blois is among the dead. Baldwin is reinforced by knights arriving by sea and defeats another Egyptian force at Jaffa. The First Crusade comes to an end; many of the Crusaders return to Europe. (*See* **First Crusade**)

1103

Baldwin begins a siege of Acre, the wealthiest city in Palestine. (*See* **Crusader States**)

1104

MAY: A Genoese fleet helps Baldwin capture Acre. The city becomes an important port for Italian merchant fleets. (*See* **Maritime States**)

1105

27 AUGUST: Another Egyptian army is defeated by the Western army at the Third Battle of Ramleh.

1107

Beirut falls to Baldwin. (*See* **Crusader States**)

1108

Sidon falls to Baldwin. Norwegian king Sigurd I aids in capturing the city.

1109

12 JULY: Tripoli is captured by the Crusaders.

1112

Tancred dies.

1113

The Hospital of St. John, which was organized before the First Crusade to provide aid to pilgrims to Jerusalem, is made an independent entity and is aligned with Rome by Pope Paschal II. (*See* **Military Orders**)

1115

With the help of local Muslims, Norman Crusader Roger of Antioch, nephew of Tancred, blocks an attempt by Il-Bursuqi to recapture Syria at the battle of Danith.

1118

Byzantine emperor Alexius I Comnenus, who helped initiate the First Crusade when he asked for aid from the West, dies. (*See* **Byzantine-Latin Relations**)

Burgundian knight Hugh of Payens arrives in Jerusalem.

Raymond of Le Puy takes control of the Hospital of St. John and introduces a military aspect to its charitable roles. Knights of this order are known as Hospitallers. (*See* **Military Orders**)

Saragossa, a Spanish city occupied by the Moors, falls to Alfonso I of Aragon. (*See* **Reconquista**)

2 APRIL: Baldwin dies while on campaign in Egypt, his army having marched unopposed up along the Nile River. Baldwin of Le Bourg becomes the new king, Baldwin II (14 April). (*See* **Crusader States**)

1119

The Order of the Temple is established by Hugh of Payens, Geoffroi de Saint-Omer, and several like-minded knights to defend pilgrims traveling to the Holy City. They become known as the Templars. (*See* **Military Orders**)

27 JUNE: Latin troops led by Roger of Antioch are defeated at the Field of Blood by Muslim troops led by Ilghazi, who had come into the area in response to appeals from Aleppo. By August the two sides have fought to a virtual stalemate.

1123

Baldwin II is captured while fighting Muslims around Aleppo.

MARCH: While attendees at the First Lateran Council concentrate mostly on Church reform, they also declare the remission of sins of Crusaders and the protection of their property while they are serving in the East.

1124

In exchange for cash and several fortresses, Baldwin II is ransomed from the Muslims and released.

7 JULY: With the help of a Venetian fleet of more than one hundred ships and after nearly five months of siege, Tyre is captured by Latin forces. The Venetians gain valuable trading privileges, and Tyre becomes an important port for international trade. (*See* **Maritime States**)

1125

Alfonso I of Aragon raids into Andalusia. (*See* **Reconquista**)

MAY: A large Crusader army led by Baldwin II defeats Il-Bursuqi of Mosul's Muslim forces at the Battle of Azaz, which quiets conflict for a time on the northern border of the Crusader States. (*See* **Crusader States**)

1127

Zangi becomes the governor of Mosul, is successful in several battles against the Latins, and gains control of northern Syria and Iraq. (*See* **Muslims**)

1129

The Council of Troyes confirms the role of the Templars in defending pilgrims. (*See* **Military Orders**)

1131

21 AUGUST: Baldwin II dies; his son-in-law Fulk V, Count of Anjou, replaces him on the throne. (*See* **Crusader States**)

1137

Zengi, while besieging the Crusader fort of Montferrand, is attacked by but defeats a Latin force led by Fulk V and Raymond of Tripoli. The Latins are forced to retreat, although they are able to ransom their captives in exchange for Muslim possession of the fort. (*See* **Muslims**)

1139

Zengi lays siege to Damascus, but he is forced to withdraw by a large Crusader contingent.

1140s

The Crusader States build many fortresses, including those constructed by Fulk—Ibelin, Blanchegarde, Krak of Moab, and Bethgibelin—to counter the Muslim forces of Zengi. (*See* **Crusader States** *and* **Military Strategy**)

1143

10 NOVEMBER: Fulk dies after being thrown from a horse. His son Baldwin (Baldwin III) is crowned king, but Melisende, his wife, serves as regent. (*See* **Crusader States**)

1144

24 DECEMBER: Edessa, ruled by Jocelin II, falls to the Muslims under Zengi, although the Muslim ruler retires from the region to handle domestic problems. (*See* **Crusader States**)

1145

Pope Eugenius III calls for a Second Crusade to the East in response to the fall of Edessa.

1146

Zengi is murdered. (*See* **Muslims**)

Bernard of Clairvaux lends his weight to establishing a new Crusade by preaching throughout Europe.

Jews are again attacked in Germany. (*See* **Attacks on Jews** *and* **Treatment of Jews**)

1147

French king Louis VII and German king Conrad accept the call of the Pope and journey to the East. The Second Crusade begins.

OCTOBER: German Crusaders split their forces as they enter Asia Minor and are attacked and defeated by the Turks; the leading knights retire.

24 OCTOBER: Lisbon falls to Crusaders.

1148

Second Crusaders begin arriving in Jerusalem.

JULY: The Crusaders attack Damascus, but they are forced to withdraw. Bickering erupts among the leaders of the Second Crusade.

1149

The Second Crusade ends; faith in crusading is shaken in Europe.

The new church at the Holy Sepulchre in Jerusalem is consecrated.

Raymond of Antioch is killed in battle against Muslim forces led by Zengi's son, Nur al-Din.

1153–1158

Crusaders travel to Spain to help fight the Muslims there. (*See* **Aljamas** *and* **Reconquista**)

1153

Baldwin II attacks Ascalon. On 10 August the city falls to the Latins. (*See* **Crusader States**)

1154

Damascus is captured by Nur al-Din. The Muslim ruler, however, does not massacre the enemy population. (*See* **Muslims**)

1156–1157

Devastating earthquakes hit the Near East, especially Syria, temporarily halting all military activities by both sides.

1158

A military order, initiated by Cistercian monks, is founded at Calatrava, Spain, in a fortified town on the left bank of the Guadiana River. (*See* **Military Orders**)

1162

10 FEBRUARY: Baldwin III falls ill and dies.

1163

King Amalric, Baldwin's younger brother, becomes the king of Jerusalem. He leads Latin forces in an invasion of Egypt at the invitation of the Egyptians, who are facing troops sent by Nur al-Din. (*See* **Crusader States**)

1167

18 MARCH: A combined Latin-Egyptian army is defeated by Nur al-Din at Minya in Egypt. The allies manage to trap the Syrians in Alexandria, however, and after starving them in a siege, the Syrians retire from Egypt.

1169

Saladin takes the reins as leader of Syrian troops in Egypt. A Byzantine fleet and Latin army attack Damietta but fail to capture the city. (*See* **Saladin and Richard I**)

1170

The Order of Santiago is established, originally to protect pilgrims to the tomb of Santiago de Compostela from Moorish raids. (*See* **Military Orders**)

1171

Crusaders fight in the Baltic region. (*See* **Missionary Activities**)

1172

Saladin establishes the Abbasid caliphate in Egypt. (*See* **Muslims** *and* **Saladin and Richard I**)

1174

15 MAY: Nur al-Din dies.

11 JULY: Amalric dies. His young and sickly son, Baldwin IV (the Leper King), temporarily takes the throne. Raymond of Tripoli serves as regent. Among many groups vying for power, the Templars and Hospitallers choose opposite sides. (*See* **Crusader States**)

28 OCTOBER: Damascus falls to Saladin. (*See* **Saladin and Richard I**)

1177

25 NOVEMBER: While besieging the Templars and Latin troops of Baldwin IV near Mont-

gisard, Saladin is surprised in the field and defeated. (*See* **Crusader States** *and* **Saladin and Richard I**)

1179

Saladin gains a measure of revenge for Montgisard by capturing the Master of the Temple and defeating a force of Franks at the Valley of the Springs. (*See* **Saladin and Richard I**)

1180

French nobleman Guy of Lusignan marries Amalric I's daughter, Sibylla, and becomes embroiled in factional disputes in Jerusalem. (*See* **Crusader States**)

1181

Reynald of Chatillon raids a Muslim caravan of pilgrims to Mecca, angering Saladin. Reynald also sends raiding parties against other pilgrimage groups and towns.

1183

Baldwin, becoming increasingly infirm, turns over the kingdom to the control of Guy of Lusignan.

11 JUNE: Aleppo falls to Saladin. (*See* **Saladin and Richard I**)

1185

MARCH: Baldwin dies, and his young nephew becomes Baldwin V, with Raymond of Tripoli to serve as regent. The young man, however, lives less than a year as king. Sybilla and Guy are crowned. (*See* **Crusader States**)

1187

4 JULY: Saladin attacks the forces of Guy at the Battle of the Horns of Hattin. The Latins, poorly situated and ravaged by thirst, are split up by the massive Muslim army. Guy is captured, and hundreds of knights are killed. Reynald is beheaded by Saladin; captured Templars and Hospitallers are executed. Saladin then takes the cities of Tiberias, Acre, Sidon, and Beirut. (*See* **Crusader States** *and* **Saladin and Richard I**)

2 OCTOBER: Jerusalem, left with a weak defense force, is forced to surrender to Saladin. The population is ransomed and allowed to retreat; many of them go to Tripoli, Tyre, and even Antioch.

29 OCTOBER: Pope Gregory VIII calls for another Crusade in response to the loss of the Holy City.

1188

Holy Roman Emperor Frederick I (Barbarossa) publicly accepts the cross to Crusade in the East.

1189

Crusaders and Italian fleets replenish the forces defending Tyre against Saladin. (*See* **Saladin and Richard I**)

MAY: The Third Crusade begins as thousands of troops of Frederick I depart Europe and march toward the east. (*See* **Third Crusade**)

4 OCTOBER: Christian troops push back Saladin, although they suffer heavy casualties.

1190

Sybilla dies. Her heiress, Isabella, is forced to marry Conrad of Montferrat. (*See* **Crusader States**)

10 JUNE: Frederick I, while swimming in the Saleph River in Armenia, drowns. The huge German army begins to splinter; some knights return to Europe, while others continue toward Jerusalem. (*See* **Third Crusade**)

JULY: Troops under French king Philip II unite with English forces led by Richard I (the Lion-Hearted) and begin moving toward the East. The two armies split; the French leave Europe from Genoa, and the English depart from Marseilles. The armies are held up in Sicily. (*See* **Third Crusade**)

1191

20 JANUARY: The Duke of Swabia dies. More German knights quit the Crusade. (*See* **Third Crusade**)

JUNE: English king Richard I, angry at the poor treatment by the Greeks of his sister, captures Cyprus. (*See* **Third Crusade**)

12 JULY: Acre falls to Richard I and Philip II. Richard massacres Muslim prisoners. Philip returns to Europe. Richard leads his troops south toward Jerusalem. (*See* **Third Crusade**)

7 SEPTEMBER: Saladin's cavalry attacks the English at Arsuf, but the Crusaders prevail and continue marching southward. The army rests at Jaffa. Richard sells Cyprus to the Templars. (*See* **Saladin and Richard I** *and* **Third Crusade**)

1192

The Crusader army suffers many defections, particularly of French knights who have run out of funds. Richard also fears that Philip is planning to attack his lands back in Europe. Conrad is made king of Jerusalem. (*See* **Third Crusade**)

28 APRIL: Conrad is assassinated. Henry of Champagne is made king.

JULY: Richard makes an attempt to capture Jerusalem, but his army is now too small, and he is forced to retreat. Saladin attacks Jaffa, but Richard returns and ends the Muslim siege. (*See* **Third Crusade**)

2 SEPTEMBER: The Treaty of Jaffa is signed. Jerusalem remains in Muslim hands, and Ascalon is returned to Saladin; Christian pilgrims are allowed access to Jerusalem; the Crusader States are temporarily saved from Muslim invasion. Richard leaves to return to Europe. The Third Crusade ends. Richard is later captured by the duke of Austria and then held by Holy Roman Emperor Henry VI for ransom. Richard is freed in 1194. (*See* **Third Crusade**)

1193

Saladin dies. (*See* **Saladin and Richard I**)

1194

Guy of Lusignan dies. Amalric II becomes king of Jerusalem. (*See* **Crusader States**)

1197–1198

Henry VI plans a Crusade to finish his father's (Frederick I Barbarossa's) goal of capturing Jerusalem, but he dies before leaving Europe. German Crusaders, however, continue to march to Palestine and engage the Muslims, but to little effect, other than stirring up trouble.

1198

The Teutonic Order is established, evolving from a hospital for German pilgrims to the Holy Land that was founded in 1190 in Acre. (*See* **Military Orders**)

AUGUST: Pope Innocent III calls for another Crusade to begin in 1199 (which does not materialize).

1201

French representatives arrive in Venice to bargain for transportation; Venice offers to join the Crusade as a partner in the expedition. (*See* **Fourth Crusade**)

1202

The Fourth Crusade begins. Venetian doge Enrico Dandolo, in exchange for a delayed payment, convinces the Crusaders to help Venice recapture Zara. (*See* **Fourth Crusade** *and* **Maritime States**)

1 OCTOBER: The Crusader fleet sails from Venice. (*See* **Fourth Crusade**)

24 NOVEMBER: Zara is captured. Deposed Byzantine prince Alexius IV Angelus convinces the Crusaders, with the promise of men and materials, to travel to Constantinople to depose Alexius III Angelus. (*See* **Fourth Crusade**)

1203

24 JUNE: The Crusader fleet arrives in Constantinople. (*See* **Fourth Crusade**)

17 JULY: The Crusaders begin their siege of Constantinople. (*See* **Fourth Crusade**)

AUGUST: The Byzantines capitulate and put Alexius IV on the throne.

1204

JANUARY: Alexius V murders Alexius IV and leads a revolt against the Crusaders.

12 APRIL: After three days of battle the Crusaders capture the city and sack Constantinople, ending the Fourth Crusade. (*See* **Fourth Crusade**)

1209–1229

Innocent III, eager to eliminate a heretical sect called the Cathars from southern France, calls for a Crusade against them. This endeavor is called the Albigensian Crusade, and one of the most brutal commanders is Simon de Montfort (who dies in 1218).

1209

The Crusaders sack the French city of Beziers and massacre the population, the vast majority of whom are not Cathars. The remaining Cathars in the region fight heroically but by 1229 sue for peace.

1212

Two young men, Stephen of France and Nicholas of Germany, independently preach for Crusades to the East. The emotional movements that follow are known as the Children's Crusade, which end in disaster for most of the participants, many of whom die en route. The few that manage to obtain transport to Egypt are allegedly betrayed and sold into slavery. (*See* **Children's and Shepherds' Crusades** *and* **Popular Crusades**)

17 JULY: Peter II of Aragon defeats Spanish Muslims at the Battle of Las Navas de Toloso. (*See* **Aljamas** *and* **Reconquista**)

1213

Pope Innocent III calls for another Crusade.

1215

Arrangements are made at the Fourth Lateran Council in Rome for another Crusade.

1216

Innocent III dies. Honorius III becomes the Pope.

1217

The Fifth Crusade (actually a series of expeditions), aimed at taking control of Egypt first, starts. The Crusaders are led by the papal legate Pelagius and John of Brienne, king of Jerusalem. (*See* **Fifth Crusade**)

1219

Italian friar Francis of Assisi, founder of the Franciscans, travels to the Holy Land, preaches to the Crusaders, and meets with the sultan. (*See* **Missionary Activity**)

5 NOVEMBER: After nearly five months of siege, Damietta falls to the Crusaders. Aleppo is also captured. The Crusaders are then blocked from capturing Cairo. (*See* **Fourth Crusade**)

1221

30 AUGUST: The Crusaders are defeated by the Ayyubids at the Battle of al-Mansura, after the Muslims flood the field, making Crusader warfare untenable. (*See* **Fourth Crusade**)

1227

Holy Roman Emperor Frederick II, who took the cross in 1225, embarks from Europe on an expedition to recapture Jerusalem. He takes ill and is forced to delay in Sicily. (*See* **Fourth Crusade**)

1228

28 JUNE: Frederick II resumes his Crusade. (*See* **Fourth Crusade**)

1229

18 FEBRUARY: Frederick signs a peace treaty with the Muslims and regains control of Jerusalem. The Fifth Crusade ends. (*See* **Fourth Crusade**)

12 APRIL: The Peace of Paris officially ends the Albigensian Crusade.

1231

Frederick II is excommunicated and returns to Europe from Jerusalem in 1232.

1241

A Crusade against the invading Mongols is called. (*See* **The Mongols**)

1244

23 AUGUST: Jerusalem falls back into Muslim hands.

17 OCTOBER: A larger Crusader force, including many knights from the military orders, marches into Gaza and is defeated at the Battle of La Forbie by the Mamluks under Baybars I.

1245

Pope Innocent IV proclaims a Crusade at the Council of Lyons.

1248

French king Louis IX, having sworn to take up a Crusade after recovering from a serious illness in 1244, starts his expedition to the East (known as the First Crusade of St. Louis) on 12 June. (*See* **Louis IX**)

23 NOVEMBER: Seville is captured. (*See* **Aljamas** *and* **Reconquista**)

1249

7 JUNE: Louis IX captures Damietta.

DECEMBER: Louis advances on Cairo.

1250

8 FEBRUARY: Louis's brother, Robert of Artois, makes an ill-advised advance against the Egyptian troops, and the Crusaders are cut down in heavy street fighting at al-Mansura. (*See* **Louis IX**)

5 APRIL: Louis is captured. He gains his freedom by surrendering Damietta and paying a large ransom. Louis stays in the Near East for four more years, working to strengthen the Christian kingdoms and gain the release of his soldiers. (*See* **Louis IX**)

1251

A movement of the poor, known as the First Crusade of the Shepherds, begins. Their targets, however, are often the Church and the aristocracy. (*See* **Children's and Shepherds' Crusades** *and* **Popular Crusades**)

1256–1258

Venetian and Genoan interests in the Crusader States spark a civil war called the War of St. Sabas, which engulfs almost all of the Christian colonies. (*See* **Maritime States**)

1259

Byzantine troops under the command of Michael VIII Paliaologos defeat Frankish troops from the Crusader States at the Battle of Pelagonia. (*See* **Byzantine-Latin Relations**)

1260

3 SEPTEMBER: Egyptian troops defeat a Mongol invading force in Palestine at the Battle of Ayn Jalut. (*See* **Mongols**)

23 OCTOBER: Baybars I is crowned the sultan of Egypt. (*See* **Muslims**)

1261

25 JULY: The Byzantines recapture control of Constantinople.

1268

18 MAY: The Mamluks capture and sack Antioch.

1269

Louis IX undertakes a Second Crusade (Second Crusade of St. Louis), this time hoping to capture Tunis. (*See* **Louis IX**)

1270

Louis IX dies of disease, along with his son and many of his troops, while camped outside of Tunis. (*See* **Louis IX**)

1272

Louis IX's brother Charles of Anjou, the king of Sicily, obtains a peace treaty and an indemnity from the Hafsids of Tunis and ends the ill-starred Crusade. (*See* **Louis IX**)

1277

Charles of Anjou arrives in Jerusalem, having purchased the rights to the kingdom. (*See* **Crusader States**)

1282

An insurrection against Charles of Anjou, called the Sicilian Vespers, breaks out in Palermo, Sicily, forestalling his plans to launch a new Crusade to recapture Constantinople.

1286

Henry II is declared the king of Jerusalem in Acre.

1289

Tripoli is recaptured and destroyed by the Mamluks.

1291

18 MAY: Acre is stormed by the Mamluks.

ALJAMAS

What impact did *aljamas* (Muslim communities subject to Christian rule) have on the acculturation of Muslims in Spain?

Viewpoint: *Aljamas* allowed Muslims to retain their own cultural practices by providing barriers to rapid acculturation.

Viewpoint: *Aljamas* facilitated the acculturation of Muslims; granting concessions to Islamic communities made them less likely to revolt and more susceptible to subtle acculturative forces.

The *aljama,* or communal organization of Muslims subject to the Christian kings, was sometimes a quarter of a city, similar to the Jewish quarter—that is, ghetto—or it could take the form of a village wholly inhabited by Muslims. In either case it was endowed with statutes and with a roster of elected officials who administered the community, dispensed justice according to Islamic law, and dealt with the Christian royal authorities. Subject Muslims were held to be direct vassals of the Crown, unless they lived in seignorial villages.

When Muslim towns and villages surrendered during the course of the *reconquista* (reconquest) in Spain, they were given charters carefully defining their future relationship with the Christian authorities. Such arrangements envisioned considerable autonomy, the most important aspects of which were the right to practice their religion undisturbed; to have their own *qadi* (religious judge), who would adjudicate cases of Muslim against Muslim according to Islamic law (Muslim versus Christian cases were almost always litigated in Christian courts); and to be responsible for collecting taxes owed to the Crown or lord without outside interference. However, the limits of autonomy were constantly in flux. Direct royal control was frequently invoked, especially when Muslims revolted or were considered to represent a threat to security.

Shifting political conditions inevitably affected the degree to which these Muslims were exposed to the ambient Christian culture. There were no "cultural isolates," not in medieval Spain nor anywhere else. Some contact was bound to occur whenever different cultures shared the same land; that much was dictated by the need for economic exchange that perforce was carried out in the Romance languages of the conquerors. Muslims were also inevitably drawn into the secular court structure, both as litigants and as witnesses in court cases. And, logically, they became quite skilled in turning civil courts to their advantage. When two Muslim villages opposed each other in court, for example, in disputes over the sharing of irrigation water, their chances for success were better if they understood the law and were able to present their cases in Castilian or Catalan. Whether such conditions acted as a safeguard for Muslim culture or undermined it is the issue here debated.

Viewpoint:
Aljamas allowed Muslims to retain their own cultural practices by providing barriers to rapid acculturation.

In the course of the late fifteenth and early sixteenth centuries, when the Christian monarchs of the Iberian Peninsula decided upon a policy of forced conversions of Muslims and Jews who inhabited their kingdoms, it appeared providential that these subject peoples had earlier been gathered into enclaves where they could easily be found and identified. These *aljamas* (Muslim communities subject to Christian rule) appear to have facilitated conversion, which begs the question of whether that had been their purpose all along. Given the overt hostility toward minorities, especially of the royal policies of Castile after the conquest of Granada, it was all too easy to assume that the monarchs had desired to develop unitary, Christian states. Thus, all their policies were aimed toward that end. Such a reading, attributing to the monarchs of earlier eras the attitudes of later royalty and churchmen, is anachronistic. In fact, even Ferdinand II of Aragon, coruler of Spain with Isabella, sought to preserve special minority communities in his own lands, all the while agreeing with her policies, which led to the destruction of similar communities in Castile. Therefore, the *aljamas* were not created purposively with the final goal of converting the Muslims and Jews. Even though *aljamas* became one agency for conversion, the historical record makes it abundantly clear that this goal was not their initial purpose.

Anytime one discusses historical phenomena in medieval Spain, there is need to take account of the particularities of time and place. That is especially true in the case of the Mozarab (Arabized Christian), Mudejar (Muslims under Christian rule), and Jewish communities. During the period of the *reconquista* (reconquest), Alfonso VI in Castile and Spanish military leader El Cid Campeador in Valencia intended to preserve the Muslim and Jewish populations. Alfonso's intent to keep intact these communities can be seen from his charters and instruments of surrender; moreover, his appointment of Sisnando Davidiz, a Mozarabic count, as the first governor of Toledo demonstrated the king's commitment. Muslims were to keep their properties, goods, and mosques—including the Friday mosque, the center of the community—in short, their *morerias* (Muslim communities). Similarly, Jews were allowed to maintain the *Madina al-Yahud* as the Jewish Quarter of

the Christian city. Until the intense interference of people from north of the Pyrenees, such *convivencia* (coexistence) was the modus vivendi. As the twelfth-century Muslim historian Ibn Bassam put it, Sisnando (acting on Alfonso's behalf) made the Muslims' loss of freedom tolerable. Alfonso styled himself "Emperor of the two Religions" (for example, Islam and Christianity) in some of his correspondence. The Cid's similar performance in Valencia indicates a kind of Castilian policy. Even well into the fourteenth century one finds Mudejar communities being preserved in Castile—and some being created—that were governed by their own laws and customs and where the citizens practiced their own religion, in spite of the tensions that that tenancy produced. Curiously, this policy reveals something significant about the Mudejar experience: their religion actually condemned them for remaining in a non-Muslim land, becoming *mudajjanun* (protected peoples). It was their duty to move to an Islamic state. Instead, the Mudejars stayed in their homes, practiced their religion (albeit with some compromises), and resisted assimilation.

In Aragon the case is even clearer—for a longer period of time—if only because it is better documented. Beginning in 1096, Mudejar communities came increasingly under Christian rule. These Mudejars were "generally obedient subjects" who lived in peace with their neighbors. All of the studies of the people within Aragon have found that Mudejars had a significant role and were important to the kings: they were, according to John Boswell in *The Royal Treasure: Muslim Communities under the Crown of Aragon in the Fourteenth Century* (1977), the "Royal Treasure." Robert Ignatius Burns in *Islam under the Crusaders: Colonial Survival in the Thirteenth-Century Kingdom of Valencia* (1973) and Mark D. Myerson in *The Muslims of Valencia in the Age of Fernando and Isabel: Between Coexistence and Crusade* (1991) have clearly demonstrated a consistent royal policy in Aragon, and later Valencia as it came under Aragonese control, which, as late as the time of Ferdinand II, continued to protect and encourage the survival of the *aljamas,* all the while as the Spanish wished for the conversion of Muslims.

Only in Navarre, however, did Mudejars seem to be considered full and important citizens. They were significant enough into the fourteenth century to be specially protected from the Crusaders of northern Europe who came to Spain to fight the Moors. Only in Majorca were Mudejars routinely reduced to slavery, and even there the monarch was not overly interested in their conversion, for it meant a change in status from slave to free.

Had there been royal intent to convert, one would expect to see steady progress in that direction from the late eleventh century onward. One should expect to see the minority communities

DIPLOMACY WITH CHRISTIANS

'Abd Allah B. Buluggin, Muslim ruler of Granada, comments on the Spanish tactics for taking back the Iberian Peninsula and on his arrangements with King Alphonso:

We had seen how the Christian [king] wanted to get his hands on the Peninsula [literally "the Island"] and how he had taken Toledo and his unfriendliness after gaining the satisfaction of receiving tribute (*jizya*) from us. Now, however, he began to seek to capture the main cities. His seizure of Toledo, we noted, resulted from its progressive decline year by year. His tactics for conquering the rest of the country were the same. His policy was not to lay siege to a fortress or to order his troops to attack a city because it would have been too difficult to achieve and because these places were inhabited by people of a different religion from his own. His policy was to exact tribute from a city year after year and to harass it with various forms of aggression until it weakened and succumbed, as Toledo had done.

The fall of Toledo sent a great tremor through al-Andalus and filled the inhabitants with fear and despair of continuing to live there. A large number of disputes arose between al-Mu'tamid and Alphonso who had asked al-Mu'tamid to cede him a number of fortresses. Al-Mu'tamid, however, would rather die than surrender to them. . . .

Alphonso now prepared for the expedition and sent his envoy ahead of him. When I confirmed this fact, I was thrown into a state of great anxiety and did not know what to do for the best—whether I should abandon the city for him to ravage or to conciliate him by paying him as much as I could afford. Great panic descended on the people and so terrified was I that I just could not believe that he would accept my money and not remain in occupation of my territory out of sheer spite for the Aledo affair and my agreement with the Almoravids.

I sincerely hoped that his envoy would be satisfied with a small payment, but he said to me: "I've not come for anything of that sort. I am here to demand the payment of tribute (*jizya*) three years in arrears. That amounts to 30,000 [*mithgals*] net. Unless you pay up, he'll soon be on his way. Then you can do the best you can." . . . So that's what I did. I sent him the 30,000 [*mithgals*] without causing anyone to lose a dirham.

Nevertheless, I deemed it necessary to conclude a new agreement with him [Alphonso] whereby he would contract not to molest any town of mine or play me false. I acted as I did for fear that he might round on me. He agreed to the proposal. "As the money has to be paid," I said to myself, "it is better to have a contractual arrangement. Should I then have need of it I will have it to hand and it can't do any harm. If, on the other hand, there came a time when it's no longer needed, sharp brown lances and fine glittering swords can take place if only God would be good enough to send me an army to repulse him. All stratagems are fair in war and if you cannot win, at least be crafty."

So he agreed to conclude a treaty because he was so eager to get his hands on the money. But I for my part had no doubt that he would play me false, yet I was like one who risks his life from some sober necessity which leaves him no choice. Alphonso's envoy then said to me: "I've been asked by Alphonso to tell you that if you would like to include in this treaty a clause entitling you to his assistance to recover some of your territory lost to Ibn 'Abbad, he will do his best to help in this way in the course of his expedition." To this my reply was: "I am not prepared to side with anyone against a Muslim. What made me conclude this treaty is the desire to protect my country and co-religionists. If you honour it, I shall achieve my end." What he had in mind was to create trouble between me and Ibn 'Abbad so as to find an excuse for attacking his territory and use my resources to do so.

Source: *'Abd Allah B. Buluggin,* The Tibyan: Memoirs of 'Abd Allah B. Buluggin, Last Zirid Amir of Granada, *translated by Amin T. Tibi (Leiden: E. J. Brill, 1986), pp. 113, 132–133.*

ALJAMAS

coming under increasing pressure, losing their rights and autonomy; a general decline in the population of the *morerias;* and gradual acculturation to Christian norms. Instead, one finds that until near the end of their existence, the *aljamas* retained their distinctiveness and independence. For example, they remained independent legal entities operating under *shari'ah* (Islamic jurisprudence); the citizens continued to speak and write Arabic, though some knew Romance languages; the free practice of religion was assured, including the right to go on the *hajj* (pilgrimage) to Mecca; and the people continued to marry and procreate, educate their children in their own traditions, and bury their dead in their distinctive way. The Mudejars went to the extraordinary length of seeking authoritative religious judgments that recognized their special situation. When they had to acculturate to Christian norms, they consented. As the use of the Romance languages advanced through their communities, they still retained cultural independence by producing some of their works, translated into the Romance tongue but written in Arabic characters. In other words, until allowed no other choice, Muslims living under Christian rule—just like the Jews of Iberia—maintained their own culture. Even after forced conversions began, many Muslims simply went along publicly while secretly keeping their own customs at home.

On a theoretical level this relationship is what one might expect: the more a subcultural group is able to retain of its heritage, the more persistent that original culture is. The presence of *aljamas,* whether *morerias* or *juderias* (Jewish communities), were impediments to acculturation. The retention of Islamic culture, which effectively regulated life within the community, produced no need for acculturation to Christian norms. When interacting with the outside world (for example, the king and his bailiffs) the Muslims usually were accorded a high degree of accommodation: the king employed translators and bilingual scribes who produced documents in both languages, and he accepted as a matter of fact the validity of their legal systems. The king did not require them to capitulate to the local bishops and their anti-Muslim policies. These factors reinforced the self-sufficiency of the *aljamas.* Being able to carry on their affairs in a predominantly Islamic milieu obviated any need to become more tightly tied to Christian culture.

Moreover, in terms of process, the presence of these communities inhibited conversion, which, like contagion, spreads person-to-person. When an effective barrier to contact across ethnic boundaries exists, conversion does not take place—in either direction. In an encounter between two religions, conversion spreads in both directions. By keeping a strict segregation of Muslim and Christian populations, the Christian monarchs were act-

ing as much out of fear of Christians converting to Islam (the dominant cultural pattern for at least 150 years before the *Reconquista* began). Especially important was the fear that *moriscos* (converted Muslims) would return to their old ways under the influence of Mudejars. One can easily discern something of the monarchs' reasoning for the isolation of these communities. It is interesting that one of the first acts when the Inquisition gained a foothold in Aragon was to arrest two Muslims for dissuading and threatening other Muslims who had received baptism. Hence, the creation and maintenance of *morerias* and *juderias* was a bulwark against conversion, physically keeping members of each religion separate from would-be proselytizers. That such "walls of separation" were maintained by royal policy indicated that conversion of Muslim and Jewish communities was not the highest priority of the kings of Castile, Aragon, or Navarre in the High Middle Ages.

Burns summarized the state of affairs succinctly:

> The Aragonese crown was according formal recognition to a religious entity, the local aljama, as a legal personality with specific rights and as an alien society in its entirety. Socially *and as a barrier to acculturation* this recognition of the public structure was much more important in its effect on the Muslim than was individual liberty of conscience. (emphasis added)

The simple fact was that the kings needed these Muslims to keep working in order for the kingdoms to survive. Depopulated land was of limited value. The easiest way to ensure the retention of these Muslim inhabitants, so necessary to continued agricultural production, was to change their world as little as possible. In the end, then, *aljamas* did far more to preserve a Muslim presence in Spain than to facilitate conversion.

–MICHAEL WEBER,
SALEM STATE COLLEGE

Viewpoint: *Aljamas* facilitated the acculturation of Muslims; granting concessions to Islamic communities made them less likely to revolt and more susceptible to subtle acculturative forces.

The *aljamas,* subject Muslim communities under Christian rule, provide a good example of what might be called "directed culture change." Muslims, like Jews, had their own special courts to hear Muslim versus Muslim cases. But over time they became more willing to plead in Chris-

ALJAMAS

tian courts. *Qadis* (religious judges) adapted their legal practices so as to better mesh with the community needs in the local economy, which was regulated within a framework of Christian law. It is obvious that if two Muslim merchants come into conflict that the *qadi* could not wholly resolve the case by *shari'ah* (Islamic jurisprudence), especially if the result of the case ran contrary to the law of the land. He wanted to keep his people out of Christian courts or at least to act in such a way that the loser did not then go to a Christian court and continue the suit. So there was a gradual erosion of the Mudejars' judicial autonomy, in a painless way, that resulted from their dwindling numbers and their increasing integration into the ambient society and economy. Note that integration in this sense in no way implies assimilation, which under the strict standards of religious segregation was an impossibility.

Another example of juridical acculturation was that the king appointed a chief *qadi* for the kingdom of Valencia to hear appeals from local *qadis*. There is no appellate jurisdiction in Islamic or Jewish law. So this was a case of the creation of a completely new institution that superficially looked Islamic but that was, in fact, designed to carry out a precept of European law. Royal courts also heard appeals, a practice acceptable to Muslims, who recognized the king (as successor of a Muslim head of state) as the source of justice.

Christian rulers replaced tribal governance of villages and other communities, whereby all decisions were made by a *sheik* (chief) and a group of elders, with a functional copy of Christian town governance: typically with a panel of two or three *adelantati*, the equivalent of Christian *jurates;* a council of elders, somewhat like a Christian town council; and a *qadi* to hear civil cases according to Islamic law, with criminal cases reserved for an appointed justiciar. Christians viewed tribal elders as a town council and invested in them the kind of legislative and consultative authority that such councils had. In Valencia such councils had—like their Christian counterparts—become elective by the fourteenth century. At the same time the status of these tribal "elders" was less and less determined by age and more by status.

This autonomy was limited and the royal bailiff could intervene in all manner of issues. Under such a system, Christian norms of governance, administration, and justice quickly made inroads into institutions and practices that became less Islamic and ever closer to Christian institutional structures.

Although subject Muslims were assured their right to live under *sunnah* (normative customs), in reality they lived under customary laws

Illumination of Alfonso VI, twelfth century

(Cathedral Library, Santiago)

that, over time, changed as a result of the need to accommodate their society to a minority situation. This situation was in part the necessary result of the need to accommodate to the new rulers, reinforced by the Christian (mis)recognition of *sunnah* as having the same status of customary law in Christian Europe.

In addition to the *aljamas* that were freestanding villages wholly composed of Muslims, the Christians also created new suburban *aljamas* that they settled with displaced persons. Such communities had a mosque and *qadi*, but the residents worked for the Christians, which deprived the community of economic coherence, and law enforcement officials (such as the *amin* or *alamí*) were appointed by the Crown and were frequently corrupt individuals chosen for their servility.

Aljama structures served as agents of acculturation. In the Christian kingdoms, public ovens for baking bread were a royal monopoly, but inasmuch as royal tax officials were not usually allowed to enter the precincts of autonomous *aljamas,* they paid a tax instead. Since they already paid the tax, Muslims were induced to use the ovens and at the same time to bake bread in the Christian style. Gradually, the feudal taste for leavened bread was adopted by Muslims in substitution for unleavened bread, which was baked at home under low temperatures in small backyard ovens. In those areas where feudal taxes were collected in grain, Muslim farmers had to shift their traditional crop balance in order to produce more wheat. In some areas of Valencia, Muslims petitioned to change irrigated land to unirrigated (which was taxed at a lower rate) so that they could produce enough wheat. Christian feudal agriculture was geared toward the production of wheat and grapes, which contrasted with the greater diversity of Muslim agriculture as traditionally practiced. Over time this agricultural diversity was necessarily pared down.

The Crown dealt with the *alamí* as the *aljama* officer in charge of the execution of justice. In a real sense the *alamí* was co-opted by the state and, although appointed from the local population, was exterior to it to the extent that he was the king's agent.

The underlying rationale (from the Muslim perspective) of autonomous communities was to retain the ability to transmit patrimony freely, so that traditional genealogical patterns (for example, cross-cousin marriages) and landholding rules (clans held agricultural fields in common, without surveyed boundaries) were preserved. Remote *aljamas* in mountainous regions functioned quite well: they tended to be more productive than comparable Christian settlements, and therefore the rulers were persuaded to leave them alone, so long as they paid their taxes. *Aljamas* that were intermixed with Christian settlements fared less well, particularly whenever Christians were allowed to purchase houses and fields in them. Such purchases, where permitted, inevitably weakened both the social and economic cohesiveness of the Muslim community. Christian purchase of land hastened the demise of communal property, which weakened the clan-based social structure. Since Christians were by practice specialized farmers (growing wheat and grapes, virtually to the exclusion of anything else), the local economy was also fatally disrupted.

Another generalized phenomenon also promoted the acculturation of subject Muslims: that was the nearly universal flight of the political and intellectual elite—first to Granada, then to North Africa. The subject *aljamas* had nei-

ther the *faqihs* (jurisprudential class) from which the *qadis* had been drawn, nor physicians who could read Arabic medical treatises, nor even teachers to instruct children in proper Arabic. The result was the progressive bastardization of religion, leading to the production of religious texts in *aljamiado* (Castilian or Catalan written in Arabic characters), as well as the distinctively untraditional enhanced religious role played by women. Medicine lost its academic cast and came increasingly to resemble folk medicine shared (perhaps with the exception of amulets and incantations of more-or-less Muslim inspiration) with Christians of the same social status. By the definitive expulsion of Moriscos (1610–1615) even those Muslims of Valencia, where their demographic weight was greatest, had become Romance speakers. Ultimately the acculturative pressures were too great and the "autonomy" of the *aljamas* too insubstantial to prevent the emergence of a distinctive Romance version of Islam, in some ways comparable to that of Bosnia centuries later.

–THOMAS F. GLICK,
BOSTON UNIVERSITY

References

John Boswell, *The Royal Treasure: Muslim Communities under the Crown of Aragon in the Fourteenth Century* (New Haven: Yale University Press, 1977).

Robert Ignatius Burns, *Islam under the Crusaders: Colonial Survival in the Thirteenth-Century Kingdom of Valencia* (Princeton: Princeton University Press, 1973).

Luis García-Ballester, *Medicine in a Multicultural Society: Christian, Jewish and Muslim Practitioners in the Spanish Kingdoms, 1222–1610* (Aldershot, U.K.: Ashgate, 2001).

Thomas F. Glick, *Irrigation and Society in Medieval Valencia* (Cambridge, Mass.: Belknap Press of Harvard University Press, 1970).

L. P. Harvey, *Islamic Spain, 1250 to 1500* (Chicago: University of Chicago Press, 1990).

Harvey, "The Mudejars," in *The Legacy of Muslim Spain,* edited by Salma Khadra Jayyusi (New York: E. J. Brill, 1992), pp. 177–187.

Mark D. Myerson, *The Muslims of Valencia in the Age of Fernando and Isabel: Between Coexistence and Crusade* (Berkeley: University of California Press, 1991).

ALJAMAS

THE AMERICAS

Was the conquest of the Americas an extension of the medieval Crusades?

Viewpoint: Yes. The crusading mentality was an essential feature of the conquest of the Americas, and the Europeans treated Native Americans the same way they treated Muslims.

Viewpoint: No. The conquest of the Americas was not crusading because there was no concerted effort to attain a specific religious goal.

On the way back from his second voyage of discovery (1493–1496), explorer Christopher Columbus expressed the hope that the garrison he had left behind in Santo Domingo would gather so much gold "that within three years the monarchs would undertake and prepare to go to conquer the Holy House. 'If I ever forget thee, Oh Jerusalem, let my tongue cleave to the roof of my mouth.'" Later, on his way home in disgrace and in chains, after the third voyage (1498–1500), he brought up the topic again: "As I hope for heaven, I swear that everything I have gained, even from my first voyage, with our Lord's help, shall be offered to him in equal measure for the expedition to Arabia Felix, even to Mecca." He wanted Spain to conquer Jerusalem and then proceed to conquer the enemy—Islam—in its homeland, Mecca, the holiest site in the Islamic world. The conquest of the Americas looked like a Crusade, at least to Columbus.

But Columbus was involved neither with the conquest of the American mainland and its indigenous dynasties nor with settling the vast new territories that Spain had opened for exploration and colonization. Soon enough, distinctive problems arose in America, right from the time that Europeans came to realize what Columbus never admitted: that the place to which he had sailed was not India but, in fact, a New World. In order to tame it, a mixture of Old World practices and new solutions was applied.

The Crusades comprised several discrete elements: ideology, military organization, civil administration, a particular kind of colonization, and a special approach to the non-Christian opponents Europeans faced on the battlefield. These elements were all present in the Spanish conquest of America, and a comparison should provide some of the answers to an old debate.

Viewpoint:
Yes. The crusading mentality was an essential feature of the conquest of the Americas, and the Europeans treated Native Americans the same way they treated Muslims.

The conquest of al-Andalus (Islamic-controlled Spain) from the Muslims and settlement of the conquered areas were certainly sources of accrued experience that the Spaniards drew upon in their colonization of the New World. Spain was the only European country that had such an experience. Both were frontier environments (the introduction of large-scale cattle herding in unpopulated areas of Spanish America drew upon Spain's experience as the only medieval European country with large herds of cattle and sheep), and both had in common the need to organize masses of subject peoples of a different culture and religion. The centuries-long peninsular Crusade, or *Reconquista* (Reconquest), moreover provided a variety of demographic situations that invited different institutional and administrative strategies. Thus, in Valencia, where Muslims outnumbered Christians three to one, Muslims were sometimes resettled in empty mountainous areas where they could be productive farmers without threatening Christian settlements.

The efforts of religious orders to convert Muslims and Jews (largely a failure with regard to the former, somewhat more successful with the latter) were the antecedents of Franciscan missionaries and missions in Mexico and California. The forced conversion of medieval Spanish Jews and sixteenth-century Muslims was but a harbinger of the later campaign to extirpate "idolatry" among the Peruvian Indians. Techniques that Spanish missionaries in the Americas used to assimilate and convert Amerindian populations were identical to those used in the sixteenth century to convert the peninsular Moriscos. The same catechisms and doctrinals were used in both places. In the New World, Franciscans and Jesuits generally favored learning the native languages so that they could preach and catechize the people and make scriptural translations available to them. In both Spain and the New World, however, there was a heavy dose of ideology. Pedro de Alcalá's Arabic manual for priests began with a diatribe against Islam. Father Ramón Pané, who wrote a book on the religion of the Tainos, a Carib Indian group encountered by Columbus in Santo Domingo, noted that, "Like the Moors, they have their law epitomized in ancient chants, and they abide closely by them as Moors do with scripture." He characterizes their religion as "evil," "false," and "deceptive." Pané says, "The island is in great need of punishing those who deserve to be punished, to teach those peoples the things of the Catholic faith, and to indoctrinate them with these teachings because they do not know how to oppose them."

Spanish conquistador Hernán Cortés, enlisting Toltec artisans to aid in the preparations for the conquest of Mexico City, remarked that the Mexican natives were "our Moriscos." Chroniclers of the conflict said that St. James had appeared to lead the Spaniards in battle, just as he had in the wars of *Reconquista* against the Muslims. Indeed, the *Reconquista* was so fresh in the mind of Cortés that, toward the end of his career, he returned to Spain in order to join the crusading expedition that Charles V sent to Tunis (1535).

There is one even closer parallel in the sixteenth century with the Spanish medieval experience. In the southern Philippines, in Mindanao, the Spaniards encountered the easternmost salient of the Islamic world: Muslim peoples whom the Spaniards reflexively called Moros and with whom they fought constantly in the sixteenth and seventeenth centuries. These Moros had assimilated the concept of jihad (just war) and deemed fighting Spaniards a just and sacred cause, sentiments that the Spaniards reciprocated. Conversion of Amerindians and *Filipinos* was held to be a sacred duty.

Some sixteenth-century Spanish apologists for the Empire and its sacred mission went so far as to claim that Spaniards were the new chosen people of God and were therefore entitled to the Universal Monarchy prophesied in Scripture, granting them rule over the entire world. There is always difficulty in establishing historical parallels. Yet, the crusading ideal was an entrenched part of the value system of Spaniards of the late fifteenth and early sixteenth centuries. Some of the conquistadors had fought in Granada. To face a new non-Christian enemy, across a sea, was part of an historically and religiously sanctioned worldview that the conquistadors embraced reflexively in the spirit of a now-familiar national narrative.

—THOMAS F. GLICK, BOSTON UNIVERSITY

THE AMERICAS

CHRISTIAN OUTRAGES

Spanish missionary Bartolomé de Las Casas, angry at the terrible treatment meted out by the Spanish conquistadors, wrote a treatise describing some of the atrocities against the Amerindians of the New World:

Thus, from the beginning of their discovery of New Spain . . . a period of twelve whole years, there were continual massacres and outrages committed by the bloody hands and swords of the Spaniards against the Indians living on the four hundred and fifty leagues of land surrounding the city of Mexico, which comprised four or five great kingdoms as large as and more felicitous than Spain. Those lands were all more densely populated than Toledo or Seville and Valladolid and Zaragoza all combined, along with Barcelona. Never has there been such a population as in these cities which God saw fit to place in that vast expanse of land having a circumference of more than a thousand leagues. The Spaniards have killed more Indians here in twelve years by the sword, by fire, and enslavement than anywhere else in the Indies. They have killed young and old, men, women, and children, some four million souls during what they call the Conquests, which were the violent invasions of cruel tyrants that should be condemned not only by the law of God but by all the laws of man (since they were much worse than the deeds committed by the Turks in their effort to destroy the Christian Church). And this does not take into account those Indians who have died from ill treatment or were killed under tyrannical servitude.

In particulars, no tongue would suffice, nor word nor human efforts, to narrate the frightful deeds committed simultaneously by the Spaniards in regions far distant from each other, those notorious hellions, enemies of humankind. And some of their deeds committed in the Indies, in their quality and circumstances, truly they could not, even with much time and diligence and writing, could not be explained. I will narrate, along with protests and sworn statements by eyewitnesses, only some portions of the story, for I could not hope to explain a thousandth part.

For instance, in Guatemala:

Another incident of unprovoked cruelty was when the Spaniards entered a large and prosperous town no better guarded than another, and in the course of two hours almost destroyed it, putting to the sword men, women, and children and the aged and infirm who could not manage to escape.

When the Indians saw that humility and the offering of gifts were of no avail to soften the hearts of the Spaniards, and that patience and endurance were useless, and that without any appearance or color of reason they would be attacked and slain, they agreed to assemble and stand together and die in a war, revenging themselves as best they could against the cruel and infernal enemies; since they knew that being not only unarmed but naked they would be opposing ferocious men on horseback so well armored that to prevail against them would be impossible, they conceived the idea of digging holes in the middle of roads, into which the horsemen would fall and have their bellies pierced by the sharp sticks with which the holes would be filled, covered over with turf or weeds. Once or twice the horsemen did fall into the holes, but not more than that, for the Spaniards learned how to avoid them. But to avenge themselves against the Indians they threw into those holes all the Indians they could capture of every age and kind. And thus children and old men and even pregnant women and women but lately in childbed were thrown in and perished. As many Indians as could be seized were flung into those holes to be mortally wounded on the sharp sticks; a pitiful sight, especially the women and children. All the remaining Indians were slain with pikes or swords, or were thrown to the savage dogs, which tore them to pieces and devoured them.

Source: Bartolomé de Las Casas, The Devastation of the Indies: A Brief Account, *translated by Herma Briffault (Baltimore & London: Johns Hopkins University Press, 1992), pp. 58–59, 69–70.*

THE AMERICAS

Viewpoint:
No. The conquest of the Americas was not crusading because there was no concerted effort to attain a specific religious goal.

Spanish explorer Christopher Columbus's mystical delusions aside, the Spaniards had both different objectives in the New World and divergent perceptions of its natives with respect to themselves. Although to a certain extent one can admit that the Amerindians, like the Muslims, were targets for conversion, there was one great difference between the two peoples: in Christian eyes, Muslims were heretics, because while claiming participation in the traditions of the Old and New Testaments, they asserted that Muhammad was the "seal," that is, the last and greatest of a long line of "prophets" extending from Abraham to Jesus. Furthermore, Islam was a proselytizing religion. By contrast, Amerindians, judged by the standard of ability to create and write a scripture, were considered illiterate by the Spaniards and therefore not sworn enemies comparable to the Muslims. Instead, the Spaniards proposed a tutelary relationship that was not unlike that of parents and children. In Mexico the Franciscans taught their native charges how to read and write and encouraged them to record their native lore (most notably botany and pharmacology) in Spanish and Latin.

In the Middle Ages there had been no pro-Muslim Christian leaders, none that protested the designation of Muslims and Jews as infidels and inferior peoples. In the New World, by contrast, priests such as Spanish missionary Bartolomé de Las Casas struck a tolerant note and argued for the humanity of Amerindians. Indeed, Las Casas, one of the great spokesmen for tolerance of the "infidel," argued that the Amerindians could not be reduced to slavery and that natural laws are common to all mankind, whether Christian or not. The Amerindians already had Christian traits, he claimed, and all that they asked was to have the Spaniards validate their natural Christianity. "At no other time," Las Casas declared in 1521, in a letter to the Council of the Indies, "and in no other people has there been such a capacity, such predisposition, and such facility for conversion." Indians resemble Christians and are endowed with Christian virtues such as humility and obedience. Above all, they are peaceful. Las Casas turned crusading ideology on its head and inquired of Spaniards: "If Moors or Turks had come with the same injunction declaring Mohammed the ruler of the world, were they to believe it?" This kind of egalitarian ideology was not present at all in the Crusades.

Looking at the European colonization of the New World as a whole, adding the English and French to the Spanish effort, one can conclude, first, that there was no concerted effort by Europeans, acting together, to attain some specific religious goal, the equivalent of the conquest of Jerusalem. Imperial and colonial rivalries took precedence over any united effort against the infidel, and none was ever proposed. In the sixteenth and seventeenth centuries neither the French, English, or Dutch—the major colonial powers next to Spain and Portugal—had any interest in linking exploration and settlement with the symbolic issues of Christianity. French interest was primarily economic and the English, although the settlers of Massachusetts, Rhode Island, and Pennsylvania—all of them seekers of religious freedom—might have had some interest in converting "infidel" Indians, they certainly had no grand schemes to advance Christianity. The millenarian fervor attending the Crusades was absent in the New World.

The Spanish Crown did not trust the conquistadors to look to the spiritual life of the Amerindians and so placed evangelization under the arm of the mendicant orders, especially the Franciscans. "For a time," according to J. H. Parry, in *The Age of Reconnaissance* (1963), "it gave masterful support to the mendicant vows of renunciation, the Christian doctrine of a compassionate deity, and the institutional authority of the sacraments. Such a missionary policy, with its logical consequences in terms of control over the native population, inevitably conflicted with the economic interests of the leading colonists, and led to long and acrimonious disputes; but the friars commanded the respect and sympathy of many of the conquistadores, including Cortés, who himself petitioned for a Franciscan mission to Mexico."

The Crusaders who captured Jerusalem and founded the Latin kingdoms in Palestine and Syria, small territories with a largely alien population that was conquered and controlled with a relatively small number of troops, at least for a while (until Saladin) enjoyed technological superiority over Arab armies. The Spanish settled America with few soldiers and thereafter governed a huge territory with a small standing army. The key to Spanish settlement was that, after a relatively short feudal period, it was civil in character, and security came not only with controlling the indigenous populations, over whom their technological superiority was tremendous, but, more impor-

Woodcut of the meeting between the Inca king Atahualpa and the Spanish, from *General History of the Things of New Spain,* **by Bernardino de Sahagun (mid sixteenth century)**

(John Carter Brown Library, Brown University, Providence, Rhode Island)

tantly, by importing virtually limitless numbers of peasants from Spain to settle the vast, newly conquered continental expanses. The denser the settlement of Spaniards, the greater the security. None of this policy bears any resemblance to the Latin kingdoms established by the medieval Crusaders.

–ROBIN FELD, SANTA MONICA,
CALIFORNIA

References

Felipe Fernández-Armesto, *Columbus* (Oxford & New York: Oxford University Press, 1991).

James Muldoon, *Popes, Lawyers and Infidels: The Church and the Non-Christian World, 1250–1550* (Liverpool: Liverpool University Press, 1979).

J. H. Parry, *The Age of Reconnaissance* (Cleveland: World, 1963).

Robert Ricard, *The Spiritual Conquest of Mexico: An Essay on the Apostolate and the Evangelizing Methods of the Mendicant Orders in New Spain, 1523–1572,* translated by Lesley Byrd Simpson (Berkeley: University of California Press, 1966).

Tzvetan Todorov, *The Conquest of America: The Question of the Other,* translated by Richard Howard (New York: Harper & Row, 1984).

THE AMERICAS

ATTACKS ON JEWS

What was the main cause of attacks on Jews during the Crusades?

Viewpoint: The main motive for attacks on Jews during the Crusades was economic in nature.

Viewpoint: The main cause of attacks on Jews during the Crusades was apocalyptic expectations on the part of Christians.

Viewpoint: Attacks on Jews during the Crusades were prompted by the desire of the Latin Christian West to eliminate them as members of a religious rather than a racial group.

The first "enemies of Christ" to be struck down by participants of the First Crusade (1096–1102) were European Jews rather than Turkish Muslims. In what has become known in some circles as the "first holocaust," the entire Jewish communities of Speyer and Worms were exterminated by Crusader contingents in 1096, while other Jewish communities were persecuted and financially extorted. Virtually from beginning to end, the crusading movement was punctuated by explosive outbursts of anti-Jewish violence. The worst outbreak grew out of the First Crusade. Neither attacking Jews nor the ideological foundations supporting such activity were ever sanctioned by the Catholic Church. At Clermont (1095), Pope Urban II probably could not have predicted that the religious fervor he unleashed would be focused on European Jewry before the participants even left the Latin West. Subsequent popes learned from this unsightly anti-Jewish chapter and made preparations for the protection of Jews before Crusades were preached. Still, even hindsight could not remove the threat to Jews that accompanied crusading completely. During the preaching of the Second Crusade (1147–1149), for example, Bernard of Clairvaux was haunted by the anti-Jewish fervor that emerged and was forced to come down hard on renegade preachers who whipped up hostility against European Jews.

Crusade-related violence against Jews (particularly during the First Crusade) has increasingly troubled scholars. Two generations ago historians of the Crusades could take some comfort in the fact that pogroms against, and sometimes the wholesale slaughter of, Jews was confined to the "rabble" of Europe—that is, the downtrodden and destitute poor who "didn't know any better." "Professional" Crusaders, the scholars argued, focused their attention solely on the proclaimed (and armed) enemies of the Church, that is, the Eastern Muslims—primarily the Turks. Recent scholarship, however, has produced a more nuanced portrait of the so-called People's Crusades. Pogroms against Jews, rather than being the agenda of only the ignorant, unwashed masses, emerged as an integral part of the crusading mentality, particularly in its earliest stages. At one time Emich of Leiningen's butchering of Jews in the Rhineland who refused to convert to Christianity could be explained away as the idiosyncrasies of an unbalanced count (after all, how normative could a man be who followed a goose that was possessed by the Holy Spirit?). Yet, the more that is learned about the People's Crusades, the more one sees a strong knightly contingent accompanying them and participating in their activities—knights who were in positions of leadership.

Attacks on Jews, particularly the attacks that resulted in the extermination of entire communities in Mainz and Worms, have become sore spots in crusading historiography. If such pogroms and mass murders were not conducted by "pseudo-crusaders" but by contingents composed of both the aristocracy and "the people," and rather than being peripheral to the movement were central, then how can such outbreaks of anti-Jewish sentiment be explained? Some scholars focused on the sociological and economic substructure upon which Jewish-Christian relations rested. Economic tensions produced by a Europe in transition have been cited by some historians as the main cause for the Jewish massacres and riots that accompanied crusading. Other historians concentrated on the religious status of European Jewry, postulating that Jews were a religious "other" in an otherwise religiously homogenized Europe and that religious bigotry was prone to transferral. Most modern historians feel that the explanation cannot be reduced to an "either/or" but rather must deal with whichever issue was salient. In other words, were economic tensions rearticulated in religious terms, or did religious issues meld with economic concerns? Particularly with questions as difficult as this, there are no definitive answers but only cogent arguments.

Historians are embedded in cultures that have pressing social concerns and cultural neuroses, and these issues vary. Scholars need to explain not only the past but also the roots that lead to the present. The treatment (much less the experiences) of minorities in medieval Europe was, at best, a minor field of historical enquiry before 1945. The attempted genocide against Jews that came to light in the aftermath of World War II (1939–1945) definitively placed its stamp on the history of Jewish-Christian relations for the whole of European history. Was the Nazi *Juden frage* (Jewish question) asked during the age of crusading? Were the ferocious attacks on Jews in 1096 really a "first holocaust" in a teleological or causative sense, one that relates in any way to the twentieth century?

Viewpoint:
The main motive for attacks on Jews during the Crusades was economic in nature.

The society that spawned the Crusades was violent and riven with economic and social tensions. With central authority distant and weak, real power was held by a caste of knights who were imbued with a warrior ethos and controlled the countryside from fearsome castles. These *milites* drew their wealth from the overburdened peasantry in the form of feudal rents. After the mid tenth century a new class of town dwellers engaged in artisanship, and trade emerged and grew in importance and power as a counterpoise to the *milites*. The consequent rise in the size and importance of towns revived the cash economy, and this change began to put pressure on both *milites* and peasantry, as both found themselves increasingly in need of cash. The only sources of currency available to them were either to sell something of value, their land for instance, or to borrow money from one of the town-dwelling merchants. Since Christian teaching forbade the practice of usury, one of the few sources of credit was from the Jews. It was in this milieu, with its potential for social conflict, that Pope Urban II issued his call for a Crusade at the Council of Clermont (1095).

Jews had several useful qualities from the point of view of rulers. Their economic activity produced reservoirs of capital that could be dipped into to fund both the secular and ecclesi-astical governments. Jews prized literacy and taught their children to read and write at a time when nearly the whole of Western society was illiterate. Also, their legal standing was tenuous. They were, in effect, the personal property of the king or emperor to dispose of as he saw fit. These facts made them vital as arms of the royal administration and as the spearhead of the local tax-gathering apparatus.

This status was both a blessing and a curse to the Jews. On the one hand, their position as royal administrators gave them some power and protection. It was also quite remunerative. On the other hand, they were utterly dependent upon the goodwill of the monarch. Also, their work as tax gatherers made them hated by the general populace; being so closely identified with the crown meant that discontent with or animosity toward the monarch, either from the common folk or the *milites,* sometimes found an outlet in violence directed toward Jews. In fact, there had been periodic outbursts of violence against Jews in France and Germany going back almost to the turn of the millennium, long before Urban's call. This violence, however, was in no way an attempt to exterminate the Jews. It was simply an expression of anger and anxiety at new economic conditions.

An example of this type of activity from a later period is the Shepherds' Crusades of the thirteenth and fourteenth centuries that degenerated not only into a series of violent attacks on Jewish communities but also upon castles and royal officials and property. These outbursts always were aimed at symbols of economic or social oppression. Throughout southern France and Aragon, mobs looted Jewish homes and businesses; they also sought out loan documents and property deeds and destroyed them. The "crusaders" sometimes squatted on Jewish property. Only at Montclus (1251) in Aragon did they actually carry out a general massacre of the Jewish population.

Both David Niremberg in *Communities of Violence: Persecution of Minorities in the Middle Ages* (1996) and Carlo Ginzburg in *Ecstasies: Deciphering the Witches' Sabbath in History* (1991) ascribe this violence in part to the social dislocation caused by the gradual return of a cash economy to Europe beginning in the eleventh century. The revival of trade, emergence of town life, and rise of a new class of middle-class businessmen and artisans caused much social tension, some of which spilled over into attacks on Jews. There was also an element of town-country rivalry in these hostilities. In the assaults on the Rhineland Jews (1096) most of the attackers were Crusaders from France, but they were joined by folk from the surrounding countryside. The burghers of the Rhineland towns were more ambivalent. In some cases they sought to protect their Jewish neighbors, and in other instances they aided the attackers.

When examining actual events in the Rhineland during and subsequent to 1096, certain facts emerge. Urban sought to mobilize the *milites,* but his call inspired many ordinary people to take up the cross. There were at least three bands of "unofficial" Crusaders that preceded the armies that Urban had envisaged, the most noteworthy of these being that led by French ascetic Peter the Hermit and French knight Gautier Sans Avoir (Walter the Penniless). Peter reached the Rhineland with a letter from French Jewry addressed to their coreligionists in Germany requesting that they offer to Peter and his people money and supplies for their journey. In this clear example of extortion the threat of violence was implicit. Indeed, chroniclers, both Jewish and Christian, report that Peter's band committed isolated acts of violence against the Jews in the Rhineland, although Peter did not sanction these attacks, and among his people there was never any program to exterminate the Jews or to force mass conversions to Christianity.

This sort of popular movement was far from Urban's original intention. Peter's band was made up mainly of peasants and others who were untrained in the arts of war and ill equipped for such an expedition. French historian Fulcher of Chartres says that only one in six of Peter's host was a fighting man. Many of these pilgrims were penniless when they set out for the Holy Land and counted on God to provide for them or on foraging from the local populations along the way. In the Rhineland, where there were established communities of Jews, this foraging activity was directed at them. Later, when Peter's band advanced into the realms of Hungary and Byzantium, they aimed their violence at fellow Christians. They ravaged the Hungarian countryside and attacked the fortress at Semlin where, chroniclers report, they inflicted four thousand casualties on the Hungarian defenders. They quickly crossed into Byzantine territory where the authorities, wary of their reputation for violence and rapine, escorted them across the Dardanelles and to the frontier with the Turks. It was during one of their raids on Turkish inhabitants that they were ambushed and decimated.

The extortionate nature of most anti-Jewish violence during the First Crusade (1096–1102) is shown in the case of Godfrey of Bouillon. Godfrey, leading a contingent of knights and peasants in the wake of Peter's larger group, vowed that he would avenge the blood of Christ with the blood of Jews. German emperor Henry IV, who was then in Italy, sent a warning to Godfrey to leave the Jews in peace. Godfrey extracted five hundred silver marks each from the Jewish communities of Mainz and Cologne, but after the warning from the emperor he insisted that he never had any intention of doing violence to them.

Another example is that of Norman crusader Tancred, who extracted thirty pieces of silver from each Jew in Palestine. This demand obviously echoed the story of Judas, who betrayed Christ for the same amount, and it reflects the widespread feeling that Jews were culpable in the death of Christ. Tancred, however, though he used the threat of violence to extort this money, did not carry out any acts of violence against Jews, nor did he seek to convert them to Christianity.

It is only Emich of Leiningen, a German nobleman, and the band of Crusaders that he gathered around him, who earnestly intended to either wipe out all the Jews that they could or to force them to convert. Emich is mentioned in both Christian and Jewish chronicles and appears sadistically violent and possibly lunatic. Christian writer Ekkehard of Aura likens him to a latter-day Saul, which implies doubts about his mental balance. Jewish chroniclers portray him as evil incarnate. He is known to have attracted many eccentrics to his standard—one contingent of followers venerated a goose that was supposed to be possessed by the Holy Spirit—and Emich is said to have claimed to receive visions from the Lord. His "army" attacked the Jews of Speyer and then moved on to Worms, where they cornered four hundred Jews sheltered in the palace of the bishop and slaughtered them all. He and his people were extremely violent, and after their actions in the Rhineland their reputation preceded them on the rest of their journey.

Albert of Aachen, another chronicler of the First Crusade, reports that many of Emich's followers saw the pilgrimage as a pleasure trip and that they intended to take whatever they needed from the locals on their journey to Jerusalem. Albert also claims that after decimating the Jewish community of Cologne, Emich's mob found much money to divide. In fact, after the massacres at Worms, Mainz, and Cologne, many of Emich's band left and went back to their homes, their purses laden with booty. Those who continued carried out their policy of pillage and violence as they made their way across Europe, attacking and stealing from Christians as well as Jews. They eventually were defeated and massacred at Wieselberg (1096) by the forces of the king of Hungary. Albert ascribes this defeat to divine judgment against them because they had massacred the Rhineland Jews out of greed and brought the Crusade into ill repute.

One does not have to look far to discover an economic motive among the knighthood for hostility toward Jews, who were an important source of loans made to the *milites* in order to finance their journey to the Holy Land. To keep his status, a knight had to maintain a suit of armor and several horses. This expense was normally borne by feudal rents that the knight collected and by monies that he received, if any, from his noble patron, as well as from booty and ransoms that he won in battle. For such a knight an expedition to the Holy Land, lasting perhaps several years, was tremendously costly. For many knights it meant selling their lands or the feudal income that they enjoyed from them, or borrowing money against the prospect of returning with booty. Sometimes the *milites* sold their lands to the Church, but in many cases they turned to Jews either for loans, using their lands as surety, or to sell their lands outright. Even before Urban's sermon many knights had fallen into debt. The possibility of these debts being foreclosed, and the consequent demotion in social status, caused anger and anxiety among the *milites*.

In preparing for the Second Crusade (1147–1149), French monk Peter the Venerable, in an epistle to French king Louis VII, advocated using the wealth of the Jews. Peter accused Jews of practicing usury and of dishonest business practices. Louis decreed that anyone who volunteered for the Crusade would have his debt to the Jews forgiven. This forgiveness applied to debts incurred before taking the cross as well as those made to finance the Crusade, and so it proved to be a great recruiting tool. In 1234, 1246–1247, and again in 1268 there were confiscations of Jewish goods in France. This wealth was to be used to finance crusading, and the confiscations were justified as having been the result of usury on money loaned to Crusaders.

In his bull *Audita tremendi* (1187) Pope Gregory VIII specified that the Jews should not be able to charge interest on loans made to those who had taken up the cross. Since this edict applied to loans made before the participants had taken the oath to go on Crusade, it was one way of escaping the toils of usury. In both of these instances Jewish moneylenders lost a good deal of money.

English chronicler William of Newburgh, writing in the late twelfth century about the preparations for the Third Crusade (1189–1192), tells the story of a group of young English knights who had taken the cross and arrived at Stamford to find a fair in progress. They saw the prosperity of the Jewish merchants and became indignant that the "enemies of Christ" should possess so much while they themselves had so little. The knights attacked the Jews with the intention of financing their journey to the Holy Land. The Jews fled to the protection of the castle, but their goods and houses were plundered by the knights and a local mob. William, along with fellow English chronicler Roger of Hoveden, says that the violence against the Jews at York (1190) was perpetrated by residents of that town who were "unable to bear their [the Jews'] opulence while they themselves were in want," and that they were egged on by some men of higher rank who were indebted to the Jews for large sums. Some had pledged their estates for the loans, were now in dire poverty, and hoped that they could eliminate their debts by eliminating their creditors. These examples show just how important the Jews were as sources of cash to finance the Crusades and why the Crusaders, both the *milites* and the peasantry, might be motivated to attack Jews.

Urban's call to take up the cross followed several bad harvests, and many peasants were in danger of losing their land. Indeed, many of them had nothing to lose and must have felt that their backs were to the wall. During the century or so leading up to the First Crusade the West had witnessed the growth of a cash economy, and this transition caused great economic dislocation and hardship. For many peasants, as for the lower ranks of the *milites,* who were feeling the pinch, the Crusade was a powerful inducement to settle up and strike out for new lands. In addition to the promised papal indulgence, there was the outside possibility of gaining an estate in the East, though more-concrete attractions were the prospects of booty and having one's debts to Jewish moneylenders canceled.

One of the strongest arguments in favor of the idea that anti-Jewish violence in the early

Crusades was the result of economic factors is that from the Third Crusade on, when the Church took over organizing the financing of the Crusades, there was virtually no such violence. After the Second Crusade this financing was much more orderly. The Church raised money from tithes and taxes as well as from the personal fortunes of some of the great magnates. Furthermore, the Church stipulated that anyone going on Crusade had to be a military man and capable of sustaining himself for two years. Consequently, there were no hordes of penniless common people accompanying the knights as there had been on the First Crusade, and there was virtually no anti-Jewish or any other kind of popular violence on later expeditions.

Christian chroniclers are equivocal about the motivation for anti-Jewish violence on the First and Second Crusades, but Jewish chroniclers emphatically blame religious fanaticism. In assessing the reliability of these narratives, one must consider when they were composed and for what reason. Robert Chazan, in *God, Humanity, and History: The Hebrew First Crusade Chronicles* (2000), questions when the narratives were written and suggests that they were not the work of eyewitnesses but were composed decades, and in some cases perhaps even centuries, later. As depictions of events they are probably reliable, but one should be careful when considering the motivations they ascribe to the participants. These chronicles are in the so-called lachrymose tradition of Jewish historiography, and the authors are anxious to portray the violence as founded upon the Christians' barbarity and irrational hatred of the Jews. The victims are portrayed as martyrs who clung to their faith unto death and thus were fulfilling their tragic role in the historic destiny of the Jewish people. These chroniclers had every reason to play down the economic motivation of the persecution.

It is impossible to look into the hearts of those who attacked the Rhineland Jews, but it would surely be wrong to impute to them such utter cynicism as to suggest that their motive was only cupidity masquerading as ideology and that the religious fervor they evinced was simply an affectation or a pose to mask their greed. However, there is no doubt that then, as now, those motivated by self-interest can find justification in ideology and that in so doing they convince particularly themselves. No doubt the religious fervor whipped up by Urban's speech at Clermont and the subsequent ecclesiastical campaign to talk the Crusade up led the common people to view Jews as legitimate targets and, along with the general atmosphere of violence, unleashed the passions of the mob. The ill will exhibited by the mob toward the Jews was more likely a mixture of fear and hatred of the alien combined

with resentment of the Jews' prosperity and the severe dislocation caused by the growth of towns and the cash economy. For both the *milites* and the common folk these factors were crystallized by their economic hardship and the need for funds for their journey to the Holy Land.

–DOUGLAS KIERDORF,
BOSTON UNIVERSITY

Viewpoint:
The main cause of attacks on Jews during the Crusades was apocalyptic expectations on the part of Christians.

Attacks on Rhineland Jews by members of various popular Crusades during 1096 were predominantly religious in nature. Popular Crusaders took the cross in an atmosphere of eschatological expectation. Belief that the apocalypse was at hand, combined with increased popular piety inspired by the Cluniac reform, as well as the revival of the clan-based blood feud, produced a religious culture convinced of its self-righteousness and its responsibility to fight in God's name. While many Crusade preachers used these ideas to promote the defeat of Muslims and the reclamation of Jerusalem, more-radical preachers harnessed the same ideas to promulgate their own visions and inspire the populace to act upon them. The result was a Crusade such as that led by Emich of Leiningen, an expedition aimed at the destruction of Jews as a prelude to an assault on Muslims. The basis of such an agenda can be traced back to the inception of Christianity.

Throughout its history, Christianity has been defined in response to social challenges. During the heretical crisis of the Gnostic movement, the Church Fathers were forced to assess exactly what they believed. In response to the Gnostic assertion that Jesus was not fully human, that his flesh was merely a visual representation of a nonsubstance, the Church affirmed its belief that Jesus was both fully man and fully God in a perfect balance. The same stimulus-response pattern can be seen in the reaction of the Church to Arianism, Donatism, Pelagianism, and Nestorianism, as well as many other heretical movements. This negative process of self-definition was not born in response to the challenges of rival Christian groups. It was present at the beginning of the "Jesus Movement," when the Jewish community was divided between those who believed that Jesus was the Messiah prophesied in Scripture and those who

Illumination from
De Universo **(1023)**
equating Jews with
heretics because they
cover their ears and
mouths and are unable to
either hear or speak the
Word of God

(from Angus Konstam, Historical
Atlas of the Crusades, *2002)*

did not. Early Christians, believing that Jesus had brought them a new law and dispensation, came to define themselves against the laws to which they previously held. In this way, Christianity, from its foundations, was defined as distinctly not Jewish.

Concepts of blood feud, vengeance, and clan honor were ingrained into the violent society that received the teachings of Christianity. The earliest European Christians came to see their newfound religion through the lens of their tribal social organization. Missionaries praised the benefits of belonging to the greatest, most powerful kinship group—Christianity. God the Father was the patriarch of this clan, and his Son was the great warrior chieftain. In submitting to this clan structure, new converts accepted promises of protection, honor, and eternal reward. In return, warriors were bound by duty to protect and, if necessary, avenge the faith. Anti-Jewish sentiment was still a predominant component of Christianity. Not only did the faithful hear Christ's message in terms of their tribal warrior culture, but they also viewed the Crucifixion as an attack on their kinship group. Their warrior chieftain had been humiliated and slaughtered by the Jews, who refused to release him at the behest of Pontius Pilate. Thus, Christ's death had to be avenged through physical retribution. If a great chieftain's life was worth the lives of ten ordinary men, the Son of God's life was worth an inestimable number of Jewish lives.

The anti-Jewish sentiment inherent in Christianity, as well as these cultural ideas about kinship and vengeance, bubbled beneath the surface of eleventh-century society, which was wracked by religious fervor evidenced by the Cluniac reform, changes in penitential practice, veneration of relics, and increased pilgrimage traffic. The Cluniacs sought to purify the Church of secular interference, from the smallest proprietary

monastery to the papacy. Divine power passed from God directly to the Pope and on to his cardinals, archbishops, bishops, and so forth, down to the lowest novitiate. Because divine power worked through this system, all of its components should be made pure. It was during this period that, for the first time, clerical celibacy became required rather than just advisable. Cloistered men and women were envisioned as the perfect Christians, those who had given up participation in the physical world in order that they might take part in building the world to come. Cluniac reform sought to purify not only the clergy but also all levels of society. It took the monastic ideal and pushed it beyond the walls of the cloister and into the secular realm. Not everyone could become a monk, but all (including warriors) should become as monk-like as possible. By monasticizing the warrior class, the Cluniac reform rerouted blood feud, vengeance, and clan violence through sacred channels and sanctified the act of killing enemies of the Church.

Enemies of the faith were seen everywhere. The period in which the First Crusade (1096–1102) emerged was rife with eschatological expectations. Christianity had been founded on millennial expectations, but eleventh-century Christians believed that Christ's return was imminent. Apocalyptic fantasies were intensified by the wild sermons of itinerant preachers such as French cleric Peter the Hermit, who wandered from village to village, dressed in sackcloth and ashes, holding a letter from God. Furthermore, "they seem to have been fascinated by the prophecy," taken from the Sibylline Oracles, "of the great Emperor who in the Last Days was to journey to Jerusalem," unite East and West, and initiate the sequence of events that would signal the reappearance of Christ. An important component of this construct was the necessary exposure of all people to Christianity. Non-Christians not only had to hear the message but also had to accept it or perish. Muslims as well as Jews were portrayed as demons who either had to be exorcised through baptism or slaughtered as agents of Lucifer. Non-Christians became the hated "other" that needed to be expunged to purify the earth and clear the way for Christ's triumphant return.

Pope Urban II's call to Crusade (1095) was directed toward the French warrior aristocracy from which he himself descended. Since the Crusade was technically a pilgrimage, however, he could not ban the general populace from taking part in it. Crusading zeal spread to all levels of society. Modern historians divide the First Crusade into two main components: the "official" Crusade, that is, the one under the auspices of the papal legate Adhemar Le Puy, and the "Popular" or "People's" Crusade. The latter was inspired by popular preachers such as Peter the Hermit, German Gottschalk, and Volkmar. These units, like the "official" Crusade, were often led by knights and nobles but contained large contingents of the poor and destitute. Unlike the "official" Crusaders, however, participants in the Popular Crusade were driven by an eschatological fervor that was whipped up and sustained by itinerant "prophets" who launched and accompanied the expeditions. These men committed the atrocities against Jewish communities in 1096.

Attacks on Jewish communities took place in the wave of violence that followed in the wake of Peter's Crusade. Inspired by his early successes, as well as radical preaching, Emich of Leiningen, Volkmar, and Gottschalk led their Crusaders to perform what was, as they saw it, the Lord's work. Peter (and Godfrey of Bouillon as well) extorted money from the Jews in exchange for the safety of their communities. The three remaining groups, however, were not interested in financial extortion. Economic factors were not central to these pogroms. Economic competition and "class warfare" might well have colored the attacks, but the degree of violence and extent of the atrocities committed do not support an economic impetus. Stabbing pregnant Jewish women to ensure the deaths of their unborn children can scarcely be reconciled with "economics" or tensions between the Christian burgher class and its Jewish competitors (which in any event predated the First Crusade).

As the Crusaders traveled through the Rhineland in 1096, they carried with them powerful cultural and religious concepts: self-conceptions based on non-Jewishness; Jews as deicides and, in a manner of speaking, regicides; and Jews as apocalyptic demons that must be converted or exterminated. Along with these concepts, these

Crusaders also possessed the deep-seated conviction that they were chosen by God, that each had been called individually to vindicate their Lord and purify His land. Killing became a sanctified act; if killing Muslims in the East was worthy of remission of sins, how much more worthy was killing Christ's immediate tormentors through their descendants? Through the millennial filter, these Crusaders believed themselves to be charged with the responsibility of bringing the apocalypse. Nowhere was the religious fervor behind these pogroms more evident than in the tour of violence led by Emich.

It is not possible to chronicle the activities of Emich and his Crusaders here; there are, however, several religious, distinctly noneconomic characteristics of his attacks on Jews that can be gleaned from the various accounts. First, Jews were offered conversion in lieu of death. By submitting to baptism, Jewish converts were assimilated into the Christian kinship group and therefore were no longer dangerous "demons." Converting Jews was also a means of initiating the apocalypse by meeting one of its important prerequisites. There was no economic advantage for the Crusaders in allowing Jews to convert—they could keep their possessions while the belongings of slaughtered Jews were free for plundering. If these attacks on Jews were economic in motivation then demanding "protection money" would make more sense than prompting baptism. Jews who refused conversion were annihilated en masse. The Crusaders' intent, which was realized in Mainz and Worms, was to slaughter every Jew regardless of age, sex, or station. What economic gain could possibly be found in the slaughtering of children or, as the Hebrew chronicles relate, stabbing fetuses in wombs? Only intense fear and hatred, the type that is never rooted in economics but is omnipresent in apocalypticism, could inspire such a level of brutality. Economically, it would have been more advantageous to allow Jews to live and to continually extort them. Emich and his Crusaders, moreover, not only targeted Jews but all symbols of their faith as well. They planned to attack the Jews of Speyer, for example, while they were at prayer in the synagogue. At Mainz the synagogue was desecrated and the Torah shredded in front of the Jewish community. Jewish cemeteries were desecrated as well. Clearly, there was no economic benefit in these crimes. Instead, they can be best understood as the externalization of an inner hatred based on eschatological expectations and religious self-righteousness.

The ultimately religious nature of the attacks on Jewish communities by the Crusaders is most poignantly revealed by the reactions and interpretations of the Jewish communities. Initially, the Jews assumed (as many modern historians have) that the Crusaders were motivated by greed and thus could be bought off. In the cases of Peter and Godfrey, this tactic worked. But it failed miserably—and with deeply tragic consequences—with Emich, Gottshalk, and Volkmar. Hebrew chronicles repeatedly relate how the Crusaders brandished crosses before them, attacked them while loudly pronouncing the name of Jesus Christ, and vocalized the highly religious nature of their retaliatory acts. Jews who refused the offer of baptism were butchered, save those who killed one another and themselves to avoid baptism and conversion. These Jews considered themselves martyrs. Economic tensions cannot even begin to explain the actions of these Crusaders or the reactions of the Jews who confronted them.

Clearly, the pogroms against Jews in the Rhineland that were prompted by the First Crusade were religious in nature—with the notable exception of Peter's contingent. These Crusaders were afire with the eschatological ideas that were instilled into or intensified within them by popular preaching. They also bore the culturally imbedded anti-Jewish ideology that was bound up in Christian self-identity. All these factors predated Urban's sermon at Clermont. The Crusade, however, provided a channel by which these men could act out their religious fantasies.

—BRENDA GARDENOUR,
BOSTON UNIVERSITY

Viewpoint:
Attacks on Jews during the Crusades were prompted by the desire of the Latin Christian West to eliminate them as members of a religious rather than a racial group.

The "Jewish Question" that resulted in such a tragic answer in the mid twentieth century had been asked in European society for centuries before the rise of German leader Adolf Hitler. The question (though posed in different terms) seems to have been first asked by St. Paul of Tarsus as he struggled to understand why so many of his fellow Jews rejected Christ. In his epistle to the Romans, Paul described Jews as being blind and deserving of retribution. His most instructive metaphor was in equating Jews with branches that needed to be pruned so that a regrafting could allow the tree of divine truth to flourish. Many Church Fathers asked the question as well and proffered disconcerting answers: Jews personified evil and hatred of God, they were the epitome of carnality, or they embodied the darker side of human nature. St. Augustine of Hippo, synthesizing the Christian and

Roman traditions and designating the status of Jews living in a society dominated by both modes of thought, created the general baseline. Jews, the Augustinian paradigm claimed, were part of God's plan. They represented the horrendous nature of what life was like before Christ and provided a portrait of the false existence that could be contrasted with the truth until the City of God and the City of Man merged and became one. Combining Roman jurisprudence with Christian eschatology, Augustine concluded that Jews had the right to live unmolested; yet, in the fullness of time that heralded the end of earthly existence, they would convert to Christianity and become full citizens, so to speak, in the kingdom of Christ.

These were the main elements that went into the formulation of what one can call the "*medieval* Jewish Question." Cast into succinct terms, "What purpose do Jews play in Christian society and when will that purpose be rendered obsolete?" Other, more specific questions were hardwired into the general query: how should Jews be treated until they no longer serve God's purpose, how will God eventually bring Jews into the Christian community, and how do humans assist God in bringing about his will? These concerns had a "medieval Final Solution." Judaism would, in the end, be finally eradicated through conversion to Christianity. In their medieval forms, both the "Jewish Question" and the "Final Solution" differ markedly from their counterparts in Nazi ideology. What made the medieval and modern versions so different was the "discovery" of race in the nineteenth century (Hitler, for example, insisted that Jews were a racial, rather than religious or cultural, group). Although medieval people were saturated with bigotry of many sorts, they knew nothing of racism since they had no real concept of race. The Jewish Question of the Middle Ages sprang from "anti-Judaism," while its twentieth-century counterpart grew from "anti-Semitism." Although both mentalities were capable of producing tragic consequences, the distinction is an important one. Medieval anti-Judaism was "inclusive," that is, it wanted to eradicate Judaism by ultimately transforming Jews into Christians. "They," in other words, would become "us." Modern anti-Semitism, on the other hand, was and is exclusive: Jews should not and cannot become "us" and need to be removed by other means. A Jew can convert to another religion; a Jew cannot convert to another race. Herein lies the difference between what some historians call the "First Holocaust" against Jews in the Rhineland in 1096 and the Holocaust against "world Jewry" in the mid twentieth century. The former focused on the spiritual extermination of a religion; the latter focused on the physical annihilation of a "race." Still, both efforts had the same goal in mind: a Jew-free society that would flourish and achieve perfection. These were two different forms of "genocide," one religious and the other racial, but both had extermination as their final objective, even if the rationality and means differed markedly.

Attacks on Jews during the age of the Crusades need to be placed within the larger context of this "medieval Jewish Question." Crusader atrocities against Jews, most plainly seen in the Rhineland massacres during the First Crusade (1096–1102), were both exceptional and ordinary. They were exceptional in that the extraordinary situations and the heightened religious animosity accompanying a Crusade unleashed a religious rage that cannot be found during "normative" periods. They were ordinary in that the views and impulses that fueled them were part and parcel of the Christian worldview at the time. Powerful stimuli, such the launching of a Crusade or the spread of plague, could rupture the modus vivendi between Jews and Christians. Extraordinary events such as pogroms, however, drew upon the ordinary perceptions that saturated the medieval Christian worldview. In other words, the potential for a massacre at Mainz or Worms was always there, lying dormant and latent, but could be activated and transformed into a more dangerous strain of anti-Judaism by the sort of episodic "cognitive dissonance" that accompanied Crusade preaching.

Oversimplifying the treatment of Rhenish Jews by the "first wave" of Crusader armies can produce a skewed understanding of the events and motivations that can easily obfuscate the complex dynamics between Jews and Crusaders. Attacks by different armies cannot be conveniently lumped together for analysis—motives and actions varied and the differences were pronounced. The view that all Crusaders shared was that of the Jew as an outsider, but the similarities virtually ended there. Documentation is best for the Crusader contingents led by French ascetic Peter the Hermit and German count Emich of Leiningen—and the motives and results of each of these contingents are on opposite ends of the anti-Jewish spectrum. The conduct of the former group is much easier to explain than the latter. Peter's group was interested in financial extortion, motivated partly by greed and partly by the desperate need for provisions for the expedition. Anti-Jewish sentiment and the status of Jews as outsiders without full rights in Christian society made them easy targets for extortion. The actions of Peter's contingent were unfortunate but easy to explain and, comparatively speaking, much more mundane and benign than those of Emich. Greed and economic jealousy certainly played their roles in the tragic treatment of Jews, but they remain fairly superficial in understand-

"HEAR O ISRAEL"

In his biography of French king Philip II, Gesta Philippi Augusti (1196 and 1207), the monk and chronicler Rigord describes the expulsion of Jews from France:

In the year of our Lord's Incarnation 1182, in the month of April, which is called by the Jews Nisan, an edict went forth from the most serene king, Philip Augustus, that all the Jews of his kingdom should be prepared to go forth by the coming feast of St. John the Baptist [June 24]. And then the King gave them leave to sell each his movable goods before the time fixed, that is, the feast of St. John the Baptist. But their real estate, that is, houses, fields, vineyards, barns, winepresses, and such like, he reserved for himself and his successors, the kings of the French. [Some of this wealth may have been used to build the Louvre.]

When the faithless Jews heard this edict some of them were born again of water and the Holy Spirit and converted to the Lord, remaining steadfast in the faith of our Lord Jesus Christ. To them the King, out of regard for the Christian religion, restored all their possessions in their entirety, and gave them perpetual liberty.

Others were blinded by their ancient error and persisted in their perfidy; and they sought to win with gifts and golden promises the great of the land—counts, barons, archbishops, bishops—that through their influence and advice, and through the promise of infinite wealth, they might turn the King's mind from his firm intention. [The lords appealed to were the political enemies of the king.] But the merciful and compassionate God, who does not forsake those who put their hope in Him and who doth humble those who glory in their strength . . . so fortified the illustrious King that he could not be moved by prayers nor promises of temporal things. . . .

The infidel Jews, perceiving that the great of the land, through whom they had been accustomed easily to bend the King's predecessors to their will, had suffered repulse, and astonished and stupefied by the strength of mind of Philip the King and his constancy in the Lord, exclaimed with a certain admiration: *"Shema Israel!"* [that is, "Hear O Israel"] and prepared to sell all their household goods. The time was now at hand when the King had ordered them to leave France altogether, and it could not be in any way prolonged. Then did the Jews sell all their movable possessions in great haste, while their landed property reverted to the crown. Thus the Jews, having sold their goods and taken the price for the expenses of their journey, departed with their wives and children and all their households in the aforesaid year of the Lord 1182.

Source: *Jacob R. Marcus,* The Jew in the Medieval World: A Sourcebook, 315–1791 *(Cincinnati: Union of American Hebrew Congregations, 1938), pp. 26–27.*

ATTACKS ON JEWS

ing the relationship between Crusades and attacks on Jews. Emich's treatment of Rhineland Jews plunges deep beneath such a superficial veneer and reveals the true, and disconcerting, depths of Christian perceptions. His contingent was not concerned with money but with the extermination of Jews—spiritually if possible, physically if necessary.

Emich's troops did not offer safety to Jews in exchange for cash. The choice given Jews of Speyer and Worms was baptism or death. In a society that knew nothing of race but rather used religion as the category par excellence by which to group people, the option of baptism or death is instructive. Calling this "genocide" is not an anachronism, though at first glance it may seem so. Emich and his troops wanted to cleanse Speyer and Worms of Jews and had two distinct, yet related, methods at their disposal (though the toll at Worms dwarfed that at Speyer). Conversion would effectively annihilate Jews as a religious affiliation. Those who refused baptism were slaughtered, effectively removing these "stubborn" and "unsalvageable" Jews from society, albeit in a different manner. Calling this "genocide" may seem pedantic and hopelessly "whigish" to many historians, yet what other term can one apply to describe the objectives and activities of Emich's contingent (men born into a society in which religion meant what race did in the twentieth century)? Would it be anachronistic to speak of "religious genocide" for a society that had no biologically constructed concept of race? Understood in its medieval religious rather than modern racial sense, genocide is a perfectly acceptable and useful term for describing the actions of Emich's contingent, which reportedly included the stabbing of fetuses in the wombs of Jewish women to make sure no Jew survived.

Emich's slaughter of Jews in the Rhineland was exceptional in both conduct and scope. But the belief that Jews would and must ultimately be eradicated from Christian society was far from exceptional. Violence, though committed against Jews many times during the Middle Ages, was not the normative solution. The choice that Emich offered Rhenish Jews indicates the preferred course and the method of last resort. Despite the brutality of Emich's conduct, his attacks were "inclusive" rather than "exclusive" in motivation. The normative and preferred methods for eradicating Jews were conversion and, to a lesser but still prominent extent, expulsion. Consideration of efforts to convert, or to expel, Jews in medieval Europe cast considerable light on the dynamic working between anti-Jewish violence and crusading.

Offering baptism or death was a primitive and crude approach. The thirteenth century marks a watershed in the Christian relationship to the Jewish question. Converting Jews would now be a "rational" affair. Armed with a new epistemology and the systematized methodologies that Europeans forged during the twelfth-century renaissance, mendicant orders launched an aggressive campaign against Judaism in the thirteenth century. Schools, many staffed by Jewish converts, analyzed Jewish arguments against Christian doctrine and formulated systematic responses. Manuals emerged, the most famous being Raymond Martini's *Daggers of the Faith* (circa 1280), that outlined the procedures for philosophically and theologically dismantling Jewish objections to Christian doctrine. Practitioners of this new approach debated with leading rabbis in public disputations. The Inquisition began intervening in Jewish affairs once the argument was proffered that Talmudic literature constituted heresy. The Talmud was condemned and publicly burned. Soon Jewish communities in Spain were forced to listen to sermons. France and then England followed suit by adopting the policy of obligatory attendance by Jews at Christian sermons. The new approach was well organized, aggressive, and militant. Yet, the goal was essentially no different than Emich's: to ultimately rid Europe of Jews.

Expulsions of communities were another manner in which medieval Christendom dealt with its Jewish "problem." While these actions were taken in the early Middle Ages in France and Spain, they did not remotely approach the scale of post-twelfth-century expulsions. Continuous waves of expulsions, however, took place in the late thirteenth. Jews were even expelled from Italy, where the imperial tradition of rights of citizenship remained stronger than in other parts of Europe. It would not be anachronistic to note in passing that the German Third Reich (1933–1945) first adopted forced emigration as a tentative solution to its Jewish question. As nation-states continued to develop and evolve, greater attention was paid to the Jewish question. Ferdinand and Isabella (and the Spanish Inquisition) turned on Jews with ferocity. Approaches to Jews continued to harden, and in the sixteenth century the policy of "pious lashes" was formally adopted by the papacy. The *Juderia* (Jewish quarters in medieval cities) were originally a concession medieval rulers made to Jews. In the Middle Ages, segregation rather than "mainstreaming" was preferred by minorities. Segregated in the *Juderia*, Jews could enjoy, at least within its physical confines, a sort of limited self-rule. During the sixteenth century such physical confines were transformed from a protective barrier into a virtual prison: the *Juderia* became the ghetto. Rather than protecting Jews, the ghetto became a pen in which Jews were concentrated and could be targeted for conversion more effectively. High taxes, poor sanitary conditions even by medieval standards, and enforced attendance at Christian sermons were all brought to bear on Jews with full force. The way to escape these "pious lashes" was relatively simple: convert to Christianity. An inclusive spiritual, rather than racial, genocide was the goal.

Conversion, expulsion, and slaughter were the three tools with which medieval Europe tried to solve its "Jewish question." The first approach was a nearly constant one, while the latter two were by and large exceptional and episodic. All, however, focused on the same goal: elimination of Jews (but as members of a religious rather than racial group, which is an essential distinction). Crusading agitation was merely one of many triggers that brought the ever-present potential for violence against Jews into a palpable and destructive actuality. There were other initiators as well: rumors about host desecration, child murder, and the poisoning of wells. Medieval Europe had deepseated, spiritually genocidal tendencies. Crusader violence against Jews was just one strand in which this hostility took place.

–CARL HILL,
LOS ANGELES, CALIFORNIA

References

Malcolm Barber, "The Crusade of the Shepherds in 1251," *Proceedings of the Tenth Annual Meeting of the Western Society for French History, 1982* (1984).

Barber, "The Pastoureaux of 1320," *Journal of Ecclesiastical History,* 32 (April 1981): 143–166.

Marcus Bull, "The Roots of Lay Enthusiasm for the First Crusade," *History,* 78 (October 1993): 353–372.

Fred A. Cazell Jr., "Financing the Crusades," *The History of the Crusades,* edited by Kenneth M. Setton, volume 6, *The Impact of the Crusades on Europe,* edited by Harry W. Hazard (Madison: University of Wisconsin Press, 1989), pp. 116–149.

Robert Chazan, *European Jewry and the First Crusade* (Berkeley: University of California Press, 1987).

Chazan, *God, Humanity, and History: The Hebrew First Crusade Chronicles* (Berkeley: University of California Press, 2000).

Giles Constable, "The Second Crusade as Seen by Contemporaries," *Traditio,* 9 (1953): 213–279.

Allan Harris Cutler and Helen Elmquist Cutler, *The Jew as Ally of the Muslim: Medieval Roots of Anti-Semitism* (Notre Dame, Ind.: University of Notre Dame Press, 1986).

Frederic Duncalf, "The First Crusade: Clermont to Constantinople," *A History of the Crusades,* edited by Setton, volume 1, *The First Hundred Years,* edited by M. W. Baldwin (Madison: University of Wisconsin Press, 1969), pp. 253–279.

Duncalf, "The Peasants Crusade," *American Historical Review,* 26 (April 1921): 440–453.

Shlomo Eidelberg, ed. and trans., *The Jews and the Crusaders: The Hebrew Chronicles of the First and Second Crusades* (Madison: University of Wisconsin Press, 1977).

Carlo Ginzburg, *Ecstasies: Deciphering the Witches' Sabbath in History* (New York: Pantheon, 1991).

Hans Eberhard Mayer, *Geschichte der Kreuzzüge* (Stuttgart: Kohlhammer, 1965), translated by John Gillingham as *The Crusades,* second edition (Oxford & New York: Oxford University Press, 1988).

R. I. Moore, *The Formation of a Persecuting Society: Power and Deviance in Western Europe, 950–1250* (Oxford & New York: Blackwell, 1987).

David Niremberg, *Communities of Violence: Persecution of Minorities in the Middle Ages* (Princeton: Princeton University Press, 1996).

Walter Porges, "The Clergy, The Poor, and the Non-Combatants on the First Crusade," *Speculum,* 21 (1946): 1–23.

Jonathan Riley-Smith, *The Crusades: A Short History* (London: Athlone, 1987; New Haven: Yale University Press, 1987).

Riley-Smith, *The First Crusade and the Idea of Crusading* (London: Athlone, 1987; Philadelphia: University of Pennsylvania Press, 1987).

Riley-Smith, "The First Crusade and the Persecution of the Jews," in *Persecution and Toleration: Papers Read at the Twenty-Second Summer Meeting and the Twenty-Third Winter Meeting of the Ecclesiastical History Society,* edited by W. J. Sheils (Oxford: Blackwell, 1984).

Stephen Runciman, *A History of the Crusades* (Cambridge: Cambridge University Press, 1951).

Elizabeth Siberry, *Criticism of Crusading: 1095–1274* (Oxford: Clarendon Press, 1985; New York: Oxford University Press, 1985).

BYZANTINE-LATIN RELATIONS

Did poor relations between the Byzantine Empire and the western Roman Empire contribute to the failure of the Crusades and the ultimate loss of the Crusader States?

Viewpoint: Yes. Byzantine support would have strengthened the crusading movement and the Crusader States.

Viewpoint: No. The Byzantine Empire was so weak and ineffective during the Crusades that it was irrelevant to the western Europeans as either an ally or an enemy.

The Byzantine Empire was an important part of the Crusades from the beginning of the movement. Pope Urban II's appeal to the Western Church for a Crusade was at the least partially motivated by Byzantine requests for assistance against the Seljuk Turks. Relations between these two fraternal descendants of the Roman Empire were never good. Politically speaking, the crowning of Charlemagne as Roman Emperor (800) was interpreted by the Byzantines as a direct challenge to their position as legitimate heirs to the Roman Empire. Religiously speaking, papal claims to universal authority over all Christians were not well received by the Eastern Church and resulted in mutual excommunications that inaugurated the Great Schism (1054). After the disaster at Manzikert (1071), the Byzantines made overtures to the Pope about the possibility of religious reunification, or at least a thawing of relations, in exchange for military assistance against the Turks. Byzantine emperor Alexius I Comnenus was suspicious of the Crusaders when they arrived, however, particularly the Italian Normans, whom he had recently fought a war against and whom he believed had designs on his empire. Apparently, the Crusaders thought that Alexius would take charge of and fully support the expedition, they were sorely disappointed with what they saw as not only his lack of leadership and assistance but also his scheming against them. It comes as no surprise that long before the Second Crusade (1147–1149), directed at Nur al-Din, the new lords of the Crusader States were lobbying for an expedition against the Byzantine Empire.

Relations between the Byzantine Empire, the Latin settlers in the Holy Land, and western Europe worsened rather than improved. The Third Crusade (1189–1192) was a major turning point, since the Byzantine Empire allied itself with Saladin's Egypt against the Crusaders. In 1204 tensions culminated in the diversion of the Fourth Crusade (1202–1204) from its destination in Egypt and resulted in the sack of Constantinople and the conquest of the Byzantine Empire. What was left of the Byzantine imperial army focused its attention on reconquering lands seized by the West. In 1261 it recovered much of its territory. Militarily and financially, however, the Empire never reclaimed the grandeur and power it once wielded.

Historians of the Crusades have long been interested in the impact that Byzantine-Latin relations had on the movement, on the balance of power in the region, and on the strength of the Crusader States. Would a solid alliance between the Latin West and the Byzantine Empire have created a Pan-Christian powerhouse that could have defeated the Muslims? Modern historians are not alone in raising this question. The possibility of a firm Byzantine-Latin alliance was seen by many thirteenth- and fourteenth-century theorists and strategists as the sine qua non for preserving and later recovering the Holy Land.

Viewpoint:
Yes. Byzantine support would have strengthened the crusading movement and the Crusader States.

In June 1098 there was one question in particular that weighed heavily on the minds of the Crusaders who found themselves besieged and on the brink of annihilation at Antioch: where were the Byzantines? At that moment in the First Crusade (1096–1102) the remnant of the Crusader army was engaged in a desperate struggle for survival as they were surrounded by a much larger, better supplied, and more rested adversary. Adding crack, professional units from the Byzantine Empire, the most prosperous Christian state of its day, would have improved the lot of the Crusaders immensely. After several weeks, however, it was clear no such relief force would be coming to their rescue. Taking matters into their own hands, the Crusaders marched out of Antioch to fight a "winner-take-all" battle that would either break the siege or bring them to their deaths. The dramatic victory against overwhelming odds that followed forever changed the course of events of crusading and perhaps the role of Byzantium within that history. As with the battle at Antioch, the Byzantine contribution to the Crusades is one of noticeable absence. Yet, unlike this event, where the lack of Byzantine involvement did not prove ultimately disastrous, the same could not be said for the overall history of the movement. Indeed, one of the major causes for the eventual failure of crusading was the lack of a significant Byzantine contribution to the effort.

The main reason for this dearth of Byzantine support rested in the poor state of relations between the Greek East and Latin West. Tension between the two parties did not suddenly arise during the crusading era, however, but rather had been strained for centuries, stretching back to the days of the Roman Empire. At that time the prevailing situation in the Mediterranean world was one in which economic and cultural leadership resided in the East, while military and political power rested in the West. The result of this arrangement was a lingering sense of friction and resentment between the opposing halves of the empire. Each side opted for assuming a condescending sense of superiority toward the other

by emphasizing its own area of strength. Hence, the West, realizing its relative economic and cultural inferiority, felt all the more determined to accentuate its political and military power. Meanwhile, the East, smarting from being controlled by a culturally and economically inferior state, took refuge all the more in its cultural and economic dominance.

Despite their many achievements in the art of empire-building, the pragmatic Romans never found a way to break down this East-West barrier by more evenly spreading economic, cultural, and political clout throughout the Roman lands. At the same time, in the last days of the empire, new religious issues complicated and reinforced the sense of division between the two parties. The Christian Church came to be centered in Rome, and from that central location the papacy sought to be the final religious authority in Christendom on all matters of faith and morals. With its own rich theological and philosophical traditions, the East soon chafed under what it perceived to be an onerous yoke of foreign domination in matters of religion. In time, the Eastern Church challenged the theory of papal supremacy and, after the eclipse of the Western Empire, even offered a new paradigm for leadership of the Church—accommodation. What this policy meant was that final authority in the Church should rest with the ranking churchman in the leading city of Christendom, thereby having the religious situation align with, or accommodate, the political reality of the times. Since Constantinople was by the fifth century clearly the most powerful city in the Christian world, this argument essentially sought to displace the primacy of the papacy in Rome with the patriarchate in Constantinople. Of course, the Western Church had no desire to have its privileged position within Christendom displaced, and so it vehemently rejected the accommodation argument. One consequence of the ensuing dispute was the injection of religion into an already well-established tense relationship between East and West, and this disagreement only deepened the division.

The situation in the coming centuries continued to deteriorate under the weight of various disputes and conflicts. For example, disagreements about the legitimate relationship between Church and State, especially regarding the Eastern tendency to practice Caesaropapism (when the leader of state also heads the church) and doctrinal disputes over such theological and moral issues as the use of icons in Christian cere-

Mosaic of Alexius I Comnenus, the Byzantine emperor at the commencement of the Crusades, in Hagia Sophia, Istanbul

recovered, the Byzantine state seemed ripe for final conquest by these Muslim forces. In desperation, Alexius I Comnenus, the head of the Eastern Empire, sent an appeal to the West for military assistance, and Pope Urban II, the head of the Western Church, responded positively to this urgent request by organizing and dispatching the First Crusade. A common enemy and a common cause seemed the perfect recipe for repairing centuries of ill feelings and estrangement, but the historical baggage quickly proved too great to overcome. Disagreements flared between Latins and Greeks in the opening stages of the Crusade and reached a crisis point with the failure of the Byzantines to send aid during the Crusaders' desperate struggle at Antioch in the spring and summer of 1098. Whatever goodwill had been built up by the Western response to Byzantine appeals for military aid completely evaporated. Not surprisingly, in the next two major crusading campaigns the bad blood between Latins and Greeks reignited. Of particular resentment was the German experience on the Third Crusade (1189–1192) in which their army, as it marched through Byzantine lands, was openly opposed by the Eastern emperor, Isaac II Angelus. In a bold display of realpolitik, Isaac actually made a secret pact with the enemy, who were led by Saladin, to disrupt the Third Crusade in a bid to improve relations with the Muslim Near East. This act in turn contributed directly to the Fourth Crusade (1202–1204), in which the centuries of bitter relations finally culminated in a Crusader attack and subsequent conquest of Byzantium. Thereafter, what little support the Byzantine Empire had given to the crusading cause all but disappeared.

The relative absence of Byzantine aid for much of the Crusades, and at times its open opposition, proved to be a major stumbling block to the cause. First, it robbed the Crusades of a vital resource—manpower. Crusading campaigns were always conducted under conditions in which Western armies found themselves outnumbered. Not only would the addition of Byzantine forces have helped numerically, but the quality of those troops would have been a valuable asset. Inheritors of the military traditions of ancient Rome, arguably the greatest military power of the ancient world, Byzantine troops had a level of training, organization, discipline, and tradition that no Western army could then rival. The more impetuous and individualistic-minded troops from the Latin West could have benefited from the experience of having such professional units within their ranks, with Byzantine officers and soldiers showing them how to improve discipline and organization and also providing them with expert tactical guidance in dealing with their Turkish opponent.

monies, were two areas of particularly hard feelings. Added to these contentions were political concerns arising over such problems as papal frustration about the lack of Byzantine aid against the Lombard threat in the eighth century and Byzantine resentment with the subsequent decision of Pope Leo III to name Charlemagne emperor of the Christian world, in effect formally rejecting exclusive claims by the Byzantines to that office. The feuding came to a head with the formal division of the two churches in 1054 and in the years following by the invasion of Byzantine territory in Italy and northern Greece by the recently Christianized Normans from the West. Relations between the Christian East and Christian West could not have been more dismal than they were just before the advent of the crusading era.

Yet, in the closing years of the eleventh century, a new arrangement seemed suddenly possible. After Byzantium suffered a catastrophic military defeat at the hands of the Seljuk Turks at Manzikert (1071), one from which it never

Second, the active involvement of Byzantium would have provided the Crusaders with a knowledgeable ally who had many centuries of experience in dealing with the Near East. Crusading armies needed sound advice on terrain, weather, enemy tactics, local politics, and religious divisions in this region, which was in many ways so different from western Europe. Time and again, Crusaders made mistakes relating to all of these factors. Perhaps, if relations had been better, it might have been conceivable for a crusading army to deploy first to Constantinople or some other station within the Byzantine Empire where the troops could have participated in a "boot camp" for Near Eastern duty. Byzantine officers, well versed from both personal and historical experience in the particular characteristics of this warfare, could have acted as the cadre for the training program. Then, once the training regimen was completed, a combined force of newly instructed Latin knights and professional Byzantine soldiers could have marched together to achieve the goals of the particular Crusade they were on. While this scenario might seem implausible, Crusaders who campaigned in the Baltics in later centuries participated in much the same type of program. Undoubtedly, the results of such a cooperative approach would have been more effective and more enduring than was the actual case. Once territory had been seized and occupied, Byzantine advisers could have served as useful guides in helping their Western allies to navigate the interwoven network of religious, political, and cultural forces that complicated their efforts to govern in the Near East.

Third, having a more supportive Byzantine Empire could have resolved a systemic problem experienced by Crusaders in the Near East—long, tenuous, and unreliable supply lines. Basing operations out of Byzantium would have shortened those supply lines and allowed crusading armies to fight on a more even field with their enemy, who enjoyed a close network of supply bases. A more efficient logistical system would have allowed the crusading armies to be larger and to be able to conduct operations longer and deeper into the Near East. Also, the viability of the Latin States in the East would have been strengthened over the long term. Instead of having to rely solely on the habitually unpredictable, highly unreliable, and agonizingly slow assistance that came from the Western powers, the Latin States could have found a more responsive ally in the Byzantine Empire, which had a greater immediate and vested interest in Near Eastern affairs. With such additional assistance, perhaps the Latins would not have felt compelled, for example, to attempt to fight a single, "all-or-nothing" battle against Saladin in the summer of 1187 at Hattin. If the Crusaders had had a better relationship with the Byzantines, perhaps the disastrous consequences could have been minimized. With reinforcements and aid arriving more quickly from Byzantium, the principalities of Antioch and Tripoli could have been salvaged, thus making the job of the Third Crusade a more manageable affair of simply recapturing Jerusalem rather than attempting to restore the Crusader States.

Finally, a friendlier Byzantium would have removed one other recurring obstacle—the distractions that undermined the unity of purpose and effort of the crusading armies. Especially on the early Crusades, clashes and disputes with imperial troops and officials led several Crusade leaders to contemplate an outright attack on Constantinople. While at first such tensions did not erupt into a full-scale war, they soured the relationship between Crusaders and their Byzantine hosts. They also directly led to needless delays in the campaigns and to refusals of full Byzantine support, which hampered the effectiveness of these early efforts. Eventually, however, outright hostilities developed during the Fourth Crusade, and the consequences damaged the cause of crusading. Given the time, effort, and expense of organizing and conducting a campaign, the diversion of the Fourth Crusade to Byzantium massively squandered limited resources. It took the West another decade before it was able to raise a comparably sized army. There was, therefore, one less hammer blow struck against the real enemy in the Near East, who under the weight of well-placed successive strikes might have been defeated. In the century that followed the capture of Constantinople (1204), the crusading movement reached a critical crossroads. The West was unable to concentrate its collective attention on dealing with the growing strength and unity of its Muslim opponent because its efforts in part also had to be focused on defending Latin holdings in the former Byzantine Empire. An indifferent, and at times uncooperative, Byzantium proved in the end to be a needless and eviscerating distraction for the Crusaders and a much-welcomed benefit to the Muslim powers.

It is clear that the Crusades proved unable to achieve the long-term strategic goal of capturing and retaining Jerusalem in Christian hands. While there were many reasons for this failure, the lack of active, committed Byzantine support for the crusading movement must be included in this list. The Western armies were deprived of needed troops, logistical support, knowledge, and unity of focus. The combined result of these factors was to reduce the potential effectiveness of the typical crusading campaign.

–CHRISTOPHER LIBERTINI,
SUFFOLK UNIVERSITY

BYZANTINE-LATIN RELATIONS

CONSTANTINOPLE CAPTURED

During the Fourth Crusade (1202–1204), the European invaders altered their original plan to capture Jerusalem and instead assaulted Constantinople. This account is by Geoffrey de Villehardouin:

Thus their peril and toil lasted for nearly ten days, until, on a Thursday morning (17th July 1203) all things were ready for the assault, and the ladders in trim; the Venetians also had made them ready by sea. The order of the assault was so devised, that of the seven divisions, three were to guard the camp outside the city, and other four to give the assault. The Marquis Boniface of Montferrat guarded the camp towards the fields, with the division of the Burgundians, the division of the men of Champagne, and Matthew of Montmorency. Count Baldwin of Flanders and Hainault went to the assault with his people, and Henry his brother; and Count Louis of Blois and Chartres, and Count Hugh of St. Paul, and those who held with them, went also to the assault.

They planted two ladders at a barbican near the sea; and the wall was well defended by Englishmen and Danes; and the attack was stiff and good and fierce. By main strength certain knights and two sergeants got up the ladders and made themselves masters of the wall; and at least fifteen got upon the wall, and fought there, hand to hand, with axes and swords, and those within redoubled their efforts and cast them out in very ugly sort, keeping two as prisoners. And those of our people who had been taken were led before the Emperor Alexius; much was he pleased thereat. Thus did the assault leave matters on the side of the French. Many were wounded and many had their bones broken, so that the barons were very wroth.

Meanwhile the Doge of Venice had not forgotten to do his part, but had ranged his ships and transports and vessels in line, and that line was well three crossbow-shots in length; and the Venetians began to draw near to the part of the shore that lay under the walls and the towers. Then might you have seen the mangonels shooting from the ships and transports, and the crossbow bolts flying, and the bows letting fly their arrows deftly and well; and those within defending the walls and towers very fiercely; and the lad-ders on the ships coming so near that in many places swords and lances crossed; and the tumult and noise were so great that it seemed as if the very earth and sea were melting together. And be it known to you that the galleys did not dare to come to the shore.

Now may you hear of a strange deed of prowess; for the Doge of Venice, who was an old man, and saw naught (seeing he was blind), stood, fully armed, on the prow of his galley, and had the standard of St. Mark before him; and he cried to his people to put him on land, or else that he would do justice upon their bodies with his hands. And so they did, for the galley was run aground, and they leapt therefrom, and bore the standard of St. Mark before him on to the land.

And when the Venetians saw the standard of St. Mark on land, and the galley of their lord touching ground before them, each held himself for shamed, and they all got to the land; and those in the transports leapt forth, and landed; and those in the big ships got into barges, and made for the shore, each and all as best they could. Then might you have seen an assault, great and marvellous; and to this bears witness Geoffry of Villehardouin, who makes this book, that more than forty people told him forsooth that they saw the standard of St. Mark of Venice at the top of one of the towers, and that no man knew who bore it thither.

Now hear of a strange miracle: those who are within the city fly and abandon the walls, and the Venetians enter in, each as fast and as best he can, and seize twenty-five of the towers, and man them with their people. And the Doge takes a boat, and sends messengers to the barons of the host to tell them that he has taken twenty-five towers, and that they may know forsooth that such towers cannot be retaken. The barons are so overjoyed that they cannot believe their ears; and the Venetians begin to send to the host in boats the horses and palfreys they have taken.

Source: Geoffrey de Villehardouin, *"Memoirs or Chronicle of The Fourth Crusade and The Conquest of Constantinople,"* Chronicles of the Crusades, translated by Frank T. Marzials (London: Dent, 1908).

Viewpoint:
No. The Byzantine Empire was so weak and ineffective during the Crusades that it was irrelevant to the western Europeans as either an ally or an enemy.

Poisonous relations between the Latin West and Byzantine Empire are sometimes cited as an important factor in the repeated failures of crusading expeditions to the East. The Byzantines should have been natural allies of the Crusaders and of–after they were firmly established–the Latin Crusader States. Instead, tensions and animosity over spiritual, political, economic, and territorial issues prompted the Byzantines to see the Latins as a threat equaling–sometimes surpassing–that posed by Muslims. Rather than join forces with the Latins, the Byzantines more often than not hamstrung their efforts. But if the two had come together, they could have created a powerful alliance that would have secured Christian hegemony in the region. The issue is almost always cast in terms of "will" rather than "ability." The Byzantines certainly did not have the inclination to truly join forces with the Latin West. What needs to be addressed seriously, however, is the fact that the Byzantines also lacked the ability. In most respects, the Byzantine Empire was an inert military force in the age of the Crusades and had little value as an ally. Their occasional efforts to support the Latins were just as irrelevant as were their more frequent attempts to frustrate them.

Byzantine Empire is a more accurate term than *Eastern Roman Empire,* at least after the tenth century. Mehmed II's conquest of Constantinople (1453) is conventionally seen as the moment of death for the Roman Empire, but it was little more than the city of Constantinople by this time and hardly qualified as an empire. The real death of the eastern half of the Roman Empire occurred at the end of the Sassanian Wars (628). The Eastern Romans made a great showing in this extended war with Persia, but they were exhausted by it. Mutually depleting each other's resources weakened both Sassanid Persia and the Eastern Romans, so much so that neither could adequately defend itself against the Arab expansion that followed the death of the Prophet Muhammad (632). The Romans fared better than the Persians; while Persia was completely conquered, the Romans lost only about one-third of their holdings, a serious but not necessarily mortal blow. The Eastern Romans, or Byzantines (at this period it is difficult to say which is the better term),

went on the defensive until the tenth century, when they started making advances both against Muslims in the East and Bulgars in the West. Just as the remains of the Western Empire had been transformed from something Roman to something Germanic, so too was the Eastern Empire changed from something Roman into something Slavic. Both West and East scarcely resembled their Roman roots, though the Byzantines kept a much tighter grip on court ritual and were better at maintaining the physical and architectural aspects of the Roman achievement. The Seljuk destruction of the Byzantine army in 1071 (after which the emperor was humiliated by being publicly used as a footstool by the victor) brought a shocking realization to the Byzantines that they were completely incapable of meeting their defensive requirements, which prompted them to request Western assistance that ultimately gave birth to the Crusades.

There was, however, one characteristic of classical Rome that the Byzantines never lost sight of: playing one "barbarian" against the other. This strategy doubtlessly informed their request for Western assistance against the Turks. The Byzantines were already fighting the Italian Normans, as well as the Turks, and looking to the West for help made good strategic sense. As these two enemies depleted one another's resources, the Eastern Mediterranean would be made ripe for Byzantine recovery. Evidence suggests that this strategy was, and remained, the main Byzantine stance regarding the Crusades and explains much of its double-dealings. Even the Byzantine trump card, economic might and commercial superiority, was essentially surrendered to the Italian maritime republics.

That Alexius I was as frightened by the First Crusaders as he was by the Turks is evident in every aspect of his conduct. Byzantine troops (which certainly were a hazy shadow of those that defended the classical Roman Empire) kept a safe distance from combat and tended to swoop down and grab what they could after battles ended. They were incapable of stopping even the mostly unprofessional contingent of Peter the Hermit. Byzantine impotence can also be clearly seen in the course of the Third Crusade (1189–1192). Emperor Isaac II Angelus opted to side with Egyptian leader Saladin and vowed to decimate the German contingent before it crossed the Bosphorus. Byzantine skirmishes and intrigues produced virtually no results, barely even slowing the German advance, and Saladin quickly realized he was dealing with an ally that had nothing to offer but empty promises. The German contingent was neutralized not by Byzan-

BYZANTINE-LATIN RELATIONS

tine forces but by the accidental drowning of German emperor Frederick Barbarossa.

Was there anything of tactical importance that the Byzantine Empire could have offered the Latins? The Byzantines could have offered guides who knew the terrain and political dynamics of the East (and actually did so during the First Crusade), but once the Crusader States were established and the Latins settled, they acquired this ability themselves and it became a forte of the military orders. Technological contributions, however, must be taken seriously. The Byzantines made great innovations in military technology (for example, fortification construction), but these secrets were rapidly diffused and quickly become common knowledge. A friendly and committed Byzantine Empire, furthermore, could have offered the Christians its lands as a base for operations, which could have proved of utmost importance to the Latins, certainly prior to the Third Crusade. After this Crusade, sea transport rose to ascendancy, and the Latin acquisition of Cyprus offered an equivalent forward base that had nothing to do with the Byzantines (who lost the island in 1191 to English king Richard I). Byzantine fleets were unable to provide naval power that remotely equaled that of the Italian maritime republics. The Crusade of French king Louis IX adopted this strategy, and his ultimate failure on the banks of the Nile (1250) had little to do with a lack of supplies (though his lines were cut by the Muslims, they would also have been severed if Constantinople were the supply base).

The final outcome of the Fourth Crusade (1202–1204) is frequently cited as evidence of the importance of the Byzantine Empire for a regional strategy. The "shifty Greek" sat on immense resources that could have altered the power balance if they were made friendly to the West. Such a theory, however, gives the participants in the Fourth Crusade far too much credit. The Latin conquest of the Byzantine Empire had much more to do with Venetian commercial ambitions and the opportunity for would-be Crusaders to become Eastern lords than any strategic benefit. Latin domination of the Byzantine Empire, moreover, did not improve the lot of the Crusader States or the movement. If anything, it diverted resources away from the war against the Muslims to the Byzantine government in exile, which ultimately succeeded in recovering its lost territory. If the Byzantine Empire was capable of action that would strengthen the Crusader States, then one would expect that once the bulk of it came under Latin control the Crusader States would have been strengthened, which was not the case. The Venetians and

Genoese could have had a palpable impact on the security of the Crusader States or the strength of a particular Crusade. The Byzantines, while either supporting or undermining a Crusade, had no tangible impact, and the result unfolded as if the Empire had not even existed.

Relatively speaking, the Latin Empire of Constantinople had a short life. In 1261 Michael VIII Palaeologus managed to recover much of the land that was lost, although some territories remained under Latin control. But he, like his predecessors for the past two centuries, could only defend the empire through diplomacy and intrigue rather than military force. Support from Aragon, the Mongols, and Egypt was solicited, while diplomatic intrigues attempted to (and actually succeeded in) frustrating the sweeping ambitions of Charles of Anjou, which included capturing the Byzantine Empire. Michael's strategy was to court Western goodwill as much as possible. His son, Andronicus II Palaeologus, took a different approach, trying to exercise Byzantine sovereignty and apparent military might, and in the process he lost most of Asia Minor to the Turks, until he was deposed by his grandson after a long reign of forty-six years.

The sad reign of Andronicus brings into bold relief exactly how emasculated the Byzantine Empire was. By trying to make the empire stand alone instead of currying international support through deference, Andronicus pushed the realm into a tailspin from which it never recovered. The Italian maritime republics and the Hospitallers, based at Rhodes, became the Christian guardians of the Aegean. "Barbarian" Venice was no longer adequately pitted against "barbarian" Genoa, and Byzantine security completely unraveled. The treasury was bankrupted, and the economic power that served as the sole mooring for Byzantine security went adrift. The Byzantine army, as it had been for centuries, was more complicated than it was effective. Discipline among the troops and the quality of training continued to deteriorate, even by Byzantine standards. Coinage was constantly devalued, and what remained of the Byzantine army and navy was systematically dismantled by the early fourteenth century.

The painful military emasculation that the Byzantine Empire suffered under Andronicus was simply the high-water mark in a state of affairs that existed from the birth of the crusading movement in the late eleventh century. To appropriate and modify a derogatory term from the age of imperialism, the Byzantine Empire was the "sick man" of global history. It did not have the military ability to protect its borders, much less make a significant contribu-

BYZANTINE-LATIN RELATIONS

tion to regional wars and the quest for hegemony. The Byzantines were a useless ally to Muslims and Latins alike, though the former were much quicker to realize this fact than the latter. A military palsy had set into the Byzantine Empire during the eleventh century, and it proved to be a degenerate and fatal condition. Byzantine assistance, resistance, or hostility and attacks made no difference. The Byzantines were the political and military equivalent to helium on the periodic table of elements—inert.

–CARL HILL,
LOS ANGELES, CALIFORNIA

References

Charles M. Brand, "The Byzantines and Saladin, 1185–1192: Opponents of the Third Crusade," *Speculum,* 37 (April 1962): 167–181.

Brand, *Byzantium Confronts the West, 1180–1204* (Cambridge, Mass.: Harvard University Press, 1968).

W. M. Daly, "Christian Fraternity: The Crusaders and the Security of Constantinople," *Medieval Studies,* 22 (1960):

Deno John Geanakoplos, *Emperor Michael Palaeologus and the West, 1258–1282* (Cambridge, Mass.: Harvard University Press, 1959).

Angeliki E. Laiou, *Constantinople and the Latins: The Foreign Policy of Andronicus II, 1282–1328* (Cambridge, Mass.: Harvard University Press, 1972).

Ralph-Johannes Lilie, *Byzantium and the Crusader States, 1096–1204,* translated by J. C. Morris and Jean E. Ridings (Oxford: Clarendon Press / New York: Oxford University Press, 1993).

CHILDREN'S AND SHEPHERDS' CRUSADES

Were the Children's and Shepherds' Crusades class protests of the poor against the wealthy?

Viewpoint: Yes. These Crusades were expressions of class conflict fueled by the military failures of the European warrior aristocracy.

Viewpoint: No. These Crusades, although linked to the concept of apostolic poverty, were more religious than class-conscious mass movements.

Crusading was a venture that, with a few exceptions, was effectively dominated by the warrior aristocracy of Europe. This fact can be seen in the gist of Pope Urban II's address at Clermont (1095). The "founding father" of the Crusades envisioned an army of professional and well-born soldiers who would form a spiritual task force. Despite Urban's intentions, however, the Crusades also mobilized mass contingents of the lower classes, who were eager to capitalize on the spiritual (and possibly material) gains the expedition offered. Urban was prisoner to the vehicle he used to launch the Crusades. Pilgrimage was open to anyone, and thus by extension so was the "armed pilgrimage" Urban initiated. Even though crusading from its beginning was conceived as an aristocratic venture, it was capable of stirring the lower classes as well. Many historians have considered carefully the effect that class distinctions had on the movement.

Interpretations of the Children's Crusade (1212) have been subjected to a great deal of historical revision in recent years. The traditional view of bands of children inspired to save the Holy Land has been attacked by many historians. Central to the debate is exactly what chroniclers meant by the word "pueri." Traditionally translated as "children" by historians, critics have pointed out that was not the only meaning of the term and, when the entire context is considered, appears not to have been the meaning intended when used to describe these events. Rather than referring to "children," revisionist historians claim it referred to a class of landless, transient laborers who suffered greatly from the sweeping economic changes that punctuated the turn of the century. This rabble has also been cited as the reason for the hostile reaction of many clerics to the movement: rather than watching pure children take the cross, they observed a mass movement of the poor that would surely threaten the propertied classes—particularly the Church. Revisionist interpretations of the Children's Crusade have not been restricted to reassessing class origins. Recently, it has been suggested that the Children's Crusade received its name from the fact that its participants were the sons of previous Crusaders.

The Shepherds' Crusades (1251, 1309, 1320) were more directly inspired by class origins. Bands of the poor assembled to accomplish what the aristocrats could not. They attacked symbols of aristocratic pride and trumpeted the stark contrast between the simplicity and devotion of the poor and the pomp of the rich. Shepherds' Crusades were marked by unruly and violent behavior (particularly the anticlerical and anti-aristocratic forms). The poor believed that they had always been Christ's special children and it was they who would liberate his patrimony, while the sins of the rich continued to prompt failures.

Although the Children's Crusade did not result in the rampant criminal behavior that marred those of the Shepherds, both have been explained in terms of class conflict and the chasm between rich and poor. Some scholars believe, following Norman Cohn, in *The Pursuit of the Millennium* (1957), that forms of class protest, and even revolution, could only take place in the Middle Ages through religious conceptions. Thus, apocalypticism and Crusades of the masses (the two frequently overlapped) became vehicles by which to attack material inequities and class distinction—a sort of Marxism before Marx. Others have argued that this position imputes modern concepts of class animosity to the past. Poverty was always a virtue in medieval religious terms, and it would be surprising not to find such undertones in these movements. Rather than representing a catalyst for protest and assault on class structure, notions of the simplicity and virtue of apostolic poverty were not active agents of social reform but merely the language in which popular Crusades were articulated. These Crusaders wanted to succeed where others had failed rather than to reshuffle the political and economic deck in Europe.

Viewpoint:
Yes. These Crusades were expressions of class conflict fueled by the military failures of the European warrior aristocracy.

In the social and economic ferment of thirteenth-century Europe the Children's and Shepherds' Crusades stand out as manifestations of popular discontent with the rulers and governing orders of society. These episodes reveal the tensions and class antagonisms extant in northern France and Germany; they also illuminate contemporary ideas about expeditions to the Holy Land. The Crusades of the Children (1212) and of the Shepherds (1251, 1309, 1320) should be seen as part of a long-standing popular movement, as a reaction to the failure and corruption of the "official" military Crusades, and, particularly in the case of the Shepherds' Crusades, as inchoate attempts to overturn the corrupt hierarchy of European society.

The Crusades were tests of the mettle of the Crusaders. People recognized that God could smite the Muslims himself and take Jerusalem if he chose to do so, but he, in his infinite mercy, would rather offer the pilgrims a chance at redemption. Therefore, the arduous "pilgrimages" to the Holy Land were part of some greater plan. In such an interpretation the fate of the expedition is a sign of God's judgment on the participants, and the Crusade becomes a test. The performance of the individual Crusader secures, or fails to secure, his place in Paradise. In fact, in the popular view this testing of pilgrims in the crucible of the Crusade, and the possibility of gaining salvation, is really the primary purpose of the enterprise.

By the early thirteenth century the repeated failures of the Crusades and the fall of Jerusalem (1187) to Saladin were powerful evidence of God's anger with the knights. French cleric Bernard of Clairvaux had been the main ideological force behind the Second Crusade (1147–1149), and he blamed its dismal failure on the sinfulness of the knights who participated. Bernard likened the knights to the children of Israel wandering for forty years in the wilderness and said that they should be ashamed of their lack of faith. Dominican monk and professor Humbert of Romans also blamed the knights for their defeat by the Muslims. Later, English chronicler William of Newburgh wrote that the fall of Jerusalem and the defeat at the Battle of the Horns of Hattin (1187) were the results of God's judgment on the dissolute denizens of the Holy City.

From the First Crusade (1096–1102) on, commentators remarked upon the moral laxity of the knights. After suffering setbacks before the siege of Jerusalem, clerics urged the Crusader host to put "light" women out of their camp and to perform acts of penitence. Witnesses recounted tales of the vanity and pride of the knights, of their squabbles over booty, and of covetousness and lust. After taking Jerusalem (1099) there was a scramble for loot, and the new rulers of the Holy Land were accused of becoming dissolute, adopting the local lifestyle, and going soft. The corruption of the Crusaders reached its height with the debacle of the Fourth Crusade (1202–1204), in which the Crusaders were diverted, attacked the Christian Byzantine Empire, and then fell to fighting among themselves over the spoils.

By 1212 there were examples of the failures of the knights nearer to home. In the south of France a Crusade was under way, supposedly against the heretical Cathars, but some commentators noted that the purpose was equally to dispossess the count of Toulouse and to annex his land for the king of France. Some people complained that the knights who participated in this Crusade expropriated the belongings of the vanquished and took possession of their estates.

Troubadours also excoriated those who took the cross and then failed to go to Outremer. Poet and troubadour Peire Vidal criticized French king Philip Augustus for delaying his departure to the East and for attacking the lands of those who were already on Crusade—meaning King Richard I of England. One reason for this sort of criticism was that when an expedition was announced, special taxes were levied on the populace. This burden was exacted upon those who could least afford it and who then saw their taxes frittered away while those

Church of the Holy Sepulchre in Jerusalem, originally built by Constantine the Great in the fourth century and renovated by the Crusaders in 1144

CHILDREN'S AND SHEPHERDS' CRUSADES

who were supposed to be crusading stayed at home. There was widespread anger at the corruption of the clergy and friars who blessed people taking the cross and then redeemed the pledge for a monetary consideration. The Crusade, in fact, became a business proposition from which the Church, crown, nobility, and financiers all gained at the expense of the common folk who were expected to pay for it all.

Two separate expeditions in 1212 set out to accomplish what the chivalry of Europe could not. Both Stephen in France and Nicholas in Germany, the young leaders, made it explicit that they had been appointed by God to lead processions of children to the Holy Land. From the beginning, miracles were associated with these charismatic leaders, and it was well known that miracles could only be performed by the pure of heart. The commentator Reinier of Liège said that since the Crusade was a test of righteousness, these innocent children could prevail. One should note that their righteousness was a rebuke not just to the materialism of the "official" Crusaders but of the chivalry as a class. The knights claimed their privileged position

in society by virtue of their function as protectors of the people and the Church. If a movement of unarmed children could free the Holy Land when the *milites* were unable to—and their innocence could overcome the Muslims when the powerful and worldly Church could not—what real function did these upper classes serve?

Virtually all contemporary writers called the Children's Crusade a stupid and wicked idea, and some even suggested that it was a plot hatched by Satan or by Hassan ibn al-Saabah, the legendary founder of the Assassins. Remember that these writers were all clerics and that the Church shared the failure and odium of the military Crusades. Later, the Shepherds' Crusades indicted the established hierarchy of society more explicitly and were condemned by the Church even more vociferously.

Running throughout all of these episodes is the theme of the impoverished being appointed by God to accomplish his purposes on Earth. Thirteenth-century English monk and chronicler Matthew Paris, who condemned the Shepherds' Crusade, nevertheless said that the Lord frequently chose the poor and weak to do his work. Paris argued that in both the Children's and Shepherds' Crusades the leaders were appointed by God, and he indicated that their followers, because of their innocence, were "chosen" by him for the task. The anonymous author of the *Chronica Universalis Mettensis* says that the Shepherds' Crusade of 1251 intended to recover the Holy Land, a task that could not be accomplished by the chivalry of France.

The worldliness of the Church gave rise to regular criticism that manifested itself in the form of heresy. These heresies typically called for the Church and society as a whole to return to the simplicity and poverty of the apostolic life. Since, in their time as in ours, divisions of wealth mirrored the division of society into castes, criticism of wealth implied criticism of the existing social order and the avarice of Church, crown, and nobility. Poverty is the fount of all virtue. This message was preached not just by the Cathars and Waldensians but by St. Francis of Assisi. If this contention is so, then only the poor are virtuous, and if only the pure in heart are capable of wresting the Holy City from the Muslims, then it follows that children and poor shepherds have the power to do so. The implications of this thinking were radically subversive, calling into question the social hierarchy.

If this belief is only implied in the actions of the Children's Crusade, it becomes ferociously explicit in the Crusades of the Shepherds. Look at the objects of their violence and hatred. They attacked royal officials—including Jews—as well as castles, the nobility, and the clergy. They threw the archbishop of Rouen out of his cathedral and killed twenty-five clerics at Orléans. In 1251 they stormed the Dominican convent at Tours and smashed the statue of the Virgin. They burned property records and squatted on the lands of the nobility and royal officials. At Tours and Bourges local people joined in, and, in fact, everywhere the Pastoureaux (participants in the Shepherds' Crusade) went, the country people appeared sympathetic to them. What emerges from contemporary accounts is an example of class warfare. The poor and the powerless, embodied by the Shepherds, rose up against their oppressors—the knights, the Crown, and the Church. At Tours the bishop put the whole city under interdict for the help its citizens gave to the Pastoureaux, who moved down through France and crossed the Pyrenees into Spain, evidently intent upon attacking the Islamic kingdom of Granada. They were attacked and wiped out by the king of Aragon after they had ransacked several towns in his kingdom and massacred the Jewish community at Montclus.

The movements of the Children's and Shepherds' Crusades were manifestations of deep-seated discontent and even hatred of the governing classes in the thirteenth and fourteenth centuries. The spark that set off these conflagrations was the

failure, both military and moral, of the chivalry to successfully defend the Holy Land.

—DOUGLAS KIERDORF, BOSTON UNIVERSITY

Viewpoint:
No. These Crusades, although linked to the concept of apostolic poverty, were more religious than class-conscious mass movements.

The Children's Crusades (1212) and the Crusades of the Pastoreaux, or Shepherds (1251, 1309, 1320), were not isolated phenomena but a product of the complex culture that surrounded them. To the modern historian the Crusades of the poor are only the most visible crests on the turbulent cultural sea of the thirteenth century. These movements were a response to popular religious ideas, such as mounting eschatological fantasies and the ascendance of apostolic poverty as a sign of holy favor, both of which were exacerbated by the continual failure of the Christian West to conquer the Islamic East.

Eschatological ideology preexisted Pope Urban II's call to Crusade at the Council of Clermont (1095). Christianity had been, after all, founded on the belief in Christ's imminent return. Christ warned his disciples in Mark 13:33, "Beware, keep alert, for you do not know when the time will come." Ever since the composition of Revelation by St. John of Patmos, Christians had watched for signs of the end times, and many of them found them. In the twelfth and thirteenth centuries, however, these signs seemed very strong. A comet accompanied the preaching of the First Crusade (1096–1102); as soon as the Crusaders embarked for the East, quenching rains ended a severe drought. Sky signs—meteor showers, comets, eclipses, and heavenly visions, such as a sword pointing to the East—continued to be seen throughout the twelfth century. The discovery of the Holy Lance at Antioch and the taking of Jerusalem (1099) by the Crusaders were both viewed as divine portents. Another sign of the end times was the presence of popular preachers who wandered throughout Christendom. Just as Jesus had John the Baptist to clear his path when he came as the sacrificial lamb, so he had these men, dressed in sackcloth, barefoot, and often carrying letters given to them by God or Mary, to clear his way so that he could return as the Judge of all humankind. Clearly, the Lord was preparing the Earth for his Second Coming.

Not only eschatological beliefs but also ideas about apostolic poverty were important factors in the development of the Children's and Shepherds'

Crusades. From the eleventh century onward the Church undertook several attempts at reform, including the Peace of God movement, Cluniac reform, and Gregorian reform, to name a few. These reforms were based on the acknowledgment that the Church, from the pope to the parish priest, was becoming more material in nature and increasingly invested in the secular world. Like other parts of society, such as the burgher class and the nobility, the Church was more prosperous and had accumulated vast amounts of material wealth. The Church as a corporate body became accustomed to a certain level of comfort: fine clothes, rich foods, well-furnished environs, and the unquestioning respect of those beneath it. Although this description smacks of the modern idea of success, thirteenth-century men and women saw such "success" as the Church straying from the true path as laid down by Christ and his apostles.

Christ's ministry was directed toward the poor and the unloved; his wrath was aimed at those who were wealthy and who neglected people in need. Because of this orientation, poverty was revered in the Christian tradition from the beginning. Some of the most venerated Christians of the postapostolic period were those who had followed Christ's injunction to "deny himself and take up his cross, and follow me" (Mark 8:34). In an *Imitatio Christi* (imitation of Christ), both St. Anthony and Paul the Hermit left behind the wealth of their families and the support of their communities in order to seek God in the deserts of Egypt. This quest became a common topic in subsequent saints' lives, such as those of St. Martin and St. Cuthbert, to name only a couple. Through the rise of pilgrimage as a form of devotion, medieval Christians became familiar with the lives of the saints and saw in them the holiness of poverty, which was something that most of them understood intimately well. These devout men and women were not only familiar with the lives of saints but also the Beatitudes, particularly the line: "Blessed be ye poor: for yours is the kingdom of God" (Luke 6:20). Only those who were poor, untainted by material wealth, and unencumbered by the activities of the physical world would be pure enough to inherit the new Jerusalem. This belief is most touchingly seen in the *Pilgrim's Guide to Jerusalem*, written by Theoderich, wherein he discusses the poor pilgrims who built rock chairs in a field outside of the city in the hopes that these might save their places when the New Jerusalem descended from Heaven. Clearly, the poor came to believe that the Kingdom of Heaven would be theirs.

Ideas of eschatological fantasy and apostolic poverty culminated in the thirteenth-century figures of Joachim of Fiore and St. Francis of Assisi, respectively. Joachim was a Cistercian monk who developed an apocalyptic time line. His theory was founded on the idea that there were three ages of man, which overlapped each other slightly. The first was the age of the Father, which encompassed the period from Adam to Christ. The second was the age of the Son, which covered the period from Christ to around 1260. Joachim believed that from about 1260 forward medieval Christians were living in the age of the Spirit, which would eventually culminate in the apocalypse. At the center of this concept, known as Joachimism, was the idea that Christ's revelation would become clearer and more obvious on Earth as time progressed. This theory offered a popular explanation for why so many portents had been seen in the sky, as well as why so many preachers had arisen to violently preach God's will. Joachim also argued that the "holy city of Christ would not accept anything unclean." Only the most pure, and in this case the poorest, would enter the Kingdom of Heaven.

The thirteenth-century movement toward apostolic poverty is most clearly seen in the life and teachings of the Italian friar St. Francis of Assisi. The son of Peter Bernardone, St. Francis relinquished his rights to the family fortune and, stripping naked in the town plaza, professed his abject poverty in service to God and the poor. Barefoot and wearing only a tattered tunic, St. Francis not only provided counsel for the destitute and ministered to the lepers but also lived among them. It was his belief that Christianity had become too centered on the rewards of the physical world and had forgotten its humble roots. He was not alone in these beliefs, as is testified by the large following he gathered both in his lifetime and beyond. In the development of the Franciscan Order and its subsequent splitting into conventual and spiritual factions, one can see the tensions that existed in thirteenth-century religious culture. While the conventuals believed that progress entailed developing a secure, profitable infrastructure and engaging in the activities of the newly founded universities, the spirituals preached that Christ was poor and served the poor, that St. Francis was poor and served the poor, and thus the best path for the Order to follow was that of abject apostolic poverty. This division within the Franciscan Order was representative of the same tense split within society. The more the spiritual Franciscans were persecuted, the more they came to see themselves as God's chosen ones; likewise, the more destitute and persecuted people felt, the more they came to believe that they were "the chosen people of God and that all others were unregenerate reprobates."

Into this already frustrated milieu of apocalyptic expectation and self-righteous apostolic poverty was introduced popular disappointment in the crusading effort. The elation that resulted from the successes of the First Crusade was followed by the emotional devastation produced by the disasters of the twelfth century that culminated in the sack of Constantinople (1204). What had begun as a holy venture to reclaim Christ's patrimony in the East and to liberate Byzantine Christians from Islamic rule had become a wanton expedition for booty. Medieval Christians, who were conditioned by Crusade preaching to believe that their success in the East was guaranteed by their favor in the eyes of God, began to doubt the power of the Crusade leaders, both at home and abroad, to defeat Islam. Although a few bitterly voiced the opinion that perhaps Muslims were God's chosen people, most believed that Christian failures were a punishment for the impurity of those who were in charge of running the venture. The First Crusaders were remembered, rightly or not, as pure, and thus their success had been guaranteed. Especially exalted was the memory of King Tafur, the leader of a particularly savage band of warrior-paupers who allegedly wore nearly nothing, scavenged from the dead, and even cannibalized the corpses of Muslims when necessary. By the thirteenth century, medieval people were already looking back to what they perceived to be the golden age of crusading, and with each failure of a Crusade or plan for a Crusade, they became increasingly convinced that only the purest of Christians, the poor, could defeat Islam, reclaim Jerusalem, and initiate the apocalypse.

Eschatological expectations, the exaltation of apostolic poverty, and a popular desire for a successful Crusade are all evident in the Children's Crusades. Shortly after Easter a group of poor pilgrims headed south from Cologne, Germany, claiming that they were going to liberate Jerusalem from the Muslims. Along the march, Nicholas, who was young but not a child, distinguished himself as a leader. At the same time, another group of pilgrims with the same objective left Vendome, France, and headed southward, hoping to set sail across the Mediterranean Sea. Both groups left home shortly after Holy Week; in this timing there was no coincidence. Holy Week was the time traditionally set aside for dwelling not only on the suffering and sacrifice of Christ but also for preaching the Crusade. Eastertide, then, was a time of increased expectation in regard to crusading. Whether the participants in the Crusades actually heard sermons or not, these medieval Christians would have remembered sermons that they had heard in the past and the promise that they held for the liberation of the Holy Land. Combine this inspiration with the belief that they were, because of their poverty, God's chosen people, and that the End Times were near, and it becomes easier to understand the fervor with which these men, women, and yes, children, left home. These groups had no itinerary, planned no route, and packed no provisions because they not only expected to live off of the charity of strangers but also the beneficence of God. The leader of the French group told his fellow Crusaders not to worry about crossing the Mediterranean, for as God had parted the Red

A MISERABLE BUSINESS

In 1212 two separate bands of Crusaders, largely made up of religiously inspired youth, took up the cross and marched toward the East. After much suffering, one group was turned back, while the other was betrayed and its participants sold into slavery. One chronicler, writing around 1213, remarked on the Crusade:

In this year occurred an outstanding thing and one much to be marveled at, for it is unheard of throughout the ages. About the time of Easter and Pentecost, without anyone having preached or called for it and prompted by I know not what spirit, many thousands of boys, ranging in age from six years to full maturity, left the plows or carts which they were driving, the flocks which they were pasturing, and anything else which they were doing. This they did despite the wishes of their parents, relatives, and friends who sought to make them draw back. Suddenly one ran after another to take the cross. Thus, by groups of twenty, or fifty, or a hundred, they put up banners and began to journey to Jerusalem. They were asked by many people on whose advice or at whose urging they had set out upon this path. They were asked especially since only a few years ago many kings, a great many dukes, and innumerable people in powerful companies had gone there and had returned with the business unfinished. The present groups, morever, were still of tender years and were neither strong enough nor powerful enough to do anything. Everyone, therefore, accounted them foolish and imprudent for trying to do this. They briefly replied that they were equal to the Divine will in this matter and that, whatever God might wish to do with them, they would accept it willingly and with humble spirit. They thus made some little progress on their journey. Some were turned back at Metz, others at Piacenza, and others even at Rome. Still others got to Marseilles, but whether they crossed to the Holy Land or what their end was is uncertain. One thing is sure: that of the many thousands who rose up, only very few returned.

Source: Chronica Regiae Coloniensis Continuatio prima *(circa 1213), translated by James Brundage in* The Crusades: A Documentary History *(Milwaukee: Marquette University Press, 1962), p. 213.*

Sea for Moses, so would God ensure the safety of this expedition. Implicit in this belief was the notion that they would also have success in Jerusalem and would be allowed to claim it as their own, just as the Israelites had been rewarded with the Promised Land in Exodus. Like so many Crusades before this one, however, the Children's Crusades failed, with many of the participants either being drowned, sold into slavery, or returned home to the disgust of their fellow townsfolk. The Children's Crusades, then, were just another point of contention for a society frustrated by promises so long expected but never fulfilled.

These same phenomena are evidenced in the German Crusade of the Poor (1309) and the Crusades of the Pastoreaux (1251, 1320). German chroniclers mention that in 1309 a small group of pilgrims rose up with the intention of liberating the Holy Land. This Crusade took place during a period of fierce famine, which might have been the catalyst for the movement. Suffering from starvation, these men and women perhaps saw themselves as truly chosen and therefore destined to succeed. More likely, however, they saw the Crusade as their only hope in a time of desperation and so set out to Jerusalem with the intention of initiating the apocalypse and clearing the way for Christ and the New Jerusalem, which was most certainly theirs. It is in the Crusades of the Pastoreaux, however, that one sees the concepts of apocalypse and apostolic poverty writ large. By 1251 the cult of poverty was reaching its peak as evidenced in the spread of the Franciscan Order, the Poor Clares, and the Franciscan Tertiaries. The Spiritual Franciscans wandered throughout the land, wearing nothing but their worn tunics and the cords of St. Francis, and preached the virtues of abject poverty. They were not only a product of the cultural belief in poverty, but they also magnified it and delivered it to the masses through their vehement preaching. The more the poor heard how glorified their existence was, the more they came to see themselves as chosen.

All of this tumult coincided with a pastoral movement within the Church that sought a return to rural, apostolic values. Thus, in 1251 a group of poor, including those from the economic groups who had chosen poverty for religious reasons, donned the vestments of shepherds and set out on a Crusade to liberate Christian lands from the control of Muslims. Believing themselves to be chosen and therefore invincible, they attacked all those institutions they viewed to be corrupt and therefore impeding Christianity's success in the Crusades. It is tempting to see the destruction of powerful institutions as a type of class warfare; however, the Pastoreaux already saw themselves as the most powerful sector of society. Through them God reasserted the hierarchy that was established at the time of Christ. They were following God's will; their intent was to purify all in their path, acting as the scourge of God, in order to make Christianity worthy of its success against Islam. Their goals extended past any type of class dominance, since they sought the salvation and protection of Christendom. None of the crusading groups, whether sanctioned or not, were unified in thoughts or intentions; it is possible that there was an element of class hatred in the Pastoreaux movement, to the extent that such a thing existed in the thirteenth century. However, in assessing the religious cultural perspectives prevalent before and during this movement, the eschatological expectations, cult of apostolic poverty, and disappointment in previous Crusades played far greater roles than ideas of class dominance.

A direct correlation can be drawn between the commencement of popular Crusades and disappointment in the sanctioned crusading movement. St. Louis (French king Louis IX) had embarked on Crusades in both 1248 and 1269, and many believed that he was to be the Emperor of the Last Days who would conquer the East and lay his crown and scepter at the foot of the cross to signal the second coming of Christ. Just when it seemed that St. Louis would succeed in his mission, he died in Tunis in 1270. Then, in the early fourteenth century, the Pope and Philip of Taranto plotted a Crusade to take back the Holy Land. Rumors of the coming Crusade excited the populace and inflamed their hopes for success. However, by 1318 the plans for this Crusade were dead on the table. The result of these unfulfilled expectations was the Pastoreaux movement of 1320, an explosion of popular frustration. For two hundred twenty-five years, a series of promises and myths had grown up around the Crusades and the idea of crusading. When these promises seemed far from fulfillment, people took the responsibility upon themselves, believing that they could be successful where those who were too concerned with the problems of this world could not. The poor were the ones who had maintained the true vision of Christ, and, following his injunction, watched and waited for the End of Days. And it was they, God's chosen remnant, who would reclaim the East for the glory of Christendom.

All of the Crusades, whether popular or sanctioned, consisted of myriad individuals with their own beliefs, concerns, and convictions. However, the pattern followed by most of the popular crusading movements is clear. Temporal promises and religious expectations, both of which were unrealistic, continually resulted in failure and mounting tension. It is important to see these disappointments not only against a medieval popular religious backdrop but also in the context of turbulent thirteenth-century society; famine, poverty, the increasing worldliness of supposedly divine institutions, urbanization, enclosure, the loss of traditional forms of relief, and reduced stability all contributed to the cycle of popular Crusades. Most important to this movement, however, were the eschatological expectations, self-righteousness of apostolic poverty, and disappointment in institutionalized crusading that were learned by medieval people throughout two hundred years of crusading culture.

–BRENDA GARDENOUR,
BOSTON UNIVERSITY

References

Paul Alphandéry, "Les Croisades d'Enfants," *Revue de l'Histoire des Religions,* 73 (1916): 259–282.

Malcolm Barber, "The Crusade of the Shepherds in 1251," in *Proceedings of the Tenth Annual Meeting of the Western Society for French History, 1982* (1984).

Barber, "The Pastoureaux of 1320," *Journal of Ecclesiastical History,* 32 (April 1981): 143–166.

Henry Bett, *Joachim of Flora* (London: Methuen, 1931).

Marcus Bull, "The Roots of Lay Enthusiasm for the First Crusade," *History,* 78 (October 1993): 353–372.

Norman Cohn, *The Pursuit of the Millennium* (London: Secker & Warburg, 1957).

Giles Constable, "The Second Crusade as Seen by Contemporaries," *Traditio,* 9 (1953): 213–281.

Frederic Duncalf, "The Peasant's Crusade," *American Historical Review,* 26 (1921): 440–453.

Guy Fourquin, *The Anatomy of Popular Rebellion in the Middle Ages,* translated by Anne Chesters (Amsterdam & New York: North Holland, 1978).

William Chester Jordan, "Pastoureaux," *The Dictionary of the Middle Ages,* volume 9, edited by Joseph R. Strayer (New York: Scribners, 1982–1989), pp. 452–454.

Walter Klaasen, *Living at the End of the Ages: Apocalyptic Expectation in the Radical Reformation* (Lanham, Md.: University Press of America; Walter, Ont.: Institute for Anabaptist and Mennonite Studies, 1992).

Harold Lamb, *The Crusades,* volume 2, *The Flame of Islam* (Garden City, N.Y.: Doubleday, Doran, 1930).

Hans Eberhard Mayer, *Geschichte der Kreuzzüge* (Stuttgart: Kohlhammer, 1965) translated as *The Crusades,* by John Gillingham, second edition (Oxford & New York: Oxford University Press, 1988).

Michel Mollat and Philippe Wolff, *The Popular Revolutions of the Late Middle Ages,* translated by A. L. Lytton-Sells (London: Allen & Unwin, 1973).

R. I. Moore, *The Formation of a Persecuting Society: Power and Deviance in Western Europe, 950–1250* (Oxford & New York: Blackwell, 1987).

Dana C. Munro, "The Children's Crusade," *American Historical Review,* 19 (April 1914): 516–524.

Munro, "A Crusader," *Speculum,* 7 (1932): 321–335.

David Nirenberg, *Communities of Violence: Persecution of Minorities in the Middle Ages* (Princeton: Princeton University Press, 1996).

Edward Peters, ed., *Christian Society, and the Crusades, 1198–1229: Sources in Translation, Including The Capture of Damietta By Oliver of Paderborn,* translated by John J. Gavigan (Philadelphia: University of Pennsylvania Press, 1971).

Walter Porges, "The Clergy, The Poor, and the Non-Combatants on the First Crusade," *Speculum,* 21 (January 1946): 1–23.

James M. Powell, *Anatomy of a Crusade: 1213–1221* (Philadelphia: University of Pennsylvania Press, 1986).

Paul Raedts, "The Children's Crusade of 1212," *Journal of Medieval History,* 3 (1977): 279–333.

Jonathan Riley-Smith, *The First Crusade and the Idea of Crusading* (London: Athlone, 1987; Philadelphia: University of Pennsylvania Press, 1987).

Riley-Smith, ed., *The Oxford History of the Crusades* (Oxford: Oxford University Press, 1999).

Stephen Runciman, *A History of the Crusades* (Cambridge: Cambridge University Press, 1951).

Frederick H. Russell, "Crusade, Children's," in *The Dictionary of the Middle Ages,* volume 4, edited by Joseph R. Strayer (New York: Scribners, 1982–1989), pp. 14–15.

Sylvia Schein, *Fideles Crucis: The Papacy, the West, and the Recovery of the Holy Land, 1274–1314* (Oxford: Clarendon Press / New York: Oxford University Press, 1991).

Elizabeth Siberry, *Criticism of Crusading: 1095–1274* (Oxford: Clarendon Press, 1985; New York: Oxford University Press, 1985).

Theoderich, *Guide to the Holy Land,* second edition, translated by Aubrey Stewart (New York: Italica Press, 1986).

Norman P. Zacour, "The Children's Crusade," in *A History of the Crusades,* edited by Kenneth M. Setton, volume 2, *The Later Crusades, 1189–1311,* edited by Robert Lee Wolff and Harry W. Hazard (Madison: University of Wisconsin Press, 1969), pp. 325–342.

CONVIVENCIA

Does *convivencia* (coexistence) describe relationships among Christians and Muslims in Spain during the Middle Ages?

Viewpoint: Yes. A marked degree of mutual tolerance, understanding, and creative interaction among Muslims, Christians, and even Jews was a reality.

Viewpoint: No. *Convivencia* is an idealistic oversimplification of the complexities of Christian-Muslim relations in medieval Spain.

Prolonged contact and routine daily interaction among members of different ethnic or religious groups raises the issue not only of tolerance but also the degree to which such contact over the long term is creative as well as conflictive. Interaction among Muslims and Christians during the Middle Ages took place under two distinct social and political dynamics. The first was as two opposing blocs facing each other across a politically established frontier, which was quite porous, and across which the transit of manufactured goods and agricultural produce flowed, mainly from al-Andalus (Muslim Spain) to the Christian kingdoms, entailing a certain degree of cultural interaction.

That this prolonged contact produced cultural exchange is not in doubt. Much of this interaction, however, does not speak to issues of tolerance, even when Muslims or Christians adopted elements of each other's culture. For example, the olive tree has a Latin name, *olivo,* in Castilian; but both the fruit and the oil are known by Arabisms: *aceituna* (olive) and *aceite* (olive oil). This naming resulted because until the twelfth century most Christian territory lay to the north of the climatic zone favorable to olive cultivation and therefore olive products had to be imported from al-Andalus. Thus, Christians acquired the habit of referring to these products with their Arabic names. Likewise, the Muslims of al-Andalus referred to certain varieties of wheat with Latin names. These examples of acculturation are neutral with respect to interpersonal relationships. Constant warfare stimulated not only two-way cultural borrowing (of military technology, for example) but also promoted the production of propaganda designed to foment hatred and fear of the enemy.

The second area of culture contact was that between the dominant Christian society of the later Middle Ages and minority ethnic enclaves of Muslims and Jews. Américo Castro, in *The Spaniards: An Introduction to Their History* (1971), asserts that what is now considered "Spanish" culture is the result of many centuries of *convivencia* (coexistence) among Christians, Jews, and Muslims. Anthropologists speak of the "degree of enclosure" of minority cultural communities. How do groups maintain their cultural boundaries when all around them live people of another, politically dominant, culture, with whom they must interact in the course of going about their daily routines? Such commonplace interaction promoted the kind of familiarity that breeds acceptance but that also places minorities at risk and produces pressures to convert. Familiarity may breed both acceptance and contempt.

Viewpoint:
Yes. A marked degree of mutual tolerance, understanding, and creative interaction among Muslims, Christians, and even Jews was a reality.

One of the key questions of Muslim-Christian relations in the Middle Ages is, "How well and in what specific ways did the two religions interact?" In the literature on Medieval Iberia, this sociopolitical context is usually termed *convivencia* (coexistence). Spain in the eleventh and twelfth centuries was the primary place where Jews, Christians, and Muslims lived in close proximity and interacted with each other in extraordinary, as well as everyday, ways. Beyond Iberia, there were significant contacts in Sicily and the Crusader States of the Near East. Throughout this period there was usually some kind of warfare being waged, which set Islamic state against Christian state, as the broad backdrop to all social and cultural history. Hegemony was not always well delineated, and it changed frequently: Christians could appear to be headed for victory, but there were also significant signs of Islamic resurgence. In such fluid political circumstances the triumphalism of dominance could rapidly become the despondency of subjugation. Therefore, people living in such circumstances had strong reasons to learn how to relate to each other in effective ways that still respected their social and cultural differences. *Convivencia* was literally "living-togetherness."

In Iberia the locus classicus of discussion has been the city of Toledo, in particular after its conquest (1085) by Spanish king Alfonso VI. The treaty of surrender allowed the remaining Muslims, those who wished to accept the rule of Alfonso, to stay in his realm—secure in their freedom, lives, possession of property, and free exercise of their religion. However, only the *Jami'* (Main) Mosque was to remain to the Muslims; all other mosques were to be given to the king, along with the personal property of the former Muslim ruler. A head tax was to be the only serious burden of accepting his overlordship. That the king expected a loyal citizenry continuing to live in *convivencia* is further indicated by his adoption of the title "Emperor of the Two Religions." One sign of the relative ease of relations between the elites of the two religions was the initial appointment of Sisnando Davidiz as governor of Toledo. Davidiz was a Mozarab, originally from al-Andalus (Muslim Spain), who instituted tolerant policies—too tolerant in the eyes of the French and some Castilians at the court—illustrative of the

course the king intended to take. Even more significant was the employment of Abu'l Qasim ibn Khayyat, the former *qadi* (judge) who converted to Christianity and who wrote several charters for Alfonso, particularly to other Ta'ifa kings who had been closely related to the Toledan Muslim kingdom. In similar circumstances, during the conquest of Zaragoza, Alfonso VI forbade his knights to harm Muslim villages and assured the people he would respect their laws and customs. One Muslim historian, Ibn Bassam, recognized the lenient approach of Alfonso—and especially of his governor Sisnando—who, he says, "tried to make the Toledans' [i.e., the Muslims'] misfortunes bearable and render tolerable the vile condition into which they had been depressed." The career of a freelance soldier such as Rodrigo Diaz, El Cid of Spanish legend, illustrated the level of military interrelationships. The alliances and treaties that the kings of Castile and Aragon made with various Muslim lords are evidence of cooperation at the highest levels of Iberian society.

Leniency in victory and elite conversions alone do not make a social structure; however, there is ample additional evidence of the interpenetration of Islamic practices among Christians that became so thoroughly ingrained that they remained long after political dominance had swung to the kings of Castile and Aragon. In al-Andalus, Christians and Jews were governed by what is known as the *dhimma* contract: they were "People of the Book," could not be forcibly converted, and had the right to practice their religion. In spite of this leniency, by about 950 most of the original Hispano-Romans had converted to Islam. There continued to be Arabized Christians, known as Mozarabs, who not only became Arabic in language but also had adopted other elements of Islamic culture. Nearly three hundred years after they had rejoined Christian society (after the conquest of Toledo), Mozarabs continued to speak Arabic and to bear Arabic names and used formulas and documents in deeds and records of property transfers according to the practice of the Malikite school of Islamic law.

Among Christians, irrigation systems captured from the Muslims were administered as they had been "in the time of the Moors," and they continued to utilize Arabic terminology and follow Muslim customs of water allocation. Christian religious scholars not only used Islamic terminology to refer to Christian practices (for example, calling an altar a *mihrab*), but they had even been thoroughly trained in the methods of reading the Qur'an and interpreting it. Christians who had lived under Islamic dominance for the better part of four centuries even

CONVIVENCIA

RESTRICTING
THE INFIDELS

In response to a query about Muslim and non-Muslim relations, an Egyptian professor of Islamic law, Hasan Al Kafrawi, observed:

It is no longer permitted them to put themselves, with respect to their houses, on an equal footing with the dwellings of their Moslem neighbors, and still less to build their buildings higher. If they are of the same height, or higher, it is incumbent upon us to pull them down to a size a little less than the houses of the true believers. This conforms to the word of the Prophet: "Islam rules, and nothing shall raise itself above it." This is also in order to hinder them from knowing where our weak spots are and in order to make a distinction between their dwellings and ours.

They are forbidden to build new churches, chapels, or monasteries in any Moslem land. We should destroy everything that is of new construction in every place, such as Cairo, for instance, founded under the Moslem religion, for it is said in a tradition of Omar: "No church shall be built in Islam." They shall no longer be permitted to repair the parts of these [post-Islamic] buildings which are in ruins. However, the old buildings [of pre-Islamic times] which are found in a land whose population had embraced Islam need not be destroyed. They shall not, however, be enlarged by means of repairs or otherwise. In case the tolerated peoples [Jews, Christians, etc.] act contrary to these provisions we will be obliged to destroy everything that has been added to the original size of the building. [Only pre-Islamic churches and synagogues may be repaired; new ones must be torn down.]

Entrance into Moslem territory by infidels of foreign lands under the pact guaranteeing protection to the tolerated peoples is permitted only for the time necessary to settle their business affairs. If they exceed this period, their safe-conduct having expired, they will be put to death or be subject to the payment of the head-tax. [Jews and Christians of foreign lands must pay a special head-tax if they wish to remain permanently in Moslem lands.] . . .

Their men and women are ordered to wear garments different from those of the Moslems in order to be distinguished from them. They are forbidden to exhibit anything which might scandalize us, as, for instance, their fermented liquors, and if they do not conceal these from us, we are obliged to pour them into the street.

Source: *Jacob R. Marcus,* The Jew in the Medieval World: A Sourcebook, 315–1791 *(Cincinnati: Union of American Hebrew Congregations, 1938), pp. 17–18.*

Mozarabs prided themselves on their resistance to Islamicization—it appears they were able to survive successfully because of their willingness to speak Arabic.

Jewish communities were also highly Arabized in al-Andalus and, therefore, were later able to mediate between Muslim and Christian culture. One famous Jewish convert to Christianity during the twelfth century, Pedro Alfonso (Petrus Alfonsi), not only adapted Muslim astronomical tables to advance science but also represented Arabic literary styles in a Latin collection of tales called the *Disciplina Clericalis* (Ecclesiastical Discipline). Even though scholars such as Alfonso became Christians, they still continued to teach—even subjects well known in the former Islamic world but relatively unknown in their new surroundings. Jewish intellectuals (and it is they about whom scholars have the most knowledge) worked alongside Christians and Muslims. Their important role ought not be forgotten. In multiethnic Toledo the only two private libraries or bookshops whose existence is documented were owned by Jews. Likewise, Jews often helped Christian scholars translate texts from the Arabic originals; one such translator was Ibn Daud. Jewish scholars appear to have known and studied with Muslim masters.

Jewish poet Moses ibn Ezra tells a story of a curious encounter that illustrates some of the tensions of intergroup relations. He relates how in the days of his youth and in his own home, a wise *faqih* (a religious or legal scholar or jurist) had asked him to recite the Ten Commandments in Arabic: "I perceived his intention, to minimize its eloquence. So I asked him to recite the *Fatihah* of his *Qur'an* in Latin language since he spoke and comprehended it. And when he set out to translate it into that idiom he debased his pronunciation and disfigured it in its entirety. Comprehending, then, my intention he excused me from having to do that which he had asked me." This tale is revealing, for it shows that each scholar was aware of a central text of the other's religion, of the equivalence in function of those texts, and of the tie between the religion and the language it was expressed in. There is also mutual knowledge of the language of the third ethnic group, the Christians. Each of these scholars knew enough about the other's religion to be able—perhaps to want to—attack it, in spite of being friends; that neither pursued the matter further is an excellent example of how *convivencia* worked among religious scholars. For both Jews and Christians there is evidence that they were acculturated in an Islamic educational milieu, if not schooled in an Islamic institution. The tools and products of their education are displayed by their writings.

imbibed the prejudices of Muslims, referring to Latin-speaking Christians as 'Ajami (barbarians). One need not even mention all the ordinary words that came into Spanish as a result of the Arabization of the peninsula. This cultural adoption is all the more curious because

This latter episode also indicates that *convivencia* means more than mere "toleration." This living together is the product of social circumstances—not some modern idealization of the relative equality of all ethnic groups. That idea is grounded in modern ideas of cultural relativity and desired assimilation (cutting social distance so that one is fully accepted in a society). However, assimilation and acculturation (becoming accommodated to dominant cultural norms) are not the same thing. Acculturation is not instantaneous, and it may not even be completely conscious: in the case of al-Andalus, because all the ruling elite comprised mainly Arabic-speaking Muslims, interaction of Iberian natives with the dominant group necessitated communication; learning Arabic was the main vehicle of that communication. In everyday life conquered peoples went to the cities to sell food or horses, seek protection, and pay taxes; such transactions were generally conducted in Arabic. This situation was especially true for the native elite who had to communicate with the Muslims as heads of their respective communities: they needed to be increasingly Arabized to bridge the cultural gap between themselves and their new rulers. This acculturation is what *convivencia* was about; it was not necessarily concerned with reducing social distance, which is not quite so simple. The gradual character of assimilation is seen in conversion: a person desiring to convert (an outsider) first became the client of one family or person (partially acculturated) and only later was acknowledged as a full-fledged member of the *ummah* (Islamic community).

Convivencia was produced largely by the Islamic requirement that people at least respect the "People of the Book," to whom God had revealed himself in earlier times. For Muslims, however, it also included a fundamental disparagement—Jews and Christians had lost the right path that followers of Muhammad had found. On the Jewish and Christian side, though, despite resistance to assimilation, there was also a recognition that Islamic civilization was in some measure superior, with more to offer than their respective traditions alone had available. Perhaps this is why *convivencia* appears to be rather one-sided: Muslims living under Christian rule did not as frequently become "Latinized"—they either converted or emigrated. One possible reason is because Christian society had no institutional status comparable to the *dhimmi* (protected persons). The only places where Christian rulers displayed an attitude such as the Muslim one was in lands that had been conquered from Muslims. In these places—Christian Spain, Norman Sicily, and the Crusader States—there is a valuing of members of the other two Abrahamic religions.

Wherever it occurred, *convivencia* produced a complex set of interactions among the rulers and the ruled that inculcated on both sides a kind of grudging respect. It was not some modern form of toleration, and it was not actively sought out as a virtue; instead, it was simply a way of living, a structure of life, which was "just the way it is" for many citizens in medieval Iberia. It lasted as long as it did because it worked as a social system. Of course, when less practical men than the medieval kings—the bishops—were able to exercise influence, then this system disappeared because of ideological intolerance. When people who had to relate to each other on a daily basis were in charge, however, *convivencia* was the rule.

–MICHAEL WEBER,
SALEM STATE COLLEGE

Viewpoint:
No. *Convivencia* is an idealistic oversimplification of the complexities of Christian-Muslim relations in medieval Spain.

While there can be no doubt that creative interaction among Muslims, Jews, and Christians certainly took place in the Middle Ages, particularly in regard to the transfer of science, technology, literary, and artistic motifs, the existence of *convivencia* must be judged at the level of daily interaction, although tolerance in the modern sense did not exist. That does not mean, however, that normal daily interaction of a nonconflictive nature was unattainable. On the contrary, interaction among these groups normally occurred without the expectation of conflict. But nonconflictive interaction does not add up to tolerance. Instead of tolerance, therefore, one must look for other terms. First is curiosity, because peoples who are habitually incurious about others are unlikely to acquire the habits of tolerance. Second is what might be termed epistemological modesty: can a person of one religion accept the validity—at any level—of the religion of another? Third is acceptance: can persons of different religions accept the presence of other groups as their legitimate right? On all three grounds, one must reply in the negative. The only curiosity that medieval people had about other religions was to gain enough information to refute them. Christians never accepted the legitimacy of the competing Abrahamic religions. Furthermore, repeated incidences of aggression against minority religious groups and the lack of any consistent

CONVIVENCIA

Illumination of a Christian and a Muslim playing chess, circa late thirteenth century

(Bibliothèque Municipale Chateauroux)

recourse by the aggrieved parties leads to the conclusion that *convivencia* (coexistence), viewed as positive interchange, was sharply limited in scope, involving a numerically insignificant group of individuals.

David Nirenberg, in *Communities of Violence: Persecution of Minorities in the Middle Ages* (1996), has shown that coexistence, far from demonstrating pacific rules of interaction, in fact defined the level of violence acceptable to the three communities. Insofar as Christians were concerned, the religion of the minority in question determined what kind of violence was permitted. Indeed, he understands competition among different ethnic/religious groups in terms of "the economy of violence." The core of Nirenberg's argument is the role of women in interethnic competition. In this view, Jewish and Muslim communities responded to Christian prohibition of miscegenation by reinforcing sexual boundaries. Christians punished sexual contact between members of their faith with Jews more severely than with Muslims. Medieval law codes explicitly prohibited these relations between Christians and members of the two religious minorities. Competition for women was not divorced from the search for converts, however, as Jews typically sought to convert their female Muslim slaves.

Nirenberg also describes ritualized Christian aggression against Jews—the routine casting of stones on the walls of the Jewish quarter,

particularly by priests and student priests, in order "to make brutally clear the sharp boundaries . . . that separated Christian from Jew." Even a socially neutral, but religiously loaded, area such as the selling of meat became a point of conflict. Jewish butchers sold meat that was not kosher to non-Jews, incurring the active enmity of Christian butchers. The Pope himself forbade such sales.

An example of Christian anti-Jewish writing is the *Dialogue Against Jews* of Pedro Alfonso, a Spanish Christian who converted from Judaism and who wrote in the twelfth century. His original name was Moshe (Moses), and he is known for four works: the *Disciplina Clericalis* (Ecclesiastical Discipline), a collection of moralizing tales of Indian origin; the astronomical tables of al-Khwarizmi; "Letter to the Peripatetic of France," which defended the new, Arab-based sciences; and a polemical religious piece, the Dialogue against Jews, which also attacked Islam (the message—to Jews—that it is better to convert to Christianity than to Islam). The fact that Alfonso, while a declared enemy of both Judaism and Islam, was also a representative of the positive aspects of *convivencia* (by transmitting Arabic science to the Latin West) points up one of the conceptual problems plaguing the concept.

The *Dialogue* takes the form of a conversation between Peter, his new self, and Moses, his former self. For a Christian polemic, it is written in quite respectful terms, and the idea is that both science and logic favor Christianity as a religion. One way he argues against Judaism is from the Aristotelian position on incorporeality of God, which relates to the philosophical question of divine attributes as Christian, Muslim, and Jewish Aristotelians argued it. Alfonso argues that in the Talmud the rabbis heretically ascribe corporeality to God, especially attacking the Jewish mystical tradition which ascribed dimensions to God's body (mystics of all three religions ran up against this kind of critique from orthodox scholars in their own ranks). The attack on the Talmud as a spurious document was standard in Christian polemics, and both Christians and Muslims argued that Jews had abrogated their own Torah by forging certain passages some time after their divine revelation (which the other Abrahamic religions, in principle, accepted as a valid part of their own traditions).

His argument against Islam was better informed than in other such treatises, and he was the first Christian polemicist who had a decent knowledge of Islam. However, while his attack on Judaism focuses on doctrinal issues, which he attacks from a logical standpoint, his critique of Islam (in spite of his knowledge) was common slander, the typical denunciation of Muhammad as a false prophet. He stops short of calling Muhammad a pagan but implies that Islam was compromised by the survival of pagan rites, linking the Kaaba to pagan cults.

When Pedro defends Christianity, it is by an appeal to reason in support of authority—a stance typical of medieval Aristotelians of whatever religion. He invokes scientific arguments to support various aspects of Christian doctrine. His explanation of Creation and various cosmologies related to it is wholly derived from classical astronomy and astrology.

A Muslim polemicist against both Christianity and Judaism was Ibn Hazm, born in Cordoba in the decade before the fall of the Spanish Umayyad caliphate. Ibn Hazm was well informed about both Christian and Jewish theology; he was familiar with both the Talmud and the Gospels. His interest in these religions, however, was only a means towards their comparison with Islam, viewed as a creed superior to both. Jews he condemned both for the supposed abrogation of the Torah and for their faulty doctrines of prophecy (which denied status to Muhammad). He also asserted that the Christian Gospels did not have the attributes of a normative revealed text (as compared, that is, with the Qur'an) and lacked the chain of attribution that traced the scriptural text back to eyewitnesses—a standard procedure in Islamic religious theology. While he was familiar with the texts, he criticized and presented them accurately, Ibn Hazm portrayed the medieval inability to accept the theological concerns of members of other faiths as having validity, even for themselves. Dissent from Islam, in this context, was a kind of arrogant vanity entertained with infidels.

Nirenberg concludes with the gloomy assessment that "Convivencia was predicated upon violence; it was not its peaceful antithesis. Violence drew its meaning from coexistence, not in opposition to it."

–THOMAS F. GLICK,
BOSTON UNIVERSITY

References

Robert Ignatius Burns, *Islam Under the Crusaders: Colonial Survival in the Thirteenth-Century Kingdom of Valencia* (Princeton: Princeton University Press, 1973).

Américo Castro, *The Spaniards: An Introduction to Their History,* translated by Willard F. King and Selma Margaretten (Berkeley: University of California Press, 1971).

Thomas F. Glick, *Islamic and Christian Spain in the Early Middle Ages* (Princeton: Princeton University Press, 1979).

Muhammad ibn Ahmad Ibn Jubayr, *The Travels of Ibn Jubayr, being the Chronicle of a Mediaeval Spanish Moor Concerning His Journey to the Egypt of Saladin, the Holy Cities of Arabia, Baghdad the City of the Caliphs, the Latin Kingdom of Jerusalem, and the Norman Kingdom of Sicily,* translated by R. J. C. Broadhurst (London: Cape, 1952).

Salma Khadra Jayyusi, ed., *Legacy of Muslim Spain* (Leiden & New York: Brill, 1992).

Vivian B. Mann, Glick, and Jerrilynn D. Dodds, eds., *Convivencia: Jews, Muslims, and Christians in Medieval Spain* (New York: Braziller in association with the Jewish Museum, 1992).

Usamah ibn Munqidh, *An Arab-Syrian Gentleman and Warrior in the Period of the Crusades: Memoirs of Usamah ibn-Munqidh (Kitab al-I'ti-bar),* translated by Philip K. Hitti (New York: Columbia University Press, 1929).

David Nirenberg, *Communities of Violence: Persecution of Minorities in the Middle Ages* (Princeton: Princeton University Press, 1996).

CRUSADER STATES

Did the Crusader States collapse from external pressure rather than internal weaknesses?

Viewpoint: An external force in the form of the Mamluk Sultanate made it possible finally for Egypt to apply the pressure necessary to expel the Franks from the region.

Viewpoint: The Crusader States collapsed because of internal weaknesses that, though they always existed, became more debilitating in the mid thir-teenth century.

The fall of Acre (1291) put an end to the two-century existence of the Crusader States on the eastern Mediterranean mainland. The loss of Acre certainly inflamed passions, but it was not surrounded by the sense of pious shock and incredulity that followed the Battle of the Horns of Hattin (1187) a century earlier. In fact, the capture of Acre was almost expected, and with good reason, given the events that had taken place over the previous three decades. In the early 1260s the ruthless and extremely able Al-Zahir Baybars became the head of an Egyptian junta that signaled the rise of the Mamluk Sultanate and a definitive disruption in normative Latin-Islamic relationships. At approximately the same time, politics in the Latin colonies, which were always antagonistic, took a decisive turn for the worse. While the Latins were disputing rights and conducting fratricidal civil wars, Baybars was scoring major victories and accumulating impressive gains that at the least would leave his successor with optimum positioning for finally driving the Franks into the sea. Brutal raids into Galilee served as the opening salvo. In 1265 both Caesarea and Arsuf fell to Baybars's troops. The next year the important Templar stronghold at Safad was taken, followed by Jaffa, Beaufort, Antioch, Krak des Chevaliers, and Montfort over the next few years. When Baybars died (suspiciously after a polo match) in 1277, the Crusader States were no more than a narrow coastal strip commanded by Acre, which itself was now ringed by an intimidating string of fortifications. Baybars's successor Qalawun was in perfect position to deal a deathblow.

Almost all historians of the Crusades agree that the cloud formations pro-ducing the storm that pushed the Western invaders out of the region began accumulating around 1260 and continued gathering strength into the late 1280s. There is also general agreement that the Crusader States came to an end by the centralization of Islamic might through the unification of Egypt and Syria under Mamluk control and the continued decentralization and tearing of the Crusader States through acrimonious squabbling. But which of these two factors, external pressure or internal weakness, proved to be the deciding factor in the loss of Acre? On this issue debate is rife. "Externalists" often argue that conflict was omnipresent in the Crusader States and that they always buckled when confronted with a fairly unified Islamic front (Zengi, Sal-adin, Baybars, Qalawun). Once the Mamluks centralized regional Islam in an unprecedented way, it was capable of delivering enough force to dislodge the settlements with finality. "Internalists" argue that the Crusader States, though their knees weakened when confronted by sporadic Islamic unifications, always managed to regain their feet and survive (Field of Blood, Zengi's jihad, Hattin, La Forbie) before the latter half of the thirteenth century. Centrifugal forces reached their height in the Latin colonies after 1260 and produced such unseemly and cannibalistic events as the War of St. Sabbas (1256–1258), a full-fledged civil war. Internalists hold that the Latins defeated themselves long before Mamluk victories finally exterminated them.

Certainly, external pressure and internal weaknesses both played roles in the ultimate fall of the Crusader States, but neither was an entirely new development in the region, and it is only natural that posterity tries to prioritize these two salient factors. Islamic unity followed by military assault had occurred before. Economic disputes and constitutional conflict had rocked the Latin States for some time.

Viewpoint:
An external force in the form of the Mamluk Sultanate made it possible finally for Egypt to apply the pressure necessary to expel the Franks from the region.

"Acre is the chief among Christian cities in Syria," wrote the twelfth-century Muslim chronicler Ibn Jubayr. "Its greatness resembles that of Constantinople itself. It is the destination of ships and of caravans, the meeting-place of all Muslim and Christian traders." A generation later, Arab historian Ibn al-Athir described the booty gained by Saladin's soldiers when they first captured the city from the Christians in 1187: "The Muslim soldiers seized everything that the Franks had not been able to take with them, and its amount was inestimable. They found there a vast amount of gold, precious stones, silks embroidered with gold thread, fine Venetian cloths, sugar, weaponry, and every other type of good—for Acre was a post for Frankish and Byzantine traders, and for merchants from all other places around the world."

There is little mystery to the fall of Acre (1291), the last Christian-controlled outpost in the Levant; what takes more explanation, arguably, is its survival until then. Along with Antioch, Sidon, and Tyre, it was one of the chief coastal links that connected the Levant with the rest of the Western world, and as such, it was inevitably the target of military campaigns aimed at removing whatever power held sway over the region. The first Crusaders made it a key focus of their efforts, and throughout the rest of the Crusader Age various Muslim and Christian forces attempted to wrest it from the other in order to disrupt regional political realities. After the loss of Jerusalem (1187) to Saladin, Acre was made the political center of the Latin States. Because of the precariousness of its own natural position, the citizens of Acre built and maintained some of the most formidable fortifications in the eastern Mediterranean. Like most of Palestine, Acre offered only a modest, shallow, and heavily silted harbor that made embarkation difficult and life

within the city unpleasant. (Ibn Jubayr also penned a noteworthy description of the filth and stench of the city, owing to its inadequate sewer system that left tons of human and animal waste in the high-shelved harbor.) But it was much the best the region had to offer, and thus, it was highly prized and massively fortified. Indeed, the Christians who took Acre back from the Muslims in 1191 during the Third Crusade (1189–1192) were able to do so only by constructing an array of enormous siege towers that took seven months to build. When the Mamluk sultan al-Ashraf conquered the city for the final time, he needed no fewer than ninety-two artillery guns (mangonels, specifically) in order to breach the walls—whereas the great Saladin, by comparison, never needed more than ten for any battle in his entire career.

Crusader Acre was therefore as noteworthy for its precariousness as for its malodor. Throughout the Middle Ages, in general, its political fate coincided with that of Jerusalem. Because of the proximity of the two cities, the control of one necessitated the control of the other: Acre provided food and basic commodities to the capital, and Jerusalem comprised the principal regional market for the merchants of the port city. After Jerusalem fell more or less permanently into Muslim hands after Saladin's conquest—overlooking the bizarre hiatus of Frederick II Hohenstaufen's tenure as king of Jerusalem—the fate of Acre seemed sealed. Thus, it is hardly surprising that Acre ultimately fell. Cut off from much of its commercial hinterland, its economy weakened markedly and so did its morale. Desperate requests for assistance from western Europe were heard repeatedly by the thirteenth-century popes, but the pontiffs proved incapable of raising support for relief of the city.

The final fall of Acre, symbolic of the fate of the Latin States in general, must be placed in the broadest context. Acre, like all important sites under Latin control in the East, was built to weather the storms of massive military invasions that periodically broke out. If military pressure upon them was mild and sporadic, then their chances of survival were decent. When pressure was intense and sustained, however, it was only a

CRUSADER STATES

matter of time before they fell. From the beginning to the end of their existence, the fate of the Latin States was primarily dictated by events taking place in the Islamic world (Syria, Egypt, and, more remotely, Baghdad) that determined exactly how much military pressure could be applied against the Christians. Factional fighting among the Turks to the north and the fairly isolated position of Fatimid Egypt to the south gave the Crusader States a period of grace in which they could flourish. The situation changed when Seljuk leader Zengi brought a marked degree of unity to Turkish Syria. After merging Mosul and Aleppo, Zengi launched a series of campaigns against both Muslims and Christians that enabled him to carve out a sturdy principality for himself. Rhetoric of the holy war both justified his conquests and galvanized the morale of his troops in such a way that massive campaigns against the Latins could be undertaken. The effects on the Latin States were immediately palpable. After a month-long siege the city of Edessa, the capital of the first Crusader State, fell to Zengi on Christmas Eve 1144. The Second Crusade (1147–1149) was launched to salvage the situation, but it failed through a combination of tactical blunders by the Latins and the newfound strength produced by increased Islamic unity. Zengi's son Nur al-Din expanded on his father's policies by earmarking Egypt for annexation into this new Turkish state. Although the policy was a sound one, neither Nur al-Din nor his line profited from it. After Egypt was acquired, Nur al-Din died, and his mantle was passed on to—or more accurately was seized by—Saladin.

Saladin inherited the Zengid political platform of jihad (just war) and expansion. He used the holy war as a justification for consolidating his power over Egypt and Syria. The Crusader States were now tightly held in a vise, and the new sultan of Egypt simply needed to apply the pressure, which he did with staggering results that deeply shocked western Europe and led to the Third Crusade. If not for the fortuitous arrival of Italian Crusader Conrad at Tyre (1187) the entire coast would have fallen. The unity Saladin imposed was impressive, but he still could not keep his armies in the field long enough to remove the remnants of the Crusader States once they were shored up with Crusader recruits from the West. Facing the inevitable disbanding of his military machine, Saladin was forced to conclude a treaty with Richard I of England. Soon after the sultan died, power passed to his sons, and the militant Islamic unity that achieved so much in so short a period of time evaporated. The struggle for succession lasted for seven years. Divided and squabbling Ayyubid princes emerged from the ashes and gave the Crusader States a new lease on life. It was not until the

1260s that this fragmentation came to an end and put in motion the chain of events that led to the final collapse of the Crusader States.

The fall of the Crusader States was the ultimate result of one of the greatest slave revolts in history. Mamluks were slave-soldiers used throughout the Islamic world; but in Egypt they acquired a central importance. While the Syrian Ayyubids were being weakened by the Mongols, the Mamluk emirs at Cairo launched a successful coup. After consolidating their hold on Egypt, the Mamluks conquered Ayyubid Syria and created an aggressive and highly centralized military state that surrounded the Latins. In their new provinces in Syria, the Mamluks created a system of dual governors (the civil *naibs* and the military *walis*) that were balanced off one another for maximum efficiency. Mamluk devotion to jihad and expansion, combined with the unprecedented unity they imposed, would have led to a swift end for the Crusader States if not for the threat posed by Mongol penetration into the region. From the Mamluk perspective, the Mongols were a much more grave threat than the Latins and needed to be dealt with first. To avoid a dangerous two-front war, the Mamluks signed frequent truces with the Latin states. In the end it was only these truces that stood between the Crusader States and obliteration. Once the Mongol threat ended, the truces ceased and along with them the Crusader States themselves.

Unlike Saladin's achievements, those of the Mamluks were not dependent on the abilities and accomplishments of a single individual. Succession to the Mamluk Sultanate was determined by a grisly but highly efficient mechanism: rounds of bloodbaths in which the strongest rose to the top. The result was a long chain of talented and brutal leaders completely devoted to a life of war (the only life these slave-soldiers ever knew). Centrifugal forces previously sapped the strength of Islamic polities in the region and gave the Crusader States breathing space. Not so with the Mamluks; each sultan maintained and expanded upon the gains of his predecessor. Qutuz, who like all the great Mamluk sultans came to power through an act of murder, had to devote much of his attention to the Mongols, whom he decisively checked at the Battle of Ain Jalut (1260). He was murdered by his emir Al-Zahir Baybars on the way back to Egypt. Baybars's sustained assaults crippled the Crusader States: he seized Caesarea and Arsuf (1265), Safad (1266), Jaffa (1268), and Krak des Chevaliers (1271). Antioch suffered badly; the males were slaughtered, while the women and children were sold into slavery. By the time he died in 1277, Baybars left his successors with great positioning. Qalawun had to move cautiously given the Mongol threat but still made impressive gains, such as capturing the great Hospitaller fortresses of Margat and Tripoli. When he died in 1290, there was little left of the Crusader States, worn down as they were by three decades of constant military pressure.

Since the rise of the Mamluks and their assumption of leadership over the war against the surviving Christian states, the reconquest of Acre acquired special symbolic significance as the culmination of the liberation of Jerusalem. One Mamluk soldier, the memoirist Baybars al-Mansuri, recalled his reaction to the news that his petition to participate in the 1291 campaign had been granted: "I felt like one who knew the happiness of having his greatest hope realized, one who witnessed the night giving way to the dawn." He was not alone in considering the undertaking a special one. The sultan al-Ashraf, in preparing for the siege, organized an assembly of Islamic clerics who performed a recitation of the entire Qur'an at the tomb of his father Qalawun, in Cairo; while in Damascus a joint ritual took place wherein clerics publicly read the entire *Sahih al-Bukhari*—the main collection of the Prophet's *hadith*. Indeed, the retaking of Acre assumed the proportions of a special jihad. A text celebrating al-Ashraf's victory exulted: "Because of you no place remains where unbelief can hide. Indeed, there is now no hope left for the Christian religion! Because of sultan al-Ashraf we are freed from the Trinity, and the One God rejoices in our jihad. Praise be to Allah—the people of the Cross have been destroyed and the faith of the Arab Prophet has been brought to glorious victory by the Turks!"

Despite the impressive fortifications of the city, the siege of Acre was relatively short, lasting only forty-four days. On 1 May 1291 a massive Mamluk army, drawn from both Egypt and Syria, arrived at Acre. Sappers began working on the walls while artillery applied pressure. Frankish sorties unsuccessfully tried to break the siege. The evacuation of women and children from the city began to be considered after the New Tower fell on 15 May. Three days later the Mamluks penetrated the outer wall, and the Accursed Tower was abandoned. Brutal street fighting commenced. The military orders fought heroically, trying both to repel the invaders and to provide cover for evacuees boarding ships. Some boats were so overloaded with refugees that they sank in the harbor. The convents of the Hospitallers and Teutonic Knights surrendered after being told their lives would be spared, but the sultan reneged on the promise and slaughtered them. The Templars learned from this treachery and held out as long as they could. After the last towers were taken or abandoned, widespread massacre ensued, and the survivors were sold into slavery. After Acre fell, the remaining Latin cities followed suit: Tyre, Sidon, Beirut, and Tortosa. Castle Pilgrim, the last Templar stronghold on the coast, was evacuated on 14 August. The Mamluks then began the systematic destruction of all coastal fortifications to prevent any possible Frankish return.

Acre is in many ways a microcosm of the Crusader States as a whole. Only the massive breadth of its fortifications allowed it to hold out as long as it did. The same can be said of every Frankish city in the region. Fortifications in the Crusader States were designed to slow sporadic assaults, to wait out periodic storms. With the rise of the aggressive, militant, and highly centralized Mamluk state that joined both Syria and Egypt, the fall of the Crusader States was only a matter of time. The existence of the Crusader States in the latter half of the thirteenth century depended solely on truces; when the Mamluks no longer had any use for these truces, the end came quickly.

–CLIFFORD R. BACKMAN,
BOSTON UNIVERSITY

Viewpoint:
The Crusader States collapsed because of internal weaknesses that, though they always existed, became more debilitating in the mid thirteenth century.

The final fall of the Crusader States (1291) is usually explained as being caused by the collapse of the fragmented Ayyubid dynasty and its replacement by the much more centralized and militant Mamluk Sultanate in Egypt. Saladin's descendants, hopelessly squabbling with one another, were unable to marshal Islamic resources in the region uniformly and apply the necessary pressure to evict the Franks from the Levant. The potential to extinguish the Latin colonies, the argument goes, was always there. But the deep-seated divisions between Muslims made it impossible. Whenever Muslims managed to establish even the slightest degree of unity (as under Zengi, Nur al-Din, and Saladin) it resulted in disaster for the Crusader States. The Crusader States were thus extremely sensitive to pressure, especially if applied with consistency. The Mamluks applied such consistent pressure and succeeded in driving the Franks into the sea.

There is much to be said in favor of this interpretation. The Franks indeed frequently buckled beneath the weight of periodic Islamic unity. The Crusader States were established during, and thrived under, periods of regional

PROMISES AND LOUD BOASTS

Jerusalem patriarch Gerold complains in a letter about the new ruler, Fredrick II, who took command of the kingdom in 1229:

For he came, excommunicated, without money and followed by scarcely forty knights, and hoped to maintain himself by spoiling the inhabitants of Syria. He first came to Cyprus and there most discourteously seized that nobleman J. [John] of Ibelin and his sons, whom he had invited to his table under pretext of speaking of the affairs of the Holy Land. Next the king, whom he had invited to meet him, he retained almost as a captive. He thus by violence and fraud got possession of the kingdom.

After these achievements he passed over into Syria. Although in the beginning he promised to do marvels, and although in the presence of the foolish he boasted loudly, he immediately sent to the sultan of Babylon to demand peace. This conduct rendered him despicable in the eyes of the sultan and his subjects, especially after they had discovered that he was not at the head of a numerous army, which might have to some extent added weight to his words. Under the pretext of defending Joppa, he marched with the Christian army towards that city, in order to be nearer the sultan and in order to be able more easily to treat of peace or obtain a truce. What more shall I say? After long and mysterious conferences, and without having consulted any one who lived in the country, he suddenly announced one day that he had made peace with the sultan. No one saw the text of the peace or truce when the emperor took the oath to observe the articles which were agreed upon. Moreover, you will be able to see clearly how great the malice was and how fraudulent the tenor of certain articles of the truce which we have decided to send to you. The emperor, for giving credit to his word, wished as a guarantee only the word of the sultan, which he obtained. For he said, among other things, that the holy city was surrendered to him.

This same prince, who had previously very often promised to fortify Jerusalem, departed in secrecy from the city at dawn on the following Monday. The Hospitalers and the Templars promised solemnly and earnestly to aid him with all their forces and their advice, if he wanted to fortify the city, as he had promised. But the emperor, who did not care to set affairs right, and who saw that there was no certainty in what had been done, and that the city in the state in which it had been surrendered to him could be neither defended nor fortified, was content with the name of surrender, and on the same day hastened with his family to Joppa. The pilgrims who had entered Jerusalem with the emperor, witnessing his departure, were unwilling to remain behind.

The following Sunday when *"Laetare Jerusalem"* is sung [fourth Sunday in Lent], he arrived at Acre. There in order to seduce the people and to obtain their favor, he granted them a certain privilege. God knows the motive which made him act thus, and his subsequent conduct will make it known. As, moreover, the passage was near, and as all pilgrims, humble and great, after having visited the Holy Sepulchre, were preparing to withdraw, as if they had accomplished their pilgrimage, because no truce had been concluded with the sultan of Damascus, we, seeing that the holy land was already deserted and abandoned by the pilgrims, in our council formed the plan of retaining soldiers, for the common good, by means of the alms given by the king of France of holy memory.

When the emperor heard of this, he said to us that he was astonished at this, since he had concluded a truce with the sultan of Babylon. We replied to him that the knife was still in the wound, since there was not a truce or peace with the sultan of Damascus, nephew of the aforesaid sultan and opposed to him, adding that even if the sultan of Babylon was unwilling, the former could still do us much harm. The emperor replied, saying that no soldiers ought to be retained in his kingdom without his advice and consent, as he was now king of Jerusalem. We answered to that, that in the matter in question, as well as in all of a similar nature, we were very sorry not to be able, without endangering the salvation of our souls, to obey his wishes, because he was excommunicated. The emperor made no response to us, but on the following day he caused the pilgrims who inhabited the city to be assembled outside by the public crier, and by special messengers he also convoked the prelates and the monks.

Addressing them in person, be began to complain bitterly of us, by heaping up false accusations. Then turning his remarks to the venerable master of the Templars he publicly attempted to severely tarnish the reputation of the latter, by various vain speeches, seeking thus to throw upon others the responsibility for his own faults which were now manifest, and adding at last, that we were maintaining troops with the purpose of injuring him.

Source: *Dana Carleton Munro, ed., "Gerold, Patriarch of Jerusalem, to all the Faithful, 1229," in* Translations and Reprints From the Original Sources of European History, *volume 1 (Philadelphia: University of Pennsylvania, 1897), pp. 27–29.*

Islamic disunity. And the Mamluk Sultanate, based in Egypt but also controlling Damascus, Aleppo, and their hinterlands in the north, applied fairly constant pressure for three decades that ultimately concluded with the end of the Crusader States. There is, however, a corollary to this argument. When pushed hard by a centralized Egypt or Syria (or, even worse, both simultaneously), why were the Crusader States incapable of pushing back just as hard? If one acknowledges the intense pressure that the Mamluks placed on the Crusader States prior to their fall, one must also recognize the major flaws and weaknesses that made the latter so quick to crumble beneath the application of pressure any time a regional Islamic power centralized and focused its attention on the Christians.

The situation existing during the end of the Crusader States was an inversion of the conditions surrounding its genesis. In retrospect, the First Crusade (1096–1102) had all the markings of a doomed enterprise. The expedition proposed to travel to the other end of the known world, defeat Islam on its own turf, and found a colony surrounded by the enemy on all sides. The proverbial "hand of God" is one way to explain its surprising success—certainly that was how the participants reckoned their achievement. Posterity evaluated it otherwise. Fortuitously, the Crusaders arrived during an optimum, if short, window of opportunity that allowed them to burrow in. They caught regional Islamic powers both off guard and off balance. The conflict between the radically orthodox Seljuks in Syria and the heterodox Fatimids in Egypt created great instability. Conflicts and disputes among Seljuk rulers, moreover, spawned even greater disunity. Thus, much of the wind is stolen from the sails of the achievement of the First Crusade. Essentially, it was victory by default. The smashing of the "Crusade of 1101" seems to confirm this theory. Regional Islamic powers were quick to respond to the unexpected Frankish threat and, once cooperating rather than fighting, easily brushed off the next crusading host.

This interpretation of the foundation of the Crusader States (and it has much validity) has served as a powerful, if occasionally subtle, backdrop for other investigations into the history of Outremer. It introduced a tendency to evaluate the fate of the Crusader States mostly in terms of the unity or disunity of Islamic regional powers. The names Zengi, Nur al-Din, and Saladin became focal points in assessing the life of Outremer, names that were considered of much greater importance than the seemingly endless lists of Fulks and Baldwins or, in popular histories, such an esoteric surname as "Ibelin." Initially, interest in the political organization of the Crusader States was relegated to what it could reveal about European political structures. Romantic notions emerged that posited the feudal society of the Crusader States as a "fossilized" version of an early European feudalism. Far off in the eastern Mediterranean, Crusader State feudalism was inoculated against the rapid changes taking place in the West. It was the "Dodo Bird," so to speak, of European political history. Thus, in a sort of "twice removed" way, the Crusader States had significance for western European political and constitutional history.

The devastating blows that unified Islamic states inflicted upon the Latin colonies are fairly well known, but the turbulent internal divisions and conflicts within the Crusader States that coincided with these examples of Islamic unity are not known as well. Saladin's conquests within, and the Mamluk destruction of, the Crusader States can serve as the two best-case studies. In each, regional Islam achieved impressive degrees of unity that resulted in massive amounts of military pressure on the Crusader States. Each, however, fortuitously hit the Franks while the latter were in a state of disarray.

Saladin's jihad (just war) against the Crusader States has been well covered, but a crisis raged within the Crusader States on the eve of the Battle of the Horns of Hattin (1187) that was simply an acute outbreak of problems that had smoldered for decades. The rulers of the Crusader States were bitterly divided, and ambitions flared in the years prior to Saladin's victory. In the 1170s there was the first clear stirring of what historians refer to as the "baronial movement" in the Crusader States. The "founding fathers," so to speak, emerged from the oldest families in the Latin East, scions of the men who staked the first claims in the colonies. The interests of these families frequently clashed with those of the crown. Land was a precious, rare, but essential resource in the Latin East. Royal power could be strengthened best by increasing the amount of land in its direct possession. Naturally, this policy clashed with the interests of those families who were the greatest landholders in the Crusader States. In the 1170s these families began cooperating and coordinating their efforts under fortuitous circumstances: King Baldwin IV had leprosy and was rendered ineffective. Legally, these men were aggressive; they reinterpreted old laws (and apparently made new ones) that strengthened their positions. Militarily, they were quite conservative when it came to Islam. Peaceful and stable relations with regional Islamic powers were in their interest. Peace with Islam not only meant prosperity but also afforded the luxury of being able to focus attention on their immediate interests without the complication of constant battle with the

Muslims. To the dismay of both the crown and leaders of the incipient baronial movement, relative newcomers such as Reynald of Chatillon pursued extremely aggressive individual approaches to Islam. For these new players, many of whom married landed and titled women, power did not mean just consolidating what they had but attacking and plundering Muslims as well. Reynald, who rebuffed royal attempts to secure Saladin's request for the return of booty taken from Islamic caravans, is naturally the most extreme example. His relentless attacks upon Muslim caravans and his attempted invasion of Mecca are widely considered to be the most immediate reason Saladin struck with such vigor.

In the years preceding Hattin, intrigue and suspicions were rampant in the Crusader States. There were many military clashes and assassinations. Baldwin thought Raymond of Tripoli and the Prince of Antioch were conspiring to steal the throne. Two parties, those surrounding Raymond of Tripoli and Guy of Lusignan, soon clashed over the issue of royal regency and succession. When Baldwin's illness made it impossible for him to properly discharge his duties as king, he gave Guy effective administration over the kingdom. The feudal lords were divided in their reactions. A falling out between Baldwin and Guy pushed the latter into moving toward the barons. Guy ignored a royal summons to appear in court and closed Ascalon to the king. Legitimate rights to the throne then revolved around the claims of two women, Isabella and Sibylla. Both women became rallying points for factional intrigues, ambitions, and conflict. The Crusader States became enmeshed in a serious constitutional crisis, and defections from opposing sides bred even more distrust and animosity. The situation continued to deteriorate, including plans to annul the marriage of Guy and Sibylla and the actual abduction of Isabella. While Guy was preparing to attack Raymond at Tiberias, the former was trying to forge an alliance with Saladin.

Naturally, Saladin was well informed about the complete disintegration of unity among the barons of the Crusader States. Chaos among the Franks certainly played a role in bolstering his confidence enough to strike hard. Disunity among the Franks, then, most likely played as great (if not greater) a role in Saladin's campaigns as the unity the Sultan managed to impose temporarily on the Muslims. The united front that Saladin forged was always so fragile that it almost disintegrated several times. Sustaining solidarity among the emirs was a difficult task that, once achieved, was assured a short life span. Latin disarray provided Saladin with a compelling reason to achieve whatever

temporary unity he could and strike while the iron was hot. Taking all of these factors into consideration, it would seem that divisions within the Crusader States, rather than unity among Muslims, was the decisive factor in the timing of Saladin's jihad.

Even more important, divisions among the Latins played a crucial role in the Frankish defeat at Hattin. Important tactical decisions during the battle were complicated and confounded by factional divisions among the Latins. Field decisions were influenced by suspicions concerning how they would strengthen or weaken the rival faction. A case in point is the controversy that surrounded the question of whether the Latin field army should lay siege to Tiberias (which Saladin had already seized). The Latin leadership knew that Saladin's unified force could not last long, and one option proffered was to dig in around a water source and wait for the Sultan's army to fall apart. All things considered, this strategy was the most pragmatic approach. Raymond (Tiberias was his fief) favored this course of action. The other option was to march on Tiberias immediately. Guy's decision to take Tiberias seems to have been at least partly based on the fact that his main rival, Raymond, favored the conservative plan. Gerard of Ridefort, the Templar master who was shoulder deep in the intrigues and had a personal grudge against Raymond, advised Guy to move on Tiberias. The reason Gerard cited is instructive. He told Guy that Raymond was trying to goad him into making a bad and unpopular decision that would discredit him. Clearly, factional disputes and mutual suspicions played a major role in the final outcome. The result of this wrong decision was no less than the destruction of the Latin field army. If the Crusaders had waited, or forced Saladin to fight on their terms rather than the reverse, the outcome of Hattin would have been different. Echoes of these disputes thundered throughout the Third Crusade (1189–1192) and significantly hampered its ability to act efficiently.

The Mamluk Sultanate was an even greater threat, which appeared while the Crusader States were even weaker than on the eve of Hattin. Given the limited amount of land available in the Crusader States, the feudal system relied on cash and "money fiefs" much more so than western European states. Trade revenues were thus of crucial importance. An escalating inflation rate, combined with increasing defensive needs, shoved military costs into an entirely new bracket. Economic ripples created by the rise of the Mongols aggravated the situation by reducing trade revenues for the Crusader States. The Mongol destruction of Baghdad, combined with their massive territorial expansion and newfound interest in trade revenues, caused an abrupt and,

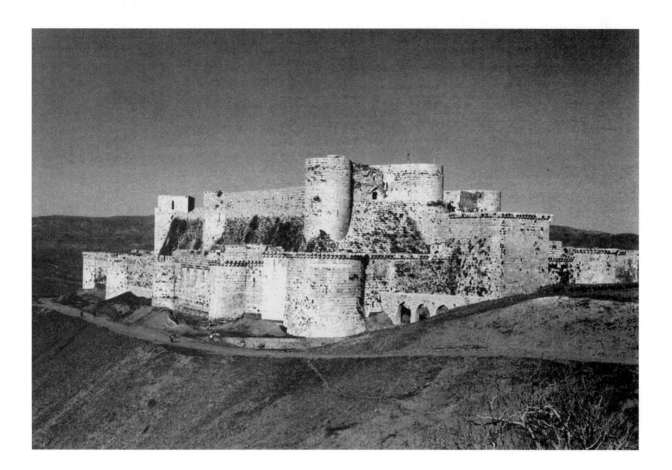

for the Crusader States, destructive change in East-West trade routes. The Mongols became the catalyst for the creation of new trade routes that reduced the importance of the Latin colonies. Although these changes did not destroy commercial activity in ports such as Acre and Tyre, they seriously diminished it. The Black Sea absorbed much of the trading activity that previously flowed through the Crusader States. Since they handled little of the shipping, there was not much they could do to control the damage being done. Italian maritime states, which dominated sea commerce, simply redirected their attention to the Black Sea (though they were still concerned with their holdings in the Latin colonies). Effects were quickly felt: many barons could no longer afford to maintain their holdings and leased them to the military orders. This difficulty brings into bold relief one of the greatest weaknesses in the Crusader States: their complete dependence on the West for sea power. Lack of a significant fleet made it impossible for the colonies to defend their most important interest, and, combined with previous losses of territory, it meant financial chaos and then military disintegration for the Crusader States. The dismal situation, moreover, made any territorial loss to the Mamluks more devastating.

Economic decline, which the Crusader States were unable to stem, was not the only factor destabilizing the colonies. Many of the prob-

lems that faced the Crusader States were common to all feudal societies. However, scarcity of land in the Latin East gave them a sense of desperation, urgency, and recklessness that is hard to match. Centralization by the crown could have strengthened the colonies, but short-sighted interests of the barons frustrated such attempts. The weak and fragmented (even by feudal standards) situation of the barons always forced them to have Western rulers arbitrate for them. Lack of manpower in the East made them even more dependent on the West in a variety of ways. Some contemporaries recognized the weaknesses. English philosopher Roger Bacon, for example, noted in the mid thirteenth century that the greatest problem in maintaining the Crusader States was their lack of serious colonization. The reason so many Crusades were launched to the East was the fact that the colonies were so weak they rarely could defend themselves. Crusades, however, were mixed blessings. Rights of conquest by the Crusade leaders allowed them to do what they pleased with lands reacquired, thus introducing constant waves of instability as land was redistributed, and, in the process, fanned the flames of factional disputes. Hopes in the Crusader States frequently hinged on the arrival of a great Western magnate who would become a strong king.

A strong monarch, however, would naturally challenge the privileges and semi-autonomous sta-

Krak des Chevaliers, Syria, built by the Knights Hospitallers in the late twelfth century

CRUSADER STATES

tus of the barons. Thus, they resented exactly what they wanted and needed. Frederick II's assumption of the crown of Jerusalem (1229) had great potential; it would have fused the fate of the Crusader States with the interests and resources of the German Empire. But the centralization Frederick tried to impose, which might have given the Crusader States just the sort of unity they needed to survive, was seen as a grave threat by the barons. The conflict that emerged between the Ibelins and the Hohenstaufen weakened the kingdom further. And the War of St. Sabbas that broke out in 1256, a civil war that tapped into the seething animosities of faction fighting, engulfed the Crusader States, and depleted valuable resources. The Latin East became a wounded animal that made easy prey.

One final weakness in the Crusader States needs to be pointed out. The overwhelming majority of inhabitants of the Crusader States were Eastern Christians and Muslims who really had no vested interest in the survival of the Frankish colony. Eastern Christians were treated as second-class citizens and were frequently regarded as heretics. Culturally speaking, moreover, they had more in common with regional Muslims. Good relations between Eastern Christians and Muslims can be easily seen in how the former were treated by the latter. Muslim conquerors, such as Zengi, distinguished between Eastern and Latin Christians and gave the former preferential treatment. Eastern Christians really had little incentive to fiercely resist Muslim invaders; Islamic victory merely signaled living under the rule of a different master, and one that might be preferable to the former. Muslims in the Crusader States achieved a modus vivendi with the Latins during times of peace, but were known to revolt against their Christian masters when Islamic invasion forces appeared. Thus, there was always an internal Islamic threat that could amplify the effects of any external one.

The Mamluks indeed imposed a long-sought Islamic unity in the region that was capable of bringing great weight to bear on the Crusader States. But this centralization and unity can be overemphasized. The Mamluk Sultanate had periods of great unity but also experienced periods of utter chaos. The history of the Bahri Mamluks, who dealt the deathblow to the Crusader States, frequently seems to be one long list of sultans who fell prey to conspiratorial activities, such as being stabbed to death in bathtubs. Its greatest strength, the lack of hereditary monarchy, was also a great weakness since succession was frequently brought about through bloodbaths and civil wars. Certainly whoever emerged as the new sultan was both brutal and competent, but the sultanate was often drained of military resources and needed to recover. If the Latin barons could have put aside their own conflicts and personal interests for the sake of presenting a unified front, Islamic unity would have crashed on the rocks of Crusader State unity. In the end, the Crusader States died of paralysis and the inability to take decisive action and the necessary steps to ensure their survival.

–MARK T. ABATE,
WESTFIELD STATE COLLEGE

References

Robert Irwin, *The Middle East in the Middle Ages: The Early Mamluk Sultanate, 1250–1382* (Carbondale: Southern Illinois University Press, 1986).

P. Jackson, "The Crisis in the Holy Land in 1260," *English Historical Review,* 95 (1980): 481–513.

Abdul-Aziz Khowaiter, *Baibars the First: His Endeavours and Achievements* (London: Green Mountain Press, 1978).

Jonathan Riley-Smith, *The Feudal Nobility and the Kingdom of Jerusalem, 1174–1277* (London: Macmillan, 1973; Hamden, Conn.: Archon Books, 1973).

Steven Runciman, *A History of the Crusades,* volume 3 (Cambridge: Cambridge University Press, 1954).

Sylvia Schein, *Fideles Crucis: The Papacy, the West, and the Recovery of the Holy Land, 1274–1314* (Oxford: Clarendon Press / New York: Oxford University Press, 1991).

CRUSADER STATES

DEFINING MOMENT

Does the modern-era conflict between the West and the Islamic Near East have its roots in the Crusades?

Viewpoint: Yes. The Crusades defined relations between Western and Islamic civilizations in an enduring way that shaped further conflicts.

Viewpoint: No. Modern relations between the West and the Islamic world were defined by nineteenth- and twentieth-century forms of imperialism and nationalism, culminating in the formation of the state of Israel and the Arab response.

Since the collapse of the Soviet Union and the end of the Cold War (1991), the conflict that has dominated international relations is that among the Western powers, Israel, and the Islamic world. Instability and turbulence are not new developments in the Near East; conflict has rocked the region with great force since the creation of Israel (1948). The al-Qaeda attack on the United States (2001), however, brought the conflict home to Americans in a forceful way. Film clips from the Gaza Strip and Jerusalem shifted to footage of the devastation unleashed in New York City. The attack on the World Trade Center towers underscored in a painful way that Americans are a part of the tension between the Islamic and Western civilizations. Optimism about peacefully resolving discord in the Near East hit an all-time low. In the past fifty years historians have tried to trace and delineate the roots of this clash; and, given the changing climate, their efforts will no doubt be redoubled. Terrorism is, however, a small, if high-profile, element of Western-Islamic relations. Though they disapprove of terrorist tactics, much of the Arab-Islamic world understands the reasons for it.

The rhetoric surrounding the modern clash between the Arab world and the West, on both sides, is peppered with the language of crusading. Historians evaluate such language in different ways. Some see it simply as rhetoric and find few significant similarities between the age of the Crusades and modern times. Crusades were religious wars, while modern conflicts in the Near East, with the exception of radical Islamic fundamentalists, are secular in nature. Arab nationalism, colonialism, imperialism, Zionism, and the state of Israel are the main ingredients in the current mix. Other historians argue that the Crusades were the ultimate roots of the modern conflict and, though the disputed issues are primarily secular in nature, they are permutations of religious concerns that dominated the first contacts between the Islamic world and the West.

Whether the causes are rooted in the twelfth century or the nineteenth century is a difficult question. Answers spring from differing views on how to measure the impact of the distant past on the immediate present and what constitutes historical continuity and change. Certainly, the Arab world feels that it has been insulted, abused, and exploited; that it has been carved up; and that it has been culturally and territorially raped by the West. The process was long, painful, and humiliating—one that culminated in the ultimate humiliation: the inability of the Arabs to deal a major blow against Israel. The Israelis, who were first seen as mere "Zionist gangs" that could quickly be disposed of, succeeded in creating a sturdy state capable of fighting and winning three-

55

front wars. To much of the Arab world, the formation of Israel and its continued existence are inextricably intertwined with the West. Israel is seen as the culmination of Western expansion that is rooted in nineteenth-century imperialism and may well be the progeny of the crusading movement.

Viewpoint: Yes. The Crusades defined relations between Western and Islamic civilizations in an enduring way that shaped further conflicts.

During the Persian Gulf War (1991), President George Herbert Walker Bush launched a "crusade" against Iraq; Saddam Hussein responded by proclaiming a jihad (just war) against the Western invaders. Such rhetoric certainly was not unique to this conflict and has punctuated the relationship between the West and the Islamic-Arab world for some time. But has invoking images of holy war been mere rhetoric, or does it rather reflect deep and enduring medieval roots that have defined modern relations between the Near East and the West? Some historians argue that the nineteenth century marked a decisive rupture in the relationship. The rise of secularism, nationalism, imperialism, and colonialism completely redefined relations between the two civilizations and jettisoned the medieval baggage that each was once burdened with. Others argue that the West is, and always has been, crusading against the Islamic world and that what essentially was a medieval religious conflict has been reconstituted using modern concepts. That the conflict between the two civilizations has escalated rather than subsided has made the issue one of the utmost importance. Some historians see historical change as a glacier-like process: so slow that its motion can hardly be detected, but overpowering in its effects. Other historians focus on "decisive events": episodes that bring about abrupt change with quick blows. Islamic-Western relations are based on the former approach; the Crusades were the foundation (but not the entire edifice) upon which the entire modern conflict is based.

Many modern and secular notions are permutations of what once was medieval and sacred. As the Western, and later Islamic, world became more secular, it recast and reconstructed many views, values, and institutions to conform to new realities. Furthermore, what is "thought" is just as important—sometimes more so—than what "is." The Positivist tradition made invaluable contributions to historical analysis by stressing the need to uncover the "hard" causes that exist beneath "soft" appearances. But the price of this approach has been

to ignore many of the irrational forces that work on the human mind—maybe chief among them being nostalgia. Imperialism and colonialism certainly define modern relations between the Near East and the West. Yet, one must take into account both the possible secularization of a much older conflict and, just as important, how participants in the new conflict assessed, and continue to see, its relation to the past.

The first substantive contact between the Western and the Islamic world was violent. The Crusaders saw the Muslims as godless heathens who were dedicated to rapine, while Muslims viewed the Crusaders as foreign conquerors kicking in the door to the House of Islam. This violent clash established the baseline by which each civilization evaluated the other. It created standards by which by all subsequent contacts and events were measured, assimilated, and given meaning. The Islamic world took great pride in the fact that its "superior" civilization expelled the Western invaders in 1291. Egyptian sultan Saladin became a great folk hero, and it comes as no surprise that in President Gamal Abdel Nasser's Egypt a feature-length film was made about the sultan's blows against the Franks. The West saw the expulsion of the Crusaders as a temporary setback, an event that would be reversed through a combination of God's will and proper timing.

Social psychologists are perhaps more useful than traditionally minded historians in measuring the impact of the Crusades on the worldviews of each civilization. They claim that all new experiences are unavoidably related in the human mind to old information to give them meaning. Experience D, for example, must be interpreted though experiences A, B, and C in order for it to make sense. Culturally speaking, experience A was the Crusades, the first substantive contact between the civilizations, and B and C were always informed by it. Social psychologists claim that this process is hardwired into human cognition, and they present a convincing case. The gist of the theory can be summed up in a popular saying: first impressions are the most important.

The idea of the exotic and irrational Muslim savage is a stereotype that has endured in the Western imagination to modern times. But among the western European elite of the Middle Ages, particularly the clergy, the concept was refined and was not quite so crude. Put in its most simplistic terms, the Christian West believed that it was "right" and that all those who deviated from its view were wrong. From the perspective of the medieval Church, Muslims were in error. The Church basically had two categories of people: those within the Church and those who should be within it. Christianity was fiercely evangelical, and its ultimate goal was to spread the "truth" throughout the world. Church leaders wanted to bring all of humanity into the fold. Conversion to Christianity, however, was supposed to be a voluntary decision severed from the use of brute force. The thirteenth century was a great turning point in Church views toward non-Christians. The canon-lawyer-turned-pope, Innocent IV, and his prize student Italian canonist Hostiensis, played major roles in developing this new view. They argued that since all humans were descendants of Adam, they were all God's children and thus under the legitimate authority of God's representative on earth, the pope. Thus, the pope had de jure jurisdiction over all people—whether they were Christian or not. He was responsible for the welfare of all people. From Innocent's perspective, the Fall (when Adam and Eve were forced out of Eden) introduced chaos and discord into the world and launched the contest between truth and fallacy.

Since religious truth had been torn apart in the human community, the natural law introduced by philosophers had to be taken into consideration. Those who did not embrace the truth still had some rights, the most important of which were property and self-rule. Innocent believed, however, that interfering with the property and sovereignty of "infidels" was not forbidden. Papal "intervention" was permissible since the pope, guardian of truth and all human souls, had global responsibilities. The barring of Christian missionaries from any region constituted a violation of natural law and required a papal remedy. If an "infidel" ruler obstructed the work of Christian missionaries, he was harming his people by denying them access to the truth. Popes were not only authorized but also obligated to launch a war to change this situation. People would not be forced to convert, but rulers would be made to allow their subjects the option. Hostiensis tweaked his master's theory: infidels did not have the right to sovereignty because of the fallacies they subscribed to and because of their inferior moral state. Non-Christians were de facto sinners and should be treated as such, which meant the loss of their rights. Innocent's view enjoyed wider support, but Hostinesis made his mark. As the Crusader period gave way to the Age of Discovery, these legal views were applied by secular conquerors to the people they dominated.

Popes became mediators among secular states that launched massive conquests against "new infidels" and used "violations of natural law" as the pretext for domination.

Innocent IV and Hostiensis's theories of dominion, of right and wrong, were powerful forces that were recast as Europe drifted to a more secular frame of mind. Christian truth gave way to the fruit of the Enlightenment. Reason was substituted for religion, and the truth was redefined. Democracy and the free market became the new "natural laws" of the nineteenth and twentieth centuries, and anyone who rejected them was, to use papal parlance, in error. The barbaric infidel who rejected Christian truth during the Middle Ages was transformed into the ignorant savage that dismissed reason and human rights in the nineteenth century. The "Popes' Burden" became the "White Man's Burden" as the relationship of the West with the non-Western world became modernized and secularized. In both cases, however, the West was "right," the rest of the world was "wrong," and it was the responsibility of the former to teach the latter the truth. Likewise, in both cases, military force played a central role in spreading the truth.

The Crusades were always on the minds of Europeans in the age of imperialism. Politicians, soldiers, and scholars all drew upon the Crusades for inspiration and justification. In 1862 the Prince of Wales, future English king Edward VII, visited the Holy Land and stayed on the very spot where Godfrey of Bouillon supposedly camped while outside the walls of Jerusalem. When German emperor Wilhelm II visited Jerusalem in 1898, he did so on horseback dressed as a Teutonic Knight and entered the city by the Jaffa Gate in the style of a triumphant Crusader lord. Less bombastic and more enlightening were the deep connections between British imperialists and their crusading past. When British prime minster Benjamin Disraeli visited the Holy Land (like many others), his experiences served as the impetus for writing the three-volume *Tancred: or, The New Crusade* (1847). Tancred, born to a family of great privilege, abandons all when he sets out for the Holy Land, in imitation of his crusading ancestor who saved the life of Richard I, the Lion-Hearted, during the Third Crusade (1189–1192). Tancred found the East to be a "career" rooted in a grand and illustrious past. Disraeli's nostalgic view of crusading, which comes through forcefully in his book, tells readers quite a bit about the irrational motives that lurked within his own expansionist policies in the East. The prime minster obviously saw imperialism as a new crusade firmly rooted in history—likewise with the French. When

THE MERCY OF ALMIGHTY GOD

Pope Innocent IV, during a 1245 council, addressed the situation in Constantinople:

Though we are engaged in difficult matters and distracted by manifold anxieties, yet among those things which demand our constant attention is the liberation of the empire of Constantinople. This we desire with our whole heart, this is ever the object of our thoughts. Yet though the apostolic see has eagerly sought a remedy on its behalf by earnest endeavour and many forms of assistance, though for long Catholics have striven by grievous toils, by burdensome expense, by care, sweat, tears and bloodshed, yet the hand that extended such aid could not wholly, hindered by sin, snatch the empire from the yoke of the enemy. Thus not without cause we are troubled with grief. But because the body of the church would be shamefully deformed by the lack of a loved member, namely the aforesaid empire, and be sadly weakened and suffer loss; and because it could rightly be assigned to our sloth and that of the church, if it were deprived of the support of the faithful, and left to be freely oppressed by its enemies; we firmly propose to come to the help of the empire with swift and effective aid. Thus at the same time as the church eagerly rises to its assistance and stretches out the hand of defence, the empire can be saved from the dominion of its foes, and be brought back by the Lord's guidance to the unity of that same body, and may feel after the crushing hammer of its enemies the consoling hand of the church its mother, and after the blindness of error regain its sight by the possession of the catholic faith. It is the more fitting that prelates of churches and other ecclesiastics should be watchful and diligent for its liberation, and bestow their help and assistance, the more they are bound to work for the increase of the faith and of ecclesiastical liberty, which could chiefly come about from the liberation of the empire; and especially because while the empire is helped, assistance is consequently rendered to the Holy Land.

Indeed, so that the help to the empire may be speedy and useful, we decree, with the general approval of the council, that half of all incomes of dignities, parsonages and ecclesiastical prebends, and of other benefices of ecclesiastics who do not personally reside in them for at least six months, whether they hold one or more, shall be assigned in full for three years to the help of the said empire, having been collected by those designated by the apostolic see. Those are exempt who are employed in our service or in that of our brother cardinals and of their prelates, those who are on pilgrimages or in schools, or engaged in the business of their own churches at their direction, and those who have or will take up the badge of the cross for the aid of the Holy Land or who will set out in person to the help of the said empire; but if any of these, apart from the crusaders and those setting out, receive from ecclesiastical revenues more than a hundred silver marks, they should pay a third part of the remainder in each of the three years. This is to be observed notwithstanding any customs or statutes of churches to the contrary, or any indulgences granted by the apostolic see to these churches or persons, confirmed by oath or any other means. And if by chance in this matter any shall knowingly be guilty of any deceit, they shall incur the sentence of excommunication.

We ourselves, from the revenues of the church of Rome, after first deducting a tenth from them to be assigned to the aid of the Holy Land, will assign a tenth part in full for the support of the said empire. Further, when help is given to the empire, assistance is given in a very particular way and directed to the recovery of the Holy Land, while we are striving for the liberation of the empire itself. Thus trusting in the mercy of almighty God and the authority of his blessed apostles Peter and Paul, from the power of binding and loosing which he conferred upon us though unworthy, we grant pardon of their sins to all those who come to the help of the said empire, and we desire they may enjoy that privilege and immunity which is granted to those who come to the help of the Holy Land.

Source: *"First Council of Lyons" (1245), from* Decrees of the Ecumenical Councils, *edited by Norman P. Tanner (London: Sheed & Ward / Washington, D.C.: Georgetown University Press, 1990), pp. 295–296.*

DEFINING MOMENT

European states were establishing consulates in the Holy Land, the French justified their pre-eminence over their competitors by pointing to the dominant role they played in the Crusades: Clermont was in France, Pope Urban II was French, Peter the Hermit was French, Godfrey of Bouillon was French, and King Louis IX was French. By implication, the Crusades and the Crusader States were French.

Crusading language was commonplace in World War I (1914–1918). The Allies saw the war as, essentially, a Crusade against the godless and tyrannical Central Powers. Yet, the idea of crusading was taken much more literally when it came to campaigns in the Holy Land. Lawrence of Arabia's (Thomas E. Lawrence) view is exemplary. Supposedly, one of his ancestors participated in the Third Crusade with Richard I, the Lion-Hearted. His college thesis was on the Crusades, and his knowledge of crusading blended seamlessly with his service in the East. Without doubt he saw himself as continuing the Crusade to the East and bringing to a successful conclusion the efforts of his ancestors by learning from their mistakes and employing modern technology. Like Disraeli's character Tancred, Lawrence saw himself quite clearly as a "new crusader" who was completing what his ancestors left unfinished.

No discussion of Crusader inspiration in World War I would be complete without addressing the expedition of English field marshal Viscount Edmund Allenby. Even if his claim, made upon entering Jerusalem (1917), that "Only now have the crusades come to an end" is spurious, it certainly reflects the real emotional tenor of his campaign. Apparently, crusading enthusiasm was so rife among the rank and file that orders had to be issued that soldiers were not allowed to call themselves Crusaders. Major Vivian Gilbert's *The Romance of the Last Crusade: With Allenby to Jerusalem* (1923) clearly roots the expedition in memories of the Third Crusade and the still palpable urge to restore the Holy Land to Christian control. Gilbert saw himself and his troops as reincarnations of the Crusaders: "What did it matter if we wore drab khaki instead of suits of glittering armor. The spirit of the crusaders was in all these men of mine . . . was not their courage just as great, their idealism just as fine, as that of the knights of old who had set out with such dauntless faith under the leadership of Richard the Lionhearted to free the Holy Land."

Historical scholarship also affiliated colonialism with the crusading past. This linkage was particularly the case with the French. Beginning with Emmanuel Rey, who published *Les colonies franques de Syrie aux XII me et XIII*

me siecles (1883), imperialism was seen as a reincarnation of crusading, and the Crusader States were considered the first European (and French) colony. Louis Madelin expanded on this theory in *L'Expansion francaise de la Syrie au Rhin* (1918), noting that the French were not only the firebrands of medieval colonialism but that they also had the best credentials for assuming the lead in the modern movement. His argument, that the French were effective and sensitive colonial powers since the late eleventh century, provided France with intellectual fuel for jockeying its way to a postwar mandate in the Near East. For understandable reasons there was a flurry of academic labors during the nineteenth century in the history of the Crusades, not only interpretive monographs but also critical editions of the sources. These works served as the building blocks for creating the "colonial theory" of the Crusades, which enjoyed great currency. Whether imperialism and colonialism were permutations of Crusade is not the main issue: what was thought, and how it affected relations between the near-prostrate Islamic-Arab world and the Western colonial powers, was more important. The West explained imperialism and colonialism as a continuation of the Crusades; the concept spread to Arab intellectuals and confirmed their suspicions that expansionist impulses were firmly embedded in the Western mentality.

Radical Islamic fundamentalists are a small minority in the Muslim world. They tend to use the rhetoric of the Crusades, but their jihads are usually intended to replicate the career of the Prophet Muhammad and his wars to end *Jahiliyya* (pre-Islamic ignorance). Secularized Muslims and Christian Arabs, however, tend to see imperialism and colonialism as modern reincarnations of the Crusades. They argue that the West, in one fashion or another, has been crusading against Islam from the eleventh century to the present. Muslim intellectual Sayyid Qutb probably put it best: "The spirit of the crusades, though perhaps in a milder form, still hangs over Europe, and that civilization in its dealing with the Islamic world occupies a position which bears close traces of the crusading spirit." Or, as an Arab Christian historian has written, the Crusades left a "festering sore that refused to heal" that made Islam more militant. Just as Europeans came to see imperialism as a secularized Crusade, so did much of the Muslim and Arab world. The conflict between Islam and the West was sacred in its original form but became secularized and is now based on nationalism.

Without doubt the major event that transformed the relationship between the Arab-Islamic world and the West was the creation of the state of Israel (1948). In order to gauge the true impact of this event, it must be placed in a broader context, one that takes seriously the legacy of the Crusades and the theories about the Crusades that existed in the nineteenth and twentieth centuries. Zionism is widely seen in the Arab-Islamic world as a new nationalistic recasting of the Western crusading mentality; that Israel was created by western European Jews is no coincidence. Israel is, in this scenario, the "last crusader state." It was created by expansionist Westerners who conquered and colonized, and it remains as dependent on Western support as the original Crusader States were. The views of some Israeli historians, such as Joshua Prawer, confirm rather than refute this theory (though they do not believe that this interpretation in any way detracts from the legitimacy of Israel as a state). In many ways imperialism, and the impact it has had on modern relations, was a secularized form of crusading. More important, the West still perceives itself to be the guardian of truth, albeit a now secularized, rather than spiritual, truth. The Islamic-Arab world still sees the West as being on a Crusade. Both of these views have shaped and continue to shape their mutual perceptions. Consequently, the Crusades are the most "defining" moment in relations between Islam and the West.

–TODD MARX, CONCORD, NEW HAMPSHIRE

Viewpoint:
No. Modern relations between the West and the Islamic world were defined by nineteenth- and twentieth-century forms of imperialism and nationalism, culminating in the formation of the state of Israel and the Arab response.

Western European and Islamic civilizations have a long history of contact and confrontation. Designating a "definitive" event that shaped their interrelations with, and perceptions of, one another is no easy task. When asking what set the tone for modern relations between the two civilizations, one must first define "modern" and exactly how the past, both proximate and remote, influences it. Many scholars have concluded that the current confrontation between the West and Islamic East is little more than a continuation of the holy wars fought against each other in the Middle Ages.

The West (now including the United States) is still "crusading" against the Islamic world, and Muslims, in turn, are still prosecuting the jihad (just war) against the West. The players, the argument goes, may have changed somewhat, but the drama is still the same one that has been performed since 1095. This interpretation is a gross oversimplification of the realities and projects modern problems, produced by current events, far into the past. The rhetoric each side uses, in fact, echoes the history of the crusading era, but beneath these statements exist causes and catalysts that are entirely different and unrelated. While using the Crusades to explain modern relations between the Western and Islamic states may not be the same as trying to fit the proverbial square peg in a round hole, it is akin to trying to fit an octagonal peg in an oval hole. In either case, however, the peg must be forced.

The Islamic world was at its zenith during the age of crusading. In many respects it was the most advanced, sophisticated, and prosperous civilization on the globe. After recovering from the initial shock of the First Crusade (1096–1102), Islam quickly responded to the threat and gained the upper hand. Although there might have been a few brief moments of fright for Islamic powers (such as the loss of Damietta, twice, in 1219 and 1249), Islam had little to fear from the Crusaders for the duration of the movement. Spain was, of course, an exception: on the furthermost extremity of Dar al-Islam, al-Andulus (the Islamic areas of the Iberian peninsula) found it difficult to resist the *Reconquista* (reconquest) and eventually succumbed. But in the eastern Mediterranean, Islam easily fended off European invasion forces and colonists, checking the former soundly and driving the latter into the ocean in 1291. Crushing the Crusader States merely confirmed for the Islamic world the nature of its superiority, while the loss of Spain had but a minimal effect on this view. The greatest blow to the Islamic world came not from Europe but from the Mongols, who raised havoc in the mid thirteenth century: they destroyed the Abbasid caliphate, conquered Iran and Iraq, and warred against Egypt. In any case, the Ilkhans and the Golden Horde both eventually converted to Islam. Islamic superiority over the Franks dovetailed with, and was explained by, religious beliefs. To the "superior" religion went superior status.

Modern Western and Islamic relations can be said to have roughly begun in the eighteenth century. The foundations for these relations were essentially based upon a complete reversal of the situation experienced during the age of crusading: western Europe was rising to ascendance as the Islamic world was in decline. Economically and militarily, the Islamic states were put increasingly on the defensive. In the nineteenth century the West systematically penetrated every region of Islamic power from North Africa to Southeast Asia. Areas under Western control introduced new legal codes inspired by the Enlightenment, while the *Shari'ah* (Islamic jurisprudence) was frequently reduced to the status of family law. Muslims throughout the world asked why the respective positions of Islam and the West had been reversed. The plethora of answers given by Muslims can be divided into two main categories: Islamic Fundamentalism (traditionalism) and Islamic Modernism. These two schools of thought have defined modern Islamic perceptions of, and reactions to, the West; this conceptual dichotomy did not exist during the Crusades but was produced in the nineteenth century.

Islamic Fundamentalism (hereafter referred to as traditionalism) was one response. It was piloted on the eve of European dominance by the traditional-thinking *ulama'* (scholarly class), who blamed the new power dynamic on decaying values within the Islamic community. Generally, traditionalists advocated a return to the incipient Islamic values that were revealed by the Prophet and a purge of foreign accretions that had seeped into religious thought. The basic beliefs of Islamic traditionalism were: the *Shari'ah* is a complete blueprint and constitution for life that requires no foreign supplements; the declining fortunes of Islam have been produced by foreign influences corrupting Islamic doctrine; and restoring the supremacy of Islam was predicated on a spiritual revolution that would restore true Islamic principles. Traditionalism, however, was far from a monolithic dogma.

There were what one can call, for lack of better phrasing, "traditionalists" and "radical traditionalists." The former group is exemplified by the creation of Saudi Arabia (1932). Many Americans are perplexed by the ambivalent relationship between the West and this "fundamentalist" state. How could it be both fundamentalist and somewhat pro-Western? First of all, "pro-Western" may be too strong a term. "Not virulently anti-Western" may be a bulky phrase, but it is more accurate. Ibn Saud, the founder of Saudi Arabia, combined traditional Islamic values and law with state-building. At least nominally basing his conduct on the Prophet, Saud created a state that was grounded on the *Shari'ah*. Domestic and foreign policy have been decisively Islamic, but Saudi Arabian policies (at least officially) have never been predicated on attacking the West. Thus, the oldest "fundamentalist" Islamic state is capable of cooperation with Western powers. The ideal has been a modus vivendi between international partners. Being an Islamic traditionalist does not equate with being the terrorists depicted in the Western media.

Radical traditionalists, although they constitute the minority, are better known to, and feared by, the West. They subscribe to all the tenets of other brands of traditionalism but add more: violent attacks are necessary to return Islam to its former grandeur; jihad, the tool for accomplishing this goal, is a duty of all Muslims; the West aspires to introduce policies that weaken the *Ummah* (community), most notably Zionism; and Islamic states that do not recognize these truths have deviated from the *Shari'ah* and thus are legitimate targets of jihad as well. This line of reasoning has been adopted by the terrorist organizations and cells that dominate Western headlines: al-Qaeda, Hezzbullah, and Islamic Jihad. These groups feel that they are currently living in a modern re-creation of *Jahiliyya* (the age of ignorance and iniquity that preceded the Prophet's revelations). Western concepts and dominance are equated with the *Jahiliyya*, which existed in pre-Islamic Arabia but on a global scale. The fundamentalist groups model their behavior on that exhibited by the Prophet (with an emphasis on his military campaigns) and feel they are reliving the drama he created.

Islamic Modernism was an alternative to the traditionalist diagnosis and cure. The great early Modernists sought to walk the line between the rejection of the West advocated by traditionalists and the wholesale adoption of Western culture advocated by secularists. Modernists also believed that Islam needed to be revitalized to meet the challenges posed by Western domination. Their approach was different; rather than clinging to the ossified faith promoted by traditionalists, they advocated a dynamic view of Islam. The backward-thinking and archaic *ulama'* made Islamic civilization stagnant. Rather than casting their gaze backward to the Middle Ages, Modernists stressed the need to look forward. Islam was to be remade in modern terms. Drawing upon Western concepts and tools was permissible so long as it did not violate the essence of the *Shari'ah*.

Jamal al-Din al-Afghani is the father of Islamic Modernism (even though many give this title to his Egyptian pupil Muhammad Abdu), and his views are particularly instructive. Afghani was a top-notch intellectual who lived at one time in all the major Islamic cul-

Illumination of Christ leading Crusaders, from *The Apocalypse* (early fourteenth century)

(British Museum, London)

tural centers, as well as in important Western ones such as Britain and France. He was extremely critical of backward-thinking Islamic leaders (one of his pupils even assassinated the Shah of Iran). Afghani claimed that the Islamic world could not bury its head in the sand and pretend the West had not grown in power, nor could it abandon Islam and fully embrace Western culture. His greatest tool for reconciling these divergent approaches and hitting upon the proper course of action was analogical reasoning. The first fruits of Western civilization, he believed, were already present in the *Shari'ah*. But a dynamic and energetically interpretive approach, rather than the slavish medievalism of the *ulama'*, was required to meet the challenge. Yet, Afghani was no pacifist. He energetically promoted jihad against expansionist imperialist powers that were invading the Garden of Islam. Afghani, moreover, was the first scholar to contrast "Islam" and the "West" as historically antagonistic categories, though he did not extend the historical context to the Middle Ages in any meaningful way. Western imperialism that began in the late eighteenth century and culminated in the nineteenth century were Afghani's focus.

Two other essential ingredients went into the mix in the nineteenth and early twentieth centuries: Pan-Arabism and Zionism. Most Arabs seem to have considered themselves loyal subjects of the Ottoman Empire, but Arab leaders sought independence. As Ottoman power waned, Arab nationalism grew. Zionism was on a collision course with Arab nationalism, even though before World War I (1914–1918) there was no significant conflict between Jews and Arabs. In 1897 the first World Zionist Congress met in Switzerland and decided on seeking the creation of a Jewish home in Palestine. Thus, Palestinians and Zionists desired an independent state on the same land (which was then under Ottoman control). Meanwhile, Jews fleeing from anti-Semitism, particularly in eastern Europe, steadily migrated to Palestine. World War I packed the region with political powder kegs as the biblical "promised land" became the "twice promised land" of the twentieth century. To enlist support against the Central

Powers, Britain made promises to both the Palestinians and Zionists. Palestine, under the British Mandate during the interwar years, underwent massive change, with both Jews and Palestinians feeling bitter and disillusioned. Hatred was rising, and resistance to a partition plan that would create Jewish and Arab states in Palestine was strong.

Colonialism, imperialism, Islamic traditionalism and Modernism, Zionism, and Arab nationalism are salient features that have defined modern relations between the Islamic world and the West. None can be said to have existed in the crusading period. On the contrary, they represented radical changes and decisive breaks with the medieval and Early Modern past. The general tenor of Islamic views toward the West at the turn of the twentieth century was a strange mixture of admiration of its accomplishments and status, on the one hand, and a suspicious distrust of its apparently godless behavior and doctrine, on the other. Such views had been boiling for some time and were accentuated by misgivings about Zionism and distrust of the West generally in the early years of the twentieth century (when Palestinians and Jews alike received a fairly raw deal from the West). These seething views were quickened, however, and given a lightning rod when theoretical Zionism became a reality with the formation of the state of Israel (1948).

The creation of Israel transformed the region into a theater of perpetual war that had international implications as it became enmeshed in the Cold War. The United States initially granted de facto recognition, and the Soviet Union de jure status, to the new state. The Palestinian diaspora created a massive refugee problem that placed tremendous financial stress on neighboring Arab states, which declared war on Israel and increasingly resented the Western powers that they believed supported and sustained it. Israel came to be seen as the most recent (and blatant) installment in the Western imperialist venture to dominate and exploit Arabs. Israeli military victories added psychological stress to the financial strains the conflict introduced to the Arab world. Faith in political options declined; the only solution evident from the Arab perspective was to achieve military superiority to reverse Israeli statehood. The Cold War arms race was thus exported to the region, as the United States and the Soviet Union assisted with the military buildups of their respective clients.

Current relations between the Islamic world and the West have nothing to do with the Crusades. The formative year was 1948 rather than 1095. The creation of Israel was not like Athena, sprouting fully grown and fully armed from the head of Zeus. It was the product of new forces that emerged in the nineteenth century, continued to intensify during the early twentieth, exploded at midcentury, and has since increasingly produced global effects. The modern conflict bears little resemblance to the medieval one; somewhat similar rhetoric is all that they share.

–CARL HILL,
LOS ANGELES, CALIFORNIA

References

Vivian Gilbert, *The Romance of the Last Crusade: With Allenby to Jerusalem* (New York: W. B. Feakins, 1923).

Albert Hourani, *The Emergence of the Modern Middle East* (London: Macmillan, 1981; Berkeley: University of California Press, 1981).

Hourani, *Islam in European Thought* (Cambridge & New York: Cambridge University Press, 1991).

James Turner Johnson and John Kelsay, eds., *Cross, Crescent, and Sword: The Justification and Limitation of War in Western and Islamic Tradition* (New York: Greenwood Press, 1990).

Abdallah Laroui, *The Crisis of the Arab Intellectual: Traditionalism or Historicism?* translated by Diarmid Cammell (Berkeley & London: University of California Press, 1976).

Louis Madelin, *L'Expansion française de la Syrie au Rhin* (Paris: Plon-Nourrit, 1918).

Peter Partner, *God of Battles: Holy Wars of Christianity and Islam* (London: HarperCollins, 1997).

Rudolph Peters, *Islam and Colonialism: The Doctrine of Jihad in Modern History* (The Hague & New York: Mouton, 1979).

Emmanuel Rey, *Les colonies franques de Syrie aux XII me et XIII me siecles* (Paris: Picard, 1883).

Edward W. Said, *Orientalism* (New York: Pantheon, 1978).

DEFINING MOMENT

DISILLUSIONMENT

Did the failure of Louis IX's military campaigns in the thirteenth century begin a period of disillusionment among the Crusaders?

Viewpoint: Yes. The failure of Louis IX's campaigns marked the end of the traditional Crusades and inaugurated a long period of disillusionment.

Viewpoint: No. Although the campaigns of Louis IX prompted some criticism, support for the Crusades remained strong, while the methods for conducting them underwent revision.

Crusading had its critics from the beginning to the end of the movement. Only a few, however, ever challenged the validity or possibility for success of the enterprise. Most critics focused on either the moral conduct of Crusaders or what were seen as institutional abuses. The most common explanation for the failure of a Crusade in the classical period (1095–1291) was as divine punishment for sins, though papal avarice gained ground as a strong second—God chastised the sinful Crusaders and would not grant them victory even in such a noble venture. This interpretation was precisely how French king Louis IX viewed the failure of his expedition to Egypt: the lack of success was not blamed on poor tactics, nor supply problems, nor the outrageous behavior of his brother Robert, but as punishment for his own personal sins.

The First Crusade of Louis, or Seventh Crusade (1248–1254), was the best-planned and -equipped Latin force ever to set out for the East. The king squeezed all the resources possible from his kingdom and the Church. Aware of the problems that had faced the Fifth Crusade (1217–1229), he planned his campaign meticulously. Its failure came as a devastating blow to the hopes of Christendom. His second campaign, to Tunis (1270), though equally well planned, resulted in little more than Louis's death from disease in camp. The dismal results of these campaigns have been linked by some historians with the fact that they were the last major Crusades to the East and are seen by some scholars as marking a watershed in declining crusading enthusiasm. Disillusioned and disgusted, western Europeans began to view crusading to the Holy Land as futile. Songs of troubadours, taunts hurled at preachers (for example, that Muhammad was more powerful than Christ), and other pieces of evidence reveal a rapid decline in crusading enthusiasm among Europeans.

Other historians have challenged this view. They argue that a willingness to Crusade to the East not only survived the defeats of Louis but even weathered the fall of Acre (1291) and the destruction of the Crusader States. Salvaging the Holy Land, and after 1291 recovering it, remained an obsession in western Europe even if the means of doing so rapidly diminished. Citing discussions at councils, attempts to launch expeditions, and an entire literary genre dedicated to crusading theory, scholars argue that disillusionment with and disinterest toward crusading is an untenable thesis. Norman Housley, in *The Later Crusades, 1274–1580: From Lyons to Alcazar* (1992), contended that "crusading to the Holy Land continued to be discussed, promoted, and carried out for many decades to come after Lyons, something that would be inexplicable if enthusiasm had reached the low-water mark claimed by some historians." The Second Council of Lyons (1274) is a central event in the debate, marking as it did a decisive shift in crusading strategy and organization. Some believe that the meeting was a tacit recognition that crusading was a dead letter and that it began the age of plans that never materialized. Others argue that it signaled a formal strategic change in how Crusades were to be conducted and that some historians misinterpreted this shift as disillusionment.

Viewpoint:
Yes. The failure of Louis IX's campaigns marked the end of the traditional Crusades and inaugurated a long period of disillusionment.

Around 1266 Humbert of Romans, minster general of the Dominican Order and an enthusiastic advocate of crusading, wrote a comprehensive forty-six-chapter work that was in essence a textbook for effective Crusade preaching. It was filled with examples of sermons and uplifting anecdotes to inspire would-be Crusaders to make that all-important vow. He instructed his readers to combine hymns with wondrous stories of the pious actions of Charlemagne, Roland, and other great military heroes of Christian tradition. He advised that stories of miracles often produced good results. Humbert also included a long list of things that any effective Crusade preacher needed to know. For instance, a preacher should understand the geography of the Holy Land and was urged to consult maps. Humbert furthermore provided a reading list so that preachers could expand their understanding of Muhammad and Islam, suggested that they read the Qu'ran and understand how to refute it, and urged them to master the technical minutiae governing the formalities of the vow and indulgence. Humbert's effort represents the views of an excellent preacher, a devotee of crusading, and a man optimistic about the military aspects of the work of God.

Almost a decade later Humbert wrote another work, the *opusculum tripartium,* which was associated with the reworking of crusading strategy undertaken at the Second Council of Lyons (1274). In this text Humbert noted that hostility among the masses to launching a new Crusade was fairly widespread, and, to combat this sentiment, he outlined seven objections to crusading that preachers might find among their targeted audiences and how to overcome them. He described these objections as: spilling blood is contrary to Christian values; the amount of Christian blood shed in Crusades is unacceptable, even if taking Muslim lives is licit; the Islamic heartland is too strong and any attack on

it is bound to fail; protecting Europe may be worth such casualties, but not retaking Palestine; it is inconsistent to fight only Muslims when there are many other infidels that pose equal threats; missionary efforts to convert, rather than kill, Muslims yield better results; and crusading is against the will of God, and that is why he punishes expeditions with consecutive defeats. The argument that Humbert was setting up straw men is untenable. He went to great pains to investigate and compile evidence. Furthermore, the first, second, and sixth criticisms (as well as others not listed here) can clearly be found in the works of other scholars, such as English philosopher Roger Bacon. Additional sources, moreover, testify to the ridicule that audiences heaped upon the preachers who tried to get them to take the cross.

As scholarship of the crusading movement matured, historians became increasingly aware of the importance of 1274—a year that many believed was of greater importance than 1291 (when Acre fell for the last time). Palmer A. Throop, in *Criticism of the Crusade: A Study of Public Opinion and Crusade Propaganda* (1940), suggested that by 1274 the commitment of the Latin West to crusading was broken. A series of failures (those of French king Louis IX being exceptionally painful) left Christendom "profoundly discouraged, sceptical and disgusted" with the prospect of launching another expedition to the East. A fine study by Elizabeth Siberry, *Criticism of Crusading: 1095–1274* (1985), vigorously attacked the "Throop thesis." Yet, her work covers only the period between the First Crusade (1096–1102) and 1274. Her conclusions are extremely convincing for these years, but her subject ends precisely when Throop's begins. Thus, it is premature to jettison the Throop thesis based on evidence from before 1274, the year that roughly marks the shift in concern between Humbert's crusading works. The evidence indicates that Throop was correct. Critics can, and do, cite the plethora of crusading projects that theorists concocted to preserve or recover the Holy Land. Precious few of these efforts, however, got off the drawing board, and their actual (rather than theoretical) target shifted and became what was then called Romania.

DISILLUSIONMENT

A HEART FILLED WITH GRIEF

Templar Ricaut Bonomel mourns the loss of Arsouf after Mamluk sultan Baybars I captured the city in 1265:

My heart is so full of grief that it would take little more to make me kill myself at once or tear off this cross which I took in honor of Him who was crucified. For neither cross nor my faith protects and guides against the cursed Turks. Rather it seems, as anyone can see, that to our hurt God wishes to protect them.

With one bound they [the Turks] have conquered Cesarea and taken by violence the strong castle of Arsouf. Oh, dear God, they have taken the lives of too many knights, foot-soldiers, and burghers who were within the wall of Arsouf. The Kingdom of Syria has lost so much that (I wish to tell the truth) henceforth it will be without power.

Thus he is mad who seeks to fight the Turks since Jesus Christ does not deny them anything. For they have conquered and will conquer Franks, Tartars, Armenians, and Persians. And they conquer us here everyday because God, who used to watch over us, sleeps and Mohammed works with all his might and inspires the deeds of Melicadefer [Bibars].

After having done so much, I do not believe he [Bibars] will stop. He has sworn and said publicly that no Christian will remain in this country and that he will make a mosque out of the Church of Saint Mary. And since her son, who should be grieved, is pleased and so desires it, we, too, should be pleased.

Source: Ricaut Bonomel, "Ir' e dolors s'es e mon cors assezo," edited by V. de Bartholomaeis, as found in Palmer A. Throop, Criticism of the Crusade: A Study of Public Opinion and Crusade Propaganda *(Amsterdam: Swets & Zeitlinger, 1940), pp. 178–179.*

Louis IX's expedition to Egypt (1248–1254) was by far the best-planned and -equipped general Crusade ever launched. Thus, its failure must have come as a bitter disappointment to Christendom. Louis's effort was the last great Crusade based on the original model. After the defeat at al-Mansurah (1250) many friars who preached the Crusade were taunted by cries that Muhammad evidently was more powerful than Christ. Other examples of discontent can be added: Italian monk and chronicler Salimbene di Adam's humorous record of similar jeers; troubadour Austorc d'Aurillac's song about worshiping Muhammad instead of Christ; and Templar knight Ricaut Bonomel's poem about Muhammad fighting for Egypt while Christ dozed. A paralysis of crusading morale set in. Many subsequent would-be crusading monarchs undoubtedly

learned valuable lessons from Louis: for instance, one could tax their kingdom to near ruin and still suffer humiliating defeat in the Holy Land. The apparent futility of the endeavor, probably more than any other reason, caused monarchs and barons to balk at a new expedition to the Holy Land.

Louis's second Crusade (1270) is instructive in this regard. News of this projected expedition met with a cool response. French chronicler Jean de Joinville, who wrote about the life of the crusading saint, opted not to go on the Crusade, and he indicated that his response was a common one. There has been a variety of explanations concerning why Louis's focus shifted away from an assault on Egypt to one against Tunis. One possible explanation is that even he came to believe that the venture would fail and decided to use the host to strengthen the position of his younger brother and new king of Sicily, Charles of Anjou, against the Hafsids. That Louis's second expedition achieved little more than his death certainly did nothing to sustain or resurrect enthusiasm for another Crusade to the East. Saving the Holy Land seemed farther away than ever, and failure bred everything from indifference to contempt. These changing views surely explain the differences between the first and second works by Humbert.

That enthusiasm for crusading to the Holy Land waned does not mean it did so for the movement as a whole. Efforts were redirected to areas that produced better results. As early as 1254 English king Henry III proposed to have his vow to Crusade in the East commuted to the Spanish theater. The stock in crusading in eastern Europe was on the rise, while that to the Holy Land was in decline. Previously seen as a "bargain basement" theater that did not have the prestige of crusading in Syria, expeditions to eastern Europe became much more popular. The Teutonic Knights were harbingers of this shift when they redirected their focus away from the ailing Holy Land and toward the conquest, pacification, and conversion of Prussia and the Baltic area. The appearance of Mongols in eastern Europe made the theater even more important and hence more prestigious than ever before. Besides, crusading armies in this region, as well as in Spain, made tangible gains that eluded warriors in the Levant. Crusading in eastern Europe was also less costly and arduous than in the eastern Mediterranean. Mounting costs involved in the latter made most Latin kings reluctant to take the reins (and responsibilities) of being the new Louis. Such reluctance on the part of European monarchs to take the initiative and act decisively to save the Holy Land offers the best explanation for the failure of a general Crusade to materialize after the death of Louis (1270). Many obstacles that previously hindered such expeditions had been solved; for example, the perennial conflict between papacy and empire ended after the Battle of Benevento (1266). However, Europeans focused more on alternatives—crusading in the Holy Land was crushed beneath the cumulative weight of successive failures.

Even the emergence of a committed Pope, such as Gregory X, a former Crusader, could not resurrect the movement. Most men came to understand that traditional crusading was obsolete. Calls for Crusades to the Holy Land took on the appearance of fund-raisers, whose revenues were raided by secular rulers or redirected to efforts in Italy or eastern Europe. After the papacy of Innocent III, the financial apparatus of crusading became more fluid and could be directed to areas of greatest importance. It is significant that this redirection of funds took on even greater consistency after Louis's death, though not to say that there was no longer any interest in the Holy Land. On the contrary, there was a greater degree of planning than ever before. The proliferation of a new genre (recovery treatises) was significant. Many of these works were sincere efforts at working out problems in the East, but many of them were dedicated to using projected Crusades to secure other ends. For example, the principal objective of treatises written by advisers of French king Philip IV was an increase in royal power. Armenians naturally favored an initial landing in their homeland that would benefit them.

Furthermore, if European monarchs were truly committed to saving or recovering the Holy Land, they would have acted decisively. Naturally, one can point to the costs involved, as well as disruptions of international relations in western Europe, that prevented bringing their plans to fruition. Yet, these obstacles faced every generation of Crusaders, and the mixture of optimism and commitment resulted in action. As optimism waned, action followed. Taking the cross to the East became a drama that more often than not resulted in the commutation of vows. There were of course "little Crusades" launched to the East after 1274, but they produced equally little. Alternatives to armed expeditions grew in importance. Chief among these alternatives was the possibility of peaceful conversion, resulting in the flourishing of schools for missionaries that taught Arabic and philosophical methods for disputing the tenets of Islam. Men such as Roger Bacon, Catalan mystic Ramon Llull, and Spanish Dominican monk Raymond of Peñafort saw peaceful conversion as a tool that could succeed where armed conflict had failed.

Previous military disasters in the history of the Crusading States—Field of Blood (1119), the Horns of Hattin (1187), and La Forbie (1244)—prompted great responses in the West. Thus, it seems strange that the response to the Mamluks driving the defenders of the Crusader States into the sea was so muted. In part, this reaction is probably because news of the defeat was far from shocking; in fact, it was expected. Plans were made for assistance, such as immediate financial aid, enforcing a naval blockade, and developing a new Crusade. Attempts were even made to take advantage of the Mongol offer for an alliance that would restore the Crusader States. All this planning amounted to little since few men were committed to acting. There are many possible explanations: escalating costs, political turmoil in western Europe, and so on. But Throop's explanation still deserves consideration, and it has the added virtue of explaining why obstacles in previous years were overcome but many of the same ones were not after 1274. All of Christendom wanted to regain the Holy Land, but few believed it was possible at the time, and even fewer were willing to take the risk. Recovery of the Holy Land continued to spark the imagination and pull at the spiritual heartstrings of Christians, but actual crusading activity was permanently redirected to other theaters that enjoyed success rather than failure. Perhaps the sole inheritors of the traditional model of crusading were the kings of Cyprus, though they could not rely on much western aid. The "Crusade" (1365–1367) of Peter of Cyprus was spectacular, but also unique and short-lived. He sacked Alexandria (1365) and rattled sabers about liberating the Holy Land, but his agenda seems to have been more in line with trade issues than resurrecting the Crusader States. Thus, one can conclude that by the middle of the fourteenth century even Eastern Christians had given up any true commitment to securing the Holy Land.

–CARL HILL,
LOS ANGELES, CALIFORNIA

Viewpoint:
No. Although the campaigns of Louis IX prompted some criticism, support for the Crusades remained strong, while the methods for conducting them underwent revision.

In 1940 Palmer A. Throop published his important study *Criticism of the Crusade: A Study of Public Opinion and Crusade Propaganda*. This influential volume suggested that criticism of crusading steadily increased from the late twelfth into the early fourteenth centu-

Illumination of Louis IX,
shown with halo, being
taken prisoner on his
retreat to Damietta; from
*The Life and Miracles of
St. Louis* (fifteenth
century)

(British Library, London)

ries and was commensurate with the frustration generated by successive failures. Most disappointing of all was French king Louis IX's great expedition to the East (1248–1254), which, despite an auspicious start, ended in disaster. By 1274 (which historians see as a significant year for the history of the movement), western Europeans were thoroughly disillusioned with the prospect of a successful Crusade to the East. Although Throop (and permutations of his thesis) still has supporters, much of his argument has been scrapped. Elizabeth Siberry's *Criticism of Crusading: 1095–1274* (1985) and Norman Housley's *The Later Crusades, 1274–1580: From Lyons to Alcazar* (1992) have been particularly important in this regard. Approaching the subject of possible "disillusionment" with the eastern Crusades must begin with an evaluation of the work of these two scholars.

Siberry's study met Throop's work blow for blow and seemed to get the better of the battle. First of all, Siberry demonstrated that criticism of crusading existed from the beginning of the movement and thus was not specifically a response to failures. Particular Crusades that floundered were criticized, but rarely the movement as a whole. Although such critics always existed, they were perpetually in the minority and had a variety of reasons for launching their

criticisms—such as axes to grind with the papacy. One finds the following forms of criticism: noncombatants interfered with the expeditions, as did the moral chaos introduced by women; vows were broken or commuted too casually; the poor moral qualifications of most Crusaders often doomed ventures to defeat since God would not grant victory to such pompous asses; and the practice of vow redemption made crusading a cash cow that popes and kings were all too eager to milk. Sprinkled among these critics one finds the rare pacifists. Most aggressive critics, moreover, such as troubadours or particular clerics, already had an antipapal bias, and, since the papacy had so thoroughly cast its lot with crusading, the failure of such ventures made good press for their causes. However, most critics launched their attacks not to discourage crusading to the East but to offer constructive criticism. More often than not criticisms of the Crusades were aimed at improving rather than discrediting the movement. Housley specialized in the "post-classical" period of crusading, an epoch that covers several centuries after the fall of Acre (1291). Naturally, there were other theaters that appear immune to the Throop thesis, yet, as Housley and others have pointed out, the Holy Land was the subject of much strategic and theoretical study as well. The entire first chapter of Housley's book provides overwhelming evidence demonstrating that enthusiasm for crusading to the Holy Land remained high not only after the failure of Louis's Crusades but well beyond the fall of Acre.

There are three main lines of argument that have kept the gist of the Throop thesis alive. The first is that criticisms of crusading became more common and vociferous beginning in the middle of the thirteenth century (Siberry is surely correct that much of it was constructive criticism that marks no significant change from previous critiques and that it was not opposed to crusading on principle). The second is that despite all the rhetorical posturing, no general Crusade departed from Europe for the East after the failure of Louis's second crusade (1270). The third is that Europeans began exploring a variety of options to crusading, chiefly conversion preached by specially trained missionaries, and this shift indicates general disillusionment with military activity. What the thesis and its variants fail to acknowledge is that crusading to the East underwent massive change beginning in 1274, which had little to do with waning enthusiasm or diminishing commitment. Before dealing with this revolution in crusading strategy, one must consider these three props that tenuously held up the basic features of the Throop thesis. A significant weakness in Throop's study is revealed in the work's subtitle "public opinion." It is highly doubtful that modern conceptions of public opinion existed in the Middle Ages, and if they did, there is not enough evidence to reconstruct it. Rather than using quantifiable evidence, medieval historians must rely on qualitative sources when gauging reactions to policy.

English philosopher Roger Bacon has often been cited as the textbook example of a man utterly disillusioned with crusading. Some scholars have suggested that he served as the model for the "critic" that Humbert of Romans warned Crusade preachers about. Bacon certainly was one of the most outspoken men of his age (and he paid the price in full). He viewed the failure of Louis IX's first Crusade (1248–1254) as a disgrace that stained all Christendom. Likewise, he roasted the Teutonic knights for the apparent avarice that overwhelmed their mission in the Baltic; without a doubt, he believed they did more harm than good, and he suggests the same might be the case regarding the military orders in the East. He preferred converting instead of killing Muslims; every Muslim slain by the sword, to Bacon's mind, was a man condemned to the fires of hell before salvation was an option.

Bacon believed that God had revealed a master science to humanity that could transmute all matter, including human bodies and souls, into another substance. But when it was abused by men who made themselves gods of the pagan pantheon, God retracted it until the final days, which Bacon was convinced he was living in. Once the philosopher's egg was created (as Alexander the Great did under the tutelage of Aristotle), the bodies and souls of men could be transmuted by tapping into celestial emanations amplified by magical words (sermons). Just as the alchemist could transmute lead into gold (the principle and mechanics for Bacon were the same), the initiate could transmute a Muslim, Jew, or pagan into a Christian. Ultimately, this process was the basis for Bacon's preference of conversion over Crusade, but he also believed that not all Muslims would be susceptible to such missionary transmutation. At precisely this point many historians became confused about Bacon's view of Crusades. Bacon was no pacifist; he argued that those Muslims who could not be converted should be utterly destroyed. He believed that traditional crusading had been rendered obsolete and ineffective (he was not alone by any means on this score). His reasons for believing so, however, were beyond idiosyncratic and qualify as unique. Bacon argued in 1266 that Louis could conquer the Holy Land by employing the services of twelve natural philosophers armed with mirrors. Like a medieval Robert Oppenheimer (the American physicist who headed the team that built the first nuclear bomb), Bacon believed that his enemies could be obliterated with a "push of the button" that would destroy entire armies without shedding a drop of friendly blood. The poster boy of the Throop thesis thus becomes a man who simply wants to reshape crusading in accordance with what he believed to be "scientific advances." If Humbert of Romans used Bacon as his model for the conscientious objector to crusading, he seriously misunderstood what the Franciscan friar had in mind. Although Bacon found the traditional means of crusading to be obsolete, he planned to increase Islamic bloodshed and optimistically believed that twelve men could save the Holy Land.

Once one looks past Bacon's odd spin on the subject (astral alchemy and Acre being defended by a chain of burning mirrors), one finds that his criticisms are constructive and reflect optimism rather than disillusionment. During the second half of the thirteenth century there were massive reassessments of crusading strategy that can easily be misconstrued as disillusionment. Bacon's stance on missionary activity as a viable alternative to constant armed conflict was just a quirky take on a general trend occurring at the time. Spanish Dominican monk Raymond of Peñafort, Catalan mystic Ramon Llull, Bacon, and others believed that missionaries trained in foreign languages and logic could make great gains in peacefully absorbing many Muslims into the Christian faith, but it was an alternative strategy that would supplement crusading rather than serve as a substitute. Most of the great advocates of missions to Muslims were also supporters of crusading. The mendicant orders are instructive in this way. Yes, they were among the greatest advocates of comprehensive missionary work, but that also played a major role in Crusade preaching. Clearly, most men of the day did not see the two ventures as incompatible; on the contrary, they complemented one another. Those who could be converted should be; those who resisted should be smashed.

Apparent objections to the concept of crusading on principle are fairly easy to push to the side because they were so rare. They reveal sporadic exceptions rather than any general rule. To Bacon one could add eschatological thinkers such as the Joachites (to whom Bacon was much more than sympathetic), who generally believed that military force was unnecessary since God planned on converting the enemies. The failure to launch a major Crusade after the death of Louis is a more serious problem. Were all Crusades planned for the East from the 1270s on little more than pious posturing? Increasing costs and the inability of Crusaders and monarchs to meet them is but one factor in explaining this turn of events. Political turbulence in western

DISILLUSIONMENT

Europe increased rather than diminished in the late thirteenth century. Papal defeat of the Empire would seem to have signaled a window of opportunity for crusading, but this chance was quickly quashed by the equally acrimonious appearance of Spaniards claiming rights to southern Italy.

Bacon was not alone in believing that the large-scale traditional Crusade had been rendered obsolete. The fact that many men lost confidence in the viability of the old model does not necessarily mean there was disillusionment with the movement. Crusading, like any institution that exists for centuries, was dynamic and adaptable. Western Europeans learned over the years that mobilizing and launching a massive international army was a slow and crude approach that needed more precision. "Proper timing" became a key phrase in crusading strategy. One feature of this strategy was making the movement more professional. Stationing permanent (if small) garrisons in the East was part of this policy. Recruitment no longer worked solely in terms of preaching the cross; secular military musters supplemented preaching tours. The use of mercenaries (though always present) gradually increased in the thirteenth century. A key component of the newly emerging strategy was the *passagium particulare* (preliminary passage). These contingents were envisioned as professional expeditionary forces, small and more mobile, that would establish a crusading beachhead and maintain it until the larger *passagium generale* (general passage) a massive international army, could mobilize and land. Later, the concept of the *passagium primum* (first passage) was introduced, a sort of reconnaissance that would precede the expeditionary force. Claiming that Christendom had become completely disillusioned because it failed to launch a general expedition to the East is to miss the point. Several efforts were mobilized and launched. Gregory X alone sent four expeditions. Crusading to the East did not die, it simply changed form.

There are many reasons why western Europe never managed to reestablish traditional Crusades: skyrocketing costs, international instability, Crusader activity in Romania and eastern Europe, and the efforts of monarchs to create nation-states. It would be a mistake to view the countless Crusader vows sworn by European monarchs as a pro forma ritual or publicity stunt that they never intended to make good on. To do so is to oversimplify and underestimate the sweeping changes that were taking place in Europe during the late thirteenth and fourteenth centuries. Even if there were few tangible results in the movement after the death of Louis IX, there certainly was an abundance of activity. Great interest can often coexist with marginal results. Many of the "recovery treatises" are difficult to explain otherwise. Reassessments of viable approaches continued enthusiastically, including plans for naval blockades and combining military orders. Some results were achieved in the East, even if they proved temporary. Peter of Cyprus, for example, sacked Alexandria (1365) and contemplated the recovery of the Holy Land, which remained a topic at the top of the papal agenda far into the fourteenth century. Frustration does not mean disillusionment nor disinterest. The Holy Land remained a perpetual obsession for the Latin West that, when the timing was right, flared into a flurry of activity. Western Europe was simply unable to launch a general Crusade at the time—but the enthusiasm for crusading, rather than waning, waxed.

—MARK T. ABATE, WESTFIELD
STATE COLLEGE

References

Norman Housley, *The Later Crusades, 1274–1580: From Lyons to Alcazar* (New York: Oxford University Press, 1992).

Maureen Purcell, *Papal Crusading Policy: The Chief Instruments of Papal Crusading Policy and Crusade to the Holy Land from the Final Loss of Jerusalem to the Fall of Acre 1244–1291* (Leiden: Brill, 1975).

Sylvia Schein, *Fideles Crucis: The Papacy, the West, and the Recovery of the Holy Land, 1274–1314* (Oxford: Clarendon Press, 1991; New York: Oxford University Press, 1991).

Elizabeth Siberry, *Criticism of Crusading: 1095–1274* (Oxford: Clarendon Press, 1985; New York: Oxford University Press, 1985).

Palmer A. Throop, *Criticism of the Crusade: A Study of Public Opinion and Crusade Propaganda* (Amsterdam: Swets & Zeitlinger, 1940).

ECONOMIC MOTIVES

Were the Crusades motivated primarily by economic considerations?

Viewpoint: Yes. The promise of economic gain and new markets was a key impetus for the Crusades.

Viewpoint: No. Crusaders were motivated by political considerations as well as the promise of spiritual rewards and increased social prestige.

The First Crusade (1096–1102) emerged amid a society that was simultaneously experiencing massive economic and religious change. Naturally, historians concerning themselves with the motives of Crusaders and the causes of such a widespread response to Pope Urban II's call (1095) have tried to determine which of the two factors was the more active agent and catalyst. Some historians have used the "materialist" argument derived from Marxist thought to explain the movement. German philosopher Karl Marx believed that the productive forces of any civilization were what determined all of its characteristics. When methods of production are altered, great historical change follows. Marx also believed that all other human endeavors constituted the "superstructure" that rose from modes of production and the means by which their distribution was justified. Religion, law, ethics, and art were mere extensions of the reality behind production. Historians applying this theory to the Crusades concluded that significant economic shifts—the growing monetary economy, population growth, and changing patterns of inheritance—transformed the relationship between Europeans and production. When the foundation shifts, the superstructure becomes modified. Religion, the central feature of the medieval superstructure, adapted. Holy wars of expansion were proclaimed as a means, conscious or not, to bridge the gap that emerged.

As the influence of Marxism among historians diminished, so did the number of those scholars supporting the materialist-economic interpretation of the Crusades. Massive religious upheaval and zeal became the dominant explanation. A newfound awareness of sin and the need to purge it resulted in increasing numbers of penitential pilgrimages and the "armed pilgrimage" that became crusading. The Crusades financially impoverished most men who participated in them, and the only real rewards they reaped were spiritual—which were premium by the standards of the day. The Crusader who turned a financial profit from his efforts was rare, but enthusiasm and participation remained high. Although many historians stressing the religious causes have made some room for economic gain, this cause has by and large been pushed to the periphery of the general consensus.

The materialist argument still flares up every now and then. In 1992 one scholar suggested that the Crusades arose from the need to export the surplus production of a growing Europe. The Church thus sanctioned holy war with the East to take the economic offensive against Islamic merchants and secure important new markets. The theory does not seem to have been well received, but many historians are realizing that economics and religious piety both played roles in initiating the Crusades.

Viewpoint:
Yes. The promise of economic gain and new markets was a key impetus for the Crusades.

Reconstructing the motives of Crusaders and the founders of the Crusader States is a complex task. Two general theories that emerged are the Marxist-influenced materialist theory and an explanation that rests on religious idealism. Two important preliminary points need to be addressed. First, the desire for material gain and devotion to religious idealism are not mutually exclusive; they could and often did coexist, and they strengthened rather than weakened one another. Second, "crusaders" are referred to as the large assortment of people drawn from the entire spectrum of social backgrounds and economic standing. One cannot assume that what motivated priests and paupers inspired *castellans* (castle wardens) and dukes. For that matter, one cannot assume that what motivated one count necessarily motivated another count. Venetian motives most likely clashed with all of the above. Backgrounds and interests varied, and therefore motives for committing oneself to such a venture did as well.

The materialist argument used to be much more popular and influential. It sprang from a confluence of two trends: the Marxist approach, which saw the root for all historical causation as being centered on production and attempts to control it, and the positivist neo-Rankian approach, which distrusted the rhetorical explanations posterity left behind and attempted to pierce the veneer to get to "real" causes and issues. The materialist theory of the First Crusade (1096–1102) stressed the massive economic changes that were taking place in western Europe and the financial pinch they applied to all sectors of society. Primogeniture, a new approach to inheritance, began awarding property to the eldest son, leaving a mob of belligerent and land-hungry second sons to fend for themselves and to seek their fortunes. Conquest was the only real method by which the second sons could become landed, and thus the idea of staking claims in the East was attractive. The First Crusade was a "second son" venture that directed surplus members of the warrior aristocracy to the East. The position of the poor was even worse. Since the turn of the millennium western Europe had experienced rapid population growth, an escalation of trade, and increases in the circulation of money—all of which pressed upon and strained the earlier manorial structure. These forces created a new form of "poor," a group of itinerant laborers who had no solid place in the feudal structure. The rapid response of the poor to the summons of a man such as Peter the Hermit is thus easy to explain. Pope Urban II mentioned the possibility of acquiring wealth while making his call for a Crusade at the Council of Clermont (1095), even if it was not the focus of his preaching campaign. That France was in the throes of crop failure and famine when the First Crusade was preached has been cited with approval and clinches the argument.

The riposte to the materialist argument has raised many solid objections. Archival research has revealed much that discredits material causes. First, the First Crusade was no "second son" phenomenon. Many aristocrats participating in the Crusade were landed and financially secure men. Second, Crusaders had to finance themselves and the expedition was costly. Families pulled together to shoulder the heavy economic burden and large stretches of land had to be mortgaged. It is difficult to detect any great material dividend that could be garnered from the investment. On the contrary, the effort most likely constituted a heavy financial loss. Dividends existed, but they were spiritual rather than material. Third, critics of the materialist "land grab" theory point out that few Crusaders actually settled in the East. Once the armed pilgrimage was concluded, most Crusaders returned home, implying that material gain and land acquisition were not strong or even significant motives. This argument usually concludes by noting that what was important to medieval men was not what is important to modern people.

The situation of the "poor" is easier to deal with than the aristocracy, even if the results prove less conclusive. German chronicler Ekkehard of Aura's description of the motives of participants in the First Crusade is instructive. His views are much more nuanced than the simplistic interpretation of French monk Guibert of Nogent, who saw motivation as stemming exclusively from religious idealism. Ekkehard mentioned that some Crusaders were moved by the words of prophets and celestial signs of divine approval, but he also pointed toward people "who were compelled to take such vows by all kinds of personal disadvantages." For this reason he felt it was not difficult to convince men to leave the West for the East. Furthermore, Ekkehard reported that many Crusaders took their wives, children, and whatever possessions they had with them. Their motives were desperation and the hope of starting a new and better life. That they intended to colonize the East seems quite clear: bringing spouses, offspring, and worldly goods indicates the desire to permanently relocate rather than to make a temporary pilgrimage. If this conclusion is true, as critics of the materialist theory point out, why did so little colonization take place? The question cannot be answered with any certainty, but two attractive answers are available. First, countless poor were slaughtered by the Seljuk army outside Nicaea, leaving piles of bleached bones that the second wave of Crusaders found when they arrived. Second, those poor who survived had the most horrible experiences imaginable on the journey, from constant attacks by the enemy to being reduced to cannibalism because of a lack of supplies. This situation, combined with the precarious condition of the new Latin states, was sufficient reason to reconsider colonization. Life in France might have been bad, but, as it turned out, settlement in the East was probably worse.

To approach the motives of the warrior aristocracy, one must first categorize them by rank: the great potentates who served as the leaders, their most powerful vassals and captains, and the lesser knights. Three main leaders stayed in the East and carved out states. Raymond of St. Gilles's motives were undoubtedly spiritual and do not seem tainted by materialism in any way. An elderly count of great means, he stood to gain nothing, and there is no reason to doubt his claim that he desired to spend the rest of his life serving the Holy Land. Godfrey of Bouillon's case is more difficult to deal with. He was a duke, rather than a second son, and one could rightly ask what he stood to gain by mortgaging his properties to march east. The answer is evident in his conduct from the beginning of the campaign: he spent considerable time and money politically outflanking Raymond and setting himself up as the strongest candidate for the crown of Jerusalem. His bid, moreover, paid off, and he became the first king of Jerusalem. Bohemond of Taranto's case is by far the clearest. His position was indeed strange: he was the eldest son of Robert Guiscard and found himself in the de facto situation of a second son. Bohemond played a major role in his father's expansionist campaign against the Byzantines and inherited these conquests. When they were taken from him, Bohemond lost his patrimony and was reduced to poverty. Despite some gains made in southern Italy, Bohemond's position had not improved much, and his eyes turned further east, probably toward the Byzantine Empire. The Crusade provided him with the perfect opportunity to become a great prince, and the prospect also appealed to his strong sense of religious piety as well. What more could a poor and pious disinherited aristocrat hope for than to become a great prince in the Holy Land? One contemporary source from southern Italy, admittedly hostile to Bohemond, claimed that his sole reason for taking the cross was to create a principality.

What about the captains of slightly lesser rank who remained in the East? Two prime examples are Baldwin of Boulogne, the younger brother of Godfrey, and Tancred, nephew of Bohemond. Baldwin was a younger son who was thrust into the Church and, as a result of the implications of the reform movement, did not find it to his liking. Leaving the Church and finding himself disinherited and painfully poor, he improved his situation through a marriage alliance with a notable Anglo-Norman family. Understanding the material gains he would make by joining his brother Godfrey required no imaginative leap. Tancred's situation is more muddled. Certainly he was not in the same desperate situation as Baldwin. His biographer claimed he responded to Urban's appeal because of the tension he always felt between the warrior profession he so loved and Christ's command to turn the other cheek. His activities tell a different story.

Finally, there are the lesser members of the warrior class. The salient features in their motivations seem to have been family and feudal obligations (which are far from incompatible with material gain). Jonathan Riley-Smith's fascinating study, *The First Crusaders, 1095–1131* (1997), brought to light the exploits of the Montlhery family, which was a dominant force in the new colonies and "had a stranglehold on the movement." Their kinship network was wide and included the king of Jerusalem. Cousins were everywhere: they staffed the most powerful lordships in the early Crusader States—one was an important abbot in Jerusalem, another the patriarch of Jerusalem. Marriage alliances extended the network even further. In a sense, the Holy Land seemed to form a pension system for the family. The clan's strong commitment to the movement must be related to the family's dynastic successes and ambitions. Vassals of the great potentates often followed their lords wherever they went and such obligations carried great weight. Yet, such vassals were frequently rewarded for loyal service with positions as *castellans* and other land grants to support them. Although the old argument that the First Crusade was just a mass movement of second sons is impossible to maintain, one must admit that there were many second sons who settled and became landed, such as Robert Fitz-Gerard, Robert Fitz-Godwin, and Ado of Quiersy.

One argument has been put forward that even those who settled in the Holy Land did not intend to do so at first. Rather than following an a priori plan of widespread land seizure and colonization, they adapted to circumstances. This theory seems difficult to accept. First, there was a tremendous degree of conflict between the Byzantine emperor and the Cru-

THE REWARD IS GREAT

St. Bernard, while preaching the Second Crusade (1147–1149) to the English, offers reasons for them to join:

What are you doing, you mighty men of valor? What are you doing, you servants of the cross? Will you thus cast holy things to dogs, pearls before swine? How great a number of sinners have here confessed with tears and obtained pardon for their sins since the time when these holy precincts were cleansed of pagan filth by the swords of our fathers! The evil one sees this and is enraged, he gnashes his teeth and withers away in fury. He stirs up his vessels of wrath so that if they do but once lay hands upon these holy places there shall be no sign or trace of piety left. Such a catastrophe would be a source of appalling grief for all time, but it would also be a source of confusion and endless shame for our generation. . . . Do not hesitate. God is good, and were he intent on your punishment he would not have asked of you this present service or indeed have accepted it even had you offered it. Again I say, consider the Almighty's goodness and pay heed to his plans of mercy. He puts himself under obligation to you, or rather feigns to do so, that he can help you satisfy your obligations toward himself. . . . I call blessed the generation that can seize an opportunity of such rich indulgence as this, blessed to be alive in this year of jubilee, this year of God's choice. The blessing is spread throughout the whole world, and all the world is flocking to receive this badge of immortality.

Your land is well known to be rich in young and vigorous men. The world is full of their praises, and the renown of their courage is on the lips of all. Gird yourselves therefore like men and take up arms with joy and with zeal for your Christian name, in order to "take vengeance on the heathen and curb the nations." For how long will your men continue to shed Christian blood; for how long will they continue to fight amongst themselves? You attack each other, you slay each other and by each other you are slain. What is the savage craving of yours? Put a stop to it now, for it is not fighting but foolery. Thus to risk both soul and body is not brave but shocking, is not strength but folly. But now, O mighty soldiers, O men of war, you have a cause for which you can fight without danger to your souls; a cause in which to conquer is glorious and for which to die is gain.

But to those of you who are merchants, men quick to seek a bargain, let me point out the advantages of this great opportunity. Do not miss them. Take up the sign of the cross and you will find indulgence for all the sins which you humbly confess. The cost is small, the reward is great.

Source: *"St. Bernard Seeks English Participation in the Second Crusade,"* in The Crusades: A Documentary Survey, *edited by James A. Brundage (Milwaukee: Marquette University Press, 1962), pp. 92–93.*

sade leaders over what the status of reconquered lands would be. Byzantine emperor Alexius I Comnenus demanded that the Crusaders swear a feudal vow to him and promise to restore recovered lands to his empire. He clearly believed that land acquisition was the goal of at least some of them and, based upon the reaction of the Crusade leaders, his suspicions seem well justified. They took the oath, but under coercion, and later would use this fact as the pretext for breaking it. Land seizure and state building began soon after crossing the Bosphorus. After defeating a Turkish army at Dorylaeum (1097), Tancred and Baldwin set out on their own. Tancred conducted raids and returned. Baldwin, however, never returned to Europe; he created the first Crusader State and became count of Edessa, not a bad score for a disinherited second son. Tancred certainly seems to have jockeyed for the best deal he

could get. He switched allegiance from Raymond to Godfrey, no doubt thinking he would get a better deal from the latter. If so, the gamble paid off: Godfrey became king of Jerusalem and Tancred eventually acquired Galilee and Haifa. French knight Fulcher of Chartres began as part of the entourage of Peter the Hermit, became a follower of Bohemond, then switched allegiance to Baldwin and lived out his final days as a lord in Edessa.

Recent studies, moreover, indicate that colonization might have taken place on a greater scale than previously believed, and Crusader State archaeology may well confirm this fact. Joshua Prawer, in *The Latin Kingdom of Jerusalem: European Colonialism in the Middle Ages* (1972), has pointed out that the allodial, (free, nonfeudal) properties in the region represent an initial period of massive conquest followed by land seizures—the "right of conquest." If true, this pol-

ECONOMIC MOTIVES

icy would indicate that while leaders of the First Crusade were carving out large principalities, knights of lesser means were gaining their own small holdings. When one combines this fact with an important passage from an early colonist, French priest and historian Fulcher of Chartres, the situation becomes clearer: "Those who were poor in the West, God has made rich here. He who had a few pennies possesses bezants without number; he who held not even a village now by God's grace enjoys a town."

The last factors to enter into the materialist equation are the Italian maritime states. They played an instrumental role in completing the conquest of the coast and continued to serve as the financial backbone of the colonies through sea trade. Their main objectives were expanding their trade operations and securing new commercial concessions in the region. In both ventures they succeeded. The greatest example was the Pact of Warmund (1124), in which Venice was granted one third of Tyre and great commercial concessions in exchange for their crucial role in conquering the city. The curious phrase *sicut rex* (just like a king) explicates their rights. When the monarchy later began describing itself as the executive power in Tyre, the Venetians said that it was true—except in their third. Admittedly, they may have been pious, but in a clearer sense than in any other case their chief motive was profit and continued to be so throughout the existence of the Crusader States.

The First Crusade has always been the most difficult subject for the materialist argument to tackle. Even the staunchest critics of the theory admit that economic motives increased in importance over time, particularly in the thirteenth century. Even a casual reading of the sources reveals considerable evidence: the profiteering of the "sand pirate" Reynauld of Chatillion, who tried to gain control over caravan routes and possibly Red Sea trade; the barons of the Crusader States, who were constantly bickering and squabbling over resources; the escalating trade disputes among the Italian maritime states that culminated in a civil war in which Latin fleets clashed; and the Templars and Hospitallers, who were not beyond engaging in street wars with each other over rights to mills and ovens. These facts do not mean that religion and piety had no role or were not important. On the contrary, they were central, but so were material rewards. Economic gain can piggyback with any ideology, including religion. One can be a holy warrior and still profit—or hope to profit—from the venture. The Crusade was "God's will," and as Fulcher of Chartres pointed out, it was through God's grace that penniless westerners became rich in the Crusader States.

–TODD MARX,
CONCORD, NEW HAMPSHIRE

Viewpoint:
No. Crusaders were motivated by political considerations as well as the promise of spiritual rewards and increased social prestige.

At one time in Western intellectual thought, it was fashionable to view history through essentially a Marxian perspective, finding in every event and era evidence to support the dogmatic proposition that economics were the driving force of history. In recent years such devotion to this singular interpretation of historical development has lost nearly all of its attraction. Most mainstream historians clearly demonstrate that economics, while important components in shaping the course of history, are not its sole determiner. Other forces and factors can, and do, play equal or more significant roles in the process of historical development. Yet, as with most trends, even after widespread interest in it has faded, the fad or its effects can linger on for many more years to come.

The retention of economic causation is certainly the case when one considers the historiography of the Crusades. Some scholarly circles interpret this broad historical movement in an essentially narrow way, arguing that economics were the raison d'être for crusading. Those who perpetuate this myth, or who allow themselves to be convinced by the arguments of those who concoct such historical fairy tales, end up with a skewed image of an important phenomenon in medieval history. Undoubtedly, economics played a role in the Crusades, as with most historical events, but it was not the primary basis of the movement, especially in its early centuries. Rather, the real impetus behind the movement lay closer to spiritual, political, and cultural developments that occurred in the eleventh and twelfth centuries and that were not the product of economic causes. In these areas a proper understanding of the crusading movement should be found.

The old notion that economics are the key to understanding the Crusades is in actuality erroneous on both a micro and macro level. In regard to the former, it once was widely accepted that the main attraction for individuals to participate in the Crusades was financial. Historians such as Georges Duby, in *The Early Growth of the European Economy: Warriors and Peasants from the Seventh to the Twelfth Century* (1974), constructed the plausible-sounding thesis that the Crusades provided one of the few means by which younger sons of medieval noble families could carve out estates of their own, given that inheritance laws in Europe tended to leave the

ECONOMIC MOTIVES

family wealth only to the eldest son. In this picture, drawn principally from the creative imagination of its proponents rather than from any real historical evidence, crusading was essentially depicted as a mad landgrab led by hordes of youthful, avaricious knights looking to make a place for themselves in the world. While there is no evidentiary basis for this image, it was a picture that many students and scholars adopted, and thus it had a staying power and resiliency that was as remarkable as it was unwarranted.

The problem is not only that there is no evidence to support such a depiction of crusading motivation, especially in its first few centuries, but also that the evidence completely contradicts this view. A newer generation of scholars, led by historians such as Jonathan Riley-Smith, have committed themselves to re-analyzing, or analyzing for the first time, the documentary evidence. What they discovered has truly reshaped scholarly understanding of the Crusades. First, it is clear from surviving charters that crusading was a prohibitively expensive proposition, requiring participants to amass, before they left home, a sizable sum of cash from which they could cover their expenses for an international journey that, especially in the early centuries, promised to be a multiyear deployment. Few families had such cash reserves readily available, and so the only option available was to liquidate part of their landholdings in return for hard currency. Furthermore, Riley-Smith's analysis of surviving charters of those individuals who sold property in order to finance their journey revealed that many Crusaders were not the younger sons of noble families. Fathers, brothers, and elder sons were all part of the mix that composed the typical crusading army. It was truly an activity that elicited support from a broad cross section of medieval society, not just from one particular demographic group.

What these individuals sought by participating in crusading becomes clearer not just from the actions they took to begin their journey but also from what they did at the completion of their Crusade. If the economic theory of crusading were to hold true, the vast majority of participants would have settled in the East. Instead, what the overwhelming evidence shows is that most Crusaders did the exact opposite—they returned home. While historians such as Duby might have a hard time trying to explain this widespread behavior, it should really come as little surprise. Properly understood, a Crusade was viewed by medieval Europeans as a form of pilgrimage, albeit one that had the peculiar characteristic of being armed and of requiring participants to engage in combat. In all other ways, however, Crusaders were thought to be traditional pilgrims. By definition a pilgrim is someone who visits but does not stay in some distant place, and in keeping with this time-honored aspect of pilgrimage, most Crusaders chose to return home at the completion of their duties. That this behavior was the prevailing model for Crusade activity is underscored by a constant problem the Crusader States faced—lack of manpower. Despite various efforts, including making inheritance and real-estate laws as attractive as possible in order to encourage Western immigration, the Crusader States faced recurring manpower shortages, which eventually contributed to their downfall.

Had Duby and like-minded historians been correct in their supposition that Crusaders were predominantly younger sons on the prowl for lands to acquire, the Latin East would not have faced population shortages. Perhaps with additional manpower reserves they could have successfully withstood the Islamic assaults of the twelfth and thirteenth centuries. Yet, such was not the reality. The true story that increasingly emerges from documentary evidence is that few Crusaders ever became rich from their participation or acquired new lands. For most, crusading proved instead to be a great financial expense coupled with physical hardship, and for some, it meant permanent injury or even death. To understand what motivated the vast majority of Crusaders to volunteer in such an unpromising venture, therefore, it is necessary to look beyond a simplistic view that dismisses the whole affair as being about money. Rather, whether modern sensibilities can fully appreciate it or not, the medieval notion that crusading was a spiritually enriching activity—as symbolized by the great reward, the indulgence—must be understood and respected. Beyond this spiritual impulse, other factors such as social pressures, political ambitions, and the love of adventure should be placed well ahead of financial desires as important motivations behind individual decisions to enlist in the Crusades.

On a macro level it is also more accurate to look to causes other than economic ones in trying to explain the Crusades. During the first century of crusading, the focal point remained directly centered on Jerusalem, a city of little economic or strategic importance but one that held immense spiritual value in the eyes of medieval Christians. Had the grand design behind crusading been economic, such as securing lucrative trade routes for the West or seizing resource-dense lands with which to enrich the states of Europe, the operation would have chosen different objectives from the start, such as Cairo or the port of Alexandria. Instead, crusading initially threw the limited resources of the medieval West into an operation that made little financial sense. Just as conquering Jerusalem promised to make few individuals rich, it offered little economic advantage to any ranking powers in Europe, for Jerusalem and surrounding

environs contained no significant natural resources, possessed no important industries, and controlled no lucrative trade routes. On the contrary, once captured, the defense of this dusty backwater city—located in a distant, relatively arid land—required significant financial expenditure. Thus, no rational economic argument could be made for marshaling the limited resources of medieval Europe for such an economically unpromising venture as attempting to capture and hold Jerusalem.

What the original crusading program offered on a macro level, however, were a series of advantages that had little to do with economics. From the perspective of Pope Urban II, the original architect of the Crusades, the movement provided the opportunity to achieve the political and cultural goals of bringing aid to Eastern Christians languishing under the assault of the Seljuk Turks, and to stem the tide of their advance into Eastern Europe, thus preserving the existence of Christendom. Flowing out of this objective would perhaps be the accomplishment of a decades-long ecclesiastical goal, namely the reunion of the Eastern and Western churches. On a spiritual and moral level, the Crusades offered the chance to redirect militant passions of the knightly class of Europe into what was seen as being a truly noble quest, thereby helping countless men to save their souls and improve their moral dispositions. At no time, however, could an economic argument be made for launching wave after wave of armies for the purpose of capturing such a financially poor target as Jerusalem.

As crusading evolved in the thirteenth century and beyond, the economic motive became more important on a macro level, but at no point was it the predominant concern. After the fall of Jerusalem (1187) and the failure of the Third Crusade (1189–1192) to recapture the city despite a massive effort on the part of three great monarchies in Europe, crusading organizers began to reassess their overall strategy. Jerusalem was flanked by two great centers of Muslim power, Cairo to the southwest and Damascus (and by extension Baghdad) to the east. To have any hope of capturing and holding the city for the long term, this stranglehold had to be broken. Because Cairo proved more accessible and

Aerial view of Krak de Montreal, a fortress built near Jerusalem in the twelfth century by Baldwin I and which controlled important caravan routes from Syria to Egypt appeared to be the weaker of the two centers, later Crusade architects concluded that a campaign in Egypt was a necessary first step toward ultimately achieving the strategic goal of reclaiming Jerusalem. At the same time it did not hurt this line of reasoning that Egypt was a wealthy land that controlled a lucrative trade network and so promised multiple financial rewards by its capture. Thus, here finally can be found a tangible and legitimate promise of some economic payback to crusading. Yet, it must be emphasized that these Egyptian campaigns of the thirteenth century were never undertaken as ends in themselves but only as an intermediary tactical objective on the road to the ultimate strategic objective of capturing Jerusalem. Spiritual, cultural, and political concerns still outranked the macroeconomic motive.

Crusading plans and ventures in the fourteenth century and beyond proved to be much more complicated affairs than was the case during preceding centuries. While the goal of capturing Jerusalem still stirred the emotions of many Europeans, political infighting and economic deals often stood in the way of organizing, launching, and successfully concluding crusading ventures. For example, the leading maritime ports of Italy often found themselves either opposing some new proposed plan or giving active support depending on how much an operation promised to affect their trading ventures in the Mediterranean, which included significant contact with Muslim parties. Yet, even though economic considerations became more prominent during this later era, the other traditional goals such as reclaiming Jerusalem, defending the borders of Christendom, and bringing moral and spiritual enrichment to Crusade participants remained. At no time could the claim be made that economics were the driving force behind the movement, even in these later times.

In the end, from neither a micro nor macro perspective can the contention be demonstrated that crusading was essentially an economic venture. For the vast majority of participants throughout most of the movement, crusading proved not to be some "get-rich-quick" scheme for impoverished young noblemen but rather a significant financial burden on families that chose to participate. The attraction to crusading lay elsewhere, including the belief that it brought significant spiritual rewards and perhaps increased social prestige. On a macro level the permanent obsession with Jerusalem as the strategic goal demonstrates that crusading was not an economic enterprise. Control of this city offered no financial advantage at all. As the ability of an increasingly divided Europe to successfully project its collective power in the Near East waned, intermediary tactical goals became the initial focal point of later crusades. These objectives offered plausible economic advantages, but there is no evidence to suggest that these later efforts could have found the necessary support and participation had they been conducted purely on economic grounds and divorced from a connection, however tenuous, to Jerusalem. The promise that a campaign in Egypt, for example, offered to bring the reality of a Christian-controlled Jerusalem one step closer to fruition remained a fundamental aspect of even these later campaigns of the fourteenth and fifteenth centuries. Thus, remove the economic dimension from crusading and little of its history would likely change. However, take away the spiritual, cultural, and political dimensions and crusading would not have occurred. Wars and conflicts might have been fought anyway, but they would not have been Crusades.

—CHRISTOPHER LIBERTINI,
SUFFOLK UNIVERSITY

References

David Abulafia, *Commerce and Conquest in the Mediterranean, 1100–1500* (Aldershot, U.K. & Brookfield, Vt.: Variorum, 1993).

E. Ashtor, *A Social and Economic History of the Near East in the Middle Ages* (London: Collins, 1976).

Robert Bartlett, *The Making of Europe: Conquest, Colonization, and Cultural Change, 950–1350* (London: John Lane, 1993; Princeton: Princeton University Press, 1993).

Georges Duby, *The Early Growth of the European Economy: Warriors and Peasants from the Seventh to the Twelfth Century,* translated by Howard B. Clarke (London: Weidenfeld & Nicolson, 1974; Ithaca, N.Y.: Cornell University Press, 1974).

Robert S. Lopez, *The Commercial Revolution of the Middle Ages, 950–1350* (Englewood Cliffs, N.J.: Prentice-Hall, 1971).

J. R. S. Phillips, *The Medieval Expansion of Europe* (Oxford & New York: Oxford University Press, 1988).

Joshua Prawer, *The Latin Kingdom of Jerusalem: European Colonialism in the Middle Ages* (London: Weidenfeld & Nicolson, 1972).

Jonathan Riley-Smith, *The First Crusaders, 1095–1131* (Cambridge & New York: Cambridge University Press, 1997).

ECONOMIC MOTIVES

ETHICAL PERSPECTIVES

Did the Crusades represent a distortion of the Christian message?

Viewpoint: Yes. The violence and brutality of the crusading movement violated the pacific principles of Christianity.

Viewpoint: No. The crusading movement was an expression of Christian values as understood at the time.

To many modern people the crusading movement seems to be a distortion of the central tenets of the Christian religion. Such a view of the movement was virtually (but not completely) unknown in the Middle Ages. Some medieval critics objected to crusading as an inappropriate way of dealing with Muslims, that deviated from Christian conduct and sensibilities. The abbot of Cluny, Peter the Venerable, for example, lamented that Christians confronted Muslims in armed conflict rather than with Christ's love. Thirteenth-century Franciscan friar and English philosopher Roger Bacon, though he did not completely object to crusading, reminded readers that the Holy Spirit moved the apostles to spread the message of Christ through the Word rather than the sword. But the predominant view throughout the Middle Ages was that crusading was not only consistent with Christian principles but also was a powerful expression of them.

The Reformation introduced new intellectual tools and categories for assessing the Crusades. Many reformers, drawing upon the new concept of "perspective" produced during the Renaissance, criticized crusading as a corruption of incipient Christian beliefs. The goal of many intellectuals during the Renaissance was to sift through accretions that, over time, corrupted philosophical texts. Recovering the "original truth" and saving it from the subsequent distortions and misunderstandings that corrupted it were their main objectives. Protestants took this torch and carried it into the realm of scriptural and religious truth—Crusaders became the unwitting stalking horses of papal ambition. Crusading was seen as about as "Christian" as the Spanish Inquisition. Such accretions were to be swept away as rubbish that was heaped upon religious truth by ignorant or worldly men. In sum, they argued, crusading was just another chapter in the long story of violence, the papacy, and the religious truth.

The debate continues, though it employs different language. The central issue is: should one speak of "a" Christian morality regarding violence or refer to "many" Christian moralities that changed during different time periods? Is Christianity, in other words, "relative"? Would it be unfair to contrast the militancy of Pope Innocent III with the pacifism of Pope John Paul II? Christianity, as an ideology, was a worldview that constantly re-created itself since it was interpreted through differing cultural matrices over the centuries. When does a reinterpretation differ so much from an original philosophy that it becomes something new and possibly at odds with the parent view?

Viewpoint:
Yes. The violence and brutality of the crusading movement violated the pacific principles of Christianity.

The Crusades, much like the Inquisition, have often been seen as symbolic of the generalized intolerance and violent tenor of life that characterized the Middle Ages. Some early Protestant scholars espoused this view, portraying the Crusades as another example of papist corruption that twisted the piety of men genuinely wanting to serve God. This view truly came into its own during the Enlightenment. Although much of the philosophes' criticism was rooted in anticlericalism, it focused on what they saw as a fundamental error in the understanding of Christianity. Crusades, romantic and interesting though they were, were distortions of the Christian message. For French encyclopedist Denis Diderot they were products of ignorance and "false zeal." For Scottish philosopher David Hume they were the "most durable monument of human folly" ever constructed. For English historian Edward Gibbon they sprang more from the primal impulses of the barbarian tribes that mingled with religious fanaticism. This view, though it has lost considerable ground, has persisted up to modern times. Steven Runciman concluded his three-volume *A History of the Crusades* (1951) by remarking that "the Holy War itself was nothing more than a long act of intolerance in the name of God, which is a sin against the Holy Ghost." The Crusades, for him, were really a continuation of the barbarian invasions that destroyed Rome.

Critics of the "perversion theory" have pointed toward the importance of historical context. It is unfair to measure Christian sensibilities of the eleventh to thirteenth centuries by a yardstick held by the modern world. There is something inherently ahistorical about such an approach. Christianity was and still is dynamic rather than static, and Christianities of the past need not be ours. Furthermore, demanding such congruence runs great risks of confusing the motives and perceptions of the actual participants by projecting modern views onto the past. Moral judgment then crushes an accurate understanding beneath its considerable weight. Christianity and piety in practice are relative concepts that are based on constantly shifting perspectives. Christians during the age of crusading believed that violence could be an expression of charity and love; one need not agree with them, but one should respect the validity of their view during their time. This school of thought can be called "relativist."

Arguments in favor of crusading being a perversion of the Christian message need not be based upon any real or imagined "sins against the Holy Ghost." They can be grounded upon the supposition that the main tenets of any philosophy can, and frequently do, go through a succession of changes that create something not only different but diametrically opposite. Crusading was not produced by a single, great perversion that definitively broke with Christian moral precepts. Rather, it was the sum total of generations of exegetical reassessments—or re-creations—of Christian thought. Tracing this development can be frustrating at times, much like trying to isolate all the points that make up a line, but there are some salient events that can bypass the minutiae of successive moments and still demonstrate exactly how a man of peace was transformed into a god of war.

Pride of place in this process must be given to Roman emperor Constantine I. By becoming the first emperor to convert to Christianity, he gave birth to what one historian has dubbed the "Great Oxymoron": a Christian empire. Although some pre-Nicene Christian thinkers believed that a military career did not necessarily preclude one from the community of Christ, Constantine's conversion paved the way for the "imperialization," and hence militarization, of Christianity. The "soldiers of Christ" would no longer be an army constituted solely of martyrs and monks. As soon as Constantine converted, one finds the first recognizable signs of a Christian "holy war," as all of his campaigns against opponents quickly became. War in the Roman world was hopelessly intertwined with religion; as Constantine's former military god Sol Invictus was ushered out the front door (mostly for not granting military victory), Christ was led in through the back. Imperial and Christian views merged in a variety of ways and produced a fusion between martial and spiritual values that constituted one of the most enduring legacies of the empire. Imperial interests were joined to warfare, hence the interests of the Christian empire were joined to war as well. Converts during and after the reign of Constantine supported and promoted this view and thus initiated the marriage between military service and Christian spirituality.

The works of St. Augustine of Hippo mark another major turning point in the militarization of Christianity and the degradation of its incipient pacifistic principles. As the premier architect of Western theology, Augustine's bona fides are unimpeachable, but he lived within a Christian empire, and his views were shaped by the latent inconsistencies introduced by Constantine's creation. Augustine, who had one foot firmly planted in the City of God and the other in the City of Man, built the main theological bridge between Christianity and war. This process began with his support of using force against the Donatist heretics and eventually culminated in his theory of "Just War." Augustine's vision of Christian holy war, however, did not legitimize wars of expansion. It was a remedy of last resort to right a wrong that resisted other solutions. Moreover, it was beneficial to the men it targeted and thus was a form of Christian charity, something similar to what modern people call "tough love."

Central values of the Germanic tribes were other important ingredients that went into the blend. Their militarism was not a major factor; Roman society was just as militaristic and did not necessarily need Germanic assistance in joining Christianity and violence. But Germanic martial values had important qualitative differences from those of the Romans, particularly the prominence of blood feuds, vendetta, and the value of valor in combat as a demonstration of personal prowess. Of even greater significance were the Germanic concepts of kinship, tribal obligations, and clan honor. Insult and injury demanded commensurate retaliation. An attack on one member of the group was an attack against the whole group. Just as the Romans Romanized Jesus, the Germans Germanized him. Rather than transforming him into the likeness of a Roman military god, the Germans likened Jesus to the head of a great spiritual tribe. His honor was their honor. Insults to him were insults to them. Attacks on him would be countered with attacks of equal or greater ferocity.

These twin distortions, the Roman and Germanic, mingled for centuries until being forcefully fused together in Charlemagne's new empire. His wars of expansion were holy wars in every sense of the word and equated the crushing of enemies with the glorification of God. Many bishops of the age were just as comfortable in the saddle as they were in the pulpit. Charlemagne preferred to "preach with an iron tongue" and equated the baptism of Saxons with their acceptance of political submission. Churches, such as the one in Paderborn, became operational bases for wars of conquest. Prebattle preparations took the form of liturgy. There is no reason to believe that the Carolingian military machine was not convinced it was doing God's work, but when one considers the values held by Jesus, or even Augustine, these activities seem an aberration.

The breakup of the Carolingian Empire ushered in an age of heightened chaos and violence that served as the immediate matrix from which crusading emerged. Christian wars before the turn of the millennium were waged by the laity, albeit frequently with the cooperation of the clergy. It was the "reform papacy" that endeavored to make the Church a full partner in the enterprise of European warfare. The reform program of the papacy was mainly geared toward liberating itself from lay domination. To do so the popes needed to wield the secular sword as well as the spiritual. The spectacular and often sordid events surrounding the Investiture Controversy (1075–1077) led the papacy to launch a reassessment of the theoretical relationship between the Church and war. Pope Gregory VII drew upon the work of a group of scholars clustered around his ally, Matilda of Tuscany. These men, drawing upon considerable literary sources (Augustine in particular), hammered out a coherent doctrine justifying Church-sponsored violence. Italian ecclesiastic Anselm II of Lucca, dean of sorts for the group, worked his exegetical magic on Augustine's corpus and found that God even demanded war on his behalf at times. Gregory would not have much success transforming their theories into successful actions, but his protégé Urban II did, and through the latter's efforts the crusading movement was born. The gestational period, however, was a long one; in many ways it stretched back to Constantine's conversion.

Finally, if one considers the lay response to Urban's appeal at the Council of Clermont (1095), one finds the characteristics of vendetta at the fore. While not discounting the strong penitential and liturgical dimensions, one can safely say that the First Crusade (1096–1102) was viewed by its participants as a blood feud on a scale previously unheard of. Christians believed that Muslims had inflicted insult and injury upon Christ; indeed, they were crucifying him again. His patrimony had been stolen. Eastern Christians, the spiritual kinfolk of Western Christians, were suffering unimaginable torments. They believed vengeance through vendetta was their obligation. This viewpoint goes a long way in explaining the horrors that the First Crusade unleashed. Attacks on European Jews, for example, were produced by the vendetta mentality—the dishonors and injuries that Jews supposedly heaped upon Christ drew them into the feud as well. While this outlook may be consistent with prevailing views of the time, it is extremely far removed from the precepts of Christianity as both religion and philosophy.

The relativist theory has made incalculable contributions to understanding the Crusades, particularly concerning the motives and perceptions of the participants. One should not doubt the sincerity of the war cry of the first Crusaders—"God wills it." Nor should one doubt that they saw themselves as true Christians engaged in a Christian enterprise. But study of the past cannot focus on the mind frame of a time to the exclusion of important benchmarks in change and continuity. Empathy is important, but it can mask substantive changes by deferring to the perceptions of the men one studies. Social psychologists believe that almost every act of understanding is an act of re-creation. As the mind places experiences or philosophies into its cognitive structure, it changes them, through the processes of integration, by relating them to one another and creating confluence. When does the recasting of an idea constitute an entirely new and compatible idea? Jesus' authorizing a blood feud is just one of many examples.

–CARL HILL,
LOS ANGELES, CALIFORNIA

Viewpoint:
No. The crusading movement was an expression of Christian values as understood at the time.

In the opinion of many contemporary historians, especially scholars studying Christianity, the Crusades constituted a medieval perversion of Christian belief and practice. The Crusades represented a grievous break from the evangelical doctrines of love and nonviolence. Generally speaking, these scholars trace the origin of this perversion of Christianity to the conversion of Roman emperor Constantine I and the ensuing transformation of "apostolic" Christianity into "imperial" Christianity. Some scholars, without denying the "tragic" consequences for Christianity of Constantine's conversion, push the origin of militant Christianity further back to the late first or second century, when a hierarchal-minded orthodox party rooted out the charismatic and egalitarian elements of early Christianity in the various local churches. Yet, regardless of how far back one traces the origin of the corruption of Christianity, scholars take a dim view of the theological legitimacy of the Crusades.

However, while it is certainly true that extra-Christian influences greatly contributed to the idea of Crusade, it is not true that the concept constituted a gross perversion of Christianity. Rather, it represented the attempt of medieval churchmen to harmonize something that could not be exorcized from their society, the Germanic warrior ethos, with the principles of Christian charity. As Jonathan Riley-Smith has argued, it was an attempt to transform the internecine violence of feudal Europe into a movement of self-sacrificing love whereby Christian knights would no longer risk life and limb for the sake of personal gain but rather in defense of their coreligionists and of the holy places in the East. Admittedly, the notion that martial combat, which was traditionally considered inherently sinful, could be spiritually meritorious was a theological novelty. However, this novelty was more a function of the interplay between the received ethical tradition of the Latin Church and the cultural milieu of the eleventh and twelfth centuries than some fundamental perversion of Christianity. In evaluating the theological legitimacy of the Crusades, one must keep in mind the maxim of twentieth-century Christian historian Christopher Dawson, that not everything that is Christian is medieval and not everything medieval is Christian.

The fundamental assumption of the harshest critics of the Crusades is that the New Testament idea of love precludes the use of violence in almost all circumstances. How else can one interpret Jesus' injunction that if someone slaps another person on the right cheek he is to turn and offer them his left cheek (Matt. 5:39)? Yet, the teaching on love and the use of violence is far more complicated than this injunction on its surface would seem. Certainly, pacifism was not part of the Hebrew bequest to Christianity. The Hebrew Bible teems with examples of holy violence and holy warfare. For instance, Moses tells the Hebrews that when they enter into the Promised Land of Canaan they must put to death its inhabitants, whom the Lord will deliver into their hands (Deut. 7:1–2). Of course, the New Testament does not attribute any kind of statement such as this one to Jesus. Still, in order to understand the real meaning of Jesus' injunction, one must read it in its proper context, whereupon it takes on a significantly different meaning than rendered by an isolated and literal reading.

Most importantly, one must recognize that Jesus' statement about turning the other cheek forms part of his discourse known as the Sermon on the Mount, which appears in two different versions in Matthew's and Luke's Gospels, respectively. Indeed, in Luke's account, Jesus actually delivers the Sermon at the foot of a hill. However, in both accounts of this discourse, Jesus' primary concern is the correction of the inner dispositions of his listeners. As all four Gospel accounts of Jesus' ministry indicate, egotism–the disordered love of self–constitutes the primary obstacle to the acceptance of Jesus and the coming of God's Kingdom. It is the chief sin of Jesus' fiercest opponents, the Scribes and Pharisees. It is no accident, then, that the first of the Beatitudes, which the authors of both Matthew and Luke place within the Sermon on the Mount, extols those who recognize their need for God: the poor in spirit. Jesus' disciples must be able to pray sincerely the words of Our Father, which also appears in both versions of

WAGE WAR BUT CHERISH THE PEACEMAKER

In a letter to Boniface, written in 418, St. Augustine of Hippo, whose works were often cited during the Crusades, comments on righteous military service:

Do not think that it is impossible for any one to please God while engaged in active military service. Among such persons was the holy David, to whom God gave so great a testimony; among them also were many righteous men of that time; among them was also that centurion who said to the Lord: "I am not worthy that Thou shouldest come under my roof, but speak the word only, and my servant shall be healed: for I am a man under authority, having soldiers under me: and I say to this man, Go, and he goeth; and to another, Come, and he cometh; and to my servant, Do this, and he doeth it;" and concerning whom the Lord said: "Verily, I say unto you, I have not found so great faith, no, not in Israel." Among them was that Cornelius to whom an angel said: "Cornelius, thine alms are accepted, and thy prayers are heard," when he directed him to send to the blessed Apostle Peter, and to hear from him what he ought to do, to which apostle he sent a devout soldier, requesting him to come to him. Among them were also the soldiers who, when they had come to be baptized by John,—the sacred forerunner of the Lord, and the friend of the Bridegroom, of whom the Lord says: "Among them that are born of women there hath not arisen a greater than John the Baptist,"—and had inquired of him what they should do, received the answer, "Do violence to no man, neither accuse any falsely; and be content with your wages." Certainly he did not prohibit them to serve as soldiers when he commanded them to be content with their pay for the service.

They occupy indeed a higher place before God who, abandoning all these secular employments, serve Him with the strictest chastity; but "every one," as the apostle says, "hath his proper gift of God, one after this manner, and another after that." Some, then, in praying for you, fight against your invisible enemies; you, in fighting for them, contend against the barbarians, their visible enemies. Would that one faith existed in all, for then there would be less weary struggling, and the devil with his angels would be more easily conquered; but since it is necessary in this life that the citizens of the kingdom of heaven should be subjected to temptations among erring and impious men, that they may be exercised, and "tried as gold in the furnace," we ought not before the appointed time to desire to live with those alone who are holy and righteous, so that, by patience, we may deserve to receive this blessedness in its proper time.

Think, then, of this first of all, when you are arming for the battle, that even your bodily strength is a gift of God; for, considering this, you will not employ the gift of God against God. For, when faith is pledged, it is to be kept even with the enemy against whom the war is waged, how much more with the friend for whom the battle is fought! Peace should be the object of your desire; war should be waged only as a necessity, and waged only that God may by it deliver men from the necessity and preserve them in peace. For peace is not sought in order to the kindling of war, but war is waged in order that peace may be obtained. Therefore, even in waging war, cherish the spirit of a peacemaker, that, by conquering those whom you attack, you may lead them back to the advantages of peace; for our Lord says: "Blessed are the peacemakers; for they shall be called the children of God." If, however, peace among men be so sweet as procuring temporal safety, how much sweeter is that peace with God which procures for men the eternal felicity of the angels! Let necessity, therefore, and not your will, slay the enemy who fights against you. As violence is used towards him who rebels and resists, so mercy is due to the vanquished or the captive, especially in the case in which future troubling of the peace is not to be feared."

Source: *"Letter CLXXXIX,"* The Confessions and Letters of St. Augustin, *edited by Philip Schaff (New York: Christian Literature Publishing, 1886), Christian Classics Ethereal Library at Calvin College <http://www.ccel.org/s/schaff/npnf101/htm/vii.1.CLXXXIX.htm>.*

ETHICAL PERSPECTIVES

the Sermon on the Mount, "thy Kingdom come, thy will be done on earth as it is in heaven."

To this end Jesus insists that his disciples rectify their dispositions. It is not enough that they merely avoid committing murder, but they must not even harbor hate in their hearts for their neighbor (Matt. 5:21–22). Similarly, not only must a man not commit adultery, but he also cannot even look at a woman lustfully (Matt. 5:27–28).

Like all teachers of his time and place, Jesus employs exaggerated rhetoric to make his points. Hence, in connection to his point about avoiding lust, he counsels his disciples to gouge out their right eyes or to cut off their right hands rather than find their entire bodies in hell (Matt. 5:29–30). Quite obviously, Jesus was not advocating self-mutilation. Rather, he is stating that true discipleship requires various forms of self-denial. Likewise, when he states that one should turn the other cheek to an assailant, Jesus is not prohibiting his disciples from defending themselves from physical attack. Instead, he is warning them to avoid every form of mimetic rivalry. They are to avoid all literal and figurative clashes of egos. They are not to give in to the *libido dominandi*. However, Jesus is certainly not condemning the military profession per se.

In *Letter 189*, addressed to the Roman commander Boniface, St. Augustine of Hippo identified several New Testament passages that indicate that military service is not at all displeasing to the Christian God. In the *Letter*, Augustine first points to Jesus' healing of a Roman centurion's servant and his glowing praise of that centurion's faith (Matt. 8:8–10; Luke 7:6–9). Next, the bishop of Hippo points to the story of another centurion. The Holy Spirit leads the apostle Peter to the righteous Gentile Cornelius, and the centurion and his entire household receive baptism (Acts 10). Finally, Augustine attaches a great deal of importance to what John the Baptist does not say to the soldiers who receive baptism from him. John tells them to harass no man and to be content with their pay; he does not instruct them to leave the military profession (Luke 3:14).

Of course, on the whole, ancient Christian authors looked much askance at the military profession. The only soldiers of God or Christ that many of them recognized were martyrs and those who had dedicated themselves to lives of prayer and mortification; for example, monks and hermits. By and large, ancient Christian authors associated soldiers with all kinds of vice. Augustine's *Letter 189* is proof of the prejudice against soldiering. The bishop of Hippo clearly believed it necessary to convince his friend Boniface that he could be a military man and a faithful Christian.

Nonetheless, one must keep in mind that prior to Constantine's conversion, military service meant soldiering in the Roman imperial legions, which were steeped in the trappings of paganism. It is no wonder then that Christian writers of the first through third centuries thought ill of the military profession. Moreover, there was another reason soldiers were not only unpopular with early Christian authors but also with most noncombatants from antiquity up to and through the early modern era. While on campaign, pre- and early modern soldiers frequently engaged in pillaging. For many villagers and townsmen, soldiers were no more of a welcome sight than locusts. Finally, one must also keep in mind that over the course of Christian antiquity there developed a certain clerical elitism—an attitude that religious service was the spiritually superior state of life. In particular, ascetics (who were not always technically clergy) came to be seen as the ideal, or model, Christians. Given, then, the milieu of the soldier, how could one be a "complete" Christian and serve in the military?

Regardless, one must also be aware that despite the rhetoric of their clergy, Christians probably served in the Roman legions prior to Constantine's conversion. With the accession of a Christian emperor, military service undoubtedly became less problematic for Christians of all ranks. Certainly, Christian bishops had no problem celebrating the victories of the Christian emperors of late antiquity. To be sure, some historians construe this acquiescence as proof of the Christian Church's co-option by the Roman state. Yet, only the most romantically minded historian could honestly imagine that the apostles Peter and Paul would have reacted with anything but joy if Emperor Nero had laid down his imperial insignia at their feet and sought baptism. Is it conceivable that Peter and Paul were less theocratic in their thinking than their pagan contemporaries and would not have prayed for the victory of Christian Roman legions against the pagan Parthians and Alemanni?

In the early medieval West, ecclesiastics continued to view the military profession with suspicion. Nothing better captures the incompatibility that they perceived between sanctity and the military profession than the remark, attributed to the soldier-turned-monk St. Martin of Tours, that as a soldier of Christ, he was not permitted to fight. Eventually, however, as evangelization of various Germanic kingdoms progressed, Western churchmen gradually began to look at military combat in a different light. For as Christian kings, the Germanic warlords assumed responsibility for the defense of the Church against violent pagans, and they extended the Christian faith into the pagan territories that they conquered.

As Carl Erdmann has argued, in *The Origin of the Idea of Crusade* (1977), with the collapse of the Carolingian dynasty and the series of foreign inva-

ETHICAL PERSPECTIVES

sions that hit Europe in the ninth and tenth centuries, churchmen grew even more appreciative of righteous combat. Increasingly, they advanced the notion that the physical defense of churches, shrines, and monasteries pleased God and his saints. With the near total collapse of royal authority in large parts of France, clerics were forced to seek physical protection for their institutions and for their peasant dependents from the knightly class itself. Again, as Erdmann has contended, through the Peace of God movement, clerics first attempted to Christianize the warrior's way of life. These clerics, especially the monks of Cluny, encouraged knights to fight good wars for God and his people against the despoilers of the churches and of the poor and to avoid shedding innocent Christian blood. Over the course of the tenth century, the conviction developed among the Cluniacs and other monastic reformers that the laity had a real and necessary role to play in the life of the Church, and one of those roles was that of the good Christian knight.

Furthermore, Erdmann noted that the promoters of the Peace of God, Cluniacs and non-Cluniacs alike, were themselves linked to the eleventh-century ecclesiastical reformers, who sought not only the reform of clerical morals but also of the laity. Of these reformers, none was more intent on reaching out to the warrior class than the former Hildebrand, Pope Gregory VII. As H. E. J. Cowdrey has observed, in *Pope Gregory VII, 1073–1085* (1998), at various points in his pontificate, Gregory called upon princes and ordinary knights to provide military aid to the Roman Church as the *fideles* (faithful) of St. Peter. More importantly, according to Cowdrey, Gregory wanted to see warfare purged of unworthy aims and motives and imbued with a righteous intention. Two Gregorian partisans, Bishop Anselm II of Lucca and Bishop Bonizo of Sutri, sought a theoretical basis for such holy warfare in the writings of St. Augustine of Hippo and other patristic authors. In the summons to holy war against Henry IV of Germany contained in his *Liber ad amicum*, Bonizo quotes from Augustine's aforementioned *Letter 189* to Boniface as proof of his own proposition that fighting for dogma was permissible for a Christian. Essentially, Bonizo argues in *Liber ad amicum* that if it is permissible for a Christian to fight at all, then it is permissible for him to fight for religious truth.

Cowdrey also observed that, for Gregory, the warrior who struggled to rectify the inner intention of his combat elevated it above reproach. From the Pope's perspective, such righteous combat constituted an *imitatio Christi* (imitation of Christ). In letters from 1074 that concern his proposed campaign to rescue the Byzantines from the advancing Seljuk Turks, Gregory sounded the theme that

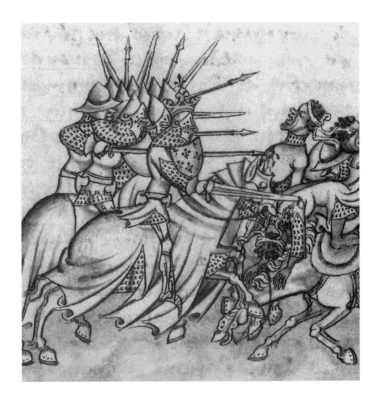

just as Jesus laid down his life for his brothers in an act of self-sacrificing love, so too the Christian knights of Europe should be willing to lose their lives in battle for their oppressed coreligionists in the East.

Riley-Smith's work has revealed that this notion of warfare as an act of love was an important feature of the Crusade propaganda of senior churchmen in the late eleventh and twelfth centuries. Many times these churchmen presented going on Crusade to their lay audience as taking up their crosses and following in the footsteps of Jesus. Quite correctly, Riley-Smith noted that Augustine's theology of the just or charitable repression of error contributed mightily to the development of the idea of Crusade as an act of love. Equally astutely, this historian has shown that such propaganda edited out Augustine's notion that love for the enemy should motivate such violence. Instead, churchmen of the High Middle Ages stressed violence as an expression of fraternal love for the Eastern Christians and as an act of loyalty to Jesus, the feudal lord whose patrimony the "pagans" had seized unjustly.

From Riley-Smith's vantage point, this concept of holy violence was a manifestation of the same impulse toward service to others that motivated the establishment of hospitals and the preaching of the Augustinians, Premonstratensians, and mendicants. Indeed, one should not forget that the one medieval figure most associated with love of neighbor, St. Francis of Assisi, went on Crusade. Thus, far from arising from a fundamental perversion of the Christian message, the idea of Crusade was at least in part a

Fifteenth-century illumination of Christian knights killing Muslims in battle

(British Library, London)

manifestation of a general spiritual renewal of the High Middle Ages.

Undoubtedly, such an expression of self-sacrificing love as Crusade would have struck second-century Greek theologian Justin Martyr as odd as it does many modern Christians. Nonetheless, the fundamental cause of this disconnect between medieval Christians and those of other eras is cultural. Medieval Christians did not hear or read the Gospel injunctions to "love one's neighbor as one's self," and to take up one's cross and deny one's self, within a cultural vacuum. On the contrary, their culture, which extra-Christian elements heavily influenced, equipped them with interpretive tools far different from those of the second or twenty-first centuries. In a world where the Germanic warrior ethos exercised a strong influence, putting one's life at risk in combat far from home for the sake of another seemed to some consonant with Jesus' demand to take up one's cross and follow him. To many contemporary Christians living in the postindustrial West, it does not. However, this view does not mean that medieval Crusaders were necessarily less Christian than their modern counterparts.

–JOHN A. DEMPSEY,
FRAMINGHAM STATE COLLEGE

References

E. O. Blake, "The Formation of the 'Crusade Idea,'" *Journal of Ecclesiastical History,* 21 (January 1970): 11–31.

James A. Brundage, *Medieval Canon Law and the Crusader* (Madison: University of Wisconsin Press, 1969).

H. E. J. Cowdrey, *Pope Gregory VII, 1073–1085* (Oxford: Clarendon Press / Oxford & New York: Oxford University Press, 1998).

Carl Erdmann, *The Origin of the Idea of Crusade,* translated by Marshall W. Baldwin and Walter Goffart (Princeton: Princeton University Press, 1977).

John Gilchrist, "The Erdmann Thesis and the Canon Law, 1083–1141," in *Crusade and Settlement: Papers Read at the First Conference of the Society for the Study of the Crusades and the Latin East and presented to R. C. Smail,* edited by Peter W. Edbury (Cardiff: University College Cardiff Press, 1985), pp. 37–45.

Peter Partner, *God of Battles: Holy Wars of Christianity and Islam* (London: HarperCollins, 1997).

Jonathan Riley-Smith, "An Approach to Crusading Ethics," *Reading Medieval Studies,* 6 (1980): 3–19.

Riley-Smith, "Crusading As An Act of Love," *History,* 65 (June 1980): 177–192.

Riley-Smith, *The First Crusade and the Idea of Crusading* (London: Athlone, 1987; Philadelphia: University of Pennsylvania Press, 1987).

I. S. Robinson, "Gregory VII And The Soldiers Of Christ," *History,* 58 (1973): 169–192.

Frederick H. Russell, *The Just War in the Middle Ages* (Cambridge & New York: Cambridge University Press, 1975).

FIFTH CRUSADE

Why did the Fifth Crusade end in failure?

Viewpoint: The Fifth Crusade failed because of the logistical inability of medieval armies to wage wars in faraway regions.

Viewpoint: The Fifth Crusade failed because of conflicts between ecclesiastical and secular powers and the challenge that territorial interests presented to the universal objectives of the reformed papacy.

The Fifth Crusade (1217–1229) marked the last major expedition to the East initiated and launched by the papacy. Organizationally speaking, it was far more sophisticated than any of its predecessors. Pope Innocent III, who planned and promoted the campaign, learned a great deal from the lessons of the Fourth Crusade (1202–1204) and intended to give the new Crusade a better chance of success through a massive reassessment and revision of crusading apparatus. That planning did not save the Fifth Crusade, however, from becoming rife with dissension, paralyzed by leadership problems, and racked by a shortage of resources. The campaign oscillated between extended stalemate and rash advance. Despite the conquest of the important city of Damietta (1219), the expedition failed in the end.

A variety of reasons have been proffered to explain the failure of the Fifth Crusade. Some historians have pointed toward a declining commitment to, and waning enthusiasm for, crusading among western Europeans. Some believe that increasing internecine conflicts within the West gobbled up the resources and attention of rulers who, though still interested in the status of Jerusalem, focused more attentively on domestic issues. Others have cited poor tactical decisions made in the field, the inability of the papacy and empire to work in concert, or the differing views of the Crusader State aristocracy and the Westerners who took the cross. Frequently, the debate has focused on the strong personalities and shortcomings of the main participants: Pelagius, the intransigent papal legate whose influence steadily increased as the campaign wore on; John of Brienne, king of Jerusalem, whose incompetence as a leader vastly outweighed his command of military tactics; and Holy Roman Emperor Frederick II, whose continuous delays left troops on the ground chronically stranded and ineffective.

The following two assessments of the Fifth Crusade tackle the problem from different angles. The first focuses on structural problems that were hardwired into medieval military logistics. The second espouses a more traditional approach by focusing on the ideological context surrounding the Crusade. Both agree, however, that the reasons leading up to the failure of the Fifth Crusade were not unique to it. Thus, studying the failure of the Crusade in many ways is to study the failure of the movement. The two views differ, however, in their dating of the end of the Fifth Crusade. The first marks the end with the surrender of the main Crusader army between Damietta and Mansurah in 1221. The second holds that the Fifth Crusade ended in Jerusalem in 1229 when Frederick recovered the city through a negotiated settlement with the Egyptian sultan.

Viewpoint:
The Fifth Crusade failed because of the logistical inability of medieval armies to wage wars in faraway regions.

The failure of a particular Crusade is merely an episode in the long-continuing conflict over the Holy Land. Historians, however, have often judged success and failure almost entirely in terms of individual Crusades, ignoring the fact that Crusaders occupied portions of the Near Eastern mainland for almost two hundred years. They have assessed the success or failure of each Crusade on many grounds, but probably a majority have focused on what they have seen as an increasing alienation from the Crusade on the part of Westerners in the late twelfth and early thirteenth centuries. Many also believe that there was increasing disenchantment with the role of the Church in European society, growing tensions between the papacy and secular rulers, and a deepening rift in Western society concerning religion. Other historians have challenged the idea that the Crusade was less popular as the twelfth century ended and the thirteenth century advanced. Without denying the existence of profound problems in European society associated with the social and economic changes that marked this period, they argue against any major ideological rift among Westerners. Instead, they try to understand the place of the Crusade in the Latin mind. They are far from agreeing with one another, but most would argue that the Crusade arose from a combination of political circumstances and religious idealism.

Latins inherited a tradition of defending their frontiers from the expanding forces of Islam as well as barbarian tribes. They came to see themselves as heirs of the Roman Empire in a cultural sense and regarded Muslims as invaders of the empire they shared with the Byzantines. This view fit quite well into the ideas of the Church reformers, who, from the late eleventh century, worked to separate the Church from lay control and who desired to restore the unity of the Church under the leadership of the papacy. Shortly after the call by Pope Urban II for what is referred to as the First Crusade (1096–1102), preachers of the Crusade were proclaiming the need to liberate the holy places where Christ lived and died. Both of these approaches, however, have often ignored the ordinary realities that influenced decision making. Relying heavily on narrative accounts, they reflect attitudes of the clerical authors who wrote about the Crusades. Such an approach

has biased the analysis of the actual conditions under which Crusades were fought. Failure or success depended as much or more on adequate troops and supplies, as well as the effective leadership of an often uncertain and divided military force, as on religious motives or attitudes toward the enemy. Indeed, those who view the Crusades as religious wars often consider that they were directed against Islam, but the brunt of the argument always relied on the idea of liberation of the Holy Land and paid much less attention to the religious views of their enemies. The Fifth Crusade (1217–1229) provides an excellent opportunity to demonstrate the process of decision making and to show how conditions beyond the control of the participants played a decisive part in the outcome.

The Fifth Crusade—the number is arbitrary but conventional—was one of a series of campaigns aimed at restoring the Latin Kingdom of Jerusalem and recapturing Jerusalem after the disastrous losses to Saladin in 1187. It was born out of frustration and failure, following the small gains made by the Third Crusade (1189–1192), which succeeded in maintaining the hold of the Latins on portions of the mainland, and the diversion of the Fourth Crusade (1202–1204) against Constantinople, which siphoned off Western forces and divided the commitment of leading Western nobles to the liberation of the Holy Land. The Fourth Crusade was probably responsible for a wave of popular reaction that coalesced in the so-called Children's Crusade (1212), which might have received its name because of the involvement of some sons of participants in the Fourth Crusade. Pope Innocent III, who had failed in his effort to direct the Fourth Crusade to its original goal, announced his plan for a new Crusade in 1213, appointed preachers, and summoned a council to meet in 1215, where the Crusade was a major topic.

When Innocent died in 1216, plans for the new Crusade were well under way. At the Fourth Lateran Council he appended his plan, "Ad liberandem," to the decrees of the council. This plan, which was undoubtedly discussed at the council and reflected the views of the participants as well as those of the Pope, is the most extensive and detailed Crusade plan produced by any Pope up to this time. Already, the young German king and future Holy Roman Emperor, Frederick II, had taken the Crusade vow, as had the penitent and aging King John of England. Philip II Augustus of France, who had taken part in the Third Crusade, did not take the Crusader vow and remained somewhat aloof from the preparations, even objecting to some of the decisions made by the Pope and council on the ground that they infringed on royal rights. Still, many French nobles took the Crusade vow, while preachers enjoyed great success in the lands along the Rhine River as well as in England. Under papal direction, they worked to reconcile warring factions and to induce leading nobles to take the vow. Innocent led this peace effort at the council, though without great success. He was, in fact, working toward this end in northern Italy when he died in Perugia.

The cardinals chose as his successor Cardinal Censius, who took the name Honorius III. This experienced administrator was well equipped to pick up where Innocent had left off. Honorius lost no time in announcing that he planned to follow Innocent's timetable for the Crusade. The task, however, was difficult because a key figure, Frederick, had not yet consolidated his political position in Germany. Indeed, even after the defeat of his rival, Otto IV, at the Battle of Bouvines (1214) by Frederick's ally and supporter, Philip II Augustus, Otto and his allies remained a formidable threat. In England, King John, who had been allied to Otto, died in 1216. Thus, none of the major rulers were prepared to depart for the East on time in 1217. Only Hungarian king Andrew II planned his departure for this time. The Rhenish and English contingents delayed their departure until the spring of 1218, expecting to be led by Frederick.

The first contingents arrived in Acre on the northern Palestinian coast in the late summer and early fall of 1217. First to arrive was Duke Leopold of Austria, an experienced Crusader, who led a group largely from Austria and Germany but included some warriors from other parts of Europe. In September, Andrew arrived. After consulting with John of Brienne, the ruler of the remnant of the Latin Kingdom, they decided on a show of force in northern Palestine and Lebanon. This decision certainly suited John of Brienne and the local barons, whose position was none too secure. In part, their objective was aimed at solving a severe food shortage by raiding grain supplies in the region around al-Fulah. They met little resistance. The Muslim forces withdrew and made no attempt to engage them. The Crusaders also scouted the area around Mount Tabor, a key fortress in the area southwest of the Sea of Galilee. They returned to Acre and, after a short stay, launched an attack on Mount Tabor. The mountain, which rises sharply from the plain, was well fortified and was defended by some two thousand troops. It represented a serious threat to Acre. In early December 1217 the Crusaders made their ascent. Although they had surprised the garrison, John of Brienne decided to break off the attack. A second attack,

two days later, was also indecisive, and the Crusaders returned to Acre. Despite this lack of perseverance, Sultan al-'Adil decided to withdraw his forces from Mount Tabor. Although Andrew left, the arrival of Rhenish troops in the spring of 1218 permitted the Crusaders to turn their attention to their chief objective, an attack on Egypt designed to split the Muslim forces and deprive them of the wealth of that land. The decision was now made to launch the attack against Damietta, at the eastern mouth of the Nile, which gave direct access to Cairo.

On 24 May 1218 the Crusader fleet began to move southward toward Damietta, landing on the coast to the west of the Damietta Nile and east of the al-Azraq Canal. (It should be noted that the geography of the area has changed dramatically between the thirteenth century and the present. Among other changes, the present city is just south of where it was in 1218 and the coastline is further north.) The Crusaders elected John of Brienne as their leader. This decision was necessary because they did not owe allegiance to any common ruler. The first task of the Crusaders was to destroy the tower from which a chain stretched across the Nile to prevent ships from moving up the river. Since the tower stood offshore, it could only be attacked from the river, requiring siege machines mounted on ships. The attack proved a major challenge. Progress was slow until, with newly designed machines, the Chain Tower fell on 25 August.

The way was now open to cross the river and cut the city off from the main Muslim camp to the south. The death of al-'Adil on 31 August threw Saladin's empire into confusion. The sons of al-'Adil divided the empire. Al-Mu'azzam gained Syria; al-Ashraf ruled Iraq; while the richest prize, Egypt, went to al-Kamil, thus laying the foundation for rivalry among the brothers and their supporters. When al-Kamil learned that many Crusaders were leaving in the aftermath of the victory at the Chain Tower, which was not unusual since Crusaders from the West normally spent less than a year in the East, he decided to attack their camp. Despite the element of surprise, the Egyptian forces were defeated. Al-Kamil continued to try to prevent the Crusaders from crossing the Nile to lay siege to Damietta. The Crusaders also found themselves prey to weather and disease. The papal legate, Cardinal Pelagius, rallied their spirits during this period and encouraged them to take practical measures to strengthen their position, but morale continued to be low as they entered 1219. Things were also going badly for the Egyptians. Al-Kamil learned of a conspiracy against him. He moved his forces away from Damietta and thus opened the way for the Crusaders to cross the river. Damietta was still well fortified, and the Crusaders were unable to do more than isolate the city. Al-Kamil, meanwhile, put down the rebellion and launched an attack against the Crusaders on Palm Sunday, 1219. It was repulsed chiefly through the leadership of Leopold, Duke of Austria, but the effort to take the city was frustrated when Leopold departed with many of his followers.

The dependence of the Crusaders on reinforcements from the West dictated most of the decisions reached in the following months. They launched a direct attack on the city, but it failed. It was during the ensuing lull that one of the most charismatic figures in history, Francis of Assisi, arrived in the Crusader camp. Francis, the founder of a religious order called the Order of Little Brothers (the Franciscans)—who were devoted to poverty—preached a message of conversion and peace. In his sermon to the Crusaders he warned that the battle they planned for the next day would fail. In fact, it was a near disaster, saved only by the strong action of the Knights Templar, the Hospitallers, and the Teutonic Knights, supported by John of Brienne. Francis also carried his message to the Muslim camp, preaching before the Sultan. Though often dismissed as ineffectual, it seems likely that al-Kamil read Francis's message as offering the possibility of a negotiated settlement, a course that he favored because he wished to devote his major efforts to making himself sole heir to Saladin's empire, eliminating his brother al-Mu'azzam, who ruled Syria. In fact, there was a period of truce and negotiations at this time. Al-Kamil offered to return the city of Jerusalem as well as Crusader fortifications west of the Jordan but this offer was rejected because, without the key forts across the Jordan and south of Jerusalem, the city was too vulnerable. Al-Kamil could not surrender these forts without giving up his own ambition to rule Syria. With the negotiations ending in failure, the stalemate continued. Crusade leaders knew, however, that the city would eventually fall unless al-Kamil launched a major effort. His attempt to relieve the city in late October 1219 failed. Shortly after, the Crusaders entered the city through an unmanned tower. The defenders of the city had simply starved to death. The booty was enormous and served to replenish the dwindling resources of the city. The conquest, however, resulted in a conflict between Pelagius and John over rule of Damietta and anger among the rank and file over the division of spoils. Pelagius felt the full brunt of their anger. In fact, however, he was merely following papal instructions aimed at securing the position of the Church. The conflict was, for a time, damaging, until a compromise was reached placing the city under the rule of John until Frederick arrived. His coming, already delayed for two years, was now anticipated. The share of booty allotted to common soldiers was also increased. In the weeks that followed, it was clear that John and his supporters understood that their difference was with the Pope, and they presented their case in Rome.

Tensions over leadership were endemic in medieval armies, which often lacked a clear line of command. Decisions were usually made in council, and those whose views were rejected sometimes withdrew their support. For this reason, one should not read too much into such disagreements. Of course, personalities played an important role, but the issues were defined by conditions on the ground, which furnished the basis for disagreements. The main problems were logistical. Supply lines were long. Men and supplies had to travel by sea, a voyage that was possible only during the spring and fall because of the danger of storms at other times. Crusaders were expected to pay their own expenses. Many relied upon the leaders of their contingents, but money was always short. Pelagius's control of money raised by the Crusade tax on the clergy, which he seems to have carefully saved for major expenses, was a bone of contention. As funds grew scarce, his influence increased. The continued absence of Frederick deprived the Crusade of effective leadership and no doubt added to the dissension among those present. Uncertainty fueled debate.

Study of arrivals and departures shows that military decisions were strongly influenced by the number of troops available. After the fall of Damietta, there was a substantial reduction in the number of Crusaders in Egypt. With high mortality rates from disease and military action, the lack of replacements sapped the morale as well as the ability of the Crusaders to mount an effective campaign. John of Brienne departed to deal with matters in Syria and Palestine, where al-Mu'azzam harassed the remnant of the Latin Kingdom. With the arrival of reinforcements from northern Italy and a force sent by Frederick, announcing his plans to join the Crusade, Pelagius wanted to move quickly against the enemy. But many Crusaders were reluctant to gamble. They felt that their forces were still too weak. The arrival of Duke Louis of Bavaria, representing Frederick, in the spring of 1221 brought matters to a head. Pressure to launch an attack on the main Muslim forces increased. The morale of the Crusaders depended on action. Although the duke was under imperial orders to await Frederick's arrival, he was a realist. He decided to undertake a reconnaissance in force southward along the Nile toward Fariskur. In

IN THE SERVICE OF THE DIVINE COMMANDER

Pope Innocent III called for a new Crusade in 1215, initiating a movement that became the Fifth Crusade (1217–1229). Some selections from his proclamation are included here:

Lest, however, we seem to impose upon the shoulders of men heavy and unbearable burdens which we are unwilling to put a finger to, like those who only say, and do not do; behold we, from what we have been able to spare beyond our necessary and moderate expenses, do grant and give thirty thousand pounds to this work; and, besides the transport from Rome and the neighbouring places that we have granted, we assign in addition, for this same purpose, three thousand marks of silver which have remained over to us from the alms of some of the faithful; the rest having been faithfully distributed for the needs and uses of the aforesaid Land, through the hand of the abbot of blessed memory, the patriarch of Jerusalem, and the masters of the Templars and Hospitallers. . . .

Since, indeed, those who with right judgment remain in the service of the divine Commander ought to rejoice in a special privilege: when the time of the expedition exceeds one year in length, the crusaders shall be free from taxes and talliages and other burdens. Upon their assuming the cross we take their persons and goods under the protection of the blessed Peter and of ourselves, so that they shall remain under the care of the archbishops, bishops and other prelates of the church. Special protectors, nevertheless, being deputed for this purpose, so that, until most certain news shall have been obtained either of their death or of their return, their possessions shall remain intact and unassailed. And if any one presume to the contrary he shall be restrained by ecclesiastical censure. . . .

Moreover we excommunicate and anathematize those false and impious Christians who, against Christ Himself and the Christian people, carry arms, iron, and wood for ships to the Saracens. Those also who sell to them galleys or ships and who, in the pirate ships of the Saracens, keep watch or do the steering, or give them any aid, counsel or favour with regard to their war machines or to anything else, to the harm of the Holy Land; we decree shall be punished with the loss of their own possessions and shall be the slaves of those who capture them. And we command that on Sundays and feast days, throughout all the maritime cities, this sentence shall be renewed; and to such the lap of the church shall not be opened unless they shall send all that they have received from such damnable gains, and as much more of their own as aid to the aforesaid Land; so that they may be punished with a penalty equal to the amount of their original fault. But if by chance they be insolvent, those guilty of such things shall be otherwise punished; that through their punishment others may be prevented from having the audacity to presume to act similarly. . . .

We therefore, trusting in the mercy of almighty God and in the authority of the blessed apostles Peter and Paul, from that power of binding and loosing which God conferred on us, although unworthy, do grant to all who shall undergo this labour in their own persons and at their own expense, full pardon of their sins of which in their heart they shall have freely repented, and which they shall have confessed; and, at the retribution of the just, we promise them an increase of eternal salvation. To those, moreover, who do not go hither in their own persons, but who only at their own expense, according to their wealth quality, send suitable men; and to those likewise, although at another's expense, go, nevertheless, in own persons: we grant full pardon of their sins. Of this remission, we will and grant that, according to the quality of their aid and the depth of their devotion, all shall be partakers, who shall suitably minister from their goods towards the aid of that same Land, or who shall give timely counsel and aid. To all, moreover, who piously proceed in this work the general synod imparts in common the aid of all its benefits, that it may help them to salvation.

Source: *Ernest F. Henderson, ed.,* Select Historical Documents of the Middle Ages *(London: George Bell & Sons, 1910), pp. 337–344.*

FIFTH CRUSADE

preparation, the legate recalled John and his forces. On the Egyptian side there was growing concern. Al-Kamil was joined by his brothers. He decided to renew his offer of peace terms, but both the Pope and the emperor had forbidden any treaty. Frederick was still expected to arrive. The Crusader army began to move southward and on 18 July reached Sharamsah. The Nile flood was due in less than a month. At this point, no decision had been made about advancing further, but the mass of Crusaders and the legate, probably misled by the lack of serious resistance, wanted to advance, while John counseled withdrawal. Nevertheless, the army moved further south into a narrow triangle of land formed by the Nile and a small stream that entered the river near Baramun. The Crusaders were now in a position where further advance was blocked by a canal between al-Mansurah and Lake Manzalah. They could easily be cut off by the rise of the Nile waters. The decision to retreat, taken about 26 August, was too late. Also, the Nile flood reached a higher level than in previous years. The Sultan opened the sluices to run water into the fields, adding to the discomfort of the soldiers. After a series of indecisive skirmishes, the Crusader army negotiated its surrender on 29 August 1221. Al-Kamil, who had never wanted to fight a campaign that jeopardized his own plans, was willing to agree. The Crusaders would abandon Damietta and exchange prisoners. The truce would last eight years. Those who remained in Damietta were bitterly disappointed, but there was no leader willing to undertake a further campaign. Frederick had not arrived. It was not until 1229 that he went on Crusade, after he was excommunicated by Pope Gregory IX in 1228 for failure to fulfill his Crusade vow. He then followed the direction that had been rejected during the Fifth Crusade. He reached a settlement that was essentially the same as the peace agreement that al-Kamil had offered earlier. As experience would show, it proved to be illusory. Jerusalem remained in Western hands for only about fifteen years.

The failure of the Fifth Crusade to attain its objectives evoked criticism from many quarters. It did not, however, dampen interest in the Crusade. Contemporaries explained this failure largely in terms of their own experience. The clergy lamented that God had not found them worthy of victory. Some blamed Frederick or the Pope, but both men agreed to work together for a new Crusade. Modern scholars have often looked for the reasons for failure in ideological conflict, but there were none. There were merely recriminations. The reasons for failure were not in conflicts over ideas but the result of problems of leadership that were endemic to medieval warfare and, above all, to

problems of manpower and logistics caused by the effort to wage war at such a great distance.

–JAMES M. POWELL,
SYRACUSE UNIVERSITY

Viewpoint:
The Fifth Crusade failed because of conflicts between ecclesiastical and secular powers and the challenge that territorial interests presented to the universal objectives of the reformed papacy.

Explaining the failure of any particular Crusade, by contemporaries who participated in it and by many modern historians alike, frequently degenerates into finger-pointing. This trend began in earnest with the disillusioning end of the Second Crusade (1147–1149)–the first of what became a long line of "failed crusades." Although the failure to recapture Edessa was the result of a single, but devastating, strategic blunder, treachery on the part of the Byzantines or the barons of the Latin East (or both) became the explanation of choice among European people who traveled thousands of miles to take part in a humiliating and unqualified defeat. On the European home front, an explanation for the failure of all particular Crusades to the East is summed up in the phrase *peccatis exigentibus hominum* (the sins of men). According to this formula, God granted overwhelming victories to the pure and afflicted moral degenerates with chastising failures. If a Crusade failed, it was because the particular Crusaders were lascivious men puffed up with pride, hiding their avarice behind a veneer of piety and holy service.

Of all the Crusades to the East, the Fifth Crusade (1217–1229) provides the best case study for examining the problems that confronted these expeditions and dragged them into continuous failure. The Fifth Crusade marks the last major Crusade launched by the papacy to the East and was the most meticulously organized and mature expedition of its kind. It was planned by Pope Innocent III, who, having presided over the disastrous Fourth Crusade (1202–1204), went to great pains to cure crusading of all its ailments. In short, the Fifth Crusade offered the best effort that thirteenth-century Europe could muster to save the Holy Land. Its failure underscores, in bold relief, the overall failure of the Crusades.

A popular way of explaining the failure of the Fifth Crusade has been to focus on the personal conduct of the main participants. In a way, this approach is a modification of the medieval explanation, the "sins of the men," by transforming it into the "shortcomings of the leaders." The villain of the piece varies from historian to historian. Some have focused on Holy Roman Emperor Frederick II's continuous efforts to dodge the Crusade through a long series of delays that amounted to an almost perpetual deferment of his vow. Thus, Frederick is to blame since his selfish machinations deprived the host of desperately needed leadership and resources. Some have focused on the weakness of the elderly Pope Honorius III, who inherited the project after Innocent's death (1216). If Honorius had only applied more pressure to the Emperor, rather than indulging him, then Frederick's hand would have been forced and the Crusade made viable. Cardinal Pelagius, the papal legate, has received the lion's share of criticism. Steven Runciman, in *A History of the Crusades* (1951), for example, described him as "singularly lacking in tact," a "haughty" and "unpopular" man who managed to antagonize all parties whenever he tried his hand at mediation. His increasing prominence as leader of the Crusade—largely by default—led to heightened dissension within the ranks that paralyzed the expedition at times and pushed the host into poor tactical decisions at others. The king of Jerusalem, John of Brienne, who butted heads with Pelagius in a series of spectacular confrontations, has received considerable criticism as well. Not only was he convinced that his views were always right and all alternatives were wrong, he actually "abandoned" the Crusade in progress, even though he was its nominal leader, to pursue personal interests in Armenia.

Personal character flaws among the participants probably were aggravating factors of great magnitude but, in the end, cannot in and of themselves explain the rifts that literally pulled the Fifth Crusade apart. Excessive concentration on specific personalities has obscured (though has not completely concealed) the ideological and political matrix in which the protagonists were embedded. The Fifth Crusade, like almost all Crusades, was planned, launched, and waged amid a conflict that cast its long shadow over the whole of western European international politics: between the reformed papacy and the Holy Roman Empire in particular and the Church and emerging territorial states in general. The incompatible and rival interests of ecclesiastical and secular powers prevented a true synchronization of their respective resources, one that was the sine qua non for such a massive undertaking as a Crusade to the East. The greatest problem facing the Crusades was the two main, yet mutually exclusive, goals of the reformed papacy. On the one hand, it wanted to liberate itself from secular domination and declare its temporal, as well as

spiritual, supremacy in all matters. On the other hand, its commitment to recovering Jerusalem and the Holy Land increased its dependency on secular powers. To reconcile these goals, the papacy needed not only a successful Crusade but one that was under its control. Inconsistency bred frustration and perpetual animosity.

Innocent III correctly recognized that one of the greatest obstacles to launching a Crusade to the East, at least on the home front, was the incessant squabbling among European powers. Establishing relative peace within Europe was the essential first step toward successful organization of the Crusade, and the papacy offered itself as an honest broker. The main hot spots at the time were the civil war in the Empire and the wars between England and France. Legates promoted reconciliation and urged the combatants, at the least, to put their conflicts on the back burner for the sake of Christ's patrimony. The papacy, however, seemed less willing to place its own political interests as a secular lord on the back burner. Chief among these interests was the papal objective to bifurcate the German Empire into separate kingdoms: Sicily (technically a papal fief) and Germany proper. The two kingdoms ran the risk of being consolidated under the crown of Holy Roman Emperor Frederick II—who was supposed to be the leader of the Fifth Crusade. If this unification were to happen, then the papacy would once again find itself sandwiched within a two-front war when hostilities resumed (which they certainly would) between pope and emperor. Thus, any partnership between the secular and religious heads of the Crusade would be a tenuous one, punctuated by mutual suspicion.

Imperial-papal tensions can be seen at work in the ambivalent reaction the papacy had to Frederick's decision to take the Crusader vow. Both Innocent and Honorius knew Frederick well and personally, the former as his childhood protector and the latter as his tutor. Likewise, both used extreme caution when measuring him as man or emperor. Emperors and popes alike laid claim to authority of a universal type and saw themselves as sanctified and rival heads of Christendom. Thus, authority over Crusades was often a bone of contention that had implications going far beyond control over a military campaign. Frederick's decision to take the cross did not have papal preapproval; his announcement was a "surprise" and was interpreted by the papacy, probably correctly, as having deeper meanings that reached to the roots of Christian authority and smacked of an aspiring Caesaro-Papism. But Frederick's vow could work more than one way and, like dynamite, had to be handled with caution. On the one

Fifteenth-century illumination of the papal legate Pelagius waiting to disembark at Damietta

(from Angus Konstam, Historical Atlas of the Crusades, *2002)*

the nascent title for the king of Jerusalem: "Advocate of the Holy Sepulchre." The title is extremely reminiscent of the "wild-west" atmosphere that predated the Cluniac and Gregorian reforms. The Crusader States in many ways remained an ossified replica of the religio-political organization of late eleventh-century France, despite the nuances produced by the religious diversity of the region. Proprietary churches and monasteries remained ubiquitous there long after becoming an abominable relic of an uncouth and spiritually immature age in the European heartland. The Church, in the Crusader States, continued to be viewed by rulers as a department of state and tended to be treated as such. Taking this climate into consideration, one can assess the behavior of John of Brienne more empathetically. He was a noble from Champagne who, despite his advanced age and years of royal service, had nothing to show for it. His marriage to the queen of Jerusalem was a great opportunity for salvaging a failed career. Given his age, he needed to move quickly, and the Latin East provided the perfect environment. Coming face to face with a firebrand of the reformed papacy such as Pelagius, however, could and did introduce stumbling blocks.

Pelagius's appointment as papal legate by Honorius has been criticized by many scholars, but really he was a man well suited for the job. Keeping in mind that the specter of the Fourth Crusade informed many of the decisions made during the organization of the Fifth Crusade, one can better appreciate his qualifications for being papal legate for the Crusade. Despite accusations of being tactless, Pelagius was a veteran statesman whose qualities gave him an excellent chance for keeping the Crusade on target while safeguarding the interests of the reformed papacy. The firmness that he so often demonstrated should not be confused with an uncompromising rigidity. Once Crusades hit the ground they tended to be run by committee, and Pelagius demonstrated a marked degree of flexibility in dealing with this situation. So long as concessions did not violate the essentials of his mission, he was relatively open to them. The concessions that John of Brienne had in mind, however, would have constituted a violation, and this stance led to clashes between the king and the legate.

Crucial to understanding John's situation is the fact that he was a territorial monarch and not a Crusader. He was more interested in preserving and extending his own personal power in the region than scoring a resounding victory for the papacy or Empire. Although John might have been both resentful and suspicious of Pelagius's increasing prominence in the Crusade, the first substantive breach between the two men

hand, it could trump papal authority by staking a major imperial claim to crusading and hence Christian leadership (a tactic that some of his predecessors experimented with). On the other hand, reneging on or delaying fulfillment of the vow would leave the emperor exposed to the tender mercies of a papacy that could easily use it as an offensive weapon against Frederick. That was exactly what Pope Gregory IX did. Yet, Honorius, despite his tacit concerns, was willing to give Frederick the benefit of the doubt and actually adopted conciliatory and accommodating approaches to him. The issue eventually exploded, but it was set on a delayed fuse. For the time being, both Pope and emperor cooperated.

The reformed papacy did not see the Empire as its only threat. On the contrary, it viewed the relationship between ecclesiastical and secular authority, and the dangers it posed, in the broadest of terms. While falling considerably short of playing a "zero-sum game," the papacy viewed any sign of secular power encroaching on the primacy of ecclesiastical authority as a hazard. Essentially, it was this conflict, rather than one of mere incompatible personalities, that pitted the papal legate Pelagius and John of Brienne, king of Jerusalem, against one another.

One of the greatest ironies of the Crusader States is that, though created by a movement launched by the reformed papacy, they boasted the most "unreformed" model of church organization in the Latin world, which can be seen in

FIFTH CRUSADE

occurred in response to the sultan's offer of a treaty. In exchange for a Crusader withdrawal, the sultan was prepared to part with the city of Jerusalem and several fortresses west of the Jordan. The Crusaders were divided over whether to accept the offer. The deal would restore Jerusalem but leave it in a strategically precarious state. John and Pelagius found themselves in opposing camps. After weighing the situation, John probably found the deal attractive since it would permit him to become a real, rather than nominal, king of Jerusalem. His interests were territorial and local. Pelagius, as legate, was the defender of papal interests and policies, and these conflicted with John's more immediate concerns. The ultimate rejection of the offer indicates that the majority most likely opposed it—with good reason. King John, however, probably viewed his defeat as one guaranteed by Pelagius's interference, one that infringed upon the royal prerogative to pursue whatever action was best for the crown.

After the conquest of Damietta (1219) John and Pelagius clashed with even greater ferocity. The issue now was control over the newly acquired city. John's perceived right of conquest collided with the ideal of Christian universalism defended by Pelagius. By the terms of his mission Pelagius was charged with presiding over the division of land conquered by the Crusade. As a papal venture, the division of spoils was to be handled by the legate. John's perspective was quite different: the Crusade was an auxiliary force, albeit a massive and desperately needed one, that was to facilitate the strengthening and eventual recovery of a territorial Crusader State. Since the expedition was essentially a royal venture, Damietta was to be incorporated into his kingdom. Pelagius's challenge was an egregious example of clerical interference in a secular affair. Complicating the issue yet further was the possibility that the Crusade was an imperial venture under the auspices of the still-absent Frederick. Certainly this view was not the papal perception, but it was probably held by the German advanced guard that Frederick sent and was present in camp. Pope and emperor, moreover, were still at least nominally working together, and that cooperation mingled imperial and papal interests. Frederick's interests, at this point, were Pelagius's as well. A compromise finally emerged from the confusion: John received control over the city until Frederick's arrival.

Did the conflict between John and Pelagius lead to the unraveling of the Fifth Crusade? This conclusion does not seem to have been the case. Certainly it created a wide array of problems and complications. When measured against such issues as racing to conquer Egypt before the inundation of the Nile or the continuing absence of Frederick, however, disputes between John and Pelagius rank low on the roster of difficulties impeding the Crusade. But the clash between the two men was not simply one of personalities. On the contrary, it was a conflict between the worldviews they represented, those of territorial monarchy and a universal papacy. When personalities were particularly strong, they simply magnified a problem that was always there.

Sometimes crusading could absorb the impact of this conflict, and at other times it buckled beneath its weight. If one defers to convention and marks the end of the Fifth Crusade at 1221, then the former situation is the case. From this vantage point the Crusade failed but not because of clashing interests of popes and monarchs. If, however, one views Frederick's campaign as part of the Fifth Crusade rather than as an addendum to it, a different picture emerges that is more consistent with the latter scenario. The Fifth Crusade, like most, was constituted of a series of waves, and the portion of this Crusade led by its designated leader—even though his arrival was belated in the extreme—should be considered part of it.

Honorius's approach to Frederick, which some have characterized as weak, was in fact a conciliatory and pragmatic one that proposed a genuine partnership between pope and emperor. Although Honorius reminded Frederick of the ultimate consequences that could follow a breach of the vow, he also realized that the emperor faced a wide array of problems, from Muslims in Sicily to Lombards in northern Italy, which defied easy solutions. Universal emperors had universal problems. Honorius backed away from hard-line claims of papal primacy and made a spectacular show of good faith by giving way on the Sicily issue. To some individuals in papal circles, such as the bishop of Ostia, who would soon become Pope Gregory IX, it seemed as though Honorius was giving away the store. Gregory's main objective was to get it back.

Gregory was cut from different cloth than Honorius. The primary goal of his pontificate was to establish, with unprecedented clarity, the supremacy of the papacy over all other powers—particularly the empire. This objective completely changed the significance and even desirability of the Crusade. Rather than doing whatever was possible to facilitate Frederick's departure, Gregory saw the advantages that the emperor's failure to do so would present. Ironically, from Gregory's perspective, strangling the Crusade served papal interests better than its successful prosecution. A successful Crusade would be a propaganda victory for the empire. Gregory began by linking the Crusade to a wide array of disputed issues between papacy and

Empire in his preliminary correspondences with Frederick. His true casus belli surfaced when Frederick, after finally departing for the East, fell sick and disembarked at Otranto for convalescence. Disease was rife rather than fictitious, and Frederick's companion, the landgrave of Thuringia, died from it en route. Gregory refused to receive the imperial ambassadors who came to explain. Frederick was excommunicated. Attention now shifted from Frederick the Crusader to Frederick the tyrant, who made an art form of despoiling the Church. Frederick's excommunication paved the way for a papal invasion of Sicily.

When Frederick resumed the Crusade, he was in an extremely difficult position. Not only was he an excommunicate—which hampered his ability to draw on further human and financial resources for the expedition—he was also facing an impending papal invasion of his lands that tapped into the rebellious inclinations of many of his subjects. Haste characterized his actions. His strong views of imperial and royal authority made dealing with the barons of the Latin East difficult in any circumstances (he was now king of Jerusalem as well as a Crusader), but he did not have time for constitutional niceties that would delay his Crusade and thus his return home. Diplomacy certainly occupied much of his time, but with the Egyptian sultan rather than his own subjects. John of Brienne, whose claim to the throne of Jerusalem had been thwarted by Frederick, joined forces with Gregory and stood at the head of the papal army intending to evict Frederick from Sicily. Frederick's Crusade became a diplomatic rather than a military one. The "victory" that he secured in reality brought the treaty negotiations, conducted with the sultan years earlier, to a successful conclusion.

In an age limited by primitive military organization, a campaign on the scale of a Crusade needed to draw upon the very marrow of the resources in existence. To do so, western Europe could not afford to be a house divided. Given the feudal structure of society, there would always be a measure of chaos and conflict. But the clash between *saeculum* and *sacerdotium,* what today is referred to as Church and State, was a deep-seated and destructive one that drew in and accentuated all other disputes. In an ideological sense, the issue was one of conflicting theories of leadership and primacy. Personalities did not create this problem but did provide the matches that ignited the powder keg. In a practical sense the interests of ter-

ritorial monarchs increasingly palsied the movement. Particular and localized interests conflicted with, and ultimately defeated, the universal and sweeping agenda of the papacy.

–MARK T. ABATE,
WESTFIELD STATE COLLEGE

References

David Abulafia, *Frederick II: A Medieval Emperor* (London: John Lane, 1988).

Joseph P. Donovan, *Pelagius and the Fifth Crusade* (Philadelphia: University of Pennsylvania Press, 1950).

Thomas F. Madden, *A Concise History of the Crusades* (Lanham, Md.: Rowman & Littlefield, 1999).

Hans E. Mayer, *The Crusades* (Oxford & New York: Oxford University Press, 1988).

James M. Powell, *Anatomy of a Crusade: 1213–1221* (Philadelphia: University of Pennsylvania Press, 1986).

Jean Richard, *The Crusades, c. 1071 – c. 1291,* translated by Jean Birrell (Cambridge & New York: Cambridge University Press, 1999).

Jonathan Riley-Smith, *The Crusades: A Short History* (London: Athlone, 1987; New Haven: Yale University Press, 1987).

Helmut Roscher, *Innocenz III. und die Kreuzzüge* (Gottingen: Vandenhoeck & Ruprecht, 1969).

Steven Runciman, *A History of the Crusades*, 3 volumes (Cambridge: Cambridge University Press, 1951).

Elizabeth Siberry, *Criticism of Crusading: 1095–1274* (Oxford: Clarendon Press, 1985; New York: Oxford University Press, 1985).

Christopher Tyerman, *The Invention of the Crusades* (Toronto & Buffalo: University of Toronto Press, 1998).

Thomas C. Van Cleve, *The Emperor Frederick II of Hohenstaufen, immutator mundi* (Oxford: Clarendon Press, 1972).

Van Cleve, "The Fifth Crusade," in *A History of the Crusades,* volume 2, edited by Kenneth M. Setton, second edition (Madison: University of Wisconsin Press, 1989), pp. 377–427.

FIRST CRUSADE

What was the most significant motivational factor in the massive lay response to the First Crusade?

Viewpoint: The most significant motive of the participants of the First Crusade was a quest for the spiritual benefits of the expedition.

Viewpoint: The most significant factor energizing the First Crusade was the widespread belief that the apocalypse was beginning: the world was ending, and possession of Jerusalem was the essential culmination of prophecy.

Viewpoint: The most significant motive of the Crusades was religious revenge against those who attacked Christ, his people, and his patrimony.

The motives behind the massive lay response to the First Crusade (1096–1102) have been debated since the Council of Clermont (1095) concluded. Twelfth-century French chronicler Albert of Aix recorded a story that St. Ambrose visited an Italian priest and asked him why the response was so great. The priest responded by reciting all the explanations he had heard circulating: piety, vanity, greed, and so on. Albert's contemporary, French monk Guibert of Nogent, described it as a spiritual movement of men and women rejecting the world and preparing themselves for its end. German chronicler Ekkehard of Aura emphasized that Europe was so racked with trouble that people were quick to leave for any reason, though he also described the massive religious enthusiasm and portents that surrounded the expedition. The debate has continued up to modern times.

It was once fashionable to explain the motives of the First Crusaders in economic terms. Changing patterns in inheritance among the aristocracy created cadres of "second sons" who desperately needed to acquire new lands. A population explosion, combined with crop failure, underscored the predicament while also explaining the massive and unexpected response of the lower classes. From the functionalist perspective, the Crusade allowed western Europe to purge itself of surplus population. Some historians have viewed the motivation in terms of love for plundering expeditions. Steven Runciman, at the end of his three-volume *A History of the Crusades* (1951), essentially considered the Crusades to be a continuation of the barbarian invasions. Other historians have stressed different salient motives. For some scholars, the Crusaders responded to new conceptions of sin and how the newly emerging "lay vocations" were able to do forms of God's work (rather than being done just by monks). Some have stressed the eschatological and apocalyptic dimensions of the movement and have seen the First Crusade as the actions of men convinced the world was ending. Since Jerusalem was to be ground zero in the apocalypse, it was only natural that thousands set out for the East. Others have seen the Crusaders' reaction to Islamic aggression as a "blood feud," a concept endemic in western Europe. Christ, their spiritual Lord, along with their Eastern coreligionists, had been despoiled by their enemies. The response was clear—massive retaliation.

The Italian priest whom Albert of Aix described, whether he was a living person or not, probably represents the reality well. Humans are motivated by many concerns, and when they pull together in great numbers for action, motivation becomes murky. The First Crusade had thousands of participants; no single explanation can reveal why all of them set out for the East. Still, "something" powerful triggered this massive response. The main factor inspiring this movement will continue to be disputed. Twenty years before the Council of Clermont, Gregory VII tried to launch a similar expedition and received little response. When Pope Urban II proclaimed the Crusade, the answer was thunderous. What was it that was so different among the targeted audiences that produced such drastically different results?

Viewpoint:
The most significant motive of the participants of the First Crusade was a quest for the spiritual benefits of the expedition.

Living in the generation before the First Crusade (1096–1102), Fulk III, Count of Anjou, had a long reign of fifty-three years. Like many men of his position, Fulk oscillated between barbarous acts of violence and expressions of deep religious piety. The omnipresent fear of the fires of hell underscored the gap between these two aspects of his life. The possibility of being plunged into perdition was an occupational hazard for warriors in the eleventh century. Fulk's long reign necessitated a great deal of sinning and consequently inspired several efforts to purge himself of it. He made the pilgrimage to Jerusalem four times, and on the last trip, when he was of advanced age, he walked naked, while being flogged by a servant, in the streets to Christ's tomb.

Norman Crusader Tancred, a high-ranking leader who ultimately became a lord in the East, had similar concerns about his martial lifestyle. According to his biographer Ralph of Caen, Tancred:

> burned with anxiety because the warfare he engaged in as a knight seemed contrary to the Lord's commands. The Lord, in fact, ordered him to offer the cheek that had been struck together with his other cheek to the striker. . . . The Lord urged him to give his tunic and cloak as well to the man who would take them away; the needs of war impelled him to take from a man already despoiled of both whatever remained to him. . . . But after the judgment of Pope Urban granted remission of all their sins to all Christians going out to fight the gentiles, then at last, as if previously asleep, his vigor was aroused, his powers grew, his eyes opened. . . . For before his mind was divided, uncertain whether to follow in the footsteps of the Gospel or the world.

Here is a sort of spiritual-psychological profile of the aristocratic warrior of the late eleventh century—at least of the sort that responded to the summons for the First Crusade.

The mentality of men such as Fulk and Tancred is foreign to the modern mind. Even stranger to posterity (though common for the time) was French lord Thomas of Marle (de

Coucy), who supposedly hanged men by their testicles, literally beat money out of them, and who later participated in the First Crusade with distinction. Eighteenth-century Scottish philosopher David Hume compared skepticism and its attack on dogma with the sling David used to bring down Goliath. Such an approach has informed many examinations of the motives of the First Crusaders. Distrusting the dogmatic conception of the Crusade as principally being a penitential pilgrimage prompted by pious reasons, many historians have looked for more mundane motives. Material gain, either through mass plunder or staking claims to lands of the conquered, is now a tired theory even if it was once popular—and still is for some historians. Denying altogether the existence of material profit for some Crusaders would be oversimplistic. Tancred is a case in point; while curing himself of his spiritual bipolar disorder, he made himself a great lord. Yet, Crusaders returning home richer than when they departed was a rarity. Spiritual and material profit, however, are not mutually exclusive. The First Crusade was a movement that cut across country and class; finding "the" motive for it is futile, but one can determine "a" major motive, one that accommodates all participants without really disqualifying any.

Having hailed from the French warrior class, Pope Urban II knew well their mentality and concerns. This background may be why he succeeded so stunningly in launching his expedition to the East, while his predecessor Gregory VII failed so miserably. Sin was part of the air that the warrior class breathed. A wide chasm separated the realities of life among the warriors and the idealistic expectations and demands of the Church. Aristocratic warriors circumvented this chasm in a variety of ways: pious donations, funding new religious houses, and making penitential pilgrimages. Urban, however, built a sturdy bridge across it by initiating an armed pilgrimage that made war part of this traditional and popular penitential act. This activity appealed to warriors on a variety of levels, for it gave their profession more spiritual justification, and it made a pilgrimage perfectly tailored to their lifestyle and status. Entering Jerusalem triumphantly on horseback as a conqueror was of more interest than doing so barefoot and humbly.

Twelfth-century French abbot Guibert of Nogent gave a clear definition of what the First Crusade was and why it had such appeal to the warrior class: "God has instituted in our time holy wars, so that the order of knights and the crowd running in their wake might find a new way of gaining salvation. And so they are not forced to abandon secular affairs completely by choosing the monastic life or any religious profession, as used to be the custom, but can attain in some measure God's grace while pursuing their own careers, with the liberty and in the dress to which they are accustomed." Guibert's description of what the Crusade truly offered the warrior class matches well the predicament that Tancred faced and his "awakening" from a confused slumber that was prompted by the news of Urban's proposed pilgrimage. Previously, the thorough purging of sin that resulted from a pilgrimage entailed a temporary transformation of one's status from lay to religious. Before the Church reform, monks were seen as the only true Christians, since the laity, living in the world, was constantly bombarded by irresistible temptations. Pilgrimages bestowed great spiritual benefits on participants for two main reasons: first, it signaled a temporary change of one's status (becoming a sort of monk for the duration of the journey); and second, the difficulties associated with the journey were seen as satisfactory penance for sins. Violence of any sort was prohibited until Gregory made it licit for pilgrims to fight in self-defense against the assortment of brigands and cutthroats that infested pilgrimage routes. Armed pilgrimage, however, posited the violence that the warrior aristocracy was addicted to, not as a concession in extreme situations during pilgrimage but as its central activity. Thus, the First Crusade was a pilgrimage more suited to the warrior ethos. Militant Christianity was not only the main reason the response was so great, but also why crusading became a tradition. In short, crusading replaced the old form of pacifistic pilgrimage among the European warrior class.

Pilgrimage, penance, and the spiritual rewards they offered were costly. Rather than finding throngs of second sons striking out toward the East, one finds well-established lords mortgaging their properties to raise sufficient cash for the pilgrimage. Entire families pulled together and alienated property to send members on Crusade. Most of the warriors who returned with anything of value did not carry cash, but relics: hay from the manger, a sliver from the true cross, a shred of cloth from the Virgin's veil, or even a small piece of rubble from the Holy Sepulchre. Many warriors spiritually prepared themselves for the journey by making amends with those whom they had previously injured. Lord Nivelo of Fréteval, for example, a *castellan* (castle warden) and despoiler of the Church par excellence, renounced forced claims on local religious estab-

TAKING THE CROSS

Ekkehard of Aura comments on groups who responded to Pope Urban II's call for a Crusade at the Council of Clermont (1095):

The West Franks could easily be induced to leave their lands, since for several years Gaul had suffered, now from civil war, now from famine, and again from excessive mortality; and, finally, that disease which had its origins in the vicinity of the church of St. Gertrude of Nivelle alarmed them to such an extent that they feared for their lives. This was the nature of the disease. The patient, attacked in any part of the body by invisible fire, suffered unspeakable torment for a long time, and without remedy, until either he lost his life from the agony, or he lost both the torture and the afflicted limb at the same time. There are to this day living witnesses of this disease, maimed either in hands or feet by the scourge.

Of the other nations, some peoples or individuals acknowledged that they had been called to the land of promise not only by the proclamation of the Pope, but also by certain prophets who had lately arisen among them, or by signs and revelations from heaven; others confessed that they had been constrained to take the vows by reason of embarrassed circumstances. Indeed, the majority set out encumbered with their wives and children and all their belongings.

But for the East Franks, the Saxons, the Thuringians, the Bavarians, and the Alemanni this trumpet call sounded only faintly, particularly because of the schism between the empire and the papacy, from the time of Pope Alexander even until today. This, alas, has strengthened our hatred and enmity against the Romans, as it has theirs toward us! And so it came to pass that almost all the Teutonic race, at first ignorant for the reason for this setting out, laughed to scorn the many legions of knights passing through their land, the many companies of foot soldiers, the crowds of country people, women, and little ones. They regarded them as crazed with unspeakable folly, inasmuch as they were striving after uncertainties in place of certainties and were leaving for naught the land of their birth, to seek with certain danger the uncertain land of promise; and, while giving up their own possessions, they were yearning after those of strangers. But although our people are more perverse than other races, yet in consideration of the promise of divine pity, the enthusiasm of the Teutons was at last turned to this same proclamation, for they were taught, forsooth, what the thing really meant by the crowds passing through their lands.

Source: August C. Krey, The First Crusade: The Accounts of Eyewitnesses and Participants *(Princeton: Princeton University Press, 1921), pp. 41–42.*

lishments and rendered satisfaction for his previous conduct. He described himself as a man born into a class that glorified oppressing the weak. Nivelo remembered that his father did likewise when he began the family fortune by squeezing peasants for what they had. He was a "tyrant" who, whenever "knightly ferocity" stirred him, gathered his soldiers and plundered villages. He declared that he was abandoning this domination and making the armed pilgrimage for the salvation of his soul. In all the charter evidence pertaining to the First Crusade, one finds nothing but expressions of piety and spiritual hopes, as well as the relinquishing or risking of property to support participants.

The purging of sin as the main motive for an armed expedition to the fringe of the known world may seem strange to many modern readers; modern sensibilities tend to see killing as a sinful act in itself rather than as a solution to sin. That it seems odd, however, does not make it any less true. People in the late eleventh and early twelfth centuries were obsessed with sin and methods for removing it. Holy sites, above all Jerusalem, had long been destinations for those who wanted to clean their spiritual slates. Conduct on pilgrimages before 1095 was to be humble and ascetic; garnering the full spiritual benefits while retaining class status on Crusade was appealing to warriors. The familiar phrase—"for the remission of sins"—is ubiquitous in the evidence pertaining to the Crusade and tells scholars much about what motivated participants the most.

–TODD MARX, CONCORD, NEW HAMPSHIRE

Viewpoint:
The most significant factor energizing the First Crusade was the widespread belief that the apocalypse was beginning: the world was ending, and possession of Jerusalem was the essential culmination of prophecy.

Historians have trouble with the causes of the First Crusade (1096–1102)—the phenomenon they seek to "explain" is so strange and so anomalous. It does not happen often in the history of any civilization that great armies, called by religious leaders on short notice, in which leadership was an afterthought, have advanced so far into the territory of a long-standing foe and conquered so much terrain that they then colonized. Early Islam (seventh and eighth centuries) provides probably the last time anything remotely similar occurred, and even that period stands out as rare. The presence of unusually

large numbers of noncombatants, even women and children, in the Crusade, however, sets this expedition apart from any earlier such phenomenon. Twelfth-century French abbot Guibert of Nogent claimed the Crusade was the work of divine forces through his people, "the deeds of God through the Franks." Moreover, this religious war set in motion a series of several widely varying "holy wars" over the course of the next three centuries. Given the great historical importance of these religious wars, both to the region that spawned them (Europe) and the lands they conquered (western Asia), the Crusades have drawn the attention of historians. In particular, scholars have discussed at length the question of origins: what motivated these people to set out on so perilous a journey to accomplish so novel a quest?

By far the most unusual aspect of these holy wars, prominent in the First Crusade and arising autonomously on subsequent occasions, was the presence of (largely) unarmed enthusiasts–the "poor" (1095–1096), children (1212), and shepherds (1251, 1321)–who believed that they would take Jerusalem from the hands of the infidels. Crowds of commoners (men, women, and children) by the thousands followed charismatic prophets in a mass movement to Jerusalem. This early contingent of unarmed Crusaders, along with their later avatars (children, shepherds), stand out as a unique phenomenon in recorded history. No other nation produced an army of people who thought they could conquer the heart of the enemy's lands without the use of force.

There seems to be a wide variety of explanations for this phenomenon, although they can be broken down into functionalist and idealist camps. On the one hand, functionalists believe that all significant (and certainly all effective) human motivation is purposeful–it serves a function and accomplishes a goal. Thus, they view the motives of the major players—the Pope and the warrior aristocracy—in terms of their material interests. Pope Urban II's call to "Crusade" (1095), therefore, was a masterstroke that accomplished three colossal deeds: he asserted his claim to the papacy for his "reforming party" (over the emperor's candidate); he declared the papacy's claim to Catholic (universal) supremacy over an Eastern Church, with which his party had broken some forty years earlier (1054); and he got the turbulent and restless aristocracy to export their violence and leave Christian Europe in peace. These knights, primarily younger sons, in turn saw an opportunity to find new regions to dominate in the way their eldest brothers ruled local dominions; they understood their religious role in classic "feudal" terms of their fidelity to their liege lord, God, in whose service they humbly fought.

As for the anonymous mobs who made up the "People's Crusade," functionalist historians conclude that their numbers and significance were greatly exaggerated. Indeed, they were probably not genuinely unarmed nor "poor," but hooligan mobs who attacked Jews and terrorized the countryside. They were more likely a collection of undisciplined foot soldiers in search of booty than a religious phenomenon and historical anomaly. In this perspective, the role of Peter the Hermit becomes secondary at best. He appears as the agent of the Pope, whose rational calculations led him, independently, to set in motion this great campaign, and Peter's poor deranged followers suffered the natural results of their imprudent haste. As for the excesses of the Crusaders in slaughtering first the Jews, then the Muslims, and even exotically dressed Christians in the Holy Land, they represent a combination of greed and bloodlust not uncommon in spirited military campaigns with weak command structures.

The greatest strength of the functionalist paradigm is also its weakness as an historical explanation: if this Crusade made so much sense, it should have happened more often. Why had no one, or so few, tried such an obviously beneficial masterstroke before, and why, all of a sudden, did Urban and the fighting warriors of Europe do so? What made Europe ripe for this galvanizing Crusade when, at the beginning of the same century, a far more shocking series of events—in which the caliph of Cairo, Al Hakim, deliberately destroyed the church of the Holy Sepulchre and forced Christians living under his rule to convert (circa 1010)—a papal encyclical from Sergius IV was incapable of rousing even the slightest response from this same society?

The idealist camp argues that deep religious passions motivated the Crusaders, even the seasoned warriors, and that the expedition was not a colonial war with a religious veneer but a religious war with colonial consequences. Warriors were touched by Christianity, hemmed in by the constraints of the peace movement, forced to curtail their violence against their fellow Christians, and, increasingly—over the course of a century of *Reconquista* (Christian reconquest of Spain), Norman invasion of England, and *drang nach Osten* (German drive to the east)—made to turn their violence against their religion's enemies, the pagans, infidels, and heretics who did not benefit from the protection of the peace. Men were concerned with the state of their souls; were torn between the demands of Christ to turn the other cheek and those of the world to defend one's rights with might (Tancred); and were enthused by the belief that, in channeling their violence against the Muslims and taking Jerusalem, they were doing God's work, and that he

would pardon them all their sins if they would undertake this holy violence. The crowds that followed Peter and the other popular leaders seemed animated by the same spirit of sacrifice and divine mission. Religious enthusiasm and belief played a definite role in these events. Indeed, some of the best historical sources come from the serious canonical thought these events provoked. Yet, this religious enthusiasm stays in the background, an atmosphere in which people pursued their desires while irresponsible leaders aroused uncontrollable crowds. They were scarcely Christianized knights serving their feudal Lord. Alone, the clergy might have had serious religious motives. Such an explanation acknowledges the religious without giving it a further role in explaining specific developments more aptly described in functionalist terms, as in the slaughter of the Jewish communities. The logic ascribed to the Normans by Guibert—why should we go to kill our enemies abroad when we have not yet killed them here?—seems logical enough. No need for religion here.

The most dramatic version of the idealist explanation places apocalyptic millennialism at the core of the event. The terrible famines and dramatic signs and wonders of the early 1090s had produced an atmosphere of prophecy that typically inspired charismatic prophets and false messiahs in medieval Europe. Indeed, charismatic preachers abounded: barefoot, preaching hermits with armies of followers; a gosling girl whose goose showed the way to another crowd; Charlemagne appearing in the skies leading a heavenly host; and a candidate for the last emperor who led his troops in the slaughter of Jews. The description that Guibert gives of Peter the Hermit, the visionary hermit and Jerusalem pilgrim—he carries a letter from heaven; crowds flock to him bearing gifts that he redistributes; he becomes their master; they seek his possessions for relics; and even clerics are taken in by his message—resembles no figures more closely than the false Christs and pseudoprophets of earlier times. Two key variables distinguish these late-eleventh-century charismatic leaders from earlier ones: instead of Europe as locus of redemption, they preached a pilgrimage to Jerusalem—for the Day of the Lord was about to take place; and in all earlier cases, the ecclesiastical authorities, especially those who retrospectively tell the tale, depict them as enemies of Christendom, as false prophets and heretics. Guibert, however ambivalent he might be about Peter (and ultimately he describes him as a failure), nonetheless gives full approval to the early preaching of this "saintly man." As for the mass pilgrimage to Jerusalem, it had already occurred twice before: the first in 1033 (recorded by French chronicler Radulfus Glaber) and the second in 1064 (as found in the *Vita Altmanni*). In each case, a belief that Judgment Day was at hand set large crowds of

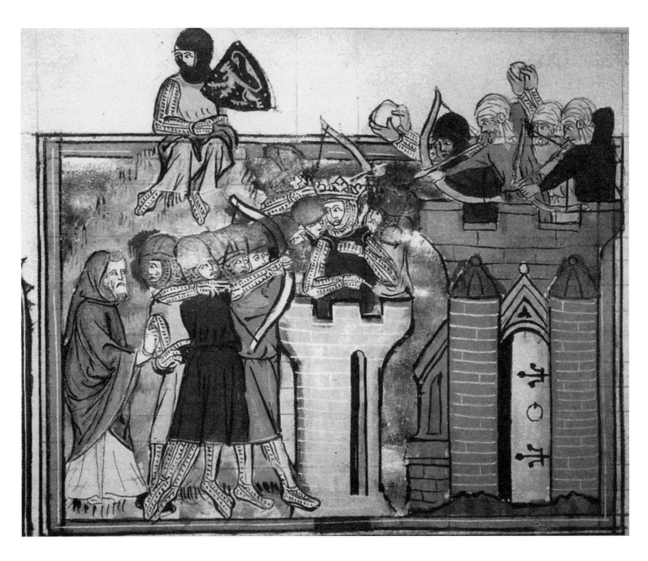

people, from the most powerful to the lowest, on the road to the city where these great events were expected to occur. While the Pope meditated on the emperor's request for help, a mass movement began among the precise populations his reforming party had so powerfully excited over the previous generation.

Moreover, in the apocalyptic version, these "poor" were following Christ in the manner he had preached—in peace, weaponless, and with entire families hastening to their redemption. This movement hardly means that all, or even the overwhelming majority, of these pilgrims belonged to this category of pacifist. Their poverty was not a stigma, as the aristocracy, lay and clerical, so often viewed it, but a sign of sanctity, of being pleasing in God's sight. At least some of them were Franciscans *avant la lettre*. Surely the temptation to slide into a triumphalist violence never left them, and it spilled out into a series of ever-more-violent episodes that produced everything from massacres of Jews to raids on villages and towns to the fearsome, naked, cannibalistic Tafurs. Historians hostile to the "People's Crusade" emphasize, as did the chroniclers, their undisciplined violence. One must be cautious, however, about attributing

to all the behavior of some. Few participants, even mad millenarian visionaries, set out without weapons to take the Holy City from a rival religion on the assumption that God wanted them to slaughter his enemies at random. It seems far more likely that the critical mass of people, as they set out for the promised land, did so in the belief that before their collective Christ-like behavior, guided by God's signs and prophets, the sea would split and the gates of Jerusalem would fling open to greet them. As such, the Crusade of the "poor" constitutes one of the most extraordinary episodes of apocalyptic possession by an entire society in recorded history.

Pope Urban II, in this version, is a Johnny-come-lately who wakes up to the ferment that has been sweeping Europe since summer and into the fall, and he convenes the Council at Clermont (1095), where he rouses the entire population of Europe, including the knights. He takes the pacific apocalyptic enthusiasm of the pilgrims and gives it a martial spirit, in much the way that the reforming papacy had taken the enthusiasms of the peace movement and given them an authoritarian and belligerent spirit with which they had attacked the emperor throughout the previous forty years. In so doing, Urban transgressed a wide range of Christian taboos, going well beyond the tolerance and encouragement that had marked most theological pronouncements on the necessary violence of this fallen world. Crusaders received a plenary pardon for undertaking the mission, and were they to die in the process—in battle—heaven would straightaway take them up (*Song of Roland*). Violence and killing were no longer an unfortunate necessity. It was sanctified, holy, and beloved of God. The war cry "God wills it!" says everything about the sense of mission, but it can encompass everything from Christ-like and loving sacrifice to the martyrdom of the hero, surrounded by the corpses of those he has slain in his zealous if suicidal rage (as did Roland).

"No," answer the functionalists. There was nothing new about the canonical legislation. All the theories of warfare had already been developing since the Christianization of the Roman Empire and the theological ruminations of St. Augustine of Hippo. Urban might have broken new ground, but it was not far afield from earlier positions. Canon law had, according to this reading, already countenanced forms of holy war, and the discontinuity between pilgrimage and holy war were not nearly as dramatic as some historians, such as Carl Erdmann, in *The Origin of the Idea of Crusade* (1977), had depicted. For these scholars the Crusade was at once a pilgrimage and a military expedition, a powerful fusion that emerged seamlessly from earlier developments and made good sense to Urban's warriors. As for the millennial scenario, one does not know what Peter or any of the other preachers told their audiences, since no chronicler recorded it, and speculation on such unknowable facts lies beyond the means of the responsible historian. Certainly little explicit millennial material appears in the unusually ample documentation (for this period) on the event.

This approach systematically downplays the perspective of the radical forms of Christianity that had fermented in western European Christianity since the turn of the millennium—mass pilgrimages, apostolic communities, peace revivals, and public penitential processions. This world, which drew its inspiration from the Sermon on the Mount and the Pauline letters, saw immense differences between the two religiosities. Pilgrims were penitents, and in their most spiritual condition traveled without arms, without mount, and even without shoes. On the apocalyptic pilgrimage of 1064, an event of capital importance often ignored by historians of the Crusade, aristocratic pilgrims refused to fight even when they were attacked. Before the First Crusade, a fighting pilgrim was an oxymoron. In

apocalyptic terms, the two movements—the pilgrimage of the poor and the holy war of the knights—represented opposing poles of the continuum between transformational and catastrophic active apocalypticism. In one, terrible violence and destruction purges the world of evil, with the holy warrior as God's chosen instrument of his wrath; in the other, the world sheds its violence through penitential conversion to the path of peace and reconciliation. And the only time that these two polar opposites combine, or pass rapidly from the one to the other, is the cauldron of apocalyptic expectations.

This eschatological interpretation sits poorly with most historians for two reasons. First, both millennialism (heaven on earth) and apocalypticism (end of the world) had been officially banned from Christian theology for more than seven centuries and never appeared openly (for example, in writing) among responsible churchmen after that time. For Urban to embrace such proscribed beliefs defies logic and credulity. Second, most historians consider millennialism the belief system of fringe groups of doubtful sanity and reason and would hardly associate one of the most successful military campaigns in history with so foolish a mindset. Furthermore, few of the reports of Urban's speech, and none of the chronicles on the Crusade, bring up such issues explicitly. It seems far more likely that this apocalyptic prophecy was added on by a rare man, such as Guibert of Nogent, for personal reasons after the Crusade, and neither apocalyptic expectations nor millennial hopes played any significant role in the Crusaders' piety.

What was the original call? To take the earthly Jerusalem, and by freeing it, to bring down the heavenly—to bring on the millennium. The city was taken (1099) and a king was crowned, but neither did the heavenly city descend nor the earthly millennium commence. A decade later, Guibert, working from the "pragmatics of disappointment," tried to save both the apocalyptic rhetoric of Urban's speech and the apocalyptic timetable of his contemporaries: he shifted his account from an active triumphalist millennial scenario, in which Christians marched straight toward their glorious redemption, to a passive catastrophic one (normally favored by ecclesiastics), in which God and Antichrist fight out the ultimate battle and men are the objects rather than subjects of the final resolution. Urban had not falsely promised the millennium, and the apocalyptic future lay just over the horizon, which was a comforting ecclesiastical "reading." As for the other reports of Urban's speech, they chose to pass over such an embarrassing—and theologically forbidden—millennial prophecy.

Thus, in the millennial analysis, the First Crusade began as a "Last Pilgrimage" and became a "Last War" (Armageddon) before reentering the world of normal time (the twelfth century) as a temporal success and a millennial failure. It would take another generation before another Crusade "took off" (1147), attempting to mimic this earlier effort, again inspired by signs and prophecies. Only at that point could anyone have thought of it as the "first" of anything. From a vantage almost a millennium later, scholars would better understand the movement if it were called the "first last Crusade."

–RICHARD LANDES, BOSTON UNIVERSITY

Viewpoint:
The most significant motive of the Crusades was religious revenge against those who attacked Christ, his people, and his patrimony.

The overwhelming and enthusiastic response to the appeal that Pope Urban II made at the Council of Clermont (1095) is something of an enigma. In terms of theological justifications of violence, the First Crusade (1096–1102) should have taken place twenty years earlier. Urban's predecessor, Gregory VII, tried to launch similar expeditions to the East, and despite the plethora of exegetical arguments proffered by his supporters, the projects were stillborn. Gregory might have made a good theological case for his "proto-crusade," but evidently it was not one capable of tapping into and releasing the seething religious fervor that had so recently developed among the warrior aristocracy of eleventh-century Europe. What did Urban propose that was so different from Gregory's plan, and why did so many Christian warriors respond to his appeal?

Although Urban drew considerably from Gregory's project, he cast the Crusade in different terms. Gregory had adopted for the Papal See a tactic that had long been employed by bishops outside of Rome: calling upon vassals to give armed protection for a cathedral and its interests. Thus, Gregory asked men to take up arms in defense of the bishop of Rome rather than of Christ per se. Urban's message was different. It was a war in defense of Christ, one that had as its objective the liberation of his patrimony as well as of his people, who were being oppressed in the East. Urban probably had in mind a sort of Augustinian "just war." If so, it does not seem that this argument is what his audience heard. What the warriors heard was a message that was much simpler than intricate theological arguments and justifications, one that had more to do with a man such as the fifth-century Salian

Frank king Clovis than St. Augustine of Hippo. It was to be a spiritual blood feud that would recover the property of their Lord Christ, seek revenge for the humiliating insults heaped upon him, and deal a violent blow to those tormenting members of the "Christian tribe" in the East. The knightly class transformed just war into something they understood much better: the vendetta. Evidence supporting this conclusion comes in two major forms: the actions of the Crusaders and writings that reflect their views after the Crusade was under way.

The merciless pogroms against Jews provide compelling evidence that the First Crusaders saw the expedition foremost as a blood feud. A salient feature of the vendetta mentality was its emphasis on generalizations and resistance to specifics. Time, for example, was extremely generalized. Decades could pass—even generations—before an injury was satisfactorily corrected through an act of equal or greater violence. Frankish bishop Gregory of Tours offers several examples of how blood feuds, which had been smoldering for years, could suddenly and unexpectedly flare up in violence. Likewise, a vendetta need not target the specific individual who caused dishonor to the clan; his fellow clan members or descendants could be targeted as well. The words that the *Chanson d'Antioche* (Song of Antioch) places in the mouth of a man crucified next to Jesus have all the characteristics of the blood-feud mentality: "It would be most just if you (Christ) should be avenged on these treacherous Jews by whom you are so tormented." Jesus responds by prophesying that the men who would avenge him have not yet been born. The prophecy mingles Jews and Muslims, portraying them as fellow kin of a rival clan that has done grave injury to the Lord Christ. This view is by no means consistent with what Urban had in mind; it is, however, perfectly consistent with the views of the vendetta-minded warriors of the day, which is why the first victims of the First Crusade were European Jews rather than Muslims. From the perspective of the Crusaders there was little difference between the two. Furthermore, this mentality also explains why outbreaks of anti-Judaism occurred whenever a Crusade was preached, despite continuous attempts by the Church to prevent or quash them.

Jewish sources confirm this view. For example, one Jewish author wrote that the Crusaders justified their actions in terms of vendetta: "You (Jews) are the children of those who killed the object of our veneration. . . . and he himself had said: 'There will yet come a day when my children will come and avenge my blood.' We are his children and it is therefore obligatory for us to avenge him since you are the ones who rebel and disbelieve in him." This statement clearly indicates Crusader belief in a feud that began in the distant past and had been passed down through the generations. Others wrote that the Crusaders did not understand why they should travel across the world to punish Muslim enemies of Christ when there were Jews, guilty of inflicting even greater shame upon the Lord, residing in Europe. The choice that the Crusaders gave Jews—convert to Christianity or die—is consistent with the vendetta mentality. Conversion meant submission and a change of "spiritual clan" status. Refusal to convert meant continuing allegiance to the enemy clan, which could only be responded to through violence. Crusader desecration of Jewish cemeteries and synagogues was avenging a past shame with current shame, with the latter erasing the stain of the former. The financial demands Crusaders placed on the Jews, furthermore, probably had more to do with the concept of *wergild* (literally "man money," a monetary payment to restore honor or compensate for injury) and the need for supplies than simple avarice. The shame of Christ crucified became more acute at the turn of the millennium as the image of Jesus as victor gave way to Jesus nailed to the cross. This transformation probably fueled the drive for spiritual vendetta against Jews. The sheer magnitude of the atrocities committed is difficult to explain in any other context.

Vengeance also stands out as the greatest theme in how the Crusaders described their victories against Muslims. In September of 1098 the Crusaders wrote home that "The Turks, who inflicted much dishonor on Our Lord Jesus Christ, have been taken and killed and we Jerusalemites have avenged the injury to the supreme God Jesus Christ." Blood, in other words, had washed away a past humiliation done to what the Crusaders saw as their greatest lord. Baldric of Bourgueil's rendition of a sermon preached outside Jerusalem is also instructive:

> Rouse yourselves, members of Christ's household! Rouse yourselves knights and foot-soldiers, and seize firmly that city, our commonwealth! Give heed to Christ, who today is banished from that city and is crucified. . . . I address fathers and sons and brothers and nephews. If an outsider were to strike any of your kin down would you not avenge your blood-relative? How much more ought you to avenge your God, your father, your brother, whom you see reproached, banished from his estates, crucified. . . .

The language is that of a kinship group that has suffered injury and dishonor. Far removed from the ethereal abstractions of theologians, the Crusaders interpreted the message by filtering it through the lens of their own culture and made it concrete. The sharp judicial categories for just war elucidated by Augustine gave way to the visceral dynamics of tribal custom. Hence, it was the "obligation" of Christ's "household" to seek vengeance for theft and

dishonor that put these men en masse on the road to Jerusalem. Such terms belong to the dialect spoken by the warrior aristocracy rather than the language of a universal church. The extended family (fathers, sons, brothers, and nephews) were summoned to restore honor through violent retaliation—a long-standing practice that predated church reform by centuries. This kinship group, however, was defined along spiritual rather than blood lines. Christians, in a manner of speaking, became a "super-tribe" that would seek vengeance for past and present injuries on a sweeping scale.

Any assessment of the massive response that Urban's appeal elicited must take the significance of Jerusalem into account. The expedition certainly was presented as a pilgrimage. But the simple joining together of a penitential pilgrimage with warfare only scratches the surface of what caused the massive religious swells that the Council of Clermont unleashed. Pilgrimage, after all, had been a long-established form of penance. Why would so many men at the same time embrace it so quickly and with such fervor? Urban's message struck a nerve with the warrior aristocracy, one that is only partially explicable in terms of penance. Penance cannot explain the widespread persecution of Jews which, though Urban did not intend it to be so, was a central feature of the First Crusade rather than an epiphenomenon.

The centrality of Jerusalem in the First Crusade is beyond doubt, as is the fact that it ranked at the top of Crusader motivation. But the Holy City had many meanings for the men of the age. Discovering which particular one was most prominent in the minds of the First Crusaders is a difficult task. Certainly these meanings were not mutually exclusive; in fact, they dovetailed quite nicely. The behavior and recorded perceptions of the Crusaders, however, implies that the vendetta mentality exerted a particularly powerful influence. Jerusalem was Christ's patrimony that had been unjustly seized by infidels, and it, along with God's honor, needed to be reacquired through violence. Naturally, no medieval person would visit the holiest city on Earth, whether in a violent or peaceful manner, without transforming the trip into a pilgrimage. Yet, the attacks on European Jews and the ruthless manner in which Jerusalem was sacked have little to do with pilgrimage—armed or otherwise. Spiritual vendetta is what best characterizes the expedition, and worship at the Holy Sepulchre, though by no means negligible, was a motive of secondary importance.

How did an Augustinian just war become transformed into a spiritual blood feud? It is possible that Urban intentionally fused these concepts. After all, unlike Gregory, Urban was from the French warrior aristocracy and knew well its spiritual and cultural idiom, though certainly the answer cannot be found in the views of a single man. The most likely explanation lay in the differing spiritual sensibilities of the Church hierarchy and the warrior class. In many ways, the Christian religion was born in suffering and humiliation. From the beginning the Catholic Church embraced this concept, seeing a stoic strength in spirits steadfastly enduring physical abuse. Beginning with Roman emperor Constantine I, Christ was likened more to a god of conquest than a suffering servant—at least from the perspective of warriors. Yet, on the eve of the First Crusade, Christ the victor was yielding once again to the Christ who suffered on the cross. Undoubtedly, this new image created a sweeping cognitive dissonance in the spiritual views of the warrior class, which became acutely aware of the fact that Christ suffered just as much as he had conquered. As his children and spiritual descendants, the warrior class was obliged to wipe this humiliation clean through the spilling of blood and recovery of property and honor.

–MARK T. ABATE, WESTFIELD
STATE COLLEGE

References

Carl Erdmann, *The Origin of the Idea of Crusade*, translated by Marshall W. Baldwin and Walter Goffart (Princeton: Princeton University Press, 1977).

Jean Richard, *The Crusades, c. 1071 – c. 1291*, translated by Jean Birrell (Cambridge & New York: Cambridge University Press, 1999).

Jonathan Riley-Smith, *The First Crusade and the Idea of Crusading* (London: Athlone, 1987; Philadelphia: University of Pennsylvania Press, 1987).

Riley-Smith, *The First Crusaders, 1095–1131* (Cambridge & New York: Cambridge University Press, 1997).

Riley-Smith, "The Motives of the Earliest Crusaders," *English Historical Review*, 98 (1983): 721–736.

Steven Runciman, *A History of the Crusades*, 3 volumes (Cambridge: Cambridge University Press, 1951).

FIRST CRUSADE

FOURTH CRUSADE

Was the Fourth Crusade really a Crusade?

Viewpoint: Yes. Although the Fourth Crusade was diverted, it was planned and launched by the papacy as a Crusade and should be considered as such.

Viewpoint: No. Once the Fourth Crusade was diverted from its proclaimed objective, it ceased to be a legitimate Crusade.

The Fourth Crusade (1202–1204) was the first expedition to the East launched by the great crusading Pope Innocent III. Although its purpose was to continue repairing the massive damage done to the Crusader States by Saladin's jihad (just war), its immediate objective was much more ambitious than that of the Third Crusade (1189–1192). Rather than trying to roll back an Islamic presence on the coastline and interior of the Latin settlements, the Fourth Crusade aimed to bring the war to the heart of the Islamic threat itself—Egypt. Another important feature that distinguishes the Fourth Crusade from its immediate predecessor was the complete absence of Western kings on the expedition. Rather than being a "crusade of kings," the Fourth Crusade marked a return to the roots of crusading by being the business of the nobility. What distinguishes it from all Crusades, however, is the fact that it became a veritable loose cannon. Rather than attacking Egypt, it turned upon and conquered the Byzantine Empire without so much as wounding a single Muslim.

Controversy has marred the interpretations of the Fourth Crusade from the time the Crusaders left port. One modern historian even dubbed it the "Unholy Crusade." Historians are divided in their explanations of how the Crusade was diverted. One school of thought holds that the Fourth Crusade fell victim to a conspiracy—or confluence of conspiracies—that doomed the venture before it began. A roster of villains has been suggested: Enrico Dandalo, the elderly and manipulative Venetian doge who wanted to secure economic hegemony of his city at any cost and who, as legend has it, was tortured and blinded years earlier by the Byzantines; a group of conspirators who plotted at the court of Philip of Swabia, an excommunicate personally despised by Innocent III; or Alexius IV Angelus, a deposed heir to the Byzantine throne, an exile residing in the West, who used the Crusade as a tool to recapture his patrimony. All of these theories can be unified under the general rubric of "directing intelligence." In this scenario the Fourth Crusade in fact hit its target, but the target was not the one Innocent and most of the Crusaders believed it to be.

Against the "directing intelligence" theory one can posit the "diversion by accident" interpretation. Laying aside grandiose conspiracy theories, historians subscribing to the latter explanation believe that a sequence of unexpected problems blew the Crusade off course gradually. Overestimation of the number of Crusaders needing transportation by sea combined with insufficient funds to put the Crusade far into the red before it even set sail. The chaos that ensued, correctly assessed by the sharp eyes of Venetian opportunists, resulted in a Crusader-Venetian partnership that blended the altruistic and dubious goals of all the participants. The Zara campaign, the decision to reinstate a deposed emperor, and the ultimate sack of Constantinople (1204) were all ad hoc solutions to problems facing the Crusaders, rather than some a priori plan hatched by conspirators. The allure and simplicity of a conspiracy theory simply blinds scholars to the mundane structural problems that hamstrung the project.

Some historians refuse to recognize the Fourth Crusade as a Crusade at all. What pushes them in this direction is not a reluctance to become embroiled in a seemingly endless controversy or the desire to dodge a thorny question. Rather, they question the entire validity of a Crusade that not only failed to reach its destination but also attacked fellow Christians and whose participants were censured with excommunication for doing so. Thus, these scholars argue that the Fourth Crusade was a Crusade only while on the drawing board or, at the least, ceased to be a Crusade while sailing in the Adriatic.

Viewpoint:
Yes. Although the Fourth Crusade was diverted, it was planned and launched by the papacy as a Crusade and should be considered as such.

History has had more than its share of peculiar moments, and the events of what has come to be called the Fourth Crusade (1202–1204) should surely rank among them. One of the major goals of the crusading movement was to bring aid to Christians living in the Near East in their fight against Islam. It is rather ironic, therefore, and some might even say tragic, that the fourth major effort of the movement ended with the attack on, and temporary destruction of, the Eastern Christian state of Byzantium while bringing no harm to Islamic power in the region. The unusual events of this Crusade not only sparked controversy in its own day but also have continued to be a source of debate for historians. Many scholars, for example, have devised or assented to elaborate theories that attempt to explain the diversion of the Crusade to Constantinople. While some argue for a conspiracy, others contend the diversion was simply the result of a series of accidents. Still others propound an intermediate position, namely, that the course of the Crusade was determined by a combination of devious scheming and fortuitous opportunity. Other historians, however, have refused to be caught up in this seemingly insoluble debate and, to end the discussion, argue simply that the expedition should not be considered a Crusade at all. While it may never be possible to discover the real cause of the diversion, on the question of whether it was a Crusade a reasonable answer can be offered. Given the balance of evidence, the Fourth Crusade should be considered a crusading campaign, albeit a bizarre, and perhaps in many ways inexplicable, one.

As many historians would agree, a Crusade was a religiously motivated war fought at the behest of ecclesiastical authority with the intention of recovering lost Christian territory or defeating enemies of the Church, for which participants received the spiritual reward of the indulgence for their vow of service. While this definition is perhaps somewhat cumbersome, it is important to remember that the era of crusading spanned several centuries and involved many theaters of operations. As such, any workable definition of crusading must be broad enough to encompass activities ranging in time from the twelfth to sixteenth centuries and in place from Syria to Spain. While it might not be a perfect fit, the Fourth Crusade does fall within the broad parameters of this definition.

When Innocent III became pope in January 1198, he had two major goals for his pontificate. He wanted to recover the holy city of Jerusalem, which had been lost to the Muslims in 1187, and he wanted to reunite the Eastern and Western Churches, which had been formally divided beginning in 1054. Almost immediately, Innocent began preparations to achieve these two objectives. Innocent issued an appeal for a new Crusade in August 1198. While the response to his request was at first tepid, by 1202 a sizable number of soldiers had taken the cross and were beginning to head to the East. Many of these Crusaders assembled at Venice, but still more sought ports of departure in other parts of Europe, especially southern France. It was only the army that gathered at Venice, however, that in the end diverted to Constantinople. The others, who were the majority of Fourth Crusade participants, remained faithful to Innocent's original plan and journeyed to Syria. However, because there is little surviving documentation for the activities of this latter group and a relative abundance of written material relating to the former group, historians have tended to use the term Fourth Crusade to refer exclusively to the soldiers who set sail from Venice. This emphasis is unfortunate, for as historian Donald E. Queller has persuasively argued, this "neglected majority" should also be credited for their participation in the Crusade. Then there would be no need to question whether the Fourth Crusade was really a Crusade, for the

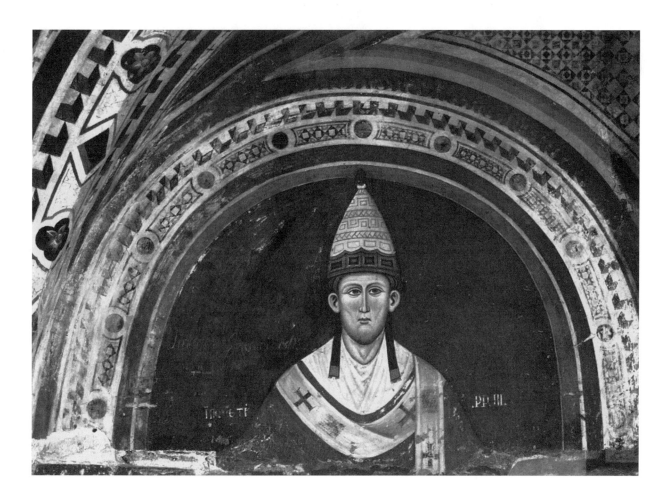

activities of the forgotten majority clearly meet the criteria of the definition of crusading. This conclusion is not offered as a dodge of the original question but rather as an important reminder of the totality of events that constituted the actual Fourth Crusade. However, because the misconception of limiting the Fourth Crusade to the Venice expedition is so prevalent, it is necessary to demonstrate how even the activities of the "notorious minority" should still be considered a Crusade.

Ecclesiastical authority initiated the Fourth Crusade, and representatives of that authority remained with the army and gave sanction to its activities, however grudgingly, until the operation came to an end in April 1204. Innocent III appealed for Crusade participants as early as the summer of 1198 to fight Muslim forces on the Syrian front with the hope of ultimately reclaiming Jerusalem. Those who eventually went on Crusade, whether they left from Venice or from other ports, did so at his urging, expecting to receive an indulgence in return for the fulfillment of their vow of service. Thus, by the summer of 1202 there is no question that this Crusade was in motion because all the elements—ecclesiastical approval, religious motivation, war for the reclamation of lost Christian territory, vow of participation, and indulgence— were present.

While Innocent devoted himself on a strategic level to the daunting task of raising sufficient troops and funds for his Crusade, he did not become directly involved in the tactical planning of the operation. In retrospect this decision was undoubtedly a mistake, for in his absence others took the initiative in mapping out the specifics of the expedition. Among the crusaders at Venice were a small number of high-ranking knights and Venetian merchants who privately questioned the wisdom of launching a direct attack on Syria and instead secretly began to plan a more indirect route to Jerusalem. Capture Egypt first, they reasoned, and Jerusalem would fall more easily into Christian hands. Without control of the important power base of Egypt, any Muslim counterattack would necessarily falter, and Jerusalem would thus be secured. As French chronicler Geoffrey of Villehardouin, one of the key eyewitnesses to the Crusade, makes clear, Innocent was not privy to this discussion of strategy and was informed only after the final decision to attack Egypt had been made. Villehardouin's claim is reliable since he was a participant in the secret meetings of this inner circle of crusading leaders. Likewise, when these same leaders soon after agreed to adjust the plans and to attack the Christian city of Zara on the Dalmatian coast as a prelude to the Crusade, Villehardouin is clear that Innocent again was not a party to the decision.

Detail of a fresco of Pope Innocent III, organizer of the Fourth Crusade, from a monastery at Subiaco, Italy

FOURTH CRUSADE

When the Pope learned of this new plan, he expressly condemned it and threatened to excommunicate anyone who would participate in what he viewed as an unjust attack against fellow Christians. Had the expedition ended with the sack of Zara (November 1202), it would be difficult to argue that it constituted a Crusade. The army had not fought any ostensible enemies of the Church, and instead of enjoying ecclesiastical approval and earning the spiritual reward of the indulgence, it had incurred ecclesiastical censure and won the grave sentence of excommunication.

Innocent, however, was determined to see his plans for recovery of the Holy Land realized, and so when word came that the army was preparing to head east once more, he agreed to rescind the sentence of excommunication, although not for the Venetian merchantmen, whom he ultimately blamed for compelling the army to attack Zara. The Crusade, one might say, was back on. Yet, given the now obvious disposition of some of the key leaders of the expedition, Innocent was not so naive as to trust that such a brazen violation of the spirit of crusading would not happen again, so he expressly forbade these Crusaders from attacking any other Christians. Once more his warnings would be ignored.

This time the leadership of the Crusade was distracted by the prospect of becoming involved in a dynastic struggle in Constantinople. As Villehardouin reports, these leaders argued that this new diversion truly coincided with the spirit of crusading because it promised to bring help to a fellow Christian, Alexius IV Angelus, so that he could reclaim his rightful position as Byzantine emperor. It also promised, they argued further, to make the eventual offensive against the Muslims more effective, for in repayment of their services the rightful Byzantine emperor, once restored to power, would give extensive support to the Crusader army. How much the leaders really believed in these altruistic arguments is questionable. Their real interests seemed to be far more mundane, namely securing personal riches from the diversion rather than performing acts of charity. Far more important, however, was what the soldiers believed, for they represented the vast majority of the Crusade, while the leaders were but a handful of individuals. The sources reveal that the army eventually bought into the high-sounding moral justifications that the leaders pitched to them, but not without much initial resistance.

By the spring of 1203 not only had the mood of Innocent soured toward this part of his crusading operation, so too had the dispositions of the rank and file of the army sailing with the Venetians. Dissent and outright desertion, which began at Zara, now threatened to end the expedition altogether. Only through sheer guile, and

significant intimidation as well, did the leaders convince the core of the army to remain together and to make the temporary diversion to Constantinople before pressing on to Syria. Resorting to moral and religious justifications, these leaders argued that it was an act of Christian love and justice to help restore an unjustly deposed Christian emperor to his throne. On the other hand, they also threatened that the army would never get to Syria if its members refused to go along with the diversionary scheme, for the Venetians would deny them the use of their ships. Since the Fourth Crusade was a completely seaborne operation, this was no idle threat, because these ships represented the only means of transport to the East. Because the desire to fight in the Holy Land was so strong, as was the fear of not being able to fulfill their vows, the majority of soldiers reluctantly agreed to follow along with the wishes of their leaders. While not pleased with the proposed alteration in plans, the ranking ecclesiastical members of the army realized that they could do little to prevent it, and so they also acquiesced to the plan with the hope of later being able to use their influence to get the Crusade back on course.

At this point, although such a change of plans clearly ran counter to Innocent's express wishes, the revision still called for the army to sail for Syria once the dynastic problems in Constantinople were favorably resolved. Because Crusade leaders threatened to terminate the expedition if the diversion was prevented, rank-and-file soldiers, along with their ecclesiastical representatives, felt compelled to go along with the scheme. Otherwise, there would be absolutely no hope in fulfilling the vows they had taken and in carrying out Innocent's charge of bringing relief to the Holy Land. Thus, without this traditional crusading spirit that pervaded the vast majority of soldiers, the leadership would have had nothing with which to manipulate them, and so an attack on Constantinople would almost undoubtedly not have occurred.

The proposed temporary diversion to Constantinople turned into a nine-month operation akin in some ways to a military siege. What began as an effort to depose an unjust usurper of the Byzantine throne unraveled into open warfare between Greek and Latin forces. By the time the dust settled in May 1204, the crusading army possessed the imperial city and was poised to crown a Latin emperor of Byzantium, to divide up the empire among Western magnates, and to forcibly reunite the Eastern and Western Churches under papal authority. Innocent's dismay at the diversion momentarily turned to joy when the first reports reached him concerning the changed situation in Byzantium. Although he vehemently had opposed the operation, he thought the resulting consequences seemed providential. The two Churches had once more been reunited, while the initial reaction from the Islamic world was one of grave consternation at the prospect of Western forces now based permanently so close to Syria. Innocent's happiness, however, would not last. As more detailed reports filtered in, Innocent realized the violent attack and subsequent division of the empire under what was seen by the Greeks as foreign occupation would ultimately undermine the two great goals of his pontificate. News that his papal legate Peter of Saint-Marcel had commuted the vows of all members of the army meant that, Muslim fears notwithstanding, there would be no relief brought to the Holy Land, for without vows to fulfill, there was no incentive for soldiers to travel to the Syrian front. In effect the commutation officially ended the Crusade. Also, when it became clear that the reconciliation of the Churches had been brought about by mere force of arms, Innocent realized the union, based as it was on compulsion and growing resentment, would not endure. With the great hopes of his pontificate now in ruins, Innocent once more angrily denounced what the army had done. Yet, it could not be reversed, and so Innocent's anger finally turned to resignation to make the best of what he saw as a bad turn of events.

The Pope's anger and disapproval, however, should not be viewed as invalidating the Fourth Crusade as a crusading operation. While he was clearly displeased with the Venetian part of the enterprise, he also realized that the real blame for the diversion rested with the secular leaders of the Crusade, whom he repeatedly singled out for censure. He was well aware that the rank-and-file members and the ecclesiastical representatives had been coerced into following along, believing that this action was the only way to insure final passage to Syria and so to fulfill their vows. Thus, apart from the actions and motives of the leadership, all elements of a true crusading enterprise were still present in this operation. The original expedition, although not the diversion, had been initiated by papal decree. Soldiers took vows to participate in the hope of receiving the spiritual reward of the indulgence. The army ultimately acquiesced to the diversion and subsequent attack on Constantinople based on religious and moral justifications and on the belief that the leadership would thus guarantee passage to Syria. Finally, the papal legate, in his capacity as vicar for the Pope in his personal absence from the army, commuted the vows of the Crusaders after the conquest of Constantinople. Although Innocent later had serious misgivings when he heard what his legate had done, it was too late to reverse what was in effect an ecclesiastical sanctioning of the attack by his own spokesman.

INTO THE HANDS OF GOD

Chronicler of and participant in the Fourth Crusade, Geoffrey de Villehardouin describes the appeal of deposed Byzantine ruler Alexius IV Angelus for the help of the Crusaders to recapture Constantinople:

A fortnight after came to Zara the Marquis Boniface of Montferrat, who had not yet joined, and Matthew of Montmorency, and Peter of Bracieux, and many another man of note. And after another fortnight came also the envoys from Germany, sent by King Philip and the heir of Constantinople. Then the barons, and the Doge of Venice assembled in a palace where the Doge was lodged. And the envoys addressed them and said: "Lords, King Philip sends us to you, as does also the brother of the king's wife, the son of the emperor of Constantinople.

"'Lords,' says the king, 'I will send you the brother of my wife; and I commit him into the hands of God— may He keep him from death!—and into your hands. And because you have fared forth for God, and for right, and for justice, therefore you are bound, in so far as you are able, to restore to their own inheritance those who have been unrighteously despoiled. And my wife's brother will make with you the best terms ever offered to any people, and give you the most puissant help for the recovery of the land oversea.

"'And first, if God grant that you restore him to his inheritance, he will place the whole empire of Roumania in obedience to Rome, from which it has long been separated. Further, he knows that you have spent of your substance, and that you are poor, and he will give you 200,000 marks of silver, and food for all those of the host, both small and great. And he, of his own person, will go with you into the land of Babylon, or, if you hold that that will be better, send thither 10,000 men, at his own charges. And this service he will perform for one year. And all the days of his life he will maintain, at his own charges, five hundred knights in the land oversea to guard that land.'

"Lords, we have full power," said the envoys, "to conclude this agreement, if you are willing to conclude it on your parts. And be it known to you, that so favourable an agreement has never before been offered to any one; and that he that would refuse it can have but small desire of glory and conquest."

The barons and the Doge said they would talk this over; and a parliament was called for the morrow. When all were assembled, the matter was laid before them.

Source: "On What Conditions Alexius Proposes to Obtain the Help of the Crusaders for the Conquest of Constantinople," Geoffrey de Villehardouin, De la Conqueste de Constantinople par les Barons Francois associez aux Venitiens, l'an 1204 (1204), in Villehardouin and De Joinville, Memoirs of the Crusades, translated and edited by Frank Marzials (London: Dent, 1908), pp. 22–23.

FOURTH CRUSADE

Thus, while the Fourth Crusade should not be viewed as a typical Crusade, its aberrant elements should not disqualify it from being ranked with other such endeavors. The majority of participants had taken the cross with sufficient religious motivation and followed through with their commitment in the way that they felt would provide, under the unusual circumstances, the best opportunity for fulfilling their vows. Only those responsible for orchestrating the diversion of the Crusade, first to Zara and then to Constantinople, should be viewed as not fulfilling their vows.

–CHRISTOPHER LIBERTINI,
SUFFOLK UNIVERSITY

Viewpoint:
No. Once the Fourth Crusade was diverted from its proclaimed objective, it ceased to be a legitimate Crusade.

Over the last decades of the twentieth century, Crusade historiography experienced great leaps that fundamentally altered the perception of the movement in both general and specific terms. Many of these gains suggest that the traditional "numeration" of the Crusades is arbitrary at best and extremely deceptive and misleading at worst. Traditionally speaking, Crusades have been numbered "One" through "Five," corresponding to the five major expeditions that the papacy launched to the Holy Land from the late eleventh to the mid thirteenth centuries. This standard view also incorporated some addenda Crusades labeled by descriptive modifiers rather than numbers: the "Peoples' Crusade" (1096), the "Crusades of St. Louis" (1248-1254, 1269-1272), the "Albigensian Crusade" (1209-1229), and so on. Recent scholarship, however, has added many smaller Crusades, such as the "Crusade of 1101," the "Crusade of 1128," and the "Mongol Crusades" (1240s). The French historian Jean Richard has even referred to the "Crusade of Frederick II," which was usually seen as an odd postscript to the Fifth Crusade (1217-1229), as the "Sixth Crusade" in his recent survey of the movement, *The Crusades, c. 1071-c. 1291* (1999). The number of Crusades has increased, and, short of inventing some sort of decimal system to make the reality beneath the conventional construct clear, one is saddled with an inherently faulty numerical system. But one's understanding of the breadth and complexity of the movement still groans beneath the weight of this burden and will most likely continue to do so.

Many Crusades have been added to the conventional paradigm, but none have been deleted. Surely to do so, even with considerable justification, would introduce more confusion than clarity to discussing the Crusades by upsetting a commonly recognized numerical sequence. Still, if some "real crusades" did not make the official cut for the traditional roster, it is entirely possible that a "pseudo-crusade" might have slipped into it. If there was ever a prime candidate for the latter scenario, it was the so-called Fourth Crusade (1202-1204).

The Fourth Crusade began as a recognizable Crusade, but it was hijacked by the Venetians during its departure—probably in collusion with the Swabians. Rather than providing promised support to the Holy Land, the Crusade became a tool of naked Venetian economic ambition and dynastic intrigue that ended in the sack and partition of the hopelessly enfeebled Byzantine Empire (1204). Fruitful analysis of the relationship of the Fourth Crusade to the movement as a whole inevitably drags one into that academic quagmire dubbed the "what were the crusades?" question. The traditionalist-pluralist debate has no relevance to defining or categorizing the Fourth Crusade; traditionalists would say that its goal made it a Crusade, and pluralists, citing its organization if nothing else, would agree. Regarding the Fourth Crusade, the question of definition needs to be recast: If an expedition promoted and launched as a Crusade had its destination rerouted so far off course that participants could not fulfill their sworn vows, then can it really be considered a Crusade? Even if it is considered as such, was it one worthy enough to lay claim to a "number" of its own when so many other Crusades, which fit the definition much better, are reduced to numerical filler?

Even the most cursory examination of the evidence reveals that many of the protagonists came to question the venture of which they were part. Crusading armies were always, both before and after the Fourth Crusade, tidal in nature. Contingents ebbed and eddied in accordance with the localized and fragmented logic governing Crusade recruitment rather than flowing in accordance with a universal timetable. The Fourth Crusade, however, has the singular distinction of "desertion" being a general norm rather than a series of isolated incidents for the duration of its course. Desertions from the Fourth Crusade, moreover, were not produced by the garden-variety motives present in other Crusades. Men did not break or defer their oaths simply because their wives were having babies or cousins were moving in on an inheritance. Most of the men who deserted the Fourth Crusade did so because they personally felt that the expedition was no longer a Crusade. Deserters unable to figure this reality out on their own had it spelled out for them by the papacy through the thunderous condemnations that roared throughout the Adriatic and rippled across the Mediterranean. There was something patently absurd about running the risk of excommunication for participating in a venture initially designed to reward participants with the remission of sins.

A quick glance, then, would seem to reveal justifiable grounds for reducing the Fourth Crusade to a Crusade in name only: the majority of participants felt it went wrong and voted with their feet, while the papacy, at least during the campaign, felt the same way. If this renunciation was both the long and short of it, one could chalk up the misnomer "Fourth Crusade" to an early categorical mistake perpetuated by academic inertia. Yet, paradoxical as it may seem, the men who "deserted" the Crusade offer the strongest evidence in favor of it being a Crusade.

The "neglected majority" argument holds that the general perception of the Fourth Crusade has been shaped by the well-documented activities of a relatively small group of men (the notorious minority) who not only departed from Venice but also remained with this particular host through the Zara campaign and all the way to the conquest of Constantinople. This focus would be the equivalent of measuring the conduct of a modern battalion based upon the behavior of one deviant platoon. If one adds up the Crusaders who originally departed from other ports and those who deserted the main body in progress, it amounts to a tidy sum of men—more, in fact, than the number of men who ultimately laid siege to Constantinople. Furthermore, the argument goes, these other Crusaders were leery of not fulfilling their vows and thus formed separate contingents to discharge their obligations. Since the main narrative accounts of the Fourth Crusade focused exclusively on the Venetian contingent, the record is deceptively lopsided. The "neglected majority" was thus the silent majority that had no eloquent spokesman such as Geoffrey de Villehardouin to record its deeds. Rather than illicitly dividing an empire, they did their duty stoically and then returned to relatively quiet lives back in western Europe.

Lopsided evidence, however, is something entirely distinct from a virtual lack of it. The "silent majority" theory rests almost exclusively on argument from silence and suppositions. If a neglected majority of Crusaders in fact appeared in the Holy Land to fulfill their vow, in contradistinction to the dubious events unfolding in Constantinople, it certainly would have shown up in the historical record, whether the participants had an accomplished publicist

or not. The only testimonial that gives some voice to this argument is that penned by chronicler Ernoul-Bernard, who simply states that some Crusaders arrived in Palestine in 1203, but they found little to do since a Christian-Muslim truce was still active. They seem to have thrown themselves into local Christian disputes and then set sail for home in the autumn of 1204. Rather than providing evidence for the visible nucleus of a forgotten rival Crusade, Ernoul-Bernard's testimony suggests that a wayward contingent of Crusaders, traveling on their own, arrived in the Holy Land only to find that there was no Crusade to speak of. After traveling such a distance they took the grand tour, medieval style, and returned home.

There probably existed many sworn Crusaders who would have liked to participate in a parallel Crusade that actually intended to hit its target. Crusaders departing from different ports would not have had their goals mutated by the chaos that led to the "Zara Crusade," and those Crusaders who became disgusted with the Venetian enterprise might well have wanted to fulfill their original vow if an opportunity presented itself. But everything that is known about Crusader armies indicates that such military operations were precarious even with the best leadership that the medieval world could offer. Fringe Crusade contingents, fragmented and isolated, would have been aimless and ineffective; men of the time surely would have realized this fact. Rather than positing the existence of something as grandiose as a Crusade that left no real written record, one should consider a more realistic scenario: those who made it to the Holy Land acted as armed pilgrims but not necessarily as participants on the sort of "armed pilgrimage" that constituted a recognizable Crusade to the East, and that many of those who "deserted" probably realized (correctly) that the Crusade was dead in the water and returned home before additional physical and financial suffering occurred.

The actions of the "notorious minority," on the other hand, are fairly clear. One could also label them the "reluctant minority" since they only acquiesced to the diversions out of sheer desperation to get the Crusade off the ground. Caught in an intricate web of circumstances—territorial and trade disputes, dynastic ambitions, and financial difficulties—they conducted a raid on the port city of Zara as a sort of "payment in kind" for passage provided by Venice. Pope Innocent III was outraged and applied the brakes to the Crusade immediately (how else can one view the excommunication of a Crusade army?). Not wanting the Crusade to completely unravel, the Pope was open to granting second chances, but he was ignored again and the result was the sack of Constantinople.

The idea of a neglected majority that redeemed the mess that the Fourth Crusade degenerated into is a comfortingly romantic one, but the reality was much more crass. This majority was probably neglected by contemporaries because the men ceased to be participants. Rather than providing proof that a real Crusade took place, they bear testimony to the fact that most of the participants did not see the diversion to Constantinople as a Crusade and opted not to feed the fiction. Nor did the Pope until, making the best of the situation, he eased his mind by convincing himself—at least temporarily—that union between the Eastern and Western Churches had been achieved through a dark serendipity. The notorious minority represents all that was left of the Crusade, and thus stands alone as the only legitimate measure of the Crusade's status or achievements. They did not receive that hallmark of crusading activity—the indulgence. It comes as no surprise that when Innocent was organizing his second expedition to the East, the Fifth Crusade, he reminded the Venetians that they still had not fulfilled their vows for the Fourth Crusade. This device was no mere rhetorical ploy to secure their participation. Their vows had not been fulfilled because,

strictly speaking, no Crusade took place during the years designated as the Fourth Crusade.

–TODD MARX, CONCORD, NEW HAMPSHIRE

References

Charles M. Brand, *Byzantium Confronts the West, 1180–1204* (Cambridge, Mass.: Harvard University Press, 1968).

John Godfrey, *1204: The Unholy Crusade* (Oxford & New York: Oxford University Press, 1980).

Donald E. Queller, *The Fourth Crusade: The Conquest of Constantinople, 1201–1204* (Philadelphia: University of Pennsylvania Press, 1977).

Queller, "The Fourth Crusade: The Neglected Majority," *Speculum,* 49 (1974): 441–465.

Queller and Gerald Day, "Some Arguments in Defense of the Venetians on the Fourth Crusade," *American Historical Review,* 81 (1976): 717–737.

Jean Richard, *The Crusades, c. 1071–c. 1291,* translated by Jean Birrell (Cambridge & New York: Cambridge University Press, 1999).

GREGORY VII

Was Gregory VII the founder of the crusading movement?

Viewpoint: Yes. Gregory VII's plan for an expedition to the Middle East as well as his approach to holy war against rival Christian powers marks the beginning of the crusading movement.

Viewpoint: No. Gregory VII's proposals for holy war were qualitatively different from crusading. He did not view a Crusade as an armed pilgrimage, and he did not promise any spiritual rewards.

Gregory VII was one of the most controversial popes of the Middle Ages. His pontificate aimed at nothing less than restructuring the order of the Christian world. From the rubble of the old Carolingian order—one that posited the emperor as the ultimate head and guardian of Christendom—Gregory proffered a new view of Christian society and spent the entirety of his turbulent career trying to make it a reality. The "Gregorian Reform" sought to establish the papacy, in its role as the earthly representative of St. Peter, as the rightful head of the Christian world. Secular rulers, particularly German king Henry IV, saw this move as a direct attack on their temporal and spiritual authority. The debate on investiture had tremendous implications for royal government. High-ranking ecclesiastical figures played prominent administrative roles in royal government, and "investing" them with their office was an important prerogative for rulers. Furthermore, kings such as Henry saw themselves as divinely appointed guardians of the Christian world. Gregory's challenge was a spiritual impeachment that would essentially remove the sacerdotal dimensions of royal authority.

In his bid to tame secular rulers and bring them under papal authority, Gregory and his supporters revolutionized Christian concepts of warfare. Previous popes had included spiritual benefits in fighting for papal objectives, but such activities were sporadic. In trying to justify their clashes with secular rulers, the Gregorians forged a coherent doctrine of Christian warfare that outlined spiritual compensation. The main function of the warrior class was to fight for the papacy. In essence, the proposal laid the foundations for the laity to become the "vassals of St. Peter." Most of the energy and effort of the Gregorian party was focused on Christian opponents, but in 1074 Gregory proposed an expedition against the Seljuk Turks in the East to assist the Byzantines and liberate them from oppression by infidels. The responses to Gregory's summonses were virtually nonexistent.

Gregory was a crucial figure in the development of the crusading movement. Yet, his proposed expedition defies simple categorization. The plan contained many features of crusading but lacked important (some would say definitive) ones. Was Gregory's plan a "crusade"? If the expedition was carried out, would it have been a genuine crusade, a "protocrusade," or a kindred-but-distinct form of holy war? He hoped to liberate Christians, yet full remission of sins for the warriors was not promised. Pushing on to Jerusalem was a possibility for participants, but the expedition was not billed as a pilgrimage. Once again, the problems associated with defining a crusade complicate an important issue in the origins and development of the movement.

**Viewpoint:
Yes. Gregory VII's plan for an expedition to the Middle East as well as his approach to holy war against rival Christian powers marks the beginning of the crusading movement.**

Few historiographical changes have exhibited such an about-face as the transition from the positivist to postmodernist approach. For decades the tradition of Rankian positivism (that objective historical truths exist) received a vigorous challenge from historians who based their methodology in a more literary cast of mind. What was thought and said became just as—some would argue more—important as what "really was the case." If reality exists, they argued, it is overrated, while "perceptions" of it are undervalued. The idea of "historical truth" (for example, that something concrete happened and can be given an equally concrete description and explanation) was partially crushed beneath the weight of the "it's all an imperfect reconstruction that has no solid grounding in reality" school of thought. Historians who have a distaste for new fashions (or fads) tend to see this debate as a latter-day sophism (the great-grandfather, if you will, of all "-isms"). Twentieth-century French historian Michel Foucault's long shadow, some contend, oppressed historical inquiry with the deep-seated and quixotic need to target "author" and "discourse." Others believe that Foucault and like-minded scholars have done a great service to scholarship by underscoring the overwhelming importance of language and discursive reformulation and reinterpretation. Since its main sources are texts, history itself is a text and is thus governed by literary conventions. History, in other words, is just as much the product of "authors" describing events as the agents who brought about the actions themselves.

The effect that this postmodern approach has had on crusade historiography can be amply demonstrated through two prime examples. Christopher Tyerman, in *The Invention of the Crusades* (1998), argues that the Crusades (as the term is understood) did not exist for most of the twelfth century. The Third Crusade (1189–1192) was the real "first crusade" from an institutional perspective. Before this period there was no solid line of demarcation between pilgrimage and what posterity now calls a Crusade. The word "crusade" (of relatively modern origin) produced an optical illusion of sorts; anachronistically, it was a concept born in the late twelfth century that was projected back upon its early ancestors. "Discourse" thus produced a perceptual, but not

actual, reality. A second example can be gleaned from Jonathan Riley-Smith's magisterial analysis, *The First Crusade and the Idea of Crusading* (1986). Tyerman and Riley-Smith are essentially in agreement that the "first crusaders" did not know that they were in fact Crusaders. Riley-Smith, however, argues that the idea of crusading was created shortly after the first expedition ended, primarily by the hand of three Benedictine clerics in northern France. These clerics were great "redactors" who reinterpreted the events with comfortable hindsight and invested them with a theological significance that the participants were by and large unaware of. Pope Urban II launched an expedition, but it fell to others to establish the concept of crusading. Other historians argue that crusading was a popular movement that was later harnessed, reinterpreted, and refined by ecclesiastical authors. Thus, the origins of crusading bear a striking resemblance to "three-card monte," the game in which the hand moves faster than the eye to conceal the identity of a card. Viewing the origin of crusading from this perspective is a useful tool.

Crusading certainly has a complex genealogy; assigning "paternity" to the movement is a daunting task. Ultimately, looking for "the author" of crusading will be in vain. In many ways, crusading was produced by a variety of time-specific events and ideas that collided under the right circumstances, produced sparks, and (surprisingly) ignited a "movement" that lasted for centuries. Thus, the "founder" of crusading was Western European society. If crusading can be likened to a text, then its author was "anonymous." So maybe Foucault, the veritable poster boy of postmodernism, was correct. In addition to emphasizing the "author" and "text" in historical analysis, Foucault also utilized what he styled as a conceptual "archaeology." Time, like earth, has layers that can be sifted through. A concept such as crusading, complex as it is, has foundational bedrock upon which it stands. The founder—the ultimate "author" of crusading— was Pope Gregory VII, a figure who frequently has the word "crusade" next to his name. Twenty years before the Council of Clermont (1095) Gregory proposed an expedition, which he would personally lead, to free the Eastern Christians from Muslim domination and then, if possible, push on to liberate Jerusalem. The quotation marks surrounding Gregory's proposed crusade mostly underscore the confusion that exists in defining crusades in general. It is not necessarily to remove the quotation marks from this often used phrase, nor should they be added when discussing Urban II (though it may well be warranted). What is important are the ultimate roots of a movement rather than the details of an institution (if one focuses on the creation of crusading as an institution, an excellent case could be made for Pope Innocent III). The roots of crusading can be found, however, in the pontificate of Gregory; if anyone can be dubbed the "founder" or "author" of crusading, it is he.

Riley-Smith described Urban's message at Clermont as "conventional in the sense that it was not unlike many put forward by Church reformers at the time." The novelty that Urban introduced was Jerusalem as the goal of the expedition, which explains why "the laity's response was far more positive than it had been to earlier summons of this sort." Some historians argue that this joining of military expedition and pilgrimage to Jerusalem was what gave birth to and defined crusading, and if anyone can be credited with forging the movement, it must be Urban. However, the First Crusade (1096–1102) was really the only expedition that proffered Jerusalem as its specific goal. Thus, Urban can be said only to have "initiated" the expedition that became the First Crusade (which certainly targeted Jerusalem but not the movement itself, which had multiple targets). So for the purposes of a "genealogy" of the movement, the goal of liberating Jerusalem cannot be considered the base or sine qua non. Urban's invention of the "armed pilgrimage" was rather the vehicle upon which a preexisting concept rode to actualization.

Carl Erdmann amply demonstrates in *The Origin of the Idea of Crusade* (1977) how Gregory significantly shifted the Christian concept of "spiritual warfare" to "physical warfare" by melding the personae of St. Peter and his earthly representative in the papacy. If popes were engaged in a physical conflict with their enemies, then so was St. Peter and, by association, Christ. Any papal war would then, by definition, be holy and draw upon the services of all true Christians. Historian I. S. Robinson described this transition as "revolutionary." Ecclesiastical critics of Gregory were quick to pounce on what they saw as a novelty. War in the spiritual Christian sense was peace and prayer; Gregory had created an abomination by making Christian warfare a synonym for what took place on the battlefield. There had been precedents for popes directing holy wars (for example, against Muslim and Norse raiders in the ninth century, or against the Normans in Italy and Muslims in Spain during the eleventh century) and even promising spiritual benefits in exchange for military service. The "standard of St. Peter" was increasingly assigned to armies that popes supported against their enemies. Yet, it was Gregory who energetically promoted a liberation of the Church from secular rulers and tried to institutionalize the concept of papally directed holy war. He transformed the pre-Gregorian episodic

Illumination of Pope Gregory VII (circa eleventh century)

(University Library, Leipzig)

history of papal warfare into a broad policy and a means for reformist ends.

The Investiture Controversy (1075–1077) was the crucible in which Gregory's views of holy war were forged. Most of Gregory's attention to papal holy war was directed at Christian secular opponents, primarily, but not only, against Henry IV of Germany. An exegetical think tank of sorts emerged at the court of the Countess Matilda of Tuscany, who was a great Gregorian sponsor and protector, that sifted through patristic authorities and particularly the work of St. Augustine to formulate a coherent doctrine of such holy war. The result was the argument that God could directly authorize and command men of arms to intervene in the world in his name. As Robinson has pointed out, the "sword of St. Peter," which usually referred to the use of spiritual sanctions, increasingly came to be a term signifying the use of military force. Gregory began referring to "knights of Christ" or "knights of St. Peter," who owed their spiritual lord a military service—one that was transferable to the lord's earthly vicar. Robinson and Riley-Smith both note that Gregory's view drew upon the long-established custom of saints having their interests physically protected by local warriors. Almost a century before Gregory's "knights of St. Peter" there was mention, for example, of the "knights of St. Martin," who physically defended their regional saint and cathedral. Gregory, though he certainly drew upon this tradition, did not slavishly mimic it. "The knights of St. Martin" reflected the localized, fragmented, and fractured nature of the pre-reform Church that tried to survive in a society violently bursting apart at the seams. Gregory's summons for aid was both qualitatively and quantitatively different than these local defensive associations: qualitatively, Peter was the saint upon whom Christ built his church and the saint who controlled the keys to heaven; quantitatively, he represented the universal, rather than a particular, Church and thus commanded a broader loyalty. Defending the interests of St. Peter was not rooted in local geography or conditions but rather in the communal interests of all who called themselves true Christians. Thus, his plea and the conceptual infrastructure supporting it were universal rather than particular, and they paved the way for a mass movement.

The most compelling argument against Gregory being the "founder" of crusading rests on the virtual nonexistence of a lay response to his summons. He opened the way for a mass movement but did not bring one into existence. If (a word historians are loathe to use) Gregory's call had received an enthusiastic response, then he most likely would be seen as the true founder of crusading. If his proposal succeeded, how else would posterity describe his military expedition designed to liberate Eastern Christians from Islamic domination, one that promised "eternal life" to its participants and proffered the possibility of driving on to and liberating Jerusalem, other than as a "crusade"? Granted, the concepts are not sharply delineated, but the main features (save the pilgrimage vow) appear to be in place. Gregory called upon all Christian soldiers to defend and pursue a universal Christian interest. Petrine authority, after all, had summoned a host to be hurled against Islam for the protection of Christians—an effort that would be rewarded with spiritual benefits. The reason this expedition is referred to in scholarship as a *crusade* (always italicized) is because it bears some (but not all) of the salient features of what now bears that name. The main rebuttals to Gregory's crucial role as "founder" can be divided into two main schools of thought (that frequently overlap). The first can be described as the "it was a fleeting and incoherent idea" school of thought. The second is the "if it was not a pilgrimage then it wasn't a crusade" line of reasoning. Both rebuttals have some substance, but when placed within the larger context, they buckle beneath the weight of evidence.

In a sense, Gregory's proposed expedition against Muslims was "fleeting" in that it lacked resilience. Gregory's proposal for this expedition

both began and ended in 1074. News of the massive Byzantine defeat at the Battle of Manzikert (1071) no doubt hit the Latin world with good timing and, absorbed as it was into the emotive environment surrounding the Investiture Controversy, was firmly incorporated into a preexisting paradigm of spiritual conflict. "Enemies of Christ" and "liberation," rubrics that enjoyed great currency in reforming circles, were permeable categories in such a climate, promoting conceptual and tangible mingling. Gregory intended to lead the expedition to relieve the East in person as its principal "commander and priest." Gregory's proposed expedition had coherence but was organized differently than Urban's Crusade twenty years later.

The charge of Gregory's "crusade" being "fleeting" has some truth, though the word choice is questionable. "Adaptable" seems a more fitting description. His primary objective was the liberation of the Church. Turkish oppression against Eastern Christians began a slow fade in importance as Gregory's clashes with Western secular powers intensified. The Pope's relationship with Philip I of France was rapidly deteriorating; Gregory was even considering the use of military force against him. By January 1075 Gregory was gathering facts to assess how much support he would receive from local French warriors if this papal-royal cold war turned hot. The following year the papal position became even more complex as the relationship between Gregory and Henry bottomed out. Henry, moreover, was to be the intended caretaker of Europe during Gregory's absence while leading his "crusade." Thus, Gregory's incipient crusade to the East was redirected against the more immediate threat posed by Christian rulers in Europe. It was in the attempt to recruit troops for his conflict with Henry that Gregory continued to construct the concept of crusading.

The "it wasn't a pilgrimage" argument has much more substance. The greatest difference between the proposed expeditions of Gregory and Urban was the latter's status as a formal penitential pilgrimage to Jerusalem (and naturally the respective responses to the proposals). Is pilgrimage to Jerusalem the sine qua non of "crusade"? The history of the movement would suggest not (even "traditionalists" do not insist on Jerusalem as "the" destination, but only the Holy Land, broadly speaking). The First Crusade, in fact, was the only Crusade that specifically targeted Jerusalem. Strictly speaking, transforming the "exception" into the "rule" can only breed confusion. Gregory's expedition, moreover, was aborted during its early development because of a rapidly declining political environment. It was quickly redirected toward more proximate (and thus more dangerous) opponents. Yet, when he focused his attention more cogently on the East (if only for one year) he mentioned Jerusalem, which had a specific spiritual appeal. It would be difficult to think of "going to Jerusalem" without thinking of "pilgrimage." Thus, the main difference between the two proposals is that one did not have sufficient time to unfold, while the other did, and the latter drew upon the experiences of its predecessor.

Time and experience were not the only significant differences between the "crusades" of Gregory and Urban. Both proposed expeditions were to give assistance to persecuted Christians, grant spiritual rewards to participants, and most likely conclude at the walls of the holy city of Jerusalem (the former probably, the latter definitely). Both, moreover, employed feudal concepts that urged the warrior aristocracy to perform as spiritual vassals to a more sublime lord. Organizationally speaking, however, these two "crusades" could not be more different. The chief difference does not lie in only one being a formal pilgrimage. Rather, it can be found in the respective roles that Gregory and Urban played. Gregory's crusading model made the pontiff the supreme "commander and priest" of the expedition, leading the "vassals of St. Peter." In other words, all participants would declare their allegiance to Gregory and the reform papacy by becoming "crusaders." Gregory's proposal demanded subordination of the laity to a universal and omnipotent papacy. The problem was that the warrior aristocracy could be (and often was) deeply pious while remaining suspicious of grandiose claims of Petrine authority. Urban's model was more subtle and stressed partnership rather than subordination. Having been born into the French warrior aristocracy, Urban had an intuitive understanding of the mind-set of the knightly class that Gregory lacked. Feudal service to Christ had greater (and less politically charged) appeal than service to St. Peter. Vassals of Henry responded to Urban's summons at Clermont, something that would be impossible to achieve for Gregory's organizational model. Warriors hostile to the reform papacy (such as Godfrey of Bouillon and his brother Baldwin of Boulogne) answered the call, as did men sympathetic to the reformist agenda, such as Raymond of St. Gilles.

Without doubt, Urban launched what is referred to as the First Crusade. Yet, the idea was already there, twenty years before Clermont, and its principal architect was Gregory. Urban certainly placed his stamp on the movement and, in Aristotelian parlance, served as the "efficient cause" that brought the theoretical movement into historical reality.

–MARK T. ABATE, WESTFIELD STATE COLLEGE

Viewpoint:
No. Gregory VII's proposals for holy war were qualitatively different from crusading. He did not view a Crusade as an armed pilgrimage, and he did not promise any spiritual rewards.

Carl Erdmann, in *The Origin of the Idea of Crusade* (1977), correctly observed that Gregory VII was more war-like than any pope before him. Prior to his papal election, the duties of the various offices that he held in the Roman Church familiarized the former Hildebrand with the business of war. Like many bishops of the eleventh century, the bishop of Rome was a territorial prince with troops to command and defensive fortifications to maintain. In a special way, his duties as archdeacon of the Roman Church involved Hildebrand in the military affairs of the *terra sancti Petri* (lands of St. Peter). Moreover, as H. E. J. Cowdrey has noted in *Pope Gregory VII, 1073–1085* (1998), in the course of his pontificate, Gregory frequently summoned princes and ordinary knights to the military service of St. Peter. Nevertheless, despite his obvious enthusiasm for holy war, one cannot single him out as the founding father or the first great theorist of the crusading movement. Admittedly, many individual elements of the idea of crusade are present in his correspondence. Still, many concepts were not new with Gregory, and he never brought them together in such a way as to rouse his contemporaries to action.

In the course of his pontificate, Gregory issued invitations to two kinds of holy war: a defensive war against non-Christians (for example, the Seljuk Turks) and a war against wayward Christians (such as Philip I of France and Henry IV of Germany). By and large, his interest in waging war against non-Christians was confined to 1074 and involved coming to the assistance of the Byzantine Empire, which was then hard-pressed by the assaults of the Seljuk Turks. At first glance the Eastern campaign that Gregory proposed bears a resemblance to what Pope Urban II advocated at the Council of Clermont (1095). Very likely, Gregory's proposal in some way influenced his successor's thinking. However, upon closer inspection, significant differences between these two proposals come to the fore.

Gregory seems to have first raised the prospect of a military expedition to the East in a letter of February 1074 to Count William of Upper Burgundy. Interestingly, Gregory's main purpose for writing to William was to find out if he would be willing to join a coalition army com-

EXCOMMUNICATION OF KING HENRY IV

In 1080 Pope Gregory VII, who was attempting to strengthen the power of the papacy and eliminate the authority of kings to invest local bishops, excommunicated his rival, German king Henry IV, for the second time:

Among them, especially, Henry whom they call king, son of Henry the emperor, did raise his heel against your church and strive, by casting me down, to subjugate it, having made a conspiracy with many ultramontane bishops. But your authority resisted and your power destroyed their pride. He, confounded and humbled, came to me in Lombardy and sought absolution from the bann. I seeing him humiliated, having received many promises from him concerning the bettering of his way of living, restored to him the communion. But only that; I did not reinstate him in his kingdom from which I had deposed him in a Roman synod, nor did I order that the fealty from which, in that synod, I have absolved all those who had sworn it to him, or were about to swear it, should be observed towards him. And my reason for not doing so was that I might do justice in the matter or arrange peace—as Henry himself, by an oath before two bishops, had promised me should be done—between him and the ultramontane bishops or princes who, being commanded to do so by your church, had resisted him. But the said ultramontane bishops and princes, hearing that he had not kept his promise to me, and, as it were, despairing of him, elected for themselves without my advice—ye are my witnesses—duke Rudolf as king. This king Rudolf hastily sent an envoy to intimate to me that he had been compelled to accept the helm of state but that he was ready to obey me in every way. And to make this the more credible, he has continued from that time to send me words to the same effect, adding also that he was ready to confirm what he had promised by giving his own son and the son of his faithful follower duke Bertald as hostages. Meanwhile Henry commenced to implore my aid against the said Rudolf. I answered that I would willingly grant it if I could hear the arguments on both sides so as to know whom justice most favoured. But he, thinking to conquer by his own strength, scorned my reply. But when he found that he could not do as he had hoped he sent to Rome two of his partisans, the bishops, namely, of Verdun and of Osnabruck, who asked me in a synod to do justice to him. This also the envoys of Rudolf pressed me to do. At length, by God's inspiration as I believe, I decreed in that synod that an assembly should take place beyond the mountains, where either peace should be established or it should be made known which side justice the most favoured. For I—as ye, my fathers and masters, can testify—have taken care up to this time to aid no party save the one on whose side justice should be found to be. And, thinking that the weaker side would wish the assembly not to take place, whereas justice would hold its own, I excommunicated and bound with the anathema the person of one—whether king, duke, bishop or ordinary man—who should by any means contrive to prevent the assembly from taking place. But the said Henry with his partisans, not fearing the danger from disobedience, which is the crime of idolatry, incurred the excommunication by impeding the assembly. And he bound himself with the chain of the anathema, causing a great multitude of Christians to be given over to death and of churches to be ruined, and rendering desolate almost the whole realm of the Germans. Therefore, trusting in the judgment and mercy of God and of his most holy mother the ever-virgin Mary, armed with your authority, I lay under excommunication and bind with the chains of the anathema the oft-mentioned Henry—the so-called king—and all his followers. And again, on the part of God Almighty and of yourselves, I deny to him the kingdom of the Germans and of Italy and I take away from him all royal power and dignity. And I forbid any Christian to obey him as king, and absolve from their oath all who have sworn or shall swear to him as ruler of the land. May this same Henry, moreover,—as well as his partisans,—be powerless in any war-like encounter and obtain no victory during his life. Whereas I grant and concede in your name that Rudolf, whom, as a mark of fidelity to ye, the Germans have chosen to be their king, may rule and defend the land of the Germans. To all of those who faithfully adhere to him I, trusting in your support, grant absolution of all their sins and your benediction in this life and the life to come. For as Henry, on account of his pride, disobedience and falseness, is justly cast down from his royal dignity, so to Rudolf, for his humility, obedience and truthfulness, the power and dignity of kingship are granted.

Source: *Ernest F. Henderson,* Select Historical Documents of the Middle Ages *(London: George Bell & Sons, 1910), pp. 388–391.*

posed of papal allies that could, if necessary, put on a show of force to dissuade the Norman prince, Robert Guiscard, from continuing his encroachment on papal lands. Once Guiscard was properly cowed by the show of strength, Gregory suggests that the faithful followers of St. Peter could then proceed to Constantinople to help the Byzantines.

Subsequently, in March of 1074, the Pope issued a broader appeal to Latin Christians to come to the aid of Eastern Christians, whom a "pagan" people were then slaughtering by the thousands. In a letter in December, Gregory informed Henry of the warm response to his earlier appeals for military aid for the Byzantines and of his own willingness to serve as the expedition's *dux* (commander) and pontifex (prelate). Gregory intimates that those who expressed a willingness to fight the "enemies of God" in the East raised the prospect of advancing all the way to Jerusalem. Gregory imagines that if such an expedition were to take place, Henry could serve as the custodian of the Roman Church during his absence. In a subsequent letter to Matilda of Tuscany, the Pope reveals his ardent desire to go overseas to bring relief to the Christians then being slaughtered by "pagans," and he asks for her aid and counsel for this project. He imagines that Henry's mother, the empress Agnes, will join the campaign and bring Matilda along with her.

Although Urban also seems to have emphasized the suffering of fellow Christians in his appeal at Clermont and held out the prospect of marching on Jerusalem, significant differences exist between Gregory's call for military aid for Byzantium in 1074 and the one made by Urban in 1095. First, Gregory did not employ the pilgrimage motif. What Gregory probably had in mind was not an armed pilgrimage but a military expedition modeled on Pope Leo IX's campaign of 1053 against the Normans in southern Italy. Second, and significantly, Gregory did not attach any specific reward to joining his campaign. Granted, at the conclusion of his letter to William, Gregory assures the count that he can expect a manifold reward from the chief of the apostles, Peter, and Paul, for coming to Italy and continuing from there to the East. Yet, he does not mention any spiritual rewards for helping the Eastern Christians in his general admonition of March 1074, nor does he do so in his messages to Henry and Matilda about this expedition. Apparently, in between these missives, the Pope sent another general admonition north of the Alps to invite followers to join his proposed campaign. Perhaps this, or other, as yet unknown, admonitions contained promises of specific spiritual rewards for aiding the Byzantines against the "pagans." As it stands, however, it does not seem that the Pope offered a specific reward for participating in this military campaign, which for several reasons never materialized.

Moreover, it would be a mistake to assume that Gregory saw Muslims only as enemies of Christianity. In 1076 the Pope sent an extraordinary letter to the emir of Mauritania, an-Nasir. Shortly before Gregory wrote to the emir, Latin-rite Christians of the Mauritanian town of Bougie had sent their bishop-elect, Servandus, to Rome for consecration. Apparently, an-Nasir had also petitioned Gregory for Servandus's consecration. The emir evidently sent gifts to the Pope, including many freed Christian slaves. Gregory's response is surprisingly warm in content and tone. In it, the Pope ascribes the emir's gestures to the inspiration of the common Creator of all men, whom both Christians and the emir's people worship and adore in their different ways. At the conclusion of his message, Gregory professes his sincere love and best wishes for the emir and prays that at the end of his earthly life the emir might come to rest in the bosom of Abraham. Although in other correspondence he writes quite negatively about the "Saracens," this letter demonstrates that, as on many other subjects, Gregory's thinking on Christian-Muslim relations lacked theoretical consistency.

As the history of his pontificate shows, Gregory was much more interested in seeing wayward Christians, especially European princes, reprimanded by the material sword of the faithful than Muslim emirs. For instance, in the fall of 1074, the Pope clashed with Philip over the despoiling of French pilgrims bound for Rome and of Italian merchants in France. In a 10 September 1074 letter to the French bishops, Gregory threatened that unless Philip amended his evil ways, the Pope would employ every means to have him stripped of his kingdom. Two months later, Gregory asked William VI of Aquitaine to pressure his king to accede to the papal demands. In January 1075 the Pope discreetly inquired of Abbot Hugh of Cluny about how many royal vassals would side with him in an armed conflict with Philip.

Like his plan to march against the Turks, the Pope's campaign against Philip never materialized. For whatever reason(s), Gregory backed away from his confrontation with the French king. Of course, his extended confrontation with Henry ended quite differently. In this struggle Gregory came the closest to calling a Crusade. As Cowdrey has noted, from 1077 to 1080, Gregory increasingly invested the German civil war between Henry and Duke Rudolph of Rheinfelden, which broke out in part because of the initial rift between the Pope and the king in 1076, with the trappings of a holy war. Gregory developed the notion that the righteous party would triumph, enjoy success in this life, and gain the remission of sins and blessings in the next life through the intercessions of Saints Peter and Paul. When in 1080 the Pope finally declared Rudolph the more righteous candidate for the German throne, he granted the duke's followers the forgiveness of their sins. In a March 1081 letter to his German allies, Gregory made the same offer to any magnate willing to enter the service of St. Peter against Henry.

One must bear in mind, however, that Gregory's actions were not entirely unprecedented in papal history. In the ninth century, Pope Leo IV promised eternal life to any warrior who died fighting the Arab marauders who were then harassing Rome. Likewise, in the same century, Pope John VIII made a similar promise to warriors who died fighting the Vikings. More significantly, in 1053, Pope Leo IX apparently absolved the sins of the troops that he led into battle against the Normans at Civitate.

In addition, unlike the indulgence offered to Crusaders by Urban at Clermont, Gregory's grant of absolution to Rudolph's men did not involve any kind of vow and was not connected in any way to the idea of pilgrimage. Rather, in his confrontations with both Philip and Henry, Gregory requested military aid, or a promise of future assistance, in the name of St. Peter. Gregory called upon the *fideles* (faithful vassals of St. Peter) for their military service. While Urban also infused his appeal at Clermont with feudal themes, it was much broader and was not specifically tied to service to the papacy. More important, perhaps, Urban did not ask his audience to take up arms against a Christian king.

Another significant problem with attributing the idea of Crusade to Gregory involves his own legislation on warfare. As Cowdrey has pointed out, Gregory never bothered to bring the Church's law concerning warfare into line with his own concept of righteous military service to St. Peter. In particular, the legislation of his November synod of 1078 and of his Lenten synod of 1080 retained the traditional notion that the military profession was inherently sinful. Furthermore, as late as 1080, Gregory required the bestowal of penances, along with the grant of absolution, on Guiscard and his troops, who were then embarking on a campaign to restore the Byzantine pretender, Michael VII, to power in Constantinople.

Of course, yet another major problem with crediting Gregory VII with the idea of crusading involves the very nature of the development of that concept. Recent scholarship, most especially that of Jonathan Riley-Smith in *The First Crusade and the Idea of Crusading* (1986), has made it increasingly clear that the notion had not crystallized even by the pontificate of Urban. Rather, the concept of crusade only began to form after the experience of what is termed the First Crusade (1096–1102) and after reflection upon that experience by its participants and by subsequent ecclesiastical authors. Thus, if one cannot fully credit Urban with founding the Crusades, how can one credit Gregory?

Undoubtedly, Gregory's pontificate acclimated people, especially knights and barons, to the idea of a papal call to arms. Moreover, his attempts to invest the military profession with a more religious spirit also undoubtedly contributed to the acceptance of the notion that a certain type of combat could be pleasing to God and spiritually efficacious. Nevertheless, one cannot ignore the major discrepancies between his invitations to holy war and those offered by Urban at Clermont. Perhaps the best indication of the discrepancy that existed lies in the response to those appeals. For, whereas Gregory's most vocal summons to holy war against Henry went largely ignored, the response to Urban's call greatly exceeded the Pope's expectations. Urban not only struck a different note from Gregory, he played a different tune.

–JOHN A. DEMPSEY, FRAMINGHAM STATE COLLEGE

References

H. E. J. Cowdrey, *Pope Gregory VII, 1073–1085* (Oxford: Clarendon Press / Oxford & New York: Oxford University Press, 1998).

Cowdrey, "Pope Gregory VII's 'Crusading' Plans of 1074," in *Outremer: Studies in the History of the Crusading Kingdom of Jerusalem Presented to Joshua Prawer*, edited by B. Z. Kedar, H. E. Mayer, and R. C. Smail (Jerusalem: Yad Izhak Ben-Zvi Institute, 1982).

Carl Erdmann, *The Origin of the Idea of Crusade*, translated by Marshall W. Baldwin and Walter Goffart (Princeton: Princeton University Press, 1977).

Jonathan Riley-Smith, *The First Crusade and the Idea of Crusading* (London: Athlone, 1986; Philadelphia: University of Pennsylvania Press, 1986).

I. S. Robinson, "Gregory VII and The Soldiers Of Christ," *History,* 58 (June 1973): 169–192.

Christopher Tyerman, *The Invention of the Crusades* (Toronto & Buffalo: University of Toronto Press, 1998).

INVENTING THE CRUSADES

Were there any genuine Crusades before the thirteenth century?

Viewpoint: Yes. Although not as clearly defined as in the thirteenth century, all the military expeditions to the East prior to this period were Crusades.

Viewpoint: No. Crusading was a concept that emerged in the early thirteenth century and has been projected by historians onto earlier periods.

In her classic 1974 article "The Tyranny of a Construct," E. A. R. Brown launched a frontal assault on the existence of medieval "feudalism" and by extension on how historians of the Middle Ages approach their subjects. What historians mean by feudalism (there was and is a panoply of definitions) was based on a concept forged by seventeenth-century lawyers, refined by Enlightenment philosophers, and codified by scholars and teachers in the nineteenth century. The article concluded with a veritable call to arms: "The tyrant feudalism must be declared once and for all deposed and its influence over students of the Middle Ages finally ended. Perhaps in its downfall it will carry with it those other obdurate isms—manorial, scholastic, and human—that have dominated for far too long the investigation of medieval life and thought." For a generation of historians confronting postmodernism and the impact that "discourse" has on mutating "reality," and for medieval historians who were already somewhat uncomfortable with the inconsistencies in understanding feudalism, Brown's short study had a profound impact.

Similar inconsistencies disturbed historians of the Crusades for some time. A decade before Brown's article was published, Hans Eberhard Mayer noted in *Geschichte der Kreuzzüge* (1965) that there was no solid or generally accepted definition of "crusade." Like "feudalism," "crusade" is a term of fairly modern origin that was not known to medieval people. Discrepancies between terms and realities did not produce a move to dethrone a conceptual tyrant among Crusade historians as it did among historians of feudalism (at least not at first). Rather than debating whether the word should be retained or scrapped, historians tried to forge more concise and clearly delineated definitions—traditionalists argued for the centrality of Jerusalem, while pluralists stressed papal authorization and the use of crusading apparatus. The picture that emerged was of a dynamic movement that expanded and was refined throughout the twelfth century and became systematized in the thirteenth. As Latin Europe became more sophisticated, complex, and mature, so did the crusading movement. This point was one that traditionalists and pluralists could firmly agree upon.

An entirely new venue was added in 1995 when Christopher Tyerman published "Were There Any Crusades in the Twelfth Century?" Heavily influence by Brown's article and the debate on the existence or nonexistence of feudalism that has raged ever since, Tyerman argued that until the late twelfth century, crusading was not a clear movement or institution but rather a nexus of fragmented concepts and customs. In his subsequent study, *The Invention of the Crusades* (1998), Tyerman expanded on his thesis and traced the thirteenth-century developments that led to the definition of crusading, as well as the historiographic tradition that from the sixteenth to the twentieth centuries established the modern concept of crusading. This process has constantly been re-creating or "reinventing" the concept of crusading, and it "has not ended yet."

Viewpoint:
Yes. Although not as clearly defined as in the thirteenth century, all the military expeditions to the East prior to this period were Crusades.

One of the challenges that all historians face is attempting to assign some starting or ending point for great movements in history. To ask questions such as "when did the ancient Classical world end" or "when did the Middle Ages begin" is to get some sense of the magnitude of the problem. Movements in history, even at the most revolutionary moments, tend to be evolutionary processes with long- and short-term causes that merge and blend with their effects, making definitive signs of a new beginning hard to discern. Because it is nearly impossible to fix these time markers with absolute accuracy, historians typically choose some reasonable, if somewhat arbitrary, date to act as a divider between eras. For example, 476 is often used by historians to date the fall of the Western Roman Empire and the end of the ancient Classical world because in that year the last true Roman, Romulus Augustulus, held the title of emperor in the West.

Of course, this date is not really a definitive marker but merely a convenient reference point that serves as a tool to help bring greater order and understanding to a jumble of historical events. Just as those who in 475 would not have sensed that they were living in the last full year of the ancient Classical world and would not have known at what precise point a new era in history dawned, so too historians—even with the benefit of time and perspective—seldom can so decisively distinguish clear dividing points of history. Indeed, some historians argue that for several decades or more prior to the fall of the nominal emperor Romulus Augustulus, the ancient Classical world had already in effect ended. Others scholars, such as Belgian historian Henri Pirenne, argue that the ancient Classical world soldiered on for a couple of centuries more and was only brought to a close by the conquests of Islam along the Mediterranean basin.

Regardless of which interpretation is closer to the true answer, the point here is that pivotal markers in history are typically hard to nail down. Yet, while this arrangement may be the prevailing situation, one of the clear exceptions to this general rule of historiography is the genesis of the crusading movement. While the end-

ing point may be hard to ascertain, there is no doubt as to when the movement began. In fact, it can be pinpointed not just down to a particular year or month but to an actual date, 27 November 1095, for on that day Pope Urban II made the first crusading appeal. It is ironic then that in recent years some historians, such as Christopher Tyerman, in *The Invention of the Crusades* (1998), have attempted to challenge this traditional date and argue for a later, more gradual beginning that only blossomed in the thirteenth century. While a bold and intriguing thesis, this historical interpretation is simply untrue and should not be allowed to confuse what is in reality one of the few undeniably clear starting points in history.

From one perspective there may seem to be some basis for this argument by Tyerman and others that there was no real crusading prior to the thirteenth century. It was only then, so the argument goes, that the Roman Church fleshed out the full theological significance and juridical justification for the indulgence, for without the concept of the "Treasury of Merits," defined by Hugh of St. Cher around 1230, the validity of the indulgence seemed dubious at best. Before the thirteenth century there was no uniform formulation of crusading rites and privileges, but such codifications became standardized after 1200. Also lacking prior to the thirteenth century was a standardized approach to preaching the Crusades and a centrally controlled mechanism for assigning preachers to this task. Yet, by 1230 it was clearly the prerogative of the Friar Minors to carry out this role, and their sermons revealed a level of sophistication and intellectual training that all previous Crusade sermons lacked. Furthermore, crusading only reached its full application during the thirteenth century, when it became a clear mechanism for the Church to deal with various enemies, both heretical and political, besides the traditional Islamic foe in Spain and the Near East. Finally, only in this century did elements such as vow redemptions, popular participation, clerical taxation, and rationalized financing methods become standardized practices.

An observer in 1291 might come to the realization, as Tyerman has, that something was visibly different with crusading at this point in history than when it first started in 1095, and such an observation would be accurate to some degree. By 1291, the traditional date given for the end point of the Holy Land crusading era, the Crusades had achieved a degree of recognizable structures, organization, definitions, and

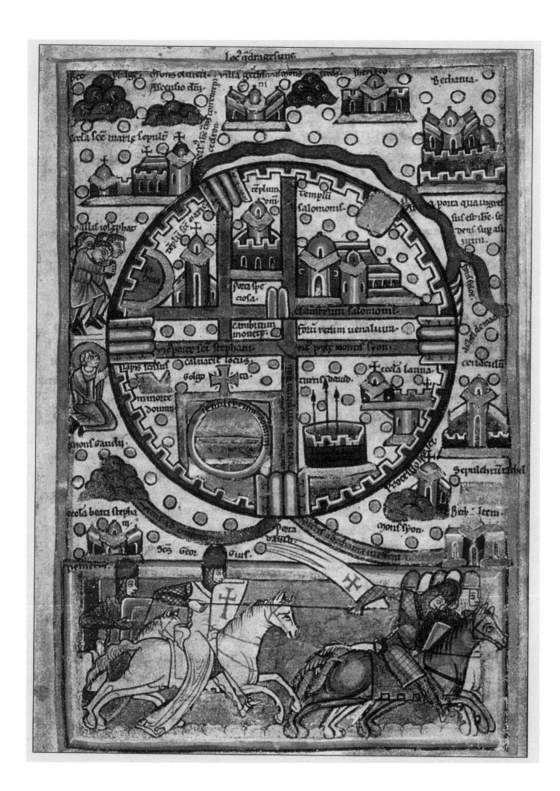

Twelfth-century map of Jerusalem showing Saint George and Crusader knights pursuing defeated Muslims

(Koninklijke Bibliotheek, The Hague)

terminology that had simply been lacking in its first years. That same observer would, however, unlike Tyerman, probably explain the differences in terms of the natural growth and development of an institution rather than to see it as a new institution altogether. While much had changed, the core ideas of crusading remained essentially unchanged, thus providing a vital continuity. Because of this continuity, the 1291 observer would not have seen himself involved in a movement that was distinct from that which his more distant predecessors of First Crusade (1096–

1102) fame had participated in, but rather he would have believed that he was sharing in the same institution and was part of a common brotherhood. His sense would be far more accurate on this point than that of the twenty-first-century historian.

Crusading from its first moments was clearly not just some new holy war that arose at the end of the eleventh century but something that went radically beyond any previous historical experience of religious warfare. It was a truly unique phenomenon in its most essential elements. The project that Pope Urban II first unveiled on 27 November at the Council of Clermont (1095) was clearly revolutionary, so much so that contemporaries who were present at his speech or heard accounts of it later claim that the audience spontaneously responded to his appeal with an enthusiastic chant, "*Deus lo volt* (God wills it)!" The subsequent actions of those first Crusaders, as they came to grips with nearly three years of unimaginable hardships and privations, also reveal that they were clearly not just traditional religious warriors. What set them apart was that Urban had fashioned them under the mold of the traditional penitential pilgrim. In his mind the venture that he proposed was to be a pilgrimage to visit—and therefore, as a necessary prerequisite, to capture—Jerusalem. The only difference was that these pilgrims would for the first time need to be armed and to be prepared to fight a war along the way. All future Crusaders, whether in the twelfth century or thirteenth century or beyond, also saw themselves as pilgrims. For example, Robert of Clari, one of the eyewitness chroniclers of the Fourth Crusade (1202-1204), continued to use the term "pilgrim" to refer to Crusaders, along with some newer terms that had by then become available to specifically describe a participant, such as: *crucesignatus, croisie, crozada,* and *croisier.* These terms proved to be more descriptive than the traditional words for Crusaders and crusading, such as *peregrinus, peregrinatio,* and *iter.* Canon law of the thirteenth century used these newer terms to more precisely distinguish Crusaders from normal pilgrims. Yet, this practice was not a new statement on the part of Church law—that Crusaders were no longer viewed as pilgrims—but rather an attempt to accurately define what type of pilgrim a Crusader was. In this scholastic age, when definitions and explications became the rage in intellectual circles, it is hardly surprising that Church law developed more-precise terms and definitions that would apply only to Crusaders, who were, after all, always understood to be special types of pilgrims, rather than to continue to use generic terms relating to all pilgrims.

At Clermont the mechanism for volunteering for a Crusade was established for the first time. Those who wanted to join the campaign had to make a vow to complete the journey and had to take a cross made of cloth as a symbol of that promise. This Crusader vow was in fact identical to one a pilgrim made before setting off on a pilgrimage. Here again Urban was clearly revealing his image of what a Crusader was to be. Not accidentally, all future Crusaders continued this practice of making a vow. While it is true that this process was elaborated in the thirteenth century—such as standardizing the practice of vow redemptions or developing more formulaic methods of taking the cross—it also remains true

that there was an essential continuity. Whether in 1095 or 1295, a person had to make the vow and accept the symbol of the cross in order to be recognized as having committed himself to be a Crusader. The exact words or ceremonies used in these rituals might have changed, but the basic concept remained.

This continuity was also the case with a centerpiece of Urban's call to arms at Clermont. To entice soldiers to volunteer for this extremely perilous mission, Urban offered them for their services a reward of unparalleled value, the indulgence, which was viewed as a guarantee of eternal salvation. The indulgence thereafter became one of the crucial hallmarks of a crusading campaign. Later popes reworked the indulgence so that by the thirteenth century it was possible to earn either a partial or a plenary indulgence, depending on the level of sacrifice a person made in supporting the crusading cause. For example, it was possible to earn part of an indulgence just for donating money to a Crusade or by supplying a soldier to take one's place on the campaign, whereas in Urban's original conception only actual participants who completed the journey or died along the way could merit this reward. Also, Urban never provided a theological or theoretical justification for the indulgence: it would take nearly a century and a half for that concept finally to be worked out by the Roman Church. Yet, the indulgence, however well or ill defined, remained at the core of all crusading campaigns, starting with the First Crusade.

Finally, the call to Crusade and its stated objective remained a function determined by the ecclesiastical hierarchy. Only a prelate, and more precisely, the pope, had the authority to launch a legitimate Crusade, a tradition that began with Urban at Clermont. While it might have served the interests of political leaders in Europe at various times to use the mechanism of crusading to raise troops for some politically ambitious purpose, such efforts never really materialized because contemporaries recognized only a papal prerogative in launching a Crusade, for the pope was the ultimate keeper of the indulgence, which was the key attraction for participants. At the same time, the papacy alone set the strategic goal for crusading. In 1095 that goal was singular in nature—the capture of Jerusalem. By the thirteenth century there had occurred an expansion in the strategic aims of the movement beyond a narrow focus on the fate of Jerusalem. The threat of heresy in southern France and the danger of imperial control of central Italy also became legitimate and urgent concerns of the papacy. Yet, even though future popes, such as Innocent III, found it necessary to expand the reach of crusading into new areas and for new purposes, the fact remained that the cause of crusading remained an ecclesiastical prerogative. Whether launched to reclaim lost Christian lands or to defeat enemies of the Church, crusading retained its fundamental nature as a program instituted and guided by papal directive for ecclesiastical needs. In this more general sense, nothing had changed from what began in 1095.

In the end, it is beyond doubt that crusading was a firmly established phenomenon well before the thirteenth century. All the characteristics that made crusading a distinctive form of religious or holy warfare were established when Urban made the first crusading appeal. Those characteristics included the pilgrimage framework, the vow, the indulgence, and papal direction and guidance. While Tyerman and others are correct in noticing that thirteenth-century Crusades were not identical replicas of their earlier counterparts, they are badly mistaken in the conclusion that they draw. It was not a new movement that suddenly arose in the thirteenth century—marked by novel levels of standardization and formalization in such areas as preaching, recruitment, and rites—but rather the same movement that merely grew in sophistication as it matured.

–CHRISTOPHER LIBERTINI,
SUFFOLK UNIVERSITY

Viewpoint:
No. Crusading was a concept that emerged in the early thirteenth century and has been projected by historians onto earlier periods.

Historians frequently refer to a "crusading movement" that officially began in 1095. This movement is often categorized, implicitly or explicitly, along the lines of the stages of human life (a method of categorization that was dear to medieval men). "Conception" occurred shortly after the defeat of the Byzantine army at Manzikert (1071); "labor" began at the Council of Piacenza (March 1095), when Byzantine ambassadors asked Pope Urban II for assistance against the Turks, and the Pope responded favorably; and "delivery" took place at the Council of Clermont (27 November 1095). The First Crusade (1096–1102) was the movement's "infancy," while its extended "adolescence" spanned the twelfth century, with the Third Crusade (1189–1192) marking the general end of its acute growing pains. "Maturity" was reached during the early thirteenth century and "middle age" set in after the

fall of Acre (1291). There is no general agreement whatsoever on the moment of "death."

In recent years the case has been growing for reshuffling these stages and the years to which they correspond. Some historians, most notably Christopher Tyerman, in *The Invention of the Crusades* (1998), have called for viewing the twelfth century as an extended gestational period for crusading. If there is something one can call the "crusading movement," its true birth pangs began in the late twelfth century rather than the late eleventh century. This theory has made considerable sense out of many of the anomalies that historians of the Crusades have recognized for some time, chief among these being the great difficulty in distinguishing between pilgrimage and Crusade during the first century of the "movement." Rather than constituting a sui generis activity with clear ideological and institutional features, the "Crusades" of the twelfth century were really inchoate bundles of religious, cultural, and political views combined with general dispositions and habits. The "articulation" and "refinement" of crusading in the twelfth century were ad hoc and unsystematic responses to challenges facing, and changes within, western European society. Tyerman argued that the Crusades were not born in the late eleventh century but rather were "invented" sometime between the late twelfth and early thirteenth century.

When Urban proclaimed the First Crusade, he introduced the novel concept of an armed pilgrimage. That this joining of the sword and the pilgrim's satchel was new is beyond dispute. But almost everything else about the venture he launched was far from new; in fact, most of it was quite old. Killing pagans for the glory of God was a venerable enterprise, one that can be seen clearly in Charlemagne's Saxon wars (772–777). In fact, this practice even predates these conflicts, which clashed with the sensibilities of many ecclesiastical theorists, who were not sure that killing in war was not homicide. Yet, lay practice outran canonical theory, and warfare was often considered a sanctified act. Papal practice did as well, and it was not unheard for a pope to give an army he supported (or one that supported him) the "banner of St. Peter." Pilgrimage was also a venerable tradition; it was a path, though arduous, by which people could purge themselves of previous sins through the greatest act of penance. Urban certainly joined holy war and pilgrimage, but there is no evidence that he intended to create a new tradition. Charter evidence suggests that none of the first Crusaders saw the expedition in terms other than pilgrimage. It was not even made clear that they had to accompany an army or even fight. Modern historians fail in attempts to make a distinction between Crusaders and pilgrims because, at least at the time, there were no "crusaders." There were only pilgrims who might or might not carry arms—might or might not fight the infidel.

As Jonathan Riley-Smith has so eloquently demonstrated in *The First Crusade and the Idea of Crusading* (1987), the First Crusade was given its significance after the fact. The horrendous conditions of the expedition, combined with the stunning victory that could only be "divine" in origin, prompted a trend to give the armed pilgrimage greater meaning. Three French monks took raw accounts of the expedition, reworked them, and created a grand chapter in Christian providential history. One of these men, French monk Guibert of Nogent, described the expedition as a means by which the bellicose class made a strong bid for salvation without becoming monks. Certainly these chroniclers began an ecclesiastical tradition, but it was far from the beginning of a defined movement. They were strands of thought that shared similar features but defined, and instituted, little. The warrior class began its own traditions, primarily though the *chansons des geste* (songs of deeds). The *chansons* fused the martial valor of the warrior class with deep expressions of religious piety; they transformed the armed pilgrimages that are called Crusades into a unique path of salvation that God created and reserved for them. Most likely there was cross-fertilization between these two new traditions, the ecclesiastical and the lay, that served as sieves for older traditions. Still, they were two distinct trends: the monastic one that saw the expedition as an important chapter in the universal history of divine providence, and the warrior aristocracy one that saw the armed pilgrimage as a palatable method for achieving personal redemption.

Rather than referring to a twelfth-century crusading movement, one should speak of a twelfth-century bundle of traditions that lacked cohesion and definition. For at least the first half of the twelfth century one could "take the cross" not only without papal sanction but also without ecclesiastical initiative. The phrase "movement" implies some degree of uniformity, but what actually took place was fragmented and prismatic. "Crusades" occurred without reference to the papacy; popes sometimes called for "crusades" and found little response. Bands of armed pilgrims appeared in the East and provided the fledgling colonies with military muscle, while participants visited sacred sites. In 1107 Norwegian king Sigurd I ran the gamut of holy war throughout the Mediterranean: striking Muslims in Spain, attacking Sicily, and then assisting with the conquest of Sidon in the East. Antioch prince

Bohemond I recruited men for a strike against Muslims and Byzantines and used the language of spiritually compensated holy war in the first decade of the twelfth century. His project was nearly identical to what ultimately became the Fourth Crusade (1202–1204). Thus, even the concept of armed pilgrimage seems of limited value in describing the explosion of holy war that took place, even though it serves as a better definition than any other. The Venetian fleet that secured Tyre (1124) had "taken the cross" and carried the banner of St. Peter that the Pope had given them, but the men did not seem to be pilgrims, and they raided the Byzantine Empire en route. The First Lateran Council (1123) issued decrees that protected Crusaders going to the East or Spain and made provisions for sanctions against those who took the vow and then procrastinated. A council at Pisa (1135) decided that those who fought papal enemies within Europe would receive the same indulgence as those who fought in the East. But there was no vow, and it certainly was no pilgrimage, even if the venture was seen as penitential. During recruitment for the Second Crusade (1147–1149) Pope Eugenius III did not want German monarch Conrad III to take the cross to the East; the Pope had Conrad's German troops earmarked for deployment against his enemies in Italy. French monk Bernard of Clairvaux, however, managed to secure the German monarch's participation in the expedition to the East despite the Pope's plan. Other examples could be compiled, but the conclusion would remain the same: conceptual chaos.

Spiritually meritorious holy war is the only common denominator found in this supposed "adolescence of a movement." "Crusaders" departing for the East often had no connection to the papacy. Fulk of Anjou, for example, fought and prayed his way through the East, though he was no pilgrim but rather an aspiring potentate. Spiritual compensation was offered for a variety of military expeditions against Muslims and Greeks in the East, against the Moors in Spain, against papal enemies in Italy, and during the Second Crusade against pagans in eastern Europe. Indulgences were granted to men who never took a vow. Crosses stood alongside papal banners. Charters did not distinguish between Crusaders and pilgrims. There was an utter lack of a contemporary term that describes what was going on; rather, a plethora of labels was used for Crusaders—*iter, via, expeditio, passagium, profectio, peregrinatio,* and so on. These scattered but interrelated terms had currency throughout the Crusades, but it is only in the thirteenth century that they really begin to be used side by side with ones that suggest formalization and consistency: *crucesignatus, crosier,* and *crozada*—words that finally led philosophers of the

ANSWERING FOR EDESSA

In response to the fall of Edessa (1144), Pope Eugenius III issued a call to arms:

We exhort therefore all of you in God, we ask and command, and, for the remission of sins enjoin: that those who are of God, and, above all, the greater men and the nobles do manfully gird themselves; and that you strive so to oppose the multitude of the infidels, who rejoice at the time in a victory gained over us, and so to defend the oriental church—freed from their tyranny by so great an outpouring of the blood of your fathers, as we have said,—and to snatch many thousands of your captive brothers from their hands,—that the dignity of the Christian name may be increased in your time, and that your valour which is praised throughout the whole world, may remain intact and unshaken. May that good Matthias be an example to you, who, to preserve the laws of his fathers, did not in the least doubt to expose himself with his sons and relations to death, and to leave whatever he possessed in the world; and who at length, by the help of the divine aid, after many labours however, did, as well as his progeny, manfully triumph over his enemies.

We, moreover, providing with paternal solicitude for your tranquillity and for the destitution of that same church, do grant and confirm by the authority conceded to us of God, to those who by the promptings of devotion do decide to undertake and to carry through so holy and so necessary a work and labour, that remission of sins which our aforesaid predecessor pope Urban did institute; and do decree that their wives and sons, their goods also and possessions shall remain under the protection of our selves and of the archbishops, bishops and other prelates of the church of God. By the apostolic authority, moreover, we forbid that, in the case of any thing, which they possessed in peace, when they took the cross, any suit be brought hereafter until most certain news has been obtained concerning their return or their death. Moreover since those who war for the Lord should by no means prepare themselves with precious garments, nor with provision for their personal appearance, nor with dogs or hawks, other things which portend licentiousness: we exhort your prudence in the Lord that those who have decided to undertake so holy a work shall not strive after these things, but shall show zeal and diligence with all their strength in the matter of arms, horses and other things with which they may fight the infidels. But those who are oppressed by debt and begin so holy a journey with a pure heart, shall not pay interest for the time past, and if they or others for them are bound by an oath or pledge in the matter of interest, we absolve them by apostolic authority. It is allowed to them also when their relations, being warned, or the lords to whose fee they belong, are either unwilling or unable to advance them the money, to freely pledge without any reclamation, their lands or other possessions to churches, or ecclesiastical persons, or to any other of the faithful. According to the institution of our aforesaid predecessor, by the authority of almighty God and by that of St. Peter the chief of the apostles, conceded to us by God, we grant such remission and absolution of sins, that he who shall devoutly begin so sacred a journey and shall accomplish it, or shall die during it, shall obtain absolution for all his sins which with a humble and contrite heart he shall confess, and shall receive the fruit of eternal retribution from the Remunerator of all.

Source: *Doeberl,* Monumenta Germania Selecta, 4, *translated by Ernest F. Henderson in* Select Historical Documents of the Middle Ages *(London: George Bell & Sons, 1910), pp. 333–336.*

Enlightenment to coin the term "crusade" and its cognates. In short, there was a great deal of activity but no consistency, and even fewer signs of an organized movement. There were traditions related to the First Crusade, as well as habitual—even ritualized—activities rooted firmly in them. But traditions do not constitute a movement—at least until they are seized, reworked, refined, and forged into something controlled and consistent. The evidence suggests that this transformation did not happen until the thirteenth century.

Italian ecclesiastic Gratian's *Decretum Gratiani* (circa 1140) goes far in underscoring the lack of a real concept of crusading. A canon jurist, Gratian attempted to synthesize, define, and codify church law. "Issue 23" examined war and violence but did not, even casually, address what today is called crusading, which should come as no surprise, since crusading as modern historians understand it did not exist in the mid twelfth century. What it addressed, however, was a panoply of traditions: holy war, papally authorized uses of violence, and military force as a means to a spiritual end. War was not necessarily sinful, particularly when sanctioned by Christ's earthly representative (the pope). Gratian's focus, however, was the suppression of heresy rather than the conquest of infidels through military force. Half a century after the Council of Clermont (1095), and dead center in what is referred to as the adolescence of the movement, crusading did not even warrant an honorable mention in the *Decretum*. Gratian's work was important to crusading; but rather than refining the concept in the twelfth century, it provided material for building it in the thirteenth.

Pope Eugenius III's encyclical *Quantum praedecessores* (1145) is no longer considered the crusading breakthrough that it once was, even if it was important as a model for later encyclicals. Today it seems more like bootstrapping—the pulling together of concepts expressed in previous papal letters and decrees that promoted the still-inchoate idea of redemptive papal military expeditions. Of greater importance is that it began a pattern that was the central dynamic in the elaboration of crusading traditions. Developments in crusading concepts followed a fairly consistent and recurring chain of events: disaster in the East, Eastern requests for assistance, popes responding by drawing upon floating traditions rather than firmly fixed institutions. The fall of Edessa (1144) was the nominal impetus for the Second Crusade. That this Crusade became a three-front war in the East, Spain, and eastern Europe is often seen as the broad application of an already well-defined institution. A more likely explanation is that the Second Crusade expanded because of the amorphous and promiscuous nature of holy-war traditions upon which it was based. Fortunately for the history of the Crusades, these activities were not yet a movement; if they were, the disastrous failure of the Second Crusade might well have ended it. The fact that it was not yet clearly defined gave it a certain resiliency. The finger-pointing and criticisms that emerged had no institution to target, and, consequently, disillusionment had no firm fixture to attach itself to. The crusading movement survived the disastrous and humiliating failure of the Second Crusade because, realistically speaking, it did not yet exist and thus could not be dealt any deathblow.

The Battle of the Horns of Hattin (1187) and the subsequent loss of Jerusalem (1187) drastically changed this situation. Traditions spawned by the First Crusade now had a solid core that attracted and drew them together. The need to recover Jerusalem brought everything back to the heart of the Clermont message (1095), and the failure to recover it and achieve hegemony in the Holy Land was the first active agent in transforming a bundle of traditions into a coherent movement. The shift can be seen in both the lay and papal reactions to Hattin. *Crucesignatus* became a widely used term as armed pilgrims came to redefine themselves. Pope Gregory VIII's *Audita tremendi* (1187) marked a decisive break with the mild recapitulations of Eugenius that preceded it. The Third Crusade, which traditionally has been seen as a sort of high-water mark for the movement, was in fact its beginning, its true infancy. Conditions changed drastically, and the network of traditions responded by beginning to solidify. All that was required to transform it into a full fledged "movement" was a man who could codify, implement, define, and authorize the conceptual compost pile that had existed for a century—someone who could take the inchoate and amorphous concepts of the past century and forge it into an institution. That it was the first great lawyer-pope, Innocent III, arguably the most powerful and influential pontiff of the Middle Ages, who accomplished this act is to be expected. What is today considered "crusading" was not created by the scholarly think tank created by Pope Gregory VII or the sermon delivered by Urban II at Clermont. It was the invention of an early-thirteenth-century lawyer-pope who responded to the changes of the late twelfth century, seized upon a primordial blend of ideas and habits, and forged them into a tool that would promote Petrine Supremacy.

Exaggerating the influence of Innocent III on the "crusading movement" is almost impossible. He was no innovator but rather an energetic and committed compiler of traditions that he transformed into concrete laws and institutions. His bull *Quia major* (1213) and the Church decree issued under his leadership, *ad liberandam* (1215), mark the most decisive shifts in crusading history. That they were formulated in the wake of a crusading disaster (the collapse of the Fourth Crusade) and on the eve of a finer and more organized expedition (the Fifth Crusade, 1217–1229) provides a solid line of demarcation between amorphous tradition and a newly emerging movement with coherency. With it one finds a host of systematic refinements that shape what is considered "crusading" to the modern mind: primacy of papal proclamation, centrality of the plenary indulgence, formalization (but not necessarily standardization) of the vow, mechanisms for broad taxation to underwrite expeditions, prorated redemptions in exchange for support, the professionalization of preaching and recruitment, and the crusading bull constituting ground zero in the growing differentiation of Crusaders and garden-variety pilgrims. Innocent made crusading and Crusaders distinct categories that differed from other forms of holy war and holy warriors. What he forged was the closest concept one can find in the Middle Ages to the modern view of "total war," a tag that defines crusading better than any other at one's disposal. Total Christian commitment directed by pan-European authorization, or at least the appearance of such, was virtually pulled from the sleeve of the most powerful and enterprising pope of the Middle Ages, Innocent III.

These issues may seem academic to many readers, and with good reason: study and interpretation of the past is academic. Eighteenth-century French writer Voltaire once said that history is little more than the collective tricks that the past plays on the present. This definition is an overstatement of the case, but the claim has some validity. Piercing presumptions, both those of contemporaries and of modern interpreters, is essential in the task of making sense out of the past and understanding the causative roots of movements and institutions. More often than not, the past is much more complicated than posterity is willing to admit. English physicist and mathematician Isaac Newton, for example, did not "discover" gravity by sitting beneath an apple tree. It was his long wrestling matches with what German astronomer Johannes Kepler left unfinished and the intricate equations that took place in his tightly shuttered home that produced the model of the solar system. Urban II's founding a movement or Holy Roman Emperor Frederick I's (Barbarossa) being a full-fledged Crusader are similar oversimplifications. Sometimes origins of great things can be mundane, and nothing is more mundane than a bureaucratic pope with a strong legal background creating what romantic soldiers and passionate clerics should have created much earlier. The Crusades were a movement, but one that began in the late twelfth and early thirteenth centuries. Crusading was certainly revolutionary. But as twentieth-century historian of science Alexandre Koyre said about the Scientific Revolution, well-prepared revolutions are still revolutions that signify radical breaks. The "crusading revolution" of the early thirteenth century was such a well-prepared revolution, and many modern historians confuse the long period of preparation with the revolution itself. If there was a "founder" of crusading, it

was not Urban II or Peter the Hermit. It was a man named Lothario dei Conti di Segni (Innocent III), whose grandparents were most likely children when Urban II made his concluding remarks at the Council of Clermont.

–MARK T. ABATE,
WESTFIELD STATE COLLEGE

References

E. A. R. Brown, "The Tyranny of a Construct," *American Historical Review*, 79 (1974): 1063–1088.

James A. Brundage, *The Crusades, Holy War, and Canon Law* (Aldershot, U.K.: Variorum / Brookfield, Vt.: Gower, 1991).

Brundage, *Medieval Canon Law and the Crusader* (Madison: University of Wisconsin Press, 1969).

J. Gilchrist, "The Erdman Thesis and the Canon Law," in *Crusade and Settlement: Papers Read at the First Conference of the Society for the Study of the Crusades and the Latin East and Presented to R. C. Smail,* edited by Peter W. Edbury (Cardiff: University College Cardiff Press, 1985).

Hans Eberhard Mayer, *Geschichte der Kreuzzüge* (Stuttgart: Kohlhammer, 1965), translated as *The Crusades,* by John Gillingham, second edition (Oxford & New York: Oxford University Press, 1988).

Maureen Purcell, *Papal Crusading Policy: The Chief Instruments of Papal Crusading Policy and Crusade to the Holy Land from the Final Loss of Jerusalem to the Fall of Acre 1244–1291* (Leiden, Netherlands: Brill, 1975).

Jonathan Riley-Smith, *The First Crusade and the Idea of Crusading* (London: Athlone, 1987; Philadelphia: University of Pennsylvania Press, 1987).

Christopher Tyerman, *The Invention of the Crusades* (Toronto & Buffalo: University of Toronto Press, 1998).

INVENTING THE CRUSADES

JIHAD

Did the Islamic concept of jihad (just war) influence the development of Crusade ideology?

Viewpoint: Yes. The notion of jihad influenced the Crusaders' sense of mission, urgency, and spiritual reward.

Viewpoint: No. The crusading movement was purely Christian in origin and development.

In Arabic, *jihad* has multiple meanings, and the term is often misconstrued by people in the West. The root meaning of jihad is "to struggle," and this fight can take many forms. There can be the spiritual jihad, in which the individual Muslim must confront his or her own personal demons; the moral jihad, in which society struggles against poverty or illiteracy; or the military jihad, in which the faithful fight a defensive war against aggressive forces that invade or threaten the Islamic world. An Islamic jihad and a Christian Crusade share many similarities, but the chief difference can be found in the respective views toward war exhibited by the founders of the two religions. As one historian has written, the difference between Jesus and Muhammad is much like that between Indian nationalist leader Mohandas Gandhi and South African leader Nelson Mandela. Both had similar goals—they just pursued them by different means.

Muhammad's view of the military jihad was shaped by the experiences of the early *umma* (community). Certainly, armed struggle against the infidel became a sacred task, but it was not expected to be offensive; rather, it must be defensive. Jihad was to battle oppression, but once the oppressors initiated violence, the followers of Allah were to prosecute the armed struggle energetically and relentlessly. Although Muhammad did not seek bloodshed, he certainly would not shy away from it to serve Allah's will. Islam, one of the most moral of world religions (despite common Western stereotypes), used jihad as an instrument of charity as well. A great imperative of jihad was to protect the weak who could not fend for themselves physically. After the Prophet's death (632) the jihad continued and, particularly after contact with Zoroastrian doctrines of holy war that followed the conquest of Persia, became more complex and codified. The origins of Christian Crusade cannot be pinpointed with the precision of jihad. Yet, the two struggles share many similarities, including the recovery of lost property, defensive war against infidel aggression, spiritual rewards for participants, and the concept of warfare as a means of distributing charity.

These similarities have caused some historians to look at the concept of jihad more closely when examining the origins of the Crusades. Did jihad make an essential contribution to the rise of the crusading mentality? Some scholars claim that Christians came into contact with jihad while facing Muslims on the battlefield, absorbed the concept, and then recreated it in Christian terms. Others have cited parallel development, rather than cultural borrowing, to explain the similarities. Both religions shared militant values of the Old Testament; both were originally tribal societies that experienced blood feuds; and both were monotheistic, Abrahamic institutions that stressed protection of the weak. Given the similar values, views, and historical experiences, it is understandable how each religion arrived at comparable forms of holy war independently. At the heart of the debate is how to explain similar institutions in different civilizations. Is cultural borrowing the rule rather than the exception? Or is parallel development a more convincing explanation?

Viewpoint:
Yes. The notion of jihad influenced the Crusaders' sense of mission, urgency, and spiritual reward.

In order to claim that the Muslim notion of jihad (just war), which is the duty to fight nonbelievers, influenced the medieval Christian concept of Crusade, one need not adduce explicit quotations by Christian Crusader ideologues, such as French monk St. Bernard of Clairvaux, to the effect that Christians fought the Muslims with their own ammunition. Such an admission would have been the equivalent of praising the motives of Islam, which is the last thing a Christian could expect his leaders to do. It is important to understand that not all historical puzzles can be resolved with one document. In some cases, such as this one, explicit documentation would not be expected to be available for study. The resolution of the problem, therefore, rests on the logic of the situation and the presence in Christian society of all of the resources necessary to produce the conclusion proposed.

In Islamic theology, holy war is both a duty incumbent upon the believer and a collective obligation imposed on a community of Muslims when confronted with unbelief. Jihad cannot be applied against unbelievers, Christians or Jews, if they submit to Islam (in which case they may accept the status of "protected peoples" accorded to the "people of the book"—those who share with Muslims the same "Abrahamic" scriptural traditions—and practice their religion undisturbed). If they do not submit, however, the Muslim community is obligated to war against them.

With respect to holy war as a duty, there is no doubt that, as early as the mid ninth century Christians understood that they had a similar, if not identical, duty to defeat the enemies of God. That obligation was advanced by Spanish priest Eulogius of Cordoba in his defense of the voluntary martyrdoms of Christians in the 850s. All of the elements of jihad are present: the apostles had been ordered to fight the enemies of God, believers must "prepare to make war against unbelievers," and those who die are martyrs whose sins will be forgiven.

In the twelfth and thirteenth centuries, under the direction of French monks, the idea of Crusade was applied to the *Reconquista* (reconquest of Spain) in political language grafted onto a preexisting notion of the imperative to defeat the infidel, a notion that was influenced by a Christianized conception of jihad. At a decisive moment during the Battle of Las Navas de Tolosa (1212), just when Castilian king Alfonso VIII feared for his life, an archbishop fighting with him said, "Sire, if you go to your death, all who die with you will go up with you into paradise." The notion of holy war as a means for attaining eternal reward in Heaven is highly developed in Islamic theology and is not attributable to the Christian theological tradition. In the Qur'an, God promises great rewards and mercy to those who fight against unbelievers and especially to those who, in such battles, die as martyrs. These sentiments were echoed by medieval aristocratic writers such as Spanish prince Don Juan Manuel, who explained that the meaning of Christians having suffered at the hands of the Muslims was to create a context for a just war "so that those who should die in it, having fulfilled the commandments of the Holy Church, might be martyrs." He further argued that those who die fighting Muslims are preferred in salvation when compared to sinners who do not perish in combat against the Moors. The former are "true martyrs, and have no other pain to bear save that death which they take upon themselves." The notion of taking death upon oneself is an expression of the sense of duty that is a necessary component of jihad.

Alfonso's archbishop was a model of the armed religious warrior in Europe—fairly common in Spain, but uncommon elsewhere—where the traditional admonition by the Church against the bearing of arms by priests and monks was generally heeded. One outstanding feature of crusading in Spain was the adoption of the apostle St. James the Elder as a kind of patron of the *Reconquista*. Christian knights yelled "Santiago" when going into battle, just as Muslims invoked the name of Muhammad; this warrior, *Santiago Matamoros* (St. James the Moorslayer), allegedly made many miraculous interventions on the battlefield. On one occasion he appeared to King Ramiro I and said: "Our Lord Jesus Christ divided between all the other apostles . . . and me, all the other provinces of the earth, and to me alone he gave Spain for me to watch over and protect her from the hands of the enemies of the Faith. . . . And so that you may doubt nothing of this that I tell you, tomorrow

JIHAD

Illumination from a thirteenth-century Persian text of the 134 of Baghdad's standard bearers

(Bibliothèque Nationale, Paris)

will you see me go into battle." What distinguished crusading from other pious exhortations to battle for the faith is that it was explicitly authorized by God; the same is true of jihad, of course. Thus, in Spain, St. James, the opposite of Muhammad, was God's representative in a holy war against Islam.

The influence of jihad on the crusading spirit is just where Muslim influence should be validated. Of course, there were deeply held elements of Christian theology, tradition, and practice that could be marshaled to the support of the crusading project. However, at the level of commitment—of mission, urgency, and the certainty of reward—one can detect the influence of jihad as a reactive adaptation to Muslim behavior that Christian knights had observed on the battlefield. Why would the Christians not have emulated it? Not to have done so, not to have countered the Muslims precisely at the source of their religious zeal, not to have attempted to go them one better would have been to place themselves at a strategic disadvantage.

–THOMAS F. GLICK,
BOSTON UNIVERSITY

JIHAD

Viewpoint:
No. The crusading movement was purely Christian in origin and development.

The concept of just or holy war in the West developed organically from different cultural elements present in society prior to the First Crusade (1096–1102), including, but not limited to, the dichotomy between the pious penitent and the Gideon-like warrior; ideas of vengeance and duty that looked back to the kinship systems of barbarian Europe; renewed spiritual fervor, which included increased human agency; and the increased importance of pilgrimage in society. These elements, however, did not coalesce into a coherent ideology of holy war. The catalyst for the development of Crusade ideology was Pope Urban II's speech at the Council of Clermont (1095), wherein he harnessed these cultural trends and inflamed the spiritual passion of the warrior class by combining pilgrimage with revenge and reward. Although a perceived threat to Christendom was necessary to set this process into motion, the actual concept of Islamic jihad (just war) was not vital to the development of crusading ideology in the West.

The idea was ingrained in medieval culture, inherited from a combination of the concepts of Hebrew holy war and Roman "just war." Part of St. Augustine's vast legacy to the medieval world was his formulation of the Christian concept of war. He postulated that war was the consequence of and remedy to sin; it was waged against a group that had sinned against either man or God. The goal was the correction of sin, and in this way, war was a charity to sinners and was a way to avenge an injury, either to society or to God. The impetus in such cases had to be pure; the decision to fight was to be made by a just authority out of love and charity, not greed or lustful vengeance. This paradox of spiritual love and physical violence is also evident in the Pauline tradition. On one hand, the apostle taught that one must love his or her neighbor, forgive all sins, and be pacifistic toward enemies, of which the ideal Christian should technically have none. On the other hand, the warrior Gideon was idealized, his fervent defense of faith held up as an example to all. The tension between these two strains in Christian ideology was integral to the development of the concept of holy war in medieval Europe.

Christianity, which was ambivalent toward war, was brought into late-medieval Europe by saints, missionaries, monks, priests, and soldiers, where it was assimilated into a violent society that was based on kinship networks and blood feuds. A kinship network was composed of clans, each of which contained at its center a powerful extended family. Because of the war-like structure of tribal society, powerful clans attracted warriors from outside the family unit to help maintain dominance in their geographical area. Warriors not only brought bravery and weapons to the clan but also received protection in return for their services. In a society where a person outside of the clan structure was likely to perish, the value of this protection cannot be underestimated. Although membership could not prevent murder, it ensured that the murdered clansman would be avenged. Homicide was seen as damaging to the clan not only in terms of its physical prowess but also in terms of its honor. To be attacked was to be disrespected and challenged; no affront to the clan could go unpunished. Not all men within a clan were considered equal. In retaliation for the murder of their chief, warriors might kill ten of the opposing clan's men. Obviously, this system entailed great losses on all sides. In response to this bloodshed, the weregeld (blood-money) system was developed, in which a lost life was paid for with money instead of blood.

These concepts of blood feud, vengeance, and clan honor affected the way that barbarian converts to Christianity interpreted their new religion. They applied the earthly social structure with which they were familiar to their relationships with God the Father, God the Son, and the rest of the Christian world. Through their tribal filter, the barbarian converts saw God the Father as the greatest clan patriarch—their chief ancestor, who demanded service and respect from his subjects. In this same context, Jesus became the warrior chieftain, leader of the Christian clan's armies. By joining the Christian tribe, new converts received the protection of a powerful God and the promise of spiritual booty in the world to come. In return for these rewards, barbarian Christians were held by the same obligations that bound their contracts with the earthly clan: fidelity to their heavenly chieftains, protection of Christian clan property, and revenge upon any insult to the Christian faith. Although these were not teachings in any way sanctioned by the Church, they were deeply ingrained in barbarian culture. As the centuries passed and more elaborate social structures came into play, the basic concepts of loyalty, vengeance, and blood feud remained an integral part of medieval European culture and would play an integral role in the development of Crusade ideology in the eleventh century.

By the mid eleventh century, medieval European culture was experiencing intense cultural change, especially on the religious level. These changes directly impacted the development of

Crusade ideology. Institutional change came in the guise of Cluniac Reform, a movement concerned with purification of the Church that extended from the pontiff down to the members of the most remote monastery. Cluniac reformers sought to purify not only the institution of the Church from the intrusion of secular political power but also the clergy from accretions of improper behavior that had come to be accepted over a period of time. It was during this reform that celibacy became mandatory for all clergy; up until that point, sexual exploits by the priests were frowned upon, but not necessarily kept secret and certainly not strictly punished. Proponents of these reforms also sought to purify secular members of the Church as well. Monasticism was considered the ideal form of Christianity; cloistered men and women gave up the physical world in order to come into closer contact with the spiritual. Although they lived apart from society, they served the vital social role of praying for the masses. Not all men and women could become members of religious orders; nevertheless, the laity could be monasticized (made more pious) by increasing the spiritual dimensions of their lives. Reformers enjoined all Christians to submit to someone else's authority and to dedicate their every action to God. In this way all acts, no matter how trivial, became a form of prayer. Secular jobs became sacred ones; just as the cobbler became the cobbler of Christ, the knight became the knight of Christ. Because the knight's job was to kill the enemies of his lord, killing became, in essence, an act of faith.

Changes in penance and the rise of pilgrimage were also integral parts of the spiritual revival of the eleventh century. Medieval Christians went to confession with contrition in their hearts and confessed their sins. After they had performed a penitential act, the priest absolved them of their sins until the Day of Judgment, when Christ would mete out otherworldly punishments for earthly wrongdoings. During the eleventh century, however, the punishment aspect of confession changed. Penitents were no longer forced to wait helplessly for the punishment of God. Through penance on Earth, purgatory—and perhaps even hell—could be avoided in the afterlife. In this way medieval Christians gained the personal agency to change their spiritual destiny, and, in a way, to beat God to the punch by punishing themselves. Many men and women sought to reduce their heavenly debt while still on Earth through the penitential act of pilgrimage, which was considered an imitation of Christ, of his wandering and his Passion. A pilgrimage, then, was not only a form of penance but also a journey to God.

The meteoric rise of pilgrimage as an act of penance was concomitant with the increased

adoration of saints and their relics. Medieval Christians believed that, whether dead or alive, saints were God's agents on Earth. Although their bodies died, their souls remained active at the site of their burial—whether it be a tomb, altar, or reliquary casket. Saints were a gateway between Heaven and Earth; a supplicant was able to communicate his or her needs to the saint as intercessor and receive his or her wish from God. Visiting a saint's tomb, then, was a path to favor, which however, did not come without a price. A pilgrim not only endured the suffering of the journey in order to communicate with the saint but also brought offerings. This reciprocal relationship between supplicant and saint is reminiscent of the gift-giving culture of barbarian Europe. The exchange of gifts signified a type of tribal pact in which each party had certain obligations to the other. The saint mediated with God on behalf of the supplicant; the supplicant pledged to provide quality housing, sumptuous tapestries, candle wax, and so on for the saint. To neglect a saint's care was to invite his wrath, not only against the direct offender but also against all of those within the saint's jurisdiction. Great care was therefore taken to keep saints and their geographical surroundings pure and in good order.

The spiritual changes had a concerted impact on the development of the Christian concept of holy war. Cluniac Reform encouraged spiritual purity and vigor and transformed every member of society, even warriors, into vassals of Christ. Medieval Christians were encouraged to recognize their individual roles in the Christian drama that was playing out in Europe. Men and women had not only the agency to control their spiritual destinies through penance and pilgrimage but also the obligation to take part in the spiritual world that surrounded them. The act of pilgrimage and the cult of relics also reinforced the reciprocal relationships that medieval Christians felt with their God through his saints. The eleventh century, then, was a period of spiritual vibrance and determined, personal responsibility to God.

This cultural phenomena predated Urban II's call to Crusade at the Council of Clermont (1095). Nevertheless, each of them played a role in the concept of holy war that crystallized during the First Crusade. Urban's plan of action was accepted with such vigor because it drew upon powerful cultural concepts imbedded in medieval European society. Urban directly targeted French feudal warriors for the Crusade. He enjoined them to take up the cross and become true knights of God. In this way he followed the ideals of the Cluniac Reform and consecrated the

JIHAD

STRIVE HARD TO PLEASE GOD

In the aftermath of the First Crusade (1096–1102) Islamic scholar 'Ali ibn Tahir Al-Sulami wrote a treatise concerning the need for jihad (just war) against the Crusaders:

These are clear proofs from the Book (of God), the *sunna* and the consensus (of the Muslims) of the obligation (of going on) the *jihad* in sufficient numbers to their lands, and an illustration of its becoming one of the obligations on prominent persons in the countries mentioned, from the doctrines and formal legal opinions of jurisprudents. It is true and clear that the *jihad* against this group and their objective is incumbent on all who are capable and have no horrible illness or chronic malady, or blindness, or weakness from old age. As for those who are excluded from these, either rich or poor, having two parents, either owing a debt or owed a debt, they are obliged to go out to fight in this situation, and to set out to put an end to the fearful consequence of weakness and reticence. Now in particular, with the fewness of the enemy and the (far) distance of their support, the agreement of the lords of the people of these neighbouring countries and their making common cause . . .

Prepare—God have mercy on you—to strive hard at the imposition of this *jihad* and the obligation to defend your religion and your brotherhood (of Muslims) with aid and support. Take as (your) booty an expedition which God (who is exalted) has arranged for you without great effort or (even) the exertion of a cheek, which has come to you. Take it with the good fortune granted by God (who is praised) from nearby and this mundane world. You will gain it from a finest winner, and (will also gain) a glory of which the clothes (will) remain on you for many ages to come. Beware with all watchfulness that you avoid disgracing yourselves or you will arrive at a fire with its flames, which God (who is exalted) has made an evil place and the worst final destiny.

The obligation on your prominent persons to fight the *jihad*, which you doubted, has been realised for you, (and) in particular (for) those who God (who is praised) has singled out for the governorship over this country. So if it is obligatory for him, (then) its being incumbent on others of you is certain because of God's entrusting him with matters of guardianship, obliging him to rule the people in his power and above all to defend Islam and its essence from being conquered.

Nay, rather it is necessary for him to commit himself—may it please God—to fighting hard against the enemies of God (who is praised) in their countries every year, and (to) driving them from them, as is incumbent on every *amir* and *imam*, so that the word of God will always be the highest, and the word of those who blaspheme (will be) the lowest, and so that the desires of the enemies of the religion of God will be too weak to concern (themselves) with something like that (which they have led to) again . . .

Know for certain that this enemy's attack on your country, and their achieving what they have over some of you is a warning from God (who is praised) to those of you that remain, so that He may see if you will refrain from disobeying Him, so that He will help you against them and calm your fear, or persist and insist, so that He will give them victory over those of you that escaped. God (who is praised) afflicted you several times with various sorts of vengeful measures and you persist in disobeying Him, and He warned you time after time, and you rebel against the punishment falling upon you which corresponds to your deeds. They (the Franks) acted as they did because of (the Muslims') blame of God (who is praised) as a warning to others of them (the Muslims), and they (the Muslims) lied about the deeds of He who is praised, and He warns them (the Muslims) and only increases them (the Franks) in great tyranny. Now He warned you with a punishment the like of which He did not warn you with before, paying attention to you, albeit that your crimes are not like the crimes which preceded them. If only you would desist from sin, otherwise He will make you fall into the hands of your enemy as a matter of serious vengeance, destructive extermination and removal. God hasten your waking up from the sleep of neglect of the places of His punishment and place you among those who fear the speed of His power and the imminence of His punishments, acting according to what He ordered and prohibited in the rulings of His book, who limit (themselves) by rooting out (their bad qualities) and repenting to the point of knocking on His door. For He hears prayer and answers when He wishes.

Source: *Niall Christie, "A Translation of Extracts from the Kitab al-Jihad of 'Ali ibn Tahir Al-Sulami (d. 1106)" <http://www.arts.cornell.edu/prh3/447/texts/Sulami.html>.*

knighthood, sanctifying their activities, especially killing, as a part of God's work. Eliminating the enemies of God was an act of prayer; to die in the line of service was to gain the crown of martyrdom. It was not just an option for these men to serve; it was their spiritual duty. Urban, who had grown up in the warrior class and understood how to motivate them, extolled the virtues of blood feud and vengeance in the name of Christ. He reminded the warriors of their Eastern Christian brethren, who were suffering under the unlawful rule of the Muslims. Even though they were in a distant land, the Byzantines were still members of the Christian kinship group and necessarily had to be defended. The honor of Christendom was dependent upon their liberation. Not just Christian subjects, but also land, were at stake. Just as Byzantine land had to be recovered as part of Christ's holdings, so also did Jerusalem have to be reclaimed as the jewel of Christ's patrimony. Jerusalem was his land, gained with his death, and his vassals had allowed it to be stolen from him by the infidels. Outsiders had attacked the Christian clan's members and landholdings; vengeance was the only answer.

By invoking the liberation of Jerusalem, Urban transformed the expedition into a pilgrimage, complete with plenary indulgences for all who successfully completed the journey. The Crusade, then, conformed to the radical eleventh-century idea of performing extreme earthly penance in order to avoid heavenly wrath. This violent pilgrimage was also the opportunity to reclaim holy sites despoiled by the Muslims, such as the city of Antioch and the Holy Sepulchre at Jerusalem, and sanctify them once again. The relics that presided over these areas, especially Jerusalem, had suffered defilement long enough and had to be liberated before they unleashed their vengeance upon Christendom for their unmitigated suffering. It was the duty of Christians to protect and honor their saints and, if necessary, to kill for them.

The paradox of the Christian warrior loomed large; the dichotomy between Paul and Gideon had not (and has not) been resolved. It is fair to say, however, that it was this dichotomy, present in Urban's plan for the East, that attracted so many followers. Current cultural ideas about spirituality, personal agency, and duty to God were combined with martial concepts of righteousness, vengeance, and Christian supremacy. Preachers, paupers, warriors, and prostitutes could all find a direct, personal reason to become involved in the Crusade. Urban did not invent the idea of holy war; he did, however, make it accessible to medieval Christians and, perhaps unknowingly, provided them with a channel through which they could vent their darkest fears and highest spiritual aspirations.

Urban did not call his plan to help the East and rescue Jerusalem a "Crusade," nor did he call it a "holy war." His speech, however, acted as a catalyst to set Crusade ideology in motion. Although the threat from a foreign religion, such as Islam, was necessary to prompt a united reaction from Christendom, the Western idea of holy war was not initially predicated on the Islamic jihad. Medieval Europeans were aware of Muslim advances on Rome, as well as the fall of the Byzantine forces to Seljuk Turk caliph Alp Arslan at the Battle of Manzikert (1071). They were also familiar with the struggles of the Christian north in Spain against the forces of the Muslim south. The Muslim threat, however, was not enough to force Europe to create a reactionary concept of holy war. Elements of what became Crusade ideology were inherent in eleventh-century society, waiting for the catalyst to set them into motion—Urban's call for men to take up the cross—and it was effective not only because of the message it delivered but also because of the context in which it was delivered.

–BRENDA GARDENOUR,
BOSTON UNIVERSITY

References

M. Bonner, "Some Observations Concerning the Early Development of Jihad on the Arab-Byzantine Frontier," *Studia Islamica,* 75 (1992).

Américo Castro, *The Structure of Spanish History,* translated by Edmund L. King (Princeton: Princeton University Press, 1954).

J. Gilchrist, "The Papacy and War Against the Saracens, 795–1216," *International Historical Review,* 10 (1988).

James Turner Johnson and John Kelsay, eds., *Cross, Crescent, and Sword: The Justification and Limitation of War in Western and Islamic Tradition* (New York: Greenwood Press, 1990).

Hugh Kennedy, *The Prophet and the Age of the Caliphates: The Islamic Near East from the Sixth to the Eleventh Century* (London & New York: Longman, 1986).

Peter Partner, *God of Battles: Holy Wars of Christianity and Islam* (London: HarperCollins, 1997).

Jonathan Riley-Smith, *The First Crusade and the Idea of Crusading* (Philadelphia: University of Pennsylvania Press, 1986).

JIHAD

LOUIS IX

Were the Crusades of Louis IX motivated more by political pragmatism than religious idealism?

Viewpoint: Yes. The First Crusade of Louis IX allowed him to strengthen his domestic position, and his Second Crusade was designed to assist Charles of Anjou in maintaining control of Sicily.

Viewpoint: No. The Crusades of Louis IX were prompted solely by religious zeal and weakened rather than strengthened his political position.

French king Louis IX was one of the greatest crusading monarchs during the classic period of the Crusades. He led two major crusading expeditions and was eventually canonized. Scion of two great lines of Crusaders, the kings of France and of Castile, Louis took the cross for the first time at age thirty in response to the loss of Jerusalem (1244). His first campaign (1248–1254) was a model of organization and finance. Following the framework of the Fifth Crusade (1217–1229), Louis invaded Egypt and seized Damietta (1249), where his pregnant wife gave birth to John Tristan, who died years later on his father's second expedition (1269–1272). Pushing on to Cairo, the death of the Ayyubid sultan seemed a portent of even greater things to come. Yet, disaster was to follow. In a fatal blunder, the vanguard led by Louis's brother Robert of Artois pursued the enemy into the narrow, winding streets of al-Mansurah before the army had completed fording the river. Ambushed by the Mamluks in the streets and with no room to move, the advanced guard was cut down nearly to a man (1250). The victory revitalized Egyptian morale and changed the course of the campaign. Starvation and disease set into the Crusader camp as their supply line was cut, and epidemic swept through the ranks. The Crusaders were forced to retreat, fighting their way back to Damietta like the men of the Fifth Crusade. Halfway back to the city they were captured, and Louis was forced to pay a sizable ransom for his release.

Louis's second expedition was originally slated for Egypt as well but was redirected in 1270 to Tunis. The reason for this change of course has been the subject of much speculation. When the Crusaders landed they made camp at the ruins of Carthage. Disease struck the Crusaders immediately and swiftly spread through the ranks. Both Louis and his youngest son were among the casualties. Louis's brother Charles of Anjou, the new king of Sicily, arrived shortly after Louis's death and assumed control. Rather than undertaking a military strike, Charles opted for a negotiated settlement and ended the Crusade.

The redirection of the Second Crusade of Louis has led many historians to reassess the king's motives as a Crusader. Some have suggested that the "Tunis crusade" was launched to help the king's brother Charles of Anjou rather than to shore up the defense of the Holy Land. Others have concluded that such a theory overestimates the influence Charles had over Louis and that the decision was made by the French court for strategic reasons. Part of the debate revolves around the motivation of crusading monarchs. Were there practical and politically charged motives for the Crusades that were reshaped through and promoted by the religious rhetoric of crusading? Was Louis committed to crusading as an implement by which to strengthen the Capetian dynasty or was he rather a man who would sacrifice anything (the financial health of his kingdom and his life) for the recovery of Jerusalem? Was he a political pragmatist or religious idealist?

Viewpoint:
Yes. The First Crusade of Louis IX allowed him to strengthen his domestic position, and his Second Crusade was designed to assist Charles of Anjou in maintaining control of Sicily.

As the only formally canonized monarch of the Middle Ages, French king Louis IX has always represented something of a mystery. His sainthood, after all, is a catechetical assertion of medievalists, yet few of them would be willing to argue seriously in its favor. He held an extraordinarily high position in the eyes of his contemporaries, and he continues to be regarded as a great king by modern writers; but it is difficult to see precisely why. As a ruler, Louis was a particularly dedicated, detail-oriented administrator who made an explicit commitment to the pursuit of justice; he struggled to root out corrupt judges, to regularize and professionalize royal government, and to create a fair system of taxation for his subjects. But he lacked charisma, social vision, and any discernible idealism apart from a rather pompous pietism; he was violently anti-Semitic and is the only medieval king known to have personally attacked his own Jewish subjects; and as a Crusader, he failed twice—once on a colossal scale, the second time farcically.

Much of Louis's great reputation results from his activities as a Crusader. As the only medieval king to go on two Crusades, however, he deserves criticism for not having learned the lesson absorbed by every other royal Crusader—namely, that no Crusade ever benefited either the Christian communities in the Holy Land or the Western kingdoms that sponsored the campaigns. Both of Louis's Crusades were disastrous endeavors. The First (1248–1254) resulted in his being captured at Damietta. After his ransom he devoted three years to spending the huge Crusade treasury he had built up in Cyprus in order to fortify and resupply the leading cities of the Crusader States. Although a noble venture, it bears pointing out that virtually all of those defenses collapsed the first time the Muslims opposed them. His Second Crusade (1269–1272), which came at the end of his life, was stopped almost as soon as it began.

Crusading was certainly in Louis's blood. No fewer than six of his immediate predecessors or their family members had gone on Crusade. As a representative of both Christian piety and chivalric culture, it was clearly expected of Louis that he would, at some point in his reign, take the cross almost regardless of circumstances. Personal factors played a role, too. His mother, the Queen Regent Blanche, was an aggressive, powerful personality who clearly dominated Louis's childhood and adult psyche. He grew up both idolizing and hating the influence she held. Blanche was zealous in her determination to defend Christianity and to champion the struggle against Islam, ideas that she had grown up with during her childhood in Castile, the central stage of the Spanish *Reconquista* (reconquest). Taking control of the government in Paris after the death of Louis's father (1226) while Louis was still a young boy, Blanche proved to be an effective administrator and an avid champion of justice (as she understood it); but, above all, she wanted to preserve and extend all royal prerogatives. Hence, Louis was raised to be a believer in Christian truth, to be responsible for the preservation of justice, and not only to be certain of his own unique responsibilities but also to be consciously on guard against attempts to undermine his rights. It was the combination of these characteristics that created within him this extraordinary mixture of high idealism and the most picayune obsession with detail and procedure.

In 1244 Louis decided to go on a Crusade. The impetus behind this decision was as much personal as political. Certainly, the condition of the Crusader States in the East was dire. They had lost many lands to Turkish armies, and, indeed, by the 1240s, Christians were in control of only a half-dozen coastal cities. There was also the political issue of the German emperor Frederick II, who had scandalized the Church and the French throne by his own bizarrely successful Crusade. Hence, the Church and Louis had to do something. It was clearly unacceptable to have the kingdom of Jerusalem remain in the hands of the Hohenstaufen Antichrist, but Louis had personal motives as well. In 1243 he became gravely ill and was on the verge of receiving last rites when he recovered. Louis regarded this episode as a divine action. Despite his earlier sins and failures, he had been given by God another opportunity to do right. He took the Crusader vow in 1244, which represented the first decisive act of his personal rule and was a sort of emancipation proclamation that initiated his political independence from his mother and regent. Although Louis was already thirty years old and married with children, politically he was still a minor of sorts under the firm grip of Blanche. The Crusade vow allowed Louis to seize full control over the French government, an act that Blanche tried to confound but in the end could not prevent.

The high moral connotations and pious enthusiasms associated with crusading also gave Louis a demonstrable rationale for reshuffling the political deck in his kingdom. The reforms that Louis instituted throughout France to support the Crusade constituted an administrative revolution that extended royal reach in an unprecedented way. Of particular importance were the *enquenteurs* (royal investigators who inspected the activities of royal officials in the provinces). They could intervene in local affairs and impose fines on negligent or corrupt officials. The plight of the Holy Land also gave Louis a compelling justification to reassign the positions of seneschal (agent in charge of a lord's estate) and bailiff to more-trustworthy officials. The economic demands of the Crusade gave Louis the perfect pretext for tightening his control over the economic resources of the kingdom, particularly the ability to fine-tune financial understandings with exempt religious institutions. After all, it would take nothing short of the plight of Jerusalem to justify confiscations of properties of Cluny by a royal bailiff. All of these actions were justified by the Crusade, and when the expedition came to an end, Louis reintroduced them as permanent administrative features of his government. Piety evidently yielded great political dividends.

The Crusade was formally announced at the Council of Lyon (June 1245) by Pope Innocent IV. This expedition was the first royally led Crusade since the Third Crusade (1189–1192). From the start, Louis approached it with enthusiasm. He spent three years drawing up detailed plans for the campaign, raising money, and in a first for Crusade history, preparing a supply chain that extended across the Mediterranean Sea. He built and stocked a network of warehouses with food, weaponry, clothing, and materials. The main storehouse that Louis built was on Cyprus, and it was massive. According to extant records, Louis built up a Crusade treasury of more than 1.2 million livres (a sum roughly three times the king's own annual income) and stockpiled approximately four years of supplies.

Strategically, the aim was to take Egypt first, which by the 1240s had become standard procedure for the Crusades. Egypt, after all, was desirable in its own right as the main grain-producing region in the Western world, but it was also the ideal staging post to launch an attack on the Holy Land. All Crusades since the late 1190s had aimed at first securing control of Egypt, or at least of the Nile Delta. Moreover, overtaking Egypt should have been easy—the country was surrounded by deserts that were not easily crossed, and thus throughout history she had been insulated from foreign attack. Hence, her cities were unfortified. Any force that was able to take the delta towns, such as Alexandria, then had a secure base for proceeding up the river and gaining control of all the other towns up to the first cataract. Bad weather and local conflicts forced Louis and his army to remain in Cyprus longer than he had wished, but he was finally able to sail directly for Egypt in late May 1249. Within a few days, however, his army was defeated and Louis captured. Louis might have been at fault—some hasty battlefield decisions made by overzealous generals seemed to have caused the confusion that resulted in the French forces being divided among different spits of land between the fanning streams. Evidence suggests that the goal of Louis's campaign against Egypt was colonization as well as conquest. It seems as though the new ruler of Egypt was to be his brother Robert of Artois, whose excessive zeal in moving on Egypt rapidly led to the disaster at al-Mansurah (1250). Capetian dynastic ambitions thus played a role in the expedition, even if its central importance is open to debate.

Louis's capture triggered another Crusade, the so-called Shepherds' Crusade (1251). This popular phenomenon was led by a curious charismatic lay preacher who went by the self-styled title of the Master of Hungary. Like earlier lay Crusade evangelists, the Master of Hungary drew wide crowds from the peasantry with calls for spiritual and social reform that were tinged with apocalyptic expectations. Claiming to have received a letter from Heaven that selected him for this particular task, the Master developed the idea that he had been chosen to lead a campaign that would free Louis from captivity and lead to the liberation of Jerusalem. The Master believed that the failure of all earlier Crusades was a result of spiritual rather than military factors. The sinfulness of the Crusaders ensured their failure; hence, any successful Crusade could only come about through the participation of the spiritually pure. And who is more pure than a shepherd? Drawing on biblical imagery dating back to the ancient Israelites, the Master argued that God repeatedly identified shepherds as the ideal spiritual actors. Hence, after the failure of so many Crusaders drawn from the nobility, ecclesiastical hierarchy, mercenary professionals, and naval militias, the time was clearly right for the rise of God's chosen campaigners: a Crusade of shepherds. He proved to be surpris-

ingly successful, but the Master was smart enough to realize that even a spiritually pure group of shepherds would only succeed against the massed forces of Islam and the Antichrist with some backing. Hence, his message emphasized the importance of targeting the liberation of Louis himself as the first step of the Crusade. Therefore, the Master decided to lead his force (which, according to some witnesses, numbered as many as 30,000) to Paris, in order to receive the blessing and financial support of Louis's mother, Blanche.

The Shepherds' Crusade ended as a fiasco, as did Louis's creditable efforts to refortify the Christian-ruled territories in the East. Louis emerged from the experience a determined penitent, convinced that his own sinfulness and shortcomings as a monarch had brought on the waste, carnage, and humiliation of his Crusade adventure. He resolved to rectify matters by committing himself to the pursuit of personal purity and the establishment of justice in his realm. Whether or not these were worthy aims depends on the precise definitions Louis gave to the notions of purity and justice.

According to Geoffrey de Beaulieu, Louis's personal confessor, the king's second and final Crusade came about because Louis had received an embassy from the Muslim ruler of Tunis, who was allegedly interested in converting to Christianity. Rather than send missionaries, Franciscans, scholars, and a handful of bishops to guide the man further into the Christian fold, Louis decided instead that a Crusade was called for. So he gathered about six thousand men in order to wrest the Muslim ruler's lands from him. They embarked from Aigues Mortes in mid 1270, but Louis and most of his men suffered an outbreak of enteric (intestinal) fever and died before they could reach the African coast. Geoffrey suggests that Louis had hoped that by seizing Tunis he might weaken Mamluk power in Egypt, which would in turn loosen the Islamic grip on the Levant. If this suggestion is true, Louis's actions can only be read as strategic idiocy in service to his own rank hypocrisy.

There is, however, an alternative explanation, one rooted more in spiritual hypocrisy than strategic idiocy. Louis had already supported his brother Charles of Anjou in his bid to become ruler of Sicily, and the gamble paid off. Charles became head of the papal Crusade against the Hohenstaufen and in the process eventually became the king of Sicily. The Hohenstaufen suffered a decisive defeat at the Battle of Benevento (1266), and German prince Conradin, the last representative of the line, was captured and executed in 1268. Charles began pursuing a policy of peaceful relations with Egypt and through marriage alliances was jockeying for the position of king of Jerusalem as well. A general assault on Egypt, the logical focal point of any general Crusade at the time, would have hindered rather than helped Charles's scheme. Tunisia, on the other hand, was a target that would have bolstered the position of the fledgling Angevin kingdom. Hohenstaufen supporters fled to, and received sanctuary in, Tunis; Charles's grip on his new kingdom would be more secure by uprooting this cluster of resistance. Economically, Tunisia was firmly within the commercial orbit that fed the prosperity of Sicily. If the ends of a Crusade can be seen, even remotely, as elucidating its motives, then the manner in which Charles brought an end to Louis's Tunisian expedition after the crusading saint's death speaks volumes. The Angevin-Hafsid peace treaty, signed with a crusading host close by, reinstated the tribute that Tunisia traditionally paid to Sicily, secured important trade concessions, and resulted in the expulsion of Hohenstaufen supporters in Tunisia.

–CLIFFORD R. BACKMAN,
BOSTON UNIVERSITY

Viewpoint:
No. The Crusades of Louis IX were prompted solely by religious zeal and weakened rather than strengthened his political position.

Motivation of Crusaders has long been a subject of lively debate. Some historians have stressed the religious and ideological allure of crusading, painting portraits of self-sacrificing idealists committed to conducting what they saw as the greatest labor that could be rendered to God. Many have emphasized the possibility of economic and, in the case of rulers, political gains. Such historians have spent a great deal of time unearthing the real motives beneath the veneer and trappings of crusading rhetoric. The points made by both sides are strong. Crusading was a movement that drew thousands of people from various backgrounds, and naturally their motives were just as varied. Holy war was the activity par excellence in which spiritual goals and worldly conditions always mingled and frequently collided.

All Crusaders placed themselves at great personal and financial risk. Besides the possibility of being killed in combat, Crusaders faced long months, and sometimes years, of disease and hunger. The costs incurred campaigning on the other side of the known world were staggering and easily amounted to several years' income for most Crusaders. The risks and costs were even greater for European monarchs who placed not only their lives in jeopardy but also their kingdoms. In terms of material gain there was little to garner but much to lose in undertaking a Crusade. Maybe the common drama of kings delaying departure or commuting their crusading vows reflected second thoughts many monarchs had after taking their oaths. Certainly, taking the cross added to royal prestige, but the price was high, as can be seen in the warm reception English king Richard I, the Lion-Hearted, received upon returning from the East. Still, some historians suspect that royal politics loomed large in the motiva-

tion of crusading monarchs. Even the "crusading saint" French king Louis IX has been suspected of having ulterior motives for his Crusades: they were tools by which Louis attempted to strengthen the organization of France while promoting the interests of his brothers Robert of Artois and Charles of Anjou. Beneath the pious gestures were pragmatic dynastic concerns. The situation was the other way around: deeply pious concerns were promoted by pragmatic decisions.

On both the paternal and maternal sides, Louis came from a long line of Crusaders. Every generation in his father's line had produced at least one notable Crusader since the First Crusade (1096–1102). His ancestors on his mother's side led the *Reconquista* (reconquest) in Spain, and his maternal grandfather was the hero of the Battle of Las Navas de Tolosa (1212). Before taking his vow, Louis had already demonstrated interest in the welfare of the Holy Land, not only in the form of generous financial contributions but also by using campaigning in the East as a form of punishment for barons he clashed with politically. Louis's decision to take the cross was prompted by a confluence of two events. The first was news of the loss of Jerusalem (1244), which was later accentuated more gravely by the disaster at La Forbie (1244). The second was the nearly fatal illness that struck the young king. Upon regaining consciousness he took the Crusader vow. Despite his previous interest in the Holy Land, his decision caught all by surprise. The most heated reaction to the news was that of the queen mother, Blanche of Castile, who did everything possible to sweep the vow aside and prevent him from leaving for the East (including physical restraint on the eve of departure). Enlisting the support of the bishop of Paris, Blanche reminded Louis that a vow sworn during an illness was not valid. Louis responded by swearing it again.

Politically, the timing of Louis's proposed Crusade was bad. Naturally there were concerns about the king's fragile health and whether or not he could survive the long journey. The French barons were rather rebellious and Louis had just recently finished clashing with them. Even worse were the turbulent relations with Henry III of England, who was rattling his sabers over possession of Poitou, Normandy, and Anjou. The Anglo-French truce regarding these possessions was nearing its end, and Henry made it quite clear that he planned to take decisive action. The only possible political gain Louis could have made by undertaking a Crusade at this time was emancipation from the domination of his mother, Blanche. One historian has pointed out that even though Louis had already come of age (he

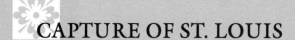

CAPTURE OF ST. LOUIS

Chronicler Jean de Joinville, who accompanied Louis IX (St. Louis) on his first Crusade (1248–1254), describes the capture of the king in Egypt:

Now I will leave off speaking of this matter, and tell you how the king was taken, as he himself related it to me. He told me how he had left his own division and placed himself, he and my Lord Geoffrey of Sargines, in the division that was under my Lord Gaucher of Chatillon, who commanded the rearguard.

And the king related to me that he was mounted on a little courser covered with a housing of silk; and he told me that all of his knights and sergeants there only remained behind with him my Lord Geoffrey of Sargines, who brought the king to a little village, there where the king was taken; and as the king related to me, my Lord Geoffrey of Sargines defended him from the Saracens as a good servitor defends his lord's drinking cup from flies; for every time that the Saracens approached, he took his spear, which he had placed between himself and the bow of his saddle, and put it to his shoulder, and ran upon them, and drove them away from the king.

And thus he brought the king to the little village; and they lifted him into a house, and laid him, almost as one dead, in the lap of a burgher-woman of Paris, and thought he would not last till night. Thither came my Lord Philip of Montfort, and said to the king that he saw the emir with whom he had treated of the truce, and, if the king so willed, he would go to him, and renew the negotiation for a truce in the manner that the Saracens desired. The king begged him to go, and said he was right willing. So my Lord Philip went to the Saracen; and the Saracen had taken off his turban from his head, and took off the ring from his finger in token that he would faithfully observe the truce.

Meanwhile, a very great mischance happened to our people; for a traitor sergeant, whose name was Marcel, began to cry to our people: "Yield, lord knights, for the king commands you, and do not cause the king to be slain!" All thought that the king had so commanded, and gave up their swords to the Saracens. The emir saw that the Saracens were bringing in our people prisoners, so he said to my Lord Philip that it was not fitting that he should grant a truce to our people, for he saw very well that they were already prisoners.

So it happened to my Lord Philip that whereas all our people were taken captive, yet was he not so taken, because he was an envoy. But there is an evil custom in the land of paynimry that when the king sends envoys to the sultan, or the sultan to the king, and the king dies, or the sultan, before the envoy's return, then the envoys, from whithersoever they may come, and whether Christians or Saracens, are made prisoners and slaves.

Source: "Joinville's Chronicle of the Crusade of St. Lewis," in Ville-hardouin and De Joinville, Memoirs of the Crusades, translated by Frank Marzials (London: Dent, 1908), pp. 211–212.

was thirty and married), the queen mother was still acting as regent. If the phrase "tough old bird" was ever applicable to a mother, it was doubly so for Blanche. It has been suggested that Louis's vow paralleled that taken by his sister Isabella in her rebellion against their mother. After rejecting a marriage proposal supported by Blanche, Pope, and emperor, Isabella fell into illness and swore a vow of chastity after recovering. On the other hand, this act could also merely indicate the deep spiritual piety that brother and sister shared. After all, Louis spent an enormous sum of money purchasing the Crown of Thorns and building a costly cathedral (Sainte-Chapelle) in which to house it. In any case, the political situation was not good and would probably be destabilized with Louis crusading in the East for years. The surprised reaction of Louis's subjects and the violent reaction of his mother can partially be explained by the political balance sheet that indicated no gain and potentially great losses.

Louis was remarkable in the ways in which he solved problems facing the venture. The easiest problem to deal with was the rebellious nature of his vassals. His solution can be seen in the gifts he gave to them at the Christmas court: robes that had the Crusader cross sewn upon them. International relations were much more problematic. Pope and emperor were, as usual, at one another's throats. Invasion by the English remained a threat—a several-year absence of the French king would provide a great opportunity for England to recover its Continental possessions. Protections the Church extended to men taking the vow could prove ephemeral, as the experience of Richard I at the hands of French king Philip Augustus demonstrated during the Third Crusade (1189–1192). Much of the resources of western Europe were being funneled to eastern Europe to deal with the Mongols. King Haakon IV Haakonsson of Norway, who took the Crusader vow earlier, opted not to join forces with Louis for an Eastern expedition. Quickly it became obvious that Louis would have to rely on his own resources for his own Crusade.

That Louis made a study of, and learned many valuable lessons from, the Fifth Crusade (1217–1229) is apparent. He was determined to produce the best-organized and well-funded Crusade yet (and he succeeded). The task was a formidable one, particularly since the financial burden would fall almost exclusively on France and the French Church. Logistics and supplies were areas in Crusade preparation that Louis revolutionized by creating a well-supplied (and costly) forward base in Cyprus. In addition to the problem of supplies, Louis also recognized one of the greatest obstacles to crusading was cash flow and solvency. Louis planned on subsidizing Crusaders and being in a position to continue lending money throughout the campaign. The financial demands that the expedition placed on the kingdom proved to be enormous, as did the strain. In fact, all public works throughout the realm had to be halted.

The cost of the Crusade puts the entire venture into perspective. It has been estimated at £1,500,000 (not counting what participants paid out-of-pocket or Louis's hefty ransom), when royal revenue was about £250,000 (most of which was marked for domestic use). Eventually, the church managed to provide about two-thirds of the money, but this contribution still left an enormous remainder that would be difficult for the French Crown to absorb. Churches reluctant to part with their money were occasionally dealt with by force. No friend to either Jews or heretics, Louis took from both groups to help fill the war chest. The king also drained whatever he could from the towns and the royal demesne (land attached to a manor). Archives were checked for any possible sources of revenue that had been forgotten. Louis also began enforcing the *licentia eligendi,* the face-to-face royal permission for the election of bishops and abbots. This policy allowed Louis to extend vacant offices and access those funds. To cut corruption and augment efficiency, Louis used mendicants as investigating officials who became the watchdogs of crusading revenue. There were moral dimensions to fund-raising as well: Louis did not want to use any "dirty money" from ill-gotten gains that would stain the piety of the venture. The financial stress of the Crusade was so great that it resulted in a massive reorganization of the French political structure. The cash Louis amassed by these means was impressive even if, in the end, he was forced to take loans from Italian bankers.

Following the strategy of the Fifth Crusade, Louis planned to strike Egypt. His actions in Egypt imply that he planned on a permanent Christian settlement there rather than simply degrading Islamic military might. It is almost certain as well that he intended for a Latin Egypt to be under the control of his brother Robert of Artois, who certainly seemed to think so. This belief, combined with a brash and aggressive personality, goes far in explaining Robert's reckless conduct that led to Robert's death in the Egyptian campaign. Suggesting that Louis's objective in conquering Egypt was to provide his brother Robert with a kingdom, however, stretches credulity. It does not explain his previous interest in the

fate of the Holy Land, and it seems like a high price tag to attach to brotherly love and concern. As can be seen in his purchase of the Crown of Thorns, money was not an issue for Louis when it came to pious causes. Egypt, moreover, was the backbone of regional Islam, and most people recognized that Christian security in the region was dependent on crushing the sultanate. Men, such as thirteenth-century English chronicler Matthew Paris, were out of touch with the true tactical concerns of crusading in the region. Matthew was of the opinion that crusading should be restricted to recovering the Holy Land and disapproved of Louis's refusal to exchange Damietta for Jerusalem. The Egyptian campaign was no mere landgrab, however, and its goal was not to make a French prince into an Egyptian king. Louis's actions after his release by the Egyptians goes a long way in demonstrating his concerns and goals in the region. Rather than returning to France immediately, he spent four years in Palestine stabilizing the government and building fortifications. When he finally returned home, he left, at his expense, a garrison of one hundred knights to help defend the Holy Land. Louis continued to send about £4,000 per year to the Holy Land to subsidize its defense.

The deep spiritual connotations of Louis's Crusade are underscored by his reaction to the failed expedition. It pushed him into a state of deep personal crisis. Convinced that the failure was the result of his own personal sins, his religious devotion increased and his entire life took on the trappings of one grand penitential performance. According to one scholar: "He dressed and ate simply. He dedicated himself to the poor. He desired death. He sought to make good kingship a kind of expiation for his offences which, he believed, had brought shame and damage on all Christianity." One would have thought that he had already suffered enough. Dysentery, typhus, scurvy, and a host of ailments afflicted the Crusaders and decimated their ranks. He was captured by the enemy and lost a brother. The last thing one would suspect would be a second campaign, but Louis's creation and use of the ideal Christian monarchy as a surrogate for a successful Crusade was not to last.

Louis informed Pope Clement IV of his decision to launch another Crusade to the East in September 1266. In the winter of 1267 he made the decision public; Louis, his three sons, and several barons took the vow. His brothers Alphonse of Poitiers and Charles of Anjou also made preparations to join the Crusade. Louis's original crusading plan seems to have been in line with the strategy of his first:

sail to Cyprus and then invade Egypt. The sultan Baybars I believed this was the case; after he was informed by spies of Louis's plan, he immediately destroyed the fortifications of Ascalon and Damietta. The plan changed in 1270, and the Crusade was rerouted to Tunis, ruled by the Hafsid dynasty that had fairly good diplomatic and commercial relations with Christians of southern Italy. The decision to change the destination of the Crusade has resulted in a great deal of speculation on the causes. Of several theories, one is that the Crusade was rerouted to strengthen the newly formed dynasty of Charles of Anjou, a theory that stresses pragmatic politics over religious zeal. A second theory was that a Crusade to Tunis would strengthen the Latin position for an eventual assault on Egypt.

Charles of Anjou had just reaped great benefits from the papally sanctioned political Crusade that finally succeeded in ousting the Hohenstaufen from southern Italy and Sicily. Charles, head of this Crusade, replaced Manfred and became king. Tunis had good relations with the Hohenstaufen and served as a haven for that dynasty's exiled supporters. The argument has been proffered that the Crusade to the East was redirected in 1270 in an effort to solve Charles's problems with Tunis and to bring the Hafsids into line with the new dynasty's point of view. A Crusader army camped at the Hafsids' doorstep would strengthen Charles's negotiating power with Tunis. The final conclusion of Louis's Crusade has led some historians to give great credence to this theory. After Louis died from sickness in the Crusader camp, Charles arrived and took control of the expedition. Rather than attacking the Hafsids, he made a treaty with them under the watchful eye of the Latin army. Thus, the final results of the Tunis Crusade were a hefty war indemnity, ratification of trade concessions, an increase in Tunisian tribute payable to Sicily, and the agreement that Hohenstaufen exiles would no longer be harbored in Tunis. This treaty cuts a striking contrast with Louis's alleged last words as he lay dying: "Jerusalem . . . Jerusalem."

Using the final results of the expedition to explain its causes, however, is pure *post hoc ergo propter hoc*. Just because the Crusade, in the final analysis, seems to have served no one's ends but Charles of Anjou's, does little in telling us about its causes. Most of the facts—at least before Louis's death—suggest the contrary. First of all, the cost of the Crusade seems difficult to reconcile with the marginal gains a show of force against the Hafsids would garner. Making the French economy groan beneath the weight of such expenditure seems to be an excessive act to help Charles of Anjou (who was already doing quite well in any case). Rather than being a tool for dynasty building, the Crusade was more likely to be a tool for dynastic dismantling (which almost turned out to be the case). Having been on a failed Crusade before, Louis was painfully aware of the dangers he faced. He had already lost a brother in his first expedition, and he was taking great risks by bringing his remaining brothers and sons on the Tunis Crusade. Such an undertaking ran the risk of ending his line, and at Tunis this event almost happened. Louis's eldest son, Philip (the royal heir), nearly died of disease in camp, and his youngest son, John, did. Louis's poor health meant he could easily die as well, which ended up being the case. Such risks are difficult to reconcile with securing political leverage for Charles. Even more significant, Charles originally asked Louis not to attack Tunis for fear of disrupting negotiations that were underway with the Hafsids. His initial support for Louis's campaign seems to have been the result more of his obligation to his brother than the reverse. That Charles finally became the sole beneficiary of the Crusade is easy to explain: he arrived after Louis's death and clearly did not want to push on with the expedition. Opportunism seems to have marked his subsequent activities rather than the culmination of a plan. It would have been suprising if Charles did not use the army for leverage before it disbanded.

The second theory, that Louis decided to move on Tunis to strengthen Latin positioning for an assault on Egypt, seems much more likely. Securing Tunis would provide a forward base that could even exceed the value of that in Cyprus or, when combined with it, create the foundations for a two-pronged assault. The possibility of expanding an economic blockade of Egypt might also have played a role. While Latin fleets blocked sea shipping, a pro-Christian and anti-Egyptian Tunis could deprive the sultanate of much land traffic. There were two possible ways of securing Tunis. First was the rumor that the Hafsids were considering converting to Christianity. News of this development probably played an important role in Louis's decision to reroute the Crusade. If it was found that the rumor had little validity (as was the case), then Louis could secure Tunis through force (which he eventually planned to do). His decision was probably informed by the disastrous results of the Fifth Crusade and that of his own debacle in Egypt years earlier. Once the role that Tunis could play in an assault on Egypt was brought to his attention, he seems to have embraced it. Thus, the geopolitical situation seems to provide a more compelling explanation for redirecting the Crusade than any desire to assist Charles of Anjou.

From beginning to end of his career, Louis IX's administration and life were defined by his commitment to the plight of the Holy Land. His efforts to extract as much revenue from France as possible to finance his Crusade resulted in permanent changes to the organizational apparatus of the French monarchy. His financial and personal sacrifices to the movement are difficult to explain by any reason other than extreme religious piety. Louis's means in pursuing his objective were fairly pragmatic, but the objective smacks of spiritual idealism. After being burned so badly by the failure of his first expedition, it is difficult to conceive of any worldly benefit he could have gained from trying again. The reasons for his second expedition are fairly clear. Louis never felt that he had fulfilled his vow, and his commitment to the Holy Land remained forever writ large across his personality. After his first failure he spent four more years in the East providing whatever assistance he could and then made generous yearly donations to the Crusader States. Yet, this commitment, even when combined with living the life of penance and of a perfect Christian king, did little to heal the spiritual scars that his failure inflicted. Historians do well in considering the worldly motives of Crusaders, for such incentives were frequently present. But one must not project one's own cynicism back upon the past. Sometimes one must yield to the fact that deep religious piety was occasionally the sole motivating factor. Such a motive, in its purest and most unadulterated form, was probably the exception rather than the rule, but one must yield to exceptions when they arise. Louis's contemporaries acknowledged his piety through his canonization. It was he, alone among the great Crusade leaders, who not only launched and led two major expeditions but was also made a saint as well.

–MARK T. ABATE, WESTFIELD STATE COLLEGE

References

William Chester Jordan, *Louis IX and the Challenge of the Crusade: A Study in Rulership* (Princeton: Princeton University Press, 1979).

Jean Richard, *The Crusades, c. 1071–c. 1291,* translated by Jean Birrell (Cambridge & New York: Cambridge University Press, 1999).

Richard, *St. Louis: Crusader King of France,* edited by Simon Lloyd (Cambridge & New York: Cambridge University Press, 1992).

Jonathan Riley-Smith, *The Crusades: A Short History* (London: Athlone, 1987; New Haven: Yale University Press, 1987).

Steven Runciman, *The Sicilian Vespers: A History of the Mediterranean World in the Later Thirteenth Century* (Cambridge: Cambridge University Press, 1958).

Margaret R. B. Shaw, ed., *Chronicles of the Crusades* (Baltimore: Penguin, 1963).

LOUIS IX

MARITIME STATES

Did the Italian maritime republics strengthen the Crusader States?

Viewpoint: Yes. The Crusader States were economically and militarily sustained by the Italian maritime republics.

Viewpoint: No. The Italian maritime republics were actually agents of destabilization that weakened the Crusader States.

The Italian maritime republics were city-states that depended on trade for their existence and prosperity. During the general period of western European growth and expansion that punctuated the eleventh century, the republics focused their expansionist activities on the sea. This focus inevitably brought them into conflict with Islamic powers; the wars of Genoa and Pisa in North Africa and those of Venice in the eastern Mediterranean against the Muslims predate and serve as a prologue to the First Crusade (1096–1102). Probably for commercial reasons, the greatest Italian maritime republics all responded to Pope Urban II's call for Crusade.

The Italian republics compensated for the most glaring tactical weakness of the First Crusaders: their lack of appropriate sea power. Land sieges of important and well-fortified coastal cities could and did succeed, but a counteroffensive by Egyptian fleets would certainly make them difficult to hold. Genoa and Pisa were the first republics to assist in the First Crusade. Venice appeared later and played an instrumental role in the conquest of the extremely important coastal city of Tyre (1124). By and large, the "rights of conquest" that the maritime republics claimed were trade concessions that promoted their commercial penetration into the region. Since the eastern Mediterranean was of such commercial importance to the Italian republics, these maritime states had a vested interest in their survival and prosperity. In many ways they became the engines that drove the financial fate of the colonies. Moreover, their efforts to obtain commercial hegemony in the region led to their successful efforts at establishing dominance on the seas. Italian control of the seas played a crucial role in provisioning and supporting the nascent Crusader States, which as far-flung colonies remained dependent on assistance from western Europe.

Yet, there was a darker side to the Italian presence. Their primary interest was commerce, and they were more than willing to conduct trade with Muslims as well as Christians. Despite attempts to ban Christian traffic in war matériel to the Muslim states, the Italian republics followed the profitable law of supply and demand whenever possible. Moreover, trade disputes among the republics could assume massive and far-reaching dimensions. Italian republics often engaged in armed conflict with one another over resources. Episodes such as the Fourth Crusade (1202–1204), which Venice diverted from assaulting Islamic Egypt against its own Christian competitors (Byzantium), and the War of St. Sabas (1256–1258), in which Venice and Genoa provoked a wide-scale civil war over a single church and its holdings, rocked the movement and the colonies to their foundations.

That the maritime republics had an enormous impact on the history of the Crusader States is beyond question. What is debatable, however, is whether, once tallied, this impact strengthened or weakened the precarious position of the colonies.

Viewpoint:
Yes. The Crusader States were economically and militarily sustained by the Italian maritime republics.

Enrico Dandalo, the infamous Venetian doge who played an important role in the disintegration of the Fourth Crusade (1202–1204), personifies in many ways the relationship between the Italian maritime republics and the crusading movement. His interests in the eastern Mediterranean stretched to, but did not revolve around, the plight of the Holy Land. Like the United States centuries later, the business of Venice was commerce and trade. Commercial hegemony and profit margins in the East, rather than spiritual redemption, were the concerns of Dandalo and the republic he represented. The Venetian approach to the Fourth Crusade was extremely business-like. The republic was contracted to equip the Crusaders with a fleet for transportation. As is well known, there were not enough Crusaders to properly pay the Venetians for their labor. Rather than dismissing the loss as a spiritual write-off, Dandalo and Venice devised an alternative payment plan. Venice would join the Crusade as a full partner and allow the Crusaders to "work off" the remainder of the debt by militarily assisting the republic in strengthening its commercial presence en route. Extracting anything of value from a failed investment, while making possible gains, was what guided Venetian policy during the Fourth Crusade. The dynamic can be encapsulated in Dandalo's response to objections raised by the papal legate Peter Capuano. The doge reminded Capuano that as legate his concerns were only spiritual and not organizational or tactical. The legate was basically told to mind his own business and not to interfere with the worldly aspects and practical details of the expedition. Pope Innocent III's excommunication of the Venetians seems to be the ultimate testament to the chasm that separated the objectives and policies of the republic from those of Crusaders.

Dandalo, both then and now, is frequently portrayed as the villain of the piece. Rumor and reality merged to paint a sinister portrait of the doge. Did he intentionally allow too many ships to be built in order to place the Crusader host in his debt and thereby create an unwilling mercenary army that would serve Venetian interests?

The Byzantine Empire had recently made the commercial position of Venice in its lands complicated and was becoming far too friendly with Genoa. Did he have a deep-seated hatred of the Byzantine Empire that could only be satisfied with its destruction? The *Chronicle of Novgorod* claimed that Dandalo was tortured and blinded by the Byzantines, thus infusing him with a hatred of the Empire and a resolute commitment to destroying it (though French chronicler Geoffrey de Villehardouin believed the man was blinded in a brawl).

Proper assessment of the relationship between Italian maritime republics and the Crusades needs to begin by adopting an antiromantic stance. Contemporaries liked to believe—even though many realized it was not the case—that crusading was a selfless act of spiritual devotion. To a certain extent this belief is true: the strongest and most resilient motive of Crusaders was spiritual. For most participants, crusading was not a "for profit" enterprise. Technically, however, the Italian republics were usually not "Crusaders" but merchants whose interests frequently paralleled (though sometimes clashed with) those of the crusading movement in general. Chivalry and piety had nothing to do with the activities of the maritime republics. Commercial consolidation and expansion were their prime directives, and all their efforts were devoted to promoting these ends. As eighteenth-century Scottish economist Adam Smith pointed out, greed can have positive effects. To truly appreciate the contributions that the maritime republics made to the preservation of the Crusader States, one must first recognize the paradox that frames the question: personal interests and greed sometimes promote the general good and interests of a society.

A century before Pope Urban II launched the First Crusade (1096–1102) at the Council of Clermont (1095), the Italian maritime republics already had begun personal wars against the Islamic states. Venice, Genoa, and Pisa were in the thick of a war of trade expansion with the Muslims in the Mediterranean region. Genoa and Pisa focused their attention on Islamic North Africa, while Venice made impressive inroads into the trade networks of the eastern Mediterranean. Any widespread assault on Islamic states in the region would have interested all of them. The republics were a force to be reckoned with on the sea; since their livelihood was based on maritime trade, they threw all of their resources into the creation of impres-

THE VENETIANS PROTECT THEIR SHIPS

French chronicler Geoffrey de Villehardouin describes Venetian activities during the attack against Constantinople in 1203–1204:

Then the Greeks bethought themselves of a very great device, for they took seven large ships, and filled them full of big logs, and shavings, and tow, and resin, and barrels, and then waited until such time as the wind should blow strongly from their side of the straits. And one night, at midnight, they set fire to the ships, and unfurled their sails to the wind. And the flames blazed up high, so that it seemed as if the whole world were a-fire. Thus did the burning ships come towards the fleet of the pilgrims; and a great cry arose in the host, and all sprang to arms on every side. The Venetians ran to their ships, and so did all those who had ships in possession, and they began to draw them away out of the flames very vigorously.

And to this bears witness Geoffry the Marshal of Champagne, who dictated this work, that never did people help themselves better than the Venetians did that night; for they sprang into the galleys and boats belonging to the ships, and seized upon the fire ships, all burning as they were, with hooks, and dragged them by main force before their enemies, outside the port, and set them into the current of the straits, and left them to go burning down the straits. So many of the Greeks had come down to the shore that they were without end and innumerable, and their cries were so great that it seemed as if the earth and sea would melt together. They got into barges and boats, and shot at those on our side who were battling with the flames, so that some were wounded. . . .

They endured thus in labour and anguish till daylight; but by God's help those on our side lost nothing, save a Pisan ship, which was full of merchandise, and was burned with fire. Deadly was the peril in which we stood that night, for if the fleet had been consumed, all would have been lost, and we should never have been able to get away by land or sea. Such was the guerdon which the Emperor Alexius would have bestowed upon us in return for our services.

Source: "Villehardouin's Chronicle of the Fourth Crusade and the Conquest of Constantinople," in Villehardouinn and De Joinville, Memoirs of the Crusades, translated by Frank Marzials (London: Dent, 1908), pp. 54–55.

Western European knowledge of the East might have been primitive at the time, but at the least, Urban recognized the importance of sea power—even for a campaign that would be fought mostly on land. The three greatest maritime republics made important, if somewhat belated, contributions to the First Crusade: Genoa first, followed by Pisa, and then Venice. Thus, the Italian maritime republics helped to solve the difficult problem of conquering and securing key coastal sites. Yet, one must immediately puncture any inflated notion that their activities were done for the glory of God. The Italians simply took advantage of new allies in their preexisting commercial war with Islam.

The Latin colonies that the First Crusade created always led a fragile and tenuous existence. They constituted a coastal strip with large appendages stretching inland. The strongest Christian ally in the region, the Byzantine Empire, was almost as hostile to the Crusaders as the Muslims were. Moreover, after the initial conquest ended and the "pilgrimage" was over, the colonies were deprived of the bulk of their military strength that allowed them to be established in the first place, as the Crusaders returned home. The "feudalization" of the region gave the colonies a system of military defense, but it was one that constantly needed to be supplemented with Western recruits. Colonization took place but not on the scale needed to meet defensive requirements. Crusades were a temporary, rather than constant, phenomenon. The Crusader States, from their inception, were dependent on Western assistance. Pilgrims coming to worship at the shrines often provided support, as did the plethora of "small Crusades" that took place between the First and Second (1147–1149) Crusades.

Venice provides the most suitable example for a case study of the relationship between the Crusader States and Italian maritime republics. The important role that the republic played in the acquisition of Tyre (1124) needs to be placed within the larger context of its trade activity in the eastern Mediterranean. Venice appears to have been replicating, by and large, the strategy that secured it such great commercial concessions within the Byzantine Empire. Thus, its role in the conquest of Tyre does not mark any radical break with its existing policies. Rather than being Crusaders, the Venetians were merely expanding upon activities they had already been involved in decades before the Council of Clermont. Venice provided the Byzantine Empire with two valuable services: sea transport for imperial purposes and military assistance against its enemies, such as the Normans. In exchange, Venice received important privileges and trade concessions in the empire.

sive fleets. The importance of the Italian republics for crusading can easily be seen in Urban's approach to recruitment for the First Crusade. By and large, Urban envisioned the expedition as primarily being a French affair, but he took care in sending a stream of letters trying to enlist the support of the maritime republics.

MARITIME STATES

Opportunities presented by the creation of the Crusader States were attractive to the Venetians for obvious reasons: it allowed them to get in on the "ground floor" of new Christian states that promised great financial dividends. The *pactum warmundi* (Pact of Warmund) of 1124 outlines the salient features that became the hallmark of the Italian presence in the Crusader States. The agreement secured for Venice terms similar to those it previously acquired in the Byzantine Empire in exchange for military assistance. The terms were a bit better though—going beyond duty-free status and the right of extraterritoriality—probably because of the implied rights of conquest. The republic became integrated into the nascent feudal structure of the region. The nature of this relationship came to be one of the most important dynamics that shaped the history of the Crusader States.

Venice, as well as the other maritime republics that carved out similar niches, had a vested interest in the security and health of the Crusader States. They were vassals of a peculiar sort since they could bring to bear the considerable military and economic might of their states when needed. Vows of loyalty were not what bound them most strongly to the fate of their overlords but rather material gain. Most of the leading magnates and higher vassals of Outremer had familial connections to western Europe, but the resources that these relationships allowed them to draw upon were insignificant compared to those of the maritime republics, whose vitality was enmeshed with the condition of the eastern Mediterranean. In a manner of speaking, the Italian maritime republics—granted for different reasons—were more forcefully committed to the preservation of the Crusader States than any other European power. For France and England, for example, preserving the Christian presence in the Holy Land was a costly spiritual luxury that dropped in importance as conditions in the West changed. For the maritime republics, conditions in the East were always of the greatest importance.

A common criticism that historians (and contemporaries) have leveled against the maritime republics is the remarkable degree to which they interjected their own conflicts and rivalries into the Crusader States. The accusation is a valid one, but it can easily be overemphasized. Territorial and commercial conflicts among the maritime states destabilized the region at times, but they were not the only, or even the most common, agents of destabilization. Feudalism was an unstable form of government organization. The War of St. Sabas (1256–1258), for example—probably the most catastrophic civil war in the history of the Crusader States—was precipitated by Venetian-Genoese rivalry. But how did a conflict between two mercantile states over a church engulf nearly the entire colony? The conflict between Venice and Genoa was merely a casus belli that ignited and amplified preexisting tensions among the lords of the Crusader States. Barons and military orders all chose sides. Tension between Tripoli and Sidon, for instance, certainly preexisted the Sabbas affair—the conflict only provided a tangible reason for opening hostilities that were rooted in old animosities between the states. The powder keg was already there; Venice and Genoa simply lit the match. The Italian republics, moreover, were not the only agents that introduced Western problems and rivalries into the region. Did not English king Richard I, the Lion-Hearted, and French king Philip II introduce their own tensions and allegiances into the Third Crusade (1189–1192), resulting in a situation as calamitous as Sabbas? What about the activities of Holy Roman Emperor Frederick II in claiming the crown of Jerusalem? The dependency of the colonies on the West, combined with confusing networks of familial relations and external loyalties, introduced constant instability to the region. The Italian republics are guilty as charged—but so is everyone else.

Maybe the problems that a Richard or Frederick introduced can be excused on the grounds that they "saved" the Holy Land or at least bettered its position. If this argument is the case, however, one must be even more understanding when it comes to the maritime republics. The Italians were a constant presence that provided steady, long-term support for the Holy Land rather than isolated and sporadic (if pious) campaigns. Constant, long-term, and committed support was precisely what the Crusader States needed. While the Italian republics are susceptible to charges of pursuing policies to secure their own interests, once again, they were not unique in this regard. Almost all the feudal lords in the region acted with a fair degree of autonomy and pursued their own interests. Likewise with the military orders; they frequently acted just as independently as the maritime republics. The Templars and Hospitallers were capable of full-blown conflict with one another over rights to ovens and mills. Condemning the maritime republics for such conduct is extremely anachronistic; it demands that Venice and other maritime republics adhere to modern notions of nationalism and fulfill romantic expectations of what defined loyal warriors of Christ.

Transport and supplies were other crucial services that the Italian republics provided to the Crusader States. The Italians were not the only ones who possessed the only fleets that were useful to the Crusaders: ships from France, England, Spain, Sicily, and other countries all played a role in the movement. The Italian republics, however, contributed great fleets that consistently promoted the goals of the colonies rather than providing only sporadic aid. The Italians not only established military dominance on the seas but also provided the colonists with essential supplies from the West. Wheat and pork were staples that the Crusader States imported from Europe. The Crusader States had commercial and diplomatic contacts with Islamic powers (they were enmeshed in the trade and, despite hostilities, frequently arrived at a modus vivendi with the enemy). Naturally, warhorses were of great importance to the Crusader States, but they could not be procured locally and had to be imported from Europe. Islamic military tactics were much different than those of Europeans. Muslims favored mares that moved quickly but could bear little weight. The Crusaders, on the other hand, fought on stallions that could easily support the weight of a fully armed knight. Such horses, which were in constant demand in the Crusader States, could only be acquired by breeders in western Europe. In addition to supplying such essentials as food and stallions (and of course transmitting information), the Italian republics also generated hefty amounts of revenue that were sorely needed by the colonists. In the money that these states generated for the colonies one can find what perhaps was the greatest contribution to maintaining the Crusader States.

Land, the main source of revenue and military power in the Middle Ages, was always limited in the Crusader States. Cash played a role that was much more pronounced in this region than in the feudal societies of Europe. The terrain of the Crusader States was favorable for cash crops, such as grapes for wine, that could be exported. Its position in the center of the important trade routes linking Europe and the Far East also held great financial promise. The duty-free status that the Italian republics enjoyed can easily obfuscate their economic value to the Crusader States. At first glance it seems to suggest that the King of Jerusalem was deprived of revenue. Yet, "duty-free" meant that while the republics were immune to royal taxation, the Easterners with whom they traded were not. Rather than siphoning cash from the royal purse, the republics made it burst at the seams. Tax exemptions prompted the republics to expand trade as much as possible; that policy, in the process, increased the taxes the crown collected from nonexempt factors the Italians traded with. These optimum terms, moreover, gave the republics a powerful incentive to divert as much trade as possible through the Crusader States rather than to

rival ports, such as Constantinople and Alexandria, that were less profitable. The eagerness of the Italians to capitalize on these terms may help explain the shifting patterns of the East-West trade routes. Acre and Tyre, for example, became great trade centers, and this status doubtless was the result of the efforts of the Italians. The revenue that this trade generated was of the utmost importance to the crown. With land as scarce as it was in the region, the crown now had the resources to create many "money fiefs" that substituted customs duties and the like for land grants.

The Italian maritime republics thus made several contributions to the survival of the Crusader States that could not be offered by any other power. They supplied the colonies with desperately needed products from the West that could not be easily obtained in the East. They provided the colonies with sorely needed revenue as the republics laid the foundations for making cities such as Acre and Tyre thriving ports of global importance. They dominated the seas and thereby protected the Crusader States from attacks along the coast, while maintaining their all-important maritime pipeline to the West. The well-being and fate of the Crusader States were intimately linked to the sea—and the Italian republics were the masters of that sea. The damage that the maritime republics did to the health of the Crusader States can easily be misconstrued and blown out of proportion. Yes, they frequently conducted policies that served their own interests, but so did the majority of the barons in the Crusader States, as well as members of military orders. Yes, they forged alliances with and provided services for Muslims in the region, but so did the majority of the nobles and military orders. Yes, they interjected their rivalries and European problems into the fragile balance that kept the colonies in existence, but so did almost every major leader of a crusading expedition. To vigorously attack the important role that the republics played in the survival of the Crusader States is to point out the shortcomings of feudal organization itself. Yes, the modern nation-state would have made the Crusader States a more solid and stable political unit with much better chances for long-term existence, but that system had not been invented yet.

Doubtless, spiritual concerns were peripheral to the Italian maritime republics' interests. Like Dandalo, financial profits rather than spiritual gains were their priority. The crucial contributions the republics made to the acquisition and preservation of the Crusader States need to be placed within their appropriate contexts. Doing so necessitates disavowing any romantic notions one might hold about crusading. Their ultimate goals were not the same as those of the Crusaders—though the immediate objectives of all parties frequently merged. Essentially, the republics became an important part of the crusading movement via serendipity. Their commercial and military campaigns against Islam predated the Crusades and then dovetailed with them. They were more allied to, than part of, the movement. In the final tally their drive for commercial expansion significantly weakened Islamic power in the region while bolstering that of the Crusader States. Furthermore, even if motivated by profit, the plethora of valuable services that they provided for the Crusader States played a major role in the two-century survival of a colony that could not exist on its own.

—TODD MARX, CONCORD, NEW HAMPSHIRE

Viewpoint:
No. The Italian maritime republics were actually agents of destabilization that weakened the Crusader States.

When the Mamluks finally succeeded in "driving the Franks into the sea" and thereby definitively terminated the existence of the Latin Crusader States in the East, Christendom diligently reassessed its Eastern policies in an effort to modify its approach to prosecuting the war against Islam. How could the situation be remedied? Such reassessment had been taking place since the Second Council of Lyons (1274), but the fall of Acre (1291) gave the issue much greater immediacy. The Council inaugurated a new age of crusading theory that was dominated by treatises written by "experts" (though this genre became a common one in which people without any real expertise tried their hand). The old stock explanation for military failure against Muslims—that defeat was divine punishment for Christian sins—continued to enjoy wide currency. More worldly and routine shortcomings, however, gradually received greater attention. Some scholars focused on the failures of the military orders, some on papal avarice, and some on Byzantine intrigues. A common denominator among those theorists who knew the issues best, that is, who had personal experience in the Holy Land, was the debilitating effects that the greed of the Italian maritime republics, principally Venice and Genoa, had on the health of the Latin colonies. Some scholars even saw the republics as the greatest single impediment to degrading Islamic power in the region and strengthening the Crusader States.

Assessing the effects of the Italian maritime states on the preservation of the Latin colonies seems, at first glance, an easy task. Control of the coast had always been important for Christian security in the East and, after the Battle of the Horns of Hattin (1187) and the Third Crusade (1189–1192), the sine qua non for the survival of the Crusader States. The rulers of the Crusader States were completely dependent on aid from the West: troops, financial support, profits from pilgrimage traffic, and trade. By the end of the twelfth century the supply of these items hinged upon sea routes. The Italian maritime republics had the greatest fleets and were the forgers and guardians of the sea pipeline that allowed the Crusader States to exist while surrounded by enemy forces. They were partners in maintaining a strong Christian presence in the region; without their services the Crusader States would have either withered slowly or been quickly crushed. Thus, the contribution the maritime states made seems clear and of the utmost importance: they allowed the Crusader States to survive.

How, then, can one evaluate the vociferous condemnation of the maritime republics by learned and informed crusading experts? Most historians of the Crusades agree that the presence and activities of the Italian republics in the East were a mixed bag of benefits and liabilities. Frequently, the advantages that the Venetians and Genoese conferred upon the Crusader States have been judged to outweigh the admittedly troublesome problems they introduced or fanned. The reverse is the case: the benefits the maritime republics provided the rulers of Outremer were precious few, and those that existed were completely nullified by the wholesale disruption the Italian states introduced.

Venice provides the most instructive example for analysis since it was the most powerful of the Italian maritime states. Participants in the First Crusade (1096–1102) almost exclusively traveled to their destination by land, so sea passage and transport was not an issue (though in later Crusades it became one of great magnitude). Sea power, however, played an important role in securing the fortified coastal cities. The first great benchmark of the Venetian role in crusading was the *pactum warmundi* (Pact of Warmund), an agreement made in 1124 between the Patriarch of Jerusalem and the Venetian republic designed to secure the latter's assistance in the conquest of the important port of Tyre. In exchange for its valuable contribution, the Venetian republic received one-third of the city and countryside, significant commercial concessions, and a generous degree of autonomy within its holdings. Recognizing this arrangement and confirming Venetian rights in Tyre became a prerequisite for the coronation

Relief of a medieval galley on a headstone at the Crusader port of Aigues-Mortes, France

of a king. Venetian interests were above all commercial, and the revenues they produced were highly valued by rulers of the Crusader States. In the decades that separated the conquest of Tyre and the crushing defeat Muslim sultan Saladin inflicted upon the colonists, the significance of sea power diminished (but did not entirely disappear) in tactical importance. Hattin and its aftermath changed that status and inaugurated a period in which control of the coast was a strategic concern that dwarfed almost all others in comparison.

Appreciating the role that Venice played during the first hundred years in the history of the Crusader States must be placed within the context of the decentralized nature of feudal politics and warfare. The relationship between the Venetians and rulers of the Crusader States was more that of a partnership than that of a superior and subordinate. Rights of conquest and other forms of military compensation that existed before the birth of the modern nation-state gave politics and war flavors that would stun the palate of a modern statesman. Venice willingly assisted in the conquest of Tyre because the activity promoted its objective of commercial expansion in the eastern Mediterranean. In a sense this goal was little more than the mutual division of spoils. Comparing Venetian interests with those of French aristocrats Godfrey of Bouillon or Raymond de Saint-Gilles during the First Crusade would introduce a degree

of confusion that would render the situation impervious to sound and cogent analysis. In essence, the Venetian fleet that played such an important role in the conquest of Tyre was not a "Crusader" fleet. Rather, it was the campaign of a commercially expansive state that seized upon an opportunity to extend yet further its penetration into the eastern Mediterranean. Land grants and concessions were the main forms of compensation, and that is precisely what Venice secured. In a manner of speaking, Venice functioned as a "vassal" to the patriarch of Jerusalem and the absentee king, who was in captivity.

What distinguished the role of maritime states such as Venice in the feudal structure of the Latin East was its status as a sovereign state rather than that of an individual or family. Feudalism was an economic and political form of social organization that could work in favor of or against the goals of a king. Steven Tibble's work, *Monarchy and Lordships in the Latin Kingdom of Jerusalem, 1099–1291* (1989), on the feudal structure of the Crusader States is quite revealing on this issue. According to Tibble, royal power waxed or waned in accordance with the "fluid" or "rigid" nature of feudal organization. Kings enjoyed the right of capitalizing on "feudal incidents" to reshuffle the political deck in their favor (for example, unexpected deaths, lack of male heirs, and minority rules). Feudal rights were defined by the man and the family; when tragedy struck, it signaled opportunity for a lord. Claims of a sovereign maritime state introduced a marked sense of "rigidity" to the feudal structure because claims did not end with an unexpected death or the end of a family line. This policy drastically circumscribed the effects of the royal "trump card" in feudal politics. Lordships held by families could potentially revert back to the crown and assist with consolidating power. Technically, holdings of maritime republics were those of a sovereign state and beyond absorption by kings. Royal policy in the East eventually focused on centralizing power at the expense of the large holdings of the feudal barons. Consolidation of resources under the crown, as well as the establishment of diplomatic and tactical unity, would have strengthened the position of the Latin States. Venice and the other maritime republics were not the only vassals that resisted this tendency, but as sovereign states they proved to be chestnuts more difficult to crack than even the most powerful families of the East. In this sense, their presence was a continuing obstacle to the centralization of power that proved to be a source of weakness in the defense of the realm. The maritime republics were a pernicious block to the slow, but important, process of creating nation-states.

Another debilitating effect that the maritime republics had on the Latin colonies sprang from the former's individual approaches to foreign policy with the Islamic states. "Private" foreign policy was rather commonplace in feudal societies but was more pronounced in the Latin East. The clash between Saladin and the Crusader States, for example, was partially produced by Reynald of Chatillon, the lord of Antioch, who in defiance of royal wishes raided Islamic caravans, disrupting an already uneasy truce. He provided Saladin with the perfect casus belli for breaking the peace. Although Reynald's policies clashed with royal ones, he still had the strength and security of the region at heart, even if this goal translated into actions that contradicted the immediate objectives of the crown. Reynald spent years in a Damascene prison; the source of all his wealth and power was intertwined with the fate of the Crusader States. The Italian maritime republics, however, were interested in the Crusader States only for the profits that they could yield. Although they most likely had a spiritual interest in the Holy Land being within the political orbit of Christendom, their religious piety more often than not yielded to the pressure of profits. The havoc that such an approach inflicted on the defense of the Crusader States can be best exemplified in the attempts at establishing a blockade to deprive those Islamic states bordering the Latin colonies of war materials.

A Christian-enforced trade embargo had long captured the interest of crusading strategists. Although naval blockades of Islamic ports became an almost universal strategy for "prepping" Crusades of recovery after 1291, the concept was well known to Crusade theorists and organizers before the fall of Acre. Raising such a naval blockade was tactically sound, but completely unrealistic: the Italian maritime republics were the only powers capable of enforcing it. These states, such as Venice, however, frequently pursued a policy of cordial relations with Egypt because of its trade value. Crusader plans that focused on the complete conquest of Egypt interested the Italian republics—for rather than placating Muslim rivals in exchange for good terms, they would be able to completely replace them. Venice, for example, was delighted with Holy Roman Emperor Frederick II's plan to conquer Egypt and was more than willing to cut the region off commercially. Barring a conquest of Egypt, maritime republics valued trade concessions from Muslims more than the prospect of an effective method for degrading Islamic military power, which would complicate political relations between the Italians and Egyptians and thus have vast commercial consequences.

The Venetians were content with selling weapons to one side and bandages to the other. It could be argued that the war between Christians and Muslims in the region created markets and trade demands that Venice thrived on. Would the prospect of winning the battle in the Holy Land be possible with a naval blockade radically altering the balance of power? Crusading theorists after the fall of Acre were convinced that this was the case. Victory in the Holy Land was predicated on the crushing or absorption of Egypt, which was militarily strong only because the commercial profits it yielded were funneled into its war machine. The Italian republics made such a blockade impossible. Pope Innocent III, arguably one of the most powerful medieval popes, made securing the Holy Land one of the main focuses of his pontificate. Yet, even he had to yield to Venetian pressure that emerged against the proposal to ban the shipping of war matériel to the Muslims. The Italian maritime republics contributed to the demise of the Crusader States in their uncompromising willingness to provide Muslims with all the supplies needed for pushing the Crusaders into the sea. During the Mamluk era in Egypt these supplies were of even greater importance. The Mamluk military machine (indeed, society in general) relied on a constant resupply of slaves. Italian fleets played an instrumental role, regardless of any formal ban prohibiting it, in providing the sultanate with the slaves it needed. Genoa, in fact, made manning Mamluk armies with slave recruits a commercial specialty. Many of the slave soldiers who eventually helped to defeat the Crusader States were probably delivered to Egypt by Italian slave traders. Fidenzio of Padua, one of the first great Crusade theorists, along with Pope Nicholas IV, who adopted his theories, argued that a non-Italian fleet needed to be created to enforce the embargo since the maritime republics, the supposed guardians of such an enterprise, were the most consistent impediment to making one successful. Rather than placing the wolf in charge of protecting the sheep, it was more advisable to create a new fleet that would spend its time enforcing the embargo rather than relying on the existing guardians, who constantly circumvented it.

Perhaps the most notorious example of an Italian republic placing its own trade interests over the welfare of the Holy Land was the Fourth Crusade (1202–1204). As is well known, the Fourth Crusade was redirected from its target (Egypt) toward Christian powers that were interfering with Venetian commercial hegemony. The "opening act" of the Fourth Crusade was the "Zara Crusade," which was no more than a Venetian-orchestrated strike upon a rebellious port, designed to drag the city back into the commercial orbit of Venice. The "grand finale" was the sack and conquest of the Byzantine Empire. The Byzantines had been circumscribing Venetian trade concessions within the Empire and were flirting with the Venetian arch rival, Genoa. The Fourth Crusade left Egypt completely unmolested—in fact, not a single Muslim was killed—and resulted in the restoration of Venetian commercial primacy in the region.

The Italian maritime republics also weakened the Crusader States by constantly throwing their personal rivalries into the fragile balance of the Latin East. Their trade rivalries on the seas, and their relations to patrons in the West, could produce or inflame causes for civil war in a federation of states surrounded by enemies dedicated to eradicating them. The devastating effects such conflicts had on the Latin East can be easily observed in the War of St. Sabas (1256–1258) that rocked Acre. Rivalries among the maritime trading states had caused problems prior to Sabas (and not only among Italian republics, as the scuffles between Montpellier and Marseilles show). Genoa and Pisa faced one another with troops and siege engines. Previous conflicts between maritime

republics over trade concessions and properties, however, are dwarfed by the Sabbas affair.

Acre strongly resembled the Italian cities in that it was bursting at the seams with the towers and walls that made civil wars in the republics such a complicated business. The fortifications at Acre were designed to protect Christians against Christians internally, as well as to protect Christians against Muslims externally. In effect, the Italian maritime republics were exporting not only the causes but also the means for aggressive and destabilizing wars over trade issues. The War of St. Sabbas was ignited in a dispute concerning a cluster of properties that sat between the Venetian and Genoese holdings in Acre. Apparently, each republic had reason to believe that the Pope had granted them these properties. In 1256 the Genoese, after enlisting the support of their former rival Pisa, invaded the Venetian quarter. Arbitration reconciled Venice and Pisa in 1257, leaving Genoa in a weaker position to force its claims. The barons of Outremer began casting their lots in the conflict, backing either Venice or Genoa. After losing their important holdings in Tyre, Venice attacked Genoan interests in Acre. Hopes of arbitration evaporated as Genoa and Acre suspected any peace overture as masking a conspiratorial attack prompted by the other side. The war over a few holdings quickly spread beyond Tyre and into Tripoli. It also pitted Tripoli in battle against Sidon. The scale of the conflict escalated to dizzying heights. Back in Acre, siege engines within the city caused utter devastation. Venetian and Genoese fleets clashed all along the coast. Finally, by 1270, French king Louis IX negotiated an uneasy settlement between the two powers, but by then the Crusader States were crushed by both the structural damage and resilient political divisions caused or compounded by the conflict. The Latin East never fully recovered from the wounds inflicted in the War of St. Sabas.

On a more subtle level, the most damaging thing that the maritime republics provided to the Crusader States was their services, which masked the greatest weakness of the Latin colonies: their lack of sea power. The colonies were little more than coastal enclaves and their hinterlands, for the bulk of their existence; Crusader State security and prosperity depended on the sea. If the maritime republics had not offered such a convenient and cost-effective solution to this problem, the rulers of Outremer would have been forced to create their own fleets, which would have pursued and enforced the interests of the Crusader States rather than those of other Mediterranean trading republics. Such fleets could have enforced the trade embargo on Egypt. Rulers in Outremer could have dominated their own seas, bolstering their profits while establishing their own commercial presence and military hegemony throughout the region. Such a course of action might well have created a viable and autonomous colony that could have been able to survive and prosper.

–CARL HILL, LOS ANGELES, CALIFORNIA

References

Eugene H. Byrne, "The Genoese Colonies in Syria," in *The Crusades and Other Historical Essays: Presented to Dana C. Munro By His Former Students,* edited by Louis J. Paetow (New York: Crofts, 1928), pp. 139–182.

Andrew Ehrenkreutz, "Strategic Implications of the Slave Trade between Genoa and Mamluk Egypt in the Second Half of the Thirteenth Century," in *The Islamic Middle East, 700-1900: Studies in Economic and Social History,* edited by A. L. Udovitch (Princeton, N.J.: Darwin Press, 1981), pp. 335–345.

John Godfrey, *1204: The Unholy Crusade* (Oxford & New York: Oxford University Press, 1980).

Angeliki E. Laiou, *Constantinople and the Latins: The Foreign Policy of Andronicus II, 1282–1328* (Cambridge, Mass.: Harvard University Press, 1972).

Joshua Prawer, *Crusader Institutions* (Oxford: Clarendon Press / New York: Oxford University Press, 1980).

Jean Richard, *The Latin Kingdom of Jerusalem,* translated by Janet Shirley (Amsterdam & New York: North-Holland, 1979).

Jonathan Riley-Smith, "The Venetian Crusade of 1122–1124," in *I communi italiani nel regno crociato di Gerusalemme: atti del Colloquio "The Italian Communes in the Crusading Kingdom of Jerusalem": (Jerusalem, May 24–May 28, 1984),* edited by Gabriella Airaldi and Benjamin Z. Kedar (Genoa: Università di Genova, Istituto di Medievistica, 1986).

Steven Tibble, *Monarchy and Lordships in the Latin Kingdom of Jerusalem, 1099–1291* (Oxford: Clarendon Press / New York: Oxford University Press, 1989).

Daniel Waley, *The Italian City-Republics* (London: Weidenfeld & Nicolson, 1969; New York: McGraw-Hill, 1969).

MILITARY ORDERS

Did the Islamic *ribat* (military religious communities) serve as the model for the Christian Crusaders?

Viewpoint: Yes. The *ribat* served as a stimulus for the concept of monastic warriors, which was then refashioned and shaped by Latin Christian culture.

Viewpoint: No. The rise of the military orders was purely Christian in origin and was a continuation of the papal reform movement.

The Order of the Temple, the first Christian military religious order, was formed in 1119 when a band of knights took the monastic vows of poverty, chastity, and obedience and dedicated themselves to the protection of pilgrims along the dangerous roads of the newly formed Crusader States. They received support from both the Patriarch and king of Jerusalem; the latter provided them with a section of the Temple Mount from which the order derived its name. French monk Bernard of Clairvaux, the most powerful churchman of the period, took up the Templar cause as well by lobbying for the new order, writing their rule, and promulgating a grand defense of their vocation. The order was confirmed at the Council of Troyes (1129) and subsequent papal bulls clarified their status. Because of the precarious condition of the Crusader States the military role of the Templars soon expanded, and other orders, such as the Hospital of St. John, followed the Templar example and developed military wings. Eventually, the military orders became the backbone of Latin defense in the East and possessed massive resources in the West to fund their activities. The Templars and Hospitallers eventually ranked among the most powerful institutions of the Middle Ages. Military orders came to play crucial roles in all three main crusading theaters: the eastern Mediterranean, Spain, and eastern Europe.

The military orders were innovations in an age that was extremely suspicious of novelty of any sort. Some men had doubts as to whether combining military and religious lives was feasible. One critic went so far as to call this "new knighthood" a "new monstrosity." Nearly all men saw it as a hybrid, but generally speaking, support for the new vocation was widespread. Beginning in the early nineteenth century some historians began questioning whether the rise of the military orders could be explained in a purely Christian context. There seems to be something inherently un-Christian about monks who kill. Islamic influences were explored. In 1818 the Austrian historian Joseph von Hammer suggested that the Templars were influenced by the Shi'ite Assassins. A more popular Islamic institution discussed as a possible influence were the *ribats,* religious-military communities that arose on the Islamic frontiers to fight the infidel. Little is known about their organization or the men who lived in them, but they appear generally to have been temporary associations. Opponents of the *ribat*–military order theory claim that the rise of the Templars and the diffusion of their vocation to new orders are explicable in Christian terms. The religious tenor of the late eleventh and early twelfth centuries was aggressive and militant. Rather than rising from Islamic origins, the military orders sprang from the same religious and social forces that produced the First Crusade (1096–1102).

Viewpoint:
Yes. The *ribat* served as a stimulus for the concept of monastic warriors, which was then refashioned and shaped by Latin Christian culture.

Ribats were fortified collective retreats, somewhat like monasteries, that arose along the frontiers of the Islamic empire from the eighth century on to protect the kingdom and also to serve as forward positions for mounting raids into enemy territory. Not all *ribats* had military functions, but those that did were garrisoned by ascetic warriors who did not have to be monks in any formal sense. Soldiers went there but so did private individuals hoping to win heavenly rewards through such military service. The men in the communities were celibate, and, while not fighting, inmates engaged in ascetic religious exercises. Although many historians have made clear that a *ribat* warrior was not literally like a Christian both in Islamic Spain and in North Africa *munastir,* an Arabic word derived from the Latin word for monastery, was a synonym for *ribat.* In both areas *munastir* survives in place-names—a famous fortification called Munastir in Tunisia; in Spain, two Almonacids (a deformed form of *al-munastir*) in Aragon and an Almonesir in Valencia; and various *munastirs* cited in medieval Arabic sources. The significance is that medieval Muslims noted the similarities between *ribats* and monasteries, and they associated the former with holy war: an Islamic hadith (tradition) says that jihad (just war) is "the monasticism of Islam."

In Islamic Spain the eleventh and twelfth centuries were the great age of *ribat*-based warfare, culminating in the rule of the Almoravid dynasty (1086–1146). The Almoravids originated with a Sanhaja Berber tribesmen who had gathered in a *ribat* on an island in the Senegal River around a mystical reformer named Ibn Yasin. The movement that he led was called *al-murabitun* (Latinized as Almoravid) or "those who live in a ribat."

The argument for Muslim influence on Christian military orders is based on chronology, geography, and inferences drawn from functional similarities between the two institutions. There is no direct, documented evidence, but Christian military orders arose in the twelfth century in Spain and Palestine, two areas with a militarized frontier with Islam. The Hospitallers attended to the needs of poor and sick Christians arriving in Jerusalem. Somewhat later (1119) the Templars, calling themselves the "little soldiers of Christ," began by protecting pilgrims from Muslim attacks along the

routes to the holy city. Both orders also took part in the *Reconquista* (reconquest of Spain), particularly in Aragon and Catalonia, where they proliferated in the first third of the twelfth century. The earliest *ribats* in Islamic Spain were in the northeast of the peninsula, particularly in southern Catalonia and the Ebro Valley, an active frontier area in the ninth and tenth centuries called the Upper March by the Arabs: a Rapita at Balaguer, north of Lleida; a Rebato to the northwest of Barcelona; another to the northwest of Tarragona; Sant Carles de la Rapita near Tortosa; and several on the Valencian coast. After the fall of the Almoravids, native Spanish military orders sprang up, further to the west. The kingdom of Granada—with an active, embattled frontier facing the Christians from the mid thirteenth century to 1492—is peppered with *ribat* place-names, many of which, however, appeared to have no military function but were simply communal residences for devotees of mysticism, similar to the North African *zawiyas.*

In 1158 a Spanish military order was founded at Calatrava, a fortified town on the left bank of the Guadiana River, just north of Ciudad Real. This site had been a key frontier post in the years after the Almoravid collapse, controlling the approach to Toledo from the south, and it had been garrisoned by Templars in 1147. In the early 1150s, fearing another Berber onslaught, the Templars announced that Calatrava could not be held and handed the castle back to the Crown. In the words of the General Chronicle: "They could not stand against the great power of the Arab, for they were not adequately equipped to stop them. Moreover, the king had not found any among the great men of Castile that would . . . face the dangers of that place." A group of Cistercian monks from Navarre occupied the site in 1158, the founding date of the military order. Like the Islamic *ribats,* the order of Calatrava and those of Santiago and Alcántara (both founded in Spain in the twelfth century) were intended to engage in holy war on the frontier, especially in the most dangerous and exposed areas. When Calatrava (now called Old Calatrava) fell into the hinterland with the southward advance of the frontier, the order moved its headquarters south to New Calatrava, again on the frontier.

In the nature of warfare, enemies routinely adopt the successful techniques and styles of their opponents in order to improve their chances of fighting them successfully. Besides the military orders, Spaniards adopted other military customs and techniques from Muslim usage. Christians copied the characteristic tactics of the Muslim warrior-monks of the *ribats,* particularly the organized raid, which they called by two terms taken from Arabic, *algara* or *rebate*. The first term comes from the Arabic *al-ghara*, which means an incursion into enemy territory for the purpose of taking booty. The second is from *ribat* itself, that is, the tactic favored by *ribat*-based warriors. King Alfonso X the Wise of Castile states in his law code, the *Siete Partidas,* that "Algaras . . . are another way of making war which the ancients found fruitful in causing harm to one's enemies; because [it consists in] traversing the land and stealing that which is found there."

Medieval Spanish knights rode like Muslim *Zanata* (a nomadic Berber group), with short stirrups, a fairly low saddle, and a palate bit that enabled the horse to turn far more quickly than by pulling at the sides of its mouth. Heavily armored European feudal knights rode with long stirrups and used a saddle with a high cantle to withstand a lance thrust in close battle but that was unwieldy in the less formal raiding style that Muslim border warriors favored. Christians appropriated Muslim military gear and weaponry, such as the *azagaya* (a kind of lance) and the *algarrada* (a machine for hurling rocks). On occasion they even dressed like Muslim knights. Emulation of the flexible offensive/defensive tactics of *ribat* warfare would have been completely within the tradition of open cross-cultural borrowing in military life. Raiding soldiers were called *Almogavers,* from *mughawir,* "they who fight in *gharas,*" or *algaras.* Christians could only conceptualize this kind of warfare by using the Arabic terms. Therefore, although evidence for the influence of the *ribat* on Christian military orders is inferential, there are too many similarities and coincidences to allow one to dismiss the case.

–THOMAS F. GLICK,
BOSTON UNIVERSITY

Viewpoint:
No. The rise of the military orders was purely Christian in origin and was a continuation of the papal reform movement.

In 1820 Jose Antonio Conde, in *Historia de la dominacion de los arabes en España, sacada de varios manuscritos y memorias arabigas,* opened the debate on whether or not the Christian military orders that emerged during the early crusading period were influenced by the Islamic *ribat.* Rough institutional analogy, combined with the assumption that a fusion of religious and military lives was alien to the Christian mentality, was all Conde could offer

in support of his theory. Still, it received considerable attention if for no other reason than it was just as difficult to prove as to disprove the thesis. More than a century later, amid great debate over the meaning of "Spaniard" taking place during Francisco Franco's regime (1936–1973), the argument was developed more fully by the great Spanish scholar Américo Castro, who was at ground zero in an historical debate over the nature of modern Spanish identity. Castro was the firebrand of the *convivencia* (coexistence) theory that posited that the Spaniard was the product of deep cultural blending and synthesis among Jews, Christians, Muslims, and their respective cultures and traditions over centuries. The result was an entirely new culture that was a hybrid, identical to none of the parent cultures but sharing similarities with all. The opposing camp was led by Claudio Sanchez-Albornoz, who proffered the "eternal Spaniard" thesis, which focused on a breed of man sired by the best characteristics of Roman and Germanic societies. According to this theory, the true Spaniard had his dynamic nature temporarily muted by Islamic domination. Sanchez-Albornoz argued that the eternal Spaniard was exceptionally resilient, resisted the allures of the alien culture that was currently in ascendance, regrouped, reconquered the homeland, and resumed his existence virtually without skipping a beat.

Castro's case for the Islamic *ribat* being the model for the Christian military orders was thus a small chapter of the theoretical construct that was his life's work. Understanding the strong Spanish context of this debate is essential for comprehending the subtle dynamics at work in the academic skirmishes surrounding the *ribat*–military order connection. The influence that Castro had, and still has, on historians of Spain is almost beyond calculation. It is no coincidence that the advocates for the *ribat*–military order argument are exclusively historians of the western Mediterranean in general and of Spain in particular. Historians of the Crusades and the Crusader States in the East are virtually unanimous in rejecting such an influence. The Templars, the first Christian military order and the one that certainly provided the model for the others that followed, originated in the East. Thus, one way of describing the context for this debate is that scholarly (or cultural) neuroses peculiar to Spain and the implications of *convivencia* were exported across the Mediterranean.

There is, however, an alternative way of describing the context: many historians of Spain, following Castro's lead, are more conversant in the theories and tools of the social sciences. This stance is taken in a seminal article written by Thomas F. Glick and Oriol Pi-Sunyer, "Acculturation as an Explanatory Concept in Spanish History" (1969), a work that revitalized and gave anthropological support to the *ribat* theory of the origins of the military orders. The introductory quote by French anthropologist Claude Levi-Strauss sets the tone: "If anthropology and history once begin to collaborate in the study of contemporary societies, it will become apparent, that . . . the one science can achieve nothing without the help of the other." Glick applied the theory of "stimulus diffusion" developed by the great American anthropologist Alfred Louis Kroeber to Castro's proposal of a *ribat*–military order connection. According to the theory of stimulus diffusion, a culture that is attracted to a foreign institution, but cannot absorb it "as is" because of cultural incongruence, absorbs the alien "stimulus" and reinvents it in accordance with its own values. When stimulus diffusion is applied to the *ribat*–military order connection the following picture emerges. Christian society in the eleventh century needed such a species of holy warrior because of prevailing military conditions. Christian religious principles clashed with those Islamic ones that served as the foundation for the *ribat*. Contact with the concept of *ribat* then served as a "stimulus" that was "re-created" in Christian terms, producing the foundations for the military orders. Because of the subtle means by which this process occurs, it is difficult to detect in the documentary record. Combining the methods of the historian and anthropologist à la Levi-Strauss, however, permits the scholar to delve deeply into the documents. As Glick pointed out, "In such a case, moreover, the anthropologist would expect precisely *not* to find that documented institutional continuity upon which medievalists so depend."

Such a theory is difficult to attack if the critic plays by the rules it has set. Part of the proof of the theory is that documentary evidence probably does not exist. Thus, it is not surprising that many historians of the military orders have suspected the use of spectral evidence of a sort by those trying to prove a connection. Elena Lourie, however, in her article "The Confraternity of Belchite, the Ribat, and the Temple" (1982), attempted to weave documentary evidence into the theory. The Belchite confraternity established by Alfonso of Aragon in 1122 is posited as a missing link of sorts between Islamic *ribats* and Christian military orders. The confraternity certainly shared characteristics with both *ribats* and the Templars. Moreover, it was established in a frontier society where *ribats* were known to exist. Still, the Belchite was not unique and equally resembles various lay confraternities that formed and disbanded in France. Rather than being a missing link that provides documentary evidence for the *ribat*–military order connection, the Belchite appears to be a garden variety lay society that dedicated itself to a religious cause. They were not monks, and there is no evidence that connects them in any way to the Templars. Alan J. Forey, author of *The Military Orders from the Twelfth to the Early Fourteenth Centuries* (1992) and one of the leading historians of the military orders, was Lou-

rie's harshest critic. A heated exchange began between the two scholars.

The strongest underlying assumption of the *ribat*-military-order theory is that Christian principles, unaided, could not have resulted in a combination of the religious and military vocations. Thus, it must have been an alien idea. If one cannot find any evidence in the institutional development of the Templars that links the order to the *ribat*, can one at least find evidence suggesting that some contemporaries found the concept to be inherently un-Christian and alien? Probably the most striking example (though it does not refer to the Templars directly) was a comment made by the archdeacon of Huntington in 1145, that combining the life of a monk and a knight was a monstrous merging of purity and corruption. A more ambivalent sense of unease can be found in the responses of some men when the Templars were actually becoming an order. The first Templars seemed a bit uneasy with their status, and their appeals to French ecclesiastic Bernard of Clairvaux for guidance suggest that they had been the recipients of some criticism. That Bernard took so long to respond to their requests before writing his great tract defending the Templars, *In Praise of the New Knighthood* (circa 1130–1140), has been seen by some as indicating the Cistercian abbot's own misgivings about the concept. Before considering Bernard's view, let us briefly consider two exemplary twelfth-century critics of the order and the possible reasons for their cautious approach to the "new knighthood."

The first criticism is that penned by "Hugh Peccator," an otherwise anonymous author. It took the form of a letter addressed to the first Templars. According to Hugh, one of the Devil's chief strategies in spreading sin is to encourage men to undertake good works and then subtly sabotage them. This argument suggests that Hugh did not necessarily see the proposed lifestyle of the Templars as an abomination but that he wondered if it were possible to live it faithfully. The religious life was a high ideal that was difficult to achieve and maintain; Hugh seems to have had his doubts that it could be sustained by men who, even though they might have the best intentions, not only inhabit the world beyond the cloister but also fight in it. The fury of warfare clashed with the life of inner contemplation that was the hallmark of the religious. Hugh certainly saw the military function of the Templars as an insurmountable obstacle to reaching the perfect religious life, but this stumbling block does not mean that they could not lead a lesser form of religious life. The Templars were not an abomination but rather a lesser form of the religious—a sort of "monasticism lite." Hugh's third criticism focused on the divinely ordained division of labor in the world. How could a body function, he asked, if each member duplicated the purpose of the other? Hugh had reservations about mingling

JUST WARRIORS

In the following letter, French ecclesiastic Bernard of Clairvaux defends the notion of Christian knighthood:

The knight of Christ, I say, may strike with confidence and die yet more confidently, for he serves Christ when he strikes, and serves himself when he falls. Neither does he bear the sword in vain, for he is God's minister, for the punishment of evildoers and for the praise of the good. If he kills an evildoer, he is not a mankiller, but, if I may so put it, a killer of evil. He is evidently the avenger of Christ towards evildoers and he is rightly considered a defender of Christians. Should he be killed himself, we know that he has not perished, but has come safely into port. When he inflicts death it is to Christ's profit, and when he suffers death, it is for his own gain. The Christian glories in the death of the pagan, because Christ is glorified; while the death of the Christian gives occasion for the King to show his liberality in the rewarding of his knight. In the one case the just shall rejoice when he sees justice done, and in the other man shall say, truly there is a reward for the just; truly it is God who judges the earth. . . .

When the battle is at hand, they arm themselves interiorly with faith and exteriorly with steel rather than decorate themselves with gold, since their business is to strike fear in the enemy rather than to incite his cupidity. They seek out horses which are strong and swift, rather than those which are brilliant and well-plumed, they set their minds on fighting to win rather than on parading for show. They think not of glory and seek to be formidable rather than flamboyant. At the same time, they are not quarrelsome, rash, or unduly hasty, but soberly, prudently and providently drawn up into orderly ranks, as we read of the fathers. Indeed, the true Israelite is a man of peace, even when he goes forth to battle.

Once he finds himself in the thick of battle, this knight sets aside his previous gentleness, as if to say, "Do I not hate those who hate you, O Lord; am I not disgusted with your enemies?" These men at once fall violently upon the foe, regarding them as so many sheep. No matter how outnumbered they are, they never regard these as fierce barbarians or as awe-inspiring hordes. Nor do they presume on their own strength, but trust in the Lord of armies to grant them the victory. They are mindful of the words of Maccabees, "It is simple enough for a multitude to be vanquished by a handful. It makes no difference to the God of heaven whether he grants deliverance by the hands of few or many; for victory in war is not dependent on a big army, and bravery is the gift of heaven." On numerous occasions they had seen one man pursue a thousand, and two put ten thousand to flight.

Thus in a wondrous and unique manner they appear gentler than lambs, yet fiercer than lions. I do not know if it would be more appropriate to refer to them as monks or as soldiers, unless perhaps it would be better to recognize them as being both. Indeed they lack neither monastic meekness nor military might. What can we say of this, except that this has been done by the Lord, and it is marvelous in our eyes. These are the picked troops of God, whom he has recruited from the ends of the earth; the valiant men of Israel chosen to guard well and faithfully that tomb which is the bed of the true Solomon, each man sword in hand, and superbly trained to war.

Source: Bernard of Clairvaux, *"In Praise of the New Knighthood,"* translated by Conrad Greenia, from Bernard of Clairvaux: Treatises Three, *Cistercian Fathers Series 19 (Cistercian Publications, 1977), pp. 127–145, in "Military Orders: In Praise of the New Knighthood (Liber ad milites Templi: De laude novae militia)," ORB: The Online Reference Book for Medieval Studies* <http://orb.rhodes.edu/encyclop/religion/monastic/bernard.html>.

the labors of those who traditionally prayed and those who traditionally fought. Hugh viewed their vocation as a hybrid, but after presenting his warnings he wished them well in their pursuits. That Hugh's letter was fixed to the Templar rule indicates that in the end it supported rather than objected to their vocation. Guigo de Castro, the prior of La Grande Chartreuse, who had an exceptionally learned command of monastic life, wrote a similar letter (circa 1130). Guigo had some concerns and doubts, but he eventually accepted the concept as a valid vocation.

Less receptive were the criticisms of the abbot Isaac L'Etoile, who, like Bernard, was a Cistercian. In a play on the title of Bernard's treatise justifying the Templar vocation, *In Praise of the New Knighthood,* Isaac referred to it as the "new monstrosity." Even more damning was his description of it as the "Order of the Fifth Gospel," a phrase that strongly indicates the abbot's belief that such a vocation was utterly alien to Christianity. The weapons of the truly religious were words and prayers, which were scarcely compatible with the swords and lances brandished by the Templars. Like French monk

Peter the Venerable, Isaac contrasted the gentle words of Christ and the apostles against the massacres and pillaging of the Christian warrior aristocracy. Isaac then raised warnings much like those voiced by Hugh Peccator and Guigo: good intentions can produce sinful results, and a violent life in the world may destroy the inner state of peace that is the hallmark of the religious life.

These reservations, followed by cautious acceptance, can be interpreted as evidence of stimulus diffusion that is more compelling than the Belchite confraternity. Both Hugh and Isaac had misgivings concerning the new hybrid. Isaac's response is more conducive to applying the theory. The "Order of the Fifth Gospel" can be seen as a perceptive reaction to the infiltration of an alien concept that Isaac recognized as patently un-Christian. Though he was never comfortable with the concept, he at least came to terms with it. Hugh and Isaac can be seen as "reconstructing" the alien stimulus using Christian concepts, with the doubts they expressed representing the fossilized footprints of an Islamic institution walking into Christian religious history. It can also be interpreted as the normal Christian reaction to "novelty" of any sort (and the Templars were without doubt novel). Innovation was always a traumatic experience for medieval society, particularly when it came to the foundation of any new religious order (the mendicants in the early thirteenth century being an excellent case in point). Innovation frequently is, but need not be, produced by cultural borrowing.

Proximity and contact are the sine qua non for stimulus diffusion and cultural borrowing of any sort. Is there any evidence supporting the proposition that such contact occurred? Naturally, the question is difficult–nearly impossible–to answer adequately. It is known that under the Almoravids, *ribats*, from which this Berber dynasty received its name, were a common fixture in the military landscape of Spain. In Spain, moreover, there was much contact between Muslim and Christian warriors, both fighting with and against one another alternately. If the first military order arose in Spain, then the argument for stimulus diffusion would be stronger. But it emerged in the East, where there is no evidence whatsoever for the existence of *ribats* at that time. In fact, the evidence implies there would not have been *ribats* in Syria and Palestine. The concept of jihad (just war) had cooled considerably in the region for some time, and an excellent case can be made for the Crusaders serving as the stimulus for a renewed emphasis on jihad beginning with Zengi, the Moslem Seljuk governor of Mosul. Critics of the *ribat* theory have pointed this fact out with great clarity. In all fairness, however, they have failed to point out that many Frenchmen had already fought against Muslims in Spain on the eve of the First Crusade (1096–1102). Thus, it is possible that contact with the *ribat* took place in Spain,

its stimulus was reworked in Christian terms, and it took root on the other side of the Mediterranean.

The theory draws upon much evidence that clashes with a wealth of hard evidence that indicates purely Christian origins. At its root, the debate really revolves around whether Christianity, in the early twelfth century, was capable of creating military orders without alien influences. There is a long trail of concrete evidence that shows that this development was not only possible but also probable. Stimulus diffusion goes far in explaining the deepest Christian roots of the military orders, but this stimulus did not originate from the Islamic world nor did it diffuse in the late eleventh and early twelfth centuries. It was the mutual exchange of stimuli and re-creations that took place between the Christian and Germanic worldviews in the early Middle Ages. Although neither crusading nor military orders necessarily or immediately followed from this cultural confluence, it created the original "hybrid" that bridged the gap between Christian pacifism (which had already been steadily waning since the conversion of Roman emperor Constantine I) and Germanic tribal militarism. The Germanic warrior became sanctified, and virtually all his wars became holy. Still, our subject is not holy war per se but the participation of monks in it. The synthesis of Germanic and Christian worldviews goes far in explaining the general contours of religious violence in the medieval mentality. But monks were supposed to be isolated from that view if, for no other reason, they were to be kept from society in general. Like the crusading movement, the immediate cause of the military orders is to be found in the Cluniac and Gregorian reforms. Both of these movements introduced great innovations that, in turn, eventually parented the military orders.

Cluniac reform revolutionized the Christian concept of sin and lay responsibility for it. Previously, a sharp line of demarcation separated monks and laity. They formed a symbiotic relationship that revolved around the divinely ordered division of labor in the world. Monks were the original "soldiers of Christ" who used prayers as weapons to fight evil in the spiritual realm. Because of the difficulty in leading the perfect Christian life and the harsh reality of human weakness, these monastic soldiers of Christ were the only perfect Christians, and it was their prayers and intercession that freed the laity from the unbearable weight of its sins. The Cluniac reform, while still recognizing that monks were the only perfect Christians, demanded that the laity bear more of the weight of its own sins. The layman could not be a perfect Christian, but he could be a better Christian and assume more responsibility for his sins. As this new view filtered into lay circles, an awareness and fear of sin proliferated. The laity needed outlets by which to purge

Templar castle of Peñíscola in the kingdom of Aragon

itself of the sins it accumulated. Pilgrimage traffic increased, and its penitential nature served the laity well and served as the greatest springboard for launching the First Crusade. Along with the rearticulation of the nature of lay sin came the need for new ways of purging it. Traditionally, such purging was done by monks carrying out the "work of God," that is, prayer in the cloister.

As the concept of sin expanded, so did perceptions of the work of God that combated it. Lay vocations, if conducted in the proper way, could become a form of God's work. The objective was not to transform the entire laity into monks but to have them become a bit more "monk-like." The First Crusade was the finest expression of this new approach to the work of God. The soldiers of the world, in the First Crusade, became temporary soldiers of Christ. French theologian and historian Guibert of Nogent, who considered the Crusade an important and divinely initiated innovation, saw the connection between these two works of God. Holy war offered a new form of salvation situated between the lay and monastic existences. Before this time the only option was to join the cloister, a difficult proposition for most of the laity. Now, with the new divinely ordered holy wars, the layman could follow his own vocation while adopting monastic characteristics. This transformation can also be seen in how the Crusaders were supposed to conduct themselves while on the expedition—they were to shun all vices, abstain from sex, and essentially live in accordance with religious austerity for the duration of the campaign. This partial "monasticizing" of the laity was the original hybrid that eventually made the Templar vocation permissible.

Intertwined with these changes was Pope Gregory VII's reassessment of the function of the laity in Christian society. It would be no exaggeration to say that Gregory, more so than any other single individual, dragged the soldier of Christ (or the soldier of St. Peter) out of the cloister and onto the battlefield. Synthesizing theology and the feudal political model, Gregory saw the warrior aristocracy as the earthly vassals of their spiritual overlord St. Peter, who was represented on Earth by the pope. The primary (perhaps sole) function of the warrior was to render military service to the vicar of St. Peter, to raise the iron sword that would complement the spiritual sword wielded by the pope. Along with these spiritual duties came spiritual rewards. Reactions to and controversy over Gregory's new creation dwarfed that which would surround the Templars a generation later. Henrican supporters in the early sixteenth century saw it as a reversal of the world order. The peace that Christ imprinted upon the soul of the knight became the brand of violent fury in the hands of Gregory.

Monasticizing the laity and transforming the spiritual soldier of Christ into a physical warrior of Christ were the bedrocks upon which the Christian military order was constructed. Proponents of the *ribat* theory can say that is all well and good, but it gets us no further in understanding how the rise of monks who kill got around the greatest Christian stumbling block: the prohibition against clerics shedding blood. Furthermore, it can be argued that the Christian contradictions inherent in the military orders are underscored by the prohibition against monks participating in Crusades. Even Bernard of Clairvaux, the Templars' greatest supporter, prohibited monastic participation in Crusades. All of this is true concerning clerics—but the knights in military orders were not clerics but rather lay brothers. Rather than subverting the clerical ideal, the military orders respected and drew sharp distinctions between their tonsured clerics who handled the orders' spiritual business and the lay brothers in lower orders who conducted military operations.

This fact takes much of the wind from the sails of the *ribat*/stimulus-diffusion theory of the rise of military orders. First of all, it demonstrates that there was really nothing inherently un-Christian (by the standards of the day) about their function. Clerical restrictions did not apply to men who were not clerics. Second, it goes far in explaining many apparent criticisms of the early Templars. Peccator's criticism that the Templars' military vocation interfered with their spiritual perfection simply states that he wished they had set their sights higher by pushing beyond the status of lay brethren and entering higher orders (which would have included a prohibition against shedding blood). Bernard expressed the same sentiments. His disappointment with the first Templars was that they were not pursuing the highest form of spiritual life but were satisfied with a middling existence—surely one that was better than that led by secular knights blinded by pomp, pride, and sin, but one that cut a pale comparison with that led at Clairvaux. Like the Crusade itself, the military order represented an alternative path to salvation and spiritual existence situated between the extremes of the lay and religious vocations.

Jerusalem had a unique importance and appeal to Christians of the time. Not only was it the greatest conduit that linked the spiritual and physical worlds, but it was also the city par excellence in which one could experience rebirth. Penitential pilgrimages to Jerusalem were rooted in this concept, signaling as they did a spiritual rebirth that enabled people to start life anew. Pilgrimage traffic, however, was but one way in which the medieval Christian could start a new life with the assistance of the Holy City. Some Christians chose to live the remainder of their lives in Jerusalem. Ademar of Chabannes is an excellent example. After suffering great disgrace when caught forging the pedigree of a saint, this monk set out for Jerusalem to begin a new spiritual life. Many Christians also went to Jerusalem for the purpose of dying. Thus, there were two main ways in which Jerusalem changed the lives of men. The first was temporary, in the form of a pilgrimage. The second was permanent and based on the desire to live the rest of one's days in the most spiritual terrain the Earth had to offer. Sometimes the former surprisingly led to the latter. Some men who intended to make a pilgrimage to Jerusalem had an epiphany and decided to remain. This change of course seems to have been the case with the first Templars. Unlike the majority of Crusaders, these men opted not to return to Europe but to spend the rest of their days serving God in the land where he became incarnate and experienced the Passion.

The original task of the Templars was defensive rather than offensive. Unlike the *ribat,* the original Templars were not devoted to expanding the frontiers of their faith. Though the Crusaders had conquered the Holy Land, they by no means secured it. Outside city walls and all along the roads, bandits, brigands, and Muslim forces preyed upon travelers. The first Templars devoted themselves to protecting pilgrims along these dangerous expanses of hostile landscape that separated one shrine or city from the next. The original Templars bear all the marks of knights who could not resist the spiritual allure of the Holy Land and dedicated their lives to serving its interests. The seminal arrangement that began the chain of events that would lead to the creation of the first military order was between these knights and Warmund, the patriarch of Jerusalem. Long before Bernard wrote them a rule, the first Templars took the standard monastic vows of poverty, chastity, and obedience. In exchange for providing the charitable work of securing safe passage for pilgrims, the patriarch made provisions for the remission of their sins. One need not cross the religious frontier to find an alien stimulus for such an undertaking. At this point the Templars' venture was far from unique. It was little more than a lay confraternity that devoted its attention to protecting a religious institution. Rather than comparing it with the *ribats,* one would be better off comparing it with the plethora of nearly identical Christian confraternities that had sprouted up for centuries. To cite but a few examples of a common activity: the bands of men who gathered to enforce the dictates of the Peace of God (989); the oath ten nobles swore to defend the interests of a monastery in Bordeaux; the oath a band of knights swore to the bishop Wazo of Liege to protect his church from oppressors (circa 1040s); and of course the confraternity of the Belchite. Lay warriors swearing to protect a local religious institution was common rather than unique.

The key phrase is "nearly identical" when comparing the Templars with the other militant lay confraternities that sprouted up throughout the Latin West. Such confraternities were rarely permanent and represented no tangible, enduring break with secular life. The original Templars—no doubt drawn to a life of religious service in, and inspired by, the Holy Land—wanted to abandon the secular life altogether and permanently. Drawing upon the confraternity model from their homeland, they formed a permanent confraternity devoted to defending the interests of the Holy

City. Not wishing to return to a secular life, it makes sense that they sought advice for how to go about living a more religious life, asking for a "rule" by which to govern their behavior. Stimulus diffusion is not the theory one should use, at this point, to understand the transition of the Templars from a lay confraternity to a religious order. The functionalist theory serves the purpose much better. The need for a highly disciplined military force in the Holy Land (and monasticism was the most disciplined product of the Middle Ages) that provided permanent rather than sporadic assistance was exactly what the fledgling Crusader States required to exist. This need was acutely understood by the new king of Jerusalem.

Michael the Syrian, a most trustworthy chronicler of the origins of the Templars, claimed that the king of Jerusalem swayed the first Templars away from a cloistered contemplative life and toward an active military one. The functionalist approach provides a compelling alternative explanation for the rise of the Templars that accommodates all the facts that the stimulus diffusion theory ignores. In this scenario, Burgundian nobleman Hugh of Payns and thirty like-minded knights were men who experienced a spiritual epiphany in the Holy Land. Rather than garnering spiritual benefits and returning to Europe like most knights who journeyed to Jerusalem, these men felt the spiritual allure of the Holy Land with full force and decided to abandon worldly lives for the religious existence. Although not completely certain, it appears that Hugh and his companions first wanted to embrace the cloistered lives of monks in higher orders. The king of Jerusalem, painfully aware of the precarious state in which the original Crusaders left the fledgling colonies, suggested that an active life of charity would serve God better than the solitary life of a cloistered monk. Isolated contemplation went far in securing the salvation of the individual who practiced it, yet active expressions of charity in the world assisted the spiritual rejuvenation of many. In biblical parlance, what greater deed could one do than sacrifice personal desire for communal need?

Bernard of Clairvaux's view of the Templars encapsulates the essence of the new order. Powerful, cautious, and particularly suspicious of "novelty," one could not ask for a more efficient and aggressive guardian of the Christian worldview as it existed (as French philosopher Peter Abelard, who was condemned by Bernard at the Council of Sens in 1140, unfortunately discovered). Bernard certainly saw the Templars as a new development in Christian society but one that was strongly consistent with its principles. He had long railed against the sinful and pompous nature of knighthood. Generous portions of his *In Praise of the New Knighthood* provided a roster of complaints, from the flashy colors and long sleeves they wore to the near moral bankruptcy. In a play on words, Bernard claimed they were not *militiae* (knights) but rather *malitiae* (evildoers). He argued that they killed for vanity, glory, and plunder. To Bernard's mind, precious little of the values promoted by Church reformers touched these men. The austerity, simplicity, humility, and piety that a rule could bestow upon these knights aspiring to the status of lay brethren would mark a true shift from *malitiae* to true knights of Christ. Bernard pointed out that the Templars would be the great role models for the secular knighthood, imparting upon them through example the true nature of "fighting the good fight" in physical as well as spiritual terms. Rather than signaling a rupture of Christian sensibilities at the time, the creation of the Templars was in many ways their culmination. It was the final and quite logical conclusion to Church efforts to reform and partially "monasticize" the warrior aristocracy of Europe.

–MARK T. ABATE,
WESTFIELD STATE COLLEGE

References

Malcolm Barber, *The New Knighthood: A History of the Order of the Temple* (Cambridge & New York: Cambridge University Press, 1994).

Américo Castro, *The Structure of Spanish History,* translated by Edmund L. King (Princeton: Princeton University Press, 1954).

Jose Antonio Conde, *Historia de la dominacion de los arabes en España, sacada de varios manuscritos y memorias arabigas* (Madrid: Imprenta que fue de Garcia, 1820–1821); translated as *History of the Dominion of the Arabs in Spain,* by Mrs. Jonathan Foster (London: Bohn, 1854–1855).

Alan J. Forey, *The Military Orders from the Twelfth to the Early Fourteenth Centuries* (Toronto & Buffalo: University of Toronto Press, 1992).

Thomas F. Glick and Oriol Pi-Sunyer, "Acculturation as an Explanatory Concept in Spanish History," *Comparative Studies in Society and History,* 2 (1969): 136–154.

Elena Lourie, "The Confraternity of Belchite, the Ribat, and the Temple," *Viator,* 13 (1982): 159–176.

Lourie, *Crusade and Colonisation: Muslims, Christians, and Jews in Medieval Aragon* (Aldershot, Hampshire: Variorum, 1990; Brookfield, Vt.: Gower, 1990).

MILITARY STRATEGY

Did the Crusaders have a coherent military strategy for securing the Holy Land?

Viewpoint: Yes. The Crusaders developed coherent, dynamic strategies that shifted emphases and adapted to changing conditions over time.

Viewpoint: No. The Crusades had no coherent and effective strategy, which was the reason for their successive failures and the ultimate loss of the Holy Land.

The Crusades were the most difficult and demanding wars of the Middle Ages. International armies were dispatched from western Europe to the East and fought their enemy on the fringe of his civilization's heartland. Few have doubted, then or today, the military prowess of the European warrior class on the battlefield. One contemporary Muslim remarked that "a Frank on horseback could punch a hole through the wall of Babylon itself." Yet, many historians today believe the Crusaders' sense of strategy, what there was of it, lagged far behind their immediate battlefield performance. On the ground Latin Western armies were capable of making sound tactical decisions such as recognizing prime ground or identifying which enemy flank was weakest, but some historians believe that their sense of strategy virtually ended there. Their approach to warfare was much like the chaotic nature of their feudally organized armies. In many ways it was the mirror image of the Islamic approach to warfare, which followed the general rule that battles are won or lost before they are actually waged—that they are won by strategy rather than brute military force.

Did the Latin West and the barons of the Crusader States have a "grand strategy"—a panoramic, holistic, well-studied, and soundly formulated long-term plan for winning a series of campaigns and achieving a well-defined objective? Scholars should not expect one of the caliber formulated by the Roman Empire or Napoleonic France, both of which were much more sophisticated and centralized states than anything medieval Europe had to offer. Transport, logistics, and supplies were all primitive endeavors in the Middle Ages. Crusading, moreover, was an international effort—launched by frequently bickering monarchs—that was mediated and given some leadership by the papacy. Some historians explain the fall of the Crusader States and the sclerosis of the movement as being produced by the lack of resources and ability to maintain a permanent Christian presence in the region. Others, often noting that the Islamic world had similar structural weaknesses, feel that Europe had sufficient resources (even if just barely) to succeed in the East, but that it lacked a grand strategy to guide and apply its efforts effectively.

Whether the Crusaders had a grand strategy or not, their approaches to the campaigns changed over time. This development is only to be expected of a military movement that spanned two centuries. The targets of the Second Crusade (1147–1149), for example, were Edessa and Damascus, while the goal for the Fourth (1202–1204) and Fifth (1217–1229) Crusades and the First Crusade of Louis IX (1248–1254) was Egypt. Certainly, this reorientation constitutes adaptation to changing conditions, but adaptation does not always indicate the existence of a grand strategy. Historians who believe the Crusades had no substantive strategy tend to see such changes as visceral, knee-jerk responses to immediate threats. Historians who believe the Crusades had a coherent and dynamic strategic approach to the Holy Land see them as well-thought-out adjustments.

Viewpoint:
Yes. The Crusaders developed coherent, dynamic strategies that shifted emphases and adapted to changing conditions over time.

Historians have posited a variety of theories to explain why crusading to the East ultimately failed and why the Crusader States eventually crumbled. One of these explanations is that the West really had no coherent strategy for definitively securing the Holy Land and that the barons of Outremer had even less of one. Mercurial Crusaders and Latin inhabitants of the East pursued a policy of moderately organized military chaos. Certainly, they were enthusiastic and committed, but their primitive grasp of strategy made it impossible for them to succeed in the pursuit of such a complex and formidable venture. Latin knights were quite adept at cavalry charges and splitting heads with battle-axes, but the strategic sophistication needed to win the war eluded them. This view has been produced by too casual a reading of the evidence and a narrow approach to the selection of evidence.

To place the subject in its proper perspective, one must first make a distinction between "tactics" and "strategy." One must guard against erroneously assuming that these terms are synonyms. Tactics refers to the techniques employed by a commander to win a particular military engagement. Can high ground be gained before battle begins? Can the enemy be flanked? Can supply lines be cut? Which wall of a fortified city is weakest? These and other similar questions constitute tactics. Strategy is something related yet distinct; it approaches the conflict from the long-term, rather than immediate, perspective. The questions it addresses are somewhat different: What natural boundaries can be exploited to promote long-term occupation? Which of the various threats should be targeted first? Can a truce buy enough time to significantly increase the strength of friendly armies without doing likewise for the enemy? How will a particular campaign affect the power balance thirty years later? Are financial resources sufficient to secure objectives? If not, where can revenues be found? Strategy here will presuppose an intensive effort to reconcile available resources and ultimate goals. Usually the two terms seemed contradictory, and the best examples of strategic thinking, then as now, are aimed toward narrowing the chasm between them.

The view that the Crusades and the Crusader States had no coherent plan has come about from misunderstandings about these distinct terms and what they represent. Military histories, with a few exceptions, have focused on tactics and have, by and large, ignored strategy. The greatest military historians of the Middle Ages tended to view the Crusades as an epiphenomenon of medieval warfare, worthy of a chapter or two and some hefty footnotes. When their attention turned to the East, they focused on particular battles or campaigns and dissected tactics without really considering the totality of military operations. Historians of the Crusades generally have done likewise: the "major crusades" receive lavish descriptions of military tactics, both the failures and successes. Emphasis has been on battle tactics at the expense of any possible strategy for winning the war. Attention has been drawn to the "flashy" or "sexy" subjects: the First (1096–1102), Second (1147–1149), and Third (1189–1192) Crusades. In recent years some historians have pointed toward the "little crusades" that took place in the interim. Charles Oman, in *A History of the Art of War: The Middle Ages from the Fourth to the Fourteenth Century* (1898), pointed out that there was a great deal of military activity between the Second and Third Crusades, "but they are not of any special tactical importance." Oman was certainly correct, but his conclusion merely underscores the problem—that interest in warfare in the Latin East is dedicated to the minutiae of particular battles and utterly ignores the larger context in which the battle is embedded. From this perspective it is only natural that the Crusades and the Latin colonies in the East would appear to have had no strategy. If one expands analysis beyond a particular battle or a series of particular engagements, however, the salient features of complex strategies can be discerned. The existence of strategies, rather than a single strategy, is a crucial distinction to keep in mind. There was no universal, eternal, immutable crusading strategy for the East, but there were coherent, dynamic strategies that shifted emphases and adapted to changing conditions.

One cannot pretend either that there was a grand strategy undergirding the First Crusade. It is difficult indeed to refute Christiansen's description of the First Crusade as a chaotic international raid that somehow managed to succeed when it should have failed. No cache of evidence from 1095 to 1102 exists for historians seeking to find a strategy. The first order of business for the original Crusaders (at least those not planning to return to Europe) was conquest and consolidation, which was accomplished through a combination of wholesale slaughter and negotiated peace. Certainly it was a feudally organized assault, even if religiously inspired. As these Crusaders settled in, however, several issues—how to maintain, strengthen, and even expand their holdings—became of paramount importance. At this point the analysis of strategy must split into two distinct but interrelated categories: that of the Crusader States and that of the Crusading movement to the East. The latter's goal was always to assist the efforts of the former.

One particularly glaring dearth in the resources of the barons of the East was manpower. Colonization never took place on the scale required to achieve complete dominance in the region. Thus, the strategy that the lords needed to formulate and implement had to achieve security and promote occupation with limited access to soldiers. Their solution was to establish a strongpoint defense rather than create an iron-clad perimeter around their borders. Nor did they need to pull the solution from midair since fortified sites capable of dominating local communities were already part of war-torn Europe. The backbone of occupational strategy in the Latin East, from the third decade of the twelfth century on, was to pock the landscape with castles, walled communities, and towers. In the first decades the strategy was to capture such sites already in existence. Beginning in the third decade they started creating their own fortifications. The Latin barons, simply put, began radically altering the landscape to suit their needs, constructing havens that geography denied them. Much of the land the Crusaders came to occupy had surprisingly few castles. A few (quite impressive) ones existed, constructed by either Byzantines or Arabs. When a modern tourist visits Israel today, however, most of the castle ruins he or she will see were created by the Crusaders. Further north, where the Byzantines and Arabs clashed with greater force, there were many fortified sites. The great numbers of castles constructed by the Crusaders were the bedrock of their strategy that reconciled, as well as possible, their resources and objectives.

Although historians recognize that castles were of utmost importance, there has been considerable debate on their particular function. Some have seen them as constituting a fortified chain along the frontiers that created an interlocking perimeter to ward off invasion. Others have refuted this theory, claiming that it cannot explain the great presence of castles in the interior, far from the border, nor can it explain the relative lack of castles on some borders. They argue that castles were fortified sites that dominated a local region, served as safe havens for lords, and were administrative centers that handled the exploitation of resources. Foreign policy and strategy, in other words, did not go far from a particular lord's own backyard. As is the case with many debates, the reality is situated between the two. Castles on the frontiers were strategically placed (as can be seen in the special attention given to repairing damage done to them), but they were no Maginot Line (a post–World War I defensive line built by the French to protect their country from German invasion). Rather than being viewed as an insurmountable obstacle, the castles were seen as the "first" ring of defense that might or might not stop, but would at least slow, an invasion force. What about castles away from the borders? There is little doubt that these interior castles and fortified towers served as points to dominate and exploit local resources, but this function is far from being at odds with playing an important role in the overall defense of the entire realm. They served as "second" rings of defense that enemies had to tackle if they penetrated the first ring. Castles frequently complemented the geography. There were many natural barriers that helped protect the region (for example, deserts and mountain ranges), and castles were frequently strategically placed to pick up the geographical slack.

To place this strategy in its proper context, one must abandon modern notions of military strategy such as the decisive battle, total war, or unquestioned regional supremacy. Cutting down a palm grove may not make much sense to the modern mind, but it had great strategic implications for the Crusaders and their Muslim opponents. Wars were primarily won or lost by successful or failed sieges of strong points. Field armies generally protected these sites and harassed the enemy. Skirmishes and raids were the main functions of soldiers, though the occasional pitched battle took place and could completely alter the balance of power when and if it was decisive. The professional standing army did not exist. Armies were temporary associations, for both Muslims and Christians, that disbanded once specified terms of service expired. War was also more susceptible to the ravages of climate—it was by and large a seasonal endeavor. A massive invasion force could be defeated simply by delaying it. Fortified sites always had water sources that could carry them through an entire campaigning season. Stockpiles of food were accumulated, though these, at times, could be exhausted. Sieges could be time-consuming, and Crusader State strategy was predicated on this fact. The first ring of fortified sites would "wait it out" as long as they could. When they succumbed, fortified sites in the interior would do likewise. Hopefully this defense would slow an invasion force to the point that it would be

Illumination of Nur ad-Din, sultan of Syria and Egypt, defeating Raymond of Antioch's army in 1149; from *Les Passages faits Outremer* (circa 1490)

(Bibliothèque Nationale, Paris)

promoted expanded colonization. Defensive and offensive stances can be continuously argued, but in either case the closing in on Ashkelon demonstrates a strategy that transcended the specific interests of regional lords and reveals decisive action on a frontier.

The lords of the Crusader States had a clear strategy, one that was convincingly reconstructed by Joshua Prawer, the great Israeli historian of the Crusades. The goal was simple: push the borders of the Crusader States to the deserts, which served as perfect natural barriers. Strategically, the Jordan River was the kiss of death; it was a shallow river with countless fords that resulted in a veritable highway for invaders. Extending the border to the desert, supplemented with a few key fortified sites, provided much more security. In the middle of the twelfth century the Latins realized that the dominant threat to their regional security was Egypt, which largely eclipsed that posed by the Seljuk Turks in northern Syria. From 1163 to 1169 the Latins launched five major attacks on Egyptian territory. Their assumption was correct, and those barons who opposed an aggressive Egyptian policy were disabused of that notion by the Muslim leader Saladin. Stock in the importance of the Sinai rose, as did Cairo and Alexandria. After the Battle of the Horns of Hattin (1187) all eyes were cast in the direction of Egypt. It became common knowledge among Crusader barons that their security, regardless of where they were situated, was ultimately determined by Egypt. Continued occupation of the Crusader States was now predicated on weakening or, better yet, destroying Egypt. That the Fifth Crusade (1217–1229) and the First Crusade of Louis IX (1248–1254) targeted Egypt demonstrates the adaptability of strategy. That most crusading proposals, even after the expulsion of the Latins in 1291, generally focused on Egypt merely reinforces the point.

Western European Crusades to the East were designed to relieve pressure on the Crusader States and, if possible, roll back Islamic gains. Thus, they served as extensions of the strategies employed by the barons of Outremer and could be dealt with more quickly. All of the major Crusades were responses to a catastrophe or to a failed response to a catastrophe (such as the Fifth Crusade following up on the Fourth, which in turn followed up on the Third). Smaller crusading hosts focused on providing whatever assistance their numbers could render to the barons of the East and were used both offensively and defensively. Crusades also quickly outgrew the primitive form of a feudal assault that focused on possession of Jerusalem. Advances in financing the Crusades, recruitment, and transport all made their marks. As the strategic concerns of the colonists shifted, so did the objectives of the Crusades.

forced to disband. The strategy was more than sound; it was an excellent combination of resources and objectives. Resources were limited, and the objective was occupation and survival.

Military strategy, however, is rarely just defensive. A coherent offense is also required. Here castles played an important role as well. They served as advanced bases for operations, providing invasion forces with supplies and refuge. The classic example of the Latins using the castle as an offensive weapon for expanding their borders was the treatment of Ashkelon. With the possible exception of Tyre, Ashkelon was the most important strategic site in the region. Essentially, it marked the gateway between Egypt and Palestine; it served as a major Egyptian forward base for attacks on the Crusader States. The Latin response was to construct a ring of fortified sites around it. There has been considerable debate on whether this act was defensive (quarantine Ashkelon and stabilize the southern border) or offensive (reduce and acquire the city to push the border further south). The debate is the sort that academics thrive on but strategists dismiss. Ringing Ashkelon with castles and towers neutralized the threat; the Crusaders slowly browbeat and acquired the city, which served as a Latin base for sorties further south and possibly

Egypt became the military target of Crusades after the Third, and the shift made sound strategic sense. Crusading became quite sophisticated and spawned a great number of theorists. Economic warfare increased in prominence and was seen as the essential prelude to striking Egypt and thus securing the Holy Land. Naval blockades were thought to financially reduce the power of Egypt and put it off balance before a full-scale Crusade toppled it. Stationing permanent garrisons as well as launching expeditionary forces that would precede a general Crusade also became popular aspects of strategy. As weaknesses were further evaluated and new complications emerged, crusading theory demonstrated a remarkable ability to adapt and find appropriate solutions.

If the barons of the East had coherent strategies as well as the European planners of crusading expeditions, then why did the movement ultimately end in failure? The reason is that strategy, no matter how sound and well thought out, completely outstripped the resources of the barons and the West. Good strategies attempt to reconcile goals and resources, but even the best plans cannot perpetually achieve goals that can never be truly reconciled with lack of resources. Maintaining a perpetual occupation of a strip of land on the other side of the known world was beyond the abilities of Europe at the time. Only the modern nation-state was capable of marshaling such resources. European dominance of the Holy Land was not truly possible until the nineteenth century, when English field marshal Edmund Allenby triumphantly entered Jerusalem (1917).

—MARK T. ABATE, WESTFIELD STATE COLLEGE

Viewpoint:
No. The Crusades had no coherent and effective strategy, which was the reason for their successive failures and the ultimate loss of the Holy Land.

In modern warfare Western armies typically conduct what is called "intelligence preparation of the battlefield" before committing troops to battle. This process entails thorough, prior analysis of all the uncontrollable factors that can affect a military operation, including weather, visibility, terrain, and the enemy, in order to limit as much as possible their potential harmful effects on friendly operations. The benefits of doing such exhaustive precombat analysis are many, but in particular this process forces commanders to take a systematic approach to battle by bringing more

science into the age-old art of war. In the end the chances for a successful outcome on the battlefield are improved while the risks are minimized.

Of course, medieval Western armies were unable to undertake such exhaustive preparations because they simply lacked the resources, training, experience, and organization that their modern counterparts enjoy. This fact does not mean that medieval commanders were wholly ignorant of the benefit of doing prebattle analysis or that it did not comprise part of the preparations for a typical crusading venture. However, in regard to the Crusades this type of preparatory planning seldom reached a sufficient depth to meet the formidable challenges posed by their campaigns. Indeed, just taking one example from the area of prebattle preparations—the process of strategic planning—reveals a major weakness in typical crusading operations. Throughout its long history, the crusading movement never produced a coherent, long-term strategy, and the failure to do so represented one of the major reasons why the Crusades ultimately failed to achieve long-term success.

The problems of poor strategic planning were apparent from the beginning of the movement. When Pope Urban II made his Clermont appeal (1095) and launched the First Crusade (1096–1102), it was clear that he undertook a degree of prior analysis and planning for his proposed campaign. After all, he instituted a mechanism for recruitment, set a fixed date of departure, made some provision for supply issues, selected a hand-picked subordinate to carry out his plans within the army, and established a single, strategic goal for the campaign—Jerusalem. Nearly four years later and despite horrific obstacles, his seemingly crazy scheme actually achieved its strategic purpose. Jerusalem was once more in Christian hands. On closer examination, however, it becomes quite evident that there was little correlation between the amazing success of the First Crusade and its level of initial strategic planning. The forces sent into battle prevailed essentially in spite of the strategic plan under which they operated, for the composition and strength of the enemy were poorly understood, the difficulty of the route not clearly appreciated, and a systematic process of providing reinforcements and supplies never formulated. Thus, the success rested really with the resourcefulness, spirit, and tenacity of the Crusade participants who in the end somehow made an ill-defined operational plan work. Future crusading ventures would seldom be so fortunate.

In fairness, it is necessary to point out that Urban was an ecclesiastical leader, not a military tactician, and so it is understandable that he might not have grasped the full complexities of strategic thinking. He had a clear strategic goal in mind and crafted a revolutionary mechanism by which

DESPERATE WARFARE

A passage from the writings of Ludolf of Suchem describes some of the desperate fighting in the defense of Acre (1291):

I have heard a very honorable knight say that a lance which he was about to hurl from a tower among the Saracens was all notched with arrows before it left his hand. There were at that time in the Sultan's army six hundred thousand armed, divided into three companies; so one hundred thousand continually besieged the city, and when they were weary, another one hundred thousand took their place before the same. . . . The gates were never closed, nor was there an hour of the day without some hard fight being fought against the Saracens by the Templars or other brethren dwelling therein. But the numbers of the Saracens grew so fast that after one hundred thousand of them had been slain two hundred thousand came back. Yet, even against all this host, they would not have lost the city had they but helped one another faithfully; but when they were fighting without the city, one party would run away and leave the other to be slain, while within the city one party would not defend the castle or palace belonging to the other, but purposely let the other party's castles, palaces, and strong places be stormed and taken by the enemy, and each one knew and believed his own castle and place to be so strong that he cared not for any other's castle or strong place. During this confusion the masters and brethren of the Orders alone defended themselves, and fought unceasingly against the Saracens, until they were nearly all slain; indeed, the Master and brethren of the house of the Teutonic Order, together with their followers and friends, all fell dead at one and the same time. As this went on with many battles and thousands slain on either side, at last the fulfillment of their sins and the time of the fall of the city drew near. . . . When the first Saracens took Acre they got in through a breach in the wall near the King of Jerusalem's castle, and when they were among the people of the city within, one party still would not help the other, but each defended his own castle and palace, and the Saracens had a much longer siege, and fought at much less advantage when they were within the city than when they were without, for it was wondrously fortified. . . . First the air became so thick, dark, and cloudy that, while one castle, palace, or strong place was being stormed or burned, men could hardly see in the other castles or palaces, until their castles and palaces were attacked, and then for the first time they would have willingly defended themselves, could they have come together. Fire fought against the city, for it consumed it. Earth fought against it, for it drank up its blood.

Source: *Ludolph of Suchem,* Description of the Holy Land and of the Way Thither, *translated by Aubrey Stewart (London: Palestine Pilgrim's Text Society, 1895), pp. 54–61.*

to achieve it, namely a military campaign harnessed to the popular practice of pilgrimage. Yet, beyond this linkage he did not appreciate the depth and breadth of planning such a campaign as he proposed. In this deficiency he would not be alone, for many of his successors consistently made a similar oversight.

From a strategic perspective in the late eleventh and twelfth centuries, there were several key factors with which crusading leaders such as Urban needed to come to terms. First, the strategic goal of the campaign was a city that was relatively inaccessible to Western forces. Situated in a semiarid climate and in harsh terrain deep within enemy lines, Jerusalem was a difficult target not only to capture but also to defend. Second, the objective lay closely hemmed in between two great enemy power bases, one centered in Cairo and the other immediately to the north in Damascus but ultimately located in Baghdad. Each power sat like two halves of an open vise easily positioned to clamp down, isolate, and eventually crush any Western force in control of Jerusalem. To prevent the occurrence of this eventuality, it was paramount for the West to defeat at least one of these Muslim powers, thus freeing Jerusalem from the threat of strangulation. Third, control of the coastline of the Near East was vital to any attempts to capture and hold Jerusalem over the long term, because it represented the only reliable means by which reinforcements and supplies could be brought to Western forces operating in the region. Controlling the coastline, however, would prove to be irrelevant if the West could not at the same time dominate the shipping lanes of the Mediterranean Sea. Hence, a necessary corollary to this point was having the means by which to achieve and maintain strategic control of the Mediterranean.

Fourth, the Christian state of Byzantium represented a huge potential ally in the cataclysmic struggle that the Crusades threatened to touch off between the Christian West and Islamic East. Yet, the prevailing state of relations between Byzantium and the West was severely strained because of a long history of misunderstanding and disputes. It was of utmost importance for these differences to be smoothed over, at least to the point that a workable alliance could be achieved and thus united action taken against a common enemy. Fifth, medieval Europe lacked sufficient unity to carry out such a bold plan to project and maintain Western power more than a thousand miles away in the Islamic Near East. Divided into a patchwork of competing kingdoms and principalities and gradually recovering from centuries of economic stagnation, the West in its current condition was hardly in a position to meet the strategic goal of crusading, which called for continued Western control of Jerusalem. Although this goal could theoretically be achieved at this stage of European economic development, it was necessary for medieval Europe to transform at least in regards to crusading: the various contending powers had to submit to some sort of consensus and unity of purpose. Only as an alliance could the West properly marshal and dispatch its limited, but now collective, resources in support of a clearly defined and coherent plan of battle. Sixth, the enemy's style of warfare differed greatly from that to which Europeans were accustomed, and their tactics gave the enemy a certain military advantage, for it was much more conducive to the climate and environment of the Near East. Western armies preferred close-quarter combat spearheaded by heavy cavalry outfitted with extensive armor protection. Muslim forces preferred light cavalry spearheaded by horse-borne archers whose defensive measures relied on speed and mobility rather than heavy armor. This latter style of warfare held distinct advantages in the hot, semiarid conditions, but it possessed potential weaknesses as well, especially in close-quarter combat. It was critical for Western armies to develop and adhere to sound tactics while on Crusade that would minimize the enemy's advantages and exploit their weaknesses.

Such was the strategic landscape with which crusading had to cope for much of its history, and in truth, crusading leaders were aware of most, if not all, of these strategic factors, at least to some degree. For example, there were sporadic efforts at rapprochement with Byzantium and calls for unity within Europe. There were discussions of how, and even actual attempts, to defeat one of the two Muslim power bases (Egypt), which proved to be more accessible to European forces. On occasion efforts were made at dealing with Muslim corsairs in the eastern Mediterranean, especially in the later centuries of crusading. Finally, crusading armies demonstrated from time to time the ability to adjust to the tactics of light-cavalry warfare that their enemy tended to employ. The problem remained, however, that none of these efforts were undertaken as key parts to an overall strategic plan. Rather, they typically represented patchwork solutions implemented to meet immediate exigencies and then were neglected until the next crisis or need arose.

Such an approach was truly a recipe for disaster. For example, the strategic issues of the poor geographic location of Jerusalem, relative to Europe, and its encirclement by two nearby enemy powers were well known to all involved with the Crusades. Yet, after the stunning success of the First Crusade, the West took few active measures to shore up the defenses of the newly established Crusader States. Not only was dispatching a consistent supply of soldiers to the area necessary for insuring the survival of Western-controlled Jerusalem, but it was also critical that war plans be devised and implemented that sought to remove one of the two pincers that encircled the city. Neither effort occurred with any degree of consistency or urgency, revealing a profound lack of strategic understanding on the part of crusading leaders. In regard to the former problem, when the Latin states of the East made repeated calls for increased military aid from the West, especially in the form of manpower, such calls often went unheeded. With Jerusalem in Christian hands, many political leaders of the West returned home to looking after their own affairs and so were content to let the Latin states fend for themselves.

Likewise, in regard to the latter issue, it took more than a century before crusading leaders made a real attempt to deal with the problem of encirclement. Of course, by then it was too late. The hundred years that had passed since the capture of Jerusalem (1099) and the first real crusading venture that planned to target Egypt as the tactical goal represented a major missed opportunity. With the beachhead established by the success of the First Crusade, Europe had in the course of the twelfth century the opportunity to solidify the security of Jerusalem by launching a follow-up invasion into Egypt. However, no such invasion actually transpired until the first elements of the Fifth Crusade (1217–1229) reached the shores of Egypt in 1218. By then the window of opportunity had passed, and so not surprisingly this Crusade ended in disappointment. Implausibly, it would not be until thirty years later that another serious attack was made on Egypt.

This time Louis IX, the great king of France, tried to breathe life into the strategy of securing Jerusalem by conquering Egypt, but his effort also failed, principally because his Crusade (1248–1254) committed the same tactical errors that had stymied the Fifth Crusade. In particular, both crusading armies attempted to capture Cairo by marching down the center of the Nile Delta rather than skirting it to the west or the east. This avenue of approach, however, was laden with various intervening waterways, and with water crossings under enemy fire a difficult thing to do in any age of warfare, both armies inevitably were defeated well before they reached their objective. Such a blunder demonstrates just how haphazard the crusading movement really was. Strategic lessons from one campaign were not being learned and systematically incorporated into future operational plans, and therefore the movement met with repeated failures in terms of achieving its strategic objective.

Similarly, although the style of Eastern warfare was well documented by the time the First Crusade ended, it is amazing how frequently crusading armies needed to relearn old lessons about how to deal with it. As early as the tenth century a Byzantine tactician, Leo the Wise, wrote a military treatise that detailed the way to overcome a light cavalry force armed with the bow. His wise counsels were based on centuries of Byzantine experience fighting against this type of enemy. Although early on the Crusaders had the benefit of Byzantine advisers who were well versed in the lessons that Leo had preached, these maxims—such as avoiding isolated pursuits of the swifter enemy, using terrain to anchor the flanks of one's battle lines, and using infantry to screen the heavy cavalry from enemy missiles—seemed to be new lessons that each crusading army time and again needed to relearn by trial and error. For example, during the Second Crusade (1147–1149), despite warnings to the contrary from Christian settlers in the East, it was not uncommon for individual Western knights to charge after the first mounted enemy they spotted only to find that they had futilely pursued their swifter adversary right into a waiting ambush. It was a predictable, long-practiced ploy that Leo had warned against, Byzantine advisers had alerted the first waves of Crusaders about, and the First Crusaders relearned themselves. By 1148 one would think Western soldiers well forewarned to avoid such simplistic traps, but time and again the same tactical errors were inexplicably made in this crusade as in others.

There were also other avoidable strategic blunders that continued to plague the movement. United action among the European powers, despite the best ecclesiastical efforts, never materialized as petty wars and differing national ambitions sapped potential resources from the crusading program. Rapprochement with Byzantium not only failed to occur, but crusading also actually deepened the divisions between the Christian East and Christian West. During the Third Crusade (1189–1192), for example, the Byzantine emperor, who had made a secret pact with the enemy, actively worked to sabotage the progress of the Crusade and as a result fueled Western feelings of anger, resentment, and contempt for Byzantium. That anger boiled over on the next Crusade when a Western army diverted from campaigning in Egypt and instead attacked, conquered, and then dismantled much of the Byzantine Empire. This internal feuding within Christendom only made the daunting task of trying to recapture and keep Jerusalem all the more difficult, for it needlessly diluted the limited resources that were then available in medieval Europe. Finally, no strategic naval policy was ever adopted in support of the crusading program. There were isolated moments in later centuries when some efforts were made in this direction, notably the naval alliance of Western

forces that led to the naval victory at Lepanto (1571). Such efforts, however, proved to be temporary, ad hoc measures taken to meet some sudden crisis rather than a well-thought-out and systematically executed effort to drive Muslim shipping from the Mediterranean. The fact that just six years earlier the Hospitallers conducted a defense of Malta by themselves against a massive Muslim armada underlines the incoherent nature of the overall strategic efforts that underlay the crusading movement.

Ultimately, there was one explanation to account for such repeated failures—the lack of a coherent strategy. Crusading began, and was always caught up, with the fate of Jerusalem. All the labors, sacrifices, and expenditures through much of the crusading era were focused on this one overriding strategic goal. Yet, to have any chance to take and maintain control of this city, the West needed a clear, consistently prosecuted strategy that dealt with key strategic factors. Western troops needed to be sent east in larger and more consistent waves. Egypt had to be occupied. Alliances, internally among European powers and externally with Byzantium, were required. Tactical experiences needed to be passed on to future crusading armies to prevent the disastrous consequences of reliving old mistakes and relearning old lessons anew. The Mediterranean had to be made a "Latin lake." Such a systematic approach, however, was not taken. Europeans desired to have Jerusalem in Western hands but did not translate this wish into a workable plan of action that was relentlessly and proactively pursued. Instead, the more typical approach was to take largely reactive measures, flailing away in a haphazard manner with the blind hope that all this frenzied activity would bear the desired fruit. More often than not, by ignoring sound strategic plans and actions, the only fruit borne for all this concern and effort was bitter frustration. Perhaps, however, there was one other tangible result. Benefiting from the advantage of hindsight, modern Western armies learned at least how not to conduct large-scale military campaigns.

The challenges that faced the crusading movement were quite daunting. The lack of sufficient manpower and material resources; absence of a highly advanced logistical system; reliance on relatively primitive means of transportation; and effects of distance, weather, terrain, and a formidable enemy are just some of the more prominent obstacles that stood in the way of achieving the fundamental goal of crusading: the capture and defense of Jerusalem. Yet, despite such a foreboding list, many of the deleterious effects of these obstacles could have been mitigated, or perhaps even eliminated, had the Crusaders adopted a clear, coherent strategy—at least enough of one to permit them to achieve long-term success.

History tends to shower its fame on those individuals who have been masters of grand strategy. The great generals of history acquired legendary status because of their abilities to develop and execute bold plans with daring and success against formidable odds. Yet, when one considers the history of the Crusades, few individuals stand out as bold strategic thinkers who left a lasting imprint on the movement. Although able tactical commanders, such as Bohemond of Taranto or Richard I, the Lion-Hearted of England, and innovative strategic planners, such as Pope Urban II or Pope Innocent III, appeared sporadically, crusading never benefited from a master strategist who implemented a grand design for the movement. Crusading therefore suffered irrevocably and was perhaps doomed to ultimate failure.

–CHRISTOPHER LIBERTINI, SUFFOLK UNIVERSITY

References

John Gillingham and J. C. Holt, eds., *War and Government in the Middle Ages: Essays in Honour of J. O. Prestwich* (Cambridge: Boydell Press, 1984; Totowa, N.J.: Barnes & Noble, 1984).

Norman Housley, *The Later Crusades, 1274–1580: From Lyons to Alcazar* (New York: Oxford University Press, 1992).

Maurice Keen, ed., *Medieval Warfare: A History* (Oxford & New York: Oxford University Press, 1999).

Christopher Marshall, *Warfare in the Latin East, 1192–1291* (Cambridge & New York: Cambridge University Press, 1992).

Charles Oman, *A History of the Art of War: The Middle Ages from the Fourth to the Fourteenth Century* (London: Methuen, 1898).

James M. Powell, *Anatomy of a Crusade: 1213–1221* (Philadelphia: University of Pennsylvania Press, 1986).

Maureen Purcell, *Papal Crusading Policy: The Chief Instruments of Papal Crusading Policy and Crusade to the Holy Land from the Final Loss of Jerusalem to the Fall of Acre 1244–1291* (Leiden: Brill, 1975).

Sylvia Schein, *Fideles Crucis: The Papacy, the West, and the Recovery of the Holy Land, 1274–1314* (Oxford: Clarendon Press; New York: Oxford University Press, 1991).

R. C. Smail, *Crusading Warfare, 1097–1193,* second edition (Cambridge & New York: Cambridge University Press, 1995).

MILITARY STRATEGY

MISSIONARY ACTIVITY

Was the conversion of non-Christians among the primary goals of the Crusades?

Viewpoint: Yes. The conversion of non-Christians was a major goal of the crusading movement, and missionary efforts complemented military activity.

Viewpoint: No. Religious conversion was not a high priority for the Crusaders and was seen by many as an obstacle to their immediate goals.

The age of crusading coincided with an expansion in missionary activity; the relationship between these two movements has been a fascinating subject of debate. Some scholars have argued that the two movements were really halves of the same walnut. Both were methods of dealing with the non-Christian world that worked in tandem with one another. Military force was a tool for subduing a region and preparing it for missionary activity. Conversion of conquered populations promoted peace and stability. That the mendicant orders spearheaded the new missionary movement and were great promoters of crusading has been used as evidence to further demonstrate that the ventures were closely aligned with each other. Conversion and Crusade were merely two tools, one peaceful and the other violent, for creating an increasingly Christian world. Others have seen them as two trends that coincided, joined in partnership, and then drifted apart. In this scenario, mission was a peaceful alternative to violent military expeditions, and as the latter met with increasing failure the former rose to ascendance as the best method for dealing with non-Christians. The missionary trained in languages and logic gradually replaced the crusading knight. Still other historians feel that while the Church energetically supported missionary activity, secular leaders resisted it. These historians tend to see the Crusader States in materialist terms—that the lay powers in the crusading theaters were more interested in exploiting, rather than converting, subjected non-Christian populations.

When addressing the relationship between missionary activity and crusading one must always keep in mind the different conditions in the three major theaters: the eastern Mediterranean, Spain, and eastern Europe. The Crusader States in the East were always in a precarious position and were close to the heartland of the Islamic world. By necessity they had to establish a modus vivendi with Muslims. Would intensive missionary efforts strengthen their position by increasing the number of Christians, or would it antagonize Muslims and have negative political and economic effects? Spain, on the other hand, was in western Europe and enjoyed a sort of home-court advantage. Colonizing conquered territory with Latin Christians was a much easier task in Spain than it was in the East. Spain also experienced much closer interactions between Muslims and Christians than the East. Crusading in eastern Europe was originally conceived as an effort to defend missionaries trying to convert pagan Slavic tribes. Thus, these Crusades, at least in their initial stages, were predicated on the combination of evangelization and crusading. Missionary activity, albeit on differing scales, was conducted in all three theaters. The relationship between Crusade and mission is still open to debate.

Viewpoint:
Yes. The conversion of non-Christians was a major goal of the crusading movement, and missionary efforts complemented military activity.

Crusading and missionary activity were interrelated methods by which Christendom dealt with the non-Christian world. Both essentially had the same objective: to expand the borders of Christendom and the numbers of the faithful. Crusading used military force to gain territory, and missionaries used peaceful means to convert populations. These methods worked in tandem and complemented, rather than conflicted with, one another. The close relationship between holy war and evangelism predated the Crusades by centuries. By far the best example of this partnership between soldiers and missionaries before 1095 was the Carolingian approach to expansion. Beginning with eighth-century Frankish ruler Charles Martel, conquered pagans were pacified through instruction in the Christian faith; baptism was equated with political submission. The high-water mark, however, was reached during the reign (768–814) of Charlemagne, who made no secret of his preference to "preach with the iron tongue," that is, to spread Christianity through force. His strategy was as simple as it was effective: the Frankish army would militarily smash the enemy, and missionaries would pick up the pieces, rebuild society, and make it Christian. The Church of Paderborne, Charlemagne's base of operations in the Saxon Wars (782, 792–804), is particularly instructive. It was virtually a Christian factory. After Saxon soldiers were defeated, they were disarmed and baptized there en masse. Holy war and conversion went hand in hand, and it was only natural that once crusading became the dominant form of holy war in Christendom, this trend continued.

The excessive drive for conversion was rooted in the evangelical nature of Christianity. Seeing itself as the universal spiritual head of the world, the Church classified two types of people: those who were Christians and those who should be Christians. The New Testament served as the foundation for this worldview. The apostles, inspired by the Holy Spirit, set out to bring the good news of Christ's death and resurrection to the world. Conversion of gentiles thus became the chief spiritual mandate for the early Church, and the concept continued to evolve. The life of a missionary, however, was a dangerous one. St. Boniface, for example, had his missionary career abruptly ended when he was ripped limb from limb by a Frisian mob (754). Some tribes tortured missionaries by nailing a strip of their intestines to a tree and then chasing the poor men with torches until they unraveled their innards completely. Methods for killing missionaries were as creative as they were grisly. Missionaries who were defended by armies, however, naturally lived longer lives and enjoyed more success. The marriage of mission and war was an old one indeed, in which both parties profited greatly. Missionaries received the protection they so desperately required, and expansionist armies found evangelization of the conquered a valuable tool for pacification.

The earliest decades of the movement show little sign of evangelical impulses. With the exception of forced conversions of Jews during the First Crusade (1096–1102), evidence indicating the desire to convert non-Christians is rare. In the East, Muslims were either slaughtered wholesale or forced into negotiated peace settlements. The Holy Land represented a unique theater of operations since it was seen as the patrimony of Christ and the heart of Christian spiritual life. During the thirteenth century, however, there was a marked increase of evangelical trappings in crusading activity in the East. The Fifth Crusade (1217–1229) was a clear turning point in this regard. First, there was the well-known effort of Italian friar Francis of Assisi to convert the sultan and achieve victory through preaching rather than violence. Being rebuffed, however, constituted grounds for violence. Preaching was preferable, but violence was permissible, and the two actually went hand in hand. Pelagius, the papal legate for the campaign, clearly saw conversion as a major objective of the Crusades. Oliver of Paderborne, preacher for and chronicler of the Fifth Crusade, justified the campaign on the grounds that missionaries could only gain access to potential converts in Islamic states by force. Effective preaching and military occupation were interdependent and symbiotic. Christian missionaries were well aware of the harsh penalties for preaching Christianity in Islamic lands: execution. Conversion should be a voluntary act, but gaining access to audiences need not be. The mendicant orders also intensified the relationship between Crusade and mission in the thirteenth century. Becoming experts on tactics for conversion, they created missionary schools that instructed pupils in the necessary languages and arguments for winning converts. This orientation does not, however, signal a shift away from crusading and toward peaceful solutions. Mendicants were also experts in Crusade preaching and clearly saw Crusade and mission as complementary activities.

During the mid thirteenth century the missionary effort came to the fore as a central com-

FOR JERUSALEM'S SAKE I SHALL NOT REST

The early thirteenth-century preacher James of Vitry clarified the goals of the Crusades as he saw them in a sermon:

For Zion's sake I will not be silent, for Jerusalem's sake I shall not rest, until her right shines forth like a bright light and her salvation is lit like a lamp. With these words Isaiah shows how much more forcefully and diligently we must preach the word of God to you and in particular when we preach *about Zion* and *Jerusalem,* so that the Holy Land may be freed from the hands of the enemies. We must not give *sleep to our eyes or drowsiness to your lids,* the *sleep* of negligence or the *drowsiness* of sluggishness and idleness, *or rest in our lifetimes, until we find* and recover *for the Lord the place,* where the Lord lived bodily as in his fatherland, *and a dwelling place of the God of Jacob,* where the Lord fought against the devil and defeated him.

Or, *for Zion's sake I will not be silent,* but speak for the church, and *for Jerusalem's sake I shall not rest,* but labor and preach to convert souls and enlarge the church, *until her right shines forth like a bright light,* that is [until] it is made known through my preaching, and *her salvation is lit like a lamp* in the hearts of the listeners. The lamp means Christ, whence in Zechariah it says that there was a lamp above the candle-holder, that is Christ above the church, whose flesh is likened to glass, because it is pure and fragile as glass. . . :

. . . The Lord indeed suffered the loss of his patrimony and wants to test [his] friends and find out if you are his faithful vassals. He who holds a fief from a liege lord is rightfully deprived of his fief if he abandons him, when he is involved in a war and his inheritance is taken away from him. You hold your body and soul and all that you have from the highest emperor, who has you summoned today to come to his aid in battle, even if you are not bound by feudal law. He offers you such great payment that you ought to rush willingly, namely the remission of all sins with regard to punishment and guilt, and in addition eternal life.

I remember when I once preached about taking of the cross in some church, there was a certain saintly man, a lay brother of the Cistercian order called Brother Symon, who often had divine revelations and visions of God's secret plans. When he saw with tears that many people took the cross while leaving their spouses, children, fatherland and possessions behind, he asked the Lord to show him what kind of a reward the crusaders were given. At once he saw in his mind the Holy Virgin holding her son and that she gave her son to everyone who received the cross with a contrite heart.

Source: Christopher T. Maier, Crusade Propaganda and Ideology: Model Sermons for the Preaching of the Cross *(Cambridge: Cambridge University Press, 2000), pp. 83, 85, 99.*

ponent of crusading. The views put forward by Pope Innocent IV and the great jurist Hostiensis formalized the preeminence of mission in crusading activity. The Catholic Church had spiritual dominion over all people, Christian or not, since all humans were the descendants of Adam. Non-Christians might have de facto authority in regions they politically controlled, but in the end de jure authority was held by the pope. The universal authority of the papacy meant jurisdiction over all. Thus, the papacy had the right to intervene in non-Christian societies if circumstances warranted it. Rulers who refused to accept missionaries were harming their own non-Christian subjects by denying them access to the Truth. Crusades must secure regions that turned missionaries away. Non-Christians must not be forced to convert, but they needed access to the information to make the choice for themselves. Non-Christians had certain rights, but chief among them was the right to become Christian if they wished.

Crusading in the thirteenth century, as seen clearly in the Fifth Crusade, was partially justified to clear a path for missionaries. Such activity in eastern Europe, moreover, was justified as a requirement to bring Christianity to the pagan tribes, to protect missionaries and fledgling churches, and to defend recent converts against their previous comrades. These Crusades were clearly little more than armed missionary expeditions. While the early crusading movement showed little evidence for the prominence of missionary activity, the conversion of non-Christians was a focal point as it matured.

Missionary efforts in the Crusader States in the East are difficult to assess. The geographical situation plays a large role: the Crusader States were surrounded by enemies, were in a perpetual state of siege, and existed for only two centuries. Compared to the seven-century *Reconquista* (reconquest) of Spain and the "perpetual Crusade" in eastern Europe, the effects of the missionaries' efforts (and thus an indication of their importance) are more difficult to gauge. The first order of business for the original settlers was to establish themselves. A modus vivendi between the Catholic rulers (a vast minority of the total population) and their subjects had to be achieved. This process began, after the initial conquest, with policies of accommodation. But missionary activity intensified even in the East during the second half of the thirteenth century (the same time in which missions came to the fore in the theoretical explications of crusading). As Benjamin Z. Kedar has demonstrated in *Crusade and Mission: European Approaches Toward the Muslims* (1984), during the last fifty years of the existence of the Crusader States, Christians finally became the majority, a development that is impossible to explain without deep interest in and firm commitment for converting the populace. Kedar speculates that had the colonies lasted longer they might have completed the process of conversion.

In Spain the picture is much clearer. As the *Reconquista* pushed forward, more Muslims and Jews came under Latin rule. Negotiated surrender and accommodation were the initial strategies. Threats needed to be defused and resources exploited. In the thirteenth century there was an explosion in missionary activity. Mendicants opened missionary schools that instructed pupils in everything they needed to know to become effective missionaries. Textbooks were written to serve as guides. Public disputations on religious truth were organized. Most notable, however, was the advent of forced sermons in non-Christian communities. Preachers (mostly mendicants) made the Christian case to infidels who were, quite literally, captive audiences. They were not forced to convert, but they were made to listen to sermons that explained why they should. Even Italian philosopher Thomas Aquinas made a contribution to the missionary campaign by penning *summa contra gentiles*. This new approach was more sophisticated and informed than previous ones. Mendicants advocated studying the texts and mentalities of the targeted audience to refine techniques and make them more effective. If one was going to convert Jews, know the Talmud. If one was going to convert Muslims, study the Qu'ran.

In eastern Europe, the perpetual Crusade was introduced to support missionary activities. The goal of these Crusades was not to recover territory lost to the enemy but to expand the physical and spiritual borders of Christendom. Crusaders in this theater, like Carolingian soldiers centuries earlier, served as shock troops that smashed pagan resistance and made the path clear for preachers. They protected the missionaries and churches; dealt with any rebellions and apostasy exhibited by fresh converts; and protected western European immigrants who settled in the region. The entire venture was dedicated to conquest and Christianization. Livonia, Estonia, Lithuania, and Prussia were all the products of missionary activity bolstered by intensive crusading expeditions. Without the concept of mission there would have been no Crusade to speak of in this particular theater.

Admittedly, in the earliest stages of the crusading movement there is little evidence that missionary activity ranked high on the agenda, but this situation changed. The first signs of the change took place during the Second Crusade (1147–1149) when a new front, clearly related to missionary activity, was opened in eastern Europe against the pagan Wends. Gradually, conversion became a more explicit component of crusading. As crusading reached maturity in the thirteenth century, the evangelical dimensions of crusading became clearer. Missions in eastern Europe became full-blown perpetual Crusades. In the mid thirteenth century, Crusade and mission became completely fused. Providing missionaries with access to potential converts became an important justification for the movement. Mendicants forged a two-pronged attack on non-Christians that mingled Crusade and mission. Missionary activity intensified in the Crusader States in the East as well as in Spain. In the East the increasing numbers of Christians (and the fact that in the last years of the colonies Christians outnumbered Muslims) was ample testimony to the new zealous approach to preaching. Meanwhile, missionary schools emerged, and forced sermons occurred in Spain. In the East and in Spain conversion was intensified after conquest was achieved. In eastern Europe conversion was synchronized with conquest. But in all three theaters Crusade and mission were, or at least eventually became, fused.

–CARL HILL,
LOS ANGELES, CALIFORNIA

Viewpoint:
No. Religious conversion was not a high priority for the Crusaders and was seen by many as an obstacle to their immediate goals.

The conquistadores in the New World, the true successors to classical-period Crusaders, were supposedly laboring to find gold and to make Christians. Although these objectives were not mutually exclusive, they frequently clashed. Extracting as much gold in as short a period of time as possible required the merciless exploitation of labor. Non-Christians were an attractive source of labor for such exploitation since, not being part of the Christian fold, their legal status was light on protections. Christian laborers could be and were exploited ruthlessly as well throughout the Western Hemisphere but not quite as ruthlessly as non-Christians. The last thing a conquistador wanted was the mass conversion of his labor pool. Yet, both the Spanish Crown and the Church insisted on mingling mass missionary efforts with mining activities, and the conquistadors were forced to comply. So the conquistadors created clever solutions to this problem—such as preaching to Native Americans in European languages that they could not understand.

a tour les teftes coper: se loft des xpiens
paffoit insques a tunes. et se il ni aloi
ent: il les deluerroit tour.

Comment melire jeban darc bouteil
lier de france qui faisoit le guet dau
tuns sarrazins qui requroient le baptesme.

**Illumination of a group of
Saracens requesting
baptism (fourteenth
century)**

(British Library, London)

A similar situation—tension between evangelical ideals and economic exploitation—existed
throughout the classical crusading period (1095–
1291) in each of the three main theaters: the
Levant, Spain, and eastern Europe. Crusade and
mission being the two sides of a single movement has been a popular belief, particularly since
the publication of Benjamin Z. Kedar's study of
the subject, *Crusade and Mission: European
Approaches Toward the Muslims* (1984). This
approach is certainly true from the perspective of
the official Church, which took its evangelical
duties seriously. When one considers events taking place on the ground rather than the lofty
heights of official policy, however, one finds a
different situation.

The clash between Crusade and mission in
the Levant is exemplified in the career of James
of Vitry. A former crusade preacher, Vitry developed an intense interest in converting Muslims
after he relocated to the East. He wrote letters to
Muslims encouraging them to adopt the Christian faith. He even acquired Muslim children,
baptized them, and housed them with Christian
families. James (and he was not alone) certainly
saw crusading as the ideal tool for preparing
regions for large-scale missions; once a region
was militarily secured then missionaries could
work in a relatively peaceful climate. In the end
he realized he was mistaken. James experienced
the conditions firsthand that Pope Gregory IX
complained to the Bishop of Jerusalem about:
Muslim slaves were being refused baptism
because this process could result in their being

freed. James was shocked that the Franks, and
even the military orders in the East, were hostile
to the missionary efforts. So when addressing
the question of whether conversion was a major
goal of the crusading movement, one must distinguish between Church officials and the laity.
Idealistic missionaries made great efforts to convert Muslims, but the lords of the Crusader
States were either indifferent or hostile to the
proposition. They were perfectly content with
being an aristocracy that ruled over and
exploited their non-Catholic subjects. A notable
exception was the mission to the Mongols,
which received support from Church and laity
alike. The goal here, however, was to acquire a
valuable ally (and defuse the potential of a grave
threat). Conversion of the Mongols would not
interfere with the exploitation of subjects and in
fact promised to expand the lands controlled by
the Crusader States.

Spain had more high-profile attempts at
conversion, ranging from the establishment of
missionary schools to public debates. But Spanish monarchs were generally not only content
with being "kings of the two religions" but also
were enthusiastic about it. John Boswell's study
of the Mudejars, *The Royal Treasure: Muslim
Communities under the Crown of Aragon in the
Fourteenth Century* (1977), speaks volumes about
their economic importance. Large blocks of
non-Christian communities not responsible for
paying tithes to the Church meant that kings
could move in on that surplus revenue. Muslims
and Jews had a certain *utilitas* (special uses) that

MISSIONARY ACTIVITY

180

HISTORY IN DISPUTE, VOLUME 10: THE CRUSADES

Christian subjects did not. Kings jealously guarded "their Muslims" and "their Jews." The value of non-Christian subjects to kings can be seen in a variety of ways. An excellent example was the policy regarding the finding of corpses of royal Muslims and Jews in towns: the town in question had to compensate the king financially for the loss. The need to create a large Christian population for security reasons was often solved by attracting Christian immigrants rather than redoubling efforts to convert Muslims. Crusader rulers in Spain were perfectly content with using and exploiting the Islamic *dhimmi* (protected person) system they found in place. Muslim communities received limited self-rule in exchange for cash payments.

Crusades in eastern Europe had a unique relationship with missionary activity. These Crusades originally were created to provide security for missionaries trying to convert the Slavic pagans of eastern Europe. The pacification of the tribes provided protection for newly created bishopric and fresh converts to the faith. This missionary-crusading activity began in the late twelfth century and intensified exponentially in the thirteenth. In the Baltic region a "perpetual crusade" emerged that was dedicated to carving new "Church-States" out of large swaths of pagan lands. Gradually the movement pushed into Prussia, and the Teutonic Knights redirected their activities from the Levant to eastern Europe. The Golden Bull of Rimini (1226) made the Master of the Teutonic Knights a feudal lord and paved the way for the creation and expansion of the "Order-State." This shift was of the utmost significance for the transformation of crusading in eastern Europe. Evangelization became overshadowed by political expansion and the carving out of territories. Gaining subjects became more important than winning converts. The new situation is well testified to by Bishop Christian, a man devoted to missionary activity in the area. When he died in 1245 he was thoroughly disillusioned with the "missionary crusade." He complained that the Teutonic Knights devoted themselves to material gains and interfered with rather than promoted conversions. The English Franciscan philosopher Roger Bacon felt the same way; he claimed that the greatest obstacle to converting pagans in eastern Europe was the unfettered greed of the Teutonic Knights and their merciless exploitation of the populace. The Teutonic Knights spent just as much time fighting rival Christian powers as they did pagans. There was a popular saying

among Slavic villagers: "Children cry and dogs flee at the sight of a Teutonic Knight."

Crusading and missionary efforts certainly coexisted during the Middle Ages, but claiming that the latter was a major goal of the former is to assert too much. The particulars of how the two efforts interacted varied from theater to theater. From the idealistic perspective of the Church, missionary activity was given great importance. From the pragmatic and materialist perspective of the power brokers along the frontiers, it ran the risk of interfering with their true objective—subjugation and exploitation. In the Levant, idealistic missionaries such as James of Vitry were disgusted by the resistance of local Christians to missionary efforts. In Spain, rulers were much more interested in cashing in on the status of their non-Christian subjects than converting them. In eastern Europe, where the perpetual Crusade was originally established to promote missionary activity, crusading devolved into a vicious and competitive landgrab. Theoretically, Crusade and mission were to cooperate in a joint effort to expand the borders of Christendom. The reality, however, was very different.

–TODD MARX,
CONCORD, NEW HAMPSHIRE

References

John Boswell, *The Royal Treasure: Muslim Communities under the Crown of Aragon in the Fourteenth Century* (New Haven: Yale University Press, 1977).

Robert Chazan, *Daggers of Faith: Thirteenth-century Christian Missionizing and Jewish Response* (Berkeley: University of California Press, 1989).

Jeremy Cohen, *The Friars and the Jews: The Evolution of Medieval Anti-Judaism* (Ithaca, N.Y.: Cornell University Press, 1982).

E. Randolph Daniel, *The Franciscan Concept of Mission in the High Middle Ages* (Lexington: University Press of Kentucky, 1975).

Benjamin Z. Kedar, *Crusade and Mission: European Approaches Toward the Muslims* (Princeton: Princeton University Press, 1984).

James Muldoon, *Popes, Lawyers and Infidels: The Church and the Non-Christian World, 1250–1550* (Liverpool: Liverpool University Press, 1979).

THE MONGOLS

Would a Latin–Ilkhan Mongol alliance have strengthened and preserved the Crusader States?

Viewpoint: Yes. The combined might of the Latins and the Ilkhan Mongols would have been sufficient to destroy the Mamluk Sultanate; furthermore, such an alliance would have allowed the Crusader States to gain power and expand.

Viewpoint: No. The Ilkhan Mongols were unpredictable allies, and they did not have the resources to alter the balance of power in the region significantly.

In the early thirteenth century, Mongol leader Genghis Khan imposed a remarkable degree of unity upon the nomadic tribesmen of inner Asia. The shock waves of this unification were felt from Hungary to Korea; he established the largest empire in history up to that time. After the death of the khan, his empire was divided by his descendants into regional khan-nates. The Ilkhans and the Golden Horde played important roles in the crusading movement. The former swept across the Islamic heartland, destroying the Abbasid Caliphate, conquering Iran and Iraq, and invading Syria, which brought them into direct contact with the Crusader States. The Golden Horde invaded eastern Europe and transformed the nature of crusading in that region. The ferocity of Mongol onslaughts tended to be viewed in apocalyptic terms. To many observers it seemed as though the gates of Hell had been opened and spewed forth the Horsemen of the Apocalypse. Even the Islamic world, by and large more resistant than Europe to apocalyptic expectations, saw the Mongols as harbingers of the end of the world.

The Ilkhans became engaged in a protracted war with the Mamluk Sultanate of Egypt, a highly centralized military regime that eventually put an end to the existence of the Crusader States (1291). Initially, the Ilkhans were seen as a greater danger to the Holy Land than the Muslims and thus became the focus of a great many crusading plans. The situation changed, however, as the Ilkhans recognized their inability to establish an enduring hegemony in the eastern Mediterranean. In the 1260s the Ilkhans were transformed from a grave threat to a potential ally of great power. The Ilkhans offered to forge an alliance with the Latin West to destroy the Mamluk Sultanate. After the power of Egypt was broken, the Ilkhans would restore the lands conquered by Muslim sultan Saladin to the Crusader States. Discussion of such an alliance captured the imagination of both the Ilkhans and the Latin West for five decades.

Some historians have referred to this proposed alliance as a "missed opportunity" that could have restored the Crusader States to a position of strength. Others have argued that organizing such a joint attack was logistically impossible. Even after the fall of the Crusader States, the hope of a Christian-Mongol alliance remained strong. Whether the plan was feasible or not, any hopes of acting on it came to an end in 1322 when the Ilkhans converted to Islam and ended the war with the Mamluk Sultanate.

The question of a Western-Mongol alliance is far more subjective than most others in Crusade historiography, for it deals not with varying interpretations of "what happened" but with debates on "what might have happened." Still, the subject is of great interest and importance since the Mamluk Sultanate succeeded in bringing an end to the Crusader States.

Viewpoint:
Yes. The combined might of the Latins and the Ilkhan Mongols would have been sufficient to destroy the Mamluk Sultanate; furthermore, such an alliance would have allowed the Crusader States to gain power and expand.

The Battle of Ayn Jalut (1260) set the tone for almost all assessments of the Ilkhan-Mamluk War, particularly regarding its implications for the Crusader States. Mongol leader Hulegu, the grandson of Genghis Khan, originally invaded Syria with a force that might have numbered as many as 120,000. The Ayyubids of Syria were incapable of offering much resistance to this military machine, which had already exterminated the Abbasid caliphate, conquered Iraq and Iran, and put an end to the Assassins by capturing and executing Hassan ibn al-Saabah (the Old Man of the Mountain). Hulegu's plan was to push southward and conquer Egypt, which was experiencing a turbulent shift that would end Ayyubid rule and give rise to the Mamluk Sultanate. The invasion of Egypt, however, was interrupted by the death of the Great Khan Mongke (Mangu Khan), as well as the intrigues of Hulegu's uncle Batu Khan, leader of the Golden Horde. Hulegu was forced to return to Azerbaijan with the bulk of the Mongol army, leaving a small detachment of troops in Syria under the command of his general Kitbugha, whose task was to hold Syria and prepare for the invasion of Egypt once interkhannate conflicts had been resolved. The Mamluks decided to take the war to the Mongols and negotiate with the Crusader States. Although the Latins were technically neutral, they not only granted the Mamluks free passage through their territory to engage the Mongols but also provided them with supplies. The forces clashed at Ayn Jalut. The Mamluks had nearly every tactical advantage: surprise (Kitbugha vastly underestimated the size of the Mamluk force), terrain (Mamluks had high ground), and positioning (the Mongols were facing the sun). The Mamluks are also believed to have enjoyed an overwhelming numerical superiority, though this belief has recently been challenged. In the end the Mongols were surrounded, Kitbugha killed, and the rest of

the Mongols cut down as they tried to flee uphill. Traditionally, this battle has been seen as the definitive Mamluk "check" on Mongol expansion into the eastern Mediterranean. It also allowed the Mamluks to fill the power vacuum created in Syria by the Mongol attack, clearing a path to the unification of Egypt and Syria under an aggressive and organized state.

Ayn Jalut has also been seen as a microcosm in which the strengths of the Mamluk Sultanate and the weaknesses of the Ilkhans can be observed with great clarity. The Mamluks were forging a highly centralized (by medieval standards) military machine that enjoyed the home-court advantage. Their military tactics and methods, moreover, were well suited to the environment. They could focus all of their attention on threats in the region. The Ilkhans, however, were fighting a battle on the periphery of their empire. Events in Persia were of greater concern to them; Syria, Palestine, and Egypt were secondary (though still important) considerations. The Ilkhans were frequently forced to disengage from Syrian campaigns to focus their attention elsewhere. Nor was this emphasis the only reason the Ilkhans could not maintain a constant presence. Syria did not offer enough pastureland for the Ilkhans' horses, and the cavalry was the sine qua non for effective Mongol military operations. When all of these factors are tallied, it becomes clear that the Ilkhans could not commit the necessary men for the requisite period of time to win a Syrian war. This deficiency can be seen in Ayn Jalut: the initial conquest was sudden and severe, but ultimately the area was defended by a small detachment. The same results can be gleaned from periodic Mongol returns to Syria such as those of 1280, 1299, 1301, and 1303.

There is much merit to these arguments, and it seems clear that the Ilkhans were incapable of maintaining a constant presence in Syria; but was a Mongol-Western alliance necessary for altering the balance of power in the region in favor of the Crusader States? Rather than focusing on the "lessons of Ayn Jalut" and using that battle as the paradigm by which to interpret the Mongol presence in the region, one should focus on the lessons of the Battle of Homs (1281) and the alternative paradigm it offers. This engagement has never received the attention that Ayn Jalut has enjoyed, but in many respects it reveals much more about the impact of the Mongols on the region than Ayn Jalut.

A STRANGE PARADISE

Although many historians view the story of Hassan ibn al-Saabah (the Old Man of the Mountain) as a mere myth, Venetian traveler Marco Polo offers this description of his world and that of the Assassins:

So the Old Man of the Mountain had had his garden built like Mohammed's Paradise and the Saracens really believed it was Paradise.

However, only men who were to become murderers could go into the garden. There was just one entrance, guarded by a fort able to withstand any attack. The Old Man kept at his court all the boys between the ages of twelve and twenty who showed any aptitude for battle. All these boys had heard tell that Mohammed's promised land was like this garden and they firmly believed in it.

The Old Man made these boys go into the garden in groups of four, ten, or sometimes twenty. First he had drinks prepared for them which sent them straight to sleep, then he had them carried into the garden, where they woke up. When they awoke and saw the wonderful things around them they thought they were in Paradise. Women and girls with whom they could take their pleasure at will played and sang to them. The boys had everything they wanted and for nothing in the world would they have left this paradise.

The Old Man's court was rich, splendid and sumptuous and he made the simple mountain people believe that he was a prophet.

When he wanted to have someone killed, he ordered the sleeping draught to be given to some of the boys in the garden and when they were asleep he had them brought to his castle. When they awoke to find themselves in the palace they were surprised and highly displeased. They went to the Old Man and, believing him to be a great prophet, knelt at his feet. When the Old Man asked where they had come from they replied, "From Paradise," and assured him that the paradise promised to their forefathers by Mohammed really existed, telling the Old Man of all the delights to be found there. The other boys who had not been there longed to go and would willingly have died, indeed

were eager to do so as soon as possible. So when the Old Man wanted an important person killed he put his assassins to the test to find out which of them was the boldest. He sent a fairly large group of them to a nearby province and told them to kill a man. When they had done so they came back to court—that is to say, those who were not captured and put to death. Those who returned, having accomplished the mission, were warmly welcomed by the Old Man. He knew perfectly well which of them had been the bravest because he sent spies to report back to him.

In this way the Old Man knew whom to trust when he wanted someone killed. He could send the boys wherever he wanted by telling them that he was making sure that they went quickly to Paradise. If they died carrying out their mission they would go straight there. The idea of going to Paradise made the assassins very happy, so they went off and did whatever they were asked, unafraid of death. Many kings and barons paid tribute to the Old Man and cultivated his friendship for fear of being murdered. The Old Man was aided in this by the fact that the kings were always quarrelling amongst themselves and were not united under one power.

So much for the way of life of the Old Man of the Mountain and his assassins. Now we come to his death. . . .

In about 1262, Hulagu, the Lord of the Levantine Tartars, having heard of the Old Man's horrible ways, decided to destroy him. Hulagu chose a few of his barons and sent them with a large army to attack the Old Man's fortified castle. It seemed impossible to capture and would certainly never have been taken if the people inside had been able to get food. The siege lasted three years, by the end of which time there was nothing left to eat. The Old Man of the Mountain, Alaodin, was captured and put to death with all his men, and the castle and the garden of paradise were demolished.

Source: Marco Polo, The Travels of Marco Polo, translated by Maria Bellonci (London: Sidgwick & Jackson, 1984), pp. 38–39.

THE MONGOLS

The Battle of Homs was the culmination of the Ilkhan invasion of Syria. After an expeditionary force sacked Aleppo and withdrew, a Mongol army of fifty thousand (complemented with non-Mongol contingents numbering up to thirty thousand) launched a full-scale invasion of Syria under the command of Mongke-Temur. As in the battle of Ayn Jalut, the Franks remained neutral (save a few renegades) because of the treaty in effect between Antioch ruler Bohemond VII and the sultan Qala'un. On 29 October 1281 the Ilkhan and Mamluk armies fought outside the city of Homs. The battle was even more pitched than that waged at Ayn Jalut. Both sides were convinced they were losing until Mongke was wounded and Mongol morale was disrupted. The Mamluk victory, however, was a pyrrhic one. Mamluk losses were devastating, so much so that an Armenian observer dubbed their victory a resounding defeat. The blow to the Mamluk army was crippling; Qala'un had to rebuild the Egyptian army before he could take any further action against his other enemies. A notable exception to this situation was Qala'un's assault on Armenia. The objective was twofold and of the utmost importance to the Sultanate. First, Armenia had to be punished for its cooperation with the Mongols to deter any possible repetition of Homs. Any joint activities between Christian powers and Mongols were a grave threat to Egyptian power. Second, the Armenian city of Ayas was an important hub for the slave trade. Auxiliaries could be quickly recruited from Bedouin tribes, but the backbone of the Egyptian army was the Mamluks, who could only be recruited from the slave markets. For the duration of their lengthy and effective training, Mamluks were slaves and, according to Islamic law, Muslims could not be slaves. So young slaves, mostly of Turkish origin, had to be purchased and then trained to replenish the most effective part of the Egyptian army. Although it was difficult for any medieval army to recover from massive losses, this problem was doubly so for the Mamluk military machine.

The main lesson to be learned from Ayn Jalut is that the Mongols were incapable of maintaining a strong military presence in Syria. The lesson of Homs is that the Mongols could inflict an incredible amount of damage in a short period of time. Even though they lost the battle, the Mongols dealt a crippling blow to the Mamluks, and they did it with no real Latin assistance. The Mamluk army was rendered incapable of taking any decisive military action against the Crusader States. The destruction of Qala'un's army, and the time needed to reconstitute it, provide a much better explanation than treaties for the extended lease on life

the Crusader States were granted. Additionally, it created a power vacuum in Syria. The initial Mongol conquest of Syria prior to Ayn Jalut created a similar vacuum—one that was filled by the Mamluks at the expense of the Ayyubids. Following Homs, the Mamluks were incapable of substantively filling that vacuum. Naturally, the barons of the Crusader States were in no position to do so either, but it certainly created a window of opportunity for making substantial gains in the region. If a traditional, major Western Crusade could have struck shortly after Homs, it would have found an already defeated enemy. There is every reason to believe that the entire balance of power in the region would have shifted. Nor is it beyond the realm of possibility that such a Crusader host would have been able to march on Alexandria and Cairo and in so doing create a Latin Egypt. Since Iran and Iraq now formed the center of the Ilkhan empire, Egypt could expect no help for the Islamic heartland in the Near East.

Hulegu's original proposal offered the West good terms. The Ilkhans had established their bona fides through their amazing victories against the center of the Islamic world. Of particular interest to Hulegu was Latin sea power, which, combined with a Mongol land offensive, could break the back of the Mamluk Sultanate. After victory, Hulegu planned to restore Jerusalem to Latin rule, as well as return lands previously held by the barons of the Crusader States. In effect, Outremer would once again resemble the land it was before the Battle of the Horns of Hattin (1187). That the Latin West considered a Christian-Mongol alliance to be an effective means for reconquering the Holy Land can be gleaned from the prominence it achieved in crusading theory. As the Ilkhans pointed out, the Mamluks would be wedged between, and crushed by, such an alliance. Alone, each side could win battles but not the war against the Mamluks. Together, the Mamluks would be destroyed to the mutual benefit of Latins and Ilkhans.

How feasible was this plan? The Mongols could be effective as a shock force. If a general passage could have been launched within a few years of Homs, then the Crusaders' main concerns would have been mop-up operations, building fortifications, and planning solid occupation. Synchronizing Ilkhan-Latin operations was a difficult task, but given the slow rate at which the Mamluk army could regenerate, Crusaders would have been at a great advantage. Crusading theory, moreover, had already shifted to the concept of using expeditionary forces (particular passages) that would be followed by a full-scale Crusade (general passage). The main problem facing such a joint attack was the inability of western Europe to launch a major Crusade on the traditional model in the latter half of the thirteenth century. Hence, those historians who have seen the Latin-Ilkhan alliance as a "missed opportunity" are correct. The Ilkhans offered an attractive opportunity that, mostly because of events taking place in western Europe, could not be seized upon.

If such a joint assault had succeeded, would it have resulted in exchanging an Islamic military threat for Mongol domination? The evidence suggests otherwise. The Ilkhans proposed an anti-Mamluk alliance with the Latins because they were not able to maintain a long-term presence in the region. This realization by the Ilkhans can be detected in the shifting tenor of their correspondence with the Latin West. Initially, the Ilkhans demanded nothing less than the complete submission of the West to the Mongol "mandate of heaven" that was inherited from Chinese political theory. Hulegu moderated his tone in a way that smacked of partnership rather than subordination. Furthermore, the fact that the Mongols could not maintain a permanent presence in Syria was advantageous to the long-term goals of the Crusades. Areas that touched upon vast pastureland tended to fall under direct Mongol rule. In areas with little pasture (such as Syria) the Mongols granted considerable self-rule and autonomy. Thus, the very reason the Mongols could not deal a deathblow to the Mamluks alone was also a guarantee of Crusader State autonomy. The Mongols also respected legitimate rights to territory, and their offer to return the Crusader States to their status before Hattin was probably sincere. The Ilkhans restored lands to Bohemond to which he had a legitimate claim. The Ilkhans might well have seen the Latins as future subjects of their empire, but the yoke would have been hardly noticeable to the Latins.

Historians who fail to see an Ilkhan-Latin alliance as a "missed opportunity" tend to dwell too much on the difficulties in perfectly synchronizing a joint attack. As the Mongols demonstrated at Homs, they were perfectly capable of destroying the Mamluk army, even if they were unable to capitalize on their victories. Even if their activities were timed on a loose "more or less" timetable, the Latins would have reaped great benefits. Previous Crusades crashed upon the rocks of perfectly intact Islamic armies. A full-scale Crusade, arriving within a few years of a "particular passage," that made use of Mongol military might, would have found a different situation. In the end, western Europe was unable to take advantage of the opportunity, even if the proposal was feasible.

–TODD MARX,
CONCORD, NEW HAMPSHIRE

Viewpoint:
No. The Ilkhan Mongols were unpredictable allies, and they did not have the resources to alter the balance of power in the region significantly.

The Great Khan Mongke (Mangu Khan) announced his intention to resume the grand conquest of almost "all under heaven" that his grandfather Ghengis Khan began decades earlier. His brother Kublai was to complete the conquest of China. Batu Khan, his uncle, was to bring eastern Europe under his yoke. The Middle East fell to Mongke's other brother Hulegu. Kublai's operation in China, though it radically changed the course of East Asian history, had no impact on the crusading movement. Batu's activities in eastern Europe prompted Crusades against the Mongols and complicated the position of the Crusader States in the East indirectly. Hulegu, however, completely upended the political, economic, and military scenarios in the eastern Mediterranean. For better or worse, Hulegu and the Ilkhan dynasty steered the fate of the Holy Land and the crusading movement in a new direction. First perceived as a threat (possibly even greater than Muslims) by the Latin West, the Ilkhans became projected targets for a Crusade to the Holy Land. From the 1260s and continuing into the first two decades of the fourteenth century the Ilkhans were seen as allies willing and able to assist in the destruction of the Mamluk Sultanate. Many historians have referred to this "missed opportunity" to save the Crusader States. Could the power balance in the region have been changed and the Crusader States raised to grandeur?

Before addressing such a subjective (though significant) question, it would be best to briefly outline the main effects that the Ilkhans had on the region. Most spectacular was Hulegu's destruction of the Abbasid Caliphate—the center of Islamic political and economic life for centuries. Seljuk power was smashed. Hulegu sacked Baghdad and slaughtered much of its population in 1258. The last Abbasid caliph supposedly died while rolled up in a carpet—he was allegedly kicked to death by Mongols. The Mongol conquest of Iraq and Iran introduced mass upheaval both politically and economically. Politically, the

قمنگاه تو رستم زنگ تیسی خوش

خوش آگرسوی من افتند نگاه دوست

Miniature of Hulegu, the first Il-khan of Persia (sixteenth century)

(British Library, London)

destruction of the caliphate threw the Islamic world into chaos and eased the rise of the Mamluk Sultanate by providing a compelling justification for its seizure of power. The caliphate was gone; sound, effective leadership was needed to prosecute the jihad (just war) against the Mongols (as well as the Latins). This upheaval also paved the way for unifying Egypt and Syria under the Mamluks, putting the Crusader States in a difficult position. The Mongols were now in control of the important trade routes that gave the Abbasids such power, and they redirected them away from Egypt and the Crusader States and toward Armenia and the Black Sea. Although trade in neither Alexandria nor Acre dried up completely, the shift in trade routes was a blow to both.

Armenia was quick to note the benefits that the Mongol presence might offer. The king of Armenia had cast his lot with the Mongols before they even arrived in Syria. Reactions were different among the Latin lords. Bohemond VII of Antioch, following the example of his Armenian father-in-law, submitted to Hulegu—which was considered disgraceful by many—and was quickly excommunicated by the patriarch of Jerusalem for doing so. Suspicion, confusion, and fear were the reactions of most. Initially, the Mongol threat was seen as being more grave than that of the Ayyubids. In 1260 the Mongols had control over Syria by conquest and negoti-

ated treaties with the Ayyubids. That same year, Mongol representatives arrived in Egypt to demand its submission to the Khan. Mamluk sultan Qutuz promptly executed the diplomats. By this time Hulegu had been forced to return to Azerbaijan following the death of the Great Khan Mongke. Hulegu needed to monitor succession and protect his holdings against Berke (who succeeded Batu) and the Golden Horde. A small occupational force was left under the command of his general Kitbugha, who was tasked with making preparations for an invasion of Egypt and scouting the region down to Gaza.

The Mamluks decided to move their troops north to Syria rather than to wait for a Mongol invasion of Egypt. The sultan opened negotiations with the Crusader States (who officially remained neutral) and secured right of passage for his troops. The Mamluk and Mongol forces clashed at Ayn Jalut (1260). The battle has been seen as a turning point in the history of the Crusades. Kitbugha was killed, his troops were dispersed, and the Mamluks took control of Syria. The Mongol advance into the region was checked, and the power of the Mamluks increased dramatically. Traditionally, the Mamluk victory has been explained as the result of an ambush of the Mongols by a vastly larger army. In addition to enjoying numerical superiority, the Mamluks also held the high ground and had the sun at their backs—two highly significant

THE MONGOLS

HISTORY IN DISPUTE, VOLUME 10: THE CRUSADES **187**

advantages. Recent reconsideration of Ayn Jalut has yielded somewhat different conclusions. Rather than positing a Mamluk numerical advantage of 120,000 to 10,000, recent estimates have placed the Mamluk force at 15,000 to 20,000 and that of the Mongols at 10,000 to 12,000. Rather than being a crude ambush, the Mamluk victory seems to have been the result of shrewd tactics, with Qutuz proving to be a much better field commander than Kitbugha. Following the same sort of Islamic strategy that secured Saladin's victory over the Franks at the Horns of Hattin (1187), Qutuz wanted the battle to begin by having a clear advantage in positioning. Qutuz outmaneuvered Kitbugha; the Mongols had poor field position, were lured in, and then were crushed on both flanks.

The Battle of Ayn Jalut is significant for three reasons. First, it prompted the Ilkhans to seek an anti-Mamluk alliance with the Franks. Before the defeat at Ayn Jalut, the Ilkhans viewed the Latins (as they viewed everyone) as future subjects rather than potential partners. Second, it demonstrates that the Mongols could be defeated by a force roughly equivalent in size to theirs. Vast numerical superiority was not the sine qua non for defeating the Mongols in the field. Third, and even more important, it shows the difficulty the Ilkhans had in maintaining a strong presence in the region. Hulegu considered events taking place to the East as being more important than those in Syria. Succession disputes in inner Asia required the presence of the khan and the bulk of his forces. The Ilkhan's interests and enemies were broad, and conflicts with the Golden Horde proved grounds for retreating from Syria. The Mamluks most likely could not have defeated the entire combined might of Hulegu's forces at Ayn Jalut. It also seems difficult to believe that Hulegu could have made such a commitment for any period of time.

Succession disputes and intrakhannate conflicts were not the only reasons that the Ilkhans could not fully commit to the region. Without doubt, a Mongol onslaught was as terrifying as it could be destructive. But grazing land for horses was to the Mongol military machine what petrol was to a German Panzer division during World War II (1939–1945). As David Morgan, in *The Mongols* (1986), has pointed out, the greatest and most enduring problem for the Mongols in Syria was the lack of grassland needed to maintain their horses. Essentially, this lack of fodder made any permanent Mongol occupation of Syria impossible. It also made sustained activities in the region extremely difficult, particularly when the Mamluks adapted by destroying the precious stretches of grassland upon which the Mongols were dependent. This formidable handicap, combined with the problems mentioned above, drastically curtailed the effectiveness and military importance of the Mongols in the region. The Ilkhan realization of this situation was what prompted their offer for an alliance with, and the granting of good terms to, the Latins. The offer placed on the table was the restoration of the Crusader States to the status they enjoyed before Hattin. The Mamluks would be sandwiched between Christian and Mongol forces; Mongol land operations, combined with western European sea power, could break the back of the sultanate.

Assessing what possible value the Mongol offer had for the fate of the Crusader States should be approached from two perspectives: First, would such an alliance have had much effect? Second, would a joint "Crusade" of Mongols and western Europeans have succeeded in strengthening the Crusader States?

After the Latin defeat at La Forbie (1244) the rulers of the Crusader States were rendered virtually inert militarily. On its own, the remnants of the Latin field army were incapable of little more than skirmishes and raids. The survival of the Latin states at this point rested more upon diplomatic strategy and negotiations with the Ayyubids than upon any other single factor. Scarcity of manpower and land leading up to the 1260s further hampered the situation. The Latin Empire of Constantinople (1204–1261) could hardly provide much assistance. Byzantine Epirus and Nicaea were on the offensive against the Latins and scored major victories. The Byzantine Empire was reconstituted in 1261. Military assistance from the West was diminishing. The Mamluks were a much greater threat than the Ayyubids had been since the death of Saladin (1193). Armenia energetically served as the gray eminence behind forging an Ilkhan-Latin alliance. That Hulegu was incapable of assisting Armenia and Antioch in 1264 did nothing to deter the dream of an alliance. The idea of a regional alliance among Franks, Armenians, Ilkhans, and Byzantines remained strong, but the Byzantines were never reliable allies—they often saw the Latins as a greater threat than the Muslims. They rarely delivered little more than token military support to the Crusaders and often worked with Muslims against the Latins.

Would the Ilkhans have made reliable allies for an anti-Mamluk alliance in the East? Mongke had originally ordered Hulegu to drive the Franks out of the region as well as seize Egypt from the Muslims. Ilkhan ruler Abaga, who succeeded Hulegu, unsuccessfully made diplomatic overtures to Egyptian sultan Baybars I in 1272. There was also the roster of reasons that prevented the Mongols from maintaining a sustained presence in the region. Flaring conflicts with the Golden Horde, as well as lack of grazing lands, meant the Ilkhans were incapable of substantively committing themselves to Syria. Such an alliance in the East would also surely prompt the creation of a counteralliance between the Mamluk Sultanate and the Golden Horde. The threat was a real one, as can be seen in correspondence between the Golden Horde and the Mamluks. Golden Horde leader Berke's assault on the Byzantine's Bulgarian frontier in 1265 was undoubtedly a shot over the bow to discourage such an alliance. If a Latin-Ilkhan alliance secured a new ally for Crusader objectives, it was also sure to drag in a new enemy. Pressure by the Golden Horde on the Ilkhans, moreover, was more than capable of forcing the latter to reconsider its hostile stance with the Mamluks.

Could the Ilkhans have made valuable allies in a joint "Crusade" on the traditional model? There is no doubt that the Mongols were sincerely interested in such an assault. The Ilkhans sent waves of ambassadors to the West trying to secure such a venture. But the logistical savvy needed to conduct such a massive campaign was far beyond the capacities of the age. Western Europeans found it difficult—almost impossible—to synchronize their own assaults on the East. "Crusades" were conducted in "waves" because it was rare that European powers could put aside their problems at the same time for a perfectly synchronized attack. This squabbling resulted in such dramas as Holy Roman Emperor Frederick II's arriving in the East after the Fifth Crusade (1217–1229) was essentially over. A "general passage" that would include the Mongols multiplied logistical problems ad infinitum. Joint Mongol-Crusader assaults were attempted from 1269 to 1272. Abaga and James I of Aragon planned a joint attack on Egypt. Abaga declared war on Baybars I, but a substantial part of James's fleet was destroyed in a storm en route. James then fell ill and set sail for home. Part of his host pushed on to Acre. After a month of helping to defend the city while waiting for James, they eventually disbanded. Not only was Abaga facing the Mamluk threat almost alone, he also had to fend off a renewed attack upon his lands by the Golden Horde. This attack was also what prevented Abaga from making his rendezvous with the troops of French king Louis IX to conduct an assault on Egypt. In an operation of such scale and such distances, all hinged upon precise timing, and that was what neither side could guarantee. When King Edward I of England arrived at Acre he received Abaga's apologies that the khan was incapable of joining him as agreed. All the khan could spare was a small detachment that was easily defeated in the field. If James had arrived . . . if the Golden Horde did not attack . . . if Abaga could have met up with Louis and Edward . . . then a substantive attack could have been launched against Egypt, but the chances of such a coalescence were rare and, despite several attempts, never succeeded.

Negotiations between the Ilkhans and the Latins continued. In fact, Ilkhan assistance played a major role in Crusade planning into the first decades of the fourteenth century. In the end, however, the myth of an effective alliance with the Mongols was as illusory as the myth of Prester John—that great but fictitious Christian ruler in the East who would launch an attack on Islam in concert with western Europeans. In theory, the plan seems to have been sound—Latin sea power dominating the coast and blockading ports, with the barons of Outremer fighting side by side with the combined military might of western Europe and the Ilkhan Empire. But the primitive state of logistics and transport, combined with the political problems facing the Europeans and the Mongols, made transforming theory into practice an impossibility. Joining forces with the Mongols was thus not a "missed opportunity." It was an opportunity that all parties tried to seize but failed to achieve.

–MARK T. ABATE,
WESTFIELD STATE COLLEGE

References

Reuven Amitai-Reiss, *Mongols and Mamluks: The Mamluk-Ilkhanid War, 1260–1281* (Cambridge & New York: Cambridge University Press, 1991).

Robert Irwin, *The Middle East in the Middle Ages: The Early Mamluk Sultanate, 1250–1382* (Carbondale: Southern Illinois University Press, 1986).

David Morgan, *The Mongols* (Oxford & New York: Blackwell, 1986).

Sylvia Schein, *Fideles Crucis: The Papacy, the West, and the Recovery of the Holy Land, 1274–1314* (Oxford: Clarendon Press / New York: Oxford University Press, 1991).

Schein, "Gesta Dei per Mongolos 1300: The Genesis of a Non-Event," *English Historical Review*, 94 (1979): 805–819.

MUSLIMS

Were Muslims treated better by the Crusaders than by Islamic rulers in the East?

Viewpoint: Yes. Since the Crusader States needed to secure the cooperation of subject Muslims for economic and strategic reasons, they offered a form of semi-autonomous rule that gave Muslims, as well as Jews, a higher degree of freedom.

Viewpoint: No. Muslims under Latin rule were treated as inferiors, were humiliated and degraded by Christian domination, and longed for the return of Islamic rule.

Legend has it that the blood in the narrow, twisting streets of Jerusalem was knee-deep from the butchery that the First Crusaders (1096–1102) inflicted upon Muslims (and probably many Jews and Eastern Christians) following the fall of the city on 15 July 1099. Whether such a tale is to be believed, it is certain that the Crusader conquest of Muslims in the Holy Land was one of the most brutal and violent campaigns of the Middle Ages (an age that was much more forgiving than modern times when it came to war atrocities). As the majority of the First Crusaders returned to Europe, however, those who settled in the East were forced to strike a modus vivendi with their new Muslim subjects, who vastly outnumbered them. The Crusaders adopted much of the Byzantine-Islamic political system they found and, although they made some modifications, by and large came to occupy the top of the social and economic edifice without disrupting its foundations. One of the Islamic systems they found and adopted was the *dhimmi* (protected minority) model for dealing with religious minorities (though it was now ironically applied to the Muslim majority). In exchange for submission, non-Latins were given legal protections and semi-autonomy.

Conceptions concerning the status and treatment of minorities in the Middle Ages were drastically different than our own. Today mainstreaming and equality are cardinal virtues for relationships between minorities and majorities. In the Middle Ages both majorities and minorities preferred segregation along religious, cultural, and even occupational lines. Segregation was thus not a malevolent system forced upon the disenfranchised but rather a mutually agreed-upon relationship. Segregation allowed minorities to practice their religion and adhere to their own cultural norms in designated areas that were in a way their own. Minorities had rights, but they were subjected to humiliation and exploitation in both the Islamic and Latin worlds. As James M. Powell pointed out, in *Muslims under Latin Rule, 1100–1300* (1990), toleration, though it existed in various forms, was not the principle upon which legislation pertaining to minorities was based. A more accurate description would be that it was geared toward checking the most extreme manifestations of intolerance.

Similarities existed in the Latin treatment of Muslims in Spain, Sicily, and the Crusader States, but the situation of the latter was much more precarious because of its geographical positioning. Surrounded by enemies, far from Europe and the possibility of immediate assistance, and constantly strapped for manpower, the Crusader States were in near constant danger for their two-century existence. Some historians believe that these dismal conditions forced the lords of the Crusader States to treat their Muslim subjects with extreme fairness—of such magnitude that it outshone not only how other Latins treated Muslims, but how Islamic states did as well.

Viewpoint:
Yes. Since the Crusader States needed to secure the cooperation of subject Muslims for economic and strategic reasons, they offered a form of semi-autonomous rule that gave Muslims, as well as Jews, a higher degree of freedom.

The knights, foot soldiers, clergy, pilgrims, and servants who made up the First Crusade (1096–1102) had their hearts fixed for years on a single goal—the conquest of the Holy Land. Numbering as many as one hundred thousand, if one considers both the "unofficial" Crusaders who composed the motley crew led by Peter the Hermit and the "official" Crusaders led by the barons of France, Germany, and the Low Countries, these men and women endured four years of hard travel, bloody battles, starvation, disease, indiscipline, mercantile chicanery, and a host of local treacheries in order to achieve their purpose of liberating Palestine from what they judged a brutal Islamic tyranny. (They all generally regarded these last three words as redundant.) Everything that they experienced from the time of Pope Urban II's call to arms (November 1095) to the nearly psychotic bloodletting of their climactic ransacking of Jerusalem (July 1099) catalyzed and strengthened their single-minded focus on the conquest of the Levant.

To judge from extant records, however, none of them seem ever to have considered what they might do with the Holy Land after they conquered it. Did they expect time to simply roll up, and the world to end? Undoubtedly some probably did, but the nonapocalyptic majority confronted their new predicament with calmer minds. The problem they confronted was simply defined: How was a small Latin Christian occupying force going to survive in a distant and difficult terrain whose populations had little reason to regard the occupiers with benevolence? Making their odds even worse, most of the surviving Crusaders (in general, all those who had estates and families in the West) simply returned to Europe, leaving an even smaller force to contend with matters in the East. At least three of the six main commanders of the Crusade—Duke Robert of Normandy, Count Robert of Flanders, and Count Raymond of Toulouse—departed quickly, leaving only Bohemund of Sicily, Tancred, and Godfrey de Bouillon in recognized positions of authority. By some estimates, no more than five hundred Latin knights and their retinues remained to govern a sprawl of territories—roughly five hundred miles from north to south and one hundred miles from west to east—with an overall population of nearly one million. In the face of this reality, the Crusaders constantly followed three policies: recruitment of new settlers from the West, intermarriage with subject-peoples willing to convert to Christianity, and pursuit of tolerant relations with their subjects. To achieve these ends, the four major principalities established by the Crusaders—the County of Edessa, the Principality of Antioch, the County of Tripoli, and the Kingdom of Jerusalem—developed (albeit each in its own way) as secular states instead of theocracies. Church leaders retained influential, but seldom determinative, roles in political and social policy.

In these ministates Muslims composed the clear majority of the population and were the chief focus of government action. The rest of the population was made up of Palestinian, Ashkenazic, and Sephardic Jews; "Syrians" (by which the Crusaders meant Monophysite and Jacobite Christians); Orthodox Greeks; small handfuls of Slavs, Copts, Turks, and Persians; and Latin Christian immigrants. Intermixed with these permanent residents were foreigners who regularly streamed through the region on commercial errands or religious pilgrimages. The Crusaders could only retain control over such a heterogeneous crowd by guaranteeing them widespread privileges and by staying as far as possible out of their lives: to succeed, in other words, not by winning their loyalty but by giving them no clear reason to rise up against their rule.

This policy proved to be a surprisingly successful stratagem. The political history of the Crusader States (1097 to 1291) was one of continuous effort by external Muslim powers to regain the lands held by the Westerners, but of virtually no effort by the local subjects to overthrow the Crusaders' regimes. What caused such acceptance—however grudging—by the Muslim and Jewish subjects? The Crusaders lacked, in their formal enactments, a legal concept analogous to that of the *dhimmis* (protected minorities) of Muslim law. According to that law, the *dhimmis* under Islamic control were to be recognized as partially autonomous legal and religious communities, with guaranteed rights and even a place in Allah's design for human salvation. The Crusaders had no such formal conception, but

MUSLIMS

the general policies they followed produced much the same result for the Muslims in their midst and may in fact have been in practice a more consistently tolerant reality than the Islamic social dictate. That conclusion certainly was the opinion of Muslim traveler and historian ibn al-Athir, who wrote in 1184 that the general opinion of the Muslims he met in Palestine was that they were better off under Christian rule than they had been under the Islamic princes and warlords whom the Crusaders supplanted. Other contemporaries echoed similar opinions, though perhaps not quite so explicitly. The most sophisticated Muslim commentator on the Levant during the twelfth century, 'Usamah ibn-Munqidh, described Crusader rule with almost comic dispassion—the "Franks" were, to his eyes, too inept to be truly malignant. His descriptions of Christian intolerance pale in comparison with the brutality he portrays in Muslim sultan Saladin's character. As for the Jews, they chafed against their exclusion from Jerusalem, but no contemporary family scrolls (private histories) describe the fall of the city to the Christians or detail any atrocities committed against them by the conquerors, and most of the letters surviving in the Cairo *geniza* that discuss the Crusader States at all suggest that contemporary Jews regarded Christian control of the Holy Land as an unremarkable and minor disruption of normal political and social life. The fact that Muslim and Jewish immigrants continued to settle in the Levant throughout the years of Christian control further encourages the conclusion that relations between conquerors and conquered were more workable than one might initially expect.

This conclusion is not to suggest that the Crusader States were halcyon islands of peace and friendship. Tens of thousands of formerly free Muslim farmers were reduced to the status of workers on feudal estates controlled by the conquerors, and most of the leading commercial and industrial positions in the coastal cities were reserved for the Christian merchant elites. Nevertheless, the Crusaders preserved the autonomy of the majority of Muslim villagers, who continued to farm their own lands, govern their own villages according to their own customs, and obey their own local legal and religious officials. In the cities, the Crusaders squeezed out the Syrian, Jewish, and Muslim entrepreneurs who had controlled commerce in favor of European (and especially Italian) merchants; but the actual effect of this maneuver was to increase economic opportunity for the bulk of the population, since the earlier elite had maintained religious prohibitions that preserved ethnic segregation.

With the exception of the city of Jerusalem, the Crusader States were zones of religious free-

dom considerably greater than what had characterized Muslim rule in the tenth and eleventh centuries. Christian churches underwent extensive expansion and renovation, but mosques and synagogues also increased dramatically in number (if noticeably less so in elaboration) and were often repaired or built with the help of public funds. Moreover, Christian houses were frequently opened for Muslim and Jewish religious services while the mosques and synagogues were under construction—as was the case with the Cathedral of the Holy Cross in Acre, for example. To help preserve the subject communities' independence, the Crusaders granted Muslims and Jews an array of commercial privileges and monopolies. Jewish merchants held monopolies over dye works in at least six coastal cities, for example, and had a near monopoly over the glassmaking industry in Tyre, while Muslim shippers retained exclusive control of several sea routes connecting the Levantine harbors with their western markets.

In sum, Muslim-Christian-Jewish relations in the Crusader States in the twelfth century compared favorably to those to be found anywhere else in the Christian world and within the Islamic world as well. Indeed, despite the continuation of episodic crusading, there was a general mellowing of hostility during the twelfth century toward Muslims among Christians that contrasts sharply with the bristling and increasingly persecutory stance taken toward Christian and Jewish subjects by Muslims of the Islamic states.

—CLIFFORD R. BACKMAN,
BOSTON UNIVERSITY

Viewpoint:
No. Muslims under Latin rule were treated as inferiors, were humiliated and degraded by Christian domination, and longed for the return of Islamic rule.

Whether Muslims were "better off" under Latin Christian than Islamic rule is difficult to answer. Ultimately, this inquiry strikes at a deeper, more universal, and amorphous question: what factors define quality of life? Schoolchildren in the United States learn at an early age a phrase that supposedly gives the answer: "life, liberty, and the pursuit of happiness." Later, they learn to give greater clarity to the last term, the "pursuit of happiness," which is often seen in the United States, Western states, and many non-Western states as economic security and all the prizes that the market economy awards to competent and enterprising contestants. Today, status and general "happiness," on both national and international levels, is primarily defined by economic prosperity. This definition was not always so. Naturally, wealth has always been a great concern of humans, but before the rise of modern capitalism the possession or lack of wealth was not how most civilizations measured themselves (though individuals might have). The modern understanding of liberty is, historically, a new concept, one that would have made no sense whatsoever to either a Christian or Muslim living during the age of the Crusades. There were concessions, grants, privileges, and even a primitive and limited sense of "rights," but there was no concept of liberty. All people, in both Christian and Islamic societies, had a particular niche, with some rights and many responsibilities, within a rigid hierarchical framework. Liberty and the pursuit of happiness imply the possibility of upward mobility, but this concept was virtually nonexistent in the Middle Ages.

One can do no better than to begin with twelfth-century world traveler ibn Jubayr. His remark that many Muslims were treated better under Frankish than Islamic rule has made quite an impression upon modern historians. That he had traveled so widely in lands under both Islamic and Christian rule (Egypt, Mecca, Sicily, and particularly in the Crusader States) provided him with substantial credentials for making such a judgment. Yet, he had a particularly deep-seated bias, ironically, against his fellow Muslims. Although a pious Muslim, ibn Jubayr had a low opinion of the state of international Islam, with the exception of Berber Almohades and, to a slightly lesser extent, the Muslim sultan Saladin. As he put it in his travel memoirs, "Let it be absolutely certain and beyond doubt established that there is no Islam except in the Maghrib lands." To his mind, Baghdad had become a den of impious thieves whose main pursuit was cheating strangers. Sudanese Muslims had little more reason than animals, and their women, far from wearing a veil, ran about naked. Ibn Jubayr even had little regard for the governor of Granada, whom he served as secretary. He decided to finally make the *hadj* (pilgrimage to Mecca) and begin his travels after the governor forced him to drink wine, which the pious ibn Jubayr found scandalous. It is essential to keep in mind this bias and context when using statements by ibn Jubayr (and they are not as frequent or definitive as is often supposed) that Muslims lived better lives under Latin rule. His memoirs constitute a moralistic attack on the declining values of the Islamic world, and such statements were clearly intended to let Muslim readers know that they were acting with less fidelity than many infidels. Latin Christians, whom he

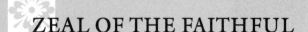

ZEAL OF THE FAITHFUL

In this call to arms, Muslim sultan Saladin comments on the zeal of his enemies and the lack of will among his own people:

We hope in God most high, to whom be praise, who leads the hearts of Muslims to calm what torments them and ruins their prosperity. As long as the seas bring reinforcements to the enemy and the land does not drive them off, our country will continue to suffer at their hands, and our hearts to be troubled by the sickness caused by the harm they do to us. Where is the sense of honour of the Muslims, the pride of the believers, the zeal of the faithful? We shall never cease to be amazed at how the Unbelievers, for their part, have shown trust, and it is the Muslims who have been lacking in zeal. Not one of them has responded to the call, not one intervenes to straighten what is distorted; but observe how far the Franks have gone; what unity they have achieved, what aims they pursue, what help they have given, what sums of money they have borrowed and spent, what wealth they have collected and distributed and divided among them! There is not a king left in their lands or islands, not a lord or a rich man who has not competed with his neighbors to produce more support, and rivalled his peers in strenuous military effort. In defense of their religion they consider it a small thing to spend life and soul, and they have kept their infidel brothers supplied with arms and champions for the war. And all they have done, and all their generosity, has been done purely out of zeal for Him they worship, in jealous defense of their Faith. Every Frank feels that once we have reconquered the (Syrian) coast, and the veil of their honour is torn off and destroyed, this country will slip from their grasp, and our hand will reach out toward their own countries. The Muslims, on the other hand, are weakened and demoralized. They have become negligent and lazy, the victims of unproductive stupefaction and completely lacking in enthusiasm. If, God forbid, Islam should draw rein, obscure her splendour, blunt her sword, there should be no one, East or West, far or near, who would blaze with zeal for God's religion or choose to come to the aid of truth against error. This is the moment to cast off lethargy, to summon from far and near all those men who have blood in their veins. But we are confident, thanks be to God, in the help that will come from Him, and entrust ourselves to him in sincerity of purpose and deepest devotion. God willing, the Unbelievers shall perish and the faithful have a sure deliverance.

Source: *"Saladin's Summons to the Holy War (Abu Shama, II, 148)," in* Arab Historians of the Crusades, *by Francesco Gabrieli, translated from Italian by E. J. Costello (Berkeley: University of California Press, 1969), pp. 214–215.*

frequently referred to as "pigs," were ibn Jubayr's noble savages who could teach civilization through hyperbolic comparisons.

When used systematically, ibn Jubayr's work is of more value in demonstrating that Muslims were much worse off under Latin than

MUSLIMS

Islamic rule. He makes such generalizations frequently, but more compelling evidence can be found in the plethora of anecdotes he provides concerning the views of Muslims under Latin control. In Sicily he met ibn al-Hajar, a prominent leader of the Islamic community. Al-Hajar suffered greatly from the suspicion that he was collaborating with the Almohades, but he eventually found his way back into Latin favor. Hajar told Jubayr that he wished he and his family would be taken as slaves and sold to Islamic lands. Jubayr was stunned by the fact that a man of such rank and wealth under the Latins would rather be a slave just to escape them. Pedantic, probably, but it certainly reflects a real distaste for living under Latin rule regardless of economic standing. In Trapani, Jubayr saw a Muslim notable searching among a pilgrimage caravan for anyone who would marry his daughter and take her to Islamic lands. Jubayr was shocked that the family and the girl were so willing to separate themselves forever just for the chance to deliver her to the Islamic world. Not all daughters were so pious. Jubayr also described the disastrous impact that Latin domination had on Islamic family life. Conversion to Christianity offered sons and daughters a means by which to undermine or escape family authority. Once the rebellious child (or wife) was baptized, she was beyond the reach of the Muslim head of the house.

In the Crusader States, Jubayr was heartbroken at the sight of pretty Muslim girls being sold to Christians at the slave markets. Visiting Acre was a miserable experience for him. It was packed with filth, pigs, and crosses, three things offensive to Muslim sensibilities. Other offenses were too many to count. The old main mosque was now a church, and the minarets were transformed into bell towers. Jubayr also noted that Muslims under Latin rule were qualitatively different than Muslims in Islamic lands; he questioned whether one could truly be a Muslim under the Franks. Jubayr's final conclusion from the lessons he learned during his travels was that the only reason a Muslim should stay in infidel lands was to rest while traveling to Islamic lands. The last thing he would have wanted was to live under Latin rule, and this conclusion is hard to reconcile with the opinion of some historians that he believed Muslims were better off under Latin rule. Memoirs such as Jubayr's, suggestive as they may be, are rather weak pieces of evidence when trying to determine whether Muslims were better off under Islamic or Latin rule. They are the biased views of individuals, more like spice than a meal, and as such are of limited value. The net must be cast wider and focus on two things in particular: the legal-economic status of Muslims living under Crusader rule and the reactions Muslims had to it.

The Crusader States in the East were created by violent conquest. The defeats of Muslims in Spain and Sicily had their fair share of slaughter, but the butchering of Muslims at the hands of the First Crusaders was almost sui generis in the scale of its viciousness. Wholesale massacre was common in the early stages of the First Crusade (1096–1102), and its effect on the city of Jerusalem is well known. Norman crusader Tancred spearheaded a new, more mature approach with the Nablus arrangement. His less bloodthirsty and more pragmatic policy sprang from two main causes. First, Tancred was an Italian-Norman who had already fought Muslims in Sicily. His experiences with Muslims on the European home front served him well in the East. Second, it seems clear that Tancred was interested in settling as well as conquering. He intended to become a great Latin lord of the East. Rather than ruling over decimated settlements, Tancred naturally preferred populated and thriving ones, which meant having living Muslims working on them. Tancred not only successfully negotiated a peaceful surrender of the Muslims of Nablus (1099) but also arranged for the return of wives and children who had fled before his arrival. Tancred tried to save some Muslims in Jerusalem when the city fell (1099) by giving them his banner to signal their protected status; the attempt failed, however, and his protected people were slaughtered by other Crusaders.

Gradually, the approach initiated by Tancred became the dominant one in the Latin East as aspiring rulers became more interested in homage and submission than indiscriminate violence prompted by religious rage. As was often the case in other theaters where Christians conquered Muslims, the Islamic elite that had the means to flee did so while much of the peasantry was stuck, although some peasants managed to flee as well, which explains several ghost towns the Crusaders found. The new Latin settlers made themselves the new regional aristocracy and replaced the Islamic elite. This action is the essential backdrop to approaching the question of whether Muslims were better off under Latin or Islamic rule in the East. To arrive at realistic answers, however, the question needs to be nuanced to accommodate the complexities of the situation. The chief factors to consider are the classes and locations of Muslims. The experience of the Islamic elite was much different from that of the peasantry, as was that of Muslims living in the cities as opposed to those living in the countryside. Saying that Muslims were taxed less by the Crusaders is a broad and bulky statement. Taxation is but one form of exploitation, and, in any case, Muslims living in Saladin's Egypt paid no taxes because of the massive revenue created by taxing non-Muslims. The experience of the Islamic elite can be dealt with quickly. They had

MUSLIMS

Ivory box made by a Muslim craftsman for a wealthy Christian in Sicily (thirteenth century)

(Museum für Islamische Kunst, Berlin)

their property and positions expropriated and divided up by the Crusaders, and it is difficult to say that they were now "better off."

The position of Muslims in the cities (a minority of the total Muslim population living under the Crusaders) is more difficult to assess than that of the elite who lost everything and fled. Mass expulsion of all Muslim inhabitants from a city was rare but did occur, for example, in Jerusalem following the First Crusade and later at Ascalon in 1153. After the Third Crusade (1189–1192) Muslim inhabitants of the old city in Acre were expelled and sent outside the gates to form the suburb of Mont Musard. So the situation of urban Muslims could radically turn without notice, resulting in a sudden loss of property and residency rights. Muslims, however, had a relatively well-defined legal status in the Crusader States. The Crusader lords in the East, much like their counterparts in Spain, adapted the Islamic *dhimmi* (protected minority) system for dealing with non-Christians. In the East the situation was more complicated since the Crusaders ruled over not only Muslims and

Jews, as in Spain, but also Eastern Christians, who were generally lumped together legally and fiscally as non-Latins. The Islamic *dhimmi* system recognized non-Muslims as a protected minority with certain rights in exchange for submission. Part and parcel of its legislation, however, was to clearly demonstrate the superiority of Muslims and the inferiority of the "protected people." When the Crusaders applied the system in the East, it made no difference to Jews or Eastern Christians, who already were subjugated minorities and had to pay the *jizya* (a minority tax applicable to all males once they turned fifteen), which proved a valuable source of revenue for rulers while simultaneously emphasizing the inferiority of the subjected *dhimmi*. Muslims in the cities, however, were hit hard when the Crusaders applied it to them. More important than the economic implications was the psychological impact: the *capatio* (the Latin version of *jizya*) symbolized their fall from the apex of social superiority to the depths of legal inferiority. The lot of urban Muslims, however, was still far superior to that of those living in the countryside.

They were essentially free, not bound to the land, and owed no personal service to a lord, but rather, they were just responsible for paying the non-Latin head tax. They were also forced to use different markets than Christians, markets which fell under a different system of taxation. Muslims could move about freely and own both land and movable possessions. Similar situations emerged in Spain and Sicily. The Crusader States differed from them, however, in completely barring Muslims from political and military affairs. Politically, they were disenfranchised. Jubayr said that, based on his observations, the Latins in the East were often fairly tolerant toward subject Muslims in the cities (the only areas he visited). Inferring, however, that they were now better off than under Islamic rule requires a substantial leap of the imagination.

Life for Muslim peasants in the countryside, who constituted the overwhelming majority of Muslims living under Crusader rule, underwent little change. Before the Crusaders arrived, Islamic Syria had already shifted from free peasants to ones who were tied to the land of a lord's *iqta* (a rough equivalent to the European fief). The concept of serfdom that the Crusaders brought was an easy fit. These rural agricultural settlements were called *casals* that, as they had been for centuries, were small self-sufficient communities (containing housing, mills, ovens, and cisterns) whose production sustained them and their lords, whether Islamic or Christian. The urban-based Crusader lords rarely appeared in the *casals* and instead tended to work through Muslim *ra'is* (middlemen), who were already in place during the period of Islamic rule, supervised the activities of the peasants and village councils, and served as mediators between rulers and the ruled (though they themselves were not free either). In many ways the change in the power structure that the Franks introduced seemed to have been scarcely noticeable to them. One could argue that although their situation was no better, it at least had not become worse, and the only real difference was who was reaping the rewards of their labor. It is always difficult to measure the opinions of those in the past who had no voice. Their opinions, however, can be gleaned from their reactions. Muslims in the Crusader States were, comparatively speaking, much more docile than Muslims in other lands living under Latin rule, but they were not necessarily content. Whenever a powerful Islamic military force invaded the Crusader States, much of the Muslim population launched a rebellion to complement it. There is also evidence pointing toward an organization in Nablus that smuggled Muslims to Islamic-controlled Damascus.

These facts are difficult to understand if the Crusader lords treated Muslims better than Islamic masters.

Cultural pride is one of those important aspects of quality of life that may be less tangible than economic prosperity, but it is no less significant. Many of the Islamic elite lost everything they had. Muslims in the cities were treated as inferiors and saw all about them the symbols of their degradation. In the *casals* of the countryside, where the regalia of Latin domination was more difficult to see, Muslims still resented Latin occupation and longed to once again fall beneath the authority of the crescent rather than the cross. The crushing of cultural pride, the loss of autonomy, and the ubiquitous presence of the symbols of inferiority inflame passions and provoke responses that have little to do with accommodating laws or economic standing.

–MARK T. ABATE,
WESTFIELD STATE COLLEGE

References

Muhammad ibn Ahmad Ibn Jubayr, *The Travels of Ibn Jubayr, being the Chronicle of a Mediaeval Spanish Moor Concerning His Journey to the Egypt of Saladin, the Holy Cities of Arabia, Baghdad the City of the Caliphs, the Latin Kingdom of Jerusalem, and the Norman Kingdom of Sicily*, translated by R. J. C. Broadhurst (London: Cape, 1952).

Hans Eberhard Mayer, "Latins, Muslims, and Greeks in the Latin Kingdom of Jerusalem," *History*, 63 (June 1978): 175–192.

James M. Powell, ed., *Muslims under Latin Rule, 1100–1300* (Princeton: Princeton University Press, 1990).

Joshua Prawer, *Crusader Institutions* (Oxford: Clarendon Press / New York: Oxford University Press, 1980).

Prawer, *The Latin Kingdom of Jerusalem: European Colonialism in the Middle Ages* (London: Weidenfeld & Nicolson, 1972).

Prawer, "Social Classes in the Crusader States: The 'Minorities'," in *A History of the Crusades,* volume 5, edited by Norman P. Zacour and Harry W. Hazard (Madison: University of Wisconsin Press, 1985), pp. 59–115.

Jean Richard, *The Latin Kingdom of Jerusalem,* translated by Janet Shirley (Amsterdam & New York: North-Holland, 1979).

MUSLIMS

ORIENTALIZATION

Was there a significant fusion of Islamic and Latin Christian culture in the Crusader States?

Viewpoint: Yes. Close interactions among Muslims and Latin Christians crystallized into a distinctive hybrid culture.

Viewpoint: No. The Latin Christians established themselves as an alien ruling aristocracy who shared a limited symbiotic relationship with the Muslims.

Conquest and armed conflict were only two of the many ways in which Christians and Muslims interacted during the age of the Crusades. An area of great scholarly interest in Crusade studies has been the aftermath of conquest and what daily life was like in lands inhabited by both Christians and Muslims. To what extent were they segregated; did their cultures integrate; what influences did they have on one another; and were such influences substantive or superficial? Most historians claim that the answers depend on both time and place, particularly the latter. Christians and Muslims (and Jews) inhabited Spain, Sicily, and the Crusader States in the East and each society experienced a different form of intercultural relations. To what extent were Latin settlers in the Crusader States acculturated and "orientalized"?

On one extreme, some French historians have argued that there was complete cultural blending and synthesis between Christians and Muslims. Latin settlers quickly adopted Islamic dress, consumed Islamic cuisine, read and spoke Arabic, hired Muslim servants, and married Islamic women. In short, they completely left their Western roots and culture behind and fully embraced oriental life, undergoing massive acculturation in the process. The result was an entirely new society formed though cultural synthesis, what some French historians have called a "new Franco-Syrian nation." The autobiography of Usamah ibn-Munqidh, a twelfth-century emir of Shaizar (a fortress city in Syria), is often cited to support this theory. On the other extreme, some historians offered the segregationist theory, most forcefully put forth by Joshua Prawer, who described Latin-Oriental relations as being defined by a system of apartheid. Supporters of this theory point toward the extremely harsh legislation passed to segregate Christians and Muslims in the Latin East, best exemplified by the statutes enacted at the Council of Nablus (1120). They also argue that a native-born intellectual such as the Syrian prelate William of Tyre (whose parents were French) knew about as much about Islam as anyone born in the West, and that the sort of intellectual cross-fertilization and cooperation that characterized Sicily—and above all Spain—never occurred in the Latin East. Christians there might have eaten couscous and worn turbans, but they certainly were not "orientalized" in any substantive way. These scholars also stress that while a plethora of Arabisms entered the Spanish language, no more than forty did so in the languages spoken in the Crusader States. Latins in the East, they argue, were far from acculturated. On the contrary, they erected formidable barriers to prevent a loss of cultural identity.

Relatively convincing cases can be made for each side, which enriches the dispute and ensures its longevity. The situation in the East, however, must not be seen as representing interactions between Christians and Muslims as a whole throughout the Mediterranean. Christian conquerors universally tried to create a modus vivendi between themselves and their Muslim subjects. The particulars of these arrangements, however, varied greatly.

Viewpoint:
Yes. Close interactions among Muslims and Latin Christians crystallized into a distinctive hybrid culture.

The "orientalization" of Crusaders who settled in one of the Latin kingdoms of the East is a fact. No culture, given long-term contact, is ever impermeable to the influence of alien cultures. The Crusaders in the Latin kingdoms of Jerusalem or Acre were no exception.

In studying the Crusades, students sometimes read the narratives of Usamah ibn-Munqidh, an Arab-Syrian gentleman who lived in Syria and had extensive contact with the Crusaders. Usamah tells many stories that indicate not only his level of acculturation but that of the "Franks" as well. He relates that he was close enough to his conquerors to converse with them regularly—one knight even invited Usamah to entrust his son to him to be taken back to France and educated in the way of the knight. Usamah realized the knight thought this action to be a sacred obligation to his friend; Usamah saw it as ridiculous—why would he send his son to an inferior civilization for training? He knew, though, that he could not say any such thing, and he politely refused the request. Moreover, Usamah recalls how the Templars allowed him to pray in the al-Aqsa mosque (built on the spot in Jerusalem where Muhammad allegedly ascended into Heaven) even though they had taken it over. One Templar even defended him from an assault when a newly arrived knight wanted to make him pray as a Christian ought.

While officially at war, Muslims and Christians worked out accommodations with each other. Iberian Muslim traveler Ibn Jubayr summed up the situation this way: "One of the astonishing things that is talked of is that, though the fires of discord burn between the two parties, Muslim and Christian, two armies of them may meet and dispose themselves in battle array, and yet Muslim and Christian travelers will come and go between them without interference . . . the soldiers engage themselves in their war while the people are at peace." Ibn Jubayr could have added Jews to this list, as Jewish travelers, such as Spanish rabbi Benjamin of Tudela, indicate in their memoirs. Of course there are stories about the First Crusaders (1096–1102) in the Outremer (Kingdom of Jerusalem) who "went

native," to the horror of later arrivals from Europe. They ate native foods, adopted native dress, and took Muslims as feudatories. Examples from Sicily could be added to this list, including al-Idrisi's great *Kitab nuzhat al-mushtaq fi ikhtiraq al-afaq*, or *Book of Roger* (circa 1140), a work of Muslim geography produced for the Christian king Roger II. Furthermore, medieval Sicily was one of the great places where Islamic medical training was slowly transmitted to the Latin West; like Toledo, it became an entrepôt for Islamic learning to filter into Christian lands. At the same time it was a place where Ibn Jubayr feared to go ashore because it was a center in the trading of Muslim slaves.

Settlers intermarried with the local population. Miscegenation with local women produced a creole class called *poulains* (Latin, *pullani*), the word perhaps deriving from Greek *pouloi* (offspring) or Arabic *fallahun* (peasants). According to French cleric Fulbert of Chartres, a settler might take "as his wife, not a woman of his own stock, but rather a Syrian or Armenian, or even, occasionally, a Saracen who has obtained the grace of baptism. . . . Men address one another in turn in the speech and idiom of different languages. The several languages of various nations are common here and one joins faith with men whose forefathers were strangers. . . . He who was a foreigner is now just like a native."

Knights and nobles lived in palaces built by local artisans and furnished in local style. Frankish men and women alike dressed in Muslim fashion: "At home a knight would dress in silks trimmed with fur, a long oriental tunic, and turban. Outdoors he covered his head with the Arab *kuffieh* and overcoat, his beard cut in oriental fashion. Many women were veiled like Muslim women and confined to the home. Local good customs were likewise adopted, including the lavish use of oriental spices, sugar, and olive oil, hardly known to the Franks before then." Most aristocrats knew some Arabic.

Institutions also were partially Arabized. Because Europeans made a distinction, unknown to Islamic jurisprudence, between civil and religious law, feudal lords took on some of the attributes of local *qadis* (judges), and feudal courts that judged civil cases assumed some of the powers of Muslim *diwans* (registers, officials), particularly in regard to taxation. The Arabic market official, the *muhtasib*, was adopted by the king of Jerusalem, who appointed a *matasep* to serve in the two quarters under his control, while the Venetians appointed another for their own quarter. Just as in Spain, the Latins of Jerusalem recognized the utility of this distinctive Muslim official who combined surveillance both of market affairs and of the streets and other public spaces.

One of the most controversial aspects of Crusader culture was the possible influence of Arabic styles and themes on the poetry of the troubadours. The first troubadour, Count William of Poitiers, was not known to have written songs before he went on the First Crusade, but when he returned to Provence he broke with previous poetical tradition and began to write poems in Arabic meter—*Farai chansoneta nueva* ("I will make a new song"), one of them began. A. R. Nykl writes in *Hispano-Arabic Poetry and its Relations with the Old Provençal Troubadours* (1946): "When the Christians became familiar with the new military tactics of the Muslims they defeated them by using the same stratagems. Against the Jihad of the Qur'an they used the Jihad of the Crusades, and Christian singers began to incite the Crusaders against the Infidels with songs similar to those which the Muslim singers used against the Kafirin [unbelievers]." Not only did troubadours use Arabic versification patterns, they also stressed the same motifs and clichés (in a literal way) used by Arab poets in their love verses. Both poetic traditions stress the plight of unrequited love, and there are too many thematic duplications to be explained away as chance occurrences.

–THOMAS F. GLICK,
BOSTON UNIVERSITY

Viewpoint:
No. The Latin Christians established themselves as an alien ruling aristocracy who shared a limited symbiotic relationship with the Muslims.

The myth that the Crusader States were a synthetic and culturally blended "Franco-Syrian nation" principally sprang from what can be called the "Frenchman's Burden." The greatest author of this myth (though myths are never the handiwork of a single individual) was Louis Madelin in *L'Expansion française de la Syrie au Rhin* (1918). He argued that the Crusades and the Crusader States constituted the origins of French colonialism in the East. Madelin believed in the innate superiority of the French and their ability to rule kindly and justly over foreign peoples for the peoples' own good. By linking the Crusader States and modern French colonies, Madelin projected an idealized interpretation of

the present far into the past. As the archetype of the benevolent colonial masters, he argued, the French had an intuitive understanding of cultural relations. Billing themselves as partners rather than conquerors, they promoted cultural blending and understanding to lay solid foundations for peaceful coexistence and mutual prosperity. Relations between the Latins and Muslims in the Crusader States were characterized more by cultural confluence than bitter clashes. Not only did the French (in both the twelfth and nineteenth centuries) allow their subjects to maintain their own culture, the French masters even adapted many aspects of it. In a way, Madelin's work provided the French with scholarly credentials for asserting that they were ideal caretakers for peoples in the Middle East following the end of World War I (1914–1918).

Like most myths, the "Franco-Syrian nation" theory was an exaggeration of real events and trends. A short list of interesting facts points in the direction of genuine cultural synthesis. Numismatic analysis yields grounds for fascinating speculation. Norman warrior Tancred, one of the original Crusaders, struck coins in the East that depicted him wearing a turban and bearing the title of emir. Even more interesting were the sarrazinas, coins minted in the Crusader States that praised Muhammad and Islam. That the barons of the Crusader States viewed Muslims in a different light than the Crusaders themselves can be best seen in thirteenth-century French king Louis IX's reaction to the sarrazina. He had them all restruck, praising Christ rather than Muhammad in Arabic. There are many—if scattered—references to Latin Christians being fluent in Arabic. Usamah ibn-Munqidh, a famous twelfth-century emir of Shaizar (a fortress city in Syria), offers a roster of anecdotes in his memoirs that strongly point in the direction of cultural synthesis. Two of the many examples in Usamah's largely anecdotal autobiography will suffice. In a bath, a Latin Christian noticed that Usamah shaved his pubic hair, as was the Islamic custom at the time. Usamah was amused when the Frank asked him to shave his pubic hair and that of his wife as well. Amusing, yes, but also instructive. What Usamah thought to be scandalous and ridiculous is revealing for our purposes. It shows how receptive a Frank could be to adopting (and eagerly) Islamic customs. A second classic example is Usamah's relationship with the Templars. Egyptian and Syrian sultan Saladin's policy was to execute any Templars captured in combat since they were a "race" that gravely endangered Muslims and since they were the "sworn enemies of Islam." Usamah, however, described the Templars as his "friends" even though he fought them on the battlefield when required. The Templars, who established themselves in the al-Aqsa mosque, opened part of it

WE ARE NOW ORIENTALS

French cleric and historian Foucher de Chartes, in the third volume of his Francorum Jherusalem peregrinantium (1124–1127), writes about the transformation of Westerners living in the Near East:

For we who were Occidentals now have been made Orientals. He who was a Roman or a Frank is now a Galilaean, or an inhabitant of Palestine. One who was a citizen of Rheims or of Chartres now has been made a citizen of Tyre or of Antioch. We have already forgotten the places of our birth; already they have become unknown to many of us, or, at least, are unmentioned. Some already possess here homes and servants which they have received through inheritance. Some have taken wives not merely of their own people, but Syrians, or Armenians, or even Saracens who have received the grace of baptism. Some have with them father-in-law, or daughter-in-law, or son-in-law, or stepson, or step-father. There are here, too, grandchildren and great-grandchildren. One cultivates vines, another the fields. The one and the other use mutually the speech and the idioms of the different languages. Different languages, now made common, become known to both races, and faith unites those whose forefathers were strangers. As it is written, "The lion and the ox shall eat straw together." Those who were strangers are now natives; and he who was a sojourner now has become a resident. Our parents and relatives from day to day come to join us, abandoning, even though reluctantly, all that they possess. For those who were poor there, here God makes rich. Those who had few coins, here possess countless besants; and those who had not had a villa, here, by the gift of God, already possess a city. Therefore why should one who has found the East so favorable return to the West? God does not wish those to suffer want who, carrying their crosses, have vowed to follow Him, nay even unto the end. You see, therefore, that this is a great miracle, and one which must greatly astonish the whole world. Who has ever heard anything like it? Therefore, God wishes to enrich us all and to draw us to Himself as His most dear friends. And because He wishes it, we also freely desire the same; and what is pleasing to Him we do with a loving and submissive heart, that with Him we may reign happily throughout eternity.

Source: *August. C. Krey, ed.,* The First Crusade: The Accounts of Eyewitnesses and Participants *(Princeton: Princeton University Press, 1921), pp. 280–281.*

Frank was a recent arrival from the West and did not understand. Thus, the Templars are seen as reprimanding a fellow Frank (who did not know any better) who was molesting a Muslim "friend" of theirs. This example can be correlated with Louis IX's decision to restrike the sarrazina. The relationship between Latin inhabitants of the Crusader States and Muslims was far different from Western views and attitudes toward Muslims. One way of explaining this reality is that Usamah and the Templars were fellow members of a "new nation."

Anecdotal evidence needs to be placed within a framework for it to make greater sense. A well-known passage from Fulcher of Chartres's chronicle describing the First Crusade and the origins of the Crusader States has provided such a framework for many historians. "We who were Westerners have now become Easterners. He who was once a Roman or Frank has in this land become a Palestinian or Galilean. . . . Already many of us have forgotten the lands in which we were born. . . . Many of us take wives not from our own kind but from Syrians, or Armenian, or recently converted Muslim women. . . . Diverse languages are spoken but a foreign language has become widely known to all groups. . . . As it was written, the lion and the cow have come together. . . . He who was a foreigner is now like a native. . . . Those who were poor in the West, God has made wealthy in the East. . . . He who did not even hold a village in the West can hold a city here in the East." Many historians have cited this passage to demonstrate the rapid acculturation of Franks and their commitment to forging a new, deeply orientalized civilization. Culturally speaking, the Franks divorced themselves from their Western heritage and embraced Eastern life in full. As Fulcher states, the invaders became natives.

This interpretation of Fulcher's remarks provides a sturdy skeleton for the synthetic, culturally blended, unique new-nation theory. Flesh can quickly be added to it. First of all, it places these anecdotes into an intriguing context. Tancred, one can assume, was now a Galilean rather than a Norman. That he was depicted wearing a turban and styled as an emir on his coins then comes as no surprise. In essence, Tancred had become an emir. Nor should one be shocked that Usamah described the Templars as "his friends." The emir and the Templars, in this scenario, shared more cultural affinities than the Templars did with recent Western arrivals. Louis's decision to restrike the sarrazina can be explained as the shock of a French monarch on seeing the indulgent approach to Muslims that these now-native Christians of a new nation demonstrated. To these examples one can add a plethora of references referring to Latins speak-

for Muslims to worship. While Usamah was at prayer, a western Christian, who did not understand that Muslims pray in the direction of Mecca, vigorously insisted that Usamah pray facing east (as was the Latin custom). The Templars intervened. They explained to Usamah that this ing Arabic; marrying Eastern women; dressing in Eastern clothing; and employing the services of Eastern cooks, physicians, and others.

If one interprets Fulcher's remarks in a different light, however, they can begin with a different theoretical skeleton. What if the first generation of colonists was a small and alien military aristocracy (which it was) whose chief interests were exploiting its newly acquired resources in the East (which is most likely the case)? In this scenario, anecdotes can flesh things out in a different way. Tancred already had experience both fighting with and ruling over Muslims in Sicily prior to his career in the Holy Land. Consequently, he realized that situating himself at the top of the already existing Islamic structure was more profitable than destroying it. The curious praise of Muhammad and Islam on the Christian-struck sarrazina can be interpreted as making the currency of the colonies more "user-friendly" to the Muslim majority that would be circulating it. Cultural sensitivity, then as now, does wonders for intercultural commerce. Tancred's turban and the sarrazina's praise of Muhammad can be seen as gestures that were designed to lubricate local commerce. Wearing Eastern clothing and consuming local cuisine could indicate acculturation, but it could also simply have been a pragmatic adaptation to the environment. Undoubtedly, intermarriage took place, but conquerors marrying pretty women from a defeated population is hardly unique. And as Fulcher pointed out, this was the case when the woman in question had already been baptized. Baptism symbolized rebirth, and in this context it was the rebirth of infidel women as Christians.

It is to be expected that Latins employed the services of Muslims, who with Eastern Christians constituted the vast majority of inhabitants in the region. It would be more surprising—actually shocking—if their services were not used on a regular basis. References to Latins speaking Arabic is another ambiguous piece of evidence for making a "cultural synthesis" argument. By and large, Arabic was the regional lingua franca, and it was natural that some Latins learned it for practical rather than cultural reasons. Reynald of Chatillon, prince of Antioch, who was fluent in Arabic, learned the language courtesy of the Islamic prison in which he spent more than a decade. Dragomen, moreover, who functioned as translators between Latin rulers and Arab-speaking subjects, were common administrative fixtures in the colonies. Syrian prelate William of Tyre, one of the most celebrated intellectuals and historians actually born in the Crusader States (to French parents), does not seem to have had any real deep understanding of, or love for, Eastern culture. Fulcher's remark about Latins forgetting their homelands, Romans becoming Palestin-

ians, and Franks becoming Galileans can also be explained in a way more convincing than rapid acculturation. Fulcher pointed to the proper way of interpreting this transformation: he who did not even have a village in the West could have a city in the East; he who was a pauper in the West could become wealthy in the East. Most settlers came from obscure backgrounds and were members of the petty nobility or were low in the ranks of powerful families. Hugh of Lusignan, in contrast, retained his name because it meant something. If many Latin settlers were quick to adopt new names ("of Tripoli," "of Tyre," "of Sidon"), it was because these titles increased their status. Their true sources of nobility and stature were rooted in their Crusader State possessions, and they acted accordingly.

Unlike western Europeans, the Latin colonists in the Crusader States were overwhelmingly city dwellers; it was within urban areas that most contacts between the Latins and the indigenous inhabitants took place. Although Jerusalem was made a "Christian only" city by the expulsion of Muslims and Jews, most cities were inhabited by members of all faiths (yet most Muslims lived in the countryside). Proximity, however, does not necessarily lead to confluence. Pragmatism dictated a marked degree of interaction, particularly in economic matters. Yet, the Latin colonists took steps to curtail the extent and depth of such interaction. Populations in the cities were residentially segregated for the most part and divided into small, self-contained communities. Different legal codes and courts governed the affairs of these groups. Laws established at the Council of Nablus (1120) took several steps to limit contacts between people of different faiths. The rules provided for specific dress that identified members of each group and passed harsh punishments for interfaith sexual contact. Christian or Muslim men caught having sex with women of the opposite religion were castrated. Similar law codes were passed in Spain but were not as harsh as those formed at Nablus. Christian men received the same punishment for the crime as Muslim men. At first glance, this policy may seem a more enlightened one than in Spain, since each group was treated equally. Yet, it also suggests a harsher policy designed to further discourage Christian men from intimate intercultural contacts. Syrian, Armenian, and Greek Christians were treated like second-class citizens and were viewed as heretics.

Expansion into the countryside and interior took place in the form of castle building or tower construction. To protect and dominate rural agricultural lands and towns, the Latins needed fortified military and administrative bases. For most small Islamic agricultural communities in the interior, Crusader conquest and domination signaled

**Illumination of a Muslim
and Christian playing the
ud and lute together,
from *Book of Chants*
(thirteenth century)**

(Escorial Monastery, Madrid)

little change. Living in the cities, Crusader lords tended to rule these communities through *rais* (local Muslim headmen), who were treated a bit better than other Muslims serfs (such as allowing them to own property) in exchange for their services. By and large, the Franks left intact the local organizational systems they inherited from Muslims. Because of the chronic manpower shortage, Crusader lords offered good terms to Europeans willing to colonize land. Rather than "integrating" with the Eastern populations, however, they took over abandoned sites or built new ones, forming small pockets of Latin culture throughout the landscape. It appears that a Muslim serf could live his entire life without ever seeing his Frankish master.

Thus, interactions between indigenous inhabitants and Latin colonists seem to have been quite superficial. All of the evidence points toward the Franks making pragmatic concessions to strengthen their position and adjusting themselves to a climate different from that of western Europe. Evidence for "synthesis" rather than segregated "coexistence" is sparse. There is one important (and rather enigmatic) exception: the *poulains* (Latin, *pullani*), or the "chickens." They appear to have been descendents of Frankish settlers who became heavily Arabized and were much like the Mozarabs of Islamic Spain. Their name is a mystery but seems to have been a derogatory label that was applied to them by settlers who did not fully embrace Eastern culture. The opinion that the Latin majority had of them, however, is instructive. They were seen as decadent, of dubious loyalty to the settlements, and as a potential fifth column. Those individuals who blended substantively with Eastern culture were held in contempt by the majority of Frankish settlers.

Taking all the evidence into consideration, the synthetic, culturally blended, new-nation theory seems untenable. The lords of the Crusader States were an alien and conquering military aristocracy who imposed their feudal system on the Eastern administrative apparatus they found. They treated their subjects with a remarkable degree of fairness for the time, but they also erected barriers, from walled cities to segregation laws, to separate the rulers from the ruled. The Muslim population was beaten into submission by the brutality of the initial conquest. From their perspective, they were dominated by foreign lords rather than being part of a new integrated nation. This reality can be seen in how quickly they rebelled when Islamic invasion forces arrived. Unlike Spain or Sicily, rulers of the Crusader States never trusted Muslims with administrative and military positions. The Crusader States were more like a cultural mosaic than a blend, and it was held together through force; it was characterized by a pragmatic coexistence between, rather than mixture of, Latin rulers and the Eastern ruled.

—MARK T. ABATE,
WESTFIELD STATE COLLEGE

References

Aharon Ben-Ami, *Social Change in a Hostile Environment: The Crusaders' Kingdom of Jerusalem* (Princeton: Princeton University Press, 1969).

Fulbert of Chartres, *The Letters and Poems of Fulbert of Chartres,* edited and translated by Frederick Behrends (Oxford: Clarendon Press, 1976).

Louis Madelin, *L'Expansion francaise de la Syrie au Rhin* (Paris: Plon-Nourrit, 1918).

Hans Eberhard Mayer, "Latins, Muslims, and Greeks in the Latin Kingdom of Jerusalem," *History,* 63 (June 1978): 175–192.

Usama ibn Munqidh, *An Arab-Syrian Gentleman and Warrior in the Period of the Crusades; Memoirs,* translated by Philip K. Hitti (New York: Columbia University Press, 1929).

A. R. Nykl, *Hispano-Arabic Poetry and its Relations with the Old Provençal Troubadours* (Baltimore: Furst, 1946).

Zoé Oldenbourg, *The Crusades,* translated by Anne Carter (London: Weidenfeld & Nicolson, 1966; New York: Pantheon, 1966).

Joshua Prawer, *Crusader Institutions* (Oxford: Clarendon Press / New York: Oxford University Press, 1980).

Prawer, *The History of the Jews in the Latin Kingdom of Jerusalem* (Oxford: Clarendon Press / New York: Oxford University Press, 1988).

Prawer, "Social Classes in the Crusader States: The 'Minorities'," in *A History of the Crusades,* volume 5, edited by Norman P. Zacour and Harry W. Hazard (Madison: University of Wisconsin Press, 1985), pp. 59–115.

Jean Richard, *The Latin Kingdom of Jerusalem,* translated by Janet Shirley (Amsterdam & New York: North-Holland, 1979).

THE PAPACY

Did the Crusades strengthen the papacy?

Viewpoint: Yes. The Crusades strengthened the papacy by providing it with a powerful and effective tool for protecting itself from secular threats and for bolstering its claims of authority.

Viewpoint: No. The failure to recover the Holy Land weakened the power of the papacy and had a negative impact on its prestige.

From the beginning of the movement, the Crusades were inextricably linked to the reform papacy. Crusade and reform sat side by side on the agenda for many Church councils. The connection among the papacy, reform, and Crusade remained strong long after the fall of Acre (1291). Renaissance mystic Catherine of Sienna, for example, blasted the papal curia for being little more than a brothel, demanded immediate reform, and connected both of these issues to the current state of the Holy Land and the possibilities of recovering it. The Crusades played a central role in the redefinition and re-creation of the papacy during the Middle Ages. Most historians see the Crusades as inaugurating a period of papal strength and authority. The long-term effects of the crusading movement on the papacy, however, are more open to debate.

The Crusades strengthened the position of the papacy in a variety of ways. Papal political and fiscal organization experienced revolutionary gains that were clearly prompted by the need to meet challenges the crusading movement posed. Crusading also gave the papacy a powerful tool to promote its territorial interests by offering an institutional and theoretically justifiable war machine that it could deploy against political enemies. Crusading gave the papacy military muscle that complemented its spiritual authority. When the interests of the papacy and a particular secular ruler merged, the deal was solidified with the proclamation of a Crusade that opened the floodgates of human and financial resources to meet their mutual objectives. The Hohenstaufen (German royal family), arguably the greatest threat posed to the medieval papacy, were finally destroyed by a Crusade (1265–1266).

Crusading also had negative effects on the papacy. Papal profiteering from Crusades was widely suspected in Christendom, even though most men did not object to crusading on principle. Crusade preaching came to be seen as a papal fund-raiser in which everyone, fit or not, was urged to take the cross and then was allowed to buy his way out with a cash settlement. Many people, particularly in the Church, felt that a crusading proclamation was simply the justification for Rome to extend its hand into the provinces, palm up, with the ultimate objective of collecting as many coins as possible. Crusading was seen as a weighty stick with which the Pope could beat down well-established immunities and rights. Some were suspicious of the "political crusades" and saw them as dubious and hypocritical papal hits against rivals. For some historians, the Crusades in the long run impeached the great spiritual position of the papacy by fanning suspicion and discontent. Joseph R. Strayer probably made the case most forcefully in *The Albigensian Crusades* (1971): "We would be living in a very different world if the Church had not weakened itself in the thirteenth century by becoming addicted to holy wars; in such a case there might not have been a Protestant Reformation."

Viewpoint:
Yes. The Crusades strengthened the papacy by providing it with a powerful and effective tool for protecting itself from secular threats and for bolstering its claims of authority.

"I loved righteousness; therefore, I die in exile." Such were the last words uttered by Pope Gregory VII as he lay dying in exile in Salerno, Italy (1085). It was truly an inauspicious end to a papal career that in its early years had shown a degree of political clout that the papacy had not enjoyed in centuries. Just eight years earlier, during a bitter struggle with German Holy Roman Emperor Henry IV over the practice of lay investiture, Gregory had achieved a resounding victory. In the early course of the dispute Gregory outmaneuvered the young emperor and forced him to do public penance for three days (1077) in his presence at Canossa, Italy. It was a truly stunning event in medieval history, for by submitting to this punishment, Henry was in effect accepting the premise that even mighty emperors were under the authority of the pope. Yet, Gregory's papal victory proved to be all too fleeting, and in the end it was Gregory, not Henry, who died in exile and political obscurity. Whatever deference Henry had shown to the Pope at Canossa was soon forgotten, as he was able to quickly reverse his political fate and place Gregory on the defensive. In the end, Henry's imperial troops underlined just how precarious papal power really was in the latter half of the eleventh century when they seized Rome (1084) in an attempt to settle the ongoing dispute with Gregory. In the wake of that invasion Gregory perished as an exile in a particularly dark moment in papal history.

Such was the state of the papacy at the dawn of the crusading era. Despite several decades of reform efforts designed to eradicate moral abuses within the Roman Church, to heal its wounded prestige, and to centralize ecclesiastical administration under the clear authority of the papacy, all that work seemed to have achieved little success. For church reformers who believed that their agenda could only succeed through the support and advocacy of the papacy, the manner of Gregory's death must have seemed like an irrevocable disaster. Yet, within ten years it was clear that papal power in Europe was in reality not in

decline but rather poised to achieve new heights of grandeur. The key to this recovery was the institution of crusading.

The lay Investiture Controversy (1075–1077) had still not been resolved by the time Urban II became Pope (1088), and he sensed that he might suffer the same fate as Gregory if he chose to press the Church's position too aggressively against the emperor. Yet, in March 1095 an event occurred that allowed the papacy to return from the brink of political annihilation—Byzantine emperor Alexius I Comnenus sent an urgent communiqué to Urban requesting military aid in his ongoing struggle with the Seljuk Turks in Asia Minor. Although relations between Byzantium and the papacy had been severely strained for decades, it is significant that Alexius chose Urban as his point of contact. Alexius must have swallowed a great deal of pride to come almost begging to the one authority in the West with whom the emperor had particularly bad relations. Yet, as a pragmatic political leader, Alexius also knew that only the Pope had sufficient international appeal among all Westerners to make him the most efficient mechanism to put out the word regarding the urgent need of the Eastern empire for troops. His request thus represented an important validation of the authority and prestige of the Pope at a critical moment in the papacy's history.

Urban's response to this imperial request was truly masterful. By November 1095 he had formulated a program that not only met the needs of the Byzantine emperor but at the same time also advanced the agenda of the Roman Church. His call for Crusade at the Council of Clermont touched a nerve with the faithful of Europe and led to an enthusiastic, overflowing response from various regions of the West. High-ranking knights, as well as commoners and peasants, flocked to the banner that Urban had raised. Almost instantly, the papacy was no longer a regional political power based precariously in central Italy but a continent-wide force that its political adversaries had to consider with greater caution than ever. In the flush of enthusiasm that surrounded crusading, especially in the twelfth century, it would have been political suicide for a monarch such as the German emperor to directly assail the papacy, the recognized leader of the movement, as Henry IV had done to Gregory VII. Crusading had thus saved the papacy from the danger of political oblivion.

About a hundred years later another Pope, Innocent III, made use of crusading not just to

Alms chest in a church in Sussex, England, placed there in 1199 by papal decree in order to increase financial support of the crusading movement

salvage the political life of the papacy but to bring the institution to a position of dominance in European affairs. It was a truly remarkable recovery from the low point witnessed with Gregory's death at Salerno. Under Innocent III the papacy was actively involved with raising armies to continue the struggle to recapture Jerusalem, to stamp out heresy in southern France, to recover Christian lands in Spain, and to convert pagans in eastern Europe. No other political leader in Europe could rival such a demonstration of power and reach. It is not a mere coincidence, therefore, that Innocent was the most politically powerful of medieval popes and also the Pope who preached more Crusades than any other. In a sense the political power of the medieval papacy rested in the fate of crusading. For example, Innocent used the popularity of crusading to increase his control of the Church by requiring the clergy to provide material support for the movement. He also took it upon himself to insure that the great kings of Europe did not dominate crusading campaigns as they had done in the twelfth century, preferring to enlist the aid of the barons, counts, and other lesser feudal lords who were more malleable. As a direct result of his whirlwind of crusading activity, Innocent succeeded not only in placing the papacy beyond the threat of its political enemies but also in positioning it as the dominant force in European affairs at the start of the thirteenth century.

In the years following Innocent's death (1216) the German emperors once more became emboldened to bring the papacy under their influence as part of a wider goal of securing control of Italy. Yet, Innocent's expansion of the crusading institution left a road map for later

popes to follow in thwarting such imperial designs. Matters between the two powers came to a head in 1239 when German emperor Frederick II, who already controlled southern Italy, began to consolidate power in northern Italy as well. Realizing that the papacy was in danger of being surrounded and eventually overwhelmed in central Italy, Pope Gregory IX preached the first so-called political Crusade. The troops that took the cross in response to Gregory's desperate appeal proved decisive in thwarting the emperor's Italian campaign. By 1241 Frederick was unable to achieve the long-standing imperial goal of controlling Rome, and so the papacy was spared a possibly disastrous fate. Without the availability of crusading at his disposal, it was a distinct possibility that Gregory would have suffered a fate similar to his namesake's. Even more significant, the potential existed that a German-dominated Rome would lead to a German-controlled papacy, centered as it had always been in Rome. Had that possibility occurred, perhaps the papacy would have been reduced to an irrelevant entity in European affairs because it would have been viewed by the other nation-states of Europe as merely a partisan organ of the German emperors rather than an independent moral authority. Its position might have come to resemble that of the archbishop of Canterbury, whose domestic role in political life became negligible once the English kings assumed control of the church in England.

It is true that power wielded by the popes through their role as leaders of the Crusades did not ensure their political position in Europe for long. While the cause of crusading remained widely popular in the later thirteenth century, the operation lost some of its original luster

RESISTING THE PAPAL TAX

In 1277, collectors of the six-year (papal) tax sent a letter to the Vatican complaining about the difficulty in raising money:

We also wish to inform you that in England the tenth is paid most unwillingly by many, both great and small, and that the Church's discipline is treated with contempt. For a great deal still remains to be paid from the first year of the tenth, more from the tenth's second year, and still more, more than half we so believe, from its third year. This is partly because of changes in the chief collectors; partly because of conflicting orders about the procedure for exaction and collection; partly because of the frequent deaths of [recent] popes, in so far as people looking for an excuse for not paying are not afraid to claim that they do not have to pay the tenth once the pope has died; and partly too because of the obstinacy of many who hold the Church's keys in contempt, showing no fear of suspensions, excommunications, interdicts or irregularities, and looking for ruses by which they can avoid paying the tenth either in whole or in part. We can see no way in which this can be remedied other than by calling on the assistance of the secular arm. With its intervention the tenth may be extracted from such people, just as the lord [bishop-elect] of Verdun has started to do. The alternative is to deprive them of their benefices. This they fear above all, so that they might pay up what they owe after being threatened, without the need to carry out the threat.

The collectors and assessors who were formerly appointed in each town are not satisfied with the immunity from the tenth which they enjoyed because of their office, on the grounds that it is not worth much. Many of them are pressing for a salary, saying that they have to bear heavy expenses because of the demands on their hospitality, and because of their assistants and servants. [They claim that] the lord of Verdun, who recently exercised that office in the kingdom of England, decreed, as his commission from the pope entitled him to do, a daily salary of three and a half shillings, to be taken from the tenth, for those supervising the collection and conducting the assessment (*taxatio*). There are also several monks appointed as collectors who hold various offices or obedientiaries in their monasteries, and who are pressing for immunity from paying the tenth on their obedientiaries or offices. Otherwise, all these people are adamant that they will never undertake this office again, nor is it to be hoped that people can be found who will volunteer for service at their own expense in such a hateful business.

. . . Nor do we wish to remain silent about the fact that all the English hold the common view that anyone who pays the tenth—both that due at Christmas and that due at Midsummer—within the octave [eight days] of the feast of St. John the Baptist, or by Epiphany, has paid sufficiently and met the due date. (Would that they at least *would* pay what they owe within the octave!) For this reason they incur all of the aforesaid [penalties], and become generally subject to the sentence of excommunication, and subsequently to that of irregularity.

Source: "A report sent to the college of cardinals in the late summer or autumn of 1277 by the collectors of Pope Gregory X's six-year tenth in England, commenting on the problems of tax collection," in Documents on the Later Crusades, 1274–1580, edited and translated by Norman Housley (New York: St. Martin's Press, 1996), pp. 21–25.

because of a series of disappointments that befell the campaigns in the Near East, starting with the failure of the Second Crusade (1147–1149). This reversal led to an eventual erosion of papal prestige as one thwarted campaign followed upon another. In a sense, the fate of Holy Land Crusades and the political power of the papacy seemed to be intertwined. At the same time, as the situation in the Near East deteriorated in the second half of the thirteenth century, the papacy faced new challenges to its political position: the rising strength of the national monarchies and the improving economic conditions of western Europe. Even without the floundering of the Crusades, it seemed only a matter of time before the papacy lost much of the political power that had reached its height under Innocent III. It simply could not compete with the new interests and ideals that often accompany periods of increased prosperity and improved government.

Just how quickly this collapse occurred is evident in the outcome of a struggle between Pope Boniface VIII and Philip IV of France at the start of the fourteenth century. At issue were the French king's attempts to independently tax and put on trial the French clergy, which the Pope vigorously protested. Perhaps not sensing the change in the political landscape of Europe or not wanting to accept it, Boniface sought to end the dispute by pressing a bold declaration of papal supremacy throughout Christendom with his papal bull *Unam sanctam* (1302). The strategy, however, backfired, and *Unam sanctam* merely proved to be the final excuse Philip needed to put the papacy in its place. Agents of the king went to Italy and, going beyond what Henry IV was able to do against Gregory VII, succeeded in briefly apprehending the Pope. Although he was eventually released, the aged pontiff perished a month later in Rome (1303). After two centuries of wielding significant political clout in Europe, the papacy seemed to be relegated to the precarious position it had held in the eleventh century.

Yet, this conclusion would not be entirely accurate. Although the Renaissance dawned in Europe in the second half of the fourteenth century and new cultural, economic, and political pursuits began to compete with religious interests, crusading once more came to the political rescue of the papacy. A new threat—the Ottoman Turks—had arisen in the eastern Mediterranean, and there was thus a renewed need for crusading. By this time, however, recapturing Jerusalem was just a pious sentiment that had little hope of actual accomplishment. Crusading was now aimed simply at preventing the collapse of Christendom's eastern frontier against the rising power of the Turks. No other European power, despite their growth in power and prestige during the last century, had the ability and authority to organize crusading activities in the eastern Mediterranean. Whether they wanted to or not, these monarchs had to make a place, however reduced, for the papacy at the table of political power in the West to insure that crusading remained a viable weapon against Ottoman incursions into Europe.

In the end it seems clear that crusading played a key role in not only preserving the political viability of the papacy but also for a time extending it. When Gregory died at Salerno, it was all too conceivable to conclude that an independent papacy might have gone with him. Yet, the call of the First Crusade (1096–1102) reversed the political fortunes of the papacy and led to an impressive rise that culminated with the vigorous reign of Innocent III. While later popes might have lacked some of the talent and energy that Innocent possessed, they found his example of expanding the institution of crusading a useful model in dealing with new imperial threats from Germany. The result was a series of political Crusades that prevented the German

emperors from controlling central Italy and, by extension, the papacy. By the fourteenth century, developments in European society were redirecting interests away from religious pursuits, and not even crusading could hold back the shifting current in European politics. Yet, the continuing need for Crusades against the Ottomans prevented the papacy from becoming entirely irrelevant in the political life of the West. Crusading was never conceived or pursued with the goal of strengthening the political hand of the papacy, but in the face of some stiff challenges during the Middle Ages, it proved for the popes to be a welcome, if unintended, consequence.

–CHRISTOPHER LIBERTINI,
SUFFOLK UNIVERSITY

Viewpoint:
No. The failure to recover the Holy Land weakened the power of the papacy and had a negative impact on its prestige.

While in its earliest phase the crusading movement might have increased the papacy's standing in the hearts and minds of many Western Christians, overall the Crusades weakened the position of the Roman Church in European society. The Crusades clearly exacerbated preexisting religious and political differences that separated Latin and Greek Christianity and made any reunion between these two branches impossible for centuries. Without a doubt, the enduring schism between Rome and Constantinople was a cause of embarrassment to the popes of the late Middle Ages. Indeed, the deleterious consequences of the Crusades for Byzantium remain a sore point in Roman Catholic–Orthodox relations. First, given that the relief of Eastern Christians from non-Christian oppression was ostensibly one of the chief purposes of the crusading movement, this result is a bitter irony. Second, the fundamental rationale behind the idea of Crusade—that violence against non-Christians can be pleasing to God—reinforced and fed popular suspicions about non-Christians already living within western Europe, which led to religious violence and over time reflected poorly on the papacy. The idea of Crusade also contributed to religious violence against nonconformist Christians in the West. In the case of the Albigensian (Cathar) heresy of southern France, the Crusade served as the very instrument of persecution. In its own indirect manner, such intramural religious violence eroded peoples' respect for the papacy as a spiritual institution. Third, the increasing financial costs of organizing Crusades, combined with the development of such a financially expedient measure as vow redemption, reinforced preexisting charges of papal fiscalism. Finally, the manifest failure of all the Crusades, except for the initial one, had a cumulatively negative effect on papal prestige and cast aspersions on papal leadership.

From its inception, the crusading movement was a cause of acrimony between Western and Eastern Christians. This conflict is a bitter irony because political and religious rapprochement with Constantinople constituted Pope Urban II's chief strategic goal for the First Crusade (1096–1102). The real origins of the schism between the Latin and Greek Churches lay in the early medieval period and were rooted in the cultural divide that developed between East and West. However, the disastrous legatine mission of Cardinal Humbert of Silva (1054) inflamed preexisting theological and political controversies between the two Churches. Partly because of strategic needs of the papacy in western Europe, Urban began early in his papacy to reach out to the emperor in Constantinople. Without question, the Pope saw Alexius I Comnenus's request in 1095 for military help as a golden opportunity to earn the gratitude of all in Constantinople.

Yet, the actual conduct of the First Crusade produced a different result (though not necessarily a totally unhappy one) than the Pope could have imagined. For while the Crusaders successfully liberated Jerusalem (1099), they did so at the cost of increasing the level of mistrust between Western and Eastern Christians. Certainly, Alexius I could not have been happy with either the behavior of the Crusaders within his territory or with their carving up of what had been Byzantine territory in the Levant into their own principalities. The Latins were not responsible for every misunderstanding and problem that arose between them and the Byzantines; still, the result of the First Crusade could hardly have been satisfying to those whom the Crusaders were supposed to have liberated.

Of course, the Fourth Crusade (1202–1204) constituted the most damaging episode of the crusading movement in East-West relations. Instead of resulting in the recapture of Jerusalem, which had fallen back into Muslim hands (1187), this expedition rather quickly degenerated into a Venetian-led assault on Constantinople (1203). This Crusade led to the virtual replacement of the Byzantine Empire with a Latin empire based in Constantinople. Although this Latin entity only lasted for a relatively brief period (1204–1261), the Eastern Christian empire never truly recovered from this Western invasion—a fact that still complicates Roman Catholic–Orthodox relations. In fairness, it

should be noted that the Crusaders attacked Constantinople (and the Adriatic port of Zara beforehand) against the express wishes of the Crusade's sponsor, Pope Innocent III. To be sure, prior to the assaults on Zara and Constantinople prominent and not-so-prominent Crusade participants refused to participate in these undertakings. Nevertheless, the Venetians' hijacking of the Fourth Crusade suggests how inadvisable it was for Innocent to have invested as much time and effort, and as many resources, as he did in such an uncertain and precarious project. One wonders if it would not have been more advisable for Innocent to commit the papacy's resources to the pastoral care of growing urban populations in Europe.

Subsequently, at the Second Council of Lyons (1274), the differences between the Roman and Byzantine Churches were temporarily papered over in an agreement born of political expediency. This "reunion" did not last long. In the aftermath of its collapse, the popes of the late thirteenth century and beyond were left to deal with an increasingly embarrassing question: why, after so many years of fighting Muslims in the East, was the Christian world itself still so badly divided?

Another problematic aspect of the crusading movement for the papacy that reared its head as early as the First Crusade concerns intramural religious violence in the West. Shortly after Urban II issued the initial summons to Crusade at Clermont (1095), anti-Jewish violence broke out in central France. This violence soon spread with the departing Crusaders to Germany and portions of eastern Europe. The worst of these pogroms seems to have taken place within the Rhineland in cities such as Speyer, Worms, Mainz, and Cologne. Admittedly, the Pope did not foresee this explosion of violence. It was not part of his idea of Crusade. Nonetheless, as Jonathan Riley-Smith has observed in *The Crusades: A Short History* (1987), both the Pope and other preachers of the Crusade couched their messages to European knights in the terms of blood feud or vendetta. This preaching tended to portray the Muslims as the savage oppressors of the knights' religious kinfolk, the faithful of the Eastern Churches. The Muslims were also portrayed as despoilers of the patrimony of their divine seigneur, Jesus Christ. It is no wonder, then, that some Crusaders lashed out at the first infidels that they encountered on their way to the East—European Jews. For Riley-Smith, this misinterpretation of the Pope's message by some Crusaders explains why they offered Jewish communities the option of either converting or being destroyed. The Jews could either become one of them or pay the price for the outrages being committed against their spiritual kin in the East. Despite the subsequent refinement of Crusade ideology and institutions, this phenomenon of anti-Jewish violence remained a feature of the movement.

Equally tragic, by the thirteenth century, popes began to employ the crusading movement against various forms of dissent from their authority within Europe. The Albigensian Crusade (1209–1229) is perhaps the most infamous example of this phenomenon. The spread of Catharism, which was really more of a dualistic Eastern religion than a Christian heresy, in parts of southern France (primarily in Languedoc) and the assassination of a papal legate there in early 1208 induced Innocent III to call for this internal Crusade. It was a long and brutal affair, and it left more than a few inhabitants of this part of France embittered with the institutional Church and the papacy.

The so-called political Crusades, which the popes of the thirteenth century waged against the Holy Roman Emperors, also elicited criticism of the papacy from certain circles in both Europe and the remaining outposts of the Latin East, which were hard-pressed at this time. There were some who grumbled aloud about the propriety of the papacy's use of money collected from local churches to pay for military campaigns against Christian princes. Undoubtedly, the cumulative effect of such taxation and the papacy's allowance of cash payments in lieu of fulfilling one's Crusade vow reinforced preexisting accusations of the fiscalism of the papal court.

One respected contemporary student of the Crusades, Elizabeth Siberry, in *Criticism of Crusading: 1095–1274* (1985), has tended to minimize the significance of those medieval written sources that criticize crusading. She has been especially dismissive of sources, such as the lyrics of troubadour poetry, that criticize the papacy's involvement in the crusading movement. By and large, she dismisses this criticism as the product of preexisting hostility for one reason or another toward the papacy, and she doubts that these sentiments demonstrate any widespread disapproval of papal involvement. However, as medieval historians have long recognized, the survival of any written body of medieval opinion is noteworthy. It may well be the case that what Siberry has essentially written off, as too small a body of evidence to merit serious attention, is really the tip of an iceberg of opinion, most of which did not make it into the sources. After all, most of those who applauded the performance of the troubadours' works were not able to register their opinions in writing. Certainly, it is worth noting (as, to her credit, Siberry does) that Pope Gregory X seems to have solicited information from those clergy whom he summoned to the Second Council of Lyons (1274) about the attitude of the laity toward the crusading movement. The Pope's measure seems to suggest that he suspected that some of the laity had objections to crusading.

Over the course of the fourteenth and fifteenth centuries, Western spirituality grew increasingly individualistic, subjective, and concerned with the performance of charitable works. While the various movements associated with this religious trend were not antipapal, their emergence reflected a certain ill-defined disenchantment with the institutional Church and the papacy. There existed a sense that the bark of St. Peter had to some degree strayed off course. For a while, prophetic voices had speculated about the advent of an "angelic" Pope who would spiritually renew the papacy. Granted, the papacy's sponsorship of the Crusade was not the cause of any disillusionment with it. The Babylonian Captivity at Avignon (1309–1377) and the Great Schism (1378–1417) were far more important factors in this regard. Still, in its own way, the crusading movement entangled the papacy in a multitude of earthly cares and sordid affairs that impeded its ability to fulfill its spiritual mission. Perhaps no feature damaged the papacy's prestige more than its manifest failure to liberate from the grip of Islam the land on which Jesus had walked.

–JOHN A. DEMPSEY,
FRAMINGHAM STATE COLLEGE

References

Norman Housley, *The Italian Crusades: The Papal-Angevin Alliance and the Crusades against Christian Lay Powers, 1254–1343* (Oxford: Clarendon Press, 1982; New York: Oxford University Press, 1982).

Jonathan Riley-Smith, *The Crusades: A Short History* (London: Athlone, 1987; New Haven: Yale University Press, 1987).

Elizabeth Siberry, *Criticism of Crusading: 1095–1274* (Oxford: Clarendon Press, 1985; New York: Oxford University Press, 1985).

Joseph R. Strayer, *The Albigensian Crusades* (New York: Dial, 1971).

Jonathan Sumption, *The Albigensian Crusade* (London & Boston: Faber & Faber, 1978).

PETER THE HERMIT

Did Peter the Hermit initiate the First Crusade?

Viewpoint: Yes. Peter the Hermit was the principal motivator of the First Crusade before the papacy asserted its control over the movement.

Viewpoint: No. Pope Urban II was the true architect of the First Crusade.

Pope Urban II is generally considered to be the true architect of the First Crusade (1096–1102) and thus the founding father of a movement that lasted for centuries. A staunch supporter of reform and a consummate diplomat, Urban hit upon the concept of armed pilgrimage that thrust the papacy into an even greater position of authority and sent many men on the road to the other side of the known world. Hailing from the warrior aristocracy of France, Urban is believed to have had an intuitive understanding of the mentality of the arms-bearing class, and he exploited this knowledge for papal ends. Drawing upon the administrative machinery of the Church and tapping into the concerns of the knightly class, Urban created a movement that began at the top of the sociopolitical hierarchy and subsequently seeped down to the lower strata. In short, it was "crusade from above"—a holy war promoted by the supreme head of the Church, whose exhortations were directed toward the great power brokers of the aristocracy.

This argument sharply contrasts with the older theory of a "crusade from below," which claims that the First Crusade was initiated by an itinerant preacher named Peter the Hermit, who also hailed from France but whose similarities with Urban end there. When Peter was not riding a donkey in Christ-like fashion, he walked barefoot. His ascetic lifestyle prohibited him from eating either bread or meat, so he ate fish. After being manhandled by the Turks while trying to visit Jerusalem, Peter returned to Europe and began preaching in public before 1095 (though what he sermonized is not certain). One man who knew him personally claimed that everything Peter said and did seemed almost divine. Even the hairs from his donkey, believed to be holy relics, were sought after by his followers. Without a doubt, Peter was able to move people in a way that eluded the bishops whom Urban recruited to preach. Some scholars have argued that Peter called for an expedition, or crusade, prior to the Council of Clermont (1095). During the early stages of his activities, Peter proffered a letter allegedly from God commanding him to lead the faithful to the East. He organized a body of preachers who spread his call to arms. His expedition set out months before the one authorized by Urban. Some historians have cited this campaign as evidence that Peter initiated the First Crusade. Supporters of the "Peter Thesis" have also added testimony from Byzantine princess Anna Comnena, author of *Alexiad* (circa 1120–1148); French chronicler Albert of Aix; the author of *Chanson d'Antioche* (Song of Antioch, circa 1130); and Eastern-born historian William of Tyre—all claimed that Peter the Hermit started the Crusades.

This debate goes far beyond which individual is credited with the genesis of the crusading movement. The two theories actually posit differing interpretations of the causes and social origins of the First Crusade. The Urban theory argues that the First Crusade originated in the papal curia and was primarily an aristocratic movement. The Peter theory claims the First Crusade was a mass religious and social movement that the papacy tried to gain control over by joining, redirecting, and giving it the stamp of official approval. The sentiment for a crusade to the East among people in western Europe was the same for either case, however. The issue is rather who tapped into these conditions to create the movement—the aristocracy or the masses.

Viewpoint:
Yes. Peter the Hermit was the principal motivator of the First Crusade before the papacy asserted its control over the movement.

The notion of a crusade was a totally unexpected and scarcely conceivable idea before the decision to recapture Jerusalem from the Muslims was made in late 1095. Not only was the concept of waging war thought to be un-Christian (as late as 1066 those engaged in the Norman conquest of England were sentenced to serve penance for their violation of the peace), but also the idea of peace was also the result of a hard-fought internal battle in Europe since the late tenth century, following the collapse in the ninth century of the Carolingian Order (the rule of much of Europe by monarchs who descended from Charles the Great, who was crowned Western Roman Emperor in 800 and who died in 814). St. Augustine had defined narrow limits for a "just war." Furthermore, no one at the time had adequate maps or much information about Jerusalem—how far from Europe it was, how long it would take to get there, and what hazards lay along the way. For many Europeans, Jerusalem was what John, in the Revelation of St. John, described at the end of the Bible:

> And he [one of the seven angels] . . . showed me the holy city of Jerusalem coming down out of the heaven from God . . . her light was like . . . the crystalline jasper stone; she had a great high wall with twelve gates, with twelve angels at the gates, and names inscribed. . . . And the city is pure gold, like pure glass. The foundation stones of the city wall are decorated with every kind of precious stone . . . jasper, . . . sapphire, . . . chalcedony, . . . emerald, . . . sardonic, . . . sardis, . . . chrysolite, . . . beryl, . . . topaz, . . . chrysopase, . . . hyacinth, . . . amethyst. And the twelve gates are twelve pearls. . . . And the city square was pure gold.

The average layperson would not have known this text, of course, but there were people who identified with the "witness" of Rev. 11 ("And I will give *power* unto my two witnesses, and they shall prophesy a thousand two hundred *and* threescore days, clothed in sackcloth") and who were moved to criticize the morals and pomp of the official church. They predicted the imminent end of the world on the basis of signs

identified in various parts of the Bible (for example, in Matt. 24.24–35; 2 Pet. 2.1, 3.10; and Rev. 11.6, 15.1, and 16). The dramatic tone of Revelation on the great struggle between Babylon—with its traders and merchants, evil sinners, wearers of "fine linen, and purple, and scarlet, and decked with golds, and jewels and pearls" (Rev. 18.16), the cowardly, the faithless, the vile, murderers, fornicators, sorcerers, idolaters, and liars of every kind (Rev. 21.8)—and those who are invited to the wedding supper of the Lamb (Rev. 19.1) inspired many who heard the words. In Rev. 14.1, John saw that on Mount Zion stood the lamb, and with him were 144,000 who had his name and the name of his Father written on their foreheads. Zion, of course, while originally a fortification within Jerusalem, in time came to be the name applied to the whole city.

That there is so little actual historical record of the *prophetae* and *gyrovagi* (wandering preachers) is in large part the result of the nature of the sources, which emanated from the Church and were strongly dismissive and castigatory of the claims of such figures. The sources tend to refer to them generically as "servants of Satan," "hypocrites," "heretics," "Manichees," and "deceivers" rather than in individual biographical detail. It is also worth remembering that in the early twelfth century, skilled Catholic preachers were rare—Guibert of Nogent comments in *Monodiae* (Memoirs, circa 1120) on the unwillingness or inability of his (clerical) contemporaries to undertake this task, and he therefore wrote some early instructions for preaching. Consequently, the clergy continually emphasized—and feared—the ability of "heretical" preachers to communicate effectively, a talent they no doubt owed both to their clerical/monastic education and the skills derived from ample practice and motivation.

Whenever times were tough in western medieval Europe, the distressed listened to such preachers, who generally rose to the developing crises; from their authoritative preaching, individuals obtained comfort and consolation. Some scholars, such as Norman Cohn, in *The Pursuit of the Millennium: Revolutionary Millenarians and Mystical Anarchists of the Middle Ages* (1970), point to a migration from countryside to new suburban areas that was promoted by the developing cloth and woolen industries of the eleventh century. This population shift deprived people of their rural religious links, pastoral care, and economic livelihood; it also made them dependent upon the ability of the nearby countryside to feed these urban centers. Yet, worsening social and economic conditions drove more people in certain areas to make this migration. The tightening bonds of rural servitude; the gradual subdivision of peasant holdings, consequent upon population growth since the end of the invasion period (Viking, Saracen, and Magyar) that followed the decline of the Carolingian empire; and the inexorable pressure of population growth on the productive capacity of rural areas drove individuals to the cities and the cloth-production areas to escape poverty, landlessness, famine, and disease. Many diseases spread when excessive rains or other factors affected food production. One such affliction was *ignis sacer* (holy fire), and it stemmed from eating bread made of rotten rye flour, stored too long in damp conditions, that was used in times of famine and poor crop yield.

Medieval transport was slow and primitive. Sudden food demands in one area could often not be supplied even though there might be sufficient crops in other areas. The Burgundian monastic chronicler Radulfus Glaber, in *Historiae* (1030–1035), described such a famine:

> And so . . . over the whole globe famine developed, and death began to threaten the whole human race because the warmth in the air came so late that there was no suitable time for sowing the corn. And when the corn was sown, so much rain fell that it became clear how difficult it was going to be to harvest the crop. . . . The cloud bursts were so frequent that the earth became flooded and for three years no ploughed land could be found suitable for planting the seed. When the harvest time came, weeds and thickets covered all the ploughland. Corn became impossible to buy. All mankind began to shrink from lack of food. . . . Some tried to escape death by eating the roots of trees and river grasses once the birds and animals had all been eaten. . . . Travellers were overpowered, cut up, cooked and eaten. . . . [Some people] dug up a kind of white earth, like potter's clay and mixed into it as much flour or bran as they could get. Out of the mixture they baked a kind of bread. The only result was that people fell into the grip of an emaciated pallor, their skins stretched and distended, their voices thin like chattering birds. So thickly did people die that bodies were piled up everywhere: at crossroads, on the grass beside the roads, anywhere—piles of five hundred bodies and more, mostly half naked or completely so.

There is much evidence in the chronicles and other sources that the 1080s and 1090s were marked by a recurrence of famine, plagues, and poor crop yields in many parts of France and the Low Countries, areas from which many Crusaders came. Chroniclers reported strange celestial phenomena that were taken to presage the coming of the end of the world. The *Hierosolymita* (Jerusalem Journey, circa 1101) of Ekkehard of Aura, written probably following his pilgrimage to the Holy Land in the company of German Crusaders, is a good example. Omens, portents, and presaged "signs" were more important to him than an assembly held by the Pope (he does not know where) at which the call for a Crusade went out.

While the lower classes were beset with problems and flocked to the preaching of itinerant clerics, the ruling elements in society (knights and ecclesiastics) had long been able to go on pilgrimages to the Holy Land (Jerusalem) and did not need any special call to do so. They always carried their weapons and employed them when necessary. The concentration of an armed pilgrimage would have been normal to them, not something requiring a special appeal.

Knights and major ecclesiastics, however, were not the first Crusaders to go on such an expedition. That honor belongs to the Peasant's Crusade organized by Peter the Hermit. The knights were supposed to set out for Jerusalem on 15 August 1096, but Peter and his band reached Cologne by 12 April of the same year—a bare five months after the Council of Clermont (1095). Peter's band, about twenty thousand strong according to some estimates—composed of women, peasants, townspeople, poor knights, brigands, and former criminals—reached Asia Minor and then was wiped out by the Turks in October 1096. Even the eminent historian Jonathan Riley-Smith, a staunch upholder of Pope Urban II as the instigator of the Crusade, admits that Peter must have been preaching "some kind of religious expedition to Jerusalem" before Clermont. It is likely that the anti-Jewish violence that broke out when these early groups of Crusaders reached the Rhineland was part of Peter's program and was no doubt assisted by the motivation of people who were in debt to Jews. Previous popes, such as Gregory VII, were unable to organize a successful Crusade, even after such a major disaster as the Battle of Manzikert (1071).

There is no evidence among the acts of the council that Urban mentioned the topic of Crusade at Clermont, which in fact was a peace council. Attendees had other business to deal with, including the marital irregularities of the king of France. The main references to Urban as the initiator of the crusading movement come from later writers—Robert the Monk in *Jerusalem History* (circa 1107); Guibert de Nogent, in *Gesta Dei Per Francos* (Deeds of God Done Through the Franks, circa 1104–1111); and Baudry of Bourgueil, bishop of Dal, in *History of the Pilgrimage to Jerusalem* (circa 1108). These writers consciously reworked earlier accounts

PETER THE HERMIT

A MAN OF GREAT VALOR

Historian William of Tyre claimed that the cleric Peter the Hermit inspired Pope Urban II to issue the call for a crusade:

He was small in stature and his external appearance contemptible, but greater valor ruled in his slight frame. For he was sharp witted, his glance was bright and captivating, and he spoke with ease and eloquence. Having paid the tax which was exacted from all Christians who wished to enter, he went into the city and was entertained by a trusty man who was also a confessor of Christ. He diligently questioned his host, as he was a zealous man, and learned more fully from him not only the existing perils, but also the persecutions which their ancestors had suffered long before. And if in what he heard any details were lacking, he completed the account from the witness of his own eyes. For remaining in the city and visiting the churches he learned more fully the truth of what had been told to him by others.

Hearing also that the Patriarch of the city was a devout and God-fearing man, he wished to confer with him and to learn more fully from him the truth concerning some matters. Accordingly he went to him, and having been presented by a trustworthy man, both he and the Patriarch mutually enjoyed their conferences.

The name of the Patriarch was Simeon. As he learned from Peter's conversation that the latter was prudent, able and eloquent, and a man of great experience, he began to disclose to him more confidentially all the evils which the people of God had suffered while dwelling in Jerusalem.

To whom Peter replied: "You may be assured, holy father, that if the Roman church and the princes of the West should learn from a zealous and a reliable witness the calamities which you suffer, there is not the slightest doubt that they would hasten to remedy the evil, both by words and deeds. Write then zealously both to the lord Pope and the Roman church and to the kings and princes of the West, and confirm your letter by the authority of your seal. I, truly, for the sake of the salvation of my soul, do not hesitate to undertake this task. And I am prepared under God's guidance to visit them all, to exhort them all, zealously to inform them of the greatness of your sufferings and to urge them to hasten to your relief."

Of a truth, thou art great, O Lord our God, and to thy mercy there is no end! Of a truth, blessed Jesus, those who trust in Thee shall not be brought to confusion! How did this poor pilgrim, destitute of all resources and far from his native land, have so great confidence that he dared to undertake an enterprise so much beyond his strength and to hope to accomplish his vow, unless it was that he turned all his thoughts to Thee, his protector, and filled with charity, pitying the misfortunes of his brethren, loving his neighbor as himself, he was content to fulfill the law? Strength is a vain thing, but charity overcometh. What his brethren prescribed might appear difficult and even impossible, but the love of God and of his neighbor rendered it easy for him, for love is strong as death. Faith which worketh by love availeth with Thee, and the good deeds near Thee do not remain without fruit. Accordingly Thou didst not permit Thy servant long to remain in doubt. Thou didst manifest Thyself to him. Thou didst fortify him by Thy revelation that he might not hesitate, and breathing into him Thy hidden spirit, Thou madest him arise with greater strength to accomplish the work of charity.

Therefore, after performing the usual prayers, taking leave of the lord Patriarch and receiving his blessing, he went to the seacoast. There he found a vessel belonging to some merchants who were preparing to cross to Apulia. He went on board, and after a successful journey arrived at Bari. Thence he proceeded to Rome, and found the lord Pope Urban in the vicinity. He presented the letters of the Patriarch and of the Christians who dwelt at Jerusalem, and showed their misery and the abominations which the unclean races wrought in the holy places. Thus faithfully and prudently he performed the commission entrusted to him.

Source: *Dana Carleton Munro, ed., "Urban and the Crusaders,"* Translations and Reprints from the Original Sources of European History, *volume 1, revised edition (Philadelphia: University of Pennsylvania Press, 1897), pp. 20–22.*

PETER THE HERMIT

(chiefly, the *Deeds of the Franks and Other Jerusalem Pilgrims,* circa 1100–1101, written by a follower of the Norman prince Bohemond I; and the account by Fulcher of Chartres, chaplain to Baldwin of Boulogne, who wrote *Gesta Francorum Jerusalem Expugnantium* or The Deeds of the Franks Who Attacked Jerusalem, circa 1101) precisely because they were "acephalous"—to use Robert's phrase—without a head or principal beginning, that is, the Clermont episode. The *Deeds of the Franks and other Jerusalem Pilgrims,* for example, notes only that "when the time had already come, of which the Lord Jesus warns his faithful people every day, and especially in the Gospel where he says 'If any man will come after me, let him deny himself and take up his cross, and follow me,'" without mentioning the council.

Medieval historians sought to chronicle not what actually happened but what they felt ought to have happened according to the will of God. They believed that the climactic capture of Jerusalem (1099) required a thorough rewriting, in the most polished manner, in order to give the great event a central importance and symmetry in world history. Each of these rewriters chose to record Urban's Crusade speech at the end of the Council of Clermont as they thought it ought to have sounded, and as a consequence there are not only many, but entirely different and mutually contradicting, versions of this speech. According to Greco-Roman historiographical practice, speeches were invented in order to create persuasive likelihoods that illustrated the general theme the historian was pressing. They were not meant to be verbatim records of actual speeches. Even chroniclers such as William of Malmesbury and Ordericus Vitalis, writing two or three decades after the First Crusade and about subjects not connected with the event (William wrote a history of the kings of England, and Ordericus wrote an ecclesiastical history of England and Normandy), felt obliged to include a highly wrought version of Urban's speech. For much the same reason, one cannot pay literal attention to such documents as the letters allegedly dispatched by Urban in connection with his organization of the Crusade. Often, with poor manuscript authority and imprecise dating, these documents can easily become assimilated into the class of *excitatoria* (documents forged to encourage intellectual, and other, attention to the problem of maintaining crusading momentum).

Other medieval writers credited a less exalted cleric with starting the crusading movement. No lesser authorities than Anna Comnena, William of Tyre, and Albert of Aix assign primacy for initiating the First Crusade to Peter the Hermit. Anna, the daughter of the Byzantine ruler Alexius I Comnenus, claims that Peter had visited the Holy Sepulchre (the basilica located at the site where Jesus was allegedly placed in the tomb) and had been mishandled by Turkish Saracens; as a consequence of this treatment, he decided to stir up a popular movement designed to permit a triumphant return to the Holy Land to liberate it from the Turks. Peter claimed he was inspired by a divine voice; in other versions of the story he was allegedly encouraged by Christ, who visited him while he was asleep in the Holy Sepulchre, to secure a letter from the patriarch that could be taken back to Europe and used to arouse interest in a military expedition to the Holy Land in defense of the sacred sites. Anna clearly saw the Crusade as a popular movement. She wrote: "The upheaval that ensued as men and women took to the road was unprecedented within living memory." Recent historical work suggests that much of her chronicle was written by her husband, but whatever the case, it makes no mention of the Pope or the Council of Clermont as the originators of the movement. She describes the Pope, elsewhere, as the holder of a "noble office, protected by soldiers of many nationalities." Albert wrote his history more than a quarter century after the First Crusade. He provides the fullest account of Peter's activities and was obviously familiar with Lorraine and the areas of northern France where Peter was active. It is also worth noting that the popular *Chanson d'Antioche* (written in French toward the end of the twelfth century but using earlier sources), used by Cohn as a prime source for describing the views and passions of the *pauperes* (rootless poor) in the First Crusade, also records Peter as the initiator of the movement. William—highly learned, well-informed, and a resident of the Holy Land—wrote what has been described as "the best history of the Crusades" (*History of the Deeds Done Beyond the Sea,* circa 1180s). Even though the author was a leading hierarch in the Roman Catholic Church, he assigns primacy in the movement to Peter.

If one notes carefully the account given by Guibert of Nogent, the fullest and most circumstantial source for Peter's early activity, it is clear that Guibert probably knew Peter or heard him preach. One finds that Peter must have been similar to figures such as Henry of Le Mans and Tanchelm of the Netherlands, who were condemned by the church for heresy in the 1110s. Peter, a French monk from northern France (Amiens region), who was given to ascetic habits and clothing, mixed his clerical/monastic experience and training with a fluency of address and a charismatic appeal, elements denied most pastoral preaching by the shortage of trained pastors and parish churches. Both Tanchelm and Henry were immensely popular in their day and strongly criticized the established church; they held unorthodox attitudes toward marriage, the clergy, churches, and the sacraments. These preachers, along with Peter the Hermit and Robert of Arbrissel, set as their goal the rehabilitation and marriage of prostitutes or women who had had many sexual liaisons outside of wedlock, an activity that was probably not unusual when one remembers that clerical celibacy was a new idea and that it was not uncommon for priests to live with concubines—who would have been thrown out onto the streets by the campaign for clerical celibacy. In the period in which Robert and Peter preached, it makes sense that poor and disadvantaged elements in the community were aroused by criticism of the hierarchs and excited by the promise of redress and residence in a land of milk and honey in an apocalyptic end-of-the- world Jerusalem, accessible only to them and not to the rich, who were to be thrown into a lake of burning tar and pitch. Passages in Revelation that promised a thousand-year reign of the "faithful" with christ on earth might also have encouraged a secular form of premillenarianism: "and all the souls of those who were killed with the axe for the witness of Jesus and the word of God . . . lived and they reigned as kings with Christ for a thousand years" (Rev. 20.4). It is worth noting that around 1102–1105 Raymond d'Augiliers, chaplain to Count Raymond of Toulouse, described the massacre that followed the taking of Jerusalem in terms lifted from Revelation; many chronicles of the Crusades are permeated with apocalyptic allusions.

It would have required a massive groundswell of popular emotion to push the masses into an affair so far-fetched, ill-researched, ill-supplied, and inherently difficult as a Crusade to the Holy Land. Since popes and rulers were previously unable to provide such inspiration, the initiative must have derived from popular preachers who made their listeners want to go to Jerusalem to be present for the final acts in the end of world. Such scenarios can be read about in the "Play of Antichrist," written for the German court around 1175, and in Revelation. Popular preaching—coupled with the distress, famine, and dislocation induced by intraregional migration—drove large numbers of people to join the Jerusalem pilgrimage. Pope Urban II, who was forced out of Rome—according to the scrupulous English historian William of Malmesbury—by a German-appointed Antipope and harrassed by a powerful and hostile German emperor with universalist ambitions (Henry IV), sought an opportunity to display world leadership and sensed the potential heterodoxy and social revolution inherent in an uncontrolled messianic Crusade to Jerusalem. Urban therefore intervened while he was in exile in France, attending to various duties unconnected with the Crusade, and sought to place ecclesiastical and knightly leadership ahead of the groundswell of popular frenzy. While at a council he convened in Piacenza, north of Rome, in March 1095, he was contacted by the ruler of Byzantium, who asked for military aid against the Turks. This request inspired Urban's response to the popular Crusade.

It is possible that Urban delivered a ceremonial Latin *sermo* (sermon) to the assembled clerical delegates at Clermont, and he might well have touched upon topics such as violence in Europe, refurbishing the peace, assisting Byzantium, resisting the Turks in the Holy Land, seeking the union of Churches, papal leadership in troubled times, the sins of the French king, and the special virtues of the Franks—whom Anna Comnena called "Kelts." Such a short thematic speech was later remembered incompletely or inaccurately and then blown up to the status of an "end-of-conference major address" on the subject of Crusade to a vast crowd of laypeople and ecclesiastics. In his negotiations with particular secular leaders, Urban no doubt used various blandishments to induce them to cooperate in this enterprise, and was, according to William of Malmesbury, not above using the pretext of Crusade for narrower ecclesiological profit: "in the great confusion that would ensue in every province [consequent upon the proclamation of an expedition into Asia, for example, a Crusade] which would make it easy to hire auxiliary troops, Urban [hoped that he] might overrun Rome," in alliance with Bohemond I, whose secret aim was to capture the provinces of Illyricum and Macedonia. It is important to realize that, according to William, Urban's ostensible reason for coming to France in 1095 was to seek recognition from the churches "this side of the Alps"; it was only his *reposition prepositum* (more secret proposition) that induced him to follow Bohemond's advice and stir up Europe to invade Asia. Urban's alleged purpose, to use the Crusade as a blind for hiring troops to retake Rome from Wibert, the Ravennese Antipope (Clement III), is oddly out of place. Clement was forced to abandon Rome by Urban's use of Norman soldiery and extensive bribery some two years before the Council of Clermont. Somehow, though he seems to have telescoped actual events, William realized that "crusade" was a secret military ploy of Urban and not an open call. Urban's undoubted real

PETER THE
HERMIT

aims must have included arranging the union of Eastern and Western Churches; checkmating German universalist ambitions; neutralizing or diverting the Normans; refurbishing the "Peace of God" movement in Europe; ameliorating social dislocation and violence in Europe; and heading off hunger, famine, and the messianism of the poor. At a more strategic level, too, in the event of any conquests in the Holy Land, the fate of the churches there and the question of sovereignty in conquered areas would be highly contested: the papacy had to appear as the *maximus auctor* (chief initiator) of the enterprise if the clerical/Gregorian idea of "right order in the world" was to be upheld.

The Pope was not the only cleric to think this way. Glaber notes in *Historiae* that following the heresies, famines, rainstorms, and other hardships that occurred early in the eleventh century, peace and abundance reigned in France, and the bishops and magnates gathered to refashion the peace and holy faith by way of councils. Their efforts were accompanied by the appearance of comets. Soon thereafter, a multitude of pilgrims began to advance toward the Holy Sepulchre—first the poor, then those of middling position, and finally the greatest counts, kings, and bishops. In the end, many noblewomen also accompanied the men to Jerusalem.

It is, of course, probable that many of the leaders whom Urban induced to take part in his campaign might have been inspired by apocalyptic preaching, though—according to Riley-Smith—no charters (recording the arrangements by which the nobility raised funds for crusading) mention Peter the Hermit. The

French illumination of Peter the Hermit in clerical garb leading his followers and pointing to the Holy Land (fourteenth century)

(British Library, London)

Pope, perhaps early in 1096, began to preach a penitential Crusade. He stressed relic worship, holy sites, and the need to assist the Byzantines militarily against the Turks. His campaign initially aimed to absorb and redirect the preexisting, largely apocalyptic, movement associated with areas in which Peter and his assistants were active. It is difficult to establish what was an initiative of Urban and what later writers thought to be a necessary reinterpretation of events. Whether in connection with the establishment of Christian government in Jerusalem or with the recruitment of troops for later Crusades, it must have seemed to chroniclers that such a magnificent episode as the retaking of the Holy Land should be seen as an initiative of the papacy in charismatic alliance with religious and secular leaders and the people. This explanation is entirely in conformity with the image of the papacy that was developing in European minds and with papal ambitions to direct secular and religious affairs.

Later historians rewrote the story with Urban II as the initiator because the First Crusade was successful in a way impossible to predict at the outset. The Crusade therefore seemed to them to be far more important than was recognized by clerics and laymen who chronicled the Crusaders' journey. These initial histories did not demonstrate clearly enough the proper role of papal leadership. Besides, there was concern about the leadership of the new state based in Jerusalem: should it be a religious or secular state? The more powerfully the chroniclers could demonstrate papal initiative and leadership at the outset, the better claim the patriarch had to make Jerusalem a religious or papal state. Note that Godfrey of Bouillon did not call himself "King" of Jerusalem when he took power on 22 July 1099—he used only the phrase "advocate of the Holy Sepulchre" (though the term appears only in one controversial source). He recognized the primary authority of the Church: Jerusalem was like a bishopric or a monastery in the West.

That Peter the Hermit was the initiator of the Crusades was the standard view up until the nineteenth century; German historians Heinrich von Sybel and Heinrich Hagenmeyer could not believe that God would have spoken first to a hermit and only then to the pope. Without any good evidence other than this assumption, they overturned the older view. Because they were schooled in the *quellenforschung* (source research) tradition, based on the classes of historian Leopold von Ranke, their interpretation was believed by similarly source-based scholars. It is now known, however, that medieval people were different from what these modern scholars believed, and they

would have found Peter the Hermit's style of preaching far more effective than any "appeal" by the Pope. William of Tyre seems to have sensed this fact, because, having written of Peter's visit to Jerusalem before the First Crusade and of his conversation with the patriarch of Jerusalem concerning the ills of the Holy Land and the vanity of expecting help from the Greeks, he devoted a whole chapter to why God chose to visit first this needy and helpless pilgrim, lacking all the qualities that made for influence and far away from his native land, and imposed upon him such an important mission. William stressed Peter's uniqueness by having Christ visit him in "the Church of the Resurrection of the Lord" in Jerusalem; Christ speaks here not to St. Peter, as in the Gospel, but to "Peter." William's chronology leaves plenty of time for Peter to travel around Italy and north of the Alps to preach his mission— long before Urban came to Clermont. William, in fact, blends the role of Peter with a careful account of several papal councils (at Piacenza, Vezelay, Puy, and, finally, Clermont); he has Peter suggest canons at the latter council; and he climaxes his account with the by-now-traditional papal Crusade speech.

Even if Urban had sent out his Crusade appeal at the end of the Council of Clermont, it would have reached few people; the call would have been impossible to be preached throughout France, the Low Countries, England, western Germany, and northern Italy in the time available. Mobilization, when it occurred, is only comprehensible in the context of an earlier, nonpapal, preaching crusade based on the most effective and easily available "tinder": people who believed the world was coming to an end and who wished to become part of the 144,000 to be saved at Jerusalem as mentioned in Revelation.

Neither the Battle of Manzikert nor the attitude of Moslem rulers toward Christian pilgrims had much effect on the practicalities of Christians worshiping in the Holy Land: certainly neither was a casus belli, and there is no evidence of any severe worsening of the situation in Jerusalem in the 1090s. In fact, the only real downturn in the life of Christians in the Holy Land took place under the mad Fatimid caliph al-Hakim much earlier in the eleventh century.

Historians are still obliged to get things right as much as they can. In the present case, they should avoid the tendency to let the victors—the leading clergy and rulers—dictate a story that denies popular religious feeling and distress as causes of the Crusade. An exercise of such cataclysmic novelty and proportion must have sprung from deep and widespread social and religious unrest, rather than being solely inspired by Pope Urban II, a man not otherwise known to have played so charismatic a role. By reassessing Peter the Hermit's participation, one begins to see the disturbed and tension-filled countryside of Europe (especially the Low Countries, northern France, and western Germany) in a new light, to gauge the role and depth of popular religious emotion and privation, and to understand the galvanizing impact of apocalypticism and criticism of the contemporary clerical hierarchy. Thus is deepened one's sense of causation in history, replacing a rather trite notion of a single cause with a social model that reveals change and innovation on its own terms. One can learn how "the record" is capable of altering and covering up what really happened, and this insight should assist students to make more-intuitive judgments in other areas of history.

–JOHN O. WARD,
UNIVERSITY OF SYDNEY

Viewpoint:
No. Pope Urban II was the true architect of the First Crusade.

Prior to the late nineteenth century, several historians who wrote about the crusading movement ascribed the origin of the First Crusade (1096–1102) to the work of the popular preacher Peter the Hermit and not to the efforts of Pope Urban II. Undoubtedly, the roots of this thesis lay in the assertions of medieval historians Albert of Aix and William of Tyre: both men claimed that Peter inspired the Pope to proclaim the Crusade after Peter returned from a pilgrimage to Jerusalem. Even though Albert insists that he spoke to eyewitnesses to the First Crusade, no corroborating evidence exists for his (or William's) assertion that Peter influenced Urban's decision to issue a call to crusade.

Plenty of evidence, however, exists that strongly suggests that the Pope arrived at the decision to issue a summons for the liberation of Eastern Churches and Jerusalem independently of Peter and his preaching activity. Because it is not known precisely when Peter began preaching for an expedition to the East, one cannot exclude the possibility that he devised a plan for a popular Crusade independent of Urban's summons. It could also be the case that the two men arrived at the same conclusion at approximately the same time. Yet, evidence in support of the thesis that Urban initiated the First Crusade

seems to indicate that Peter's "Peasants' Crusade" was an unforeseen and unintended consequence of the papal summons issued at the Council of Clermont (1095).

Well before Peter the Hermit issued his summons to the ordinary folk of central France and the Rhineland, Urban II's thoughts were turned to a war of liberation against Islam. Early in his papacy, Urban took a keen interest in the struggle taking place on the Iberian Peninsula among the various Christian princes and their Muslim counterparts. In particular, the Pope promoted the idea of reestablishing the frontier town of Tarragona, which lay some fifty miles south of Barcelona. He erected an archbishopric there and promised the remission of sins to surrounding magnates who helped rebuild the city. So important was the restoration of Tarragona to the Pope that when he learned that Catalan knights were preparing to head east in response to his appeal at Clermont, Urban forbade them to go. He commanded them to stay at home and win the same spiritual reward by fighting the persecutors of Christians on their native land.

Jonathan Riley-Smith noted in *The Crusades: A Short History* (1987) that the idea of a war of liberation had enjoyed wide intellectual currency prior to Urban's papal election. Eleventh-century ecclesiastical reform, which was in part a spin-off from an earlier monastic movement, had conceived of its own work against the abuses of simony and Nicolaitism (a married clergy), and later against lay investiture of bishops, as a kind of war of liberation. Reformers insisted that in their campaign against these abuses they simply sought the *libertas ecclesiae* (freedom of the Church). By and large, the war that reformers waged was rhetorical and legislative. But, as in the case of the Milanese *Pataria,* it could lead to physical combat. In the last years of Gregory VII's pontificate (1080–1085) the moral struggle against ecclesiastical abuses evolved into a veritable religious civil war between the Pope and German emperor Henry IV. In his later years, Gregory, whom Urban served as cardinal-bishop of Ostia, called on the *fideles* (the faithful) of St. Peter to defend him against the armed forces of Henry and his Antipope, Clement III. As many commentators have observed, popes in the ninth century had summoned Christian knights to war (albeit against non-Christians) and promised them spiritual rewards for their military service. Thus, in a certain sense, irrespective of the figure of Peter the Hermit, there was precedent in papal history for what Urban did at Clermont.

Besides the influence of papal history, there was much in Urban's own background that could have led him to conceive of the First Crusade. Before assuming his duties as the cardinal-bishop of Ostia in 1080, the former Odo of

PETER THE HERMIT

Champagne served as grand prior of the great monastic house of Cluny. While it would be somewhat of an exaggeration to claim that the Cluniacs actively and consciously promoted holy war per se, they made a special effort to spiritualize the lives and activities of the feudal nobility with whom they came in contact; and part of this effort entailed redirecting the knightly class's bellicosity away from blood feud and indiscriminate violence toward fighting the good fight against outlaws and hostile pagans, for example, the Muslims of the Iberian Peninsula. Still, as H. E. J. Cowdrey has observed in *The Cluniacs and the Gregorian Reform* (1970), close contact with the Cluniacs could, and did, lead some feudal barons to forsake the world and their military duties and to enter the cloister. Nonetheless, Cluny, its many daughter houses, and other affiliates associated themselves with such exercises of moral violence as the Spanish *Reconquista,* and they encouraged more than a few French and Spanish knights to participate in this undertaking. Urban's concern with the restoration of Tarragona perhaps stemmed in part from his time at Cluny. Of course, it is also true that his papal predecessors Alexander II (1061–1073) and Gregory VII (1073–1085) had shown an interest in the *Reconquista*. Regardless of the exact cause of his concern for Tarragona, the future pope certainly must have absorbed a good deal from his time at Cluny about the merit of holy or righteous warfare.

Cluny was also associated with another phenomenon crucial to the formulation of the First Crusade: the idea of pilgrimage. Indeed, monastic houses affiliated with the great abbey lined the route from southern France across the Pyrenees and along northern Spain to one of the most popular pilgrimage sites of the Middle Ages, the shrine to St. James at Santiago de Compostella in northwestern Spain. The Cluniacs were by no means solely responsible for the popularity of pilgrimages in the late eleventh century or for Santiago de Compostella's appeal to the laity of all ranks. Nevertheless, they were important promoters of pilgrimage to Santiago as well as to Jerusalem, and as a Cluniac, Urban would have understood the appeal of a papal-sponsored pilgrimage to the Holy Land to the knights of western Europe.

The Pope's family background also contributed to his independent formulation of the idea of Crusade. He belonged to the same knightly class to which he directed his call. He knew how the knightly class thought. He understood their bellicose spirituality. As Riley-Smith has demonstrated, Urban's summons at Clermont, as it has come down to us, strikes all the right notes for a knightly audience. Significantly, Urban seems to have presented his proposed enterprise in the terms of a spiritual blood feud or vendetta: a concept readily understood by eleventh-century knights.

In short, given his affiliation with the papal reform movement and Cluny, as well as his family background, Urban was perfectly capable of envisioning an armed pilgrimage to the East under papal auspices for the liberation of the Eastern Churches and Jerusalem without Peter the Hermit's input. Yet, perhaps some of the best evidence against the notion that Urban somehow followed Peter's lead in calling for the Crusade involves papal-Byzantine relations on the eve of the First Crusade. After all, the Crusade's ostensible purpose was the liberation of Eastern Christianity and the holy places from heathen oppression.

Early in his papacy, Urban showed a strong desire to improve relations between the Roman Church and Constantinople, which had soured considerably when Urban's predecessor, Gregory VII, formed an alliance in 1080 with the great foe in the southern Adriatic, the Norman prince Robert Guiscard. Gregory formed this alliance as a desperate defensive measure against the impending march on Rome by Henry IV of Germany, with whom the Pope had broken relations in that same year. As punishment for Gregory's understanding with the Normans, the Byzantine emperor Alexius I Comnenus helped finance Henry IV and his Antipope's military activities against the reform papacy.

Not long into his reign, Urban set about winning the Byzantine emperor over to his side by receiving assurances from the Norman count of Sicily, Roger I, that he had no plans to revive the assaults on Byzantine territory by Guiscard, who had died in 1085. Urban then lifted the sentence of excommunication that Gregory VII had imposed on Alexius's predecessor, Nicephorus III, and he wrote to Alexius in 1089 asking that the name of the Roman pontiff be reinserted in the *diptychs* (tablets) of the Greek Church. No doubt, the Pope somehow also informed Alexius of Roger's pledge. While no theological rapprochement ensued, Urban achieved his primary goal of weaning Constantinople away from Henry IV and closer to the papacy.

Relations between the papacy and Constantinople improved to the extent that at the papal council held at Piacenza (March 1095), Alexius requested through his emissaries the military aid of Latin Christians. This request was the proximate cause of Urban's summons at Clermont eight months later to Crusade, and there is no reason to believe that Peter the Hermit had anything to do with it. By the spring of 1095 the Turkish offensive had come to a stop just shy of Constantinople. Alexius was preparing his forces for a counteroffensive, and he wanted his army supplemented with Western knights. To be sure, Western mercenaries had served the Byzantine emperors for quite some time. Thus, Alexius's request was not in itself extraordinary.

By the spring of 1095 the Pope was in the process of his own political and spiritual counter-offensive against Henry IV and Clement III. At Urban's papal election seven years earlier, the reform papacy was in difficult straits. Henry was in firm control of events in Germany, and Clement III's forces were strong in Italy. To the extent that either claimant to St. Peter's chair enjoyed the support of the Romans, the city belonged to the Antipope. Urban and his household were pinned south of Rome in Norman territory. Yet, through shrewd diplomacy and with the help of some strategic mistakes by his enemies, Urban was able to turn the tables on Henry and the Antipope by the spring of 1095. With the German emperor and the Antipope trapped in northern Lombardy and Ravenna, respectively, the Pope embarked on a tour up the Italian Peninsula. The council held at Piacenza was something of an exclamation point to his Italian sojourn.

Urban would not have needed Peter the Hermit or anyone else to point out the political advantage that the reform papacy could derive from sponsoring an expedition of knights to aid the Byzantine emperor. In the not-too-distant past, other reform popes had sponsored military ventures, such as William of Normandy's invasion of England in 1066, as a means of augmenting papal prestige in Europe. More important, in 1074, Gregory VII openly considered leading an army to the East himself to help the Byzantines, who were then hard-pressed by the advance of the Turks across Asia Minor. In the spring of 1095 papal sponsorship of a military mission to the East offered great advantages to the papal reformers both in Europe and in Constantinople. Urban might have harbored the hope that a successful military expedition to the East would speed a theological rapprochement between the Latin and Greek branches of Christianity—a development that would bring even greater prestige to the reform papacy.

It would be a mistake to think that a man as careful and prudent as Urban would have embarked on a project such as the First Crusade on the advice of a character such as Peter the Hermit. While he might not have already decided on the particulars of the military venture that he would propose at Clermont when he and his traveling party crossed into France in the early summer of 1095, he must have had good reason to believe that his idea would find a warm reception there. It is equally certain that the Pope would never have summoned the feudal classes to a religious war if he were not already certain beforehand of the commitment of some important people to the project. Urban's itinerary prior to the Council of Clermont indicates that his call for the Crusade was premeditated. For instance, while as a guest of Bishop Adhemar of LePuy, the Pope called for a council to be held at Clermont in November. It is virtually certain that Adhemar had agreed to serve as Urban's legate on the Crusade. Similarly, at the end of August 1095 the papal party was in St. Gilles, the heartland of the territory of Count Raymond of Toulouse, the chief layman on the First Crusade. Very likely either Raymond or his representative gave the Pope the necessary assurance of the count's participation in the venture. Almost immediately after Urban called for the Crusade at Clermont, Raymond announced that he would take up the cross. Given Urban's itinerary leading up to the council and his modus operandi, it is equally implausible that the Pope would have launched his Crusade extemporaneously in a rash attempt to latch onto an enterprise already set in motion by Peter the Hermit or some other popular preacher.

Again, since it is not known exactly when Peter began preaching, it is theoretically possible that his activity either slightly predated or was coterminous with that of Urban at Clermont. In any event, as the sources make clear, their respective summonses differed in at least one important detail. For, whereas Peter evidently called for a popular march to the East, the Pope, as his letter to the Bolognese demonstrates, wanted an army of knights with few noncombatants to head to the East. Given the available evidence, one can safely state that the Pope acted independently of Peter. The idea that Urban's summons was his attempt to gain control of an enterprise that Peter or some other popular preacher had already launched is far-fetched at best.

–JOHN A. DEMPSEY,
FRAMINGHAM STATE COLLEGE

References

Paul Alphandéry and Alphonse Dupront, *La Crétienté et l'idée de croisade* (Paris: A. Michel, 1995).

Karl-Heinz Bender and Hermann Kleber, *Les Epopées de la Croisade: Premier Colloque International (Trèves, 6–11 août 1984)* (Wiesbaden: Steiner, 1987).

E. O. Blake and C. Morris, "A Hermit Goes to War: Peter and the Origins of the First Crusade," *Studies in Church History*, 22 (1985): 79–107.

Marcus Bull, *Knightly Piety and the Lay Response to the First Crusade: The Limousin and Gascony, c. 970–c. 1130* (Oxford: Clarendon Press / Oxford & New York: Oxford University Press, 1993).

Claude Cahen, "Introduction to the First Crusade," *Past and Present,* 6 (November 1954): 6–30.

Norman Cohn, *The Pursuit of the Millennium: Revolutionary Millenarians and Mystical Anarchists of the Middle Ages,* revised edition (New York: Oxford University Press, 1970).

Penny J. Cole, *The Preaching of the Crusades to the Holy Land, 1095–1270* (Cambridge, Mass.: Medieval Academy of America, 1991).

Anna Comnena, *The Alexiad of Anna Comnena,* translated by E. R. A. Sewter (Baltimore: Penguin, 1969).

M. D. Coupe, "Peter the Hermit—A Reassessment," *Nottingham Medieval Studies,* 31 (1987): 37–45.

H. E. J. Cowdrey, *The Cluniacs and the Gregorian Reform* (Oxford: Clarendon Press, 1970).

Cowdrey, "The Peace and the Truce of God in the Eleventh Century," *Past and Present,* 46 (February 1970): 42–67.

Cowdrey, "Pope Urban II's Preaching of the First Crusade," *History,* 55 (June 1970): 177–188.

Carl Erdmann, *The Origin of the Idea of Crusade,* translated by Marshall W. Baldwin and Walter Goffart (Princeton: Princeton University Press, 1977).

Fulcher of Chartres, *A History of the Expedition to Jerusalem, 1095–1127,* translated by Frances Rita Ryan, edited by Harold S. Fink (New York: Norton, 1969).

Gesta Francorum et aliorum Hierosolimitanorum (The Deeds of the Franks and the Other Pilgrims to Jerusalem), edited by Rosalind Hill (London & New York: Thomas Nelson, 1962).

Heinrich Hagenmeyer, *Le vrai et le faux sur Pierre l'Hermite: analyse critique des témoignages historiques relatifs à ce personnage et des légendes auxquelles il a donné lieu* (Paris: Librairie de la Société Bibliographique, 1883).

Jonathan Riley-Smith, *The Crusades: A Short History* (New Haven: Yale University Press, 1987).

Kenneth M. Setton, ed., *A History of the Crusades,* volume 1, *The First Hundred Years,* edited by Baldwin, second edition (Madison: University of Wisconsin Press, 1969).

POLITICAL CRUSADES

Were the political Crusades against Christians a later distortion of the original concept of crusading?

Viewpoint: Yes. The political Crusades were opportunistic abuses of papal authority to counter territorial threats and to achieve hegemony in Europe.

Viewpoint: No. Crusades against Christians sprang from the same roots and depended on the same legal superstructure as Crusades against Muslims.

The term *political Crusades* has been given to a variety of military campaigns that the papacy launched against its Christian opponents in Europe, mainly during the thirteenth and fourteenth centuries. What distinguishes these particular papal campaigns from others against Christian lay powers is the fact that they were preached, organized, and prosecuted in the same manner as Crusades against Muslims. From the perspective of papal policy the political Crusades were juridical equivalents to those carried out against Muslims. The rationale behind them was that Christian heretics within Europe were an even greater threat to Christendom than were the Muslims beyond its borders.

Naturally, the "Traditionalist-Pluralist" debate looms particularly large in any discussion of these Crusades. For many Traditionalists these Crusades represent the most egregious example of the distortion and degradation that afflicted the crusading impulse and values as the movement progressed. Pluralists, though most consider these expeditions Crusades, are a bit more divided in their appraisals. Some Pluralists argue staunchly that the political Crusades were, without exception or reservation, central to the inspiration and development of the movement. Others generally define them as Crusades but find a few particular examples a bit embarrassing, ones that push the envelope far across the table and definitions along with it—such as Pope Boniface VIII's transformation of a family feud and policy disagreement into a "Crusade."

The traditionalist-pluralist controversy is not the only one that surrounds the political Crusades. Historians also disagree on the origins of political crusading. Some believe that crusading against Christians was neither explicit nor implicit in the origins of the movement. This school of thought views the political Crusades as an opportunistic redirection of crusading from being directed at Muslims to any significant lay threat to papal territorial and political ambitions. Political Crusades, therefore, were created by a new breed of popes (mostly those from a legal background) that dominated the papal see beginning in the early thirteenth century. Other historians hold that political Crusades, or at least the idea of political crusading, existed at the earliest moments in the movement and were by no means thirteenth-century aberrations of an ideal. Rather than being a later appendage to, or epiphenomenon of, the movement, Crusades against Christians were rooted in the same spiritual soil as those against Muslims. Political crusading, in this scenario, sprang from the same inspirations, experienced a palpable parallel development, and took on its final form when the full-fledged apparatus of Crusade was applied to it in the thirteenth century. "Holy civil war" was very much a part of the conceptual blend that produced Pope Urban II's expedition to the East and thus was no simple deviation from what the Crusades were.

Viewpoint:
Yes. The political Crusades were opportunistic abuses of papal authority to counter territorial threats and to achieve hegemony in Europe.

One of the greatest perceptual and procedural problems that faces professional historians is that the past simply is not easy to measure with infallible precision. Human activity of any sort, at any time, is in a constant state of flux. Causes can become confused with effects, while effects can become new causes that in turn spawn even more surprising effects. Historians try to slow the events down a bit so that sense and meaning can be derived from, or as some would say imputed onto, them. Reducing the sheer velocity of the past allows historians to draw links between events that otherwise would seem mere episodic events. Sometimes these links can be overdrawn, creating an optical illusion that "makes sense" even if it has little to do with what actually happened. Essentially, this (almost unavoidable) problem is what provided eighteenth-century French writer Voltaire with the fodder for his unforgettable quip that history is nothing but the jokes that the living play on the dead. His view has reemerged in the guise of postmodernism, an extremely literary school of thought that brands all history as an imaginative re-creation rather than an accurate recording of the past. The origin of crusading against Christians is firmly rooted in this uncomfortable scholarly predicament: Was it a modification and redirection of crusading against Muslims or was it rather a parallel crusading structure built upon the same foundations?

One of the few things that almost all historians of the Crusades agree on is that the roots of the movement can be found in the perceptions and goals of the late-eleventh-century reformed papacy. "Liberation" was the true battle cry of reformed popes: liberation of monasteries from their "proprietary patrons" or supposed lay "advocates"; liberation of churches from the oppression of local thugs; liberation of popes from Italian mobs, Norman bullies, and German monarchs; and liberation of the mother Church from all forms of pretentious lay domination and interference. Undoubtedly, the liberation of Jerusalem from Muslim rule was part and parcel of this general ecclesiastical rebellion against "tyranny." The reformed papacy was truly fighting a multifront war. All of the military efforts that the papacy was involved in to pursue this war of independence, moreover, had a deeply sanctified tenor and was thus easily qualified as "holy war."

Spiritual sanctions against Christian opponents of the papacy could, but did not necessarily, have desired political effects. Excommunication was, in a manner of speaking, an "occupational hazard" for rulers trying to preserve their sovereignty from any sort of papally sponsored spiritual imperialism. Popes wielding the spiritual sword usually found that it only cut when their objectives dovetailed with those of men who wielded the material sword. Thus, reformed popes were quickly forced to appreciate the merits of spiritual rewards for its lay allies and join them to current secular territorial disputes. This policy can be seen in Pope Leo IX's promise of spiritual rewards to those defending the papacy against Normans (1053) and in Pope Alexander II's protection of the Norman duke (soon to become king) William the Conqueror (1066). By forging spiritual and secular linkages, the reformed papacy found a weighty stick with which to beat back secular opponents. The spiritual-legalistic think tank that emerged during the pontificate of Gregory VII provided the papacy with a roster of reasons and justifications for religiously charged wars against lay powers. All they managed to prove was something known since the time of Roman emperor Constantine I: violence could be used to defend the Church. Still, their efforts could not save the embattled Pope from death in exile.

Pope Urban II was raised to the papacy amid the intense fallout from the war between the German emperor Henry IV and Gregory VII. Urban, in fact, began his pontificate inauspiciously—in exile. Despite the fact that the reformed platform was dear to his heart and that he stood dead center within Gregory's inner circle, Urban's great venture, which came to be known as the First Crusade (1096–1102), seems far removed from the papal-imperial conflict. Lay powers that opposed the reform program were represented just as well as those that were sympathetic to it—probably more so. In all the rhetoric surrounding the First Crusade there is no indication whatsoever that it bore any relation to lay Christians in conflict with the papacy. There is a multiplicity of possible reasons for this lack of linkage, but chief among them is the fact that Urban wanted to defuse the conflict and pursue a less belligerent policy of détente. The First Crusade, then, seems to have emerged during a period of retrenchment rather than advancement of the papal war of liberation against lay power.

The sheer power of the tool that Urban fashioned proved irresistible to later popes less willing to compromise with Christians in enemy camps, but this application of the crusading concept to Christian powers developed slowly and spasmodically. Conflict between papacy and empire continued to smolder and flare early in the twelfth century, but it was not until the Council of Pisa (1135) that the first partial linkage of Crusade to Christian opponents of the papacy was made. Pope Innocent II, probably as a result of a mixture of desperation and experimentation, granted the indulgence to those willing to fight against the Norman king of Sicily. Pope Eugenius III, though he did not launch a Crusade against Christian opponents, laid the foundation for popes who later would do so by severing the relationship between Crusade and a specific, devotional destination. Service for Church and Christ now seemed to be what defined Crusade, and this definition gave the movement the ability to float and drift without a specific geographical mooring. The Spanish campaign, as a result of similar circumstances, was comparable to crusading in the East. Extending the Second Crusade (1147–1149) to battle the pagan Wends in Saxony, however, created a precedent that could be used to support "crusading" against any enemy of Christendom.

Precedents are dear to lawyers in particular; thus, it really comes as no surprise that the first clearly defined Crusades against Christians were launched by the greatest of all the lawyer-popes, Innocent III. It is the height of irony that the first "political crusade" was supposedly geared toward defending the interests of a boy, young Frederick II, who was under the guardianship of Innocent (1198–1208) but who would later (as Holy Roman Emperor) become the target of political Crusades. Yet, the irony is mitigated by the fact that it was really geared toward defending papal territorial interests from a continuously encroaching German Empire. The "Crusade against Markward of Anweiler" (1199) was in reality an attempt to repel an imperial invasion of Sicily. Innocent's language is crucial to understanding the true origins of the Crusades against Christians; it bears all the markings of a use (or abuse) of case law. Markward was portrayed as "another Saladin," and an "infidel worse than infidels" who aligned himself with Sicilian Muslims against Christendom. In essence it was Crusade by analogy. Such language suggests that political crusading emerged as an offshoot of expeditions against Muslims rather than both activities rising from the same pool of ideas. Territorial ambitions and a monopoly on spiritual concessions and crusading apparatus merged to produce the greatest weapon the papacy ever wielded in

ALL CHRIST'S SHEEP

Fourteenth-century church official Marsiglio of Padua condemned Pope John XXII's attacks on Christians in The Defender of the Peace *(1324), a portion of which appears here:*

Of all that we have remarked on, the most wicked and serious harm, which cannot be passed over by anybody unwilling to be excluded from charity's law, has come about from the fact that the man holding the Roman see is casting into eternal disorder and destruction "all Christ's sheep," which he says were entrusted to him to be nourished with salutary doctrine. For putting bad in place of good, and darkness in place of light, he grants both verbally and in writing "absolution from guilt and punishment of any kind" to all who fight for a specified time, on horse or on foot, against the above-said faithful of Christ, those subjects of the Roman prince who obey him with constancy as their king, and who wish to do so. Acting personally and through orders, both verbally and in written proclamations, he declares that the latter are "heretics" and "rebels" against Christ's cross, that it is lawful to attack them in any way, and that they may be despoiled and finally destroyed. And, horrible to hear, he preaches and has it preached everywhere, by certain false so-called "brethren" eager for ecclesiastical preferment, that this is just as pleasing to God as fighting against the heathen overseas. Similarly, the said bishop grants this false pardon to those whose bodily weakness prevents them joining in the wickedness, providing that they get others to do so, for the same period of time, at their own expenses, or hand over the sum needed for this to his abominable collectors.

Nobody should be in any doubt that, according to the Catholic religion, this ridiculous and empty absolution will not benefit those fighting in this manner, but rather do them harm. He is tricking the simple in this way into carrying out his impious desires, for it is not in his power vocally to grant [these things]; indeed he leads them down and misleads them to the everlasting ruin of their souls. For those who unjustly attack and invade other people's countries, those who disturb the peace and quiet of the innocent faithful, whom they know to be true Catholics, defending their own country and observing their fealty to their true and rightful lord, those who despoil, kill or attack in other ways, are the soldiers not of Christ but of the Devil. They plunder, burn, steal, murder, fornicate, commit adultery, and perpetrate almost every other kind of misdeed. So it is patently obvious that far from earning forgiveness, they deserve to be prosecuted, and damned for all eternity. And yet they are seduced into doing this by the words and writings of a man who calls himself (although he is not) Christ's vicar on earth.

Source: Documents on the Later Crusades, 1274–1580, edited by Norman Housley (New York: St. Martin's Press, 1996), pp. 52–53.

the arena of international politics. Excommunication and interdict paled in comparison.

Innocent's other Crusade against Christians, the Albigensian Crusade (1209–1229), is much more problematic. Although it had political and territorial dimensions, it really cannot strictly be considered a political crusade. Catharism, more so than any other Christian heresy, bordered on being an entirely different religion that attached itself to Christian sensibilities while vociferously rejecting Church authority. Political Crusades were waged against men who considered themselves, and were considered by many others, as Catholic. The Albigensian Crusade was Innocent's response to a heresy that was so widespread in a particular region (mostly southern France), and one that had at least tacit support in the highest local circles, that the launching of a Crusade was seen as a response of last resort. Still, its widespread support signals a turning point of great importance in crusading against Christians: heretics within Christendom were even more threatening than infidels without. This formula reached its most clear definition long after the Albigensian Crusade in the words of the great canonist Hostiensis: crusading against heretics at home should be pursued with even greater rigor than warfare against infidels beyond the sea since the former were a more palpable threat than the latter. Since the papacy had wide powers in defining heresy, the label of *heretic* could be transferred with ease to any of its opponents. The papal see took on the spiritual significance of Jerusalem and thus became an end to which the means of Crusade was universally applicable.

This concept was applied, with exceptional vigor, throughout the thirteenth century. By playing the "Crusade card," the papacy ultimately won its drawn-out battle with the Hohenstaufen emperors and destroyed the dynasty. In 1239 Pope Gregory IX proclaimed a Crusade against Frederick II; after the latter's death successful Crusades were launched against survivors of his line until none were left. In reality these expeditions were little more than wars of territorial protection or expansion (depending on one's perspective) even if they were cloaked in the language of the reformed papacy and bolstered by the machinery of crusading organization. The papacy was the spiritual head of Christendom, but it was also the seat of a secular lordship that it was determined to maintain at the very least and expand if possible. By extending the trappings of crusading to lay powers with compatible interests, such as Charles of Anjou with regard to Sicily and the Hohenstaufens, the papacy created a virtual steamroller that

would clear a path to its political goals. By the close of the century Pope Boniface VIII launched a Crusade for personal goals, that is, against the family of two cardinals who questioned the validity of his election.

Were Crusades against Christians a relatively late mutation of crusading against Muslims, or was the concept present, in an incipient form, in the blend of ideas that produced the movement? Agreeing with the latter proposition imposes a degree of linearity that the evidence does not warrant. Some men associated with Gregory VII's circle certainly concerned themselves with the prospect of holy war against political rivals and spent a considerable amount of time devising justifications for it. But this episodic event had little to do with the origin or motivation of crusading except in the grossest general terms of advocating "holy war" (which was not unique to the eleventh century).

Rather than constituting a continuation of Gregory's approach, Urban's plan seems to have been a retreat from it. Thus, the original author of "Crusades" did not see it as a tool to use against Christian opponents of the papacy. Papal conflict with secular powers continued and, over a period of time, was fused with the apparatus supporting Crusades against Muslims. When looking for the true architects of Crusades against Christians, it is not to the eleventh century that one should turn. Rather it is toward the great lawyer-popes, beginning with Innocent III, who had visions of ecclesiastical hegemony that Gregory VII and his supporters could not possibly have dreamed of. They did this by channeling the crusading impulse and institutions against enemies that were "worse than infidels," a euphemism for any significant Christian threat to the papacy.

–CARL HILL,
LOS ANGELES, CALIFORNIA

Viewpoint:
No. Crusades against Christians sprang from the same roots and depended on the same legal superstructure as Crusades against Muslims.

Traditionally, scholars of the crusading movement have viewed the political Crusade against heretical or schismatic Christians in Europe as a later offshoot of the original idea of Crusade against non-Christians. However, the truth of the matter is far more compli-

POLITICAL
CRUSADES

cated. About a decade before Pope Urban II called for a Crusade against non-Christians at the Council of Clermont (1095), Bishop Bonizo of Sutri, a churchman involved in the Investiture Contest (1075–1077) between German king Henry IV and Pope Gregory VII, issued his own literary summons to holy war against Henry and his Antipope Clement III. Because Bonizo's summons lacks the juridical elements of a formal Crusade, most notably an indulgence for the remission of the temporal punishments of confessed sins, it would be inaccurate to call his proposed military campaign a Crusade. However, his proposal is certainly an antecedent to the idea of Crusade against dissident Christians, and its emergence out of the same late-eleventh-century milieu as

the idea of Crusade against non-Christians suggests that it might be better to think of the political Crusade as a related but distinct phenomenon from Urban's idea of Crusade and not merely as its appendage.

Bonizo issued his call to holy civil war in *Liber ad amicum* (circa late 1085 or early 1086), his history of papal-imperial relations, which was written during a veritable religious civil war between Henrican and Gregorian partisans that had been raging for some time. For three years the forces of the German monarch and the Antipope besieged the Pope in Rome before finally gaining entrance into the city in the spring of 1084. By late 1085 or early 1086 Gregory had died in exile in Salerno, and the bishop of Sutri was exiled in the territory of

Illumination of Cathars being ejected from the town of Carcassonne, from *Les chroniques de France* (fourteenth century)

(British Library, London)

the loyal Gregorian, Countess Matilda of Tuscany, having been chased from Sutri three years earlier by Henry's army as it approached Rome. Thus, it was under Matilda's protection that Bonizo issued his call to arms against Henry and Clement.

In *Liber ad amicum,* Bonizo drew upon Scripture, Christian history, and patristic literature to construct a justification for waging war against heretical Catholics. Interestingly, from his own perspective, he was not so much constructing an argument for holy civil war as he was recovering one from Christian antiquity that the passage of time hid from the view of his contemporaries. Ostensibly, he wrote his history in response to an historical question of a friend. At the outset of Book I, he reminds his friend that he had asked him this question: based on the teachings of the church fathers, "was it ever permissible or is it even now permissible for a Christian to fight for religious truth with weapons?" Using his own allegorical interpretation of two episodes recorded in Genesis involving the Hebrew patriarch Isaac, Bonizo offered his scriptural justification for such a course of action. Indeed, Abraham's banishment of his slave girl Hagar, and his son by Hagar, Ishmael, in Genesis 21, for Ishmael's taunting of little Isaac, is used by Bonizo to teach that if the sword of preaching cannot curb the violence of belligerent heretics then, the Catholic faithful may take up the material sword against unbelievers. Conversely, Isaac's patient endurance of the hostility of his Philistine neighbors in Genesis 26 is used to teach that Catholics should overcome persecution by non-Catholics through the patient endurance of such persecution.

Indirectly, Bonizo admits that his prescription for fighting for religious truth with weapons represents a departure from early Christian practice. He readily acknowledges that Jesus, the apostles, and the ancient martyrs overcame persecution through patient endurance of it. However, he argues that Roman emperor Constantine I's conversion to Christianity fundamentally altered the relationship between the Church and the Roman state. In a clear allusion to the apocryphal legend of Pope Sylvester I's baptism of Constantine, Bonizo reasons that when through peaceful means the Roman see finally converted the leader of the empire to the Christian religion, it subjected the sovereign power of the empire to its authority. With Constantine's conversion, then, emperors became members of Christ's flock entrusted to St. Peter and subject to the authority of St. Peter's successors, the bishops of Rome. Therefore, the Gregorian partisans need not patiently endure Henry IV's persecution of

their cause as Isaac had endured the harassment of the Philistines. Rather, they (or at least laymen in their ranks) could legitimately punish the German emperor and his Antipope as Abraham had punished Hagar and Ishmael.

Throughout the remaining eight books of his history, Bonizo develops different aspects of this basic argument. In Book II he cites three alleged historical precedents (all taken from sixth-century Roman writer Cassidorus's *Tripartite History*) for armed resistance against wicked public officials, one of which involves the people of Milan protecting Catholic bishops with weapons against the evil designs of the Arian emperor Constantius I. In Books II to IV he also presents his reader with historical examples of both the persecution of God's priests and his Church by wicked emperors (for example, Constantius I, Julian the Apostate, and Carolingian king Lothair II) and the veneration of God's ministers and his Church by righteous emperors (for example, Constantine I, Theodosius I, and Justinian I). The inference that he wants his audience to draw from this comparison is obvious: by his orchestration of the rebellion against Gregory VII, Henry showed himself to be the heir of the wicked emperors and not their pious counterparts, and thus was deserving of punishment.

Beginning in Book V, the Bishop of Sutri introduces his reader to contemporary model holy warriors. He praises the soldiers of the papal army, which Pope Leo IX organized, who fell at the Battle of Civitate (1053) fighting the forces of the Norman duke Robert Guiscard. Although the engagement at Civitate went poorly for the papal army, Bonizo asserts that God approved of the efforts of Leo's troops who fell in battle. Through signs and miracles (which presumably occurred at their grave sites) God showed that those who had died fighting in a righteous war had pleased him and were now numbered among the saints. All of which, Bonizo believes, was God's way of providing great assurance to future generations who are willing to fight for righteousness's sake.

More important, in Books VI and VII the author weaves into his discussion of papal-imperial relations the martial exploits of the leader of the Milanese *Pataria,* Erlembald Cotta. Indeed, he and Gregory VII are the chief heroes of Bonizo's history. Almost from the inception of their fight (circa 1056–1057), the Patarene reformers were embroiled in bitter conflict with the ecclesiastical establishment in Milan, which staunchly resisted the efforts of the *Pataria* to end the practices of simony and clerical marriage in the Milanese Church. From 1065 to 1075 violence repeatedly flared up between the forces of the *Pataria* and the conservative aristocracy. Moreover, the veritable religious civil war, which raged in Lombardy's chief city, also brought papal reformers in Rome into conflict with German king Henry IV. For, whereas the reform papacy was generally supportive of the Patarenes' reform program and its extension to neighboring Lombard cities, the German monarch was adamantly opposed to the triumph of a radical reform movement in any of the cities of his Italian Kingdom. Bonizo does not hesitate to draw attention to this fact in several places in *Liber ad amicum*. In fact, according to Bonizo, Henry was an ally of the enemies of the *Pataria* in Milan.

A close reading of *Liber ad amicum* reveals that the *Pataria* and its often violent campaign against ecclesiastical abuses in Milan and beyond were subjects close to its author's heart. Evidence in this text and other writings of Bonizo strongly suggests that he began his ecclesiastical career as a Patarene activist in Cremona and that he wrote his book in the hope of stirring Patarene knights in Lombardy to the cause of the Gregorian party against Henry and the Antipope. To this end, he reminds his audience of the martial exploits of the then-deceased Erlembald. Three times in *Liber ad amicum* he refers to Erlembald as the "soldier of God." Indeed, he was a soldier of God "like Judas Maccabeus." However, whereas Judas Maccabeus led the Jews in rebellion against the religious pollution introduced into Israel by the Seleucid monarchy in Syria, Erlembald led a "multitude of the army of God" against the "enemies of God" in Milan who had polluted the Church there through simony and clerical marriage. According to Bonizo, Erlembald simply wanted to liberate the Milanese Church from the tyranny of the aristocrats, to whom he disparagingly refers several times as the "sellers of the churches." Neither Erlembald nor Bonizo was concerned with liberating the Christian East or Jerusalem from the tyranny of Islam. Interestingly, however, although Bonizo neglects to mention it, Andrew of Strumi relates that Erlembald went on pilgrimage to Jerusalem before becoming a prominent figure in the *Pataria*. Regardless, like many of Leo IX's troops at Civitate, Erlembald too was killed in action. Shortly after Easter of 1075, he was killed during a street fight in Milan. Yet, as was also the case with the fallen members of Leo's army, Bonizo reports that miracles soon occurred at the Patarene knight's tomb.

Significantly, the bishop of Sutri waits until near the end of the ninth and final book of *Liber ad amicum* to bring forward patristic evidence in support of his proposition. Here he cites statements from early Christian fathers Augustine of Hippo, Ambrose, Jerome, Pope Gregory I (the Great), and even from Gregory of Tours. On the whole his canonical argument for holy civil war is quite weak. His citations from the works of Ambrose and Jerome are especially taken out of context and do great violence to their authors' original meaning.

Ultimately, his chief argument is that if it is permissible for a Christian to fight for any reason, then it is permissible to fight for the true faith. He contends that "if it has ever been lawful for a Christian to be a soldier for any reason, then, it is lawful to fight the *Guibertistas* (the supporters of the Antipope Clement, the former Guibert of Ravenna) in all ways." In this regard, Augustine's *Letter* 189, addressed to the Roman commander Boniface, which Bonizo draws upon in Book IX, is invaluable to him. Here Augustine assures Boniface that one can be a good Christian and a soldier.

Finally, in the peroration of his work Bonizo urges the "soldiers of the most glorious God" to fight for "truth" and "righteousness." He implores them to imitate the "most excellent Countess Matilda" who fights with all her strength against heresy, which then was sowing its seed in the Church. Of course, the heresy to which he refers is that of revolting with weapons against a legitimate pope.

As Bonizo's *Liber ad amicum* proves, long before the emergence of Catharism in Languedoc and Provence, the controversies of the eleventh-century reform era stimulated the development of a justification for the violent suppression of obstinate heretics. His work demonstrates that medieval churchmen were quite capable of devising a rationale for holy civil war without the benefit of the example of Crusades against non-Christians before them. Essentially, the political Crusades of the thirteenth and fourteenth centuries differ from Bonizo's proposal in their clearly defined juridical form. In this regard the example of previous Crusades against non-Christians was crucial. In short, then, the Crusades against wayward Christians of the High and Late Middle Ages might have been dependent upon the Crusade against non-Christians for their legal superstructure, but not for their inspiration.

–JOHN A. DEMPSEY,
FRAMINGHAM STATE COLLEGE

References

Uta-Renate Blumenthal, *The Investiture Controversy: Church and Monarchy From the Ninth to the Twelfth Century* (Philadelphia: University of Pennsylvania Press, 1988).

H. E. J. Cowdrey, "The Papacy, the Patarenes and the Church of Milan," The Royal Historical Society, fifth series, 18 (1968).

Norman Housley, "Crusades against Christians: Their Origins and Early Development, c. 1000–1216," in *Crusade and Settlement: Papers Read at the First Conference of the Society for the Study of the Crusades and the Latin East and Presented to R. C. Smail,* edited by Peter W. Edbury (Cardiff: University College Cardiff Press, 1985).

Housley, *The Italian Crusades: The Papal-Angevin Alliance and the Crusades against Christian Lay Powers, 1254–1343* (Oxford: Clarendon Press, 1982; New York: Oxford University Press, 1982).

Elizabeth Kennan, "Innocent III and the First Political Crusade: A Comment on the Limitations of Papal Power," *Traditio,* 17 (1971): 231–249.

Kennan, "Innocent III, Gregory IX and Political Crusades," in *Reform and Authority in the Medieval and Reformation Church,* edited by Guy Fitch Lytle (Washington, D.C.: Catholic University of America Press, 1981).

Karl F. Morrison, ed., *The Investiture Controversy: Issues, Ideas, and Results* (New York: Holt, Rinehart & Winston, 1971).

Peter Partner, *The Lands of St. Peter: The Papal State in the Middle Ages and the Early Renaissance* (London: Eyre Methuen, 1972; Berkeley: University of California Press, 1972).

I. S. Robinson, *Authority and Resistance in the Investiture Contest: The Polemical Literature of the Late Eleventh Century* (Manchester: Manchester University Press / New York: Holmes & Meier, 1978).

Frederick H. Russell, *The Just War in the Middle Ages* (Cambridge & New York: Cambridge University Press, 1975).

Brian Stock, *The Implications of Literacy: Written Language and Models of Interpretation in the Eleventh and Twelfth Centuries* (Princeton: Princeton University Press, 1983).

Joseph R. Strayer, "The Political Crusades of the Thirteenth Century," in *The Later Crusades, 1189–1311,* edited by R. L. Wolff and H. W. Hazard, volume 2 of *A History of the Crusades,* edited by Kenneth M. Setton, second edition (Madison: University of Wisconsin Press, 1969).

POPULAR CRUSADES

Were the Popular Crusades legitimately a part of the crusading movement?

Viewpoint: Yes. The Popular Crusades were true Crusades because the participants vowed to defend the Holy Land.

Viewpoint: No. The Popular Crusades lacked papal organization and approval.

The term *Popular Crusades* is applied to those crusading expeditions that were organized and launched at the lower rungs of the medieval European hierarchy. There is some debate on whether they should be considered legitimate Crusades or just a related form of holy war or unintended offshoot of the movement. In either case, the Popular Crusades began at the same time as the official Crusades. Without doubt, Pope Urban II had a limited view of desirable participants for the expedition to the East—namely, the warrior aristocracy and maritime republics that would provide sea support. Almost instantaneously, however, itinerant preachers such as French monk Peter the Hermit began proclaiming their own version of the Crusades, and these Popular Crusaders first reached the East.

The crusading movement was for the most part, at least after the First Crusade (1096–1102), an elitist venture dominated by lay lords, their troops, and the Church. Popular Crusades, however, continued to live on, even if sporadically. Other than the popular contingents of the First Crusade, the two main Popular Crusades that have attracted attention were the so-called Children's Crusade (1212) and the Shepherds' Crusades (1251, 1309, 1320). The Children's Crusade is now recognized as a misnomer since its participants were not really children. The term *pueri* (boys) referred to their social class rather than age; thus, the expedition ranks among the Popular Crusades of the thirteenth century. The Shepherds' Crusades were not manned solely by shepherds but were popular uprisings of the lower classes. While the Children's Crusade was relatively peaceful, the Shepherds' Crusades were extremely violent.

The debate as to whether the Popular Crusades qualify as Crusades primarily revolves around the issue of authorization, making it part of the wider "what were the Crusades" question. If papal authorization is seen as the ultimate measure of a Crusade, then the Popular Crusades of the thirteenth and fourteenth centuries would not qualify, while the expedition of Peter the Hermit would be murky. If the Crusades were something more than a particular form of expedition launched by the papacy, then the Popular Crusades would qualify. The debate is deeply rooted in the question of what defines and gives shape to any movement, the grassroots perceptions of the majority or the official versions proffered by the elite.

Viewpoint:
Yes. The Popular Crusades were true Crusades because the participants vowed to defend the Holy Land.

Class is a concept that has wreaked havoc in the historiography of the Crusades. Many theories have attempted to steer clear of it. Lower-class participation in the Crusades was once seen (and still is by some) as little more than an embarrassment. The unwashed masses, from the beginning of the movement, acted unseemly, mercurially, violently, and irrationally. Some historians argued that in many ways they tainted the history of the movement by leaving a bad taste in the mouths of readers who should be focusing on the great deeds of the elite. Western historians, however, could hardly ignore class altogether. The word and the concept were loaded: intellectual, as well as social, dynamite that left many scars on, and unresolved issues in, the European past. Marxist history, and later the new history that tried to recover the stories of the disenfranchised and adopt new methodologies, changed this orientation somewhat. The masses with no or little voice became respectable, even fashionable, subjects for historical inquiry. Virtues could be found, for example, in the English working class. But what virtues (except anachronistic Marxist ones) could be found in the violent exploits of participants in the Popular Crusades?

Scholarly attention in crusading historiography has slowly accommodated lower-class participation in the Crusades in more meaningful ways. Occasionally, there is a stunning statement that bears on them directly, such as the theory that French monk Peter the Hermit was the true founder of crusading and that the Crusades began as a mass rather than elite movement. Blame for the atrocities committed by the first Popular or People's Crusade has been spread out as recent scholarship has revealed an aristocratic, even if small, element to it. Studies inspired by the New History have been increasing in number, but the bulk of attention still falls upon kings and barons, popes and canon lawyers, and high politics and international relations. The majority of scholarly output on the Crusades still underscores the elite. Even the debate on what constitutes or defines a Crusade has been by and large an elitist subject, focusing on papal policy, Church councils, royal chanceries, canon law, juridical formulae, and theater of operations. Crusading has been seen both overtly and tacitly as an enterprise initiated, staffed, defined, and conducted by the elite of western Europe. This focus places the Popular Crusades of the lower classes in a strange position. They were either perversions of Crusades or not Crusades at all. This conclusion may well be true—if one considers the Crusades as a clearly defined and well-regulated venture of the European elite.

Modern historians are not alone in having a class-based bias in approaching the Crusades. Many contemporaries did as well, including the movement's father. Pope Urban II was clear about who he wanted to participate in the First Crusade (1096–1102): aristocratic warriors and sailors from the Maritime republics. Urban's main goal in launching the First Crusade is debatable, but the means of securing that objective, whatever it was, is obvious: he wanted to employ a body of warriors drawn from the aristocracy. Thus, the original architect designed the Crusade as an elite venture. The main tool that he chose to fashion it, however, dictated otherwise. Since the Crusade was launched as an armed pilgrimage, participation could not be restricted to one class or even one gender. Women, the poor, the elderly, the lame—all could participate. The Pope could discourage noncombatants, but he could not bar them from participation. Essentially, Urban had little control over the First Crusade. He proclaimed and promoted the expedition, but because joining hinged on making a personal and voluntary vow that was open to all, he could not control it.

There has been a tendency among some historians to exclude Popular Crusades from the movement. Viscerally, this reaction has often been prompted by revulsion toward these expeditions for not being what they were supposed to be. Rationally, papal authorization and control have been cited as prime reasons for striking these movements from the official crusading roster. For a Crusade to be a Crusade, it must have been authorized and sanctioned by the papacy, and since the Popular Crusades were not, they really were not Crusades at all but chaotic offshoots of the movement spawned by the massive unleashing of religious zeal prompted by real Crusades. This conclusion presumes too much; the greatest presumption of all is that the papacy truly monopolized and controlled the movement. On the contrary, the reality seems to have been that while the papacy could inaugurate Crusades, real control was in the hands of the laity. Crusades, in other words, were truly made by those who responded to a call, not the men who made the call. The aristocracy created elite Crusades and the lower classes created Popular Crusades. If the latter were not what they were supposed to be, it was only to the mind of the elite. The masses were capable of payback in the same

Illumination of Peter the Hermit's pilgrim army being attacked by Bulgarians; from *Les Passages fait Outremer* (circa 1490)

(Bibliothèque Nationale, Paris)

vesthier dvs le mois d' Nouembre. d'mil. mIIII. vb. Touteffoie po les dame apurils que pour pir journir tant dmiterense z qmint kebouine conuoioit se qencias par tenent Rendu quint temps et aussi pour la predication delle. dns restui Gunsier sanz sci noir. z ses qens qui furent les

premiers Comme say dit. se dep turent du sieu ou ils auoient en tirprins culx assembler le vm; jour du mois de nuire auant passauce. Lan rvi mIIII. vb. z commencer san apres la bene diction du Sunt C leurebenit z luisi que se fait on puisemeut de prire. Lesquels passereut

coin, such as the Shepherds', or Pastoureaux, Crusade (1251) in the mid thirteenth century, when the lower classes claimed an aristocratic Crusade was not what it was supposed to be and thus ended in failure. Both elite and Popular Crusades were responses to and interpretations of the same stimulus, and both should be considered genuine Crusades.

The First Crusade was an armed pilgrimage, but it was also one that was forcefully urged, according to the Pope, by Christ. Urban made this point clearly and he, in his capacity of Christ's earthly representative, promoted it. Tapping into the organizational machinery of the Church, Urban recruited through personal preaching engagements, by authorizing selected preachers, and through councils and letters. Immediately after the Council of Clermont (1095) a rival expedition emerged that will forever be associated with Peter the Hermit, who began his own preaching campaign and selected his own recruiting captains that he sent out to the masses. Although Peter was probably reacting to Urban's plan, he was by no means officially associated with it. Peter, moreover, did not draw upon the authorization of the official Church for legitimacy. He claimed to have been commissioned by Christ to organize and launch the expedition, and he brandished a letter from God as proof. Thus, two forms of Crusade emerged in the late eleventh century: an elitist one promoted by the Church and authorized by the Pope and another that was popular and authorized by God through Peter. If the People's Crusade is excluded on the basis that it was not truly papally authorized, one must first demonstrate that the papacy had a monopoly on the concept, and it alone could give authorization. Urban was ominously silent about—though undoubtedly well aware of—Peter's activity. So, to decide if the People's Crusade was a genuine Crusade (particularly at this early stage when the concept was not clearly defined), one must assess the situation based on scattered reactions to it at the time. Was it seen, in other words, by men of the day as being essentially the same as the activities Urban prompted?

Evidence indicates that this opinion was the case. Peter's warm reception by the masses is but one form of proof. More important, many members of the elite believed this expedition was a Crusade. There were, to be sure, elitist criticisms at the time that the People's Crusade was composed of bandits, brigands, murderers, and whores. This critique should be expected since the elite more often than not held the populace in contempt. However, some members of the elite viewed Peter's expedition with great regard. The French abbot Guibert of Nogent described Peter as a holy man and showed no sign of distinguishing between Urban's real Crusade and a counterfeit one springing from the masses. Many members of the lay aristocracy joined Peter's movement and led it into battle, demonstrating that at least some of them saw it as a real Crusade that did not differ from the one which was officially announced at Clermont. Byzantine emperor Alexius I Comnenus received Peter much as he did other crusading leaders, that is, with respect and suspicion. Once the official, aristocratic Crusaders caught up with Peter in the East, they treated him as a legitimate participant. Peter, in fact, was made the representative of the lower-class Crusaders and in that capacity participated in the committees that made major decisions during the campaign. The reasons for this willingness to include him are evident. The Crusade at this date was no more than an armed pilgrimage that was open to all. To exclude the popular element from it is to make a distinction that most men did not make at the time. At this point the papacy had no tangible monopoly on the Crusade and, even if it targeted the elite, it had to yield to popular participation.

The Children's Crusade (1212) is a more problematic issue to tackle. Much had changed between 1095 and 1212 that led to an increasing emphasis on the aristocratic nature of crusading. First, the poor experienced a de facto exclusion from crusading as the cost of expeditions rose. During the First Crusade the poor could readily join in because the main route was by land. Costly transport did not need to be arranged, and the poor could live off the land by raiding the locals or receiving their hospitality. Once the sea route came to dominance, it economically closed the possibility for (but did not completely shut out) the poor to participate. Holy Roman Emperor Frederick I (Barbarossa) even made it a prerequisite that a man must be able to support himself for two years in order to participate in his expedition. Second, the poor were beginning to be excluded de jure, as the Church struggled to gain increasing control over the movement. Defining and regulating Crusades began to attract the attention of more clerics.

The most significant development was the move to sever Crusade and pilgrimage, which was in the Church's interest for two main reasons. First, it made crusading more flexible in that an expedition could be directed regionally with greater precision. Second, by making Crusades something distinct from pilgrimage (beginning with Pope Alexander III), it gave the papacy greater control over who could participate in it. Pilgrimage was open to anyone; changing the relationship between it and Crusade gave thirteenth-century popes a control over the movement that eluded Urban. These popes and lawyers increasingly defined Crusade from above. Through vow redemption and prorated indulgences, the poor and noncombatants were given an alternative method for participating. The thirteenth century became the age of crusading bulls, documents written by the papacy that detailed the reasons for the expedition, its goals and targets, and the compensation that participants would receive. There are, however, nuances in this newly emerging Crusade paradigm that must be noted. Even in the age of crusading bulls, the popes were not the only ones who could initiate a Crusade. Secular rulers could decide to go on Crusade, though their decisions needed papal ratification for them to receive the official benefits. Furthermore, the new subtle distinction between Crusade and pilgrimage that was emerging was lost on many. Countless numbers of people still saw an intimate connection between the two ventures, while others continued to believe there was no essential difference.

That the Children's Crusade happened on the watch of Innocent III, the greatest of the crusading popes and a man dedicated to gaining control over them, makes it a fascinating subject for understanding the relationship between elite and popular crusading. Innocent's view of crusading as papally sanctioned holy wars in any authorized theater clashes starkly with the Children's Crusade, which followed the original model of the movement. The romantic myth of children setting out to save the Holy Land has been dispelled. The actual participants were lower-class adults referred to as *pueri* (boys). The term thus represents class rather than age. In many respects this Crusade was much like the People's Crusade. Its opening salvo can be found with Stephen, a shepherd, bringing a letter supposedly from Christ to the King of France announcing a Crusade to the Holy Land to liberate Jerusalem. In Germany a *puer* named Nicholas was allegedly visited by an angel that commanded him to enlist recruits to liberate Jerusalem. Elite reaction was mixed, but the general population received them enthusiastically. The movement swelled. Looking at the record, one is struck by the elite focus with who urged them to undertake such a task, clearly a concern with the new model of authorization and definition of Crusade. The question does not seem to have made much sense to the participants. No one authorized them—no one, that is, but Christ himself and his angels. They followed the old model, the one that they did not realize was obsolete in the minds of the elite. They clung to the idea of the Crusade's still being God's Will rather than the Pope's and thus open to individual initiative. Although they might not have found much support for this concept among the Christian elite (both lay and clerical), they found it in the grand reception given to them by the general population. Furthermore, the perception of the elite is not altogether clear for making the argument that the expedition was not a Crusade. Innocent III tried to absolve the Popular Crusaders of their vows. Chroniclers used crusading terminology to describe what was taking place regardless of their opinions about it. The elite response was ambivalent.

The First Shepherds' Crusade (1251) was a more radical and violent movement than the Children's Crusade. French king Louis IX's defeat and capture (1250) was the spark that ignited it. The Shepherds' Crusade was proclaimed and led by the Master of Hungary, who

probably was a renegade monk. Similar to the Crusade of Peter the Hermit and the Children's Crusade, authorization for the Shepherds' Crusade was not derived from the papacy. The Master of Hungary claimed to have a letter, not from Christ but from the Virgin Mary, that commanded him to organize and launch a Crusade. Peter's Crusade and the Children's Crusade were popular movements that paralleled official Church-sanctioned Crusades. The Pastoureaux Crusade paralleled but also actively challenged the elitist concept of crusading that had gained so much ground by the mid thirteenth century.

The Master of Hungary's argument was relatively simple. Pompous and proud nobles were punished in the failed Crusades for their vanity by suffering a humiliating defeat. Christ had always loved the poor and, in particular, the poorest of the poor, shepherds. Who was it, after all, that the angels first informed of the Incarnation? It was the shepherds and the humble poor, and it was therefore they who were the only hope of success in the Holy Land. Their objective was the recovery of Jerusalem and freeing the captives of Louis's failed Crusade. Scottish philosopher Roger Bacon, who personally witnessed their arrival in Paris, was puzzled that such a wise woman as Blanche of Castile, the Queen Mother, received such rabble well. Bacon's explanation was sorcery and fascination. Some modern historians have explained her embracing the movement as the result of her psychological distress with the plight of her son. A more convincing explanation is that she recognized (at first) this movement as a legitimate Crusade. The old model still seems to have had currency outside high ecclesiastical circles. Personal vows to take the cross appear to have been valid in the eyes of some, including Louis's mother. In a certain sense the movement was pro-royal although anti-elite in every other way. This support for the monarchy probably had much to do with Louis's new approach to justice and equity before departing for the East.

The decisive anticlerical tenor the movement quickly took on gave much cause for concern. Mendicants, Cistercians, and Benedictines; bishops and canons; and even university students were all considered to be perverse elitist distortions of Christ's simplicity and were attacked. Clerical opinion of them, therefore, was extremely hostile, much more so than elitist interpretations of Peter the Hermit and the Children's Crusade. English historian Matthew Paris, like Bacon, saw them as mere gangs of murderers and cutthroats. After the violent attacks on the clergy broke out, Blanche naturally turned against the Pastoureaux and gave the green light for checking them. Yet, this move did not prevent the people of Bourges, despite the opinion of the bailiffs, from throwing open the city gates and embracing them. Still, such a rabidly anticlerical Crusade could only have its lease on life extended so far. The central core was eventually hunted down and slaughtered. Does this orientation, however, mean it was not a Crusade? One fact that is hardly stressed enough, however, is that a significant portion of the Pastoureaux survived extermination and actually made it to the Holy Land. They joined the French royal forces in the East and became full-fledged official Crusaders. If they were not real Crusaders by the general definition of the time, then how can one explain their integration into the official Crusade?

What conclusions can be drawn from these three examples of Popular Crusades and their relationship to official Crusades? The most salient feature of these Popular Crusades is that they sprang from a different system of authorization (that was present for the genesis of the movement) and in a sense resemble the conflict between mystics who received direct personal revelations and the official Church with its claims to being the sole gateway between heaven and earth. The official Church monopoly on religion was challenged both within and beyond the parameters of the crusading movement. The populist contingents in the First Crusade had the luxury of having acted before the movement had a definition imposed upon it by the elite. No one really knew what a Crusade was at that time, so posterity is hardly in a position to exclude anyone or any branch. The so-called Children's Crusade took place at a categorical crossroads, and few contemporaries were sure what to make of it. Alexander III's move to sever Crusade from pilgrimage was still quite new, and the ambivalent attitude of the elite toward it reflected the still novel notion that popes had complete control over the movement. The Shepherds' Crusade, regardless of its anticlerical effects, began from the same platform. But the aftermath of Innocent III's transformation of crusading, as well as the work by the canon-lawyer-turned-Pope, Innocent IV, and his pupil Hostiensis, increasingly tightened the definition of crusading and papal control of it. Even though the official Church was defining Crusade in an elitist and centralized way, the old model continued, and it captured the imagination of those outside high secular and ecclesiastical political circles. The unauthorized Children's Crusade, in fact, might have been more consistent with the foundations of the movement than the authorized Albigensian Crusade (1209–1229).

To exclude Popular Crusades from the movement is to buy wholesale into the papal and aristocratic desire to define what crusading should be. Movements should, however, be defined by what they were rather than by what they should have been. The Traditionalist and Pluralist debate on defining Crusades by their destination need not concern us. Popular Crusades were without exception directed toward the Holy Land, so destination is not at issue. Pluralists, who define Crusades by the essentially papal criteria (did the pontiff say it was a Crusade and provide compensation accordingly?), find themselves in the strange predicament of trying to expand the definition of Crusades while simultaneously restricting them when it comes to Popular Crusades. They thus become prisoners to a formula by stressing the plenitude of papal power, a concept that Christians approached with ambivalence. What is at issue is who (if anyone) monopolized the movement. In the final analysis the decision rests on whose view one subscribes to—the literate elite and lawyers who formed the minority of the Christian community, or the majority who still viewed crusading as being an activity initiated by a personal, voluntary vow to "take the cross." Crooking the knee to the elitist view gives too much credit to a minority, assigning to it complete control over the hearts and minds of the majority, a condition that simply did not exist. Such a view excludes expeditions that were more consistent with the original goals of the movement and adds anything that could be passed off as simply a papal just war. Expeditions in which participants took a vow (public or private) to travel to and secure the Holy Land is a definition of Crusade that is more consistent with what most people probably thought at the time.

–MARK T. ABATE,
WESTFIELD STATE COLLEGE

Viewpoint:
No. The Popular Crusades lacked papal organization and approval.

Any standard work on the history of the Crusades eventually mentions ventures that are typically referred to as Popular Crusades. In one sense it is somewhat erroneous of modern historians to selectively term only some Crusades as popular, for in truth the crusading movement remained a widely popular cause throughout the Middle Ages. Even into the sixteenth century, dreams and plans for campaigns to recover Jerusalem drew the emotional, if not tangible, support of the vast majority of Europeans, indicating that even at this late stage the movement retained much of its original appeal. In this more

WRETCHED BAND OF PILGRIMS

French chronicler Albert of Aix describes the end of the Peasants' Crusade for the majority of the participants in Peter the Hermit's march to the East:

The foot-soldiers came in a body to Reinald of Broyes, Walter the Penniless, to Walter of Breteuil, also, and to Folker of Orleans, who were leaders of Peter's army, to urge them to rise in a body in vindication of their brethren and against the audacity of the Turks. But they positively refused to go without the presence and counsel of Peter. Then Godfrey Burel, master of the foot-soldiers, upon hearing their response, asserted that the timid by no means avail so much in war as the bold; and in sharp words he frequently reproached those men who prevented their other companions from pursuing the Turks to avenge their brethren. On the other hand, the leaders of the legion, unable to endure his insults and reproaches any longer, or those of their own followers, were deeply moved by wrath and indignation and promised that they would go against the strength and wiles of the Turks, even if it should happen that they died in battle.

Nor was there delay; at dawn on the fourth day, all the knights and foot-soldiers throughout the entire camp were ordered to arm themselves, to sound the trumpets, and to assemble for battle. Only the unarmed, the countless sick, and the women remained in camp. But all the armed men, to the number of 25,000 foot-soldiers and 500 knights in armor, pressed on their way together toward Nicaea, in order to avenge their brethren by provoking Soliman and the rest of the Turks to engage in battle. And so, divided and arrayed in six battle lines, with standards uplifted in each, they advanced on the right and on the left.

Boasting and shouting with vehement tumult and great clamor, they had scarcely advanced through the aforesaid forest and mountain region three miles from the port of Civitote, their halting place, (Peter being absent and unaware of all this), when lo! Soliman, with all his intolerable following, entered that same forest from the opposite side. He was coming down from the city of Nicaea to fall suddenly upon the Gauls in camp, intending at the point of the sword to wipe out and destroy them, unaware and unprepared. Upon hearing the approach and the violent outcry of the Christians, he marvelled greatly what this tumult meant, for all that the Christians had decided was unknown to him. . . .

But the Franks, unaware of Soliman's approach, advanced from the forest and the mountains with shouting and loud clamor. There they beheld the battle lines of Soliman in the midst of the field, awaiting them for battle. When they had seen the Turks, they began to encourage one another in the name of the Lord. . . .

There Walter the Penniless fell, pierced by seven arrows which had penetrated his coat of mail. Reinald of Broyes and Folker of Chartres, men of the greatest renown in their own lands, fell in like martyrdom, destroyed by the enemy, though not without great slaughter of the Turks. But Walter of Breteuil, son of Waleramnus, and Godfrey Burel, master of the foot-soldiers, having slipped away in flight through briars and thickets, turned back along the narrow path where the entire band, withdrawn from battle, had gathered together. When the flight and desertion of these men became known, all turned in flight, hastening their course towards Civitote along the same route by which they had come, but with little defense against the enemy.

And so the Turks, rejoicing in the pleasing success of victory, were destroying the wretched band of pilgrims, whom they followed for a distance of three miles, killing them even at the camp of Peter. And going within the tents, they destroyed with the sword whomever they found, the weak and the feeble, clerics, monks, old women, nursing children, persons of every age. But they led away young girls whose face and form were pleasing in their eyes, and beardless youths of comely countenance. . . .

. . . . Towards that fortress three thousand pilgrims rushed in flight. They entered the ruined fortress in hope of defense. But finding no gates or other obstacles, and anxious and deprived of aid, they piled up their shields for a gate, along with a huge pile of rocks; and with lances, wooden bows, and sling-stones, they bravely defended themselves from the enemy. But the Turks, seeing that they were having but little success in killing those inside, surrounded the fortress, which was without a roof, on all sides. They aimed their arrows high, so that, as they fell from the air in a shower, they would strike the bodies of the enclosed Christians, destroying the poor wretches; and that all the others, at the sight of this, might be compelled to surrender.

Source: August C. Krey, The First Crusade: The Accounts of Eye-Witnesses and Participants (Gloucester, Mass.: Peter Smith, 1958), pp. 74–76.

POPULAR CRUSADES

general sense of the word, therefore, nearly all Crusades could rightly be labeled popular. Yet, on another level, it is understandable and even justifiable for historians to divide and categorize Crusades along the lines of whether they were popular or not when the word is used with a more restricted meaning. The word often refers specifically to those ventures that were fought in the name of crusading but were predominantly manned by low-ranking knights, peasants, and the poor. Often, these efforts were also organized in a spontaneous fashion without proper oversight and sanction from high-ranking Church or political officials, and they seldom achieved significant results. When the word is used in this latter, narrower sense, it becomes clear that Popular Crusades should not be considered legitimate crusading efforts at all.

In the original plan for crusading, there was little provision made for popular participation. What Byzantine emperor Alexius I Comnenus sought when he made his appeal to Pope Urban II for military assistance was a mercenary force of highly capable Western knights who could help him halt and perhaps drive back the Seljuk Turks who were menacing his southern border. In turn, what Urban thought he was initiating at the Council of Clermont (1095) was a recruitment of professional soldiers drawn from the knightly classes of the West, although he envisioned a much grander purpose for the enterprise than Alexius had suggested. For Urban the final strategic goal of the campaign was to be the capture of the religiously significant city of Jerusalem, while only one of the tactical goals would be securing Byzantium's southern border, as Alexius had desired. To achieve his more expansive program, Urban made the radical decision to organize the military campaign along the lines of the traditional devotional practice of pilgrimage. It proved to be an ingenious decision on his part because of the unique benefits a pilgrimage model gave to a military campaign that promised to be both extremely difficult and highly dangerous. What Urban had not foreseen, however, was that a war fought within the framework of traditional pilgrimage almost necessarily opened it up for participation beyond the noble class.

In hindsight the reason for this inclusion is rather obvious. Pilgrimages had for centuries been a widely practiced devotional exercise in which members from all levels of European society participated. Most often, pilgrims visited local shrines, but journeys to more distant places such as Santiago de Compostela, Rome, and even Jerusalem were not uncommon. In fact, during the eleventh century there was an explosion of pilgrimages to these more distant shrines, especially to Jerusalem, and, moreover, the participants in these long-range journeys came from

all levels of European society, including a significant number from the peasantry. By tapping into this widespread enthusiasm for pilgrimage, Urban realized that he could almost guarantee a strong response to his crusading appeal. However, at the same time, what Urban did not foresee was that while the lower classes of Europe viewed warfare as the exclusive preserve of the upper class, they believed pilgrimage to be a devotional practice open to all. Thus, in their minds the appeal for armed pilgrims issued by Urban was as much directed to them as to the knightly class, and they responded with a correspondingly robust enthusiasm. In fact, their participation easily outnumbered that of the knightly classes; during the main effort of the First Crusade (1096–1102), sometimes referred to as the Princes' Crusade by historians, these poor helped to play a decisive role in the final, successful outcome of the campaign. This Popular element of the Princes' Crusade indeed fulfilled the terms of a Crusade, and the poorer participants should thus be considered true Crusaders on a par with their more princely counterparts. The same, however, cannot be said for all aspects of the First Crusade.

Prior to the departure of the main princely army in August 1096, a large host of peasants, with a small collection of low-ranking knights at the lead, headed east in response to Urban's appeal. Along the way some contingents actually attacked Jewish enclaves in Germany, reasoning, at least ostensibly, that these Jewish residents represented as much a threat to Christendom as did the Muslims. Such sporadic attacks, although carried out by many of those who had taken the cross as an expression of their agreement to be Crusaders, should in no way be construed as representing legitimate crusading activity. The isolated pogroms carried out against Jewish communities during this Crusade, as with other crusading ventures of the twelfth century, never enjoyed official ecclesiastical sanction. In fact, such abuses, which were often conducted by the lower classes, were widely condemned by the highest echelons of Church leadership. Also, the persecution of Jews was never a stated or implied goal of the crusading movement, and so such activities cannot be rightly construed as representing Popular Crusades. They might have been popular or mob actions, but they were not Crusades.

Again, it is critical to have recourse to an accurate definition of the word *Crusade* to avoid confusions and misapplications of the term. A Crusade should be understood as a religiously motivated war pilgrimage fought at the behest of ecclesiastical authority with the intention of recovering lost Christian territory or defeating enemies of the Church, for which participants

POPULAR CRUSADES

received the spiritual reward of the indulgence for their vow of service. Clearly, the Jewish pogroms conducted by mob action while a crusading venture was underway do not meet the standards of this definition, even if some of the participants continued later on to take part in the real Crusade. There was no papal or ecclesiastical sanction for such attacks, there was no granting of an indulgence for such abuses, and there was no official ecclesiastical policy that classified Jews as enemies of the Church. The better way to understand these isolated events that coincided with the general preparations of crusading campaigns in the twelfth century is as no more than small mob actions that attempted to use the cover of crusading to carry out the perpetrators' maleficent, self-serving designs. Hence, to be accurate, historians should not apply the term *Popular Crusade* to such activities.

One final aspect of the popular element of the First Crusade should also be considered. Besides that group of peasants and low-ranking knights who attacked Jewish settlements in Germany, there were other loosely organized peasant groups that also set out for the East ahead of schedule. By July of 1096 most of these forces had reached Constantinople. When Byzantine officials surveyed the quality of this odd collection of would-be warriors, they were horrified. It bore little semblance to an army and certainly did not match Alexius's expectations of the military assistance he had asked for. Nonetheless, this band of premature Crusaders had come to fight, and with their eager zeal and lack of good order they eventually prevailed upon their wary host to give them transport to Asia Minor ahead of the main princely army. However, without the assistance of that main army, which had set out much later, this host of largely peasant Crusaders proved no match for the Turks and were summarily annihilated. In the end, were these individuals who were cut down, captured, or put to flight in northern Asia Minor real Crusaders? Although this initial wave achieved no tangible results, its participants should be considered true Crusaders. They had taken the cross and vow of service, despite papal misgivings about their appropriateness as soldiers, and they fought in support of an ecclesiastically sanctioned campaign, and as such they warranted the awarding of the indulgence. This phase of the well-known Peasant's Crusade therefore can be also termed appropriately a Popular Crusade.

The same cannot be said of the Children's Crusade (1212), perhaps the only other widely famous venture that is often referred to as a Popular Crusade. The details of this event remain somewhat obscure, but the consensus among historians is that groups of peasants from France

and southern Germany gathered together spontaneously in the summer with the intention of achieving by themselves crusading's strategic goal, the capture of Jerusalem. The early thirteenth century was a time of great interest in crusading activities. The fall of Jerusalem (1187) into Muslim hands was an event that was still not yet a generation old. While the ill-fated Fourth Crusade (1202–1204) did nothing to improve the chances of recapturing Jerusalem, the vast majority of Europeans were in no way discouraged by this failure. At the same time the more successful effort to eradicate heresy in southern France, the Albigensian Crusade (1209–1229), was already well underway, and a significant component of peasants joined this cause. Thus, caught up in this general crusading enthusiasm that permeated Europe, a group of rustics from France and southern Germany took it upon themselves to attempt the recapture of Jerusalem. Fired with idealistic visions, they concluded that the failures of recent ventures such as the Fourth Crusade were the result of the unworthiness of the nobles, whom, they believed, God was thwarting. Accordingly, they thought that God stood ready to reward the righteous with the prize of Jerusalem, and they planned to march to the East unarmed, relying on nothing but God's providence to hand this sacred city over to them. In the end, this band of peasants never found passage to the East and soon disbanded, with most of them returning home in somber disappointment.

Although the idealism of these youths captured the imagination of chroniclers, their effort never constituted a true crusading venture. There was no official crusading appeal to which they were responding. There was no sanctioned vow that they took for their participation, and there was no awarding of an indulgence for their efforts. While this rather peculiar event was thus not a true Crusade, the idealism of these participants strengthened the resolve of Pope Innocent III to call for a second major crusading campaign to the East, the end result of which was a bona fide expedition often called the Fifth Crusade (1217–1229). However, that is where the connection to crusading ends.

Other popular movements sporadically appeared in the years following the Children's Crusade, but none of these ever qualified as true Crusades either. For example, in the mid thirteenth century a spontaneous peasants' movement, sometimes referred to as the Crusade of the Shepherds (1251), occurred in France once again in response to a failed crusading venture, but it too proved to be short lived. With the failure of French king Louis IX to achieve success on his first campaign in Egypt (1248–1254) on his way to Jerusalem, these peasants concluded, much like the Children Crusaders before them, that the nobles had become unworthy to carry out God's plan and that only they, as the pure and simple, could obtain victory. This alleged Crusade, however, was no Crusade at all. It lacked all the elements that would have made it an official campaign. There were no ecclesiastical sanctions, no formal vows, and no indulgences granted. The only connection between the two was that the Shepherd Crusaders found their inspiration in the crusading movement. That, however, is not enough to grant to them the status as Crusaders any more than it would be appropriate to call a private citizen in a modern state who is inspired to clean up crime a police officer simply because there is a commonality in interest or stated goals.

The fact that participants in popular expeditions adopted the name *Crusader,* or were given the title by later historians, does not mean that they were truly participants in the crusading movement. It is also not sufficient to accord them this name simply because they might have been inspired by the cause and general public enthusiasm as they set off on their particular ventures. Crusading was an institution in medieval Europe with definite characteristics such as the vow, the indulgence, and ecclesiastical approval. It also granted to participants certain, definite legal privileges that coincided with their recognized status as Crusaders. In most cases what are termed *Popular Crusaders* were in fact not Crusaders at all, because they did not share in these institutional aspects of the movement. To use the term, therefore, in the manner that it is typically employed is to use in most cases an historical misnomer based either on a poor understanding of what a real Crusade was or on simple intellectual laziness to draw proper distinctions. In either case, mob actions should be noted for what they were and should thus be relegated to the footnotes of crusading history.

–CHRISTOPHER LIBERTINI,
SUFFOLK UNIVERSITY

References

Malcolm Barber, "The Crusade of the Shepherds in 1251," *Proceedings of the Tenth Annual Meeting of the Western Society for French History, 1982* (1984).

E. O. Blake and C. Morris, "A Hermit Goes to War: Peter and the Origins of the First Crusade," *Studies in Church History,* 22 (1985): 79–107.

G. Dickson, "The Advent of the pastores (1252)," *Revue belge de philologie et d'historie,* 66 (1988): 249–267.

Walter Porges, "The Clergy, The Poor, and the Non-Combatants on the First Crusade," *Speculum,* 21 (January 1946): 1–23.

Paul Raedts, "The Children's Crusade of 1212," *Journal of Medieval History,* 3 (1977): 279–333.

Jean Richard, *The Crusades, c. 1071 – c. 1291,* translated by Jean Birrell (Cambridge & New York: Cambridge University Press, 1999).

Jonathan Riley-Smith, *The First Crusade and the Idea of Crusading* (London: Athlone, 1987; Philadelphia: University of Pennsylvania Press, 1987).

Riley-Smith, *What Were the Crusades?* (London: Macmillan, 1977; Totowa, N.J.: Rowman & Littlefield, 1977).

RECONQUISTA

Was the *Reconquista* really a Christian reconquest of the Iberian Peninsula?

Viewpoint: Yes. The *Reconquista* was seen as a Christian recovery of the Iberian Peninsula from Muslim invaders.

Viewpoint: No. The *Reconquista* was actually a conquest of the Iberian Peninsula by the Spanish—a different people from the Goths, who lost the territory to the Muslims in the eighth century.

Many debates about Spanish history have had a polemical edge bearing on the question of "the Spanish character." As Américo Castro overstated this situation in *The Spaniards: An Introduction to Their History* (1971), "Among the peoples of the West, the Spaniard is the only one who is guided in the awareness of his past and of himself by a historiography based on fantastic notions." While one may reasonably doubt the uniqueness of the Spaniard's experience of his historiography, one still finds these "fantastic notions" informing contemporary scholarship. The so-called *Reconquista* (Christian reconquest of the Iberian Peninsula) is a case in point.

By midsummer of 711, Muslim troops of Tarik ibn Ziyad had killed the last Visigothic king, Roderick, and routed his troops. Aided by peoples living in the Visigothic kingdom, Arab and Berber armies subdued nearly all of the Iberian Peninsula by 714. Despite the initial conquest, not all of the peninsula was settled with Muslims. A narrow band of lands consisting primarily of the mountainous slopes and valleys of the Pyrenees did not remain under permanent Muslim control and reverted to local rulers. Such small and isolated Christian outposts were of little concern to the conquerors: as historian Ibn Hayyan expressed the Muslim perspective, "What are thirty barbarians perched on a rock?" Nevertheless, Christian chronicles of the ninth century attribute great significance to a revolt in Asturias of a certain Pelayo/Pelagius that occurred around 720—it was their point of view that less than a decade after the Muslim conquest, organized resistance led by Visigothic refugees had begun.

The question here is whether the extended process whereby Spanish Christians slowly pushed the Muslims southward and, eventually, out of the peninsula entirely, was *re*-conquest or just a conquest. Reconquest supposes that the same people who carried out this conquest were the same as had lost Spain. That clearly was not the case, at least in a literal sense, inasmuch as the losers of 711 were German-speaking Goths, while the winners of the Middle Ages spoke Spanish—people, that is, of two distinct and separate cultures and social structures. Viewed from a purely religious angle, reconquest has been used to describe a Crusade by medieval Christians to retrieve for Christianity lands that had been lost to the Muslims in the eighth century. This view was adopted by the Francisco Franco regime (1936–1975) that, it can be argued, used the reconquest-as-crusade to legitimize its own victory over the Spanish republicans whom it cast as godless communists—every bit as "infidel" as medieval Muslims had been. The problem for historiography has been that a whole generation of medieval historians, Spanish and foreign alike, were socialized into their fields under the general aegis of this ideologi-

241

cally tinged view of the medieval contest between Christians and Muslims. One of the problems with such a view of the reconquest is that to the extent it was indeed a Crusade, it was introduced late (twelfth century) and from outside of the country (France), both points having been something of an inconvenience to Franco-era historians. So the debate that has raged among medieval historians since around 1975, and that continues, is in part an effort to distinguish between medieval events and the perceptions of medieval people participating in them, with the outlook of present-day historians, some of whom (it has been argued) have projected their understanding of twentieth-century politics backward into the Middle Ages.

Viewpoint:
Yes. The *Reconquista* was seen as a Christian recovery of the Iberian Peninsula from Muslim invaders.

It cannot be legitimately argued that there was no continuity whatsoever between the defeat of the Visigoths by the Arab-led Berber army of 711 and the "legitimist" aspirations of the descendants of the defeated Goths to recover the territories lost. It must be admitted, however, that the notion that inheritors of the Gothic tradition viewed *Reconquista* (Christian reconquest of the Iberian Peninsula) as solely a Christian imperative seen in religious terms only, may in fact have played a role in the conquest of Al-Andalus, but not until the crusading movement began in the twelfth century. Any argument based on Christian, as opposed to "Spanish," nationalism before that time is specious.

This essay focuses on the political ideology of the medieval Spanish aristocracy: the struggle against the Muslims was a retrieval and restoration of the Visigothic kingdom, with both its political as well as religious capital in the city of Toledo. This notion of the reconquest, which toward the end of the Middle Ages had become the cornerstone in the ideology of Spanish nationalism, supposed that those Christian groups who had battled the Muslims did so in the name of the Gothic kings of Toledo who had "lost" the peninsula in the first place during the Arab invasion. Such an ideology, sometimes called "neo-Gothic" because it sought a restoration of the old Visigothic kingdom of Toledo, was a literary and historical invention. According to Peter Linehan, in *History and the Historians of Medieval Spain* (1993), the myth of the reconquest was born in the 880s, its objective being (according to the Chronicle of Alfonso III) "the recovery of Spain and the restoration of the Gothic army." A symbolic act that occurred in 883 solidified the claim that the kings of Asturias were the legitimate heirs of the Visigothic kingdom: the burial in Oviedo of Eulogius, propagandist of the Christian martyrs of Córdoba, himself a martyr. This act also makes clear that recon-

quest was both a sacred and a civil duty. From this beginning, the neo-Gothic myth, invented by historians in the court of Alfonso III, became the political program of the Middle Ages for Christian rulers.

The Christian minority living under Muslim rule—the Mozarabs—also preserved the memory of Visigothic Spain. They safeguarded the liturgy of their church and the learning of the great scholars of the Visigothic era, such as Isidore of Seville. Most important, they perpetuated the hope for a return to the legitimacy of Christian rule (although they also retained an undisguised disgust for the rulers who had lost the country).

In the late ninth century the kings of Asturias—a small Christian kingdom in Northwest Spain—began to promote the notion that the Asturian nobility was a continuation of the Visigothic royal line and that the Goths who had fled to Asturias to escape the Muslim onslaught were the legitimate heirs to the tradition of the Visigothic monarchy of Toledo. Alfonso I had symbolically transformed his modest rural capital of Oviedo into a new Toledo (*sicuti Toleto fuerat* [just as if it were Toledo]). By the eleventh century, Alfonso VI was identified as the descendant of the Visigothic king Reccared. Then Vermudo II reestablished Visigothic law (known as the *Forum Iudicum*) as the legal code of the kingdom, now with its capital in León. By the twelfth century, as the pace of the Christian attack picked up, the term "reconquest" actually came into general usage: the Christian army reconquered (*recunquisierat*) Muslim-held territory. After the reintroduction of the *Forum Iudicum,* medieval Spanish law texts and documents—both Castilian and Catalan—display a consciousness of the Visigothic origins of Spanish law. There are repeated, standardized references in medieval charters, such as "it is decreed in accordance with the laws of the Goths" or "just as we find written in the Gothic law."

Besides the issue of royal legitimacy, the other main party interested in promoting the notion of continuity with the Goths was the Church. Twelfth-century bishop of Oviedo, Pelayo (not to be confused with the Asturian nobleman, the ancestor of Alfonso I, identified by Franco-period historians as the initiator of the reconquest) wanted the Episcopal sees of the Christian Spanish kingdoms to appear as the direct successors of the Visigothic sees that, after 711, had been reallocated to reflect the altered political reality.

Thirteenth-century historians, such as Lucas of Tuy and Rodrigo Jiménez de Rada, actively promoted the notion of Gothic heritage. For Lucas, the Gothic loss of 711 had been the ruin of Spain. In Jiménez de Rada's *Historia Gothica* (Gothic History) the Gothic inheritance was transformed into a positive ethnic attribute. Such Gothic traits as ferocity were now exhibited by their rightful successors, the kings of Castile and León. In the *First General Chronicle* of Alfonso X the Wise of Castile, the rule of the Arabs was only an incidental episode in a long, continuous history of "Gothic" Spain.

In eastern Spain there were similar traditions. The Franks of the tenth century referred to Catalonia as the "land of the Goths." Ramon Berenguer the Elder, count of Barcelona, justified his right to make laws by claiming that he had inherited the authority that the Visigothic kings had previously held. Clearly, what had been a notion originally crafted for utilitarian reasons, to give meaning to a disjointed series of battles against the Muslims, had by the end of the Middle Ages become identified as the historical destiny of the Christian kings and all of their inhabitants.

There was a certain irony in the claims of a Christian Spain fragmented into several jurisdictionally and geographically discrete kingdoms to represent, singly and collectively, the unity of rule that had characterized the Visigothic state prior to 711. One of the oddities that this paradox produced was the notion of *Hispaniae* (the Spains) as if the sum total of the diverse Christian kingdoms was equally the heir to the Gothic mantle.

What emerged was a strongly ingrained conviction, expressed in the public statements of the Spanish medieval aristocracy, both lay and ecclesiastical, that the loss of Spain by the Visigoths in the eighth century was a wrong that their descendants had undertaken to right in retaking the former territories of the kingdom of Toledo from the Muslims. Of course, the overly literal expressions of neo-Gothicism, such as applying the lofty titles of royal officials to the simple retainers that served the early Asturian kings, point up the absurdity of their pretensions at the inception of the myth. But with the passage of time, myth—in this case, a religio-political belief system—has a way of acquiring reality. Whether modern historians can accept the reality of reconquest is one question; that medieval people accepted it as a program and acted upon it is beyond doubt.

—THOMAS F. GLICK,
BOSTON UNIVERSITY

SACK OF LISBON

Anglo-Norman Crusaders joined Spanish contingents in capturing Moorish strongholds along the western coast of the Iberian Peninsula. The following selection is from an English account of the fall of Lisbon in 1147:

When morning came the constables and leaders of our side went again to the King's court at about the ninth hour of the day in order to turn over the hostages and to attend to the many things necessary for the siege. Those of our boys who were carrying slings, meanwhile, provoked the enemy into advancing onto the field with the result that, being the more provoked by the slinging of stones from a distance, the enemy ventured a major attack. As our men, little by little, armed themselves, the enemy shut themselves within the suburb. They threw stones from the roofs of the houses which were enclosed by parapets, and thus they made it difficult for our men to enter. Our men, who were looking for an opening whereby they might get in, if there were such a thing, drove them back into the middle of the suburb. There they put up a strong resistance to us. Our men, little by little, increased in numbers and made a fiercer attack. Many, meanwhile, were struck by arrows and the missiles of the balistas and fell, for the volley of stones made it impossible to approach closer. Thus a great part of the day was spent. Finally, at sunset, our men got through some twisted passages which were scarcely passable even for unarmed men and, after a major encounter, occupied part of a hill. . . .

The Moors, meanwhile, made frequent sorties against our men by day because they held three gates against us. With two of these gates on the side of the city and one on the sea, they had an easy way to get in and out. On the other hand, it was difficult for our men to organize themselves. The sorties caused casualties on both sides, but theirs were always greater than ours. While we kept watch, meanwhile, under their walls through the days and nights, they heaped derision and many insults upon us. . . .

The Muslims were forced to surrender. When the German and Flemish troops arrived, they began to loot:

The men of Cologne and the Flemings, when they saw in the city so many spurs to their greed, did not observe their oaths or their religious guarantees. They ran hither and yon. They plundered. They broke down doors. They rummaged through the interior of every house. They drove the citizens away and harassed them improperly and unjustly. They destroyed clothes and utensils. They treated virgins shamefully. They acted as if right and wrong were the same. They secretly took away everything which should have been common property. They even cut the throat of the elderly Bishop of the city, slaying him against all right and justice.

Source: James A. Brundage, The Crusades: A Documentary Survey *(Milwaukee: Marquette University Press, 1962), pp. 100–101, 103.*

RECONQUISTA

Viewpoint:
No. The *Reconquista* was actually a conquest of the Iberian Peninsula by the Spanish—a different people from the Goths, who lost the territory to the Muslims in the eighth century.

The *Reconquista* (Christian reconquest of the Iberian Peninsula) was no MacArthur-like liberation (U.S. general Douglas MacArthur's recapture of the Philippines from the Japanese in 1944–1945) of a recently conquered land by the same people who had seen it taken from them. Rather, it was a new conquest by peoples who had been for the most part as tangentially related to Visigothic society as they were to Islamic society, who simply expanded their hegemony as circumstances allowed. Under the influence of a small number of (perhaps) Hispano-Gothic aristocracy and their Mozarab propagandists, an identity was created for the peoples of the North as successors to the Visigoths. With such an identity in place, it was only their natural right to reclaim what had been taken from them. However, one must ask whether this reality was the case or not.

In the eighth century it is possible to distinguish three broad zones in the Christian North, differing from one another in social organization and culture, none of which were Visigothic. Beginning at the western end of the peninsula was Galicia, where continuity of settlement had been unbroken from late Roman times and where elements of Roman social organization survived. In the center a continuous mountain belt from the Cantabrian Mountains to the Pyrenees was populated by Cantabrian and Basque mountaineers, who also represented an ancient tradition. In the east was the future Catalonia, an area only lightly garrisoned by the Muslims and which in the early ninth century came into the orbit of Carolingian political power and social organization. The bulk of the population who made up the Christian states consisted of indigenous Galicians, Asturians, Cantabrians, Basques, and others who had not been entirely assimilated into Roman or Visigothic society. While perhaps some of the aristocracy had been related to the Visigothic nobility, the traditions, however, that attribute Visigothic ancestry to Pelayo (the first Christian king in Asturias after the Arab conquest of Spain) are not contemporary and are suspect. Most likely, he was simply an Asturian who led a successful uprising against the conquerors, and "he had no conscious intent to resurrect the defunct kingdom of the Visigoths." As to the significance of his battle, the Mozarabic *Chronicle of 754,* written inside of al-Andalus, does not even mention what would have been a momentous event from its perspective. Richard Fletcher, in *Moorish Spain* (1992), summarizes Pelayo's importance succinctly: he "did not 'initiate the Reconquest of Spain from the Moors.' He founded a tiny Christian principality which could serve as a haven for refugees from the Islamic south. One day, far in the future, it would grow into the medieval kingdom of Leon-Castile. Yet nobody could possibly have foreseen that in the eighth century."

While the growth of the kingdom of Leon-Asturias is uncontestable, there was also no continuously expanding conquest of the south from the time of Pelayo. Prior to the eleventh century any conquest was in fits and starts. Even the indomitable Charlemagne was unsuccessful in his bid to capture Islamic sites in the late eighth century. At nearly the same time, during the kingships of Alfonso II (791–842) and Alfonso III (866–910) of Asturias-Leon, the war was primarily one of propaganda. The kings attempted to re-create the image of the Visigothic monarchy, reestablishing the ecclesiastical structure of Visigothic times and attempting to model their rudimentary royal administration after the more highly developed Gothic model. At this time there were also significant Mozarabic migrations to the north and perhaps the writing of the first historical work proclaiming the royal continuity, the *Chronicle of Alfonso III.* Before the eleventh century, however, not only was there no "reconquest" going on, these kings were not even able to protect their own territories. The caliphal armies under al-Mansur invaded Christian territory at will, and the caliph was able to dominate the nascent kingdoms of Leon and Asturias despite the emerging inflated rhetoric. In 997 the forces of al-Mansur were able to penetrate to the most holy site in the Christian lands—Compostela—where they sacked the town and destroyed the important pilgrimage church. In contrast, before 1045 the expansion of the Christians did not involve the capture of a single town from the Muslims.

So when did the *Reconquista* actually begin? Only after the start of the dissolution of the Islamic state, a destruction wrought by internal forces that had nothing to do with Christian resistance. Between 1008 and 1031 central power in al-Andalus dissolved. At this time the reigns of the Party Kings began; in the early eleventh century no less than twenty-three petty Muslim kingdoms, each with conflicting loyalties and alliances, came to independence—and vulnerability. With the disappearance of the formerly unconquerable Caliphate of

Cordoba, the Christians were now on more equal footing with the Islamic principalities. Once again, the Leonese-Castilian rulers, Ferdinand I (1038–1065) and Alfonso VI (1072–1109), attempted to construct a federation of states based upon the old idea of the rulers of Leon as authentic heirs of the Visigothic kings; hence, they ought to be entitled to imperial authority over all other peninsular princes. This stance was not accepted by the rulers of other Christian states. The conquest, at last, became a reality in the late eleventh and twelfth centuries—when the Islamic states were at their weakest. In the central and eastern regions the movement of conquest began in 1045, when Garcia III, king of Navarre, captured Calahorra, starting the penetration of the Ebro Valley. In the west, significant advances were made by Alfonso VI of Castile, beginning with the seizure of Coria (1079) and culminating in the capture of Toledo (1085), the first major Islamic town to fall, but the Christians were incapable of sustained, joint action.

This initial success was nearly reversed by the arrival of the Almoravids from the Maghrib. Between 1086 and 1102 they managed to recover nearly all the lands that had been Muslim Spain, unified them, and dealt a severe setback to the reconquest. As historians of Spain have recognized for a long while, the Christian *Reconquista* was in practice much more a contest for immediate secular prizes to reverse political changes than a religious Crusade.

Hence, it would be a mistake to view this conquest as some sort of concerted holy war of Christian against Muslim. The whole movement might have been given added impetus by the crusading spirit, set loose when Pope Urban II called upon the nobility to go on Crusade (1095) and fight against the Muslims. However, the warfare in Spain was not initially conceived of as a Crusade. In fact, about six years after the Council of Clermont, Pope Paschal granted Crusader indulgences to those who fought Muslims in Iberia. Apparently, prior to that time not even the kings of Spain had considered their unique warfare a holy war. Furthermore, few other Europeans actually participated in the conquest. The psychological importance of the justification of the crusading movement must not be overlooked, but it should not be overstated.

The conquest was a rather peculiar kind of warfare, and the careers of Alfonso VI and his great vassal, Rodrigo Diaz de Vivar (El Cid), illustrate the complicated nature of the conquest. Alfonso's most serious early threat came from his brother Sancho II, who deprived him of his kingship and forced both him and his brother Garcia to flee to the Muslim lords for protection. After Sancho's assassination (1072), Alfonso returned from Toledo to assume the kingship. He considered many Muslim lords his subordinates but was unable to extend his sovereignty over all the Christians. Some fought with him against the Almoravids. At various times El Cid worked for the king of Barcelona, and then for the Muslim ruler of Zaragoza, where he defended the town against both Christians and Muslims. He also fought for the Muslim ruler of Valencia until he decided to take power in that city himself. He then fought against the Almoravids, inflicting upon them their first defeat. Yet, he remained a

Castle of Segura de la Sierra, which was given to the Order of Santiago in 1242 during a period of Christian military victories in Andalusia, Spain

RECONQUISTA

somewhat reluctant vassal of Alfonso. After his death (1099) his widow and her son-in-law continued to hold the city until 1102. Similarly, the Almoravids regarded the Muslim Party Kings as enemies and fought against them as much as the Christians. In fact, the rationalization of the *Reconquista* as holy war was introduced among the Christians rather late in the twelfth century. While there were earlier territorial and political claims to Muslim lands, there do not seem to have been religious ones until 125 or so years after the actual reconquest had begun. As Vicente Cantarino has shown, in an article for *Islam and the Medieval West: Aspects of Intercultural Relations*, edited by Khalil I. Semaan (1980), these sentiments seem to have emanated from centers of thought north of the Pyrenees. In truth, most of the conquest was simply a battle to extend the power and territory of local kings and had little or no relation to religion.

The real productive period of the conquest only began when Yusuf ibn Tashufin, the Almoravid emir, died (1106); the most significant event of the renewed conquest occurred when Alfonso I of Aragon and Navarre conquered Zaragoza (1119). From this point on, the conquest continued until the important battle of Las Navas de Tolosa (1212) near Cordoba. Created during this era were the military religious orders that functioned as a kind of permanent military for the Christian kings. By 1209, under the influence of Bishop Jiménez de Rada of Toledo and with the encouragement of Pope Innocent III, the final push south was on. By now the conquest was a full-blown Crusade, with the Pope threatening excommunication of all Christian rulers who refused to enter the fray or make war on the enemy. Clearly, this phase of the *Reconquista* was significantly different from all that had gone before.

The main problem of the idea of a *Reconquista* is that many different types of warfare, in many different historical periods, waged by unrelated peoples is subsumed under an overall rubric that obscures more than it illuminates. Such constructions of history can be useful in prompting patriotic pride—but they make for bad history.

–MICHAEL WEBER,
SALEM STATE COLLEGE

References

Vicente Cantarino, "The Spanish Reconquest: A Cluniac Holy War against Islam?" in *Islam and the Medieval West: Aspects of Intercultural Relations: Papers Presented at the Ninth Annual Conference of the Center for Medieval and Early Renaissance Studies, State University of New York at Binghamton*, edited by Khalil I. Semaan (Albany: State University of New York Press, 1980), pp. 82–109.

Américo Castro, *The Spaniards: An Introduction to Their History*, translated by Willard F. King and Selma Margaretten (Berkeley: University of California Press, 1971).

Richard Fletcher, *Moorish Spain* (London: Weidenfeld & Nicolson, 1992).

Thomas F. Glick, *Islamic and Christian Spain in the Early Middle Ages* (Princeton: Princeton University Press, 1979).

L. P. Harvey, *Islamic Spain, 1250 to 1500* (Chicago: University of Chicago Press, 1990).

Peter Linehan, *History and the Historians of Medieval Spain* (Oxford: Clarendon Press, 1993; Oxford & New York: Oxford University Press, 1993).

Joseph F. O'Callaghan, *A History of Medieval Spain* (Ithaca, N.Y.: Cornell University Press, 1975).

Claudio Sánchez-Albornoz, *Spain: A Historical Enigma*, translated by Colette Joly Dees and David Sven Reher (Madrid: Fundación Universitaria Española, 1975).

E. A. Thompson, *The Goths in Spain* (Oxford: Clarendon Press, 1969).

RECONQUISTA

SALADIN AND RICHARD I

Was Saladin a better military commander than Richard I?

Viewpoint: Yes. Saladin's use of caution, stealth, and guile demonstrates that he was superior to Richard I as a military commander.

Viewpoint: No. Saladin's performance after the Battle of the Horns of Hattin in 1187, particularly his failure to seize Tyre and other strong Frankish sites, shows that he was an inferior commander compared to Richard I.

Sultan Saladin's victory at the Battle of the Horns of Hattin on 4 July 1187 was as impressive as it was destructive to the Crusader States. In many ways it was the epitome of tactical cunning and near-flawless execution. Although all historians consider Saladin's campaign at Hattin an unqualified success, many criticize Saladin for his apparent inability or unwillingness to press on and completely exploit his subsequent position. Many believe that if Saladin had turned upon and seized, rather than bypassed, the strongest Frankish cities (such as Tyre, Tripoli, and Antioch), he could have driven the Franks into the sea. By focusing on easier prey and negotiated settlement, Saladin allowed the Crusaders to retain an important beachhead at Tyre for a new invasion and, further north, left Tripoli and Antioch in Christian control. Many feel that Saladin's failure in this regard constituted a grave tactical error of major proportions, one that ultimately led to the reversal of many of his gains.

The gains of Richard I, the Lion-Hearted, are equally impressive. Under his command one of the most formidable marches in medieval history was conducted down the coast. Difficult to bait and cautious not to stray too far from the reach of the Crusader fleet, Richard picked and chose his battles well and recovered the coast. Most criticisms of Richard's campaigns during the Crusade focus on his diplomatic blunders and inability to inflict a major defeat on Saladin. Capable of antagonizing virtually all parties in one way or another, Richard bungled the diplomatic handling of the colonists. Many feel that his "modest" military gains were negated by the instability and animosity that he introduced to the region. Many scholars have also pointed out the fact that Richard, despite the momentum he achieved, was incapable of inflicting any sort of decisive defeat on Saladin. Despite some flashy engagements, Richard was still forced to check Saladin by treaty rather than force.

Comparing the tactics and strategies of Saladin and Richard (and their execution of them) is a difficult task. Both recognized the importance of strong fortified sites. The military theories of the Islamic and Christian military commanders were different. Muslims, for example, depended on the speed and dexterity of their mares—harassing the enemy with archers and hit-and-run tactics were preferred in the field. Christians, on the other hand, mounted on stronger and aggressive stallions, favored the pitched-cavalry charge. Frequently, strategy was geared toward forcing the opponent to fight on one's terms. Some historians have argued that diplomacy played an extremely important role in Saladin's military strategy. Thus, they argue, when comparing the military tactics of each diplomacy, Saladin's strength and Richard's weakness must be factored into the equation.

Viewpoint:
Yes. Saladin's use of caution, stealth, and guile demonstrates that he was superior to Richard I as a military commander.

Comparing the abilities of Richard I, the Lion-Hearted, and Sultan Saladin as military strategists and tacticians is a complex task. Once the romantic mythologies that have sprouted up around each commander are pierced, one finds problems much more difficult than sifting through panegyric to reach reality. One needs to assess the relative merits and weaknesses of Richard and Saladin as commanders in order to render a judgment.

Although Saladin is still often (and wrongly) considered in popular histories one of the greatest military leaders of all time, his reputation as a strategist has been deflated in scholarly circles. Until 1187 Saladin was completely unable to have any real effect on the Franks: in 1177 the sultan was routed by the Franks at Montgiscard; in 1182 the clash at Forbelet produced no results, and his well-planned surprise assault on Beirut floundered. *Inconclusive* has become the descriptive term of choice when referring to all the sultan's engagements with the Franks. Even Saladin's greatest victory, the utter decimation of the Frankish army at the Horns of Hattin in 1187, is now frequently explained as being the result of Christian strategic blunders and infighting among the Latin leadership than the sultan's tactical skills. The importance of his swift conquests throughout the Frankish colonies following Hattin has been methodically dismantled by scholarship as well: Saladin bypassed the most important fortified sites inland to prey upon more easy pickings; he left important beachheads along the coast (Tyre, Tripoli, and Antioch), by which Christians would eventually reverse many of his gains; and he proved ineffectual in relieving Acre from what ultimately was a phantom siege composed of the remains of the Latin army. Despite the numerical superiority of his army, he was unable to defeat Richard's forces in the field. Although Saladin had nearly every advantage, the best result he was able to achieve was a drawn-out stalemate that finally ended with a negotiated peace that revealed his military failures. In the final analysis, according to this view, Saladin's true skill was in diplomacy, and his greatest achievement was being able to keep an army in the field for three years.

The circumstances surrounding Saladin's rise to power are the essential backdrop for assessing his campaigns against the Franks at Hattin. Saladin was a usurper who used the ideology of jihad (just war) against the Franks to justify the creation of his own dynasty. This conclusion does not necessarily mean that he was not committed to the holy war or that he was not genuinely interested in driving the Franks into the sea. He had a wide array of concerns and problems that took precedence over the Frankish presence, and, for the time being, the existence of the Crusader States served his purposes. Strengthening Egypt and consolidating his control over emirs were his immediate concerns. Yet, Saladin needed time to accomplish these goals. In addition to battling with Muslim rivals and negotiating truces, Saladin embarked upon a policy that was geared toward making Egypt an even greater economic power than it already was. His control of Red Sea trade would be bolstered by siphoning off and redirecting toward Egypt some of the trade taking place among the Christians. Thus, in the 1170s Saladin was busy courting the Italian maritime republics and with a considerable amount of success. He was also trying to attract more allies—even if just marriages of convenience—while isolating the Franks as much as possible.

A decade later Saladin had yet to score any significant victory against the Franks, even though all his activity was supposedly geared toward prosecuting the holy war. On the eve of Hattin, the scholar ibn al-Athir observes, Saladin needed a victory against Christians rather than fellow Muslims "to establish our own excuse and check tongues." Naturally, one can say that Saladin's need to hit the Franks hard was caused by political reasons. However, what war is not fought ultimately for political reasons? Taking into consideration his need for an overwhelming victory to shore up his reputation, along with capitalizing upon the vast numbers of troops he had mustered, Saladin recognized that his best course of action was to force the Franks into a pitched, open battle. His strike against Tiberias was designed to goad the Franks into just such a predicament, one that he hoped could be aggravated by the excessive heat and by denying them access to water. The plan ultimately succeeded—quite probably beyond Saladin's expectations—and the Frankish army was annihilated. Ultimately, his victory can be attributed to poor leadership among the Christians.

Most criticisms of Saladin's tactical skills focus on the events immediately following Hattin. Although there was no real Latin army to speak of that could face him on the battlefield, Saladin skirted around important fortified Frankish bases rather than seizing them and left three important coastal cities in Christian hands. Saladin, the argument goes, failed to capitalize on his victory at Hattin; in a series of fatal miscalculations he left important strategic strongpoints in Latin control and thus provided the Christians with a sound position from which to strike back in the Third Crusade (1189–1192). However, the historian William Hamblin has recently shed considerable light on the tactical rationale behind these supposed blunders. Drawing upon a military manual written by al-Harawi, a man who served as an agent of Saladin and participated in the Third Crusade, Hamblin offers a thoroughly convincing reconstruction of a campaign strategy based on guile rather than brute force. Saladin's siege of Bourzey Castle in 1188 is an excellent illustration of the sultan's use of tactics. That the siege itself was a "textbook example" of masterful strategy can be easily gleaned from al-Harawi's use of it as an example in his chapter "On attacking and besieging fortifications and related ruses and stratagems." Bourzey was acquired through sheer dissimulation. To draw attention and defenders away from the weakest point in the castle's defenses, Saladin assembled a mass of troops on the opposite and much stronger side. The ruse worked when the surprise attack struck at the true target. Bourzey was taken quickly and at little cost. One would be hard-pressed indeed to find an example of Richard the tactician that can match such a flawless operation.

In retrospect, Saladin's failure to take Tyre as quickly and as brutally as possible may well have been a mistake. Yet, as Hamblin demonstrates, the strategy the sultan was employing was sound. Sieges could be messy and costly enterprises that depleted resources and slowed advances. Al-Harawi's advice was to capitalize on the psychological advantage of a major victory. After such a decisive defeat as the one Saladin dealt to the Franks at Hattin, a well-fortified city such as Tyre might be taken with little or no bloodshed through fear and negotiated surrender. Such a strategy could deliver the city more quickly while drastically reducing or eliminating altogether casualties in Saladin's ranks. As Hamblin points out, Tyre accepted the terms, and it was only the unlucky appearance of Conrad of Montferrat'a at the city's port that changed the situation. The strategy at Tyre was sound but became nullified by an unforeseeable contingency. Saladin's objective was to maintain momentum (a tactic of perennial appeal to great commanders throughout history) and secure as many locations as possible, preferably by treaty but through force when necessary. Ideally, a domino effect would set in; the virtually impregnable fortresses he did not besiege would be ready to negotiate once they observed Saladin's giving quarter and good terms to smaller, more-vulnerable garrisons. Saladin also had a spy in Jerusalem who played a role in the quick surrender of the city. The tac-

THE HORNS OF HATTIN

One of the greatest Muslim victories during the Crusades occurred at the Battle of the Horns of Hattin (1187), named after twin hills located in present-day northern Israel. In the following excerpt the Frankish chronicler Ernoul describes some of the events leading up to the battle, especially Sultan Saladin's use of psychological warfare:

Now I will tell you about King Guy and his host. They left the spring of Saffuriya to go to the relief of Tiberias. As soon as they had left the water behind, Saladin came before them and ordered his skirmishers to harass them from morning until midday. The heat was so great that they could not go on so they could come to water. The king and all the other people were spread out and did not know what to do. They could not turn back for the losses would have been too great. He sent to the count of Tripoli, who led the advance guard, to ask advice as to what to do. He sent word that he should pitch his tent and make camp. The king gladly accepted this bad advice. When the count had given him good advice he would never take it. Some people in the host said that if the Christians had gone on to meet the Saracens, Saladin would have been defeated.

As soon as they were encamped, Saladin ordered all his men to collect brushwood, dry grass, stubble and anything else with which they could light fires, and make barriers which he had made all round the Christians. They soon did this, and the fires burned vigorously and the smoke from the fires was great; and this, together with the heat of the sun above them caused them discomfort and great harm. Saladin had commanded caravans of camels loaded with water from the Sea of Tiberias to be brought up and had water pots placed near the camp. The water pots were then emptied in view of the Christians so that they should have still greater anguish through thirst, and their mounts too.

Source: "Ernoul: The Battle of Hattin, 1187," from Medieval Sourcebook Internet website, <http://www.fordham.edu/halsall/source/1187ernoul.html>.

tics might not have been romantic or flashy, but they were sound and effective.

Criticisms of Saladin's military strategies tend to bifurcate his tactics and diplomacy, a tendency that obfuscates the holistic nature of his approach to the Crusaders. Saladin was a cautious and calculating tactician who made every effort to secure the outcome of a war long before it actually began. In 1185 Saladin was already successfully negotiating an alliance with the Byzantine Empire against the Franks. After Hattin and the mustering of the Third Crusade, the Byzantines agreed to handle" the problem posed to Saladin by Frederick Barbarossa's German wing (which was arriving well ahead of the French and English). The Byzantines were not trustworthy or effective allies in the region during the Crusades. Despite Emperor Isaac's guarantees to Saladin that he had rendered Barbarossa's army unfit to fight by a combination of military engagements and denying it supplies, the German army was still a force to be reckoned with (as can be seen with its successful siege of the well-fortified city Iconium).

Does this situation mean that Saladin's tactic of pitting the Byzantines against the Crusaders was ineffective? It is difficult to say since the German contingent of the Third Crusade turned back because of the accidental drowning of Barbarossa rather than a crushing blow inflicted by the Byzantines. Isaac certainly slowed and complicated the Germans' progress. Barbarossa's troops did have to fight their way through Byzantine territory and at one point were even considering laying siege to Constantinople. Although the Germans were by no means hamstrung, Isaac did degrade their military capacity somewhat in both troops and horses. Combined with the German losses that could be expected during their dangerous march through the hostile climate that lay ahead, the tactic—which cost Saladin nothing—would have provided some advantage.

Richard was one of the greatest field commanders that the Middle Ages produced. His inherently intuitive eye for spotting opportunities and exploiting enemy weaknesses was finely honed in the best military school of the age—in the field while taming rebellious vassals. His march down the coast during the Third Crusade will forever remain one of the most amazing troop movements of the period. He not only managed to exert tremendous control over the contingents but also demonstrated an amazing ability to adapt when his troops aggressively broke ranks prematurely to attack the enemy. The strategies of Richard and Saladin were extremely different and thus difficult to compare. Richard preferred the aggressive frontal assault, while Saladin favored oblique attack. Richard preferred demonstrations of force, while Saladin favored stealth. Richard preferred hard clash, while Saladin favored guile. Even their respective resources were dissimilar: Richard had control over the coast, while Saladin had numerical superiority. Saladin, however, demonstrated his superiority as a tactician in his ability to "prosecute the war with other means." Combat is a human activity that is always linked with other human activities; battles, in other words, cannot be divorced from the general context in which they take place. The best generals are the ones who can grasp the intricacies and implications that the interface between war and politics presents. Richard certainly did not have a subtle, or even remotely effective, touch when it came to

the politics of the Latin East. His political behavior mirrored his field conduct—frontal and aggressive. Rather than using his position to smooth over the rough edges of Crusader State politics, Richard made them much more jagged. Saladin finished the Third Crusade as a hero of Islam—not as great as if his conflict with the Franks ended on the high note of Hattin—but a hero nonetheless. Meanwhile, Richard departed the Holy Land in disguise because of the animosity that existed toward him. Saladin left unity, while Richard left greater dissension than he originally found. Indeed, the best military leaders always have a stable postwar position in mind while pursuing immediate objectives.

—MARK T. ABATE,
WESTFIELD STATE COLLEGE

Viewpoint:
No. Saladin's performance after the Battle of the Horns of Hattin in 1187, particularly his failure to seize Tyre and other strong Frankish sites, shows that he was an inferior commander compared to Richard I.

The qualities that are needed to make a great political leader are not always the same ones necessary to produce an exceptional military commander. As the course of history has abundantly demonstrated, resources, acceptable tactics, and objectives can oftentimes work at cross-purposes for the individual who attempts to be at the same time both a head of state and the head of an army. It is difficult to compare the two opposing leaders of the Third Crusade (1189–1192). While both Richard I, the Lion-Hearted, and Sultan Saladin combined the two offices of king and general, their interests in these dual functions were not the same. Saladin was far more concerned with being the consummate political leader, while Richard favored the role of military commander. Not surprisingly, therefore, when these two famed characters of the Third Crusade are rated solely as military figures, Richard proves to be the better leader.

In an interesting twist of history the pinnacle of Saladin's career had really culminated just prior to the start of the Third Crusade, while Richard's would be just beginning with his departure for the Crusade on 1 July 1190. Through shrewd diplomacy, unbridled ambition, and opportunistic military action, Saladin had succeeded in the course of two decades in uniting the Muslim world of the Near East under one leader. Rising from relative obscurity to become vizier of Egypt under Nur al-Din in March 1169, Saladin quickly revealed that he was a man of great abilities. While he occasionally clashed with Christian forces, his real focus for the first fifteen years of his career was his Muslim rivals in the region. By the time he had outmaneuvered these adversaries, Saladin found himself on top of a Muslim Syria and Egypt, which he had united into a feudal-like political organization. For the Latin East the real effect of his political maneuverings was to leave the Crusader States isolated and surrounded by a unified enemy for the first time in their history. His success in this quest for political unity was attributable more to his diplomatic genius and charismatic propaganda than to his military tactics. Undeniably, Saladin displayed some true boldness and competency during his campaign to unite the Near Eastern world under his hegemony, but as he finally turned his attention to dealing with the Crusader States militarily in 1185, his fame as a great military leader was still not firmly established.

In the deadly posturing between the two powers that followed, there was no reason why the Latin Kingdom should have been defeated by Saladin. The Christian states likely could have weathered the crisis presented by Saladin's unification of surrounding Muslim territory had they maintained a relatively simple policy: defend their key fortresses and cities while avoiding large pitched battles against Saladin's numerically superior army unless favorable opportunities presented themselves. In early July 1187, however, the king of Jerusalem, Guy of Lusignan, broke with this recipe for survival, if not success, and attempted to fight a pitched battle in which his cavalry was outnumbered three to one by Saladin's and his supply of water was wholly inadequate to support his attempted offensive at that time of year. The ensuing defeat at the Horns of Hattin in the scorching summer heat proved to be a catastrophe for the Latin East, and although Saladin must be credited for prompting his opponents to give battle on terms of his choosing, the real decisive point of the battle rested with the poor decision making of the Latin commanders.

Had Saladin's career ended there, his reputation as a military figure might have been secured. He had brought a degree of unity to Syria and Egypt; he had decimated the Latin army at Hattin; and in the months following this decisive battle he easily captured nearly all the Christian-occupied land in the Levant. Yet, his limitations as a general were soon exposed in the next phase of the war. Despite the ragged state of his opponents after Hattin, Saladin was unable to take by siege the coastal ports of Tripoli, Antioch, and Tyre. Even more inexplicably, however,

he was unable to break a siege of Acre, which was initiated in August 1189 by the pathetic remnants of Guy's army. As reinforcements from Europe trickled into Guy's small force, Saladin failed to take decisive action with his vastly more numerous army. Finally, nearly two years after the siege of Acre began, the main body of English and French soldiers from the Third Crusade began to arrive at Acre in the summer of 1191 under the leadership of Richard I and Philip II. With little prospect for relief from Saladin's army in the field, the demoralized garrison surrendered the city in July of that year. While this was a humiliating loss for Saladin and one that should have been completely avoided had he acted with bolder leadership, it might not necessarily have tarnished his military reputation beyond repair. What was to follow, however, did.

By the end of July, Philip abandoned the Crusade, leaving Richard to carry on the war with Saladin by himself, although some French Crusaders remained behind as well. Richard, the relatively new king of England, had already demonstrated glimpses of his military genius even prior to his arrival at Acre. During the sea voyage to the Levant in the winter of 1190 he had conducted a successful, if minor, operation in Sicily. Far more impressive, however, was his conquest of the island of Cyprus during the following spring. This impromptu campaign was touched off by his anger at how some English Crusaders, who had sailed ahead of him, were being treated by the Byzantine ruler of the island. Unlike Saladin at Acre, Richard acted with speed and decisiveness once he had committed himself to war, and within a month had conquered the entire island. While the capture of Cyprus from the Byzantines was not the real purpose of his Crusade, the operation proved not to be inconsequential, for it insured that the island would remain a vital base for Christian forces operating in the eastern Mediterranean for nearly four hundred years. Impressive as these earlier actions were, however, Richard's real promise as a general lay before him in the head-to-head contest with Saladin.

After the capture of Acre in July 1191, Richard began his methodical march to Jerusalem. Anticipating the tactics of his enemy, Richard orchestrated a brilliant scheme of maneuver for his forces. To ward off harassing attacks of Saladin's cavalry, which were designed to slowly bleed the Crusader army of its horses, Richard organized his foot soldiers to guard the exposed left flank of his army. To the right of this protective screen marched the cream of his force, his heavy cavalry. Finally, along his right flank, which was closest to the sea, he placed his baggage train and those foot soldiers who were in need of rest from the ongoing action that was

SALADIN AND RICHARD I

Illumination of Saladin and Richard I signing a treaty, from the *Chronica Minora* by Matthew Paris (mid thirteenth century)

(Corpus Christi College, Cambridge University)

occurring on the exposed flank. Although Richard's march south was only to cover about seventy miles, it took him fifteen days to complete the journey, a remarkably slow rate of march of approximately four and a half miles a day. While the experience of marching at such a slow pace must have been agonizing, especially given the continual harassment of enemy missiles and threat of attack, it proved to be the right tactical decision. Three years earlier a Christian army of nearly equal size was destroyed at Hattin because of inappropriate haste, insufficient supplies, and the attrition of horses. With his greater appreciation of military tactics, Richard was not going to make a similar error. Saladin found himself, despite his best efforts to entice the Crusaders to give battle on unfavorable terms, completely unable to stop Richard's march. His failure to do so allowed the Crusaders to reestablish control of the more easily defended coastline and thus insured the history of the Latin East would persist for another hundred years.

After skirmishing for two weeks, the two armies finally clashed in a full-scale battle near Arsuf on 7 September. Although Richard had intended to launch a heavy cavalry attack upon Saladin's lighter horse archers once he had reached Arsuf, his rearguard charged prematurely. If his forces had been allowed to become strung out and separated, the superior numbers and speed of the enemy cavalry would probably have led to the encirclement and destruction of his heavy knights in piecemeal fashion. Faced with this sudden development, Richard adjusted instantly to the crisis presented by his rearguard's impetuous charge and led the rest of his heavy cavalry into a coordinated attack against Saladin's force. In the ensuing action Saladin's lighter host broke contact and reorga-

nized, hoping to counterattack against the slower Crusader cavalry now strung out in pursuit. Richard, however, prevented such an ill-advised pursuit from developing and instead reorganized his own lines. It was then Saladin who was enticed to give battle on unfavorable terms. Twice he sent his cavalry charging toward the Crusader line, hoping to get the heavy cavalry to charge and to string itself out in pursuit, and twice Richard launched limited counterattacks. In the end, after suffering significant losses and unable to place his opponent in a situational disadvantage, Saladin was forced to withdraw. It was not just his dead that he left on the field of battle but also his reputation as a great military commander.

Thereafter, the Third Crusade proved largely uneventful. Saladin understandably sought to avoid another pitched battle with Richard, while Richard struggled with the decision of whether to attempt a siege of Jerusalem. After deciding for a second time against an assault on the Holy City, Richard withdrew north to the port city of Acre at the end of July 1192. His plans at this point in the Crusade seemed to be weighted heavily in favor of returning to Europe to deal with the growing French aggression against English territory on the Continent. In his absence Saladin took the opportunity to try to recapture the southern port of Jaffa, which represented a key staging point for any possible attack on Jerusalem. After three days of fighting, his forces were in control of most of the city except the citadel. Having heard of the new offensive, Richard quickly set sail at the start of August and arrived at Jaffa with a small force. Despite being heavily outnumbered, Richard drove Saladin's troops from the city and repulsed a counterattack a few days later. Given the large disparity in numbers and the positional advantage initially enjoyed by the enemy, Richard's actions at Jaffa were perhaps his finest display of his military genius.

Jaffa proved to be the final chapter of the Crusade, and in many ways the battle was a microcosm of the Third Crusade as a whole. Throughout the war Saladin held nearly all of the advantages. He possessed the clearly superior force in terms of numbers, and he also controlled the key, decisive terrain. His supply lines were much shorter and far more secure and dependable than that on which the Crusaders had to rely. While Saladin admittedly had problems trying to keep his feudal army in the field for a protracted war, Richard faced a similar difficulty, and so this argument cannot be used to explain away Richard's continued success over Saladin. In fact, the only advantage that the Crusaders enjoyed was perhaps in the area of equipment—their use of heavy armor. Yet, after a century of fighting against Crusaders, Muslim troops were well aware of the unique potentials of the enemy's style of warfare and also its unique limitations, such as the problems of trying to pursue a lighter cavalry force or operating for extended periods in excessive heat. As Hattin had demonstrated, heavy armor was not a necessary guarantee of victory by any means. While Saladin failed to find a way to neutralize or overcome the one potential edge enjoyed by his opponents, Richard proved throughout the Crusade that he could prevail against an enemy that held nearly all the tactical and strategic advantages.

In the end, pitting Richard against Saladin leaves little choice but to conclude that Richard was the far better military tactician. Facing a numerically superior enemy who enjoyed internal lines of supply and acclimation to the terrain and climate, Richard was able to reconstitute a viable Latin East against insurmountable odds. While Saladin might have been his better at political leadership and diplomatic maneuvering, Richard was the clear champion when it came to operating on the field of battle.

—CHRISTOPHER LIBERTINI,
SUFFOLK UNIVERSITY

References

Ambroise, *The Crusade of Richard Lion-Heart,* translated by Merton Jerome Hubert (New York: Columbia University Press, 1941).

J. B. Gillingham, "Richard I and the Science of War in the Middle Ages," in *War and Government in the Middle Ages,* edited by Gillingham and J. C. Holt (Cambridge: Boydell, 1984).

Gillingham, *Richard the Lionheart* (London: Weidenfeld & Nicolson, 1978).

William J. Hamblin, "Saladin and Muslim Military Theory," in *The Horns of Hattin,* edited by B. Z. Kedar (London: Variorum, 1992).

Malcolm C. Lyons and D. E. P. Jackson, *Saladin: The Policies of the Holy War* (Cambridge & New York: Cambridge University Press, 1982).

Christopher Marshall, *Warfare and the Latin East, 1192–1291* (Cambridge & New York: Cambridge University Press, 1992).

THIRD CRUSADE

Was the Third Crusade a success?

Viewpoint: Yes. The Third Crusade was successful because the Crusaders managed to recapture strategic sites on the Mediterranean coast and check the advance of Saladin.

Viewpoint: No. The Third Crusade was unsuccessful because the Crusaders failed to recapture the Kingdom of Jerusalem, and they left Latin-controlled areas in a weakened state.

The Third Crusade (1189–1192) was the response to the crushing defeat that Muslim sultan Saladin had inflicted upon the Crusader States in 1187. After Saladin virtually destroyed the entire army of the Latin East, he swept through the Crusader States to expand and consolidate his victory. Although he did not take three cities of great importance (Tyre, Tripoli, and Antioch), he seized most of the region, including Jerusalem. The response in the West was substantial. Pope Urban III died after receiving the news, and his successor Gregory VIII immediately issued the crusading encyclical *Audita tremendi*.

The Third Crusade is sometimes referred to as the "Kings' Crusade" since, unlike the first two Crusades, several monarchs took the cross. King William of Sicily quickly dispatched a fleet to assist the beleaguered colonists. The kings of England and France both took the cross, but their departure was delayed by feudal intrigues between the two kingdoms. In the meantime, the remnant of the Crusader State army laid siege to Acre with little result. German emperor Frederick I (Barbarossa) set out for the Holy Land. After some clashes with Byzantine forces, Barbarossa drowned while fording a river (1190), with the result that much of his force disbanded and returned home.

When English king Richard I, the Lion-Hearted, and Philip II Augustus finally reached the Holy Land, they joined the siege of Acre and brought it to a successful conclusion. Relations between the two monarchs were tense. Philip sailed back to France shortly after the fall of Acre. Assuming almost complete command of the Crusade, Richard marched down the coast in a spectacular military movement and recovered most of the coast. Pressed to return home as quickly as possible (where the French king was, despite his promise not to, attacking English land), Richard finally concluded a truce with Saladin, in which they recognized Christian control of the Mediterranean coast from Acre to Jaffa, agreed upon the destruction of the fortifications of Ascalon, and made provisions for Christians to visit Jerusalem.

Viewpoint:
Yes. The Third Crusade was successful because the Crusaders managed to recapture strategic sites on the Mediterranean coast and check the advance of Saladin.

More often than not the First Crusade (1096–1102) has been seen as the only successful Crusade ever sent to the East. Political fragmentation among the emirs of the eastern Mediterranean during the late eleventh century created a short window of opportunity that allowed the First Crusaders to establish a Latin presence. A fortuitous confluence of Latin enthusiasm and Turkish disarray resulted in the capture of Jerusalem (1099) and the creation of the Crusader States—resounding victories that would never be repeated on such a scale. Increasing Muslim unity in the region, combined with escalating squabbles and dynastic disputes among western European rulers, enfeebled the movement shortly after its birth. Subsequent Crusades might have slightly bettered the situation of the barons of Outremer by temporarily reshuffling (or at least disrupting) the balance of power in the region, but none can be said to have succeeded in its primary objectives. No amount of reassessment or fancy interpretive footwork could possibly redeem the Second Crusade (1147–1149). The Fourth Crusade (1202–1204) "missed" its target and resulted in the sack of the Byzantine Empire. The Fifth Crusade (1217–1229), despite initial successes in Egypt, resulted in long, drawn-out stalemates that culminated in the eventual surrender of the Crusader host. In addition, French king Louis IX was captured in his failed expedition against Egypt (1248–1254).

The Third Crusade (1189–1192) has been seen as the most significant crusading failure. It neither recaptured Jerusalem nor restored Latin primacy to the region, but it made sound gains by recapturing the coast and resuscitating the near-dead colonies. Still, the Crusader States were left in such a precarious position that another Crusade was clearly needed. Thus, the Third Crusade must be reckoned a failure. Unable to decisively defeat Muslim sultan Saladin on the battlefield, Richard I, the Lion-Hearted, was forced to broker a negotiated truce that relegated the plight of the Holy Land to the status of a festering wound that eventually proved fatal.

A wide array of reasons has been cited to explain the "failure" of particular Crusades and of the crusading movement as a whole, but if the history of these expeditions to the East is nothing more than a long list of failures, with the notable exception of the First Crusade, then how can one explain the two-century existence of the Crusader States? Could the Latins have lost every battle and yet still won the war for two hundred years? The alternative explanation—and one that probably corresponds to the realities—is that one must reassess the criteria for evaluating the success of a Crusade.

Using the First Crusade as the yardstick by which to measure the accomplishments and shortcomings of crusading obfuscates the dynamic nature of the movement. Such an approach assumes that Crusader objectives and strategies were static and that they stubbornly resisted adaptation to changing conditions. It also fails to take into account the exigencies and realities of medieval warfare. In terms of strategy, Crusades were not sui generis campaigns but rather garden-variety medieval military expeditions (though the distance and duration of crusading campaigns made them exceptional in terms of logistical problems). Holy wars, in the final analysis, are still wars; they are fought, won, and lost by military commanders and their troops. Rather than being governed by the teleological mechanics of salvational history, they are shaped by the men, tactical objectives, and logistical limitations of the day—just like any other war. Spiritual objectives needed to give way to tactical ones; any assessment of the success or failure of a Crusade must keep these priorities straight. Possession of Jerusalem and complete hegemony in the Holy Land cannot be the standard by which a Crusade is deemed a success or a failure. Richard I, covering his eyes with his shield while in sight of Jerusalem so that he would not see the holy city he could not take, cuts a tragically romantic picture. More mundane—but much more important—were the muddy fields that made the task impossible, as well as the fact that a fortified coastal city such as Ascalon was of much greater tactical importance than the strategically irrelevant Jerusalem, which was an extremely difficult city to take and which offered precious few strategic gains to compensate besiegers for their costly effort (in effect, the only gains it offered were confined to the realm of morale and propaganda). If Richard had opted to lay siege to Jerusalem and succeeded, the Third Crusade might well have gone down in history as a success. That course of action might have made the campaign a true failure and drastically shortened the life span of the Crusader States.

The Battle of the Horns of Hattin (1187) is naturally the best place to begin any analysis of the Third Crusade. The importance of the battle can scarcely be exaggerated; it decimated the native Latin army and paved the way for Saladin's blitzkrieg that almost drove the

Christian colonies into the sea. Of equal significance, however, is how unique the engagement was in terms of medieval military history. Medieval warfare was not characterized by great decisive battles that granted comprehensive territorial dominance to the victors. This battle was the exception rather than the rule. The complete destruction of an army that left the battlefield under the thumb of the victor was a rarity. Hattin was the product of a conjunction of particularities: Saladin's brilliant ploy, bad decisions made by Latin leadership, and local geographical handicaps. The result was that the fate of the Crusader States was staked on one throw of the dice when the norm of medieval warfare was to conservatively hedge bets. Herein lies one of the main reasons that so many historians deem the Third Crusade a failure. At least tacitly, many modern historians look for an "anti" or "counter" Hattin that restored the pre-1187 status quo. In other words, perfectly repeating a rare occurrence has become the bar that one expects the Third Crusaders to have raised themselves up to. The ostensible goal of the Third Crusade was to check Saladin's advance and save the colonies from perishing completely. Recovering Jerusalem and restoring the pre-Hattin balance of power were like a dessert—nice but not necessary. The real objective was survival rather than dominance, and it is from this perspective that the gains and shortcomings of the Third Crusade should be approached.

Essentially, success or failure in any campaign must be evaluated in terms of the strategy that guides it. Strategy can be defined as a practical synthesis of means and ends, objectives and resources—that perennial logistical clash between desire and circumstance. Viewing the movement in these terms, the First Crusade was exceptional in that its proposed objective was a specific city. In this sense, the First Crusade was sui generis; if one insists that its objectives define "Crusade" and the ultimate measure of the movement, then there was only one real Crusade—that of the late eleventh century. With Pope Eugenius III and the Second Crusade, one finds that crusading strategy had already been radically altered. Rather than focusing on control over a particular city, the objective became regional defense. This policy marks the end of crusading as an "armed pilgrimage" in the strictest sense of the phrase and begins the real "militarization" of the Crusades (meaning making it more professional in a strategic sense). When Pope Gregory VIII responded to the news of Saladin's victories with the crusading bull *Audita tremendi*, he followed the lead of Eugenius rather than Pope Urban II; the expedition hinged upon checking Islamic advances in the region rather than on acquiring or retaining Jerusalem. Strategic details on how

to secure this objective would be left to the acumen of the secular commanders.

Saladin's conquests shattered the Crusader States. With the important exception of Tyre, the Christians lost the entire coast south of Tripoli by 1190. The County of Tripoli was reduced to the city and a few castles garrisoned by the military orders. The Principality of Antioch suffered a similar fate. Jerusalem was completely lost. The political situation was just as dismal. Loyalties of the barons of Outremer were divided between Guy of Lusignan and Conrad of Montferrat. The Byzantine emperor decided that the Crusaders were a greater threat than Egypt and began conspiring with Saladin against the Latins. Politically and militarily, the participants of the Third Crusade had their work cut out for them just in extending the life of the colonies.

The gains made by the Third Crusade began in earnest with the arrival of Richard I, the Lion-Hearted. En route to the remnants of the Crusader States, Richard had already made a contribution of great value by seizing Cyprus from the Byzantines and bringing it into the Latin sphere. Important both economically and militarily, the joining of Cyprus to the Crusader States was one of the most important bricks that went into laying the foundation for a renewed Latin presence. Richard then landed at Acre, where Guy of Lusignan was laying siege to the city with the remnant of the army of the Latin East. Diplomatic feelers were immediately extended. Upon arriving at Acre, Richard sent an envoy to Saladin's camp to inquire about the possibility of negotiated settlement to the conflict. Saladin declined the offer, claiming that a meeting of kings was not appropriate until a truce had already been formulated (but he was willing to reciprocate by sending his brother al-Adil as an envoy to Richard).

This initial contact between the two commanders underscores an important point that has eluded many historians of the Crusades: the role of diplomacy. Negotiated truces are by no means as romantic as a pitched cavalry charge. Viscerally, truces seem like "cheating" in the age of chivalry and leave a bad taste in the mouth of posterity. Yet, negotiations played a role just as important in medieval warfare as the cavalry charge. If one looks at the entire course of the Third Crusade, from both the Christian and Islamic perspectives, the significance of negotiations can be seen clearly. In fact, events on the battlefield were frequently used as diplomatic bargaining chips; skirmish victories and field assessments strengthened or weakened a commander's hand in the tents in which negotiations were discussed. Thus, if one claims that the Third Crusade was ended with a truce, one must also admit that it actually began with the offer of one. Rather than representing attempts to cut losses in futile situations, negotiated truces were one of the main tools used in securing campaign objectives. In other words, they constituted an important part of successful strategies rather than hasty compensation for failed ones.

Richard probably did not expect much to come about from this first diplomatic exchange. More likely, it served as an opportunity for commanders to meet and size each other up. Successful negotiations required leverage, and little had happened before Richard's arrival. The king of France, the local barons, and the military orders had been pounding the walls of Acre, but their efforts had little effect on the garrison and its morale. If the steady bombardment of the city walls had any psychological effect on the defenders, it was surely offset by the arrival of reinforcements from Saladin. What transformed the situation were events taking place on the sea. Crusader ships blockaded Acre's harbor, denying the defenders access to supplies. Thus began a commonplace strategy that frequently decided the fate of a medieval siege: waiting for the city to run out of food and war matériel while continuing to apply pressure. The monotony of waiting would occasionally be interrupted by the Franks launching probes against the city walls hoping to create and then exploit a breach, or Saladin's troops trying to force their way to the city with supplies. On 4 July, the four-year anniversary of Saladin's victory at Hattin, envoys from the Acre garrison were sent to negotiate terms—which the Crusaders promptly rejected. Yet, on the same day Richard sent envoys to Saladin to investigate again the possibility of a negotiated settlement. Desperation among the defenders of Acre provided a useful bargaining chip for a new round of negotiations. When Saladin refused, Richard made terms with Acre's garrison, and the city surrendered on 7 July. Having control over Acre and its supplies, as well as dominance on the sea, now provided improved terms for brokering a deal.

Thus began the first serious direct negotiations between Richard and Saladin. Discussions revolved around the timetable by which Saladin needed to make good on the terms that the Acre garrison had made in his name. The garrison's lives would be granted in exchange for a sizable financial indemnity, the freeing of Christian prisoners, and the return of the true cross. Richard responded to the breakdown in these negotiations with the most notorious act of the Third Crusade: the wholesale slaughter of the Muslim prisoners and their families. Morally, the act was reprehensible in its degree of barbarity and heartlessness, but the slaughter cannot be explained away as a senseless fit of rage on Richard's part—it certainly seemed as though Saladin was drag-

ging his feet, a ploy to buy time that the king of England could not afford. French king Philip II was heading back to Europe, not only depriving Richard of military strength but also laying open English possessions to the tender mercies of his rival while he was thousands of miles away. Richard had to move quickly. Setting out from Acre and beginning the reacquisition of strategic sites needed to restore the Latin colony would be impossible to do with so many Muslim prisoners. Saladin knew this fact, and Richard appears to have thought the Sultan's stalling was a tactical ploy. Furthermore, since these were the first direct negotiations between the commanders, they were both feeling each other out. The lessons each learned from his opponent influenced all further negotiations. Richard set a harsh tone—he was not to be toyed with.

On 22 August, Richard led his troops out of Acre and began one of the most amazing movements in medieval military history. His initial goal was to push his way down the coast past the important port of Jaffa and then move southeast to Jerusalem. Richard's forces marched down the coast parallel to the Crusader fleet. Discipline within the ranks was near perfect despite constant raids launched by mounted archers, skirmishes, and pressure on the rear guard. The feat was an impressive display of strength that paved the way for a new round of negotiations. Richard and al-Adil met on 5 September to discuss once again the possibility of a peaceful settlement. Richard was not in a generous mood and demanded a complete restoration of the Latin kingdom. Al-Adil saw the demand for what it was: an invitation to take to the field so that each side could make a more accurate assessment of the other. Near Arsur, the forces of Richard and Saladin fought the first major Christian-Islamic field battle since the crushing defeat at Hattin. Saladin's forces were defeated, but the casualties were light on both sides.

Less dramatic, yet more important than the Battle of Arsur, were the nonviolent events that immediately followed it. Arsur proved to be a Christian victory, but by no means was it a decisive one. Wisely, Richard decided not to push east toward Jerusalem but chose to further secure Jaffa. Richard realized that coastal bases were of the utmost tactical importance. While the Crusaders were consolidating their hold on Jaffa, Saladin moved south to Ascalon (the maritime gate between the Crusader States and Egypt) and began dismantling the fortifications of the city. The significance of these symmetrical moves, the bolstering and destroying of fortifications, is great. Security throughout the Crusader States was based more upon a strong point than perimeter defense. This strategy was why the creation and destruction of fortifications was of

GOBLETS OF DEATH

In flowery prose, Arab chronicler Imad ad-Din describes the Crusaders bravely defending Jerusalem:

There were in Jerusalem at the time 70,000 Frankish troops, both swordsmen and archers, and champions of error armed with lances, their pliant points quivering, ready to defend the city. They challenged (us) to combat and barred the pass, they came down into the lists like enemies, they slaughtered and drew blood, they blazed with fury and defended the city, they fumed and burned with wrath, they drove us back and defended themselves, they became inflamed and caused us harm, groaned and excited, called for help in a foreign tongue, entrenched themselves and acted like men enraged with thirst, whirled about and crossed, advanced and retreated, rolled about and grieved, cried out and yelled in the conflict, immolated themselves in their tragedy and flung themselves on death. They fought grimly and struggled with all their energy, descending to the fray with absolute resolution, they wielded the sockets of their spears to give their thirsty points the water of the spirit to drink; they dealt with those that had lost their nerve, and passed round the goblets of death; they hurled themselves into battle to cut off limbs, they blazed and set things to fire, they clustered together and obstinately stood their ground, they made themselves a target for arrows and called on death to stand by them. They said: "Each of us is worth twenty, and every ten is worth a hundred! We shall bring about the end of the world in defence of the Church of the Resurrection, we shall despise our own safety in desire for her survival." So the battle continued and the slaughter with spear and sword went on.

Source: *Francesco Gabrielli, ed. and trans.,* Arab Historians of the Crusades *(Berkeley: University of California Press, 1969), p. 154.*

much greater concern to commanders than flashy field engagements. Fortified sites were administrative and defensive centers that maintained local control rather than broad and sweeping dominance, but they still were strategic keys to almost all conflicts. Field armies were certainly important but mostly because of their symbiotic relationship with fortified sites. Medieval military commanders were reluctant to take great risks and launch spectacular but dangerous engagements because troops were too valuable to squander. A more accurate assessment of power in a particular area was who controlled which strong points and how good their fortifications were. The construction or destruction of fortifications, then, was of greater tactical significance than the outcome of a normative field engagement. Arsur was not decisive and did little to alter the circumstances for potential negotiations. Once again Richard and al-Adil met to discuss terms. Richard proffered a plan for marrying his sister to al-Adil that implied a form of power sharing, but the suggested conversion of the sultan's brother to Christianity seemed a dubious term to meet.

After these negotiations broke off, Richard began the march toward Jerusalem. For a variety of reasons—chief among them the distance of the Holy City from the coast—Richard turned away from Jerusalem in favor of moving on the strategically valuable Ascalon. The city was of inestimable value as both a defensive buffer for the Crusader States and as an advanced base for taking the war to Egypt. Richard spent four months repairing the damage Saladin had done to the fortifications. New rounds of negotiations ensued, but Richard's situation was complicated and undermined by the diplomatic advances Italian Crusader Conrad of Montferrat made to Saladin.

In late July, Richard returned to Acre, and Saladin seized the opportunity to take the city, which was still in the process of being refortified. Essentially, Saladin's reacquisition of Jaffa was the only real Islamic victory scored against the Third Crusaders, and it was short-lived; Richard retook the city with relative ease. Militarily, Richard was scoring great victories, but these were offset by political disaster within the Christian forces. The deep-seated animosity between Richard and Conrad of Montferrat ended when the Assassins (Muslim followers of Hassan Ibn al-Saabah) struck down the latter. Yet, Conrad's assassination brought more problems than solutions, since many people suspected that Richard was party to the plot. The episode drove even deeper the wedge between the English on the one hand and the French and native barons on the other.

Both Saladin and Richard needed a settlement. It was by no means easy for Saladin to keep an army in the field for such an extended period of time, and the continuous successes of the Crusaders no doubt had a substantive effect on the emirs. Richard's position was sound and growing stronger. Richard, for his part, needed to return home as quickly as possible to deal with the intrigues of his brother John and King Philip. He was also ill. The political situation among the Latins, furthermore, was deteriorating at an alarming rate. Both commanders wanted a negotiated settlement from the beginning of the campaign, but now both men needed one quickly. What is usually considered to be the "meat and potatoes" of the Third Crusade—the military engagements—seems to have been a series of confrontations designed to bolster negotiating power. The Third Crusade was fought more by strategic leverage and negotiations than by battles. Saladin was prepared to accept the map as redrawn. Both commanders were willing to acknowledge a sharing of Jerusalem that could accommodate both Christian and Muslim immediate needs. The real bone of contention during the last and most serious rounds of negotiations was Ascalon; neither side was willing to cede it to the other. That Richard and Saladin were so willing to accommodate each other on the issue of Jerusalem—but so staunchly refused to budge of Ascalon—reveals what the military commanders saw as true priorities. In the end, Richard gave in on the issue and in so doing brought the Third Crusade to a close. If there is in fact any validity to the argument that the Third Crusade was a failure, it has little to do with the fate of Jerusalem or the interior. The greatest drawback to the achievements of the Third Crusade was its inability to secure Ascalon. Yet, the city's fortifications were demolished in accordance with the settlement, so even this failure was mitigated. With the short-lived exception of Jaffa, the Crusaders did not lose a battle, and Saladin's forces were incapable of checking Richard's "reconquest."

The Third Crusade has been seen as a failure primarily because it was not a "counter-Hattin" that restored the pre-1187 balance of power. A symmetrical restoration of the Crusader States, however, is simply too high a benchmark for measuring the success or failure of the campaign. It assumes that a rarity in medieval warfare—the pitched and decisive battle—is the sine qua non for success. Strategy and achievement must remain paramount in assessing warfare (holy or otherwise), and in this sense the Third Crusade was an almost unqualified success. Its objectives—checking Saladin's advance and preserving the colonies—were achieved. One cannot fault the Crusaders for not achieving "targets of opportunity," regardless of how dear they may have been to the hearts of Christians. The Third Crusade redrew the map, and Saladin accepted it; it recovered much of the coast and allowed the Latins to entrench themselves; and it added the important island of Cyrpus to the colonies. Furthermore, the Crusaders really did not lose a battle, except for the minor setback at Jaffa. To say that Crusader gains came about "just by treaty" is to oversimplify and overromanticize the subject. Most wars end with peace treaties. The battles of the Third Crusade were for the most part low-intensity wrangles designed to secure the best peace possible. Finally, one of the most convincing proofs of the success of the Third Crusade is that it transformed a near-dead colony into one that lived for another century.

—MARK T. ABATE, WESTFIELD
STATE COLLEGE

**Viewpoint:
No. The Third Crusade was unsuccessful because the Crusaders failed to recapture the Kingdom of Jerusalem, and they left Latin-controlled areas in a weakened state.**

As with many aspects of life, war is a complex phenomenon. What may appear as success at one level may not translate into success at another. This dichotomy is certainly the case with the Third Crusade (1189–1192). From one perspective, English king Richard I, the Lion-Hearted's efforts in the Holy Land produced tangible results that halted and partially reversed the string of defeats suffered there by Christian forces since the Battle of the Horns of Hattin (1187). Without his effective intervention, the history of the Crusader States might have been brought to a premature end a century earlier than their final loss in 1291. Yet, at a deeper level and a more long-term perspective, the events of the Third Crusade ushered new and disturbing forces into crusading, which suggest that Richard's Crusade produced in the end a strategic defeat for Christendom. From this viewpoint, then, the ultimate conclusion for the Third Crusade must be that it was a failure.

In the summer and fall of 1187 the state of Christian forces in the Near East was perhaps at its darkest moment since the desperate struggle at Antioch in 1097–1098. A bold gamble by the Latin king of Jerusalem, Guy of Lusignan, to entice Muslim sultan Saladin's larger army to commit to a pitched battle so that it could be destroyed had ended in utter failure on the heights of Hattin. The immediate effect of this lost gamble was monumental, for the heart of Guy's army, which represented nearly all of the defense forces of the Latin States in the East, had been destroyed. In the wake of this disaster Latin cities and castles in the Levant had insufficient forces to resist Saladin's army, which now attempted to exploit the success achieved at Hattin. Within months, more than fifty towns and fortifications fell to Saladin with relative ease, including Acre on 10 July, Ascalon on 4 September, and most important, Jerusalem on 2 October. The hard-won success of nearly a century of bitter struggle to reclaim the Levant for Christendom seemed to evaporate overnight. Indeed, so horrifying was the sudden turn of events that Pope Urban III was said to have died of a broken heart when he received the traumatic news on 20 October of the loss of Jerusalem.

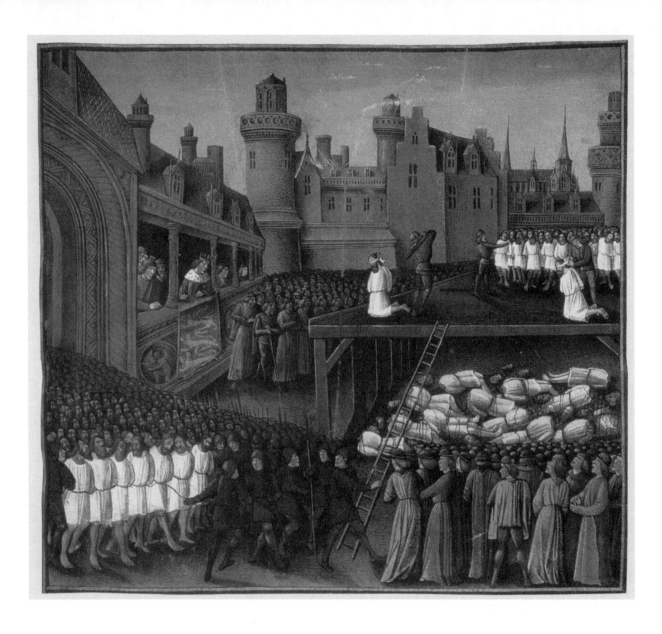

Illumination of Christians executing Muslim prisoners after the fall of Acre, from *Les Passages faits Outremer* **(circa 1490)**

(Bibliothèque Nationale, Paris)

Urban's successor, Gregory VIII, immediately committed himself to organizing and launching a new Crusade, promulgating his crusading appeal *Audita Tremendi* within days after his election, but the prospects for success of this appeal must have seemed bleak indeed. Only a few eastern cities and fortresses remained in Christian hands, and their eventual loss seemed only a matter of time. The enemy enjoyed a degree of unity and organization not witnessed since before the dawn of the crusading era. At the same time the Western world was deeply divided internally, with the great states of France and England at odds, the lands of Germany in varying states of disunity and also in opposition to the papacy, and Spain completely preoccupied with its internal crusading struggle against the Moors. To have any hope to reverse the state of affairs in the East, the West had to operate with a degree of cooperation and unity of purpose it had not enjoyed since perhaps the days of Char-

lemagne, and this unity must have seemed in the fall of 1187 a fantastic dream.

Yet, the emotional and spiritual attraction of Jerusalem still held a seductive charm among the multitudes living in Christendom at the close of the twelfth century. Thus, in response to its plight the three great monarchs of Europe and many of their leading magnates temporarily set aside their various political differences and personal ambitions and agreed to take the cross in the quest to reclaim the Holy City for Christianity. Henry II of England and Philip II of France agreed to a truce and pledged themselves to go on Crusade on 21 January 1188. Holy Roman Emperor Frederick I (Barbarossa) of Germany followed suit on 27 March. Yet, this appearance of unity and combined action was little more than that. Frederick's army marched off independently ahead of the French and English on 11 May 1189, taking the longer and more difficult land route to the East. The departure of French and English forces by sea was delayed for more than a year, caused by a rupture in the truce between the two realms during the summer of 1189, which was instigated by Henry's son Richard. It was also during this crisis-filled summer that Henry passed away, and thereafter the throne fell to his headstrong son. Although tensions and animosities between Richard and Philip remained, the two monarchs succumbed to popular pressure and finally embarked on their part of the Crusade on 1 July 1190, nearly three years after the catastrophic events of Hattin and their aftermath.

Given such a backdrop, the prospects for success of the Third Crusade had to be mixed at best. True, the crusading forces, in terms of their numbers and leadership, presented on paper perhaps the best crusading army ever assembled and thus necessarily represented a formidable challenge to Saladin. Yet, this army was more a potential than an actual threat since the three monarchs and their forces seemed incapable of conducting coordinated and concerted operations. This lack of unified action allowed Saladin to avoid facing the combined power of the Crusaders and thus negated whatever advantage they should have enjoyed. At the same time, Saladin had controlled much of the Levant for three years. His army was not only entrenched, but it also enjoyed the unity of command that typically seemed to elude the grasp of crusading armies. Faced with a divided enemy whose ranks dwindled during the Crusade and enjoying superiority in terms of numbers and disposition of his own forces, Saladin held the clear advantage.

Despite the many difficulties, including the premature departure from the Crusade of two of its three leaders, one because of death and the other because of illness, the Third Crusade produced tangible results. Acre, a key port city in the north, was recaptured on 12 July 1191. The crusading army, which was now composed mainly of Richard's forces and buttressed with a contingent of French knights and a mere remnant of Frederick's once imposing host, turned south along the coastal road to Jerusalem in late August. Through expert leadership and disciplined action, Richard was able to reclaim by mid September about seventy miles of coastland for the Crusaders, including two key cities in the south, Jaffa and Ascalon. Almost as suddenly as Christian fortunes had turned for the worse in the East after the Battle of the Horns of Hattin, it seemed now that Richard had resurrected them almost overnight. There was once more a viable Latin Kingdom, albeit a greatly truncated one. If the story ended here, it would be difficult to dismiss the Third Crusade as a failure.

However, there was another, more significant side to the story, and from this perspective the Crusade was a strategic loss. The real objective of the Crusade remained unrealized because Jerusalem was still in Saladin's hands. Twice Richard approached to within twelve miles of the city, which by all accounts was poorly fortified, and both times Richard decided against an attack that would have almost certainly given him the city. His concern was not the ability of Christian forces to capture the city but rather their ability to hold onto it over the long term, given the weary state of his soldiers and events back in Europe that increasingly attracted his attention. In the end he settled on a half measure, shoring up the defenses of the newly reclaimed Latin territory and on negotiating a truce with Saladin. Although the truce recognized Christian control of the coastline from Tyre, north of Acre, to Jaffa, it left Jerusalem in Saladin's possession. By agreeing to such terms Richard had secured his impressive tactical victory, but he had also accepted a strategic defeat.

Crusading from its inception had always revolved around, and drawn its inspiration from, the plight of Jerusalem. Until the Third Crusade, all major crusading ventures had ended in or passed through this city because at its most fundamental level a Crusade was an armed pilgrimage. Vows had to be taken by Crusade participants that could only be redeemed by visiting the holy shrines in Jerusalem, and the failure to complete this journey of faith was believed to bring serious spiritual penalties upon the vow taker. In light of this belief, and driven on by the mystical attraction that Jerusalem held for many Europeans of this era, earlier Crusaders had endured unimaginable hardships in order to make their way to Jerusalem. To have stopped short of this goal would have been for them nothing less than complete failure.

Yet, at the end of the first full century of crusading, a new paradigm was being put forward by the leaders of the Third Crusade. A successful Crusade was one that did not culminate necessarily in a particular religious experience but one that simply achieved tactical military objectives. Such was the new definition of success that Richard was legitimizing when he took leave of the Holy Land in early October 1192 with Jerusalem still in enemy hands and his own pilgrimage vow to visit its shrines unrealized. Of course, it would be unfair to single out Richard in this regard, for his crusading partner and political rival Philip, citing health problems, had left the Crusade a year earlier with his vows similarly unfulfilled. Giving credence to this new model of successful crusading, Pope Celestine III agreed to commute Philip's vow and even gave him the palm and cross as symbols of his having fulfilled his crusading duties. Whatever benefit this commutation might have brought to Philip's soul and psyche, the real effect it had on the crusading movement was nothing less than disastrous. The practical effect of Philip's and Richard's stopping short of fulfilling their vows was to redefine the essence of crusading. No longer was it primarily a pilgrimage conducted under the auspices of a military campaign, but now it was to be primarily a military operation with only the outward trappings of a pilgrimage.

Not surprisingly, the major crusading ventures launched in the wake of the Third Crusade no longer were aimed directly at recapturing Jerusalem. Following Richard's lead, later crusading commanders concluded that the seizure of Jerusalem made little tactical sense. The real problem lay in defeating important Muslim power bases in the region. Hence, the Fourth Crusade (1202–1204) targeted the rich lands of Egypt and its treasure-filled capital at Cairo. The argument for this objective may have made for sound military and economic strategy, but it was a religiously and emotionally uninspiring objective that held little interest for the rank-and-file Crusader. Thus, once Jerusalem was displaced as the direct focal point of crusading, the movement meandered into a series of errant misadventures. The Fourth Crusade, for example, never reached the shores of Egypt but rather changed course to attack the Byzantine capital of Constantinople. The reasoning for this diversion was at one level a tactical calculation. The leadership concluded that a temporary but successful campaign in Byzantium would translate into a more effective campaign later on in Egypt, one that never materialized as the Crusade culminated instead with the conquest and partition of the rich Byzantine Empire. While this diversion was a shocking development, in some ways it should have been anticipated. Once crusading was severed from its direct connection with Jerusalem, why should not one military rationale be substituted for another in the selection of objectives for a crusading campaign even if it meant in this case attacking a fellow Christian city?

In like manner the other great crusading operations of the thirteenth century that followed the Fourth Crusade all sought exclusively military solutions to a war that was in reality more than just a typical military operation. The Fifth Crusade (1217–1229), for example, succeeded in accomplishing what the Fourth failed to do—reach Egypt. Although the Crusaders achieved some initial success, notably the capture of the key port city of Damietta, their leaders turned down a peace offer in early 1219 from their Egyptian opponents that would have traded Christian control of Damietta for Jerusalem and its surrounding territory. The decision

to refuse the deal again rested solely on a military calculation. Holding Jerusalem without subduing Muslim power in either Egypt or Syria was considered to be pointless, for the long-term viability of a Christian-controlled Jerusalem could not be assured without defeating one or the other of these centers of Muslim power. Yet, the long-term status of Jerusalem was never intended to be the concern of crusading proper. Rather, that was something to be worked out by those Crusaders and other Westerners who decided to settle in the East after the Crusade had ended. In other words, it was to be a state matter to be solved by whatever Latin kingdoms were carved out in the region. In contrast, the Crusade had been designed to offer to the warrior class of Europe a chance to participate in a special type of pilgrimage that doubled as a military campaign whose immediate goal was the recapture or direct defense of Jerusalem. Richard's dissembling on the road to Jerusalem had changed all this orientation, making crusading in essence merely a military campaign; the ramifications of his decision proved to be a watershed moment in the history of crusading.

The obstacles that faced a typical crusading venture were immense. Armies were drawn from disparate and often contending regions of Europe. They lacked clearly defined organization and leadership and were expected to operate in a hot climate thousands of miles from home in the heartland of their enemy. Their logistical support was constantly tenuous, and the ability to bring in replacements or reinforcements was always a haphazard affair. On top of all this, the Crusaders were always attempting to conduct offensive operations while being the numerically smaller force, which is usually a grievous violation of the most basic principles of war.

From a military perspective the movement made little sense at all. In fact, crusading in the East might appear to be more a suicide mission than a rational military enterprise. Yet, interest and participation in Crusades continued to be strong throughout the twelfth and thirteenth centuries. What attracted the typical Crusader to this seemingly futile enterprise was the aura of Jerusalem and the ideology of pilgrimage. Only this goal impelled these soldiers on when they had faced such dire circumstances as at Dorylaeum (1097) or at Antioch (1098). Their vows could only be fulfilled in Jerusalem. Commutation in crusading's earlier days was not an option. The hardships were so unique and extreme that something special had to bind participants to the task at hand, and something intangible had to be offered to them as a reward in order to motivate them to risk all on the road to victory. Cairo or Constantinople did not offer such an enticement. Jerusalem did. To grant the crusading indulgence for campaigns that never reached Jerusalem set the precedent that the all-or-nothing approach of the First Crusade was no longer necessary. Yet, without such an attitude it is hard to envision how crusading could ever be successful given the overwhelming odds it faced.

Not surprisingly, crusading campaigns following the Third Crusade never achieved significant results. The efforts increasingly lacked focus and lacked the kind of extreme dedication that was required to prevail in such a war. In this light then, the Third Crusade must be seen as a strategic defeat. The failure of the three armies to operate in unison was perhaps the greatest missed opportunity in the history of crusading. That Richard twice marched on Jerusalem without taking the city perhaps was the second greatest missed opportunity. The end result was that crusading was put on a new trajectory, one that would necessarily end in defeat. The armies of Europe thereafter pursued strictly militarily strategic targets in what was in essence a war based on spirit, emotion, and faith. It was a policy made acceptable by the actions of Richard I and, to a lesser extent, Philip II. It also was a policy that ushered in the eventual demise of crusading, for once the movement had been "liberated" from its necessary connection to Jerusalem, there was little incentive to continue to attract the masses of Europe to venture all in an essentially losing proposition.

–CHRISTOPHER LIBERTINI,
SUFFOLK UNIVERSITY

References

Hans Eberhard Mayer, *Geschichte der Kreuzzüge* (Stuttgart: Kohlhammer, 1965); translated by John Gillingham as *The Crusades,* second edition (Oxford & New York: Oxford University Press, 1988).

Joshua Prawer, *Crusader Institutions* (Oxford: Clarendon Press / New York: Oxford University Press, 1980).

Jean Richard, *The Crusades, c. 1071–c. 1291,* translated by Jean Birrell (Cambridge & New York: Cambridge University Press, 1999).

Jonathan Riley-Smith, *The Crusades: A Short History* (London: Athlone, 1987; New Haven: Yale University Press, 1987).

Kenneth M. Setton, ed., *The History of the Crusades,* 6 volumes, second edition (Madison: University of Wisconsin Press, 1989).

R. C. Smail, *Crusading Warfare, 1097–1193,* second edition (Cambridge & New York: Cambridge University Press, 1995).

TRADITIONALISTS AND PLURALISTS

What is a Crusade?

Viewpoint: Crusades were military expeditions that had as their ultimate goal the recovery or defense of Jerusalem and the Holy Land from Islamic occupation.

Viewpoint: Crusades were military expeditions against a variety of opponents (including some Christians) in multiple locales that were sanctioned by the papacy and shared organizational features and recruitment methods.

Studies of the past are frequently pocked with controversy and disagreement, and the Crusades are no exception. Defining the subject has proven to be so complex that it has eluded general scholarly consensus. The controversy began in earnest when the great German historian of the Crusades, Hans Eberhard Mayer, pointed out with consternation that the scholarly definition of a Crusade was ambiguous at best. Although he was the first to pose the question in concrete terms, Mayer aligned himself with the generations of historians who preceded him by emphasizing the centrality of Jerusalem and the Holy Land. Crusades, for Mayer, were ultimately defined by their destination. Jerusalem and the Holy Land were the sine qua non of a Crusade; if a "Crusade" did not have these as its objective, then it was not really a Crusade. This approach has become known as the Traditionalist school of Crusade historiography.

Although Mayer's conclusion made no radical departure from previous scholarship, many historians responding to the central question he raised did. Rather than emphasizing destination, a new generation of Crusade historians began to focus more on a set of fundamental organizational features that transcended specific geographical location, particularly the presence of papally sanctioned preaching and recruitment, conferment of Crusader status, and granting of the indulgence. Organization apparatus that the papacy monopolized is the measure of the movement. For these Pluralists, papal prerogative was essentially what determined whether a particular expedition was a Crusade, regardless of its destination. A holy war was a Crusade if a particular pope decided to make it so.

Claiming that the Pluralist response to the Traditionalists is revisionism or that it simply represents a younger generation of scholars sharpening their teeth on the bones of their elders would trivialize what is arguably one of the most important and fundamental questions of Crusade history. Each camp has valid points that can be traced back to the ambiguous language that constituted the crusading lexicon. The word *Crusade* itself was not one used by the men who organized and took part in these expeditions. Thus, in the end it really comes as no surprise to find that modern historians have some difficulty in defining it.

Viewpoint:
Crusades were military expeditions that had as their ultimate goal the recovery or defense of Jerusalem and the Holy Land from Islamic occupation.

Describing a Crusade as a holy war, while accurate, borders on uselessness. All wars in the Middle Ages, in one way or another, were holy since they universally synchronized the liturgical and the strategic and blended the will of God and conflicts among men. The war cry of the First Crusaders, "God will it," would have made just as much sense to a Carolingian infantryman as it did a knight on a Crusade.

Unfortunately, historians cannot use the contemporary definition because medieval vocabulary did not contain the modern word *Crusade;* nor did it have a standard word to describe what present-day scholars mean by the term. Crusading terminology employed a variety of words to describe the enterprise: journey, trip, path, expedition, a going forth, passage, or pilgrimage. There is an inner coherence to these words: they all indicate going to some place, not just any battlefield. Sometimes the trip included the destination: the Holy Land and its omnipresent synonym "across the sea." Language, however, can at times be a confusing measure of the realities that lie beneath it. Depending on the specific time period, the word *pilgrimage* could refer to what seems to have been a Crusade even when there was not a shrine present at the destination.

The best way to approach the problem is to view it from the ground, that is, from the perspective of those men who organized and participated in the event. Most historians designate Urban II's 1095 address at Clermont (and the immediate events leading up to it) as the beginning of the crusading movement. The joining together of a military expedition and penitential pilgrimage that took place there seems to be ground zero in crusading.

The pilgrimage Urban envisioned was primarily but not solely intended as a French pilgrimage. He launched it from France and personally preached it in France alone, but he did not want to exclude participants from other areas in western Europe. On the contrary, international participation was welcomed and, in the case of Italian city-states that could provide valuable maritime contributions, actively solicited through correspondence. The notable exception to this rule was Spain. Urban had been a staunch advocate of the Christian war against the Moors in Spain. Concerned that

enthusiasm for the pilgrimage to Jerusalem among Spaniards would drain the reconquest of its vigor, Urban specifically urged Spanish warriors to fulfill their vows in their own homeland. Spaniards fighting Moors in Iberia would receive the same spiritual benefits as men who made the pilgrimage to Jerusalem. This situation would seem to imply that Urban, if he were not a Pluralist, at least was not a Traditionalist. Spain was a theater of operations that was equated with the Crusade to the East.

This is an important and difficult juncture at which the historian must slow the clock to measure cause and effect in their proper context. Urban's pontifical concerns were certainly pluralistic, and the plight of Spain was in many ways just as important to him as that of Jerusalem. One can say with equal certainty that Urban did not want to siphon off military resources in Iberia to further fuel the conquest of Jerusalem. What one cannot say with certainty—or even probability—is that Urban launched an armed pilgrimage against the Moors in Spain. Crucial to understanding Urban's apparent extension of the crusading indulgence to Spain is the nature of his version of a Crusade. It was based on the solemn vow to undertake an arduous act of such proportions that it would serve as a satisfactory penance for sins. Penance, however, could take on a variety of forms that had nothing to do with the city of Jerusalem itself. Urban's granting of equivalent spiritual rewards to these Spaniards was not so much an extension of the Crusade as a commutation of the vow, that is, the agreement to substitute one penitential act with another. Both mixed violence with penance, but that does not mean that the campaigns were equivalents. Significantly, one finds no evidence that the reverse happened; one discovers no French, Italian, German, or English Crusaders making an armed pilgrimage to Spain. The pilgrimage was nontransferable, though its rewards could be received through commutation and the performance of an alternative penitential act.

Urban's view and approach can be placed squarely in the Traditionalist camp, but the same cannot be said of all popes through the classical age of crusading. If the original spread of Crusade-like rewards was owing to commutation rather than expansion, then many popes made an art form of trying to break down this distinction. *Divina dispensatione,* the encyclical penned by Eugenius III that inaugurated the Second Crusade (1147–1149), proposed a three-front assault against Muslims in the East, Muslims in Spain, and pagans in eastern Europe. Yet, he, like all popes who most closely fit the Pluralist model, constantly needed to

WITHOUT SHAME

In 1282 the Sicilians revolted against French rule, and two years later Pope Martin IV proclaimed a Crusade against them and their chief supporter, Peter II of Aragon. The following decree touches upon a key question underlying the debate between Traditionalists and Pluralists: did mounting a holy war against fellow Europeans qualify as a Crusade?

May the Lord arise, and proclaim His cause, not unmindful of the taunts which the foolish ones make the whole day through. For surely it is His own cause, to combat the wickedness of those who have provoked serious conflicts amongst the Christian people, distracted the Catholic princes, and obstructed God's pious concerns, particularly that of the Holy Land, which Holy Scripture attests is dearer to Him than anything else? Those by whom the sacrosanct Church, His bride, is so gravely injured, so greatly oppressed, to the extent that her own realm and special land, the kingdom of Sicily, is being invaded? Those through whom the island of Sicily, no small part of the said kingdom, is incited to rebellion and held in occupation, while the kingdom's other regions are disturbed with various conspiracies, and numerous attacks are launched there on the Church . . . ?

Truly, these Sicilians are without shame. Forgetting the fidelity which they owe us, the Church and the king, they presumptuously and audaciously engaged in rash rebellion against us all. They have launched into such madness as to raise Peter, the former king of the Aragonese, to be their leader and lord. He is an idol, a new Baal, in so far as he has been made into a devourer of his own worshippers, but by the virtue of the All Highest he will be devoured along with them. . . .

Confident of the mercy of the same Almighty God, and of the authority of His blessed Apostles Peter and Paul, we grant to all Christ's faithful, wherever they come from, who assist ourselves, the Church or the king of Sicily, against the former king of the Aragonese, the Sicilians, their accomplices and allies, and all others in the kingdom, or any part of it, who are attacking ourselves, the Church and the king of Sicily, should any one or more of them die engaged in this manner in God's cause, the same forgiveness of those sins for which they are truly contrite, and which they have confessed, which has been customarily granted to those crossing over in aid of the Holy Land.

Source: *Norman Housley, ed. and trans.,* Documents on the Later Crusades, 1274–1580 *(New York: St. Martin's Press, 1996), pp. 25–27.*

"dowry of the Virgin," no doubt an attempt to bolster its religious importance and make it competitive with the allure of Christ's patrimony in the East. Spain already had important religious shrines as well as Muslims to fight, making it a theater more naturally and easily equated with the Holy Land.

As the ecclesiastically created apparatus for crusading to the East grew, it was extended, with much credit going to canon lawyers, to other theaters. Much of this expansion was because of the most popular tool used by medieval scholars: the analogy. Through analogy other wars, which were certainly holy, could be equated with a Crusade and thus be made meritorious enough to qualify for the same spiritual compensation given to those who made the journey to the East. Moreover, several popes who promoted Crusades in multiple theaters did not view them as equivalent to that of the Holy Land. Crusading indulgences were, in a manner of speaking, prorated; for example, Gregory IX, one of the great crusading popes, pointed out that men who participated in political Crusades did not receive the full remission of sins that crusading to the East granted. Many of these Crusades, moreover, were billed as preliminary actions that would culminate in a Crusade to the East. This situation seems to suggest that beneath all the fancy footwork there was the realization, even among popes pursuing a plural policy, that Crusades in other areas somehow had to be linked to efforts in the Holy Land for a proper pedigree. As far as organizational features and benefits are concerned, the line of demarcation becomes blurred and sometimes even collapses. If one defines a Crusade solely from the perspective of papal policy forged by jurists, then the Pluralist case is fairly strong and, in fact, gets stronger as the movement progresses. However, if one follows this logic to its end, one must also concede that the Crusade of Pope Boniface VIII (1294–1303) was a genuine Crusade, even though it was little more than an ecclesiastically organized attack against the rival Colonna family who had been feuding with Boniface's relatives.

Another way of trying to define what a Crusade was, though one more difficult than examining papal policy, is to gauge the reactions of the laity to a variety of activities that were promoted by the Church as Crusades. One certainly cannot measure public opinion of crusading activity with complete accuracy, but scattered bits and pieces can provide some illumination. Monks at the monastery of St. Albans saw the Crusade against Frederick II of Sicily in the early fourteenth century as nothing more than an exercise in papal greed. Troubadours, like modern artists such as Bob

refer to and compare expeditions to other theaters of operations with those to the Holy Land—almost as if a Crusade outside of the Holy Land could not stand on its own feet. It would not be overly cynical to suspect, as some historians do, that the movement began to take on the appearance of three-card monte at this point, with hands trying to move faster than the eye. Eastern Europe miraculously became the

Dylan and Joan Baez, were quite fond of incorporating political commentary and criticism into their music (known as *sirventes*). Several of them are known to have participated in Crusades, and many of them claimed in no uncertain terms that such service was a meritorious form of penance. Quite a few did criticize Crusades launched by the papacy against Christians, events that clearly meet the criteria set by Pluralism. Their criticisms, however, are only of limited value since troubadour *sirventes* were frequently tailored to the views of their patrons. On the other hand, some seem to have been expressing what their personal consciences dictated, and they came from a wide array of backgrounds.

Criticisms of crusading can be a valuable tool for defining what a Crusade was if one credits the laity with having an important and active role in its creation and continuation. There is no doubt that papal authorization was a prerequisite for a Crusade to occur. However, was that the only requirement? The greatest difference between Gregory VII's failed protocrusade of 1077–1085 (a struggle with the Holy Roman Empire) and Urban II's successful Crusade of 1096–1102 was that the former pursued only papal objectives without really including the laity and its concerns while the latter essentially transformed the project into a papal-lay partnership. In the late eleventh century the laity recognized this dichotomy and continued to do so throughout the movement. Criticisms of crusading to the East focused primarily on the specifics of a particular Crusade rather than the concept itself. This situation arose because the laity—and many members of the clergy who were not in the papal inner sanctum—recognized the validity of the movement even though they deplored abuses of it. Crusades against Christians, however, regardless of papal sanction, were frequently criticized on principle. In other words, some contemporaries did not see them as genuine Crusades regardless of the trappings the papacy dressed them in.

The greatest strength of the Pluralist interpretation is the indisputable fact that thousands of men participated in campaigns in Europe that were preached, organized, and justified in the same manner as the expeditions to Jerusalem. This situation would seem to indicate that the majority of contemporaries saw these wars as Crusades. However, it is equally true that men of the age did not see these Crusades as being of the same stature, importance, or significance as the Crusade to Jerusalem. The Holy City seems to have been the crusading goal though other expeditions modeled on it could and were still popular. European Crusades did not have the same financial burdens or last as

long; the investment of time, money, and effort was smaller but yielded similar dividends—facts that go far in explaining their popularity. Yet, contemporaries saw them as qualitatively different, and it is reasonable for modern historians to follow their lead when trying to define the word *Crusade*.

However, if European Crusades were not Crusades, then what were they? Their origins can be found in the tradition of commuting vows. The first such commutation of Crusader vows was authored by Urban II himself, but this was clearly just commutation rather than the creation of a dual armed pilgrimage. Eugenius III (1145–1153) marks a watershed in what seems to have been the institutionalization of commutation to such a point that the original vow was no longer needed. In so doing, Eugenius launched a parallel tradition with permeable borders. As other papal holy wars progressed and utilized the apparatus of crusading, the line of demarcation between them became less clear. Popes, particularly from the time of Innocent III (1198–1216) on, unleashed the machinery of crusading upon their opponents. The twin movements became almost indistinguishable. One can still detect visceral responses, among the laity and papacy alike, which show that the line of demarcation was still there, if increasingly difficult to detect. The laity did not consider European Crusades to be of the same caliber as Crusades to Jerusalem. In addition, popes constantly used Jerusalem as the ultimate referent in crusading language and discussion of the indulgence. If European Crusades were in fact Crusades, they were still dependent on the tradition of Jerusalem.

–TODD MARX,
CONCORD, NEW HAMPSHIRE

Viewpoint:
Crusades were military expeditions against a variety of opponents (including some Christians) in multiple locales that were sanctioned by the papacy and shared organizational features and recruitment methods.

In any study of the past it is good to remember that history is in essence the continuing record of real people and actual events, not a series of academic definitions derived from the theory-laden realm of the lecture hall. Yet, academic definitions do serve a very useful function. They help us to organize and structure that record of the past so that some rational sense may be brought to what otherwise would be a sprawling, unintelligible mass of information. When faced, for example, with trying to make sense of so vast and complex a subject as the Crusades, it is particularly useful to begin with a concern for defining key terms, especially the term *Crusade* itself. As many historians would agree, a Crusade was a religiously motivated war-pilgrimage fought at the behest of ecclesiastical authority with the intention of recovering lost Christian territory or defeating enemies of the Church, for which participants received the spiritual reward of the indulgence for their vow of service. If this definition is accurate, one important implication flows from it. A range of military operations that were not specifically conducted in the Holy Land and that spanned across several centuries beyond 1291 must be included within the sphere of legitimate crusading activities. At the same time, this definition is sufficiently narrow that it excludes many other manifestations of mere holy war. The real question, however, is whether this definition can be substantiated. An examination of the key elements of a typical crusading enterprise will demonstrate that this Pluralist approach is the most appropriate manner in which to understand events of the past relating to the Crusades.

The idea and institution of crusading took its final recognizable shape in late 1095 when Pope Urban II made his first appeal for armed knights to march on pilgrimage to reclaim the Holy Land in the East. His initial call to arms and subsequent actions clearly revealed that what he was organizing was something that went far beyond any previous notion of the historical experience of holy war. Urban consciously united his war plans with the Christian tradition of pilgrimage, thereby transforming his holy warriors into pilgrims as well. This approach was not, however, some mere idle or semantic redefinition on his part. Rather, it was a conscious juridical classification that carried with it real and profound consequences. By designating his Crusaders as pilgrims, Urban deliberately opened to them all the traditional privileges of pilgrimage, including moratorium on personal debt, the right of safe passage, and the promise of spiritual reward. Unlike the holy warriors who preceded them, Crusaders were instantly made part of an institution, with all its ramifications. In other words, participants throughout the history of the Crusades were instantly made members of a recognizable fraternity in a way that the typical holy warrior could not sense. This situation was decisive in setting Crusades apart as a special and distinctive form of warfare.

As a result of this decision of Urban to unite holy war to pilgrimage, there were several key aspects of crusading that took on an institutional form. The proffered spiritual reward that pilgrims traditionally enjoyed for their journeying had always been ill defined, but for the Crusaders that same prize became for the first time clearly defined as the indulgence, a specific ecclesiastical act whereby the temporal punishment of confessed sins was forgiven. Any previous holy warrior would have assumed that he qualified for some type of spiritual reward for his fighting, but none would have ever conceived of that reward in such specific and juridical terms. The indulgence was an institutionalized reward for institutionalized warriors.

Closely tied to the indulgence was the vow of participation that Crusaders had to make in order to qualify for the reward. This vow paralleled the promise pilgrims traditionally made prior to setting off on their journey. In both cases the promise constituted an enforceable moral and juridical obligation on the person involved to carry out the proposed endeavor until completion. The receipt of the promised spiritual reward rested directly upon this vow and its successful fulfillment. As with the pilgrimage vow, the act of taking the Crusader vow involved the participant's adoption of some symbol of the journey that was about to be undertaken. This symbol became a visible reminder of the solemn promise that the participant had made to complete the journey. In the case of the Crusaders the special symbol that all claimed was the cross, a symbol that united all participants within the same institution regardless of the location or time period in which they fought.

A further institutional element that Urban incorporated into his crusading program was the dispatch of preachers and papal legates to serve as representatives of the Church during the recruitment process and later during the campaign itself. The audiences who heard these official ecclesiastical messengers came to understand the common core message. They were being asked to participate as pilgrim warriors in a cause to reclaim lost Christian territory or to defeat an enemy of the Church in return for a promised indulgence. It was also clear to them that the call to arms was coming ultimately from the highest echelons of the Church hierarchy, even if secular lords and kings were to play dominant roles in the actual execution of a Crusade. So this ecclesiastical initiative or leadership would remain yet another conspicuous trait of what constituted a Crusade.

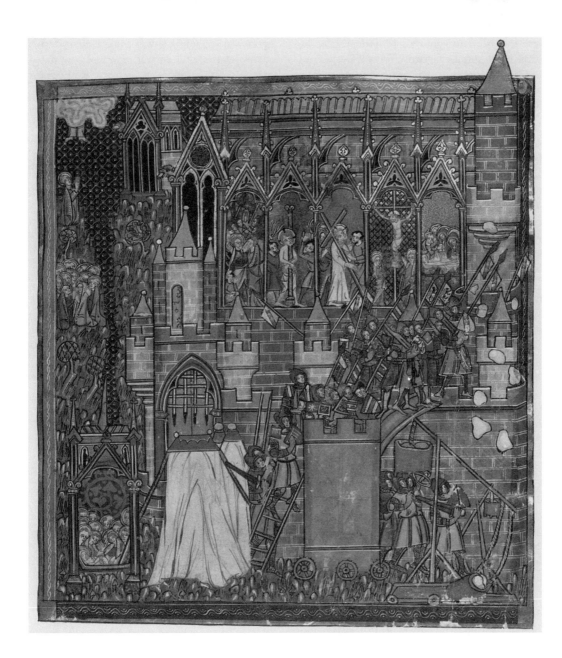

Illumination of the Crusader assault on Jerusalem in 1099. Scenes of Christ's passion are in the background

(Bibliothèque Nationale, Paris).

Because some of these key characteristics specifically marked a Crusade, it would not be accurate to attempt to make the word *Crusade* synonymous with holy war in general. Rather, these elements made Crusades a highly specialized form, or subset, of holy war, and thus the crusading definition excludes many historical holy wars from being categorized as true Crusades. This exclusion would include such holy wars as Charlemagne's war against the Saxons (782, 792–804), the Christian struggle in Spain to drive out the Moors prior to 1095, Pope Leo IX's conflict with the Normans in southern Italy (1053), and even Robert Guiscard's expulsion of the Byzantines from southern Italy (1071).

At the same time, the definition is certainly broad enough to include within its general parameters several military campaigns fought in theaters of operations other than the

Holy Land or at time periods later than 1291. Of course, crusading purists would not agree, arguing that the only real Crusades were those launched between 1095 and 1291 with the specific intention of reclaiming the Holy Land. Such scholars, however, ignore that even from the start of the movement the conception of crusading was at once more expansive. For example, as Urban II sent out crusading appeals throughout Europe in the months following his inaugural crusading address made at Clermont in November 1095, he specifically directed the knights of Spain not to answer the call for service in the East. Rather, he desired that they remain in their own country and perform their crusading service against the much more immediate threat of Muslim forces on the European continent. He promised in return that such soldiers fighting in the Spanish theater would qualify for the crusading indulgence just as if they had gone to Jerusalem. Clearly, in Urban's mind the two efforts were part of the same, larger institution of crusading that he was in the process of establishing and of which he was the principal architect.

Because of Urban II's pioneering work, subsequent popes found that they had an established institutional model with which to operate whenever they deemed it necessary to organize new crusading ventures, whether directed specifically at the Holy Land or more generally at other theaters of operation in which the Church or its people were threatened. Not surprisingly, when Pope Eugenius III had to confront the disaster of the loss of Edessa in 1144, he set about organizing a new major Crusade. Yet, by now other problems faced Christendom that seemed to suggest the need for a broader crusading solution. In Spain there was the continuing war for reunification that appeared to need fresh recruits, while in eastern Europe the continuing presence of hostile pagan peoples beyond the Elbe River seemed to warrant the infusion of crusading armies to pacify and Christianize the region. Accordingly, the crusading encyclical issued by Eugenius in 1147 treated the Spanish and eastern European Crusades as equivalent to the Holy Land Crusade. All the hallmarks of a traditional Crusade were present in these two additional theaters of operation, including the granting of the same indulgence for a similar vow of service and the dispatch of papal legates in order to represent ecclesiastical interests during the campaigns.

Pope Innocent III continued the process of expanding the institution of crusading. In eastern Europe he made the Crusade in essence a perpetual enterprise by granting an indulgence indefinitely for Christian soldiers who fought against enemies of the Church there. Thereafter, campaigns of pilgrim warriors in the Baltic region became an annual tradition. At the same time, Innocent faced a growing problem of heresy in southern France that preaching and ecclesiastical reforms seemed unable to stem. As a last resort, Innocent made the decision in 1208 to use the mechanism of crusading to bring an end to the religious and political instability in the region caused by the presence of the Cathar heresy. Once again vows, indulgences, and papal legates were all part of this venture that historians have come to term the Albigensian Crusade (1209–1229). Later still, Innocent III and several of his successors deemed it appropriate to preach Crusades against the papacy's traditional political rival, the Holy Roman Emperor, whose political designs in Italy threatened to rob the Church of its long-cherished independence. Again, soldiers who fought against this enemy of the Church were recruited by papal preachers and took vows of service in return for an indulgence.

In the centuries following the reign of Innocent III the situation in Europe and the Near East continued to evolve and change, yet the idea and institution of crusading persisted. By the end of the thirteenth century the papacy concluded that the crusading institution was no longer an effective mechanism to check German imperial designs in Italy and thus had to look to other means to frustrate the political ambitions of Holy Roman Emperors in the region. By the start of the fourteenth century the need for a Crusade against heretics in southern France had long since passed as the presence of Catharism had now been eradicated. The conversion of the peoples of eastern Europe and the Baltic area to Christianity essentially brought an end to crusading in that region by the end of the fourteenth century. In Spain the centuries-long effort to drive Muslim power out of the Iberian Peninsula finally came to a conclusion in 1492, thus ending the need for crusading activity in this theater of operation as well. However, in southeastern Europe, the Near East, North Africa, and the waters of the Mediterranean the continued presence and thus threat of Muslim forces perpetuated the need for further crusading activity in these theaters. The fall of the last Crusader possessions in the Levant in 1291 had redirected, not ended, the focus of crusading in this part of the world, from an attempt to recover the Holy Lands to a desperate defense of southeastern Europe and Mediterranean shipping lanes. Even as late as 1578 a clearly identifiable crusading army was still carrying the fight against Muslim power in the Mediterranean, this time in a failed effort to wrest the coastline of Morocco from the control of the Ottoman Turks. Yet, even then the hallmarks of vow, indulgence, and ecclesiastical sanction as represented by the presence of papal legates clearly showed that crusading was still a viable institution at the close of the sixteenth century, nearly three centuries after Christian armies had been driven out of the Levant.

In the end, while historians may continue to debate definitions, theories, and their appropriate applications, it is important to remember the opinions and attitudes of the actual makers of history. From 1095 to at least the end of the sixteenth century the spirit of crusading lived on in the minds and hearts of various Europeans. Whether soldiers fought in the Levant, Spain, the Baltics, North Africa, or Italy and whether they faced the Seljuk Turks in the twelfth century or the Ottoman Turks in the sixteenth century, all of those who took the vow of service at the behest of the Church in return for the grant of an indulgence saw themselves as true Crusaders. While service in the Holy Land might have retained a certain preeminence in terms of prestige, it did not prevent soldiers who fought in other theaters from identifying themselves as being part of that special fraternity today known as crusading. In their own minds they were every bit as much Crusaders as those first Crusaders who laid the very foundations of the movement by their heroic deeds performed in the Holy Land at the close of the eleventh century. The popes themselves not only sanctioned this sentiment but also institutionalized it by time and again granting soldiers who fought at their behest in theaters other than the Holy Land the same privileges and rewards originally established for Holy Land Crusaders. Accordingly, in the minds and actions of all those associated with the crusading phenomenon, the idea and institution of crusading was clearly something grander and more expansive than the more restricted effort directed specifically at controlling the Holy Land until the end of the thirteenth century. Thus, to attempt to exclude these other non–Holy Land and post-1291 ventures from the annals of crusading would reflect an arbitrary decision of historians, not the realities of history.

–CHRISTOPHER LIBERTINI,
SUFFOLK UNIVERSITY

References

Norman Housley, *The Avignon Papacy and the Crusades, 1305–1378* (Oxford: Clarendon Press / New York: Oxford University Press, 1986).

Housley, *The Later Crusades, 1274–1580* (New York: Oxford University Press, 1992).

Jean Richard, *The Crusades, c. 1071–c. 1291* (Cambridge & New York: Cambridge University Press, 1999).

Jonathan Riley-Smith, *The Crusades: A Short History* (New Haven: Yale University Press, 1987).

Riley-Smith, *What Were the Crusades?* (London: Macmillan, 1977).

Christopher Tyerman, "The Holy Land and the Crusades of the Thirteenth and Fourteenth Centuries," in *Crusade and Settlement,* edited by Peter W. Edbury (Cardiff: University College Cardiff Press, 1985).

TRADITIONALISTS AND PLURALISTS

TREATMENT OF JEWS

Did the Jews have a more stable position under Islamic rule than Christian rule?

Viewpoint: Yes. The position of Jews in the Muslim world was much better than in Christian regions because Islamic law made clear provisions for the treatment of monotheistic minorities.

Viewpoint: No. The Jews were subjected to as much violence and exploitation in the Near East as in the West.

In an important article, "Islam and the Jews: Myth, Counter-Myth, and History," Mark R. Cohen outlined both the history and historiography of the comparative treatment of Jews in the Islamic and Latin Christian civilizations of the Middle Ages. In the nineteenth century, European Jewish historians created two interrelated hypotheses concerning medieval Jewry. First, the Jews experienced a "golden age" of toleration, economic prosperity, and cultural growth in Islamic lands. The second was the "lachrymose" interpretation, which posits a long, painful, and unremitting Jewish trail of tears that torturously winds throughout the history of medieval Christian Europe. Taken in tandem, the vision of an extremely tolerant Islam was contrasted with that of an inherently intolerant Christianity. This myth was countered with a revisionist and equally grandiose countermyth that reshuffled (and occasionally inverted) the "golden age" theory. It focuses on the assumption that Islam was inherently and unavoidably anti-Jewish and that in the best-case scenario Jews were just as mistreated under Islamic rule as under Christian domination or, even worse, they suffered more.

Recent reassessments of this myth and countermyth argument have greatly enriched the understanding of both the experiences of medieval Jewry and the Christian and Islamic societies. That Jews were to varying degrees "second-class citizens" in both civilizations is beyond question. Issues for debate, however, are many. Were Jews more readily and easily assimilated into Islamic society? Were persecutions of Jews less frequent and violent in the Islamic world? Was Christianity more anti-Jewish than Islam?

Many historians participating in or commentating on this debate, either overtly or tacitly, have acknowledged its implications for broadening the understanding of twentieth-century problems facing Jews. Some scholars have speculated on the possibility of long-term, deep-seated connections between the massacres of Jews in the Rhineland during the First Crusade (1096–1102) and the attempted genocide against Jews conducted by the Nazis during World War II (1939–1945). Likewise, some historians have focused on the Islamic treatment of Jews as the essential context in which to view current tensions between Israel and the Arab world.

Viewpoint:
Yes. The position of Jews in the Muslim world was much better than in Christian regions because Islamic law made clear provisions for the treatment of monotheistic minorities.

Jews, like Christians, as possessors of Scriptural traditions that Muslims also venerated, were accepted in the Islamic world as "people of the book," or "protected people." If they paid their taxes and pursued their religious life discretely, they were granted considerable autonomy. Because Islamic civilization was largely secular (paradoxically, in view of the nature of Islamic law, which made no distinction between civil and religious realms), non-Muslims were able to participate in Arabic culture. Jews embraced Arabic language with enthusiasm and wrote both prose and poetry in conformity with the norms of Arabic style.

The first great convergence of Jewish and Arab interest was in commerce. In the marketplace there was no discrimination: Jewish and Arab merchants entered into partnerships and served each other as business agents. The great importance of business to the well-being of the Jewish community, and the success of Jews in commerce, was inevitably a source of stability. According to S. D. Goitein, in *A Mediterranean Society* (1967–1993), "The minority groups . . . seem to have been loyalist by conviction; a stable though oppressive government was preferable to disorder and turmoil." And, of course, disorder and turmoil were just what a community that was preeminently commercial did not want. In the long run, loyalty (and prompt payment of taxes) paid off, reinforcing the inclination of Muslims to obey the dictates of Islamic law with regard to the "people of the book."

Both Jewish and Muslim secular leaders were frequently medical doctors, such as the twelfth-century Jewish philosopher and physician Moses ben Maimon (Maimonides). Jewish and Muslim physicians studied with one another, and Jews were not suspected—as they notoriously were in Christian Europe—in any way of taking advantage of their Gentile patients. Jews were appointed to positions in Muslim hospitals and served with distinction. In Europe, Christians were constantly admonished not to entrust their medical problems to Jewish doctors, just as they were not supposed to work for, or rent housing from, Jews. In the Islamic world, Muslims rented from and owned properties in partnership with Jews.

There was some anti-Jewish violence in the Islamic lands, but it was sporadic, local, and generally recognized by Muslim authorities as being contrary to religious law. Forced conversions were occasionally ordered by rulers (in Egypt, Fatimid caliph al-Hakim demanded the forced conversion of non-Muslims, but the effort was directed mainly against Christians; in North Africa and Spain, the Almohads threatened Jews and Christians with death unless they converted, sparking a massive flight of Jews from their realm).

There was considerable convergence in the religious beliefs of the two peoples. Islamic belief, like Judaism, had a "rabbinical" cast, insofar as it was both legalistic and formalistic; religious scholarship took the form of studying scripture, codes of religious law, and commentaries. Muslims studied the Qur'an and hadith (sayings attributed to the prophet Muhammad); Jews had the Torah, Talmud, Mishnah, and other texts that dealt with religious law and duty. Mystics of both faiths revolted against religious pedantry. Arab mystics were known as Sufis, and the works of the great Jewish mystical philosophers of Islamic Spain—Yehuda ben Shemuel ha-Levi, Solomon ben Yehuda ibn Gabirol, and Bahya ben Joseph ibn Pakuda—all resembled Sufi spirituality. Ibn Pakuda was from Zaragoza, where he flourished in the first quarter of the eleventh century. He was, in essence, a Jewish Sufi. The Sufis rebelled against the reduction of religion to a series of legal provisions promulgated by Muslim jurisprudents; Ibn Pakuda opposed the punctiliousness of rabbinical Judaism with regard to the written law. He was aware he might have been overly influenced by Muslim ideas, but he persisted in blending Sufi concepts with Jewish tradition. He even quoted sayings of Muhammad and phrases from the Qur'an—examples of specific Islamic influence in his work. Ibn Pakuda depicts man's struggle with impulses and instincts as something like a jihad (just war). Ibn Gabirol was also from Zaragoza; he was mainly a religious poet, whose great work of philosophy, *M'kor hayyim*, widely diffused in Latin as *Fons vitae* (Fountain of Life, circa 1050), was based on neo-Platonic metaphysical concepts having to do with the relationship between form and matter, the kind of discussion commonly found in neo-Platonic Muslim philosophers such as Ibn Sina (Avicenna).

Even religious writers who were not mystics were imbued with Arabic spirituality, to the point that Sa'adia ben Joseph, the great rabbinical scholar from Egypt who wrote in Arabic, used Arabo-Muslim terminology to express basic points of Judaism: in his writings he calls the Torah *shari'ah*, the standard Arabic word for Islamic religious law; the Hebrew Bible he calls *Qur'an;* the prayer leader *imam* (the equivalent

TREATMENT OF JEWS

of Hebrew, *hazzan*); and so forth. Sa'adia did not confuse Islam with Judaism; his integration in the scholarly world of Arab Muslim culture influenced both his language and the way he conceptualized religion.

Such a high level of acculturation in no way characterized the situation of Jews in medieval Europe, where few ever mastered Latin well enough to fit into European high culture where, in any case, they were not welcome. Communal autonomy had to be constantly negotiated in Europe, unlike the situation in the Islamic world where the underpinnings of autonomy were ensured through religious law enough so that the majority seriously promoted the emergence of a rather pacific, stabilized pluralism that lasted until the twentieth century.

–THOMAS F. GLICK,
BOSTON UNIVERSITY

Viewpoint:
No. The Jews were subjected to as much violence and exploitation in the Near East as in the West.

Comparative history can yield interesting insights into the past, but it can also introduce confusion and occasionally create optical illusions. In comparing the experience of Jews under "Islamic" and "Christian" rule, one sees that Jews were treated in roughly similar manners. The "Islamic world" never was—nor is it today—a monolithic entity with completely homogenous views and uniform practices. Thus, one should speak of particular Islamic societies rather than of a general Islamic world. One can legitimately study the treatment of Jews in Abbassid Baghdad; in Fatimid, Ayyubid, or Mamluk Egypt; or during the Taifa, Almoravid, and Almohad states in Islamic Spain. One cannot, however, lump them together to derive a singular set of general axioms that is valid for all. The same statement can be made about the position of Jews in the "Christian" world. The Jewish experience in northern Europe, the western and central Mediterranean, or the Crusader states cannot be lumped together.

On a similar note, one must also pay close attention to different time periods. The Jewish experience was not static in either civilization. Confining one's study to the Middle Ages, the comparative treatment of Jews by Muslims and Christians is a subject that spans roughly eight centuries. Like modern anti-Semitism, medieval anti-Judaism waxed and waned in accordance with constantly changing social, political, and

economic matrices that these societies were rooted in. Complicating the issue even further are the differing timetables in which economic and political growth or decline occurred. Both civilizations had nascent periods of growth and crystallization, as well as apogees, and experienced violent periods of disruption. These cycles were not synchronized. For example, during the eleventh century one finds social and political conditions that can hardly be compared in each civilization. The Islamic world enjoyed strong economic growth and prosperity, while its political situation had a marked degree of stability. Western Europe was characterized by a massive upsurge in religious fervor amid a landscape of political chaos destabilized even further by the Investiture Controversy (1075–1077). Comparing the vicious attacks on Jews in the Rhineland that occurred at the end of the eleventh century with the stable situation of Jews in Baghdad at the same time is akin to matching the "worst of times" in one civilization with the "best of times" in the other. Assessing whether one civilization was more tolerant than the other requires a broader analysis.

Two suitable case studies can be found in the late-eleventh-century butchering of Jews in the Rhineland and in the late-eleventh- to late-twelfth-century Berber persecution of Jews in Islamic Spain. Arguably, the former was the darkest chapter in Jewish history before the mid twentieth century. Entire communities were slaughtered. The vicious heights that these attacks reached can be seen not only from the extermination of Jewish communities but also through such reports as the stabbing of pregnant Jewish women in the abdomen to kill fetuses or the malevolent quip of one Crusader that he would not leave Europe until he killed a Jew. But this "first holocaust" was a violent tearing of the delicate fabric of Christian-Jewish relations. Far from normative, it represented a rupture in the modus vivendi that was produced by equally abnormal conditions. Acute apocalyptic anxieties combined with the complete unfettering of militant religious fervor to produce disastrous results. Yet, this massacre sprang from no "policy" toward Jews. Both the Church and the German king moved quickly to protect Jewish communities. Rather, the Rhineland attacks constituted a violation of such policies. Actuality clashed with theory and resulted in a chilling, bloodthirsty (but sporadic and short-lived) mass slaughter of Jews. Subsequent Crusades also produced heightened antagonism toward Jews for similar reasons, but as was the case with the First Crusade (1096–1102), these attacks were produced by ruptures in the normative relations between Jews and Christians.

The Almoravid and Almohad Berber invasions of the Iberian Peninsula violently smashed the stability of Spanish Jewry. Freshly converted to and fanatical about their own austere interpretation of Islam, the Almoravids upended the benign treatment of Jews in Islamic Spain. Although not as bloodthirsty as the Teuton count Emich's Crusader contingent in the First Crusade, the Almoravids were just as capable of crushing Jewish communities (the most poignant example being the destruction of the Jewish community in Granada). In North Africa, however, the Almohads gave Jews the same options that Emich offered in the Rhineland: conversion or death. Maimonides, writing to Jews in Yemen, claimed that no nation had ever harmed Jewry as much as the "nation of Ishmael" (Islam). Persecution of Jews under the Almoravids was so severe that it prompted a wave of Jewish apocalypticism. Some Jews comforted themselves with the notion that the unbearable tyranny of Islam was soon to be divinely swept away. Yehuda ben Shemuel ha-Levi claimed that the yoke of Islam and that of Christendom were equally painful and disastrous. Faced with the option of living under either Almoravid or Crusader rule, Levi opted for the latter. He immigrated to the Crusader States in the East, where he died in 1141. The Almoravid persecu-

tion of Spanish Jewry, however, was merely the overture to the more devastating assault conducted by the Almohads later. Basically, there were two Jewish responses to the fanatical (even by Almoravid standards) campaign against Jews launched by the Almohads: conversion or emigration. The Almohads brought a temporary end to Spanish Jewry at the time.

Neither case can be considered indicative of the normal relationship between Jews and the "civilization" in question. In both cases, an established and relatively quiet modus vivendi had been overturned. Jews and Christians in Mainz and Worms, for example, had a much different relationship with one another before and after the preaching of the First Crusade. Under the Taifa kings, Andalusian Jewry enjoyed an incredible degree of stability and prosperity that was violently upended by the Berbers. In both cases, religious change seems to have been the main causal factor in rupturing interfaith stability. Both Jewish communities suffered at the hands of men possessing a radical degree of religious fanaticism who were also engaged in holy wars. Generally speaking, Jews were considered to be "resident aliens" in both civilizations. Their alien status was defined by religious affiliation. During periods of explosive religious fervor and seething tensions—such as during the First Crusade and the

Illumination of Castilian Jews taking the road to exile (early fourteenth century)

(British Library, London)

TREATMENT OF JEWS

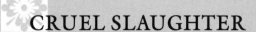

CRUEL SLAUGHTER

As Rhineland warriors prepared for the Crusade to the East in 1096, they fell upon and slaughtered the defenseless Jewish residents of several German cities. The following account is from the twelfth-century French chronicler Albert of Aix:

They started upon their journey, as they had vowed, and arrived in a great multitude at the city of Mainz. There Count Emico, a nobleman, a very mighty man in this region, was awaiting, with a large band of Teutons, the arrival of the pilgrims who were coming thither from diverse lands by the King's highway.

The Jews of this city, knowing of the slaughter of their brethren, and that they themselves could not escape the hands of so many, fled in hope of safety to Bishop Rothard. They put an infinite treasure in his guard and trust, having much faith in his protection, because he was Bishop of the city. Then that excellent Bishop of the city cautiously set aside the incredible amount of money received from them. He placed the Jews in the very spacious hall of his own house, away from the sight of Count Emico and his followers, that they might remain safe and sound in a very secure and strong place.

But Emico and the rest of his band held a council and, after sunrise, attacked the Jews in the hall with arrows and lances. Breaking the bolts and doors, they killed the Jews, about seven hundred in number, who in vain resisted the force and attack of so many thousands. They killed the women, also, and with their swords pierced tender children of whatever age and sex. The Jews, seeing that their Christian enemies were attacking them and their children, and that they were sparing no age, likewise fell upon one another, brother, children, wives, and sisters, and thus they perished at each other's hands. Horrible to say, mothers cut the throats of nursing children with knives and stabbed others, preferring them to perish thus by their own hands rather than to be killed by the weapons of the uncircumcised.

From this cruel slaughter of the Jews a few escaped; and a few because of fear, rather than because of love of the Christian faith, were baptized. With very great spoils taken from these people, Count Emico, Clarebold, Thomas, and all that intolerable company of men and women then continued on their way to Jerusalem, directing their course towards the Kingdom of Hungary, where passage along the royal highway was usually not denied the pilgrims. But on arriving at *Wieselburg,* the fortress of the King, which the rivers Danube and Leytha protect with marshes, the bridge and gate of the fortress were found closed by command of the King of Hungary, for great fear had entered all the Hungarians because of the slaughter which had happened to their brethren.

Source: *August C. Krey,* The First Crusade: The Accounts of Eyewitnesses and Participants *(Princeton: Princeton University Press, 1921), pp. 54–55.*

Berber invasions—their status could be, and was, temporarily revoked. Stability among the Jewish communities returned only when religious tensions eased.

If such persecutions were ruptures between Jewish minorities and their host civilizations, then one should consider what the normative relationship was like and was based upon. Both civilizations had common assumptions about the place of Jews in their societies (though interpretation and application varied drastically). Islamic societies defined the position of Jews in a much clearer manner. Their status in the Islamic world was theoretically defined in religious law. Essentially, the Pact of Umar (circa seventh century) laid out the provisions for a peace treaty between Muslims and subjected "people of the book" (for example, Jews and Christians). In exchange for payment of special taxes and political submission, Jews became *dhimmi* (protected people) who enjoyed a fair degree of self-rule in their own quarters. Stipulations existed, however, that clearly marked the inferior rank of Jews and their status as outsiders. Jews were never to have political authority over Muslims. They were not to carry arms, make public displays of their religious practices, or possess synagogues that were larger or more ornate than mosques; were not to construct new synagogues; were to act humbly and live in equally humble dwellings; were to wear distinctive clothing or a colored badge that identified them as Jews; and were to adhere to sumptuary laws and to display submissive modesty at all times. They were also subjected to occasional public degradation that reinforced notions of their humble status and reminded all of their inferior condition. So long as they lived in accordance with these terms, Jews were not to be molested. The contract, however, could be revoked at any time. Theory and practice naturally diverged—and usually in the favor of Jews. The rougher strictures were not always rigorously enforced, and Fatimid Egypt, for example, was notoriously lax in applying them.

The Christian approach to Jews was much more amorphous (at least in its earliest stages). There was no precise equivalent to the Pact of Umar, and treatment of Jews was not rigorously codified in religious law. Fourth-century Church father Augustine of Hippo's views on the status of Jews in Christian society is the closest functional equivalent one can find to the Pact of Umar. Synthesizing Christian perceptions with the dictates of Roman law, Augustine viewed Jews as citizens of sorts residing within a Christian empire. Jews were not to be subjected to violence, have their synagogues burned, or be forced to convert to Christianity. These rights were to be respected as long as Jews did not criticize or act aggressively toward Christianity. Like the Islamic view, Jews were not to be in positions of power over the faithful. As in Islamic areas, this policy was frequently ignored. What complicated the status of Jews in the Augustinian paradigm, however, was their unique eschatological purpose. Jews were God's tools for reminding Christians of the degraded condition that humanity was locked into before the coming of Christ. One effect of this concept was the ritualized public humiliation of Jews. Potentially more explosive, however, was the belief that Jews would convert to Christianity at the end of the world. Thus, during episodes of apocalyptic expectations (not a rare occurrence in the Middle Ages), the protected status of Jews was frequently swept aside. The accusation of deicide (that Jews were responsible for the execution of Christ), though it was never official Church policy, often had powerful effects on the popular mind. It was a potent ingredient in the mixture of Christian perceptions of Jews that proved explosive when unstable conditions emerged.

These general views of Jews have more similarities than differences. Both Islamic and Christian societies viewed Jews as aliens but tolerated their presence. They felt the need to visibly subordinate Jews within their societies, and both civilizations were susceptible to considerable discrepancies between theory and practice. Neither can be considered more tolerant regarding Jews. In the early Middle Ages, Islam can be said to have had more clearly defined practices that implemented the general theory. Somewhat standardized provisions for the treatment of Jews in Christendom was a later development; it really began in the twelfth century and became increasingly more delineated in the thirteenth. An important difference between theory and appli-

cation was the decentralized nature of Islamic religion and the centralized nature of the Latin Church. Islam never had an official "church" or "priests." Different "schools" of religious law were dominant in different regions, and these had palpable effects for the treatment of Jews. There were no real priests—let alone popes—in the Islamic world. Religious scholars served as interpreters of laws and were not always in agreement. The Latin Church promulgated religious policies that were theoretically binding throughout western Europe. In the twelfth and thirteenth centuries, uniform policies regarding Jews were issued by Church councils. Implementation, however, was ultimately the prerogative of secular rulers who enforced or ignored them in accordance with their own immediate interests.

Rulers in both civilizations frequently made use of Jews. By providing important services, many Jews reaped great rewards, but these relationships could also prove catastrophic. The anti-Jewish riots in York (1190) are a case in point. Some English Jews played an important role in handling the debts to the crown of knights and a nascent middle class. This role placed them in the uncomfortable position of being the royal stalking-horses regarding foreclosures while the Third Crusade (1189–1192) was being organized. William of Newburgh dubbed them the "royal usurers." After fleeing to a royal tower, the Jews committed mass suicide. In the Islamic world many rulers were known to sacrifice a favored Jewish courtier to appease animosity among mobs or to defuse criticisms by religious scholars who objected to deviations from the *dhimmi* contract. In December 1066 in Granada a popular uprising against a prominent Jew resulted in his crucifixion at the main gate, followed the next day by a mob attack on the Jewish quarter. Mamluk Egypt was also racked by popular uprisings against Jews. If they never reached the scale of Crusader attacks on Jews, it was probably because Christians also lived as a protected monotheistic people in Islamic lands and absorbed much of the animosity directed at non-Muslims. With the exception of Spain and Sicily, Jews were the only such minority in western Europe and thus became the only real outlet for venting outbursts of religious rage. Spain, which had a situation more like that existing in Islamic societies, never experienced massacres on the scale of those in the Rhineland. Islamic societies occasionally had pogroms that approached the magnitude of that led by Emich. In 1465 the Jewish community in Fez was completely slaughtered by participants in a rebellion against the Merinids, which certainly was not indicative of the Islamic treatment of Jews. But Emich was not indicative of the Christian treatment of Jews. Both incidents represented brutal deviations from a roughly equivalent modus vivendi.

Dangerous rumors occasionally circulated in Christian communities about Jews desecrating the host. Similar accusations, however, were known to occur in Islamic states. In 1438, for example, Jews in Morocco were accused of pouring wine into the lamps of a mosque (a clear functional equivalent to host desecration). Anti-Judaism was certainly present in Christian artwork and music, but it was a salient theme in the poetry of the Spanish Muslim Abu Ishaq in Elvira (which played a role in mobilizing mobs against Jews). The sinister Jewish physician became the villain of a literary genre in Islamic lands. If one speaks of the waves of Jews expelled from European states in the late thirteenth century (though they usually returned within a few years), one must also mention the purges of Jewish officials that took place throughout Iran and Iraq in the last decade of the century.

Neither Christianity nor Islam was inherently more tolerant of Jews. Both civilizations had provisions for the toleration and protection of Jews that exhibit equally sketchy track records. They were capable of allowing Jews to live in their societies—but only on their own terms. Both were prone to violent outbursts against Jews under certain circumstances. The historical debate surrounding the comparative treatment of Jews in the medieval Christian and Islamic worlds is pregnant with modern concerns. In the mid twentieth century, the revelation of the Holocaust and the formation of the state of Israel raised the stakes and gave the issue a pressing modern importance. One of the greatest handicaps facing the subject is what Herbert Butterfield described as the "Whig" interpretation of history: many historians tend to emphasize certain parts of the past to explain the exigencies of the present. Neither civilization really persecuted Jews more than the other when all of the evidence is tallied. In the end, ha-Levi was probably right: domination of Jews in the Middle Ages was an equally bitter experience under both Christians and Muslims.

–MARK T. ABATE,
WESTFIELD STATE COLLEGE

References

Mark R. Cohen, "Islam and the Jews: Myth, Counter-Myth, and History," *Jerusalem Quarterly,* 38 (1986): 125–137.

Cohen, "The Neo-Lachrymose Conception of Jewish-Arab History," *Tikkun,* 6 (May–June 1991): 55–60.

Cohen, *Under Crescent and Cross: The Jews in the Middle Ages* (Princeton: Princeton University Press, 1994).

S. D. Goitein, *Jews and Arabs: Their Contacts through the Ages* (New York: Schocken Books, 1955).

Goitein, *Letters of Medieval Jewish Traders,* translated by author (Princeton: Princeton University Press, 1973).

Goitein, *A Mediterranean Society: The Jewish Communities of the Arab World as Portrayed in the Documents of the Cairo Geniza,* 6 volumes (Berkeley: University of California Press, 1967–1993).

Joshua Prawer, *The History of the Jews in the Latin Kingdom of Jerusalem* (Oxford: Clarendon Press / New York: Oxford University Press, 1988).

Norman A. Stillman, comp., *The Jews of Arab Lands: A History and Source Book* (Philadelphia: Jewish Publication Society of America, 1979).

Stillman, "Myth, Countermyth, and Distortion," *Tikkun,* 6 (1991), pp. 60–64.

Kenneth R. Stow, *Alienated Minority: The Jews of Medieval Latin Europe* (Cambridge, Mass.: Harvard University Press, 1992).

TREATMENT OF JEWS

URBAN II

What was Pope Urban II's main objective in launching the First Crusade?

Viewpoint: Urban II wished to liberate Eastern Christians and the city of Jerusalem from Islamic rule.

Viewpoint: Urban II wanted to achieve a rapprochement between the Eastern and Western Churches and to strengthen the position of the papacy in western Europe.

Viewpoint: Urban II's launch of the First Crusade was part of a broad counterstrike against Islam in Spain, Sicily, and the eastern Mediterranean.

When Urban II was elected to the papacy in 1088, he found himself at the head of an energetic reform movement, one that aspired to make the Pope the universal head of all Christendom. This bid for power was both turbulent and dangerous; Urban began his pontificate in exile. His qualifications for weathering this storm (and launching the First Crusade, 1096–1102) were impressive. He had a comprehensive understanding of reform ideology, ecclesiastical politics, and the mentality of the warrior class. His father was most likely a vassal of the count of Champagne. Urban attended the excellent cathedral school at Reims before joining the Benedictine abbey at Cluny. His career there was stellar, culminating in his appointment as grand prior. Urban then was made cardinal-bishop of Ostia and became enmeshed in the Investiture Controversy (1075–1077). The fact that he was made papal legate to Germany at such a sensitive and dangerous time is ample testimony to his abilities. Urban was an excellent successor to take up Gregory VII's projects, and though he shared his predecessor's enthusiasm and energy, he demonstrated a greater flare for political acumen and subtlety.

That the First Crusade was intimately connected to these events and the papal reform movement is beyond doubt. But what exactly Urban wanted to accomplish most—the objective at the center of his crusading policy—has been the subject of some debate. Was he merely following Gregory VII's plan to march toward the East to liberate Christians, and possibly Jerusalem, from Islamic domination? Was he using the Crusade as a tool by which to reconcile the Eastern and Western Churches and heal the schism? Was it an attempt to roll back Islamic gains throughout the Mediterranean? Most likely all these issues played a role, but which one proved to be the decisive factor is still debated. Descriptions of the Council of Clermont (1095) are not to be too readily trusted. The first problem with using these sources to delineate papal policy is that they can confuse the "pitch" with the goal. If Urban were trying to use the warrior aristocracy for papal ends, then he could hardly say so. The second problem is that different accounts of the council emphasize varying aspects. The third problem is that all these accounts were written after the successful conclusion of the First Crusade, and the end was universally read into the beginning. Combining these accounts with letters Urban wrote, however, has been instrumental in clarifying the matter.

The three theories presented in this chapter focus on different possible salients in Urban's Crusade policy. The first is generally spiritual: Western charity and protection had to be extended to Eastern Christians, and the Holy City of Jerusalem had to be wrested from Islamic control. The second is generally political: the Crusade was designed as a tool for reconciling the Eastern and Western Churches and thus constituted diplomacy under the guise of armed pilgrimage. The third is purely military: Islam had encroached upon the Christian world on every border, and the launch of a massive holy war throughout the Mediterranean world was needed.

Viewpoint:
Urban II wished to liberate Eastern Christians and the city of Jerusalem from Islamic rule.

At the threshold of the twelfth century, Europe and the Western Church together faced several challenges that threatened to undermine, and perhaps even destroy, their way of life. There was the military threat posed by Islamic armies on the border frontiers of Christendom both in Spain and Anatolia. If Christian resistance on either the eastern or western border collapsed, it was quite possible that much of the interior would be overrun by a renewed surge of Muslim conquest and European culture consequently would be swept away. Politically, Christendom was fragmented into a series of competing principalities, each led by a warrior aristocracy imbued with a seemingly unquenchable thirst for combat. With no real external foes to oppose since the pacification of the Vikings and Magyars in the tenth century, these warrior elites turned against each other to satisfy their cravings for war and their ambitions for increased power and wealth. The result was a climate of endemic violence that, while waged among the feudal hierarchy, nevertheless had as its real victims the poor and the Church, who were often caught in the crossfire.

Religiously, the West faced a dual crisis. Since 1054 the Churches of the East and West had formally separated from each other, ending a thousand-year legacy of Christian unity in the Mediterranean world. The cause of this schism had as much, and perhaps more, to do with politics as with differences in theology, yet forty years later the possibility of a mutual reconciliation still seemed both desirable and possible. The other religious crisis was more an internal, private problem for the West: the widespread climate of moral decay that had seeped deeply within the Church hierarchy and among the laity in general. While nearly all inhabitants of Europe in the eleventh century professed Christian beliefs, many failed to practice Christian morality. The inherent hypocrisy of this state of affairs threatened not only to undermine the moral authority of the Church but also to tear apart Western society.

Urban II, who became Pope in 1088, was well aware of the grave problems that the Church and the West were then facing. He was a reform-minded Pope, as the last several pontiffs had been, and as such he was a man of action, determined to meet problems head-on. Thus, when he received word from Byzantine emperor Alexius I Comnenus in March 1095 about the deteriorating state of affairs on Christendom's eastern border, Urban responded to the imperial request for military assistance with a call to arms to Western knights that has come to be known as the First Crusade (1096–1102). While historians widely agree that Urban's call was the genesis of the crusading movement, there is no consensus among them as to what the original goals and purposes were. The problem is that, aside from a handful of recruitment letters, Urban left no written declaration of war; no collection of strategic maps with graphic overlays that neatly laid out for future scholars the reasons for and goals of this military enterprise. There is, however, sufficient supporting evidence to enable a careful historian to reconstruct with reasonable certainty Urban's original war plan. Undoubtedly, Urban would have welcomed the opportunity to strengthen the central authority of the papacy, to further the progress of the growing reform movement, and to strike back at the threat of further Islamic expansion. Yet, the balance of existing evidence suggests that these goals were ancillary objectives of his crusading plans, not his immediate and ultimate concern. Rather, the fundamental purpose in launching the First Crusade was the rescue of Eastern Christians and the great Christian shrines of the Near East from Muslim control.

Urban's call for Crusade was immediately precipitated by Emperor Alexius's appeal in March 1095 for Western knights to assist in the war against the Seljuk Turks in Anatolia. For Byzantium the struggle had been going badly ever since the core of its imperial army was decimated at the Battle of Manzikert (1071) on the Armenian border. Not only did the defeat leave the Byzantine army severely weakened, but, more important, it also left the Turks in control of all of Anatolia, the breadbasket and prime military recruiting ground of the Byzantine state. Furthermore, it left Christian residents of this region under the control of a hostile Islamic force. Understandably, Alexius dreamed of recovering all or part of this lost province, which was so vital to the economic and military strength of the empire, but given the current condition of his army, he realized that this objective was impossible to achieve without military assistance from the West.

At the same time, although harder for modern historians to ascertain, there were actual or rumored problems with the traditional pilgrimage routes that Western Christians followed to visit the great holy shrines in the Near East. While Christians had been making the arduous journey from Europe to Jerusalem since Christianity's earliest days, the eleventh century marked a significant increase in the participation, frequency, and interest associated with this religious devotion. Yet, with the expansion of Islamic power not only were the shrines of the Holy Land in Muslim hands but so too were the pilgrimage routes. Passing through hostile territory presented a further hardship for peaceful pilgrims from the West, whose journey had always been a difficult and expensive proposition.

Without this concern for the fate of Eastern Christians and the holy shrines that Alexius's urgent report brought to the forefront of Urban's attention, there simply would not have been a First Crusade. Therefore, these two concerns weighed heavily on Urban's mind, as reflected in his speech at the Council of Clermont (1095) in November, and were what actually launched the Crusade. Although Urban's exact words have not survived, accounts of his address have been preserved by four eyewitnesses—Robert the Monk, Baldric of Dol, Fulcher of Chartres, and Guibert of Nogent. While there are differences in the particular wording or emphasis of each account, all four concentrate on the issues of bringing aid to Eastern Christians, protecting Western pilgrims, and recovering the holy shrines in Palestine. These accounts, for example, focus with similar impassioned rhetoric on the terrible fate of Christian brethren living under the yoke of Muslim oppression or traveling through Muslim-controlled territory on pilgrimage. The plight of Jerusalem and of the holy shrines also is prominently mentioned, whether placed within the specific wording of Urban's speech or in the wider context of a passage into which the writer inserted Urban's appeal. Given this substantial consistency among these four accounts, it is reasonable to conclude that these two issues must have been the primary concerns that Urban hoped to resolve by launching the Crusade.

That these four chroniclers were accurate recorders is buttressed by the few surviving letters that Urban sent out to different parts of Europe in order to recruit volunteers for his Crusade. In all of these documents the Pope mentions the need to free Eastern Christians from the bondage of their Muslim overlords and to rescue the holy shrines in the East, especially those in Jerusalem.

Notably absent, however, are arguments to wage a holy war against Islam, to increase the central authority of the Pope, to further the spread of the Church reform movement, or to reunite the Eastern and Western churches. While undoubtedly these outcomes would have been welcomed by Urban, judging from his own words, they did not constitute the core purpose of his Crusade.

In the same way the indulgence, which is the remission of the penalties of sins, which Urban promised to the Crusaders, was linked specifically to saving Jerusalem. Indeed, this promise represented perhaps the most appealing incentive to volunteers for the Crusade. It seemed that Urban offered potential recruits the guarantee of going to Heaven in return for their participation in the Crusade. In order to earn so great a prize, however, participants had to undertake the perilous trip to Jerusalem, for the canons from the Council of Clermont explicitly stated that the indulgence would be won only by those who reached Jerusalem or died along the way. In one surviving recruitment letter, Urban reiterates this crucial point by declaring that the receipt of the indulgence hinges on Crusaders going to Jerusalem with the sole intention to save their souls and to liberate the Church in the East. Since Jerusalem was deep behind enemy lines, evidently Urban had its recovery as his ultimate objective. Because Jerusalem was the primary objective of the Crusade, the whole movement reflected the spirit and practice of the traditional pilgrimage. Indeed, early accounts of the Crusades refer to participants as pilgrims, not Crusaders. The term "crusader" is rather anachronistic, coined centuries later to describe what historians, not contemporary participants, saw as a movement distinct from pilgrimage. Likewise, many surviving charters that recorded the sale of property by departing Crusaders to help finance their journey mention pilgrimage to Jerusalem as the key reason for disposing of their property.

The centrality of recovering Jerusalem and of bringing aid to oppressed Christians as the primary goal of the Crusade is also reflected in the actions of the Crusaders. Despite clashes with imperial troops during their march through the Balkans toward Constantinople, the crusading forces refrained from all-out warfare with the Byzantines. This restraint was remarkable, given the headstrong ambitions, fierce pride, and universal penchant for fighting that these Western knights typically displayed against each other. One should remember that the West had for generations suffered endless internecine violence waged by this same knightly class. Yet, in the face of many provocations, the Crusaders for the most part held their fire, preventing intermittent clashes with imperial scouts from escalating into all-out war. On the contrary, despite some bitter feelings about how they felt their Byzantine hosts had treated them, the Crusaders ultimately requested that Alexius march with them to Jerusalem at the head of the army and agreed to return any former Byzantine lands they captured to the emperor. Implicit here is the fact that the Crusaders realized that their mission was to assist their Eastern brothers against the Seljuk Turks, not to provoke a war against fellow Christians or amass large personal landholdings in the East.

Once they crossed into Anatolia in the spring of 1097, the Crusaders suffered many hardships and achieved some improbable successes during the next two years; yet, the core of the army did not stop its march until it had captured Jerusalem. Eyewitness accounts of the campaign clearly indicate that what continued to impel the Crusaders forward was the urgent desire to fulfill their vows by visiting the holy places in Jerusalem. Their actions thus serve as further evidence of Urban's real purpose in launching the Crusade. If the goal had been something other than liberating Jerusalem, the army almost certainly would have turned back during particularly desperate moments in the campaign, such as the battle at Dorylaeum (July 1097) or the long siege of Antioch (1098). If they had been summoned only to assist Eastern Christians, for example, then the Crusaders probably would have terminated their offensive and consolidated their surprising gains after they had freed western Anatolia (1097) or had captured the strategic city of Antioch, especially since the army had almost been annihilated twice, first at Dorylaeum and then at Antioch. Yet, the march did not end until Jerusalem had fallen (July 1099). Only then did many of the Crusaders, having made their visit to the holy shrines and thus fulfilled their vows, end their crusade and return to Europe. Their mission, as they had understood it, had been accomplished. Had the real intent of the Crusade been something different, such as waging war against the peoples of Islam, then the army would likely have continued its offensive deep into Egypt or Syria, the central strongholds of Muslim power. That was not, however, the mission Urban had enlisted them to undertake.

Despite this evidence, some historians continue to argue that Jerusalem was not part of Urban's original plan but something that developed almost accidentally within the ranks of the army over the course of the campaign. Such a position, however, fails to account for the terms of the indulgence that was promulgated at the Council of Clermont, which clearly stated the need to visit Jerusalem in order to obtain the reward. Likewise, it ignores Urban's own recruitment letters. It also fails to account for the fact that Urban's handpicked representative, the papal legate Adhémar de Monteil (Aimar de Le Puy), went on the Crusade and provided crucial leader-

ship until his death in August 1098. As Urban made clear in a recruitment letter sent to Flanders in December 1096, Adhémar spoke for Urban in his absence, and it was to him that all participants in the Crusade should be obedient. This announcement was an important delegation of authority, and it is clear that Urban did not make it haphazardly. In fact, before he made the crusading appeal at Clermont, Urban first met with Adhémar at his residence in Le Puy in August. Although what the two prelates discussed is unknown, it is hard to imagine that Urban did not brief Adhémar about his imminent plans to call for an army of knights to march to the East to free the Christian peoples and their shrines from Muslim control. Indeed, Adhémar accompanied Urban to Clermont, and at the council he was the first to take the cross. Urban subsequently installed Adhémar as the papal legate to the army. Adhémar was sent to insure that the army carried out the plan Urban had devised. Eyewitness chroniclers of the First Crusade all recognize Adhémar's contribution as one of its key leaders and guiding spirits. Historians should likewise appreciate his efforts, for without Adhémar the Crusader army, in the face of so many overwhelming obstacles, would probably never have maintained its unity nor its commitment to Urban's original war plan.

While definitive answers are nearly impossible to achieve on the topic of Urban's goals for the First Crusade, the balance of evidence supports the conclusion that he sought primarily to rescue Christians and holy places in the Near East. That his call to Crusade might advance other interests of the reform papacy, such as increasing its central authority and promoting its program of moral reform, should be viewed as added benefits, not primary intentions.

–CHRISTOPHER LIBERTINI,
SUFFOLK UNIVERSITY

Viewpoint:
Urban II wanted to achieve a rapprochement between the Eastern and Western Churches and to strengthen the position of the papacy in western Europe.

In his seminal work, *The Origin Of the Idea Of Crusade* (1977), Carl Erdmann argued that the recovery of Jerusalem was not the chief purpose behind Pope Urban II's summoning of the First Crusade (1096–1102). Rather, he contended that liberating the Holy City constituted only one important piece in the Pope's overarching goal of

IMPERISHABLE GLORY

At the Council of Clermont (1095) Pope Urban II called upon the Franks to take up the cross and help the Byzantines against the Turks, a call that initiated the First Crusade (1096–1102). Robert the Monk, allegedly in attendance, recorded this version of Urban's speech:

From the confines of Jerusalem and the city of Constantinople a horrible tale has gone forth and very frequently has been brought to our ears, namely, that a race from the kingdom of the Persians, an accursed race, a race utterly alienated from God, a generation forsooth which has not directed its heart and has not entrusted its spirit to God, has invaded the lands of those Christians and has depopulated them by the sword, pillage and fire; it has led away a part of the captives into its own country, and a part it has destroyed by cruel tortures; it has either entirely destroyed the churches of God or appropriated them for the rites of its own religion. They destroy the altars, after having defiled them with their uncleanness. They circumcise the Christians, and the blood of the circumcision they either spread upon the altars or pour into the vases of the baptismal font. When they wish to torture people by a base death, they perforate their navels, and dragging forth the extremity of the intestines, bind it to a stake; then with flogging they lead the victim around until the viscera having gushed forth the victim falls prostrate upon the ground. Others they bind to a post and pierce with arrows. Others they compel to extend their necks and then, attacking them with naked swords, attempt to cut through the neck with a single blow. What shall I say of the abominable rape of the women? To speak of it is worse than to be silent. The kingdom of the Greeks is now dismembered by them and deprived of territory so vast in extent that it cannot be traversed in a march of two months. On whom therefore is the labor of avenging these wrongs and of recovering this territory incumbent, if not upon you? You, upon whom above other nations God has conferred remarkable glory in arms, great courage, bodily activity, and strength to humble the hairy scalp of those who resist you.

Let the deeds of your ancestors move you and incite your minds to manly achievements; the glory and greatness of king Charles the Great, and of his son Louis, and of your other kings, who have destroyed the kingdoms of the pagans, and extended in these lands the territory of the holy church. Let the holy sepulchre of the Lord our Saviour, which is possessed by unclean nations, especially incite you, and the holy places which are now treated with ignominy and irreverently polluted with their filthiness. Oh, most valiant soldiers and descendants of invincible ancestors, be not degenerate, but recall the valor of your progenitors.

But if you are hindered by love of children, parents and wives, remember what the Lord says in the Gospel, "He that loveth father or mother more than me, is not worthy of me." "Every one that hath forsaken houses, or brethren, or sisters, or father, or mother, or wife, or children, or lands for my name's sake shall receive an hundred-fold and shall inherit everlasting life." Let none of your possessions detain you, no solicitude for your family affairs, since this land which you inhabit, shut in on all sides by the seas and surrounded by the mountain peaks, is too narrow for your large population; nor does it abound in wealth; and it furnishes scarcely food enough for its cultivators. Hence it is that you murder one another, that you wage war, and that frequently you perish by mutual wounds. Let therefore hatred depart from among you, let your quarrels end, let wars cease, and let all dissensions and controversies slumber. Enter upon the road to the Holy Sepulchre; wrest that land from the wicked race, and subject it to yourselves. That land which as the Scripture says "floweth with milk and honey," was given by God into the possession of the children of Israel.

Jerusalem is the navel of the world; the land is fruitful above others, like another paradise of delights. This the Redeemer of the human race has made illustrious by His advent, has beautified by residence, has consecrated by suffering, has redeemed by death, has glorified by burial. This royal city, therefore, situated at the center of the world, is now held captive by His enemies, and is in subjection to those who do not know God, to the worship of the heathens. She seeks therefore and desires to be liberated and does not cease to implore you to come to her aid. From you especially she asks succor, because, as we have already said, God has conferred upon you above all nations great glory in arms. Accordingly undertake this journey for the remission of your sins, with the assurance of the imperishable glory of the kingdom of heaven.

Source: "The Council of Clermont," Norton Topics Online: Robert the Monk, Jerusalem History <http://www.wwnorton.com/nael/nto/middle/crusade/councilfrm.htm>

URBAN II

relieving all Eastern Churches from Muslim oppression. According to Erdmann, the eventual souring of relations between the Western Crusaders and the Byzantine Empire distorted the post-1099 accounts of the First Crusade. With the "Greek betrayal" in the forefront of their thoughts, early authors wrongly portrayed the recapture of Jerusalem as the chief concern of the Crusaders.

More recently, Jonathan Riley-Smith has demonstrated that Erdmann overstated his case on this point. Riley-Smith has persuasively argued that from its inception the liberation of Jerusalem was indeed the primary objective of the First Crusade. It definitely was something more than an alluring carrot that Urban held out to the Crusaders. It was a vital objective.

Still, Riley-Smith's research has not disproved the notion that Urban ultimately saw the Crusade as a vehicle for improving relations between the Roman Church and Constantinople. The Pope probably believed that recovery of the Holy City could serve as a catalyst to political and religious rapprochement between the papacy and the Byzantine Empire. Certainly, better relations with Constantinople would have served the papacy's strategic interests in western Europe. A friendly emperor in Constantinople would be a counterbalance to the somewhat unpredictable Norman princes of southern Italy and a hostile German emperor and his Antipope. Political rapprochement with the Christian East would give the Pope maximum strategic flexibility on the Italian peninsula and beyond. Equally important, it could facilitate the healing of the religious schism between Latin and Greek Christianity that had developed during the early Middle Ages. In turn, reunion with the Orthodox Churches of the East could add to the papacy's prestige in the West and undoubtedly aid in the implementation of papal reforms in the Western Church.

The idea of using a military campaign to facilitate better relations with Byzantium was not at all unprecedented in the annals of the reform papacy. In the early 1050s the venerable Pope Leo IX sought to form a united front with the German and Greek emperors against the Norman clans of southern Italy. In the early 1050s, reformers in Rome saw the Normans as a predatory power poised to encroach on papal territory. While the growth of Norman power also posed a challenge to the territorial interests of the German emperor, Henry III (cousin of Leo IX), the Normans were an immediate threat to Byzantine possessions in southern Italy. In 1051 Byzantine emperor Constantine IX dispatched Argyros, "Duke of Italy and Sicily," to deal with the Normans. Both the Pope and the Byzantine duke tried separately to defeat the Normans and failed. For his part, Leo had assembled a papal army without much direct support from either emperor and engaged the Nor-

mans at the Battle of Civitate (1053). The Normans smashed the papal force and took Leo prisoner.

Despite this humiliating setback, the Pope did not give up on the idea of a papal-Byzantine alliance against the Normans, and neither did Constantine IX. In early 1054 Leo sent a legation, under the leadership of Cardinal Humbert of Silva Candida, to Constantinople to discuss various matters, including some thorny religious issues, with the emperor and patriarch. Although Humbert was not to blame for the mission's failure, his legation was a diplomatic and theological disaster, which he concluded by laying a bull of excommunication against the patriarch, Michael Cerularius, on the altar of the Church of Hagia Sophia.

In the years that followed, relations between the papacy and the Normans improved considerably. In large part, the strategic needs of the reform papacy were responsible for this change in relations. The premature death of the imperial protector of the reform papacy, Henry III, in 1056 and the subsequent regencies of his wife Agnes and Bishop Anno of Cologne forced Roman reformers to seek new allies who could provide military support against their enemies in the Roman and northern Italian aristocracies. Hence, in 1059, Pope Nicholas II set his seal of approval on conquests of Byzantine territory by the Norman princes Richard of Capua and Robert Guiscard in exchange for their promise of military aid. Quite understandably, this papal-Norman entente further strained the already difficult relations between Rome and Constantinople.

However, during the 1060s the reform popes learned that the Normans made poor allies. On more than one occasion these ostensible allies ravaged papal territory. As H. E. J. Cowdrey has remarked, in *The Age of Abbot Desiderius: Montecassino, the Papacy, and the Normans in the Eleventh and Early Twelfth Centuries* (1983), when Pope Nicholas II confirmed the conquests of Richard of Capua and Guiscard in 1059, Rome played its trump card with the self-interested Normans. There really was no other prize that the reform popes could hold out to the Normans as a reward for their good behavior. From the late 1060s to the 1070s, the reform Popes Alexander II and Gregory VII pursued a diplomatic divide-and-conquer strategy against the Norman princes, for, when the Norman clans were not at war with others, they were more than likely warring and plotting against one another.

In 1074, relations between Gregory VII and his ostensible vassal Guiscard had so deteriorated that the Pope excommunicated the duke of Apulia and Calabria. It is not a coincidence that Gregory took this strong measure against Guiscard at a time when he was most optimistic about the future course of the reign of Henry III's son and successor, Henry IV. Because of young Henry's professions of devotion to him early in his pontificate, Gregory believed that the German king and heir to the Holy Roman Empire would provide the same protective shield over the reform papacy's activities that his father had. Of course, much had changed, both in Germany and in Rome, during Henry IV's minority. The chief goals of the Salian House and the reform papacy had begun to diverge. When Henry reached the age of majority in 1065, his and his leading counselors' primary objective concerned the restoration of the sacral kingship of the Salian dynasty both in Germany and in its Italian territories. This policy led to clashes between the German court and Rome in the late 1060s over the course of ecclesiastical reform in the German and Italian kingdoms. In particular, the German court had little patience with the papal reformers' increasing discomfort with the investiture of bishops by laymen, which constituted a key expression of the sacral character of Salian rule.

However, upon Gregory VII's papal election, Henry IV faced a serious rebellion among the German nobility, and he could not afford any trouble with the new Pope. So, Henry told Gregory what he knew the Pope wanted to hear. Out of expediency, Henry promised his future obedience to Gregory. Reasonably confident in the German monarch's fidelity to him, Gregory floated the idea in 1074 of personally leading an army of the faithful to the East to liberate the Eastern Church from "pagan," for example, Turkish, oppression. An earlier message from Byzantine emperor Michael VII Ducas, in which he hinted that Western military help against the Turks could lead to reunion between the Latin and Greek Churches, might have inspired Gregory's proposal. Interestingly, the Pope floated his idea within the context of soliciting military help against Guiscard. In a letter of February 1074 to Count William of Upper Burgundy, the Pope suggested that after a coalition force of papal allies had cowed Guiscard from any further encroachments on papal territory, it could proceed to Constantinople to help the Byzantines against the Turks. One month later, Gregory issued a broader appeal to Latin Christians to come to the aid of their brothers in the Lord whom a pagan people were slaughtering by the thousands. In a December 1074 letter to Henry, the Pope informed him of the warm response to his earlier appeals for military aid for the Byzantines and of his desire to lead the expedition personally. He intimated to Henry that some of those who expressed a willingness to fight God's enemies raised the prospect of advancing all the way to Jerusalem. Significantly, Gregory also communicated his hope that such an expedition to the East could facilitate the healing of the religious schism between Rome and Constantinople.

For several reasons, Gregory's "crusade" never materialized. In the years that followed, rela-

tions between Gregory and Henry deteriorated. Not surprisingly, as matters worsened, the Pope's dealings with Guiscard grew warmer. When the final break between the Pope and the German king occurred in 1080, Gregory reconciled with Guiscard out of sheer necessity. Because Guiscard was the principal enemy of Byzantine interests in the southern Adriatic, this reconciliation earned Gregory the enmity of the successors of Michael VII in Constantinople. In retribution for Gregory's blessing of Guiscard's military adventures along the southern Adriatic coastline of the Balkan Peninsula, Byzantine emperor Alexius I Comnenus helped finance the military activities of Henry and his Antipope against Gregory in Italy.

In 1085 the Pope died in exile in Salerno. A year earlier the raucous behavior of Guiscard's troops in Rome after their rescue of Gregory from his encirclement by the Antipope's forces in the Castel Sant' Angelo had compelled the Pope to flee the hostility of the populace and to retreat to Norman territory. Although Gregory's immediate successor, Victor III, was not wholly ineffective, the papal reform party remained pinned south of Rome by the Antipope's forces, and they were largely (though not completely) cut off from their lay and clerical allies in northern Italy, Germany, and France.

Thus, when he was elected Pope on 12 March 1088 in Terracina, Urban II faced a difficult, but not impossible, situation. Amazingly, both through his own shrewd diplomacy and the missteps of his adversaries, the tide of events had turned decisively in Urban's favor by 1095. His efforts at rapprochement with Alexius I, which Urban began early in his papacy, constituted one of the key components of his diplomacy. Urban had solicited a promise from Count Roger II of Sicily that he would not resume the late Guiscard's offensive against Byzantium in the Balkans. Guiscard had died in 1085. Almost certainly, Urban communicated Roger's intentions concerning the Balkans to the Byzantine emperor through his representatives, whom he dispatched to Constantinople in 1089 to request the reinsertion of the Roman pontiff's name in the official prayers of the Byzantine Church. Urban had previously lifted the sentence of excommunication from Alexius that Gregory VII had imposed on Alexius's predecessor, Nicephorus III Botaneiates. Given the situation of his party, Urban's gesture toward the Eastern Christian empire made perfect sense. First, warmer relations with Constantinople would presumably end Alexius's subsidies paid to the then Emperor Henry IV and his Antipope. Second, they also would forestall Constantinople's recognition of the Antipope's claim to St. Peter's throne. Third, a friendly Eastern emperor would serve as something of a check on the ambitious Normans, with whom the papacy shared a border.

As it turned out, Urban's opening gambit was not a spectacular success. In exchange for the reinsertion of the Pope's name in the Byzantine *diptychs* (tablets), the leading churchmen of Constantinople insisted that the Pope send a profession of faith to them. Characteristically, Urban opted not to risk opening recent religious wounds and never sent the requested profession. Consequently, the papal name was not reinserted into the intercessory prayers of the Byzantine Church. Yet, Alexius's enthusiasm for Henry's cause seems to have waned, and Constantinople never recognized the German emperor's Antipope.

In the West the Pope's shrewd diplomacy yielded more-tangible results. In 1089 Urban helped arrange the marriage of the forty-three-year-old staunch papalist, Countess Matilda of Tuscany, to the seventeen-year-old Welf V, heir to Bavaria and Este. This union of two anti-imperialist houses situated on either side of the Alpine passes between Henry's German and Italian kingdoms induced the emperor to launch a disastrous incursion into Italy that left him trapped in northern Italy and cut off from Germany until 1097. In part, the formation of the first anti-imperial Lombard League (1093), representing Matilda and some of the leading cities of northern Italy, was responsible for Henry's quandary. Without a doubt, Urban had a hand in the formation of this union as well. Moreover, in 1093, Henry's son, Conrad, defected from his father's camp and joined the emperor's adversaries. Finally, in 1094 Urban secured the obedience of all of Rome through gifts of money to the last Henrican holdouts in the city. Thus, by 1095 the Pope and the emperor had reversed their roles of 1088–1089.

In order to determine what Urban hoped to accomplish by sponsoring an armed pilgrimage to the East, one must keep in mind the context in which he passed along Alexius's appeal to Western knights. That the Pope received the Eastern emperor's appeal and first sounded the call to Crusade at Piacenza (1095) is symbolically significant. The council that Urban convened constituted something of a capstone to his seven-year-long effort to restore and to strengthen the bonds of loyalty between the Roman Church and the faithful of northern Italy. Ever since the violent schism of Bishop Peter Cadalus of Parma (Antipope Honorius II) in the early 1060s, many leading churchmen and laity looked on the reform papacy and its agenda with a hostile eye. Gregory VII's zealous pursuit of religious reform in the 1070s and 1080s greatly intensified this hostility. Much more so than Gregory, Urban was willing to compromise on nonessential points and on the implementation of specific reforms with the independent-minded northern Italians. He was also shrewd enough to use their long-standing mistrust of the German monarchy to his party's advantage. Remarkably, in 1076 Piacenza had hosted an anti-Gregorian synod under the auspices of the city's bishop, Dennis. Nineteen years later the well-attended council, over which Urban presided, ratified many reform canons. Here, as well as in Milan and elsewhere on the trek that took him to Clermont and back to Italy, Urban sounded the interrelated themes of reconciliation, restoration, and liberation under the Roman pontiff. At Clermont his summons to Crusade was one component of this broader message.

Almost certainly, Urban viewed the First Crusade as a means to several ends. Within Europe itself, the Crusade was a manifestation of papal leadership over the *societas christiana* (Christian society). On several earlier occasions, reform popes sponsored military adventures as a means of boosting papal prestige. To be sure, well before his summons, Urban took the war of restoration and liberation in Spain under his wing. The Pope's invitation to holy war in the East also served to underscore the difficult circumstances of Henry IV and of his Antipope.

More important, Urban almost certainly viewed the liberation of the Eastern Churches and Jerusalem as a means of restoring, or at least repairing, the Roman Church's relationship with both Church and State in Constantinople. He likely imagined that a successful outcome of the Crusade, especially the capture of Jerusalem, would generate much goodwill in Constantinople toward the papacy, underscore what the two branches of Christianity shared in common, and blunt their theological differences. Among other things, good relations with Constantinople would give Urban greater latitude in his dealings with the Normans to his south and with the Germans to his north.

–JOHN A. DEMPSEY,
FRAMINGHAM STATE COLLEGE

Viewpoint:
Urban II's launch of the First Crusade was part of a broad counterstrike against Islam in Spain, Sicily, and the eastern Mediterranean.

One of the most perplexing questions surrounding the First Crusade (1096–1102) and the rise of the crusading movement is why, after several centuries of contact and conflict, the clash between the Latin Christian and Islamic civilizations reached such epic proportions. Although few historians argue against the centrality of Jerusalem in the First Crusade, the need to reacquire Christ's tomb alone cannot explain the birth or transmutation of this clash between civilizations. By the time Pope Urban II convened the Council of Clermont (1095), Jerusalem had been under Islamic control for 457 years. By any reckoning the Crusade was an extremely belated bid to recover lost territory, regardless of its spiritual importance. The Holy Sepulchre, moreover, had been completely destroyed by the unbalanced Egyptian caliph al-Hakim in 1009; though shocking to western Europeans, its destruction elicited no response even remotely resembling a crusade. If the First Crusade was merely a bid to recover Jerusalem and liberate Eastern Christians from Islamic domination, then why was the response so slow?

Historians have tried to answer this question by analyzing the tumultuous changes that took place within western Europe during the interim. Chief among these was the rise of the reformed papacy and its ambitious program for restructuring the religious and sociopolitical order of western Europe. This approach has generated the impression that the rise of crusading was primarily rooted in domestic affairs and, in a sense, was implicit in the nature of the reformed papacy. A closer examination of key changes taking place along the Christian-Islamic frontier, however, suggests that the main events leading up to the launching of the First Crusade were international in origin. Rather than being a "proactive" policy designed to further the goals of the papacy within Christendom, the First Crusade was "reactive" in that it was a response to palpable changes in the balance of power between the Christian and Islamic worlds.

The Latin Christian world had a long tradition of dealing with violent frontier clashes and invasions from Huns and Germanic tribes to Magyars and Vikings. Early western European perceptions of Islamic expansion were shaped by this tradition. Muslims encroaching upon Christian lands were simply seen as a new strain of "barbarian" threatening "Roman" civilization. After the initial shock of the rapid inroads that early Islamic expansion had made into the Christian world (the eastern Mediterranean, the Iberian Peninsula, and Sicily), a tolerable modus vivendi emerged. Carolingian emperor Charlemagne, for example, not only corresponded with the Abbasid caliph Harun ar-Rashid in the East but also offered support to Muslim allies in Spain. At the turn of the millennium, Christian-Islamic relations could be described as stable. Mutual interests and alliances of convenience were ubiquitous. Certainly, there were armed conflicts between the two cultures: the Byzantine Empire was trying to hold its own in the East and the "reconquest" of Spain was already well under way. But generally speaking, they were "low-intensity" conflicts that were spliced together by long periods of diplomatic and commercial exchanges.

During the first half of the eleventh century, Christian civilization simply did not feel unduly threatened by the Islamic world. In the East the Byzantine Empire had recovered some lands that it lost to Islam in Syria. Byzantine relations with Fatimid Egypt were in many ways better than its relations with western Europe. In the western Mediterranean, Christians frequently had the upper hand while dealing with the fragmented Taifa kingdoms of Islamic Spain (whose rulers often paid protection money to the Christians). This relative equilibrium, however, was overturned in spectacular ways during the second half of the century, the gestational stage of the crusading movement. Important power shifts in the Islamic world took place almost simultaneously on both ends of the Mediterranean basin. Recently converted Muslim tribesmen, the Seljuk Turks in the East and the Almoravid Berbers in the West, began to eclipse the power of sedentary and urban-minded Islamic states. As these nomadic Muslims rose to predominance, they practiced a more aggressive form of Islam that turned the tables and placed the Christian world on the defensive. Suddenly, Islam seemed ubiquitous, aggressive, and dangerous.

Ibn Khaldun, the great fourteenth-century Islamic scholar, was the first to create a complex and clearly articulated theory explicating the causes of dynastic change in the Islamic world. Central to his paradigm was the concept of *asabiyah* (group feeling) and its cyclical nature. Groups with strong *asabiyah* come to dominate those with weaker ones. *Asabiyah* was particularly virile among the nomadic groups whose culture revolved around raiding and domination. Eventually, they came to rule over the settled cultures whose *asabiyah* had weakened over time. All groups, Ibn Khaldun believed, had a natural inclination to create a dynasty, but this change is predicated upon urbanism and settled life (which sap the strength of *asabiyah*). Thus, the ultimate objective of *asabiyah* contains the causes of its decay. Nomads become settled and sedentary and eventually are targeted by new groups with stronger *asabiyah* in a recurring cycle.

Modern scholarship, though using a different vernacular, has described the process in similar terms. The Islamic world, from its origins, exhibited a deep-seated tension between nomadic and urban lifestyles and mentalities. Bedouin tribes, for example, were the most difficult to absorb into the Islamic community (and the most likely to rebel after converting to the faith). All of the early architects of Islam came from sedentary, urban backgrounds and were deeply suspicious of nomadic tribesmen.

Fourteenth-century miniature of Pope Urban II proposing the First Crusade at Clermont to assembled clergy and princes in 1095

(from Angus Konstam, Historical Atlas of the Crusades, *2002)*

Muhammad himself stressed the importance of settlement for Muslims. Islamic leaders were so distrustful of nomads that they always tried to place them under the command of those who came from sedentary backgrounds. Historian Frederick Donner has persuasively argued that one of the main causes of early Islamic expansion was the desire of the sedentary elite to domesticate the nomads by leading them far away from the desert and into newly conquered urban lands.

Islam was a powerful ideology that contributed to political centralization and settled life among nomads. These two transformations, however, were not always synchronized. Islam revolutionized tribal relations in such a way that mass mobilization was fairly easy to achieve before the inclination to adopt settled urban lifestyles set in. Religious zeal, combined with the aggressive nature of nomadic life, created an explosive mix that shattered stability.

In the tenth century, Islam began spreading rapidly among the nomadic tribes of the Turkish steppe. By 1056 the Seljuk Turks had risen to dominance in the Near East and established a sultanate that ruled Iran, Iraq, and part of Syria on behalf of the Abbasid caliphs. Subscribing to an aggressive and austere interpretation of Islam that so appealed to freshly converted nomads, the Seljuk Turks began repairing, through holy war, what they saw as a degenerating and soft Islamic world. The perennial tension between nomadic and sedentary Muslims once again flashed. After achieving political hegemony in the Abbasid heartland, the Turkish leader Tughril Beg redirected his nomadic armies toward the heretical Fatimid Muslims in Egypt and the Byzantines in a sweeping holy war, which culminated in the disastrous Byzantine defeat at Manzikert (1071)—a battle that proved to be a seminal event in the genesis of crusading. The Byzantines asked for Western military assistance against the Seljuks, and Pope Gregory VII was receptive to the idea.

In North Africa the Sanhaja Berbers began converting to Islam during the tenth century, and although their piety might have been loose at first, their affinity for jihad (just war) was particularly pronounced. During the first half of the eleventh century, great religious change occurred among the Berbers. Purer strains of Islam were introduced to the Sanhaja after a tribal chieftain returned from a pilgrimage to Mecca. Most Sanhaja Berbers rejected this new form of Islam, and the missionary who introduced it fled with a small group of followers to create a *ribat* (austere and militant religious community). Flooded with new recruits, the community grew extremely powerful and in the 1040s turned upon and absorbed the Sanhaja tribes that had formerly rejected it. During the 1070s the Almoravids (men of the ribat) became masters of Northern Africa.

At the same time, the Taifa kingdoms of the Iberian Peninsula faced increasing pressure from the Christians. In 1085 Toledo fell to Alfonso VI, and this defeat created a stir among the Taifa kingdoms, who faced a dangerous decision: solicit the assistance of the Almoravids (which might endanger themselves) or face the Christian advance alone. One Taifa king summed up the situation well when he remarked that he would "rather be a camel-driver in Morocco than a swineherd in Castile." In 1086 the Almoravid army defeated the Christians at Sagrajas—an event that Richard Fletcher, in *The Quest for El Cid* (1989), has described as "Alfonso VI's Manzikert." The papacy responded by supporting the recruitment of French soldiers to assist in facing the Almoravid threat. Meanwhile, the Almoravids turned upon and annexed the Taifa kingdoms.

During the latter half of the eleventh century a complete transformation of the Christian-Islamic border occurred throughout the entire Mediterranean. Aggressive advances by new nomadic dynasties disrupted the relatively stable status quo simultaneously in the eastern and western extremes of the basin, culminating in major Christian defeats. Christian and Muslims were also locked in battle as the Normans reconquered southern Italy and Sicily for Christendom. Success in the center of the Mediterranean, combined with reverses on each extremity, served as the larger backdrop for the Council of Clermont. A reformed papacy necessitated universal interests that culminated in a universal policy. The First Crusade, rather than being an isolated expedition, was part of a wider three-pronged riposte against what seemed to be an increasingly aggressive Islamic advance.

The reformed papacy expressed deep interest in all three of these theaters prior to the pontificate of Urban II. In southern Italy and Sicily, where Muslims had for some time been on the virtual doorstep of the papacy, the Normans became papal champions, rolling back the Islamic threat while serving as powerful allies against the German emperors. Gregory VII's reaction to the disaster at Manzikert is well known: he proposed, more than once, to organize and lead a Christian army to smash the Turks and liberate the Christians in the East. The papacy was also interested in the Christian conflict with Muslims in Spain at least since the 1060s and, after the fall of Toledo (1085), enthusiastically and optimistically promoted the *Reconquista*.

Urban II was elected Pope in 1088. His pontificate began with intense interest in and activity on both of Christendom's fronts with Islam. Manzikert heralded the virtual collapse of the Byzantine-Islamic frontier, and Emperor Alexius was anxious for Western support. Urban began negotiations with him at once and might have considered a French expedition to the East by 1089. The Western front underwent considerable change shortly before Urban's election: the loss of Toledo generated great enthusiasm, but this victory was partially muted by the Almoravid invasion in 1086. Urban took extraordinary actions in the no-man's-land fifty miles from Barcelona. In 1089 he urged the count of Barcelona to reoccupy the deserted city of Tarragona and begin colonization of the region. It was to be the "land of St. Peter" and a literal "wall" against Islam. Significantly, Urban billed the activity as a form of penance that would remit sins—he clearly was using crusading language before the First Crusade. He went so far as to suggest that men planning to make the penitential pilgrimage to Jerusalem commute their vow and contribute to the colonization of Tarragona instead. Thus, long before Clermont, Urban was offering indulgences for rolling back the Islamic threat in Spain, while simultaneously brokering a deal to assist the Byzantines in the East.

Urban's stunning decision in 1098 to grant the powers of a papal legate to King Roger II of Sicily also underscores the broad international character of the riposte against Islam. In terms of reformed papal domestic policy, such a decision (which virtually made the king head of the Sicilian Church) would seem inexplicable. David Abulafia, however, in *Frederick II: A Medieval Emperor* (1988), has offered a convincing explanation for Urban's otherwise enigmatic decision. Dealing with a conquered Muslim majority and the creation of a new Christian state "were tasks for its military conqueror." Christian recolonization required almost unfettered secular dominance, and Urban seems to have been more concerned with quelling Muslims in Sicily than pushing forward reformed Church organization.

Placing too much emphasis on the conflicting accounts of Urban's speech at Claremont can easily obfuscate the international context and causes of the First Crusade; it was designed to recruit one prong of a much wider counterattack. In other sources Urban made it quite clear that he viewed the conflict with Islam in universal terms. He praised Roger's victories in Sicily as a glorious event that "spread greatly the Church of God into Muslim territories" and saw Pisan successes against Muslims as God's grace reordering the world. Describing victories in both Sicily and Spain, Urban explained them as manifestations of a divine restructuring of the balance of power: "God, the ruler of all things, whose wisdom and strength, when he wishes, taketh away kingdoms and changeth times." Focusing on Spain, Urban remarked that "we ought to make many expressions of thanks to the mercies of God that in our time the Church has been enlarged, the domination of the Muslims has been reduced, the ancient honor of episcopal sees has been, by the gift of God, restored." Urban also drew a stark parallel between the war against Muslims in the Eastern and Western theaters: "In our days God has fought through Christian men in Asia against the Turks and in Europe against the Moors."

When considering the papal policy behind the First Crusade, one must take into account the major changes that took place along the entire Christian-Islamic frontier—just as Urban had. The entire Mediterranean basin erupted into holy war between Christians and Muslims, and the First Crusade was one particular manifestation of it. Dynastic changes and shifting balances of power in the Islamic world were main causes. The entire Christian-Muslim conflict, however, should be viewed as a "Crusade." It was the unique spiritual significance of Jerusalem and the Holy Land that made the eastern campaign an "armed pilgrimage." Be that as it may, the expedition was part of a generalized Christian holy war that responded to changes across the Mediterranean. Taken within this larger context, the First Crusade was part of a much wider policy implemented by Urban, one designed to roll back the Islamic threat, restore the honor of Christendom, and change the fates of kingdoms.

—MARK T. ABATE,
WESTFIELD STATE COLLEGE

References

David Abulafia, *Frederick II: A Medieval Emperor* (London: John Lane, 1988).

Roger Collins, *The Arab Conquest of Spain, 710–797* (Oxford & Cambridge, Mass.: Blackwell, 1989).

H. E. J. Cowdrey, *The Age of Abbot Desiderius: Montecassino, the Papacy, and the Normans in the Eleventh and Early Twelfth Centuries* (Oxford: Clarendon Press, 1983).

Cowdrey, "Pope Urban II's Preaching of the First Crusade," *History,* 55 (June 1970): 177–188.

Cowdrey, *Popes, Monks, and Crusaders* (London: Hambleton, 1984).

Carl Erdmann, *The Origin of the Idea of Crusade,* translated by Marshall Baldwin and Walter Goffart (Princeton: Princeton University Press, 1977).

Richard Fletcher, *The Quest for El Cid* (London: Hutchinson, 1989).

Albert Hourani, *A History of the Arab Peoples* (London: Faber & Faber, 1991; Cambridge, Mass.: Belknap Press of Harvard University Press, 1991).

Harry J. Magoulias, *Byzantine Christianity: Emperor, Church, and the West* (Chicago: Rand McNally, 1970).

Peter Partner, *God of Battles: Holy Wars of Christianity and Islam* (London: HarperCollins, 1997).

Jean Richard, *The Crusades, c. 1071–c. 1291,* translated by Jean Birrell (Cambridge & New York: Cambridge University Press, 1999).

Jonathan Riley-Smith, *The Crusades: A Short History* (London: Athlone, 1987; New Haven: Yale University Press, 1987).

Riley-Smith, *The First Crusade and the Idea of Crusading* (Philadelphia: University of Pennsylvania Press, 1986).

Kenneth M. Setton, ed., *A History of the Crusades,* volume 1, *The First Hundred Years,* edited by Marshall W. Baldwin, second edition (Madison: University of Wisconsin Press, 1969).

R. Somerville, "The Council of Clermont (1095) and Latin Christian Society," *Archivum historiae pontificae,* 12 (1974): 62–82.

URBAN II

VOW REDEMPTION

Did vow redemption, a knight's promise to send a substitute soldier to the Holy Land or provide a monetary pledge to Rome, hamper the crusading movement?

Viewpoint: Yes. Vow redemption weakened the crusading movement by sapping it of manpower and diverting financial resources.

Viewpoint: No. Vow redemption strengthened the crusading movement by improving its financial organization and making it more adaptable to changing conditions.

The Crusader vow was at the heart of the crusading movement because it defined the objectives, obligations, and compensation for participants. Originally modeled on the pilgrim's vow to travel to and worship at a specific site of great religious significance, the Crusader vow evolved, or, as some historians believe, devolved, into a commitment to provide military assistance to an area designated by the papacy as in great need. When Urban II launched the First Crusade in the late eleventh century, the vow represented a solemn promise made by an individual to make the arduous and dangerous journey to Jerusalem. Once made, the decision was binding, and failure to discharge its obligations in full could result in the two things that men of the age feared most: excommunication and public shame. By the early thirteenth century, men could take the vow without even intending to make the journey since it could be "redeemed" for a cash equivalent of the cost of going in person.

Some historians view vow alterations as the most devastating blow dealt to the crusading movement as a whole. By betraying the two fundamental features of the First Crusade (1096–1102), the binding promise to reach a specific objective and the oath to fight personally, vow alterations led to an irremediable breakdown of the coherence of crusading. Objectives became increasingly vague once the targeted site shifted from a clearly defined place such as Jerusalem to one determined by participants overseas. Such ambiguity opened the floodgates of abuse to lay powers and popes alike. Crusading activity, once emancipated from Jerusalem itself, could be redirected with ease to a variety of avenues. Leaders of the Fourth Crusade (1202–1204), for example, conquered Constantinople, never even crossed the straits into the Holy Land, yet returned claiming that their vow had been discharged. Likewise, popes could tap into resources earmarked for crusading to the East and use it against their own Christian opponents. Vow redemption, an even more egregious offense against Urban's original crusading plan, had a plethora of deleterious effects. Offering the indulgence to anyone willing to take the oath and then redeem it through financial contributions bestowed a dangerous liquidity upon crusading that guaranteed spiraling corruption and misappropriation of funds. Full coffers became more attractive to popes and lay powers alike than successful prosecution of the Crusade. Furthermore, vow redemption afflicted the movement with a sort of martial paralysis: men would rather pay others to fight than fight themselves, bleeding the movement of real Crusaders while glutting it with quasi-Crusaders who would never make the journey.

Other historians view vow alterations in a more positive light. Rather than initiating and augmenting a continuous debasement of crusading, vow alterations were pragmatic responses to changing conditions that allowed the movement to survive. The modifications provided the movement with a heightened degree of flexibility, both strategic and financial. Strategically speaking, divorcing the Crusade from Jerusalem as the primary and immediate objective allowed military leaders the freedom to pursue more-sound tactics in the field. Urban's original model was well suited to the environment in which it was planned and launched; Jerusalem was in enemy hands; those trying to reach it would need to cut a violent path through the landscape; and the Turkish presence—in disarray as it was—was incapable of unified resistance. As military exigencies changed, Syria and Egypt became the prime battlefields, and Jerusalem, which had no strategic value anyway, was tactically irrelevant. Likewise, vow redemption was a pragmatic response to the great hurdle that all Crusades faced: finance and supplies. The First Crusaders found themselves financially strapped, and the costs of campaigning skyrocketed as the centuries wore on. Innocent III, the Pope who perfected vow redemption, completely lost control over his first crusade to the East, and the main factor involved was lack of funds. Vow redemption allowed noncombatants to make valuable contributions to a war effort that otherwise would have come to a grinding halt.

The underlying issue addressed in this chapter is one common to major military efforts in any age: the balancing of means and end and of resources and objectives.

Viewpoint:
Yes. Vow redemption weakened the crusading movement by sapping it of manpower and diverting financial resources.

At first glance, when historians examine the many formidable obstacles that opposed the typical crusading army, vow redemptions might seem to rank rather low on the list. After all, even more-obvious factors are often not accorded as much significance as they merit when various historians attempt to explain the successes or failures of crusading campaigns. For example, it is not unusual for insufficient emphasis to be given to the lack of political unity in Europe, the primitive state of logistical support systems for long-range military operations, the debilitating factors of distance and climate, the inability to establish consistent unity of command within crusading armies, and the perpetual inferiority in numbers such armies encountered in contrast to enemy forces. Yet, all these factors weighed heavily against crusading armies and played a role in determining the outcome of military operations. Instead of this European-centered focus, many crusading scholars traditionally have tended to view the external political and military conditions of the Islamic world of the Near East as the single most important determinant of crusading success or failure. For example, the improbable triumph of the First Crusade (1096–1102) is often attributed to the lack of political unity among the Muslim principalities in the region at the end of the eleventh century. Disunited and caught by surprise by the unanticipated invasion of Western knights, the Muslim states of the Near East were unable to prevent the Crusaders from achieving their objective of Jerusalem. However, as the twelfth century progressed, the Islamic world moved toward increasing political unity, and as a result, subsequent crusading campaigns met with failure.

While there is certainly some merit to this latter line of analysis, too many historians have either neglected or not emphasized enough the former set of factors—the internal developments within the Western world and within the movement itself during the twelfth and early thirteenth centuries—which were perhaps of even greater importance in determining the fate of crusading campaigns. Of particular importance in this regard was the changing nature of the crusading vow during this period, moving from an open-ended promise to reach a specific well-defined location, to a limited promise to perform some ambiguous service in the East, and finally to the possibility of merely substituting cash payment in place of personal participation. Thus, if historians wish to fully comprehend the demise of the Crusades, understanding this transformation of the crusading vow would be a good starting point, for it represents one of the single greatest causes of their failure.

To begin with, it is important to understand the original need and role of a vow within the history of the crusading movement. When Pope Urban II decided in 1095 to answer the appeal for military assistance from the Byzantine Emperor Alexius I, he envisioned something greater and more sublime than the dispatch of a mere mercenary army as Alexius had intended. What he had in mind was the novel idea of an army of penitents marching on pilgrimage to Jerusalem and freeing fellow Christians along the way. As such, Urban based his crusading project squarely on the long-standing Western tradition of pilgrimage. Some of the most essential elements of this traditional religious practice, such as the long journey to a holy shrine, participants' self-financing of the trip, the vow to complete the pilgrimage, the penitential spirit of participants, and the spiritual reward for their efforts, were therefore carried over into crusading. It proved in some ways to be an awkward construction, at least in the sense that one of the other great hallmarks of traditional pilgrims, their peaceful, unarmed status, was suddenly being turned completely on its head. What Urban was now asking for were pilgrims who would be not only armed but also inherently belligerent. This new policy, however, would be the only essential difference between his new pilgrims and the pilgrims of old. All other aspects of traditional pilgrimage were to apply, including the penitential spirit, the visit to a holy shrine, the vow to complete the journey, and a spiritual reward for participation.

Except for the inherent tension of trying to maintain the union between the two contrary traditions of peaceful pilgrimage and violent warfare that had the potential to undermine crusading from within, in all other ways Urban's decision to arm the traditional pilgrimage to Jerusalem was perhaps nothing less than ingenious. The idea of pilgrimage, especially to Jerusalem, already had captured the imagination of eleventh-century Europeans. For a ruggedly austere yet adventurous society the idea of making the long, difficult, and potentially dangerous journey to Jerusalem, where the central mysteries of Christianity had occurred, seemed like the pinnacle of spiritual exercises. As such, during this time period it had become a widely popular activity. By linking his crusade to the practice of pilgrimage, Urban was effectively tapping into its widespread popularity and in the process ensuring a popular, enthusiastic response to his call to arms. What is more, pilgrimage's inherent connection to a specific site correlated well with a fundamental principle of military operations, namely the need for a clear, well-defined objective. Just as pilgrims knew unequivocally what the terminus of their journey must be to earn their spiritual reward, so too would Urban's Crusaders. Their mission would not be complete until they had visited the holy sites in Jerusalem, and since this city was at the time in enemy hands deep behind hostile lines, the only way his Crusaders could make their visit was to take the city by force. Furthermore, like other pilgrims, these early Crusaders also expected to gain great spiritual benefit for their efforts. In their case, however, Urban had promised the Crusaders a special spiritual prize, the indulgence. This indulgence was technically a granting of the remission of the penalties of sin, but participants interpreted it to be tantamount to guaranteeing them entrance into heaven. In an era in which salvation was a primary concern of many people, such a generous offer of winning eternal paradise seemed for many knights of Europe too good to pass up.

Finally, pilgrimage lent one other vital quality to crusading, the vow to complete the journey. Traditional pilgrims who took the promise to visit some holy shrine did not do so lightly, for they realized that this commitment was morally binding. The failure to complete this pious exercise would result not only in public embarrassment but also, more importantly, in grave personal sin. Such a heavy spiritual penalty seemed to be a just counterbalance to the great spiritual benefit pilgrims hoped to achieve by completing their journey. So when it came time to ask for volunteers for what must have seemed like an impossible mission, Urban had his knights take this pilgrim vow to complete the journey to Jerusalem. By taking such a vow, his soldiers well understood that they were incurring the same moral obligation that traditional pilgrims did. To turn back before the mission was completed was to incur public shame and spiritual punishment. The subsequent events of the First Crusade demonstrate the extraordinary level of commitment that this vow inspired within a critical mass of the army. For participants, their Crusader/pilgrim vow was not something to be taken lightly, and so they knew that all possible efforts had to be expended in order to fulfill it.

In subsequent years, later popes also found it necessary to appeal to the knightly class of Europe to undertake a distant campaign to fight the enemies of Christendom. Understandably, these popes looked back to the institutional model for crusading that Urban had initiated with the original campaign back in 1095. As such, these later efforts also wedded traditional pilgrimage to military activity, and so Crusades of the twelfth and thirteenth centuries continued to include such pilgrimage elements as the long journey, the vow to participate, and the spiritual reward of an indulgence for fulfilling the vow. Later Crusaders, therefore, continued not only to view themselves as pilgrims but also to associate themselves with the First Crusaders, whose triumph had accorded them legendary stature among these later generations of knights.

On the surface it might seem that little had changed in the practice of crusading from the time of Urban II. Yet, in reality a critical transformation had occurred. For example, when Pope Eugenius III felt it necessary in the mid twelfth century to launch a second great crusading effort, he made appeals for volunteers in 1145 and 1146 in which he promised an indulgence to all who fulfilled their vow to participate. Unlike Urban's indulgence, however, Eugenius's could be earned by anyone who journeyed to aid

TAKING THE CROSS

Viscount Amaury of Lautrec made the following vow to accompany Philip VI of France on a Crusade in the early fourteenth century:

I, Amaury, viscount of Lautrec, knight and lord de Ambricio, receive the cross and declare that, if our lord king crosses over within the specified period of time, then I will cross in aid of the Holy Land with three knights and six squires, each and all of whom, when I set out, I intend to provide with armor for his person and with one horse, once only. I beseech our said lord, the present king, that he see fit to provide me and these knights and squires with expenses and all other necessary things, and that this be promised, by the said lord, when I set out. It is my wish that, when I am overseas, I should be free of coercion on anybody's part to stay longer than I want to, but that I may return if and when it please me. I beseech our lord the king that, if I should cross over and he considers it more appropriate to my station that I fight or cross over with more knights and squires than specified above, then he be pleased to provide me with them at his costs. I wish that if, which God forbid, I should be detained by some form of illness within the said period of time, i.e. the time when the passage takes place, then I should in no way be expected to go on the passage, or to send soldiers, except of my own free will. The judgment in the case of such an illness is to rest with myself and my conscience, and I want nobody else to judge.

If our lord the king declines to abide by these terms, then I am not to be bound to carry out my vow to go in person with knights and squires, or even to send soldiers, except of my own free will, as stated above. . . .

Source: *Norman Housley, ed. and trans,* Documents on the Later Crusades, 1274–1580 *(New York: St. Martin's Press, 1996), pp. 70–71.*

Christians, whether they were in the Near East, the Baltics, or Spain. In effect, this decision severed the reward's direct link to pilgrimage, which connected visiting a particular shrine with earning the spiritual reward of the indulgence. While this change might seem to have been a minor adjustment to Urban's indulgence, which was necessitated after all by the fact that Jerusalem was still in Christian hands at this time, in fact Eugenius had created in the process a radical revision to the crusading program. There no longer was a clearly defined objective on which fulfilling one's vow and earning the indulgence depended. Now all that was required was for a participant to travel to the East and provide some sort of undefined assistance to the people and the church of that region. This policy was an incredibly ambiguous standard for earning what was viewed by contemporaries as the greatest of spiritual rewards. In effect, it was left up to the individual Crusader to determine when he had sufficiently fulfilled the terms of his vow. Not surprisingly, it was now possible for someone such as Conrad III of Germany to declare in a letter that the Second Crusade (1147–1149) was over because he had accomplished all that was possible in helping the Christians in the Latin East, even though little practical advantage for them had actually been achieved by his Crusade. As modern research in the area of management psychology has shown, ambiguous standards typically lead to ambiguous results, which became increasingly a problem for later Crusades as the nature of the vow changed.

After the Second Crusade failed to improve conditions in the Latin East, it is not surprising that a generation later the situation there completely collapsed, prompting another pope to issue a new crusading appeal. Rather than follow Urban's framework for the indulgence, Gregory VIII chose instead to follow Eugenius's. Even though Jerusalem was by now once more in enemy hands, Gregory's crusading bull of 1187 did not demand that Crusaders worship at the shrines in Jerusalem in order to fulfill their vows and so to earn the indulgence. Rather, he merely required them to take whatever relief to the East that they could. While this Third Crusade (1189–1192) succeeded in recapturing the coastline of the old Latin Kingdom, it never took back Jerusalem nor gave the West a strategic victory that might have altered the balance of power in the Near East for the long term. Had the crusading vow obligated the Crusaders to visit Jerusalem in order to win the indulgence or else face severe moral punishment, perhaps the Third Crusade might have achieved longer-term solutions to the Eastern problem. Instead, new crusading appeals were needed in 1198, 1213, and 1215, and again it was the Eugenius model of the vow and the indulgence that was followed.

The final evolution of the vow and indulgence occurred in 1215 as the West made preparations for launching the Fifth Crusade (1217–1229). Pope Innocent III went beyond the modifications made by Eugenius and offered an indulgence that was as generous as it was disastrous to the cause of successful crusading. In his concern to raise the best manned, equipped, and financed army yet to be sent on campaign in the East and also to make participation in the Crusade as inclusive as possible, Innocent decided to open the crusading vow to everyone. Those who proved unfit or unwilling to actually go on the Crusade could, nevertheless, have their vow redeemed either by sponsoring a replacement or donating money to help defray the enormous cost of the expedition. This situation represented a momentous change that perhaps ensured the impossibility of ever achieving again Urban's original crusading goal of reclaiming the Holy Land for Christendom. Innocent's indulgence program did indeed increase revenue to help defray the ever spiraling costs of crusading, and it succeeded in making the spiritual benefits of crusading available to all segments of society, not just the knightly class of Europe. However, in practical terms it also meant that someone could now take the Crusader vow and fulfill its obligations without ever leaving home. It marked a radical change in the crusading program, especially when it is remembered that the First Crusaders enjoyed no such luxury. In their case they had to spend three agonizing years undergoing innumerable dangers and privations all because they were driven on by the real concern that they might fail to complete their pilgrimage vow to visit Jerusalem. Eugenius III had already begun the process of eroding the motivational value of the crusading vow by making mere service in the East rather than the accomplishment of some specific task the determining factor of fulfilling the vow. Innocent III completed this process of erosion by now permitting individuals the opportunity to gain the spiritual rewards of crusading without having to risk its many typical hardships and dangers. While his modification of the crusading vow and indulgence might have made good pastoral sense by making the spiritual rewards of crusading accessible to all, it was disastrous as an incentive system to promote successful crusading.

In the end, as the crusading movement went on, the religious leadership of the West found its objectives increasingly at cross-purposes. The desire to win back control of Jerusalem and protect fellow Christians in the Near East ran up against what really was in some ways a competing desire, namely to make the spiritual reward of the indulgence more easily attainable. Popes after Urban II might have continued the practice of making the indulgence contingent on achieving some difficult, unambiguous standard, such as capturing Jerusalem, which sat deep inside enemy territory. Given all of the obstacles that Crusaders faced in trying to achieve such a goal, the most likely way to ensure that Crusaders gave their best efforts to accomplish such a dangerous mission was to maintain Urban's demanding and unforgiving reward system. To win the indulgence, Crusaders either had to succeed or die trying. Returning home unsuccessfully would not be an option unless the Church agreed in its mercy to commute their vows. As time went on, however, it became clear that ecclesiastical leaders began to see the Crusade in an increasingly pastoral sense. It was not just an instrument to achieve certain temporal objectives but a spiritual tool that might serve as the only practical way for the contentious knights of Europe to save their

souls through the promise of the crusading indulgence. In this light, diluting the terms of the crusading vow and indulgence might have made for good moral and spiritual policy, but it was a disastrous military and political policy that perhaps more than any other factor doomed the future of crusading. While they might have desired to see Jerusalem liberated, most Crusaders were more concerned to ensure that they would gain the benefits of the indulgence. If this goal could be done in some way that posed less personal danger and privation than fighting to the death on some long, drawn-out campaign, then, even if with regret, many would be resigned to let Jerusalem continue to languish on its own.

–CHRISTOPHER LIBERTINI,
SUFFOLK UNIVERSITY

Viewpoint:
No. Vow redemption strengthened the crusading movement by improving its financial organization and making it more adaptable to changing conditions.

The men attending the Council of Clermont in 1095, whether they realized it or not, witnessed the birth of one of the greatest revolutions in medieval European warfare: the Crusader vow. By joining together the penitential act of pilgrimage and war, Urban II forged the single most effective tool—in fact probably the only possible tool—for bringing about the mass mobilization of an international army. Today one takes such mass mobilizations for granted; the twentieth century, after all, has experienced two world wars, the deployment of many United Nations' peacekeeping forces, and several international "police actions." Yet, such actions would be well nigh impossible before the rise of nationalism and other potent ideologies that emerged in the nineteenth century. The eleventh century had no modern sense of nationalism, but in the form of the Crusader vow it found a surrogate. Urban's innovation gave medieval Europe the ability to hurl thousands of warriors toward another continent.

To truly grasp the military significance of the Crusader vow, one must first recognize the salient features of medieval military organization. Warfare, in essence, was much more a private than a public matter; if one places it in modern terms, it bears a much greater resemblance to a group of friends on a weekend hunting expedition than a standing army mobilizing

VOW REDEMPTION

for the defense of a state. Medieval men fought for and were compensated by other men and not nation-states. The reason for this situation is rather simple: the medieval mind did not recognize the communal but impersonal institutional concept of the state. All that is associated with a modern state was, to the medieval mind, a collection of obligations and privileges that were defined by personal ties between individual men. Men fought as an obligation to an individual, and because it was nothing more or less than a personal obligation, it was expected that those discharging it would finance themselves. The threads that constituted the web of obligations were many, but the most important ones were based on family solidarity and indebtedness for gifts of land or protection. Thus, medieval military mass mobilizations were constrained by two distinct limitations forged by the personal nature of warfare. First, military targets and objectives were defined by the interests of individuals or small groups of individuals rather than sweeping communal interests. Thus, wars would be restricted to fragmented skirmishes among competing interests rather than large-scale concerted action. Second, since warriors tended to be self-financed, the monetary resources for massive, extended campaigns were limited, bordering on nonexistent. Such warriors could bear the financial burden of short-term local wars in support of their lords' interests, but distant campaigns would create immense personal hardships for them.

The Crusader vow managed to transcend both of these limitations. First of all, it provided a universal rather than personal foundation for the expedition. Jerusalem had a universal appeal to men of the age. Its spiritual significance placed its fate squarely in the interest of all Christians; its importance was not encircled by local territorial borders; its value was not restricted to a small handful of men. Thus, it created a general rather than a personal obligation. Furthermore, since it was a pilgrimage site of the utmost importance, it bestowed great spiritual rewards upon those who visited it—rewards that were in many ways a form of compensation more valuable than money. Second, it unleashed a veritable flood of new financial resources that made such a long campaign possible. Pilgrimages were to be arduous and difficult, journeys that entailed discomfort and hardship from beginning to end; that, in essence, was why it was a form of penance that God found satisfactory. Such suffering certainly extended to financial hardship—that is one of the greatest obstacles for self-financed soldiers undertaking a distant and long campaign. Warriors of the age would not mortgage lands to pursue the interests of their personal lords on another continent, but they would do it for God and the spiritual rewards he would grant for such

service. Third, the rules governing pilgrimage had a precision and austerity that personal military obligations lacked. Medieval warriors' obligations were usually to serve their lords for a fixed amount of time, regardless of whether or not the tactical objective was achieved. The pilgrim's obligation was the opposite. Reaching the objective was what determined the end of the obligation rather than how much time was involved in doing so.

In this form the Crusader vow was perfectly suited to the climate that existed on the eve of the First Crusade (1096–1102). If one examines it solely from the perspective of military logistics, an impressive harmony can be seen between interests and resources that had no equivalent elsewhere in medieval campaigning. So evident was its value that similar vows were made to visit important pilgrimage sites in Spain and the Baltic, where Christians fought the infidel. The Crusader vow created a large, self-financed international army that would not stop until it secured a well-defined objective. Ironically, the objective might have been too well-defined for the Crusader vow, in its incipient form, to be of perpetual value. It certainly created a well-defined target—but only one. Once Jerusalem was in Christian hands, the Crusader vow began a process of inevitable degradation as a tool of mass mobilization. Between the First Crusade and the Second Crusade (1147–1149) members of the arms-bearing class did make pilgrimages and did assist in the defense of the fledgling Crusader States in the process. Yet, there was no mass mobilization of an international army until the Second Crusade. Eugenius III, the Pope who launched it, correctly realized that the Crusader vow needed to be modified to make it effective.

Small bands of armed pilgrims would not be sufficient to reverse Zengi's capture of Edessa in 1144 and the impending danger posed to the Crusader States. Eugenius modified the Crusader vow in two substantial ways that had a profound effect on the further development of the movement. First, the rewards for participation in the expedition were increased; rather than simply representing a satisfactory penance for the participant, the Crusade granted the full remission of all sins. Second, the Crusader vow became a pilgrimage with no specific pilgrimage site; it no longer required worship at Jerusalem or any other Christian shrine. Yet, it maintained the privileges and other trappings that marked a pilgrimage. Both of these innovations strengthened the movement in important ways. The former increased the spiritual compensation for participants and probably bolstered recruitment for subsequent Crusades (at the least more rewards could not have decreased the number of

VOW REDEMPTION

willing recruits). The latter allowed the Crusade to become more dynamic. By severing the Crusade from a single target, Eugenius's modification permitted Christendom to strike at whatever strategic site was preferable at the time. Jerusalem, which had no strategic value whatsoever, could justifiably be reduced to a "target of opportunity" when in enemy hands (which it was not in 1144). The failure of the Second Crusade cannot really be linked to the modifications Eugenius made; poor tactical decisions made at Edessa were what caused the disastrous outcome. What can be said is that if not for Eugenius's fine-tuning of the vow there might not have been a Second Crusade at all. Christendom, moreover, was also battling Muslims in Iberia and pagans in the Baltic. Eugenius's modification not only provided tactical flexibility concerning strategic targets in the East, but it also allowed the papacy remarkable freedom in deciding which theater was most in need of troops.

Pope Gregory VIII saw the wisdom in Eugenius's approach when he began organizing the Third Crusade (1189–1192) following Saladin's stunning victories in 1187. Now that Jerusalem was back in enemy hands, Gregory could have easily returned to Urban's original plan of making the expedition a Jerusalem-centered warrior pilgrimage. Instead, his crusading bull was modeled on that of Eugenius and the fact that the obligations that it imposed on the commanders of the expedition were not dependent on Jerusalem. Allowing the commanders to make their own decisions could have negative results. For example, it allowed a fairly unwilling Crusade commander such as King Philip Augustus of France to depart early, leaving Crusaders who remained in a difficult position, and return home claiming to have fulfilled his vow. But it also allowed a committed Crusader and brilliant tactician such as King Richard of England to make sound military decisions that would have been impossible if the whole campaign revolved around Jerusalem. It was through such sound tactical decisions that Richard recovered the coastline and allowed the Crusader States to survive and rebuild. And it was this flexibility that allowed Richard to forsake Jerusalem (while it was physically within his sight) in favor of taking the all-important strategic port city of Tyre. If he had not taken Tyre the history of the Crusader States might have been restricted to the twelfth century rather than extending to the end of the thirteenth century.

Eugenius's innovation and Gregory's decision to follow in his footsteps were practical responses to the shifting terrain upon which crusading stood. Both gave crusading a tactical flexibility that Urban's model could not grant. The disastrous Fourth Crusade (1202–1204) brought

Contract from 1270 in which two English knights (Payn de Chawarth and Robert Tybetot) agree to go on a Crusade with five other noblemen in return for passage, water, and one hundred marks per man

(British Library, London)

VOW REDEMPTION

to light, in bold relief, a new problem that needed a practical solution if crusading armies were to continue getting off the ground and the movement itself survive. The plenary indulgence, combined with the fact that many families had established crusading traditions that could not be ignored, guaranteed that willing recruits would respond to crusading bulls; however, willingness to crusade without financial ability could produce disastrous results such as that loose cannon that historians refer to as the Fourth Crusade. The Fourth Crusade clearly demonstrated that the traditional methods of financing crusading had become obsolete. Military and transport costs had been increasing at an alarming rate and in fact would continue to do so for centuries to come. The age of the self-financed crusading host that Urban inaugurated was over. Restructuring crusade financing was the task that fell upon Innocent III.

Innocent was a much wiser man after the Fourth Crusade. The expedition spiraled out of papal control, and most of the factors involved in this expedition were related to financial problems and those exploiting them to their own advantage. For the papacy to regain control over the movement, it must first have possession over a sizable war chest. Innocent's efforts focused on two main areas: clerical taxation and modification of the Crusader vow.

Innocent's efforts at instituting a general tax on the clergy produced mixed results. Although Innocent prefaced his decision by stating that it was an extraordinary act and would not create a precedent, many in the clergy feared precedent was exactly what it would become (and in fact they were correct). Resistance to the tax was fierce. The Cistercians, for example, refused outright, and one of the brothers claimed he was visited by the Virgin Mary herself, who warned the order of papal avarice. Churches throughout Spain complained that their resources were already being completely consumed by the continuing war against Muslims in Iberia. In a world riddled with immunities and exemptions, the idea of a comprehensive clerical tax raised thunderous objections throughout Christendom. Despite such resistance, the clerical tax did generate revenue that helped financially underwrite crusading. But it was never enough, and popes only had so much control over collecting it.

Innocent's second strategy, further modification of the Crusader vow, was far more successful. He offered the indulgence to men who were willing to take the vow but not necessarily prepared to take part in the projected campaign itself. Eugenius severed the crusading vow from making a pilgrimage to a specific shrine; Innocent went further and severed it from making a

journey at all. Men could literally Crusade by proxy without ever leaving home and still receive the indulgence. At first glance, this practice may seem like a ridiculous state of affairs. It turned Crusade recruitment into a sort of fund-raising event. On the other hand, that is exactly what the crusading movement required, and Innocent realized this need.

Theologically speaking, Innocent's innovation was sound and, in a strange way, returned to the movement's original roots by making it a universal obligation and option for penance rather than one dominated by the knightly class. The First Crusade originated as a pilgrimage, and no willing Christian could be excluded from it. Urban's call actually suffered from this specific aspect of the pilgrimage tradition by burdening it with noncombatants whose participation was accepted but certainly not welcome. Innocent found the perfect vehicle for tapping into the general enthusiastic desire to participate while channeling it into productive avenues. Men and women of all ranks and abilities, even those not physically able to make the journey, could participate by financing men both willing and able to do it. Once the vow was sworn, it could be redeemed in two important ways, both of which contributed to the individual's spiritual health and the needs of Christendom. The first was substitution, which allowed those who took the vow to finance other individuals who would fulfill it for them. For example, a sick or elderly man who wished to participate but was physically unable could send a warrior in his place. In practical terms, it provided a Crusader that otherwise would not have existed. The second was redemption that allowed the man or woman who took the vow to fulfill it by making a cash payment to the papacy that equaled the cost for the expedition. This money could then be rolled over and pooled with redemptions made by others, creating quite a war chest for financing a Crusade. Moreover, the liquidity that this policy provided allowed the papacy to put the resources of these people to the best possible use, such as providing supplies and transportation for those who would fight. In principle the idea was well received by contemporaries, though many had concerns about the abuse of such cash reserves.

Some historians have seen these modifications of the Crusader vow as representing a gradual degradation of crusading itself. This conclusion, however, is to take a static approach to the crusading movement rather than seeing it as a dynamic tradition that was capable of responding to changing circumstances in pragmatic and spiritually sound ways. Thus, the modifications really represent responses to what was the gradual erosion (rather than perversion) of Urban's original methods, which were essentially obsolete after the victory of the First Crusaders. The First Crusade, though successful, was really an international and self-financed raid on a specific site. Compared to later Crusades, its methods were crude. As crusading evolved, its strategies became more sound and precise while its costs continued to escalate unabated. The weight of crusading eventually consumed the foundations that Urban laid, and the movement would have collapsed. Rather than seizing like an engine without oil, the Crusades continued for centuries. This situation would have been impossible without the strategic and financial flexibility that alterations of the Crusader vow conferred.

–MARK T. ABATE, WESTFIELD STATE COLLEGE

References

Penny Cole, *The Preaching of the Crusades to the Holy Land, 1095-1270* (Cambridge, Mass.: Medieval Academy of America, 1991).

G. Constable, "The Financing of the Crusades," in *Outremer,* edited by B. Z. Kedar and others (Jerusalem: Yad Izhak Ben-Zvi Institute, 1982).

Norman Housley, *The Later Crusades, 1274-1580* (Oxford & New York: Oxford University Press, 1992).

Christoph Maier, *Preaching the Crusades: Mendicant Friars and the Cross in the Thirteenth Century* (Cambridge & New York: Cambridge University Press, 1994).

Maureen Purcell, *Papal Crusading Policy* (Leiden: Brill, 1975).

Sylvia Schein, *Fideles Crucis: The Papacy, the West, and the Recovery of the Holy Land* (Oxford: Clarendon Press / New York: Oxford University Press, 1991).

Elizabeth Siberry, *Criticism of Crusading, 1095-1274* (Oxford: Clarendon Press / New York: Oxford University Press, 1985).

VOW REDEMPTION

WESTERN IMPERIALISM

Were the Crusades the beginning of Western imperialism and colonialism in the Middle East?

Viewpoint: Yes. The Crusader States were the first European colony in the Middle East.

Viewpoint: No. Western imperialism and colonialism in the Middle East were products of the nineteenth and twentieth centuries.

In the nineteenth century some historians began theorizing that the age of high imperialism and colonialism was actually inaugurated by the Crusades and that the Latin settlements that existed from 1096 to 1291 in the East were the first European colonies. Crusading, it was believed, was the first chapter in the history of Western expansion and domination of the globe. The great German historian Leopold von Ranke saw crusading zeal as the ultimate impetus for nineteenth-century European imperialism. But pride of place among the colonial theoreticians of the Crusader States went to the French. The works of Louis Madelin and René Grousset, in particular, painted a portrait of a benevolent colonization in the Eastern Mediterranean that resulted in a new "Franco-Syrian nation." In France, viewing the Crusader States as a prologue to modern French imperialism became a virtual orthodoxy, and this belief had adherents in many European nations.

Although the "colonial theory" of the Crusades still has staunch supporters (particularly among French and Israeli scholars), it was subjected to increasing criticism after World War II (1939–1945). The move toward "decolonization" certainly influenced this shift, but a greater cause was to be found in the new venues of scholarship in imperialism and colonialism. One powerful argument against the colonial theory of the Crusades was the relationship between the modern nation-state and notions of nationalism (and the phenomenon historians call colonialism). Feudal societies were built upon personal ties of blood or obligation and were incapable of conceiving of, much less pursuing, true colonialism. Modern colonies, moreover, were sponsored by a mother-state, and this development cannot be said of the Crusader States. Technological factors and the incessant search for new markets that fueled the imperialist frenzy of the nineteenth and twentieth centuries had little, if anything, to do with the motives of medieval Crusaders.

While both movements can be considered wars of conquest, there was a major difference. Modern colonies were dependent on the mother-state that created and sponsored them. Crusader States, like all examples of medieval expansion, created independent realms. Describing the Crusader States as "colonies" has also been criticized on the ground of semantics. The word is not only vague but also politically and emotionally loaded, and this combination renders the term either useless or disruptive to the study of the Crusader States. Advocates of the colonial theory tend to stress the "secularization of the sacred" that caused the crusading impulse to eventually reconstitute itself in modern terms. Particulars may vary, but the phenomena are ultimately the same. The Crusaders were the first Europeans to conquer and settle a foreign land far from their borders, and this act, in the end, is the heart of colonialism.

A symposium was conducted in 1987 by an international group of Crusade scholars who addressed the colonial theory, particularly as recast by the eminent historian Joshua Prawer. The record of the symposium, *The Horns of Hattin*, edited by B. Z. Kedar (1992), is essential reading for anyone interested in the colonial theory of the Crusades. In the end, the participants seem to have agreed to disagree.

Viewpoint:
Yes. The Crusader States were the first European colony in the Middle East.

Colonialism and *imperialism* are loaded terms in the scholarly discourse concerning the Crusades. In one sense, the debate over whether the Crusader States were an early form of colonialism is part of a larger discussion on the importance of the Middle Ages for Western development. Many of the greatest European achievements and problems have been traced to incipient medieval forms. For instance, some historians argue that medieval maritime republics were capitalist; others claim capitalism is a useful term, a sort of analytic shorthand, that helps one understand the republics; and still others contend that capitalism is a modern concept that cannot be applied to medieval people without incurring the charge of anachronism. Some scholars concede a sort of "proto-capitalism" that can legitimately be ascribed to medieval merchants, while others claim the term introduces more confusion than clarity and thus defeats the analytical purpose. Many historians have applied the terms *colonialism* or *colony* to the Crusader States, and the words even appear in several book and article titles devoted to the subject.

There are almost as many definitions of colonialism and imperialism as there are historians approaching the subject. Moses Finley's article "Colonies—An Attempt at a Typology" (1976) was exactly what it claimed to be—an attempt. Many historians have lost sight of an important aspect of defining colonialism (or capitalism). Terms should outline central features of the phenomenon they represent; in the end that is what makes them useful. Imperialism/colonialism is defined here as any movement that expands beyond original borders, subjugates the population of a distant land, promotes immigration to establish a new ruling class over an indigenous people, and remains closely tied to the host civilization and continues to be dependent on it.

The crusading movement to the East, and the Crusader States it produced and sustained, were the opening salvo of European imperialism and colonialism. It began a systematic and an enduring attempt to maintain a presence in

the Holy Land and exploit its spiritual and economic resources. That the Latins expanded well beyond their traditional borders during the Crusades is beyond dispute; thus, it was something substantially different from the Norman Conquest of England (1066) or western Europe encroaching upon eastern Europe (though the latter was achieved through the machinery of crusading as well). The Levant is not contiguous to western European borders, and thus the Crusades represent something substantively different from mere expansion through conquest. It involved a massive marshaling of resources (almost all that the West could spare) to establish and maintain a settlement in what was the other side of the known world. The new lords and barons of Outremer (lands beyond the sea), after brutally subjugating the native populations, established themselves as a new ruling class. Immigration was actively supported; generous terms were offered to potential Western immigrants by the new rulers. The result was an influx of Westerners (the volume of which is still in dispute, though estimates of their numbers have been increasing). "New towns," created by European settlers, sprouted up. A most distinctive characteristic of the Crusader States, however, was their utter dependence upon western Europe for their continued existence. This particular feature offers the most convincing case for considering the Crusader States as "colonies" rather than garden-variety medieval military conquests.

The Crusader States were never self-sufficient militarily, politically, or economically. From their origins to their demise (1097–1291) they were settlements that only survived because western Europe wanted them to exist. From the military perspective, the situation is fairly clear. Cairo and Damascus (the latter often being the stalking-horse of Baghdad) could muster far greater military resources than the Latin States. The Crusader States could frequently "hold the fort," and occasionally even took the offensive, but maintaining a permanent presence in the region was clearly beyond their resources. The real war against the Muslims was conducted by western European armies that were recruited through preaching the Crusades. Denying European military muscle to the region eventually resulted in the death of the colonies. The military situation was intimately connected to the political one. The barons of Outremer constantly

LIVING IN ANGUISH OF SOUL

Christian knights garrisoning the Crusader States lived under the constant threat of Muslim attack. Patriarch Aymeric, in a letter to the French king, complains about the condition of his people in Antioch:

The deaths of the Christians are frequent and the captures which we see daily. Moreover, the wasting away of the church in the East afflicts with ineradicable grief us who, tortured internally even to our destruction, are dying while living in anguish of soul, and, leading a life more bitter than death, as a culmination of our miseries, are wholly unable to die. Nor is there anyone who turns his heart towards us and out of pity directs his hand to aid us. But not to protract our words, the few Christians who are here cry out to you, together with us, and implore your clemency, which with God's assistance is sufficient to liberate us and the church of God in the East. . . .

Therefore, the great devastator of the Christian people, who rules near us, collected together from all sides the kings and races of the infidels and offered a peace and truce to our prince and very frequently urged it. His reason was that he wished to traverse our land with greater freedom in order to devastate the kingdom of Jerusalem and to be able to bear aid to his vassal fighting in Egypt. But our prince was unwilling to make peace with him until the return of our lord king.

When the former saw that he was not able to accomplish what he had proposed, full of wrath, he turned his weapons against us and laid siege to a certain fortress of ours, called Harrenc, twelve miles distant from our city. But those who were besieged—7,000 in number, including warriors, men and women—cried loudly to us, ceasing neither day nor night, to have pity on them, and fixed a day beyond which it would be impossible for them to hold out. Our prince having collected all his forces set out from Antioch on the day of St. Lawrence and proceeded as far as the fortress in entire safety. For the Turks in their cunning gave up the siege and withdrew a short distance from the fortress to some narrow passes in their own country. . . .

After the slaughter of the Christians the Turks returned to the above-mentioned fortress, captured it, and by compact conducted the feeble multitude of women, children and wounded as far as Antioch. Afterwards they advanced to the city, devastated the whole country as far as the sea with fire and sword and exercised their tyranny according to their lusts on everything which met their eyes.

God is witness that the remnant which is left us is in no way sufficient to guard the walls night and day, and owing to the scarcity of men, we are obliged to entrust their safety and defense to some whom we suspect. Neglecting the church services, the clergy and presbyters guard the gates. We ourselves are looking after the defense of the walls and, as far as possible, are repairing, with great and unremitting labor, the many portions which have been broken down by earthquakes. And all this in vain, unless God shall look upon us with a more kindly countenance. For we do not hope to hold out longer, inasmuch as the valor of the men of the present day has been exhausted and is of no avail. But we do, in order that whatever can be done may not be left undone by us.

Above all, the only anchor which is left in this extremity for our hope is in you. Because we have heard from everybody of your greatness, because we have understood that you, more than all the other kings of the West, always have the East in mind. From that we are given to understand that your joy will not be full until you accomplish at some time what we are unable through our misdeeds to accomplish. And it is our hope that by your hand the Lord will visit His people and will have compassion on us.

Source: *Letter from Aymeric, Patriarch of Antioch, to Louis VII of France, 1164, in Dana C. Munro, ed., "Letters of the Crusaders," Translations and Reprints from the Original Sources of European History, volume 1, revised edition (Philadelphia: University of Pennsylvania, 1897), pp. 15–17.*

tried to integrate fully the crown of Jerusalem with the line of a European monarch or great potentate. This connection was seen as the panacea for all the ills in the colonies. Desire to shore up the military was not the only reason the Crusader States usually looked to the West. There were also blood relations and kinship networks that produced similar dependency and support. The potentates of the East were often from cadet branches of the great families in the West, and thus policies promoting the interests of the extended families often exerted great influence. It is also impossible to ignore how Western monarchs, such as French king Louis IX, assumed complete political control while in the East. The economic situation is more confusing but still points clearly to dependence. As trade routes in the East changed, the ports of the Crusader States took on new importance. Invaluable contributions by the Italian maritime republics were motivated by the promise of financial gain and possible commercial hegemony rather than by spiritual rewards. Italians certainly reaped respectable profits from the venture, but also, along with the military orders whose financial assets were rooted in European holdings, they played a central role in supplying and sustaining the Crusader States. One must remember that the Crusader States even depended on the West for warhorses. In each of these crucial areas the Crusader States were completely dependent on western Europe. The umbilical cord remained intact for two centuries. Thus, the Crusader States were not viable settlements that could sustain themselves. Their fate and fortune was ultimately determined in western Europe, which sponsored and underwrote their entire existence.

Many historians who reject the idea that the Crusader States were the first European colony focus on the fact that no single "state" served as the sole sponsor. The Crusade was an international joint venture of feudal states, not to be confused with the real colonial activities of separate modern nation-states in the nineteenth century. Finley was most vociferous in this regard, claiming that feudal societies by definition were incapable of true colonial ventures. Feudalism was based on personal ties rather than the impersonal mechanisms that govern modern states. The nation-state had not yet been invented in the twelfth and thirteenth centuries, even though the process had begun.

In this regard one should also note the dominance of the French during the classical period of crusading. English, German, and Italian interest and support was real, but there was, and remained, something distinctly "French" about Outremer. Still, Finley and other critics cite the lack of a *metropole* (mother-state). Also some historians looking for a *metropole* for medi-

Late twelfth-century illumination of the Christian attack on Antioch during the First Crusade

(The Menil Collection, Houston)

eval colonialism must nuance the modern model to take into consideration the peculiarities of the Middle Ages. The papacy, some have argued, discharged the *metropole* function for medieval colonialism. This argument is attractive, for it meets a significant objection by proffering a medieval functional equivalent. The papacy had an undying interest in preserving the Crusader States; it received revenue from them through Peter's Pence; it played an important role in sustaining them; it provided moral justification through the "Christian's burden" (rather than the "White Man's burden" of the nineteenth century); and it marshaled the resources only a modern nation-state could provide.

The Crusades should be considered an imperialist movement (though not identical to that of the nineteenth century) and its first fruits, the Crusader States, a colony. As Joshua Prawer noted in *The Latin Kingdom of Jerusalem: European Colonialism in the Middle Ages* (1972), in the best-case scenario they were actual colonies; in the worst, they were the venture in which Europe first expanded far beyond its borders and learned the initial lessons in colonization. Nor was there really a decisive break in this European expansion that can be considered a line of demarcation between the Crusades and modern imperialism. The Crusader States came to an end in 1291, but crusading to the East and the desire to impose domination upon the region did not.

Crusading was redirected to sea battles and offensives against the Turks—a venture that continued for centuries without a break. Europeans, moreover, had not given up hope of resurrecting the Crusader States, and plans for rebuilding them enjoyed a long life after 1291.

The age of discovery and expansion was deeply intertwined with the crusading movement. Portugal was still trying to outflank Islamic North Africa, as well as develop an economic structure based on sea trade, as it explored and colonized Africa. Spanish explorer Christopher Columbus's expeditions to the West had many motives, but one was to meet up with the mythical Prester John, a Christian king of the Far East, who would help the Latins place Islam in a vise that would apply the necessary pressure to recover the Holy Land. The conquest of the Americas was by and large a permutation of crusading. The phrase "American colonies" raises few eyebrows, even though it existed long before the "real age" of nineteenth-century colonialism. Claiming that the Crusades were a "preface" to modern colonialism may well be justified, but they are part of the same book—that of Western expansion. The modern nation-state was not what began colonialism; it finally perfected the institution and accomplished what feudal societies began but were unable to maintain.

—TODD MARX, CONCORD, NEW HAMPSHIRE

Viewpoint:
No. Western imperialism and colonialism in the Middle East were products of the nineteenth and twentieth centuries.

The claim that the Latin Crusader States in the East were the first European colony emerged from a fundamental misunderstanding of the historical nature of continuity and change. Rather than recognizing an essential break with their past, nineteenth-century Europeans connected their own imperialist movement with the Crusades and stressed continuity, claiming that the Western quest to dominate the savage non-Christian world began in the late eleventh century and continued until the job was done. Many modern historians followed the lead of their immediate ancestors. Essentially, it is a myth and, like all myths, was created to root a given people into a noble and illustrious past. First-century B.C.E. poet Virgil, for example, gave Rome an impressive pedigree by tracing its origins to the Trojan War (circa 1230 B.C.E. – circa 1180 B.C.E.). Imperialists of the nineteenth century (politicians,

military commanders, and scholars) likewise rooted colonialism firmly within the history of the Crusader States and used the rhetoric and history of crusading to justify their actions. Historians now know that the Romans did not descend from the Trojans, and one should likewise realize that late-nineteenth- and early-twentieth-century British-South African colonial administrator Cecil Rhodes had little if anything to do with the twelfth-century English king Richard I (the Lion-Hearted).

Baron Emmanuel Rey is the best place to begin. In the throes of the "New Imperialism," which produced such unseemly chapters of the Western experience as the "Scramble for Africa," Rey published *Les colonies franques de Syrie aux XII et XIII siecles* (1883). In earlier ages the work would have been described as a wonderful piece of epic poetry. However, it can be considered a textbook case of what English historian Herbert Butterfield called the "Whig Interpretation of History," which refers to the tendency to view the past solely in terms of justifying the present. Rey downplayed the religious impetus for the Crusades and saw them as an intentional colonial endeavor. Rey was not alone in this effort. The "father" of modern approaches to history, the great German scholar Leopold von Ranke, also saw the crusading mentality as the central impetus for colonialism. But Rey proved to be the greater influence on the colonial interpretation of the Crusades. He gave colonialism (the French variety in particular) what most movements and nations desperately want to find in the past: an explanation of and justification for themselves.

Rey was a pioneer, but the gist of his theory became near orthodoxy among French historians during the interwar period (1919–1939). It was the age of the "mandate" and, given the disaster of World War I (1914–1919) and the promise of a better postwar world order, it was only natural that the prehistory of imperialism received increasing attention. The moral base for crusading was transferred to that of colonialism. The history of the Crusades and the translations of texts pertaining to it gained considerable ground in the nineteenth century since they were seen as constituting a part of colonial history, a practical scholarship that emphasized utility over antiquarianism. The fact that generous funding for pursuing studies of the colonial past was readily forthcoming did not cause this shift, but it certainly underwrote it.

Rey's most accomplished student and representative during these years was Louis Madelin, who approached the subject in 1917 with his article "La Syrie franque." Madelin saw the Allied victory in World War I as signaling an opportunity for France to return to its long-lost colony in the East and rule to the benefit of all. In 1918 (an important year in the history of modern colonialism) he published *L'Expansion francaise de la Syrie au Rhin*, a compilation of earlier lectures, that clearly marked the Crusader States as the first French colonial experiment. Its basic premise, that French colonialism began with Godfrey of Boullion and continued forward and that it was beneficial to both the conquerors and conquered, was most effectively picked up by René Grousset, who made it the conceptual foundation for his three-volume *Histoire des croisades et du royaume franc de Jérusalem* (1934–1936).

Grousset argued that an *esprit colonial* (colonial spirit) emerged that strengthened and nurtured the Crusader States. Much of the tension he detected between the colonists of the Crusader States and new French arrivals was informed by the new identity that French Algerians (who evidently shared an *esprit colonial* with the barons of Outremer) were assuming and their relationship to France. Grousset, at the end of his study, noted that the Templars held Ruad (modern Arwad, an island off the coast of Syria) for years after the fall of Acre (1291) and that in 1914 the French returned there. In the 1930s much attention (including that of Grousset) was turned toward the causes for the loss of the first French colony, the Crusader States. Since they believed the two efforts at colonization were essentially the same enterprise separated only by time, some scholars believed that understanding the failures of the old attempt could help solve the problems of the new. One popular explanation centered on the conflict that emerged between the spiritual domination of crusading ideology and the nascent and more secular colonial ideology that rose alongside it.

Thus, the French were harbingers and chief architects of the "colonial theory" of the Crusades and the Crusader States. Modern colonialism certainly served as a major impetus for their concentration on this period and the relatively new interest in studying Latin settlement in the East. With the exception of Israeli historians, French historians are still the greatest advocates of the colonial interpretation of the Crusades. One could ask why the British or Germans did not emphasize the colonial nature of the Crusader States to the same degree. A possible reason is that the evidence is not there—unless one makes a strenuous effort to create it, which requires a motive. From the French perspective, the colonial argument staked historical turf in a way that it did not for the British and Germans, though their ancestors also played a significant role in the movement. This stance, however, did not deter the British, who, though intellectually not as committed as the French to defining the Crusades as a colonial enterprise, certainly did so on the level of political propaganda. After the British general Edmund Allenby triumphantly entered both Jerusalem (9 December 1917) and Damascus (1 October 1918), Vivian Gilbert published *The Romance of the Last Crusade: With Allenby to Jerusalem* (1923), which lauded Allenby's exploits; one writer remarked that the continuation of William of Tyre's chronicle could now finally be written. When German kaiser Wilhelm II had earlier entered Jerusalem (1898), he did so in the dress of a Teutonic knight. Italian scholars have also been great advocates of "medieval colonialism," though they have focused on the activities of the maritime republics that forcefully intersect with, but do not dominate, the history of the Crusades. Besides, Italian colonial ambitions, zealously unleashed with the rise of Benito Mussolini, were better served by a different and much older epoch in history, the Roman Empire, particularly regarding colonial designs on North Africa.

After World War II (1939–1945) colonialism acquired an unpleasant political and scholarly connotation. "Decolonization" was the watchword, and few nations wanted to associate any more than necessary with the demonized movement of colonialism. Still, some French historians refused to genuflect to new fashions and continued to expand on what Rey had begun. Jean Richard, one of the giants in crusading history, is an excellent example. At the turbulent crossroads in which France both wanted to yield to decolonization and yet retain its colonies, such as Algeria, Richard described the Crusades as a movement trying to found colonies and the Crusader States as the first French state overseas. But Richard proffered this view after 1948, globally, a year of great magnitude from China and India to Africa. The chief importance of this year was the creation of the state of Israel, which became a powerful and dominant voice in the colonial interpretation of the Crusades. The Israelis found themselves in a situation similar to that of the Crusader States. Creating a deep-rooted state history became an important Israeli concern.

The firebrand of the Israeli colonial theory of the Crusader States was Joshua Prawer, a French-educated historian and citizen of Israel, who was in a unique position to rearticulate the colonial theory of the Crusades. He drew upon the well-established French tradition and reshaped it from the perspective of a modern man of the West surrounded by hostile Islamic forces. Prawer elaborated upon the theories of his French predecessors, but he also made some notable alterations. Most significant was the relationship between the rulers of the Crusader States and their Eastern subjects. Madelin and Grousset emphasized cultural synthesis and cooperation between colonizer and colonized. The complete integration of peoples during French rule in Jerusalem created a new synthetic nation, and this process, by and large, was seen as the ultimate proof for the intuitive mastery of colonial sensibility that belonged to the French. Prawer turned this aspect on its head and posited a theory of rigid and intentional separation that he described as a form of apartheid. Just as Madelin's optimistic recital was rooted in the conditions surrounding the Paris Peace Conference (1919), so Prawer's more pessimistic description was rooted in the Palestinian problem. It would be going much too far to claim that Prawer's revision was an attempted justification for the Palestinian diaspora, but it was rooted in that same tendency to apply the Whig Interpretation that affected earlier French historians. At an international conference held in Israel in July 1987, commemorating the eighth centennial of the Battle of Hattin (1187), a symposium was dedicated to the question of "colonialism" and the Crusader States. Prawer presided over the concluding remarks and described modern Zionism as a colonial enterprise that was not so different from the Crusades, thus connecting Israel as an essentially Western colony with the Crusader States. Prawer's contributions were, and remain, invaluable to the history of the Crusades. Like his French predecessors, however, he had a marked tendency to write history in the present tense.

Modern colonialism and imperialism were rooted in many causes, chief among them the emergence of the modern nation-state and nationalism, two concepts that simply did not exist during the crusading period. Both movements can be said to have been expansionist, but they emerged from different motives and historical forces that are hardly comparable. Thus, the Crusades and colonialism are different. Historians must guard against the tendency to mingle promiscuously the past and present, continuity and change.

—CARL HILL, LOS ANGELES, CALIFORNIA

References

Robert Bartlett, *The Making of Europe: Conquest, Colonization, and Cultural Change, 950–1350* (Princeton: Princeton University Press, 1993).

Robert Ignatius Burns, *Medieval Colonialism: Postcrusade Exploitation of Islamic Valencia* (Princeton: Princeton University Press, 1975).

Herbert Butterfield, *The Whig Interpretation of History* (London: Bell & Sons, 1931).

"The Crusading Kingdom of Jerusalem—The First European Colonial Society?: A Symposium," in *The Horns of Hattin*, edited by B. Z. Kedar (Jerusalem: Yad Izhak Ben-Zvi: Israel Exploration Society / London: Variorum, 1992).

Felipe Fernández-Armesto, *Before Columbus: Exploration and Colonization from the Mediterranean to the Atlantic, 1229–1492* (Basingstoke, Hampshire: Macmillan Education, 1987; Philadelphia: University of Pennsylvania Press, 1987).

Moses Finley, "Colonies—An Attempt at a Typology," *Transactions of the Royal Historical Society*, 5.26 (1976): 167–188.

Vivian Gilbert, *The Romance of the Last Crusade: With Allenby to Jerusalem* (New York: W. B. Feakins, 1923).

René Grousset, *Histoire des croisades et du royaume franc de Jérusalem*, 3 volumes (Paris: Plon, 1934–1936).

Louis Madelin, *L'Expansion francaise de la Syrie au Rhin* (Paris: Plon-Nourrit, 1918).

J. R. S. Phillips, *The Medieval Expansion of Europe* (Oxford & New York: Oxford University Press, 1988).

Joshua Prawer, *Crusader Institutions* (Oxford: Clarendon Press; New York: Oxford University Press, 1980).

Prawer, *The Latin Kingdom of Jerusalem: European Colonialism in the Middle Ages* (New York: Praeger, 1972).

E. G. Rey, *Les colonies franques de Syrie aux XII me et XIII me siecles* (Paris: Picard, 1883).

Jean Richard, *The Crusades, c. 1071–c. 1291*, translated by Jean Birrell (Cambridge & New York: Cambridge University Press, 1999).

REFERENCES

1. BIOGRAPHIES

Abulafia, David. *Frederick II: A Medieval Emperor.* London: John Lane, 1988.

Bett, Henry. *Joachim of Flora.* London: Methuen, 1931.

Cowdrey, H. E. J. *Pope Gregory VII, 1073–1085.* Oxford: Clarendon Press / Oxford & New York: Oxford University Press, 1998.

Fernández-Armesto, Felipe. *Columbus.* Oxford & New York: Oxford University Press, 1991.

Gillingham, John. *Richard the Lionheart.* London: Weidenfeld & Nicolson, 1978.

Jordan, William Chester. *Louis IX and the Challenge of the Crusade: A Study in Rulership.* Princeton: Princeton University Press, 1979.

Khowaiter, Abdul-Aziz. *Baibars the First: His Endeavours and Achievements.* London: Green Mountain Press, 1978.

Richard, Jean. *St. Louis: Crusader King of France.* Edited by Simon Lloyd. Cambridge & New York: Cambridge University Press, 1992.

2. BYZANTINE EMPIRE

Brand, Charles M. *Byzantium Confronts the West, 1180–1204.* Cambridge, Mass.: Harvard University Press, 1968.

Geanakoplos, Deno John. *Emperor Michael Palaeologus and the West, 1258–1282.* Cambridge, Mass.: Harvard University Press, 1959.

Laiou, Angeliki E. *Constantinople and the Latins: The Foreign Policy of Andronicus II, 1282–1328.* Cambridge, Mass.: Harvard University Press, 1972.

Lilie, Ralph-Johannes. *Byzantium and the Crusader States, 1096–1204.* Translated by J. C. Morris and Jean E. Ridings. Oxford: Clarendon Press / New York: Oxford University Press, 1993.

Magoulias, Harry J. *Byzantine Christianity: Emperor, Church, and the West.* Chicago: Rand McNally, 1970.

3. CRUSADER STATES

Airaldi, Gabriella and Benjamin Z. Kedar, eds. *I communi italiani nel regno crociato di Gerusalemme: atti del Colloquio "The Italian Communes in the Crusading Kingdom of Jerusalem": (Jerusalem, May 24–May 28, 1984).* Genoa: Università di Genova, Istituto di Medievistica, 1986.

Ben-Ami, Aharon. *Social Change in a Hostile Environment: The Crusaders' Kingdom of Jerusalem.* Princeton: Princeton University Press, 1969.

Edbury, Peter W., ed. *Crusade and Settlement: Papers Read at the First Conference of the Society for the Study of the Crusades and the Latin East and Presented to R. C. Smail.* Cardiff: University College Cardiff Press, 1985.

Kedar, H. E. Mayer, and R. C. Smail, eds. *Outremer: Studies in the History of the Crusading Kingdom of Jerusalem Presented to Joshua Prawer.* Jerusalem: Yad Izhak Ben-Zvi Institute, 1982.

Madelin, Louis. *L'Expansion francaise de la Syrie au Rhin.* Paris: Plon-Nourrit, 1918.

Prawer, Joshua. *The Crusaders' Kingdom: European Colonialism in the Middle Ages.* New York: Praeger, 1972.

Prawer. *The Latin Kingdom of Jerusalem: European Colonialism in the Middle Ages.* London: Weidenfeld & Nicolson, 1972.

Rey, E. G. *Les colonies franques de Syrie aux XII me et XIII me siecles.* Paris: Picard, 1883.

Richard, Jean. *The Latin Kingdom of Jerusalem.* Translated by Janet Shirley. Amsterdam & New York: North-Holland, 1979.

Riley-Smith, Jonathan. *The Feudal Nobility and the Kingdom of Jerusalem, 1174–1277.* London: Macmillan, 1973; Hamden, Conn.: Archon Books, 1973.

Said, Edward W. *Orientalism.* New York: Pantheon, 1978.

Tibble, Steven. *Monarchy and Lordships in the Latin Kingdom of Jerusalem, 1099–1291.* Oxford: Clarendon Press / New York: Oxford University Press, 1989.

4. CRUSADES

Bull, Marcus. *Knightly Piety and the Lay Response to the First Crusade: The Limousin and Gascony, c. 970–c. 1130.* Oxford: Clarendon Press / Oxford & New York: Oxford University Press, 1993.

Donovan, Joseph P. *Pelagius and the Fifth Crusade.* Philadelphia: University of Pennsylvania Press, 1950.

Fourquin, Guy. *The Anatomy of Popular Rebellion in the Middle Ages.* Translated by Anne Chesters. Amsterdam & New York: North-Holland, 1978.

Godfrey, John. *1204: The Unholy Crusade.* Oxford & New York: Oxford University Press, 1980.

Grousset, René. *Histoire des croisades et du royaume franc de Jérusalem.* 3 volumes. Paris: Plon, 1934–1936.

Housley, Norman. *The Later Crusades, 1274–1580: From Lyons to Alcazar.* New York: Oxford University Press, 1992.

Lamb, Harold. *The Crusades.* 2 volumes. Garden City, N.Y.: Doubleday, Doran, 1930, 1931.

Madden, Thomas F. *A Concise History of the Crusades.* Lanham, Md.: Rowman & Littlefield, 1999.

Mayer, Hans Eberhard. *Geschichte der Kreuzzüge.* Stuttgart: Kohlhammer, 1965. Translated by John Gillingham as *The Crusades.* Second edition. Oxford & New York: Oxford University Press, 1988.

Mollat, Michel and Philippe Wolff. *The Popular Revolutions of the Late Middle Ages.* Translated by A. L. Lytton-Sells. London: Allen & Unwin, 1973.

Oldenbourg, Zoé. *The Crusades.* Translated by Anne Carter. London: Weidenfeld & Nicolson, 1966; New York: Pantheon, 1966.

Paetow, Louis J., ed. *The Crusades and Other Historical Essays: Presented to Dana C. Munro By His Former Students.* New York: Crofts, 1928.

Powell, James M. *Anatomy of a Crusade: 1213–1221.* Philadelphia: University of Pennsylvania Press, 1986.

Prawer, Joshua. *Crusader Institutions.* Oxford: Clarendon Press / New York: Oxford University Press, 1980.

Queller, Donald E. *The Fourth Crusade: The Conquest of Constantinople, 1201–1204.* Philadelphia: University of Pennsylvania Press, 1977.

Richard, Jean. *The Crusades, c. 1071–c. 1291.* Translated by Jean Birrell. Cambridge & New York: Cambridge University Press, 1999.

Riley-Smith, Jonathan. *The Crusades: A Short History.* London: Athlone, 1987; New Haven: Yale University Press, 1987.

Riley-Smith. *The First Crusade and the Idea of Crusading.* London: Athlone, 1987; Philadelphia: University of Pennsylvania Press, 1987.

Riley-Smith. *The First Crusaders, 1095–1131.* Cambridge & New York: Cambridge University Press, 1997.

Riley-Smith, ed. *The Oxford History of the Crusades.* Oxford: Oxford University Press, 1999.

Runciman, Steven. *A History of the Crusades.* 3 volumes. Cambridge: Cambridge University Press, 1951.

Setton, Kenneth M., ed. *The History of the Crusades.* 6 volumes. Second edition. Madison: University of Wisconsin Press, 1989.

Shaw, Margaret R. B., ed. *Chronicles of the Crusades.* Baltimore: Penguin, 1963.

Siberry, Elizabeth. *Criticism of Crusading: 1095–1274.* Oxford: Clarendon Press, 1985; New York: Oxford University Press, 1985.

Throop, Palmer A. *Criticism of the Crusade: A Study of Public Opinion and Crusade Propaganda.* Amsterdam: Swets & Zeitlinger, 1940.

5. DOCUMENTARY SOURCES

Ambroise. *The Crusade of Richard Lion-Heart.* Translated by Merton Jerome Hubert. New York: Columbia University Press, 1941.

Brundage, James A., ed. *The Crusades: A Documentary History.* Milwaukee, Wis.: Marquette University Press, 1962.

Comnena, Anna. *The Alexiad of Anna Comnena.* Translated by E. R. A. Sewter. Baltimore: Penguin, 1969.

Fulbert of Chartres. *The Letters and Poems of Fulbert of Chartres.* Edited and translated by Frederick Behrends. Oxford: Clarendon Press, 1976.

Fulcher of Chartres. *A History of the Expedition to Jerusalem, 1095–1127.* Translated by Frances Rita Ryan. Edited by Harold S. Fink. New York: Norton, 1969.

Gabrielli, Francesco, ed. and trans. *Arab Historians of the Crusades.* Translated from Italian by E. J. Costello. Berkeley: University of California Press, 1969.

Gesta Francorum et aliorum Hierosolimitanorum (The Deeds of the Franks and the Other Pilgrims to Jerusalem). Edited by Rosalind Hill. London & New York: Thomas Nelson, 1962.

Henderson, Ernest F. *Select Historical Documents of the Middle Ages.* London: George Bell and Sons, 1910.

Housley, Norman, ed. *Documents on the Later Crusades, 1274–1580.* New York: St. Martin's Press, 1996.

Ibn Jubayr, Muhammad ibn Ahmad. *The Travels of Ibn Jubayr, being the Chronicle of a Mediaeval Spanish Moor Concerning His Journey to the Egypt of Saladin, the Holy Cities of Arabia, Baghdad the City of the Caliphs, the Latin Kingdom of Jerusalem, and the Norman Kingdom of Sicily.* Translated by R. J. C. Broadhurst. London: Cape, 1952.

Ibn Munqidh, Usamah. *An Arab-Syrian Gentleman and Warrior in the Period of the Crusades: Memoirs of Usamah ibn-Munqidh (Kitab al-I'ti-bar).* Translated by Philip K. Hitti. New York: Columbia University Press, 1929.

Krey, August C., ed. *The First Crusade: The Accounts of Eyewitnesses and Participants.* Princeton: Princeton University Press, 1921.

Theoderich. *Guide to the Holy Land.* Translated by Aubrey Stewart. Second edition. New York: Italica Press, 1986.

Translations and Reprints From the Original Sources of European Sources. Volume 1. Philadelphia: University of Pennsylvania, 1897.

6. ECONOMICS

Abulafia, David. *Commerce and Conquest in the Mediterranean, 1100–1500.* Aldershot, Hampshire & Brookfield, Vt.: Variorum, 1993.

Ashtor, E. *A Social and Economic History of the Near East in the Middle Ages.* London: Collins, 1976.

Duby, Georges. *The Early Growth of the European Economy: Warriors and Peasants from the Seventh to the Twelfth Century.* Translated by Howard B. Clarke. London: Weidenfeld & Nicolson, 1974; Ithaca, N.Y.: Cornell University Press, 1974.

Lopez, Robert S. *The Commercial Revolution of the Middle Ages, 950–1350.* Englewood Cliffs, N.J.: Prentice-Hall, 1971.

7. GENERAL HISTORIES

Bartlett, Robert. *The Making of Europe: Conquest, Colonization, and Cultural Change, 950–1350.* London: John Lane, 1993; Princeton: Princeton University Press, 1993.

Moore, R. I. *The Formation of a Persecuting Society: Power and Deviance in Western Europe, 950–1250.* Oxford & New York: Blackwell, 1987.

Morgan, David. *The Mongols.* Oxford & New York: Blackwell, 1986.

Parry, J. H. *The Age of Reconnaissance.* Cleveland: World, 1963.

Phillips, J. R. S. *The Medieval Expansion of Europe.* Oxford & New York: Oxford University Press, 1988.

Runciman, Steven. *The Sicilian Vespers: A History of the Mediterranean World in the Later Thirteenth Century.* Cambridge: Cambridge University Press, 1958.

Stock, Brian. *The Implications of Literacy: Written Language and Models of Interpretation in the Eleventh and Twelfth Centuries.* Princeton: Princeton University Press, 1983.

Strayer, Joseph R., ed. *The Dictionary of the Middle Ages.* 13 volumes. New York: Scribners, 1982–1989.

REFERENCES

Todorov, Tzvetan. *The Conquest of America: The Question of the Other.* Translated by Richard Howard. New York: Harper & Row, 1984.

Waley, Daniel. *The Italian City-Republics.* London: Weidenfeld & Nicolson, 1969; New York: McGraw-Hill, 1969.

8. INTERNET WEBSITES

Encyclopedia of the Orient <http://lexicorient.com/e.o/index.htm>

The Labyrinth: Resources for Medieval Studies <http://www.georgetown.edu/labyrinth/>

Medieval Crusades <http://www.medievalcrusades.com/>

New Advent Catholic Encyclopedia <http://www.newadvent.org/cathen/>

ORB: The Online Reference Book for Medieval Studies <http://orb.rhodes.edu/>

Setton, Kenneth M. *A History of the Crusades,* on-line edition <http://libtext.library.wisc.edu/HistCrusades/>

9. JEWS

Chazan, Robert. *European Jewry and the First Crusade.* Berkeley: University of California Press, 1987.

Chazan. *God, Humanity, and History: The Hebrew First Crusade Chronicles.* Berkeley: University of California Press, 2000.

Cohen, Jeremy. *The Friars and the Jews: The Evolution of Medieval Anti-Judaism.* Ithaca, N.Y.: Cornell University Press, 1982.

Cutler, Allan Harris and Helen Elmquist Cutler. *The Jew as Ally of the Muslim: Medieval Roots of Anti-Semitism.* Notre Dame, Ind.: University of Notre Dame Press, 1986.

Eidelberg, Shlomo, ed. and trans. *The Jews and the Crusaders: The Hebrew Chronicles of the First and Second Crusades.* Madison: University of Wisconsin Press, 1977.

Goitein, S. D. *Jews and Arabs: Their Contacts through the Ages.* New York: Schocken Books, 1955.

Goitein. *Letters of Medieval Jewish Traders.* Translated by author. Princeton: Princeton University Press, 1973.

Goitein. *A Mediterranean Society: The Jewish Communities of the Arab World as Portrayed in the Documents of the Cairo Geniza.* 6 volumes. Berkeley: University of California Press, 1967–1993.

Marcus, Jacob R. *The Jew in the Medieval World: A Sourcebook, 315–1791.* Cincinnati: Union of American Hebrew Congregations, 1938.

Niremberg, David. *Communities of Violence: Persecution of Minorities in the Middle Ages.* Princeton: Princeton University Press, 1996.

Prawer, Jonathan. *The History of the Jews in the Latin Kingdom of Jerusalem.* Oxford: Clarendon Press / New York: Oxford University Press, 1988.

Sheils, W. J., ed. *Persecution and Toleration: Papers Read at the Twenty-Second Summer Meeting and the Twenty-Third Winter Meeting of the Ecclesiastical History Society.* Oxford: Blackwell, 1984.

Stillman, Norman A., comp. *The Jews of Arab Lands: A History and Source Book.* Philadelphia: Jewish Publication Society of America, 1979.

Stow, Kenneth R. *Alienated Minority: The Jews of Medieval Latin Europe.* Cambridge, Mass.: Harvard University Press, 1992.

10. MIDDLE EAST

Amitai-Reiss, Reuven. *Mongols and Mamluks: The Mamluk-Ilkhanid War, 1260–1281.* Cambridge & New York: Cambridge University Press, 1991.

Hourani, Albert. *The Emergence of the Modern Middle East.* London: Macmillan, 1981; Berkeley: University of California Press, 1981.

Hourani. *A History of the Arab Peoples.* London: Faber & Faber, 1991; Cambridge, Mass.: Belknap Press of Harvard University Press, 1991.

Hourani. *Islam in European Thought.* Cambridge & New York: Cambridge University Press, 1991.

Irwin, Robert. *The Middle East in the Middle Ages: The Early Mamluk Sultanate, 1250–1382.* Carbondale: Southern Illinois University Press, 1986.

Kennedy, Hugh. *The Prophet and the Age of the Caliphates: The Islamic Near East from the Sixth to the Eleventh Century.* London & New York: Longman, 1986.

Laroui, Abdallah. *The Crisis of the Arab Intellectual: Traditionalism or Historicism?* Translated by Diarmid Cammell. Berkeley & London: University of California Press, 1976.

Lyons, Malcolm C. and D. E. P. Jackson. *Saladin: The Policies of the Holy War.* Cambridge & New York: Cambridge University Press, 1982.

Peters, Rudolph. *Islam and Colonialism: The Doctrine of Jihad in Modern History.* The Hague & New York: Mouton, 1979.

Powell, James M., ed. *Muslims Under Latin Rule, 1100–1300.* Princeton: Princeton University Press, 1990.

Semaan, Khalil I., ed. *Islam and the Medieval West: Aspects of Intercultural Relations: Papers Presented at the Ninth Annual Conference of the Center for Medieval and Early Renaissance Studies, State University of New York at Binghamton.* Albany: State University of New York Press, 1980.

Udovitch, A. L., ed. *The Islamic Middle East, 700–1900: Studies in Economic and Social History.* Princeton: Darwin Press, 1981.

11. MILITARY OPERATIONS, ORDERS, AND TACTICS

Barber, Malcolm. *The New Knighthood: A History of the Order of the Temple.* Cambridge & New York: Cambridge University Press, 1994.

Forey, Alan. *The Military Orders from the Twelfth to the Early Fourteenth Centuries.* Toronto & Buffalo: University of Toronto Press, 1992.

Gillingham, John and J. C. Holt, eds. *War and Government in the Middle Ages: Essays in Honour of J. O. Prestwich.* Cambridge: Boydell Press, 1984; Totowa, N.J.: Barnes & Noble, 1984.

Johnson, James Turner and John Kelsay, eds. *Cross, Crescent, and Sword: The Justification and Limitation of War in Western and Islamic Tradition.* New York: Greenwood Press, 1990.

Kedar, B. Z., ed. *The Horns of Hattin.* Jerusalem: Yad Izhak Ben-Zvi: Israel Exploration Society; London: Variorum, 1992.

Keen, Maurice, ed. *Medieval Warfare: A History.* Oxford & New York: Oxford University Press, 1999.

Marshall, Christopher. *Warfare in the Latin East, 1192–1291.* Cambridge & New York: Cambridge University Press, 1992.

Oman, Charles. *A History of the Art of War: The Middle Ages from the Fourth to the Fourteenth Century.* London: Methuen, 1898.

Partner, Peter. *God of Battles: Holy Wars of Christianity and Islam.* London: HarperCollins, 1997.

Russell, Frederick H. *The Just War in the Middle Ages.* Cambridge & New York: Cambridge University Press, 1975.

REFERENCES

Smail, R. C. *Crusading Warfare, 1097–1193*. Second edition. Cambridge & New York: Cambridge University Press, 1995.

12. ORIGINS OF THE CRUSADES

Alphandéry, Paul and Alphonse Dupront. *La Crétienté et l'idée de croisade*. Paris: A. Michel, 1995.

Bender, Karl-Heinz and Hermann Kleber. *Les Epopées de la Croisade: Premier Colloque International (Trèves, 6–11 août 1984)*. Wiesbaden: Steiner, 1987.

Erdmann, Carl. *The Origin of the Idea of Crusade*. Translated by Marshall W. Baldwin and Walter Goffart. Princeton: Princeton University Press, 1977.

Hagenmeyer, Heinrich. *Le vrai et le faux sur Pierre l'Hermite: analyse critique des témoignages historiques relatifs à ce personnage et des légendes auxquelles il a donné lieu*. Paris: Librairie de la Société Bibliographique, 1883.

Tyerman, Christopher. *The Invention of the Crusades*. Toronto & Buffalo: University of Toronto Press, 1998.

13. PAPACY AND THE CHURCH

Blumenthal, Uta-Renate. *The Investiture Controversy: Church and Monarchy From the Ninth to the Twelfth Century*. Philadelphia: University of Pennsylvania Press, 1988.

Cole, Penny J. *The Preaching of the Crusades to the Holy Land, 1095–1270*. Cambridge, Mass.: Medieval Academy of America, 1991.

Cowdrey, H. E. J. *The Age of Abbot Desiderius: Montecassino, the Papacy, and the Normans in the Eleventh and Early Twelfth Centuries*. Oxford: Clarendon Press, 1983.

Cowdrey. *Popes, Monks, and Crusaders*. London: Hambledon, 1984.

Housley, Norman. *The Italian Crusades: The Papal-Angevin Alliance and the Crusades against Christian Lay Powers, 1254–1343*. Oxford: Clarendon Press, 1982; New York: Oxford University Press, 1982.

Lytle, Guy Fitch, ed. *Reform and Authority in the Medieval and Reformation Church*. Washington, D.C.: Catholic University of America Press, 1981.

Maier, Christoph. *Preaching the Crusades: Mendicant Friars and the Cross in the Thirteenth Century*. Cambridge & New York: Cambridge University Press, 1994.

Morrison, Karl F., ed. *The Investiture Controversy: Issues, Ideas, and Results*. New York: Holt, Rinehart & Winston, 1971.

Partner, Peter. *The Lands of St Peter: The Papal State in the Middle Ages and the Early Renaissance*. London: Eyre Methuen, 1972; Berkeley: University of California Press, 1972.

Purcell, Maureen. *Papal Crusading Policy: The Chief Instruments of Papal Crusading Policy and Crusade to the Holy Land from the Final Loss of Jerusalem to the Fall of Acre 1244–1291*. Leiden: Brill, 1975.

Robinson, I. S. *Authority and Resistance in the Investiture Contest: The Polemical Literature of the Late Eleventh Century*. Manchester: Manchester University Press; New York: Holmes & Meier, 1978.

Schein, Sylvia. *Fideles Crucis: The Papacy, the West, and the Recovery of the Holy Land, 1274–1314*. Oxford: Clarendon Press / New York: Oxford University Press, 1991.

Strayer, Joseph R. *The Albigensian Crusades*. New York: Dial, 1971.

Sumption, Jonathan. *The Albigensian Crusade*. London & Boston: Faber & Faber, 1978.

14. RELIGION

Brundage, James A. *The Crusades, Holy War, and Canon Law*. Aldershot, U.K.: Variorum; Brookfield, Vt.: Gower, 1991.

Brundage. *Medieval Canon Law and the Crusader*. Madison: University of Wisconsin Press, 1969.

Chazan, Robert. *Daggers of Faith: Thirteenth-century Christian Missionizing and Jewish Response*. Berkeley: University of California Press, 1989.

Cohn, Norman. *The Pursuit of the Millennium*. London: Secker & Warburg, 1957.

Cowdrey, H. E. J. *The Cluniacs and the Gregorian Reform*. Oxford: Clarendon Press, 1970.

Daniel, E. Randolph. *The Franciscan Concept of Mission in the High Middle Ages*. Lexington: University Press of Kentucky, 1975.

Kedar, Benjamin Z. *Crusade and Mission: European Approaches Toward the Muslims*. Princeton: Princeton University Press, 1984.

Klaasen, Walter. *Living at the End of the Ages: Apocalyptic Expectation in the Radical Reformation*. Lanham, Md.: University Press of America; Walter, Ont.: Institute for Anabaptist and Mennonite Studies, 1992.

Muldoon, James. *Popes, Lawyers and Infidels: The Church and the Non-Christian World, 1250–1550*. Liverpool: Liverpool University Press, 1979.

Peters, Edward, ed. *Christian Society, and the Crusades, 1198–1229: Sources in Translation, Including The Capture of Damietta By Oliver of Paderborn*. Translated by John J. Gavigan. Philadelphia: University of Pennsylvania Press, 1971.

Ricard, Robert. *The Spiritual Conquest of Mexico: An Essay on the Apostolate and the Evangelizing Methods of the Mendicant Orders in New Spain, 1523–1572*. Translated by Lesley Byrd Simpson. Berkeley: University of California Press, 1966.

15. SPAIN

Boswell, John. *The Royal Treasure: Muslim Communities under the Crown of Aragon in the Fourteenth Century*. New Haven: Yale University Press, 1977.

Burns, Robert Ignatius. *Islam Under the Crusaders: Colonial Survival in the Thirteenth-Century Kingdom of Valencia*. Princeton: Princeton University Press, 1973.

Burns. *Medieval Colonialism: Postcrusade Exploitation of Islamic Valencia*. Princeton: Princeton University Press, 1975.

Castro, Américo. *The Spaniards: An Introduction to Their History*. Translated by Willard F. King and Selma Margaretten. Berkeley: University of California Press, 1971.

Castro. *The Structure of Spanish History*. Translated by Edmund L. King. Princeton: Princeton University Press, 1954.

Collins, Roger. *The Arab Conquest of Spain, 710–797*. Oxford & Cambridge, Mass.: Blackwell, 1989.

Conde, Jose Antonio. *Historia de la dominacion de los arabes en España, sacada de varios manuscritos y memorias arabigas*. Madrid: Imprenta que fue de Garcia, 1820-1821. Translated by Mrs. Jonathan Foster as *History of the Dominion of the Arabs in Spain*. London: Bohn, 1854-1855.

Fletcher, Richard. *Moorish Spain*. London: Weidenfeld & Nicolson, 1992.

Fletcher. *The Quest for El Cid*. London: Hutchinson, 1989.

García-Ballester, Luis. *Medicine in a Multicultural Society: Christian, Jewish and Muslim Practitioners in the*

REFERENCES

Spanish Kingdoms, 1222–1610. Aldershot, U.K. & Burlington, Vt.: Ashgate, 2001.

Glick, Thomas F. *Irrigation and Society in Medieval Valencia*. Cambridge, Mass.: Belknap Press of Harvard University Press, 1970.

Glick. *Islamic and Christian Spain in the Early Middle Ages*. Princeton: Princeton University Press, 1979.

Harvey, L. P. *Islamic Spain, 1250 to 1500*. Chicago: University of Chicago Press, 1990.

Jayyusi, Salma Khadra, ed. *Legacy of Muslim Spain*. Leiden & New York: Brill, 1992.

Linehan, Peter. *History and the Historians of Medieval Spain*. Oxford: Clarendon Press, 1993; Oxford & New York: Oxford University Press, 1993.

Lourie, Elena. *Crusade and Colonisation: Muslims, Christians, and Jews in Medieval Aragon*. Aldershot, U.K.: Variorum, 1990; Brookfield, Vt.: Gower, 1990.

Mann, Vivian B., Glick, and Jerrilynn D. Dodds, eds. *Convivencia: Jews, Muslims, and Christians in Medieval Spain*. New York: Braziller in association with the Jewish Museum, 1992.

Myerson, Mark D. *The Muslims of Valencia in the Age of Fernando and Isabel: Between Coexistence and Crusade*. Berkeley: University of California Press, 1991.

Nykl, A. R. *Hispano-Arabic Poetry and its Relations with the Old Provençal Troubadours*. Baltimore: Furst, 1946.

O'Callaghan, Joseph F. *A History of Medieval Spain*. Ithaca, N.Y.: Cornell University Press, 1975.

Sánchez-Albornoz, Claudio. *Spain: A Historical Enigma*. Translated by Colette Joly Dees and David Sven Reher. Madrid: Fundación Universitaria Española, 1975.

Thompson, E. A. *The Goths in Spain*. Oxford: Clarendon Press, 1969.

REFERENCES

CONTRIBUTORS' NOTES

ABATE, Mark T.: Assistant professor of history at Westfield State College, Westfield, Massachusetts.

BACKMAN, Clifford R.: Associate professor of history, Boston University; author of *The Decline and Fall of Medieval Sicily: Politics, Religion, and Economy in the Reign of Frederick III, 1296–1337* (1995).

DEMPSEY, John A.: Scholar at Framingham State College, Framingham, Massachusetts.

FELD, Robin: Independent scholar, Santa Monica, California.

GARDENOUR, Brenda S.: Graduate of the University of New Hampshire and doctoral candidate at Boston University; scholarly interests are in medieval religious and medical history of the Mediterranean region.

GLICK, Thomas F.: Professor of history and director of the Institute for Medieval History at Boston University; author of *Islamic and Christian Spain in the Early Middle Ages* (1979) and *From Muslim Fortress to Christian Castle* (1995).

HILL, Carl: Independent scholar, Los Angeles, California.

KIERDORF, Douglas C.: Ph.D. candidate at Boston University writing his dissertation on the social and political history of La Plana, an irrigated plain north of Valencia, in the late medieval period.

LANDES, Richard: Associate professor of history at Boston University; director and cofounder of the Center for Millennial Studies; author of *Relics, Apocalypse, and the Deceits of History: Ademar of Chabannes (989–1034)* (1995); co-editor, with Thomas Head, of *The Peace of God: Social Violence and Religious Response in France around the Year 1000* (1992).

LIBERTINI, Christopher: Lecturer in history at Suffolk University, Boston.

MARX, Todd: Independent scholar, Concord, New Hampshire.

POWELL, James M.: Professor emeritus of history, Syracuse University; author of *Albertanus of Brescia: The Pursuit of Happiness in the Early Thirteenth Century* (1992) and *Anatomy of a Crusade, 1213–1221* (1986).

WARD, John O.: Professor of medieval history at the University of Sydney, Australia, since 1967; he has published on the crusading movement, medieval witchcraft, medieval intellectual life, and the history of the art of rhetoric; cotranslator of *The Vézelay Chronicle and Other Documents* (1992).

WEBER, Michael: Visiting assistant professor in history at Salem State College, Salem, Massachusetts.

INDEX

INDEX

atomic bomb II 228; III 10, 16; V 48–55; VI 20, 57, 136, 154, 254–255; VIII 195
   American I 260, 262–263
   Anglo-American cooperation on VI 10
   data passed to Soviet Union II 231
   development V 44
   Hiroshima and Nagasaki III 10
   impact on World War II II 268; III 11
   introduction I 4
   Soviet Union development of II 229
   "Stockholm Appeal" II 47
Atomic Energy Act (1946) I 220–221
Atomic Energy Act (1954) VII 175
Atomic Energy Commission (AEC) I 27, 29–31, 214, 220; II 82; VII 174–175, 178
Atoms for Peace I 216–217, 221; II 51
Attaturk Dam (Turkey) VII 82
Attlee, Clement VI 11, 250
Attorney General's List I 76
Auchinleck, Sir Claude John Eyre V 76, 172
Audubon Society VII 31, 258
Auden, Wystan VIII 191
Aufmarschplan I (Deployment Plan I) VIII 247
Aufmarschplan II (Deployment Plan II) VIII 247–248
Ausgleich agreement (1867) IX 137
August Revolution (1945) V 146
Augustine of Hippo X 20, 80–81, 84–85, 103–104, 229, 277
Aurul SA cyanide spill (Romania) VII 248–250, 252–255
Auschwitz I 138; III 253–254, 256; V 54, 56–57, 60, 158, 160–163, 219; VIII 94
   theories of formation V 156
Australia VI 136; VIII 33, 133, 137, 160–161, 208; IX 76, 173
   grain reserves VIII 290
   Japanese immigration to IX 162
   motivation of soldiers VIII
   World War I VIII 54, 117–123, 220
Australia (Australian ship) VIII 137
Australian and New Zealand Army Corps (ANZAC) VIII 121–122
Australia Light Horse IX 72
Australia Mounted Division IX 67
Austria I 253, 293; VI 136; VIII 18, 82, 106, 251–252, 266, 281; IX 49, 82, 93, 120, 158, 225–226
   alliance with Germany (1879) VIII 35
   Central European Model I 108
   contribution of Jews in VIII 167
   customs union with Germany forbidden VIII 283
   dam agreement with Hungary VII 101
   dams in VII 101
   East German emigration through VI 118, 121
   occupation I 108
   pre-World War I alliances VIII 225–231
   Socialists in VIII 260
   supports Slovak anti-nuclear activists VII 103
   union with Nazi Germany VIII 284
Austria-Hungary VIII 76, 95, 98, 104, 172, 178, 226, 228, 230, 266 267, 280, 299; IX 30, 64–65, 99, 102, 140, 154, 192–193, 204, 206, 225, 227, 248, 266–272
   army VIII 69; IX 134, 158
   collapse of VIII 216–217; IX 81
   invades Poland VIII 72
   invades Serbia VIII 72
   relations with Germany concerning Slavic lands VIII 94
   Socialists in VIII 257, 261
   U. S. trade with IX 22
   World War I VIII 11, 43–49; IX 133–138
      aircraft IX 13
      casualties VIII 125, 268
      defense budget VIII 44
      Jews in VIII 164
      mobilization in VIII 125
      motivation of soldiers VIII 266

   war against the United States VII 11
Auténtico Party I 91
automobile
   impact on interstate highway development II 106
   impact on United States II 109
   recreation II 108
Axis I 3; V 62–67
   defeat in Tunisia IV 144
   North African campaign V 66
   parallel war theory V 63–65
Ayyubids X 48–49, 139, 183, 185, 187–188, 274
Azerbaijan VI 255; VIII 96, 216; X 183, 187

B

B-1 bomber I 191; II 57
B-1B "Lancer" supersonic nuclear bomber VI 109, 234
B-17 bomber V 4, 5, 6, 98
B-17C bomber V 5
B-17E bomber V 5
B-24 bomber V 7, 98
B-26 bomber V 5
B-29 bomber V 3, 7, 49, 52,
B-36 bomber I 3– 8
B-52 I 189, 193
B-58 I 193
Babbitt (1922) II 109; III 177
Baby Boomers VI 24–25
Baby M II 80
Babylonian Captivity X 210
Back to Africa movement III 121
Backfire bomber VI 259
Bacon, Francis VI 195
Bacon, Roger X 53, 65, 67, 69, 79, 181, 235
Badeni crisis (1897) IX 138
Badoglio, Marshall Pietro V 178
   Italian campaign IV 144
Baghdad X 48, 52, 77, 172, 193
Baghdad Pact (1955) I 161, 277; II 146
   Iraq I 277
   Turkey I 277
Baghdad Railway VIII 212
Baia Mare Environmental Protection Agency VII 248, 253
Baia Mare Task Force VII 248, 252, 254
Baia Mare, Romania VII 247, 249, 253, 255
Baker v. *Carr* (1962) II 139, 281–282, 286
Baker, Newton VIII 17–18; IX 2
Bakunin, Mikhail Aleksandrovich VI 179
Bakuninist anarchists VI 178
balance of power VI 45
Balcones Escarpment VII 70
Baldric of Bourgueil X 105
Baldric of Dol X 105
Baldwin IV X 51
Baldwin of Boulogne X 73, 119
Baldwin, James II 90–91; III 82
Baldwin, Prime Minister Stanley V 120; VIII 168, 190
Balfour Declaration (1917) VIII 37, 41, 163, 166, 168, 208
Balfour, Arthur VIII 16, 168
Balkan League VIII 212
Balkan Wars VIII 39, 43–45, 117, 211, 214, 230; IX 226
Balkans I 289; V 68–78; VI 50, 272; VII 82; VIII 76, 80, 95, 106, 226, 228, 252; IX 27, 133, 203, 224–226, 266–272; X 281, 285
   as second front V 75– 76
   Christians in VIII 211
   genocide in VI 216
   Islamic rule in VIII 211
   Soviet influence I 304
   World War I VII 43–49
Ballistic Missile Defense (BMD) I 186, 195–203, 225
   technological problems I 199–200
Baltic Sea VII 18, 148; VIII 75; IX 144, 181; X 66, 69
   German control of IX 194
   salmon populations in VII 90
   submarines in VIII 292

INDEX

INDEX

Dulles, John Foster I 49, 69, 130, 149, 267–274, 278, 282; II 50–51, 135, 168, 208; VI 130, 153, 221, 268
    "massive retaliation" policy I 192, 211, 213
    New Look policy I 117, 211, 214
    U.S. policies in Europe I 208
Dunkirk evacuation (1940) V 123
Dunkirk Treaty (1947) I 208; VI 210
Du Pont Corporation IX 22
Durance River VII 98
Dust Bowl VII 181, 183, 185
Dutch East Indies VIII 137
Duwamish River VII 189, 191
Dwight D. Eisenhower System of Interstate and Defense Highways II 109
Dyer, Reginald IX 93
Dyer Bill IX 4
Dzhugashvili, Iosef IX 197

E

Eaker, Ira C. V 5, 98
Earth Day VII 123, 265
East Africa VIII 193
East Germany I 107, 274; VI 110–111, 115–122, 141, 178, 182, 206–212, 217, 246, 249, 251, 261, 276
    defectors VI 170
    dissidents in VI 117, 121, 211
    Dulles acceptance of Soviet influence I 273
    flight of citizens VI 141
    political parties in VI 121
    reforms I 154
    relations with Soviet Union I 253
    revolt against totalitarianism (1953) I 254
    shift in leadership VI 117
    Soviet suspicion of I 185
    strategic importance I 109
East Prussia VIII 249, 252, 280; IX 15, 158
Easter Rising (1916) VIII 154–162, 209; IV 21
East St. Louis, riot IX 7
East Timor, Indonesian invasion of VI 270
Eastern Europe VI 116, 120, 131, 148, 181, 201, 207–208, 221, 224, 226, 236, 251, 267, 281; VII 250; IV 81, 83; X 62, 67, 130, 178, 180–182, 206, 265, 301
    collapse of communist regimes in VII 101
    collapse of Soviet control in VI 216
    Crusades in X 66, 128, 270
    dissident movements in VI 229
    environmental crisis in VII 17–24
    German occupation (World War I) VIII 91–101, 176
    German occupation (World War II) VIII 91–101
    NATO expansion in VI 54
    political repression in VII 18
    removal of Soviet forces VI 110
    Soviets in VI 244–245, 250, 252
    Soviets block Marshall Plan to VI 255
    treatment of refuges VI 251
    U.S. support of dissidents in VI 3
    voter apathy on environmental issues VII 20
Eastern Orthodox Church VIII 207; X 25, 190, 208
Ebert, Friedrich VIII 257, 280; IX 32
Ebro River VII 147
Echo Park Dam (United States) VII 27, 29, 30–31
Economic Commission for Latin America (ECLA) I 20–22
Economic Opportunity Act (1964) II 276
Economic Opportunity Act (1965) II 272
Eden, Anthony I 272, 280; V 41, 290, 312; VI 11
Edessa X 48, 74, 92, 129–130, 167, 191, 270, 296–297
Edison, Thomas Alva VIII 197
Edmondson, W. T. VII 189, 192
Edward I X 189
Edward VII X 57
Edwards Aquifer VII 69–75

Egypt I 308–312, 273, 283; II 53; VI 11, 83, 137, 162–164, 172, 246, 271–27; VII 29, 82, 135, 149; VIII 31–32, 38, 168, 213; IX 96; X 24, 30, 46–51, 56, 60, 64, 66, 78, 89, 95, 107, 109, 139–142, 144–148, 155–156, 167, 170, 173–174, 182, 185, 187, 193, 239, 248, 251, 255–258, 273, 277, 282, 287, 292
    Arab-Israeli War (1967) II 150
    Aswan High Dam VII 3
    attack on Israel VI 10, 161, 163
    conflict with Israel I 159
    deportation of Jews VIII 166
    environmental control in VII 145
    Free Officers' regime II 148
    Great Britain in VIII 35
    Kafara Dam VII 3
    nuclear weapons development I 219
    Soviet alliance I 161; II 146; VI 43, 81
    Soviet-Egyptian Pact (1955) I 162
    Suez Canal I 308, 316
    Suez Crisis I 289; VI 135, 270
    Suez War I 277, 280
    U.S. resistance to return of Soviet troops VI 163
    Western Desert Project VII 2
    World War I VIII 37–42
Ehrlichman, John D. VI 24
Einsatzgruppen (special action commandos) IV 88, 131, 134, 141; V 161
Einstein, Albert VIII 167 ; IX 87
Eisenhower, Dwight D. I 35, 64, 71, 92, 102, 210–215, 274, 292, 297, 306; II 38, 45, 49–55, 64, 67, 105–106, 112, 135, 137, 200, 229, 232, 260, 280; IV 183; V 314, 92, 69, 281, 284; VI 11, 17, 35, 64, 86, 96, 130, 133, 136, 139, 153, 155, 231; IX 108–109
    appeal to Soviets VI 135
    as NATO commander-general I 208
    Atoms for Peace I 216–217; II 49, 53
    Battle of the Bulge IV 64
    Bay of Pigs invasion II 52, 54, 115
    Berlin crisis I 69
    "Chance for Peace" speech II 53
    dealings with de Gaulle VI 105
    Eisenhower Doctrine (1957) I 280–282; II 148
    foreign policy of VI 141
    Interstate Highway Act II 105
    Korea VI 146
    military career IV 65
    1952 presidential campaign I 274
    Open Skies policy II 51, 54; VI 20, 35
    planning D-Day invasion IV 68
    restraint in use of nuclear weapons I 236–237
    rollback policy I 72
    sends envoy to mediate Middle East water dispute VII 138
    space program II 242, 260
    Suez Crisis VI 80
    summit with Macmillan VI 10
    support of U.S. involvement in Korea II 211
    Supreme Allied Commander II 50
    Taiwan policy I 68
    vetos rivers-and-harbors legislation VII 259
    World War I service VIII 192
    WWII strategy in Germany VI 169
Eisenhower administration I 49, 66, 94, 110, 117, 281; VI 30, 56, 81, 92, 95, 139, 149, 238; VII 259
    "atomic diplomacy" I 211, 213, 267
    Atoms for Peace policy I 216
    concern over Soviet Middle East policy VI 239
    containment policy I 184
    defense spending VI 144
    Dulles, John Foster I 278
    East Germany policy I 271
    Eisenhower Doctrine I 282
    Hungarian uprising VI 13
    Middle East policy I 161
    military spending I 69, 192

INDEX

INDEX

Mexico III 124–131; VII 197; VIII 296, 298; IX 21, 168; X 8, 10
    cientificos (scientific ones) III 125
    criticism of Libertad Act I 98
    Cuban investment I 97
    departure of French army (1867) I 125
    land reform I 21
    mining industry III 125
    nationalization of U.S. businesses, 1930s I 130
    relations with the United States VIII 16, 18, 22
    salmon range VII 196
    water policy in VII 151–159
Michael VII Ducas X 122, 285
Michel, Victor VIII 234–235
Micronesia IX 163, 165
Middle Ages X 123–124, 130–131, 140, 152, 158, 166–168, 181, 208, 229, 236, 241–243, 250, 265
Middle East I 157–158, 161, 277; VI 53, 79, 90, 135–136, 162, 171, 188, 266, 268, 271; VIII 109, 211, 228 ; IX 27, 34, 67, 72, 91; X 199
    Arab-Israeli conflict II 145
    infrastructure I 158
    peace process I 289
    relations with United States I 278
    Soviet influence VI 160–167, 261
    Suez Canal Zone II 146
    U.S. interests I 162; VI 61
    water crisis in VII 135–141
    water policy in VII 76–84
    water shortage in VII 280
    World War I 37–42
Migratory Bird Conservation Act (1929) VII 277
Mihajlovic, Draza VI 275, 277–278
Mikva, Abner Joseph VII 121
military gap between U.S. and Soviet Union I 188–194
Military Intelligence Service (MIS) III 14–15
Military Service Act (1916) IX 58
Milites X 14, 16, 34
Millerand, Alexandre VIII 152, 255
Milliken v. *Bradley* (1974) II 293, 298
Milne, George VIII 214, 216; IX 206
Milyukov, Pavel VIII 173–174
Minow, Newton II 121, 23
Miranda, Ernesto II 284
Miranda v. *Arizona* (1966) II 281, 284, 286
Missao do Fomento e Powoamento dio Zambeze (MFPZ) VII 240
missile gap I 182–194; II 260; VI 21, 141
Mississippi River VII 27, 29, 31, 182, 211
Mitchell Act (1938) VII 202
Mitchell, William A. (Billy) IV 2; V 3, 14, 126; IX 11, 223
Mitterand, François-Maurice VI 102, 104
Mobutu Sese Seko VI 81
Mohammad Reza Pahlavi (shah of Iran) I 11, 141–146; II 97
Molotov, Vyacheslav I 36, 113, 175, 177, 238, 303; II 35; VI 101, 255, 280
    Molotov Plan I 178; II 40
    Soviet nuclear spying I 245
Molotov-Ribbentrop Pact I 110
Moltke, Helmuth von (the Elder) VIII 73, 75, 184, 248–249, 252; IX 98
Moltke, Helmuth von (the Younger) VIII 72, 114, 179–180, 182, 184, 226, 248; IX 41, 46, 52, 98–99, 101, 103, 124, 227, 263
Mongke (Mangu Khan) X 183, 186–187
Mongols X 30, 48, 52–53, 60, 66, 144, 180, 182–189
Monroe, James IX 96, 246
Monroe Doctrine (1823) I 124–125, 132; II 98, 156, 257; III 45–46, 243, 247; VI 75; IX 96, 173, 246
    as applied to Cuba VI 71
    Roosevelt Corollary (1904) III 46
Montenegro IX 267, 270
Montgomery bus boycott II 22–24, 90, 140

Montgomery, Field Marshal Bernard Law II 50; IV 64, 66, 144, 177–184; V 16, 19–25, 28, 34, 42, 44, 122–125, 129
Moors X 2, 8, 10, 41, 128, 133, 260, 265, 269, 290
Morelos Dam (Mexico) VII 152, 155, 157–159
Morgan, J. P. IX 19, 57, 248
Morgenthau, Hans J. I 266; II 8
Morgenthau, Henry III 257
    Morgenthau Plan (1944) II 210
Moriscos (converted Muslims) X 4, 6
Morrill Act (1862) III 2
Morocco VIII 32, 152, 227; IX 91, 114, 226; X 270, 278, 289
    soldiers in France IX 118
Moroccan Crisis (1905) VIII 35
Mosaddeq, Mohammad I 66, 69, 211; II 146; VI 131
Moscow Conference (1944) V 311
Moscow Olympics (1980) VI 166, 237
    U.S. boycott VI 43
Mountbatten, Lord Louis V 42, 196
Movimiento de Izquierda Revolucionaria (MIR) I 127, 130
Movimiento Nacionalista Revolucionario (MRN) I 125–126
Moynihan, Daniel Patrick II 166, 271, 276
Mozambique VI 1–7, 188, 221, 256, 261; VII 236–237, 239–240
    aid from Soviet Union VI 2
    independence VI 2
    Porgtuguese immigration to VII 237
Mozambique Liberation Front (*Frente da Libertação de Moçambique* or FRELIMO) VI 2, 6; VII 239
Mozambique National Resistance Movement (*Resistência Nacional Moçambicana* or RENAMO) VI, 2, 4, 6
Mozarabs X 2, 202, 242, 244
Mubarak, Hosni I 163, 317
Mudejars X 2, 180
Mudros Armistice (1918) VIII 217
Muhammad X 10, 29, 43, 45, 59, 64–66, 132–133, 198–199, 201, 273, 288
mujahidin (mujahideen) I 10–16; VI 2, 133, 165, 238
    U.S. support VI 229
Mundt, Karl E. I 74, 306; II 131, 211
Mundt-Nixon Bill I 74
Munich Agreement (1938) I 293, 300
Munich Conference (1938) IV 127
Municipality of Metropolitan Seattle (Metro) 188–195
Munitions of War Act (1915) IX 56
Murphy, Charles Francis III 262
Murphy, Justice Frank V 188
music
    "folk revival" II 214
    as political force II 214
music industry
    impact of television II 218
    record companies at Monterey Music Festival II 219
    sheet music production II 217
    technological advances II 216
    youth market II 219
Muskie, Edmund Sixtus VII 176, 261, 263–264, 268
Muslims X 8, 10, 17, 19, 27, 29, 33–34, 37, 43–44, 47–48, 52, 54, 59–60, 65, 69, 78, 81, 88–90, 95, 101, 105, 108–109, 117, 128, 133, 140, 149–150, 153, 159, 169, 174, 176, 179–181, 195, 209, 212, 219–220, 223–224, 238, 248, 255, 265–266, 280–281, 284, 287, 289, 292, 297
    Christian treatment of X 177
    cultural interaction with Christians X 197–203
    in Spain X 1–6, 40–45, 241–246
    Latinization of X 43
    treatment of in Crusader States X 190–196
    treatment of Jews X 272–278
Mussolini, Benito I 134; IV 14, 80; V 36, 108–109, 117, 135, 169, 175–177, 226, 233; VIII 95; IX 96, 175; X 305
    alliance with Hitler V 179
    downfall V 2

INDEX

wetlands takings compared to attack on VII 278
Pearse, Patrick VIII 155–156, 158, 162
Pelagius X 87, 89–90, 93–95, 177, 241, 244
Pender, F. G. VII 53, 55
Pennsylvania
  dams in VII 29
  signs Chesapeake Bay 2000 Agreement VII 49
Pennsylvania State University VII 262
Pentagon II 51, 67
Pentagon Papers (1971) II 177; VI 24, 26
People's Liberation Army (PLA) I 268
Pepó, Pal VII 250
perestroika I 14; II 56, 60; VI 114, 116, 245; VII 20
Perkins, Frances III 150, 200, 251
Perot, H. Ross II 194–202
  advantages to his campaign II 198
  election grassroots movement II 195
  hatred of George Bush II 199
  importance of wealth to his campaign II 202
  presidential campaign II 195
Pershing, John J. III 130, 138; V 14, 126; VIII 10–20, 21–25, 114; IX 21, 26, 29–30, 104–105, 107, 109–110
  Mexican expedition III 127
  U. S. Punitive Expedition III 129
Pershing II missiles VI 3, 20–21, 35, 101–102, 208, 229, 232, 236, 263
Persia VIII 31, 35, 41; IX 96, 226; X 29, 183
Persian Gulf VII 77, 147
Persian Gulf War (1990–1991) I 163, 195–196, 199, 217, 239; VI 58, 61, 100, 173, 235, 250, 266; VIII 168; X 56
Peru VII 74
Pétain, Philippe IV 276; V 244; VIII 150, 265; IX 26, 108–110, 114
Peter I (the Great) IX 154, 238
Peter the Hermit X 15, 18–19, 21, 29, 59, 72, 74, 101, 131, 191, 211–221, 231–232, 234–235, 237
Peter the Venerable X 16, 79, 163
Petrograd IX 197, 237, 239–240
Petrograd Soviet VIII 170, 173, 175, 178, 258; IX 201–202
Philip I (France) X 118–119, 121
Philip II Augustus (France) X 21, 33, 88–89, 144, 151, 251, 254, 257, 260, 263, 297
Philip IV (France) X 67, 207
Philippines I 51, I 295; VI 77, 80, 149, 188, 194; IX 96; X 8, 244
  Clark Field and Subic Bay I 145
  crucial to U.S. security I 85
  Insurrection (1899–1902) IX 96
  Opium War III 136
Phongolapoort Dam (South Africa) VII 245
Picasso, Pablo III 79; IX 86
Picq, Charles VIII 71, 234
Pinochet Ugarte, Augusto I 124, 128–129, 141; VI 64
Pisa X 148–150, 156
Plan XVI VIII 233–234; IX 45
Plan XVII VIII 146, 148, 182, 232–238; IX 47, 99, 101
Planck, Max IX 87
Planned Parenthood of Missouri v. *Danforth* (1976) II 222
Planned Parenthood of Southeastern Pennsylvania v. *Casey* (1992) II 79, 222, 224
plants
  African grasses VII 217
  alfalfa VII 14, 182
  Bermuda grass VII 217
  black mustard VII 217
  corn VII 181, 182
  Huachuca water umbel VII 216
  invasion of alien species in the United States VII 213
  Johnson grass VII 217
  Kearney blue-star VII 216
  Russian Thistles VII 13
  sorghum VII 181–182
  tiszavirág (Tisza flower) VII 252
  winter wheat VII 181

Platt Amendment (1901) III 47
  revocation of, 1934 III 47
Plessy v. *Ferguson* (1896) II 23, 25, 90, 136, 138, 141, 280, 290
Plum Island VII 277
Plumer, Herbert VIII 219–220, 224
Po River VII 147
Podoba, Juraj VII 103
Point Reyes National Seashore VII 178
Poison Gas VIII 239–244
Pol Pot I 44, 46, 134, 145, 289; VI 83
Poland I 109–110, 112, 152, 259, 271, 294; II 34, 36, 39, 153; V 30; VI 110, 130, 133–134, 137, 178, 181, 217, 237, 244–246, 249, 251–252, 261, 274, 276; VIII 91, 277–278, 280–281, 284; IX 44, 93, 134, 158–159, 175, 193, 238, 242
  aftermath of World War II I 173
  Baruch Plan I 27, 29, 31
  entry into NATO I 207
  environmental activism in VII 17–24
  expatriates VI 170
  German invasion during World War II V 35, 132, 179; VIII 284
  German occupation during World War I VIII 92–98
  impact of pollution on population of VII 18
  independence movement VI 110
  Jews in during World War I VIII 164–167
  martial law in (1981) VII 19
  partition VI 54
  poisoning of waters in VII 18
  postwar elections I 258
  radioactive fallout from Chernobyl VII 18
  reforms I 154
  Soviet invasion of II 32
  strategic importance I 109
  and Warsaw Pact VI 170
  Yalta Agreement (1945) I 301–302, 304
Polaris Submarine VI 11, 75
Polaris Submarine/Sea-Launched Ballistic Missile (SLBM) VI 10
Polivanov, Alexei IX 193, 243
Polish Communist Party, Tenth Congress of VII 20
Polish Ecological Club (Polski Klub Ekologiczny, or PKE) VII 18
Polish Green Party VII 20
Political parties
  history of II 199
  history of third parties II 199
  voter demographics II 199
Pollution Control Act (1915, Ontario) VII 117
polychlorinated biphenyls (PCBs) VII 147
Pong Dam (India) VII 130
Pope Pius XII IV 36, 38, 191
Popular Unity Coalition (UP) I 123, 127
Populist Party II 3, 86, 199
  aka People's Party II 196
Porter, Eliot VII 113
Portland Dock Commission VII 53
Portland, Oregon VII 52, 197
  importance of VII 53
Portugal VII 240; VIII 31; IX 49, 84; X 10, 304
  colonial rule in Africa VII 236–237; VIII 86, 89
Potsdam Conference (1945) I 239, 263; II 205; III 13; VI 155, 267
Potlatch Corporation VII 226
Potsdam Declaration (1945) III 15; V 50–51, 149, 264
Powell, Adam Clayton, Jr. II 197, 274
Powell, Colin II 100
Powell, John Wesley VII 181
Powers, Francis Gary I 66
Pravda IX 197
President's Foreign Intelligence Advisory Board (PFIAB) VI 256–257
Pressler Amendment (1985) I 218
Prester John X 189, 304
Principle International Alert Center VII 248

Prince Max of Baden IX 32
Prince Rupprecht IX 262
Princip, Gavrilo IX 225–226
Prittwitz und Graffon, Max von IX 159
Progressive Era VII 10, 47, 122, 257, 271, 273; IX 250
        women in III 197–203
Progressive movement III 204–211; VII 263; VIII
        295, 301
Progressive Party II 195–196, 209; III 177
Prohibition III 174, 198–211
Prussia VIII 71, 184, 257, 278; IX 44–45, 206, 225
        military 30, 67; X 66, 179
Pryce, E. Morgan VII 55
Public Broadcasting System (PBS) II 125; VII 184
Public Works Administration (PWA, 1933) III 150;
        VII 43
Pueblo Dam (United States) VII 14
Puerto Rico IX 96
Puget Sound VII 188–189, 191, 193–194
Pugwash Conference I 253
Punjab, India VII 133
        agriculture in VII 130
Pure Food and Drug Act (1906) III 243
Pyle, Ernie V 175
Pyramid Lake VII 169
Pyrenees X 2, 241

Q

Qalawun X 46, 48–49, 185
Q-ships IX 76, 183–188
Quadrant Conference (1943) V 236
Quai d'Orsai (French Foreign Office) V 173
Quebec, Canada, opposes water bill VII 120
Quebec Conference (1943) V 239
Queen Blanche of Castile X 140–143, 235
Queen Mary (British ship) IX 177–178
Queen Victoria IX 44, 140
        Silver Jubilee of (1862) IX 45
Quemoy I 275; II 52; VI 103, 181
        Chinese attack I 265–270
        Eisenhower administration I 211, 213
Quinn v. *U.S.* I 80
Qur' an X 41–42, 45, 49, 65, 133, 179, 199, 273
Qutuz X 48, 187

R

Rába geologic fault line VII 106
Rachel Carson National Wildlife Refuge VII 278
racism II 163; III 213–219
        American IV 217
        and narcotics legislation III 134
Radio Free Europe I 65; VI 133, 135
Radic, Stjepan IX 267, 272
Railroad Retirement Pension Act (1934) III 28
Rainbow Bridge VII 30
Rainey, Gertrude "Ma" III 82
Rajasthan, India VII 125
        agriculture in VII 130
        rainfall in VII 126
Rajasthan Canal VII 132
Rákosi, Mátyás VI 134, 276
Ramadan War. *See* Yom Kippur War I 314
RAND Corporation I 119; II 65–66
Randolph, A. Philip II 189; III 123, 184, 217
        march on Washington III 219
Ranke, Leopold von X 218, 300, 304
Rape of Nanking (1937) IV 152–153; V 153, 192; IX
        96
Raritan Bay VII 265
Rasputin, Grigory VIII 258; IX 160, 237, 239–240,
        243
Rathenau, Walther VIII 140, 166
Rawlinson, Henry VIII 272, 275; IX 36, 122
Raymond of Penafort X 67, 69
Raymond of St. Gilles X 73, 119
Raymond of Toulouse X 191, 216, 221

Reagan, Ronald I 48, 51–54, 104, 106, 149; II 56–63,
        102, 190, 199–200, 295; III 48; VI 6, 8, 13,
        17, 20, 25, 31, 33, 50, 58, 104, 109, 190–191,
        205, 208, 221–242, 256–257, 261, 270
        anticommunism II 60; VI 228–229
        election platform I 50
        invasion of Grenada II 58
        nuclear arms race I 183
        Reagan Doctrine II 58
        Screen Actors Guild president II 189
        support of anticommunist regimes II 58
        view of Vietnam War I 295
        Strategic Defense Initiative (SDI) I 195–196, 199
Reagan administration VI 17, 36, 57, 133, 221, 225,
        228–235
        Afghanistan I 10–16; VI 133, 237
        Africa policy VI 1–7
        aid to contras I 54
        arms control VI 19–20, 22
        budget deficits I 202
        Central America policies I 48–52, 54, 56
        defense spending II 57; VI 109, 226
        foreign policy VI 57, 61, 236–242
        Iran-Contra affair I 54
        Latin American I 14
        National Security Decision Directive 17 (NSDD-
            17) I 50
        National Security Decision Directives 32, 66, 75 I
            196
        Nicaragua VI 190–196
        nuclear proliferation I 15
        Soviet Union I 196; VI 44, 116, 194, 263
        zero-zero option (1981) VI 36
Reagan Doctrine VI 44, 186, 221–227
        impact on the Soviet Union VI 226
Reaganomics VI 226
Realpolitik I 285; II 169; IV 123
Reconquista (reconquest) X 1–2, 8, 101, 133, 140, 143,
        159, 178–179, 220, 241–246
Red Scare I 174; III 221–226, 229; VI 129, 156, 158–
        159
        impact on Sacco and Vanzetti trial III 233
Redmond, John VIII 154–157, 161
Reform Party (1996) II 195–200
Refuse Act (1899) VII 266, 268
Rehnquist, Justice William H. II 224, 281
Regional Center for Ecological Supervision of the
        Apuseni Mountains VII 250
Reichstag (German parliament) IV 137; V 115, 134,
        211; VIII 164, 256; IX 142
Reinsurance Treaty (1887–1890) VIII 225–226, 249
Remarque, Erich VIII 55, 59, 186, 188, 264; IX 84, 212
Rennenkampf, Pavel IX 65, 160, 242
Republic of Vietnam. *See* South Vietnam
Republic Steel VII 266
Republican Party I 272; II 51, 180, 194–195, 198; III
        118, 211
        abortion II 79
        benefits from school busing II 295
        pro-life platforms II 223
        reaction to Marshall Plan II 209
        Republican National Convention (1952) II 280
        United States presidents II 49
        Vietnam policy II 266
Reserve Mining case VII 266, 268–269
Resistance movements V 243–247
        aid to Allies V 245
        forms of sabotage V 247
        Germany's response to V 245
        impact in France V 244
        Vichy France V 247
Resources for the Future VII 259
Reuss, Henry Schoellkopf VII 266
Revolutionary Left Movement. *See* Movimiento de
        Izquierda Revolucionaria I 127, 130
Reykjavik Summit (1986) II 61; VI 33, 36, 224, 231
Reynald of Chatillon X 52, 155, 201
Reynolds v. *Sims*, 1962 II 139

Roosevelt (TR) administration
    Anti-Trust Act (1890) III 242
    Big Stick diplomacy III 46
    corollary to the Monroe Doctrine III 247
    Department of Commerce and Labor, Bureau of
        Corporations III 242
    foreign policy III 243, 245
    Hepburn Act (1906) III 243, 245
    National Reclamation Act (1902) III 243
    Panama Canal III 243, 247
    Pure Food and Drug Act (1906) III 243
    United States Forestry Service III 243
Roosevelt Corollary (1904) III 46
Roosevelt Dam (United States) VII 214, 216
Root Elihu VIII 298
Rosellini, Albert D. VII 190
Rosenberg, Alfred V 143, 216
Rosenberg, Julius and Ethel I 274; II 131, 227–234; VI
        154, 156, 158, 177
    and Communist Party of the United States of
        America (CPUSA) II 227
    arrest of II 229, 231–232
    execution of II 233
    forged documents II 230
    Freedom of Information Act II 228
    G & R Engineering Company II 229
    martyrdom II 230
    Meeropol, Michael and Robert, sons of II 228
    possible motives for arrest of II 231
    proof of espionage activity II 230
    Soviet nuclear spying I 241, 243, 246–247
    Young Communist League II 228
Ross, Bob VII 74
Rostow, Walt W. I 20, 294
    flexible response I 120
Rowlett Act (1919) IX 93
Royal Air Force (RAF) I 235; IV 163, 168; V 86, 90,
        93, 95, 124; VIII 55, 194; IX 9, 11, 217, 220,
        222
    attacks on civilians V 87
Royal Air Force (RAF) Mosquitoes V 60
Royal Canadian Navy V 80, 82, 85
Royal Flying Corps (RFC) IX 10, 38
Royal Navy (Britain) V 43, 82, 85, 118, 260; VI 75;
        VIII 132; IX 31, 48–51, 75–77, 79, 99, 139–
        142, 173, 176–177, 181, 183–184, 186, 228,
        247, 256
Ruacana Diversion Wier VII 239
Ruckelshaus, William D. VII 263, 266, 268
Rundstedt, Field Marshal Karl Gerd von 125–126, 129
Rupprecht, Prince VIII 179–180, 184, 246, 274
Rural Institute in Puno, Peru VII 74
Rusk, Dean I 160, 294; VI 71, 95–96, 101
Russia
    alliances before World War I VIII 35, 225–231
    anti-semitism VIII 164
    Constituent Assembly IX 199, 201
    Crimean War (1853–1856) VIII 33
    Council of Ministers IX 240
    Duma IX 145, 190, 201, 238, 240
    General Staff Academy IX 158
    Great Retreat (1915) IX 240
    Imperial state, collapse of IX 81, 154–161
    Jews in VIII 164, 167
    Provisional government VIII 96, 167, 170–178,
        260, 261; IX 194, 196237–243202, 240
    Socialists VIII 255, 258, 261
    Soviet IX 82
    Special Conference of national Defense IX 190
    White Army VIII 168
    World War I VIII 30, 44–45, 48, 69, 71–72, 76,
        82, 92–101, 122, 182, 208–209, 212–213,
        245–246, 251–252, 256, 277, 281, 299; IX
        27, 30, 34, 43, 45, 48–49, 60–67, 84, 91–93,
        99, 101, 105, 108, 120, 128, 133–137, 140,
        145, 163, 171, 189–195, 204, 208, 224, 226,
        228, 237–243, 250, 252–253, 267
        aircraft IX 13

    alliance VIII 11, 212, 223
    army in VIII 69, 75, 170–171
    casualties VIII 125–126, 268
    cavalry IX 72
    naval aircraft IX 181
    Supreme headquarters IX 239
    War Industries Committee IX 193, 243
    women in combat VIII 125, 129
    Zemstva Union IX 190, 242
Russian Federation VI 47, 53–54, 114
    former communists VI 55
Russian Revolution (1917) VI 176; VIII 96, 163, 170,
        211, 221, 261, 268; IX 27, 165, 168, 189,
        195–202, 208, 240
Russian Civil War (1918–1920) VI 244
Russo-Japanese War (1904–1905) IV 256; VI 40; VIII
        35, 44–45, 73, 75, 226, 228, 247; IX 127,
        154, 156, 160, 162, 168, 181, 190, 227
Russo-Turkish War (1877–1878) VIII 73, 226
Rwanda I 289; II 101, 155; VI 51, 213
    Tutsi population VI 83

S

SA (storm trooper) I 139
Sacco, Nicola and Bartolomeo Vanzetti III 228–237;
        VIII 301
    involvement with Italian anarchist groups III 233
    League for Democratic Action III 235
    New England Civil Liberties Union III 235
    protest over verdict III 231
    trial III 231
Sacco-Vanzetti Defense Committee (SVDC) III 234
Sacramento River VII 29, 272
as-Sadat, Anwar I 159, 309, 311–314; II 150; VI 162–
        164, 170
    death (9 October 1981) I 317
    making peace I 317
    objective I 316
    policies I 316
    "year of decision" I 316
Saimaa Lake, Finland VII 90
St. Augustine X 117, 135, 212
St. Francis of Assisi X 35–36
St. James Declaration (1942) V 264
St. Peter X 115, 117, 119, 121–122, 218
Saipan
    fall of (1944) V 112
Sakharov, Andrei I 146; II 104
Saladin X 10, 24, 26–29, 33, 46–49, 51–52, 56, 88–90,
        107, 154–155, 170, 188, 193, 199, 225, 254,
        256–259, 261, 297
    and Richard I X 247–253
Salish Mountains VII 171
Salmon 2000 Project VII 229–235
Salsedo, Andrea III 229–231
Salt River VII 214, 216
Samsonov, Aleksandr IX 65, 159–160, 242
San Antonio River VII 70, 256
San Antonio Riverwalk VII 71
San Antonio Water System (SAWS) 70, 74
San Antonio, Texas VII 69–70, 74–75
    recycling of water in VII 70
San Francisco VII 262
San Francisco Bay VII 178
San Luís Rio Colorado VII 153, 154
San Marcos River VII 70, 74
San Pedro River VII 216
Sandanistas (Nicaragua) I 48–51, 53–54, 94, 96, 125–
        126; II 58; VI 61, 64, 190–191, 193, 237,
        241, 265
    attempting to maintain control of Nicaragua I 56
    Civil Defense Committees VI 192
    removed from power (1990) I 51
    takeover of Nicaragua (1979) I 54, 141
Sand Dunes and Salt Marshes (1913) VII 277
Sanders, Bernard II 197, 201

demilitarization I 314
Israeli forces I 313
Sinn Féin VIII 156, 158–159, 161–162
Sino-French War (1884–1885) IX 101
Sister Carrie (Dreiser) II 239
Sit-in movement (1960s) II 27, 160; VI 25
Six-Day War (1967) I 156–157, 159, 162, 308, 314; VI
      107, 163, 171; VII 135, 140
    aftermath I 312
    Gaza Strip I 314
    Golan Heights I 314
    Sinai Peninsula I 314
    West Bank of the Jordan River I 314
Sixth Amendment II 281
Skagit River VII 223
Skawina Aluminum Works VII 18–19
Skoropadsky, Pavlo VIII 99–100
Slim, William V 3, 122, 198
Slovak Green Party VII 103
Slovak Union of Nature and Landscape Protectors VII
    103
Slovakia VII 248, 250, 252
    dams in VII 100–107
    environmentalists in VII 103
    importance of Gabcikovo dam VII 103
    nuclear reactor at Jaslovské Bohunice VII 103
    nuclear-power plant at Mochovce VII 103
    symbolic importance of Danube VII 102
Slovenia IX 136, 266–272
Smith Act (Alien Registration Act of 1940) I 77, 79, 81;
    III 11
Smith v. *Allwright,* 1944 II 141
Smith, Adam IX 54–55
Smith, Bessie III 79, III 82
Smith, Holland M. "Howlin' Mad" V 297, 299
Smith, Howard Alexander II 208
Smith, Ian VI 2, 83
Smuts, Jan VIII 85–86, 89; IX 13, 222
Smyrna VIII 214, 217; IX 208
Smyth Report I 248
Smyth, Henry De Wolf I 247–248
Smythe, William A. VII 151
Snake River 27, 29, 31, 53–54, 196–197, 220, 221,
    223–225, 227
    dams on VII 219–228
Social Darwinism III 260; IV 86, 123; VIII 60, 299;
    IX 99, 112, 209, 224, 228
Social Democratic Party I 255; VI 20, 207
Social Ecological Movement VII 20
Social Security Act (1935) III 63, 149
Socialism II 34, 60, 160; VIII 254–262; IX 83
Socialist convention (1913) III 223
Socialist Labor Party II 42
Socialist Party II 196, 199; III 222–223
    Debs, Eugene V. III 221
Socialist Unity Party (SED) VI 118, 121
Soil Conservation and Domestic Allotment Act
    (1936) III 157
Solidarity VI 110, 237; VII 17, 19, 20
Solzhenitzyn, Aleksandr VI 200
Somalia II 100, 155–156; VI 164, 271
    claim to Ogaden VI 165
    Ethiopian conflict VI 165
    imperialism I 151
    relations with the Soviet Union VI 165
Somoza Debayle, Anastasio I 48–49, 54, 126, 141; III
    51; VI 190–191
Somocistas VI 64, 191
Sonoran Desert VII 151–152
    agriculture in VII 152
Sorensen, Ted II 275
Sorenson, Theodore C. II 117
South Africa I 51; VI 1, 2, 4, 6, 50, 54, 87, 136, 178,
    215; VII 2, 5, 67, 236–237,239–241; VIII
    31, 160–161, 208
    apartheid VI 13
    Bill of Rights VII 287
    British immigration to VII 237

inequalities of water supply in VII 284
    intervention in Angola VI 7
    intervention in Mozambique VI 6
    nuclear weapons development I 219–223
    rinderpest epidemic VII 34
    use of water by upper class VII 7
    water policy in VII 286, 287
South African National Defense Force VII 7
South African War (1899–1902) IX 68
South America, introduction of species to the United
    States from VII 217
South Carolina
    laws on rice dams and flooding VII 272
    rice cultivation in the tidewater zone VII 272
    slaves cleared swamp forests VII 272
South Dakota VII 181
    dams in VII 29
South East Asia Treaty Organization (SEATO) II 52,
    264
South Korea I 86–87, 288, 293; II 37; VI 102, 147–
    149, 217, 263
    domino theory I 266
    invaded by North Korea (1950) I 208; VI 28
    invasion of I 184
    nuclear weapons development I 216, 219, 223
    U.S. intervention I 158
South Vietnam I 40–46, 290, 293–299; II 5–8, 263,
    266; VI 58–60, 92–99, 101, 138, 140, 201,
    203, 284
    aid received from United States I 158; VI 2, 66,
    142, 144
    conquered by North Vietnam I 142; VI 222
    declares independence I 290
    Soviet support I 185
Southeast Asia Treaty Organization (SEATO) I 277;
    VI 203, 287
Southeastern Anatolia Project VII 77, 83
Southern African Hearings for Communities affected by
    Large Dams VII 242
Southern Baptist Convention III 38
Southern Christian Leadership Conference (SCLC) II
    22, 26, 28, 89
Southern Okavango Integrated Water Development
    Project VII 243
Southern Pacific Railroad VII 151, 155
Southern Rhodesia VII 237, 239
Southern Tenant Farmers' Union (STFU) II 189; III
    159
South-West Africa VII 237, 239
South-West African People's Organization
    (SWAPO) VII 239
Southwest Kansas Groundwater Management
    District VII 185
Soviet expansionism I 262; II 34–35, 208, 264, 267;
    III 10
    U.S. fear of II 129, 207
Soviet intervention
    Hungary I 278, 281
    Middle East I 277
Soviet Union I 77, 91; II 9, 56–62, 64–71, 168, 171;
    III 10; VI 9, 16, 20–21, 32, 35, 49, 106, 115–
    116, 147, 149, 161, 201, 206, 208, 236, 250–
    255, 260, 264; VII 55; VIII 94, 97, 99, 277,
    285; X 55, 63
    aging leadership VI 111
    aid to China V 198
    aid to Mozambique VI 2
    Angola policy VI 41, 43, 165
    annexes Estonia VII 22
    "Aviation Day" I 192
    bomber fleet I 6; VI 50
    casualties in Afghanistan (1979–1989) I 12
    Central Committee II 59
    Central Committee Plenum II 60
    challenge to U.S. dominance in Latin America I
    125
    collapse I 11; VI 47, 50, 58, 108, 213, 224, 227,
    235, 237; VII 17, 207; VIII 139

INDEX

U

INDEX

INDEX

272–273, 276, 282; IX 12–13, 15–16, 27, 29–31, 33–34, 38, 40, 48–49, 53, 61, 65–67, 71–73, 104–110, 114, 118, 120, 122, 124, 128, 131, 190, 193, 203, 225, 231–232, 234–235, 253–254

women in VIII 296, 298

World War II (1939–1945) I 61, 91; III 11, 50, 250–257; VI 8, 27, 31, 36, 49, 77, 79, 126, 146, 179, 267; VII 27, 29, 53, 69, 90, 93, 109, 152, 168, 174, 188, 199, 202, 204, 236–237, 257, 263–264, 273, 278, 287; IX 22, 27; X 14, 272, 300, 305

African American contributions IV 221; IX 115
Allies V 27–33; VI 169
Anglo-American alliance IV 208
anti-submarine defense IX 79
Axis powers V 62–67
Balkans V 68–78
Catholic Church VIII 209
Eastern Front IV 53–60
    casualties IV 55
    Soviet advantages IV 55
effect on Great Depression III 63
homefront segregation IV 218
impact on Civil Rights movement IV 220
impact on colonial powers VI 183
Japanese internment III 102–109
Kyushu invasion III 13
labor impressment IX 114
Okinawa III 15
Operation Olympic III 14
Operation Overlord II 39
Pacific theater III 13, 214; VI 254
Pearl Harbor III 214–215
relationship of Great Britain and U.S. II 31
resistance movements V 243–247
role of tanks IV 238–251
Soviet casualties II 38
strategy: IV 104–128; Allied V 19–26; Anglo-American disputes V 34–40; Anglo-Americn relations V 41–47; atomic bomb V 48–55; Axis V 62–67; Balkans 68–78; bomber offensive V 86–100; Eastern Front IV 53–60; Italian campaign IV 143–150; Operation Barbarossa V 226–234; Operation Dragoon V 235–242; unconditional surrender V 270–277; Yalta conference V 309–316
submarines V 255–261
Teheran Conference (1943) II 32
threat of Japanese invasion III 108
Tokyo trials (1945–1948) V 263–269
unconditional surrender policy V 270–276
U.S. combat effectiveness V 278–286
U.S. Marine Corps V 295–301
War Plan Orange III 108
women's roles V 302–308; VIII 130
Yalta Conference (1945) II 39

World's Fair, Chicago (1933) III 2
World's Fair, New York (1939) II 122
World's Fair, St. Louis (1904) III 242
World Water Commission VII 280, 281
World Water Forum (2000) VII 286
World Wildlife Fund (WWF) VII 107

X

Xhosa VII 67, 242

Y

Yakama Reservation VII 60
Yakovlev, Aleksandr N. I 104, 152
Yalta Conference (1945) I 73, 110, 252, 254, 256–257, 259, 273, 285, 288, 300–307; II 39, 205, 211; V 32, 75, 88, 252, 309–315; VI 126, 153, 158, 267
    "betraying" east European countries I 59
    criticism of I 302, 306

"Declaration of Liberated Europe" I 300
Far East I 303–304
German war reparations I 300
Poland V 310–311
Stalin's promise of elections I 151
United Nations V 310, 314

Yamagata Aritomo IX 164, 167
Yamamoto, Isoroku IV 2, 6
Yamashita, Tomoyuki
    trial of V 265
Yarmuk River VII 78, 81
Yasui, Minoru V 188–189
Yasui v. *U.S.* (1943) V 188
Yates v. *United States* (1957) I 81; II 281
Yatskov, Anatoli II 230
Year of Eating Bones VII 242
Yellow Sea VII 148
Yeltsin, Boris VI 113–114
Yemen VIII 39, 41, 212
    assasination of Ahmad I 282
    civil war (1962) II 150
    pan-Arab campaign I 281
    revolution I 158
Yom Kippur War (1973) I 162, 222, 308–317; VI 41, 43, 107, 161, 163, 166, 171, 204, 268
Yosemite National Park VII 112
Young Lords II 94, 197
Young Plan (1929) IV 270; IX 92, 171
Young Turks VIII 37, 45, 211
Yugoslav National Council (YNC) IX 267
Yugoslavia I 36, 108, 273, 277, 294; II 154, 156; VI 134, 136, 175, 181, 217, 219, 226–227, 243–244, 265, 271, 273–275, 277; VII 248–249, 252–254; IX 93, 203, 208, 266–272
    collectivization VI 274
    NATO in VI 219
    "non-aligned" movement I 283
    Soviet domination until 1948 I 107; VI 54
    U.S. aid I 86
Yuma County Water Users Association (YCWUA) VII 154
Yuma Valley VII 151, 155

Z

Zahniser, Howard VII 112
Zaire VI 81
    support for FNLA and UNITA VI 1
Zambezi VII 5
Zambezi River VII 1–2, 4, 236–237, 239
Zambezi River Authority VII 245
Zambezi Valley Development Fund VII 245
Zambia 1, 4, 236–237, 239
    as British colony 4
    copper mines in 5
Zapata, Emilano III 125, 127, 129–130
Zara X 109–110, 112–113, 156, 209
Zemgor (Red Cross) IX 243
Zengi X 46, 48–49, 51, 54, 163, 296
Zepplin, Ferdinand von IX 218, 221
Zeppelins VIII 200; IX 13, 181, 217–218, 220
Zhou En Lai II 168, 172; VI 43
Zimbabwe VII 1, 4–5, 66, 236–237
    as British colony VII 4
    black nationalist movement in VII 9
    eviction of blacks from traditional homelands VII 8
    water extraction in VII 63
Zimbabwe African National Union (ZANU) VII 239
Zimbabwe African People's Organization (ZAPU) VII 239
Zimbabwe Electricity Supply Authority (ZESA) VII 7
Zimmermann Telegram VIII 296; IX 21, 245
Zimmerwald Conference (1915) VIII 256, 259, 261
Zionism VIII 41, 168, 208; IX 93; X 55, 60–63, 306
Zouaves IX 111, 115–116
Zola, Emile VIII 147
Zwick, David R. VII 268

ISBN 1-55862-454-6

90000

9 781558 624542